# APPLICATION DEVELOPMENT
Using **C#**
and **.NET**

ISBN 0-13-093383-X

9 780130 933836

## The Integrated .NET Series from Object Innovations and Prentice Hall PTR

**C#**

- Introduction to C# Using.NET
  Oberg

- Application Development Using C# and .NET
  Stiefel/Oberg

**VISUAL BASIC**

- Introduction to Programming Visual Basic Using .NET
  Wyatt/Oberg

- Application Development Using Visual Basic and .NET
  Oberg/Thorsteinson/Wyatt

**VISUAL C++**

- .NET Architecture and Programming Using Visual C++
  Thorsteinson/Oberg

**WEB APPLICATIONS**

- Fundamentals of Web Applications Using .NET and XML
  Bell/Feng/Soong/Zhang/Zhu

**PERL**

- Programming PERL in the .NET Environment
  Saltzman/Oberg

EXPERT PRACTITIONERS • SEASONED INSTRUCTORS

.NET

# APPLICATION DEVELOPMENT

## Using C#

## and .NET

MICHAEL STIEFEL • ROBERT J. OBERG

PH
PTR

Prentice Hall PTR, Upper Saddle River, NJ 07458
www.phptr.com

**Library of Congress Cataloging-in-Publication Data**

Stiefel, Michael.
    Application development using C# and .NET / Michael Stiefel, Robert J. Oberg
        p.   cm.
    ISBN 0-13-093383-X
    1. System design. 2. Computer software—Development. 3. C# (Computer program
language). I. Oberg, Robert J.   II. Title.

    QA76.9.S88 S745 2002
    005.2'768—-dc21

                                                                        2001056574

Editorial/Production Supervision: *Nick Radhuber*
Acquisitions Editor: *Jill Harry*
Marketing Manager: *Dan DePasquale*
Manufacturing Buyer: *Maura Zaldivar*
Cover Design: *Anthony Gemmellaro*
Cover Design Direction: *Jerry Votta*
Interior Series Design: *Gail Cocker-Bogusz*

© 2002 by Michael Stiefel and Robert J. Oberg
Published by Prentice Hall PTR
Prentice-Hall, Inc.
Upper Saddle River, NJ 07458

ISBN 0-13-093383-X

Pearson Education LTD.
Pearson Education Australia PTY, Limited
Pearson Education Singapore, Pte. Ltd
Pearson Education North Asia Ltd
Pearson Education Canada, Ltd.
Pearson Educación de Mexico, S.A. de C.V.
Pearson Education—Japan
Pearson Education Malaysia, Pte. Ltd
Pearson Education, Upper Saddle River, New Jersey

To the memory of

Dr. A. Edward Stefanacci, 1930-1993
*To keep an adjunct to remember thee*
*Were to import forgetfulness in me.*
William Shakespeare Sonnet 122

# CONTENTS

*M*icrosoft .NET is an advance in programming technology that greatly simplifies application development both for traditional, proprietary applications, and for the emerging paradigm of Web-based services. .NET is a complete restructuring of Microsoft's whole system infrastructure and represents a major learning challenge for programmers developing applications on Microsoft platforms. The new platform includes a new programming language C# and a major class library, the .NET Framework.

This book covers important topics in the .NET Framework for experienced programmers. You do not need prior experience in C#, because there is a self-contained treatment, but you should have experience in some object-oriented language such as C++ or Java. The book could also be read by a seasoned Visual Basic programmer who has experience working with objects and components in VB.

If you already understand C#, you may safely skip or skim Chapters 3 and 4. Chapter 5 contains important information about the interactions of C# and the .NET Framework. You may then proceed with a detailed study of the .NET Framework in Chapters 6 and beyond. For a thorough introduction to the C# language you may read the book *Introduction to C# Using .NET.*

The book is practical, with many examples and a major case study. The goal is to equip you to begin building significant applications using the .NET Framework. The book is part of The Integrated .NET Series from Object Innovations and Prentice Hall PTR.

## Organization

The book is organized into five major parts, and is structured to make it easy for you to navigate to what you most need to know. The first part, consisting of Chapters 1 and 2, should be read by everyone. It answers the question "What is Microsoft .NET?" and outlines the programming model of the .NET Framework.

The second part, consisting of Chapters 3–5, covers the C# programming language. If you are already familiar with C# you can skim these chapters, paying the most attention to Chapter 5, which covers topics such as interfaces, delegates, and events. This chapter also describes important interactions between C# and the .NET Framework. The case study, which is elaborated throughout the entire book, is introduced in Chapter 4.

The third part, Chapters 6–9, covers important fundamental topics in the .NET Framework. Chapter 6 covers user interface programming using the Windows Forms classes. Chapter 7 discusses assemblies and deployment, which constitute a major advance in the simplicity and robustness of deploying Windows applications, ending the notorious "DLL hell." Chapter 8 delves into important .NET Framework classes, including the topics of metadata, serialization, threading, attributes, application domains, asynchronous programming, remoting, and memory management. Chapter 9 covers ADO.NET, which provides a consistent set of classes for accessing both relational and XML Data.

The fourth part of the book provides an in-depth introduction to Web programming using ASP.NET and SOAP. Chapter 10 introduces the fundamentals of ASP.NET, including the use of Web Forms, which greatly simplifies the development of sophisticated Web sites. Chapter 11 covers SOAP and Web Services, which provide an easy-to-use and robust mechanism for heterogeneous systems to interoperate.

The final part of the book covers additional important topics in the .NET Framework. Chapter 12 covers the topic of security in detail, including code access security, declarative security, and the securing of Web applications and services. Chapter 13 introduces the debug and trace classes provided by .NET. Chapter 14 covers interoperability of .NET with COM and with Win32 applications.

## Sample Programs

The only way to really learn a major framework is to read and write many, many programs, including some of reasonable size. This book provides many small programs that illustrate pertinent features of .NET in isolation, which makes them easy to understand. The programs are clearly labeled in the text, and they can all be found in the software distribution that accompanies this book.

A major case study, the Acme Travel Agency, is progressively developed in Chapters 4 through 12. It illustrates many features of C# and .NET working in combination, as they would in a practical application.

The sample programs are provided in a self-extracting file on the book's Web site. When expanded, a directory structure is created, whose default root is   **c:\OI\NetCs**. The sample programs, which begin with the second chapter, are in directories **Chap02**, **Chap03**, and so on. All the samples for a given chapter are in individual folders within the chapter directories. The names of the folders are clearly identified in the text. Each chapter that contains a step of the case study has a folder called **CaseStudy**, containing that step. If necessary, there is a **readme.txt** file in each chapter directory to explain any instructions necessary for getting the examples to work.

This book is part of The Integrated .NET Series. The sample programs for other books in the series are located in their own directories underneath **\OI**, so all the .NET examples from all books in the series will be located in a common area as you install them.

These programs are furnished solely for instructional purposes and should not be embedded in any software product. The software (including instructions for use) is provided "as is" without warranty of any kind.

# Caveat

The book and the associated code were developed with Beta 2 of the .NET Framework. Microsoft has indicated that this version of .NET is close to what will be the final version. Nonetheless, changes will be made before .NET is released. The code in the examples has been verified to work only with Windows 2000. Database code has been verified with SQL Server 2000. Several examples in the database and security chapters have machine names embedded in connection strings or role names. When trying to run these examples, you will have to replace those names with the appropriate name for your machine. To make installation easy, the database examples run with user name "sa" and without a password. Needless to say, in a real system you should *NEVER* have any login id without a password or have a database application use **sa** to log into a database.[1]

# Web Sites

The Web site for the book series is:
**www.objectinnovations.com/dotnet.htm**
A link is provided at that Web site for downloading the sample programs for this book.

Additional information about .NET technology is available at:
**www.reliablesoftware.com**
The book sample programs are available at this Web site as well.

The Web site for the book will also have a list of .NET learning resources that will be kept up-to-date.

---

[1] That is just one of several steps necessary to avoid an SQL Injection attack.

# Acknowledgments

We are indebted to Mike Meehan for helping to get this project off the ground, starting at a meeting at the PDC when Microsoft announced .NET. That conversation put into motion what has become a substantial series of books on .NET technology, in which this volume is the second. We would also like to thank Jill Harry at Prentice Hall for her ongoing support with this ambitious book project.

Several people at Microsoft reviewed parts of the book: Steven Pratschner, Jim Hogg, Michael Pizzo, Michael Day, Krzysztof Cwalina, Keith Ballinger, and Eric Olsen. We thank them for taking time out from their very tight schedules to correct our manuscript. Connie Sullivan and Stacey Giard coordinated technical sessions and helped assure our access to resources at Microsoft.

Moshe Raab took precious time off from his consulting work and provided many helpful suggestions. Peter Thorsteinson, an author of another book in our series, was a valuable resource for understanding the deployment of .NET applications. Will Provost helped clarify several issues related to XML. We also want to thank all the other authors in the .NET series, because there is much synergy in a group working on parallel books, even if in the heat of writing we did not always collaborate as closely as we might have. These hardworking people include Eric Bell, Howard Feng, Michael Saltzman, Ed Soong, Dana Wyatt, David Zhang, and Sam Zhu.

As always, reviewers should get credit for improving the quality of the work; any remaining errors are the responsibility of the authors.

Robert always has a hard time writing acknowledgments, because there are so many people to thank on such a major project. I (Robert) usually thank Michael Stiefel, but this time he is my co-author, and so we are on the same side of the fence, thanking others. My wife, Marianne, has provided enormous support and encouragement for all my writing efforts. This project was especially demanding, and so her support is all the more appreciated. Thank you all, and the other colleagues, friends, and students—too numerous to mention individually—who have helped me over the years.

Michael would like to thank his wife not only for her understanding of his intellectual lack of presence while writing the book (even if he was physically present), but also for the associated behaviors, not the least of which was the repeated playing of music that one social critic referred to as "Das Lied von der Erde and other light classics." Of course I did not follow his other advice about how to write a book.

תושלב"ע

*November 23, 2001*

About this Series
Robert J. Oberg, Series Editor

## Introduction

The Integrated .NET Book Series from Object Innovations and Prentice Hall PTR is a unique series of introductory and intermediate books on Microsoft's important .NET technology. These books are based on proven industrial-strength course development experience. The authors are expert practitioners, teachers, and writers who combine subject-matter expertise with years of experience in presenting complex programming technologies such as C++, MFC, OLE, and COM/COM+. These books *teach* in a systematic, step-by-step manner and are not merely summaries of the documentation. All the books come with a rich set of programming examples, and a thematic case study is woven through several of the books.

From the beginning, these books have been conceived as an *integrated whole*, and not as independent efforts by a diverse group of authors.. The initial set of books consists of three introductory books on .NET languages and four intermediate books on the .NET Framework. Each book in the series is targeted at a specific part of the important .NET technology, as illustrated by the diagram below.

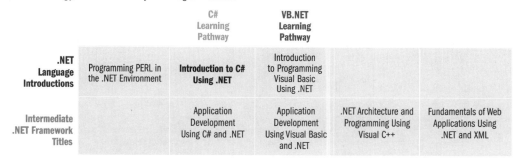

|  | | C#<br>Learning<br>Pathway | VB.NET<br>Learning<br>Pathway | | |
|---|---|---|---|---|---|
| **.NET<br>Language<br>Introductions** | Programming PERL in<br>the .NET Environment | **Introduction to C#<br>Using .NET** | Introduction<br>to Programming<br>Visual Basic<br>Using .NET | | |
| **Intermediate<br>.NET Framework<br>Titles** | | Application<br>Development<br>Using C# and .NET | Application<br>Development<br>Using Visual Basic<br>and .NET | .NET Architecture and<br>Programming Using<br>Visual C++ | Fundamentals of Web<br>Applications Using<br>.NET and XML |

## Introductory .NET Language Books

The first set of books teaches several of the important .NET languages. These books cover their language from the ground up and have no prerequisite other than programming experience in some language. Unlike many .NET language books, which are a mixture of the language and topics in the .NET Framework, these books are focused on the languages, with attention to important interactions between the language and the framework. By concentrating on the languages, these books have much more detail and many more practical examples than similar books.

The languages selected are the new language C#, the greatly changed VB.NET, and Perl.NET, the open source language ported to the .NET environment. Visual C++ .NET is covered in a targeted, intermediate book, and JScript.NET is covered in the intermediate level .NET Web-programming book.

## Introduction to C# Using .NET

This book provides thorough coverage of the C# language from the ground up. It is organized with a specific section covering the parts of C# common to other C-like languages. This section can be cleanly skipped by programmers with C experience or the equivalent, making for a good reading path for a diverse group of readers. The book gives thorough attention to the object-oriented aspects of C# and thus serves as an excellent book for programmers migrating to C# from Visual Basic or COBOL. Its gradual pace and many examples make the book an excellent candidate as a college textbook for adventurous professors looking to teach C# early in the language's life-cycle.

## Introduction to Programming Visual Basic Using .NET

Learn the VB.NET language from the ground up. Like the companion book on C#, this book gives thorough attention to the object-oriented aspects of VB.NET. Thus the book is excellent for VB programmers migrating to the more sophisticated VB.NET, as well as for programmers experienced in languages such as COBOL. This book would also be suitable as a college textbook.

## Programming Perl in the .NET Environment

A very important part of the vision behind Microsoft® .NET is that the platform is designed from the ground up to support multiple programming languages from many sources, and not just Microsoft languages. This book, like other books in the series, is rooted in long experience in industrial teaching. It covers the Perl language from the ground up. Although oriented toward the ActiveState Perl.NET compiler, the book also provides excellent coverage of the Perl language suitable for other versions as well.

## Intermediate .NET Framework Books

The second set of books is focused on topics in the .NET Framework, rather than on programming languages. Three parallel books cover the .NET Framework using the important languages C#, VB.NET, and Visual C++. The C# and VB.NET books include self-contained introductions to the languages suitable for experienced programmers, allowing them to rapidly come up to speed on these languages without having to plow through the introductory books. The fourth book covers the important topic of web programming in .NET, with substantial coverage of XML, which is so important in the .NET Framework.

The design of the series makes these intermediate books much more suitable to a wider audience than many similar books. The introductory books focus on languages frees up the intermediate books to cover the important topics of the .NET Framework in greater depth. The series design also makes for flexible reading paths. Less experienced readers can read the introductory language books followed by the intermediate framework books, while more experienced readers can go directly to the intermediate framework books.

## Application Development Using C# and .NET

This book does not require prior experience in C#. However, the reader should have experience in some object-oriented language such as C++ or Java™. The book could also be read by seasoned Visual Basic programmers who have experience working with objects and components in VB. Seasoned programmers and also a less experienced reader coming from the introductory C# book can skip the first few chapters on C# and proceed directly to a study of the Framework. The book is practical, with many examples and a major case study. The goal is to equip the reader with the knowledge necessary to begin building significant applications using the .NET Framework.

## Application Development Using Visual Basic .NET

This book is for the experienced VB programmer who wishes to learn the new VB.NET version of VB quickly and then move on to learning the .NET Framework. It is also suitable for experienced enterprise programmers in other languages who wish to learn the powerful RAD-oriented Visual Basic language in its .NET incarnation and go on to building applications. Like the companion C# book, this book is very practical, with many examples, and includes the same case study implemented in VB.NET.

## .NET Architecture and Programming Using Visual C++

This parallel book is for the experienced Visual C++ programmer who wishes to learn the .NET Framework to build high-performing applications. Unlike the C# and VB.NET book, there is no coverage of the C++ language itself, because C++ is too complex to cover in a brief space. This book is specifically for experienced C++ programmers. Like the companion C# and VB.NET books, this book is very practical, with many examples, and includes the same case study implemented in Visual C++.

## Fundamentals of Web Applications Using .NET and XML

The final book in the series provides thorough coverage of building Web applications using .NET. Unlike other books about ASP.NET, this book gives attention to the whole process of Web application development. The book incorporates a review tutorial on classical Web programming, making the book accessible to the experienced programmer new to the Web world. The book contains significant coverage on ASP.NET, Web Forms, Web Services, SOAP, and XML.

# What Is Microsoft .NET?

.NET is Microsoft's vision of applications in the Internet age. .NET provides enhanced interoperability features based upon open Internet standards. .NET improves the robustness of classic Windows applications. .NET offers developers a new programming platform and superb tools, with XML playing a fundamental role.

Microsoft .NET is a platform built on top of the operating system. Three years in the making before the public announcement, .NET represents a major investment by Microsoft. .NET has been influenced by other technological advances such as XML, Java™, and COM.

Microsoft .NET provides:

- The Common Language Runtime, a robust runtime platform.
- Multiple language development, with no language being more preferred over any other.
- The .NET Framework, an extensible programming model, which provides a very large class library of reusable code available to any .NET language.
- Support for a networking infrastructure built on top of Internet standards that allows a high level of communication among applications.
- Support for the new industry standard of Web Services. Web Services represent a new mechanism of application delivery that extends the idea of component-based development to the Internet.
- ASP.NET, which allows you to use standard programming practices to develop Web applications.
- A Deployment model that allows for versioning and the end of "DLL Hell."
- A Security model that is easy for programmers to use in their programs.

- An interoperability mechanism that enables .NET programs to access legacy code, including COM components.
- Powerful development tools.

## Microsoft and the Web

The World Wide Web has been a big catch-up challenge to Microsoft. Actually the Web coexists quite well with Microsoft's traditional strength, the PC. Through a PC application, the browser, a user gains access to a whole world of information.

The Web relies on standards such as HTML, HTTP, and XML, which are essential for communication among diverse users on a wide variety of computer systems and devices.

While complex, the Windows PC is quite standardized. While the Web is based on standard protocols, there is a Tower of Babel of multiple languages, databases, development environments, and devices running on top of those protocols. This exploding complexity of technology exacerbates a growing shortage of knowledge workers who can build the needed systems using the new technologies. .NET provides the infrastructure so that programmers can concentrate on adding value in their applications without having to reinvent solutions to common programming problems.

### Applications in the Internet Age

Originally the Web was a vast information repository. Browsers would make requests for pages of existing information, and Web servers would deliver this information as static HTML pages. Even when interactive Web applications were introduced, HTML, which combines information with the details of how it is formatted for viewing, was still used.

XML provides a standard way of transmitting data independent of its formatting. XML can thus provide ways for companies to agree on standards for documents and information flows, such as purchase orders and invoices. E-commerce can then be automated among cooperating companies (B-to-B). XML, however, only describes the data; it does not supply the actions to be performed on that data. For that we need Web Services.

### Web Services

One of the most important aspects of .NET is the support for Web Services. Based on the industry standard SOAP protocol, Web Services allow you to expose your applications' functionality across the Internet. From the perspective of a .NET programmer, a Web Service is no different from any other kind of service implemented by a class in a .NET language. The programming model is the same for calling a function within an application, in a separate component on the same machine, or as a Web Service on a different machine.

This inherent simplicity will make it very easy for companies to create and host applications. If desired, a whole application could be completely outsourced, removing issues of development, deployment, and maintenance. Or you could use third-party Web Services that did not exist when you designed your application.

## ASP.NET

.NET includes a totally redone version of the popular Active Server Pages technology, known as ASP.NET. Whereas ASP relied on interpreted script code in languages with limited capabilities interspersed with page-formatting commands, ASP.NET code can be written in any NET language, including C#, VB.NET, JScript, and C++ with managed extensions. Since this is compiled code, you can separate your interface code from your business logic in a separate "code behind" file. Although C#, VB.NET, and JScript may be left as embedded script within the Web page, managed C++ must be placed in a code behind file.

ASP.NET provides Web forms, which vastly simplifies creating Web user interfaces.

Drag-and-drop in Visual Studio.NET makes it very easy to lay out forms. You can add code to form events such as a button click.

ASP.NET will automatically detect browser capability. For high-end browsers code processing can be performed on the client. For low-end browsers the server does the processing and generates standard HTML. All this is done transparently to the developer by ASP.NET.

The combination of Web Services and compiled full-blown languages such as C#, VB.NET, and managed C++, allows Web programming to follow an object-oriented programming model, which had not been possible with ASP scripting languages and COM components.

## Open Standards and Interoperability

The modern computing environment contains a vast variety of hardware and software systems. Computers range from mainframes and high-end servers to workstations and PCs and to small mobile devices such as PDAs and cell phones. Operating systems include traditional mainframe systems, many flavors of UNIX, Linux, several versions of Windows, real-time systems, and special systems such as PalmOs for mobile devices. Many different languages, databases, application development tools, and middleware products are used.

In the modern environment, few applications are an island unto themselves. Even shrink-wrapped applications deployed on a single PC may use the Internet for registration and updates. The key to interoperability among applications is the use of standards. Since applications typically run over a network, a key standard is the communications protocol used.

## Communications Protocols

TCP/IP sockets is highly standard and widely available. Too much detail, however, has to be mastered, for programmers to be productive in writing robust distributed applications. Somewhat higher is the remote procedure call (RPC), but RPC is still very complex, and there are many flavors of RPC. Popular are higher level protocols, such as CORBA, RMI, and DCOM. These are still complex, and require special environments at both ends. These protocols suffer other disadvantages, such as difficulty in going across firewalls.

One communication protocol has become ubiquitous: HTTP. For this reason, Microsoft, IBM, and other vendors have introduced a new protocol called SOAP (Simple Object Access Protocol). SOAP uses text-based XML to encode object method requests and the accompanying data. The great virtue of SOAP is its simplicity, leading to ease of implementation on multiple devices. While SOAP can run on top of any protocol, its ability to run on top of standard Internet protocols, such as HTTP, allows it to pass through firewalls without any connectivity problems.

# Windows on the Desktop

Microsoft began with the desktop. The modern Windows environment has become ubiquitous. Countless applications are available, and most computer users are at least somewhat at home with Windows. While Microsoft has made much progress in modernizing Windows, there are still significant problems.

## Problems with Windows

Maintaining a Windows PC is a chore, because applications are quite complex. They consist of many files, registry entries, shortcuts, and so on. Different applications can share certain DLLs, and installing a new application can overwrite a DLL an existing application depends on, possibly breaking an old application ("DLL Hell"). Removing an application is a complex operation and is often imperfectly done.

A PC can gradually become less stable, sometimes requiring the drastic cure of reformatting the hard disk and starting from scratch. While there is tremendous economic benefit to using PCs, because standard applications are inexpensive and powerful and the hardware is cheap, the savings are reduced by the cost of maintenance.

Windows was originally developed when personal computers were not connected over a network and security was not an issue. While security was built into Windows NT and Windows 2000, the programming model is difficult to use. (Pop quiz: Did you ever pass anything but NULL to a Win32 LPSECURITY_ATTRIBUTES argument?)

## The Glass House and Thin Clients

The old "glass house" model of a central computer that controls all applications has had an appeal, and there has been a desire to move toward "thin clients" of some sort. But the much heralded "network PC" never really caught on. There is too much of value in standard PC applications. Users like the idea of their "own" PC, with their data stored safely and conveniently on their local computer. Without broadband connectivity a server-based application such as word processing would not perform very well. Security is also a very difficult issue to solve with thin clients. The personal computer is undoubtedly here to stay.

## A Robust Windows

With all the hype about .NET and the Internet, it is important to realize that .NET has changed the programming model to allow the creation of much more robust Windows applications. Applications no longer rely on storing extensive configuration data in the fragile Windows Registry. .NET applications are self-describing, containing metadata within the program executable files themselves. Different versions of an application or component can be deployed side-by-side. Applications can share components through the Global Assembly Cache. Versioning is built into the deployment model. A straightforward security model is part of .NET. Windows Forms technology is a new paradigm for building Windows GUI applications.

# A New Programming Platform

Let us look at what we have just discussed from the point of view of .NET as a new programming platform:

- Code can be validated to prevent unauthorized actions.
- It is much easier to program than the Win32 API or COM.
- All or parts of the platform can be implemented on many different kinds of computers (as has been done with Java).
- All the languages use one class library.
- Languages can interoperate with each other.

There are several important features to the .NET platform:

- .NET Framework
- Common Language Runtime
- Multiple language development
- Development tools

## .NET Framework

Modern programming relies heavily on reusable code provided in libraries. Object-oriented languages facilitate the creation of class libraries, which are flexible, have a good degree of abstraction, and are extensible by adding new classes and basing new classes on existing ones, "inheriting" existing functionality.

The .NET Framework provides over 2500 classes of reusable code, which can be called by all the .NET languages. The .NET Framework is extensible, and new classes can inherit from existing classes, even those implemented in a different language.

Examples of classes in the .NET Framework include Windows programming, Web programming, database programming, XML, and interoperability with COM and Win32. The .NET Framework is discussed in the next chapter and throughout the rest of the book.

## Common Language Runtime

A *runtime* provides services to executing programs. Traditionally there are different runtimes for different programming environments. Examples of runtimes include the standard C library, MFC, the Visual Basic runtime, and the Java Virtual Machine. The runtime environment provided by .NET is called the Common Language Runtime or CLR.

### MANAGED CODE AND DATA

The CLR provides a set of services to .NET code (including the .NET Framework, which sits on top of the CLR). In order to make use of these services, .NET code has to behave in a predictable fashion, and the CLR has to understand the .NET code. For example, to do runtime checking of array boundaries, all .NET arrays have identical layout. NET code can also be restricted by type safety requirements.

As we will discuss in the next chapter, the restrictions on .NET code are defined in the Common Type System (CTS) and its implementation in the Microsoft Intermediate Language (MSIL or IL). The Common Type System defines the types and operations that are allowed in code running under the CLR. For example, it is the CTS that restricts types to using single implementation inheritance. MSIL code is compiled into the native code of the platform.

.NET applications contain metadata, or descriptions of the code and data in the application. Metadata allows the CLR, for example, to automatically serialize data into a storage.

Code that can use the services of the Common Language Runtime is called managed code.

Managed data is allocated and deallocated automatically. This automatic deallocation is called *garbage collection*. Garbage collection reduces memory leaks and similar problems.

## Microsoft and ECMA

Microsoft has submitted specifications for the C# programming language and core parts of the .NET Framework to the European Computer Manufacturers Association (ECMA) for standardization. The ECMA specification defines the platform-independent Common Language Infrastructure (CLI). The CLR can be thought of as the CLI plus the Base Class Libraries (BCL). The BCL has support for the fundamental types of the CTS such as file I/O, strings, and formatting. Since the CLR is platform dependent, it makes use of the process and memory management models of the underlying operating system.

The ECMA specification defines the Common Intermediate Language (CIL). The ECMA specification allows for CIL to be compiled into native code or interpreted.

### VERIFIABLE CODE

Managed code can be checked for type safety. Type safe code cannot be subverted. For example, a buffer overwrite cannot corrupt other data structures or programs. You can only enter and leave methods at fixed points, you cannot calculate a memory address and start executing code at an arbitrary point. Security policy can be applied to type safe code. For example, access to certain files or user interface features can be allowed or denied. You can prevent the execution of code from unknown sources.

Not all code that makes use of the facilities of the CLR is necessarily type safe. The canonical example is managed C++. Managed C++ code can make use of CLR facilities such as garbage collection, but cannot be guaranteed to be type safe.

## Multiple Language Development

As its name suggests, the CLR supports many programming languages. A "managed code" compiler must be implemented for each language. Microsoft itself has implemented compilers for managed C++, Visual Basic.NET, Jscript, and the new language C#. Well over a dozen other languages are being implemented by third parties, among them COBOL by Fujitsu and Perl by ActiveState. To accommodate the use or creation of .NET data types, however, new syntax often has to be introduced. Nonetheless, programmers do not need to be retrained in a completely new language in order to gain the benefits of .NET. Legacy code can be accessed through the interoperability mechanism.

## Development Tools

A practical key to success in software development is a set of effective tools. Microsoft has long provided great tools, including Visual C++ and Visual Basic. With .NET they have combined their development tools into a single integrated environment called Visual Studio.NET.

- VS.NET provides a very high degree of functionality for creating applications in all the languages supported by .NET.
- You can do multiple language programming, debugging, and so on.
- VS.NET has many kinds of designers for forms, databases, and other software elements.

As with the languages themselves, third parties can provide extensions to Visual Studio.NET, creating a seamless development environment for their language that interoperates with the other .NET language. The tool set includes extensive support for building Web applications and Web Services. There is also great support for database application development.

### The Importance of Tools

The importance of tools should not be underestimated. Ada, a very powerful programming language, never achieved widespread use. While part of the initial vision was to create a standard Ada Programming Support Environment (APSE), most of the attention was paid to specifying the language, not the APSE. Consequently, Ada never did develop any development environment comparable to that of Visual Studio, Smalltalk, or some of the Java IDEs.

Visual Studio.NET will be highly tuned for productivity, and much training will be available. Microsoft has far more resources to throw at Visual Studio.NET than do smaller vendors in the highly fragmented tools market. Java is highly standardized in the language and API, but tools, which are required for productivity, are not standard.

## The Role of XML

XML is ubiquitous in .NET and is highly important in Microsoft's overall vision. Some uses of XML in .NET include:

- XML can be used to model data in coordination with ADO.NET datasets.

- XML is used in configuration files.
- XML documentation can be automatically generated by some .NET languages.
- XML is used for encoding requests and responses in Web Services.
- XML is used to describe and transmit data in Web Services.

## Success Factors for Web Services

The ultimate success of Microsoft's Internet vision depends on two external factors: the infrastructure of the Internet and the success of the proposed Web Services business model. The widespread use of Web Services depends on having high bandwidth widely available. This capability will probably indeed materialize within the next several years. The prospect for the business model remains to be seen.

It is important to understand that the overall .NET technology includes far more than the widely hyped Internet part. The more robust Windows platform and the very powerful .NET Framework and tools will be enduring features.

## Summary

Microsoft .NET is a new platform built on top of the operating system. It provides many capabilities for building and deploying both standard applications and new Web-based ones. Web Services allow applications to expose functionality across the Internet, typically using the SOAP protocol. SOAP supports a high degree of interoperability, since it is based on widely adopted standards such as HTTP and XML.

NET uses managed code running on the Common Language Runtime that employs the Common Type System. The .NET Framework is a very large class library available consistently across many languages. XML plays a fundamental role in .NET. All this functionality can be used to build more robust Windows applications as well as Internet applications.

# .NET Fundamentals

What kind of problems is .NET designed to solve? .NET solves problems that have plagued programmers in the past. .NET helps programmers develop the applications of the future. This chapter is designed to present an overview of Microsoft .NET by looking at a simple program rather than talking in vague generalities. While we will start discussing Microsoft .NET in detail in Chapter 6, this chapter will enable you to get a feel for the big picture right away.

## Problems of Windows Development

Imagine a symphony orchestra where the violins and the percussion sections had different versions of the score. It would require a heroic effort to play the simplest musical composition. This is the life of the Windows developer. Do I use MFC? Visual Basic or C++? ODBC or OLEDB? COM interface or C style API? Even within COM: do I use IDispatch, dual, or pure vtable interfaces? Where does the Internet fit into all of this? Either the design had to be contorted by the implementation technologies that the developers understood, or the developers had to learn yet another technological approach that was bound to change in about two years.

Deployment of applications can be a chore. Critical entries have to be made in a Registry that is fragile and difficult to back up. There is no good versioning strategy for components. New releases can break existing programs often with no information about what went wrong. Given the problems with the Registry, other technologies used other configuration stores such as a metabase or SQL Server.

Security in Win32 is another problem. It is difficult to understand and difficult to use. Many developers ignored it. Developers who needed to apply security often did the best they could with a difficult programming model. The rise of Internet-based security threats transforms a bad situation into a potential nightmare.

Despite Microsoft's efforts to make development easier problems remained. Many system services had to be written from scratch, essentially providing the plumbing code that had nothing to do with your business logic. MTS/COM+ was a giant step in the direction of providing higher level services, but it required yet another development paradigm. COM made real component programming possible. Nonetheless, you either did it simply, but inflexibly in Visual Basic, or powerfully, but with great difficulty in C++, because of all the repetitive plumbing code you had to write in C++.

## Applications of the Future

Even if .NET fixed all the problems of the past, it would not be enough. One of the unchanging facts of programming life is that the boundaries of customer demand are always being expanded.

The growth of the Internet has made it imperative that applications work seamlessly across network connections. Components have to be able to expose their functionality to other machines. Programmers do not want to write the underlying plumbing code, they want to solve their customers' problems.

## .NET Overview

### The Magic of Metadata

To solve all these problems .NET must provide an underlying set of services that is available to all languages at all times. It also has to understand enough about an application to be able to provide these services.

Serialization provides a simple example. Every programmer at some time or another has to write code to save data. Why should every programmer have to reinvent the wheel of how to persist nested objects and complicated data structures? Why should every programmer have to figure out how to do this for a variety of data stores? .NET can do this for the programmer. Programmers can also decide to do it themselves if required.

To see how this is done, look at the **Serialize** sample associated with this chapter. For the moment ignore the programming details of C# which will be covered in the next three chapters, and focus on the concepts.

```csharp
[Serializable] class Customer
{
  public string name;
  public long id;
}
class Test
{
  static void Main(string[] args)
  {
    ArrayList list = new ArrayList();

    Customer cust = new Customer();
    cust.name = "Charles Darwin";
    cust.id = 10;
    list.Add(cust);

    cust = new Customer();
    cust.name = "Isaac Newton";
    cust.id = 20;
    list.Add(cust);

    foreach (Customer x in list)
      Console.WriteLine(x.name + ": " + x.id);

    Console.WriteLine("Saving Customer List");
    FileStream s = new FileStream("cust.txt",
            FileMode.Create);
    SoapFormatter f = new SoapFormatter();
    f.Serialize(s, list);
    s.Close();

    Console.WriteLine("Restoring to New List");
    s = new FileStream("cust.txt", FileMode.Open);
    f = new SoapFormatter();
    ArrayList list2 = (ArrayList)f.Deserialize(s);
    s.Close();

    foreach (Customer y in list2)
      Console.WriteLine(y.name + ": " + y.id);
  }
}
```

We have defined a **Customer** class with two fields: a **name** and an **id**. The program first creates an instance of a collection class that will be used to hold instances of the **Customer** class. We add two **Customer** objects to the collection and then print out the contents of the collection. The collection is then saved to disk. It is restored to a new collection instance and printed out. The results printed out will be identical to those printed out before the collection was saved.[1]

We wrote no code to indicate how the fields of the customer object are saved or restored. We did have to specify the format (SOAP) and create the medium to which the data was saved. The .NET Framework classes are partitioned so that where you load/save, the format you use to load/save, and how you load/save can be chosen independently. This kind of partitioning exists throughout the .NET Framework.

The **Customer** class was annotated with the **Serializable** attribute in the same way the **public** attribute annotates the name field. If you do not want your objects to be serializable, do not apply the attribute to your class. If an attempt is then made to save your object, an exception will be thrown and the program will fail.[2]

Attribute-based programming is used extensively throughout .NET to describe how the Framework should treat code and data. With attributes you do not have to write any code; the Framework takes the appropriate action based on the attribute.  Security can be set through attributes. You can use attributes to have the Framework handle multithreading synchronization. Remoting of objects becomes straightforward through the use of attributes.

The compiler adds this **Serializable** attribute to the *metadata* of the **Customer** class to indicate that the Framework should save and restore the object. Metadata is additional information about the code and data within a .NET application. Metadata, a feature of the Common Language Runtime, provides such information about the code as:

- Version and locale information
- All the types
- Details about each type, including name, visibility, and so on
- Details about the members of each type, such as methods, the signatures of methods, and the like
- Attributes

Since metadata is stored in a programming-language-independent fashion with the code, not in a central store such as the Windows Registry, it makes .NET applications self-describing. The metadata can be queried at runtime to

---

[1]  The sample installation should have already built an instance that you can run. If not, double-click on the Visual Studio.NET solution file that has the .sln suffix. When Visual Studio comes up, hit Control-F5 to build and run the sample.

[2]  Comment out the **Serializable** attribute in the program (you can use the C/C++/* */ comment syntax) and see what happens.

get information about the code (such as the presence or absence of the **Serializable** attribute). You can extend the metadata by providing your own custom attributes.

In our example, the Framework can query the metadata to discover the structure of the **Customer** object in order to be able to save and restore it.

## Types

*Types* are at the heart of the programming model for the CLR. A type is analogous to a class in most object-oriented programming languages, providing an abstraction of data and behavior, grouped together. A type in the CLR contains:

Fields (data members)
Methods
Properties
Events

There are also built-in primitive types, such as integer and floating point numeric types, string, etc. We will discuss types under the guise of classes and value types when we cover C#.

## .NET Framework Class Library

The **Formatter** and **FileStream** classes are just two of more than 2500 classes in the .NET Framework that provide plumbing and system services for .NET applications. Some of the functionality provided by the .NET Framework includes:

- Base class library (basic functionality such as strings, arrays, and formatting)
- Networking
- Security
- Remoting
- Diagnostics
- I/O
- Database
- XML
- Web services that allow us to expose component interfaces over the Internet
- Web programming
- Windows User Interface

## Interface-Based Programming

Suppose you want to encrypt your data and therefore do not want to rely on the Framework's serialization. Your class can inherit from the **ISerializable** interface and provide the appropriate implementation. (We will discuss how to do this in a later chapter.) The Framework will then use your methods to save and restore the data.

How does the Framework know that you implemented the **ISerializable** interface? It can query the metadata related to the class to see if it implements the interface! The Framework can then use either its own algorithm or the class's code to serialize or deserialize the object.

Interface-based programming is used in .NET to allow your objects to provide implementations to standard functionality that can be used by the Framework. Interfaces also allow you to program using methods on the interface rather than methods on the objects. You can program without having to know the exact type of the object. For example, the formatters (such as the SOAP formatter used here) implement the **IFormatter** interface. Programs can be written using the **IFormatter** interface and thus are independent of any particular current (binary, SOAP) or future formatter and still work properly.

## Everything Is an Object

So if a type has metadata, the runtime can do all kinds of wonderful things. But does everything in .NET have metadata? Yes! Every type, whether it is user defined (such as **Customer**) or part of the Framework (such as **FileStream**), is a .NET object. All .NET objects have the same base class, the system's **Object** class. Hence everything that runs in .NET has a type and therefore has metadata.

In our example, the serialization code can walk through the **ArrayList** of customer objects and save each one as well as the array it belongs to, because the metadata allows it to understand the object's type and its logical structure.

## Common Type System

The .NET Framework has to make some assumptions about the nature of the types that will be passed to it. These assumptions are the *Common Type System* (CTS). The CTS defines the rules for the types and operations that the Common Language Runtime will support. It is the CTS that limits .NET classes to single implementation inheritance. Since the CTS is defined for a wide range of languages, not all languages need to support all features of the CTS.

The CTS makes it possible to guarantee type safety, which is critical for writing reliable and secure code. As we noted in the previous section, every object has a type and therefore every reference to an object points to a defined memory layout. If arbitrary pointer operations are not allowed, the only way to access an object is through its public methods and fields. Hence it's possible to verify an object's safety by analyzing the object. There is no need to know or analyze all the users of a class.

How are the rules of the CTS enforced? The Microsoft Intermediate Language (MSIL or IL) defines an instruction set that is used by all .NET compilers. This intermediate language is platform independent. The MSIL code can later be converted to a platform's native code. Verification for type safety can be done once based on the MSIL; it need not be done for every platform. Since everything is defined in terms of MSIL, we can be sure that the .NET Framework classes will work with all .NET languages. Design no longer dictates language choice; language choice no longer constrains design.

MSIL and the CTS make it possible for multiple languages to use the .NET Framework since their compilers produce MSIL. This one of the most visible differences between .NET and Java, which in fact share a great deal in philosophy.

## ILDASM

The Microsoft Intermediate Language Disassembler (ILDASM) can display the metadata and MSIL instructions associated with .NET code. It is a very useful tool both for debugging and for increasing your understanding of the .NET infrastructure. You can use ILDASM to examine the .NET Framework code itself.[3] Figure 2–1 shows a fragment of the MSIL code from the **Serialize** example, where we create two new customer objects and add them to the list.[4] The **newobj** instruction creates a new object reference using the constructor parameter.[5] **Stloc** stores the value in a local variable. **Ldloc** loads a local variable.[6] It is strongly recommended that you play with ILDASM and learn its features.

---

[3] ILDASM is installed on the Tools menu in Visual Studio.NET. It is also found in the Microsoft.NET\FrameworkSDK\Bin subdirectory. You can invoke it by double-clicking on its Explorer entry or from the command line. If you invoke it from the command line (or from VS.NET) you can use the /ADV switch to get some advanced options.

[4] Open Serialize.exe and Click on the plus (+) sign next to Test. Double-click on Main to bring up the MSIL for the Main routine.

[5] Technically it is not a parameter. IL is a stack-based language, and the constructor is a metadata token previously pushed on the stack.

[6] You can read all about MSIL in the ECMA documents, specifically the Partition III CIL Instruction Set.

```
Test::Main : void(string[])                                                    _|□|×|
IL_0000:  newobj    instance void [mscorlib]System.Collections.ArrayList::.ctor()
IL_0005:  stloc.0
IL_0006:  newobj    instance void Customer::.ctor()
IL_000b:  stloc.1
IL_000c:  ldloc.1
IL_000d:  ldstr     "Charles Darwin"
IL_0012:  stfld     string Customer::name
IL_0017:  ldloc.1
IL_0018:  ldc.i4.s  10
IL_001a:  conv.i8
IL_001b:  stfld     int64 Customer::id
IL_0020:  ldloc.0
IL_0021:  ldloc.1
IL_0022:  callvirt  instance int32 [mscorlib]System.Collections.ArrayList::Add(object)
IL_0027:  pop
IL_0028:  newobj    instance void Customer::.ctor()
IL_002d:  stloc.1
IL_002e:  ldloc.1
IL_002f:  ldstr     "Isaac Newton"
IL_0034:  stfld     string Customer::name
IL_0039:  ldloc.1
IL_003a:  ldc.i4.s  20
IL_003c:  conv.i8
IL_003d:  stfld     int64 Customer::id
IL_0042:  ldloc.0
IL_0043:  ldloc.1
IL_0044:  callvirt  instance int32 [mscorlib]System.Collections.ArrayList::Add(object)
IL_0049:  pop
IL_004a:  ldloc.0
```

**Figure 2–1**    *Code fragment from Serialize example.*

## Language Interoperability

Having all language compilers use a common intermediate language and common base class make it *possible* for languages to interoperate. But since all languages need not implement all parts of the CTS, it is certainly possible for one language to have a feature that another does not.

The *Common Language Specification* (CLS) defines a subset of the CTS representing the basic functionality that all .NET languages should implement if they are to interoperate with each other. This specification enables a class written in Visual Basic.NET to inherit from a class written in COBOL.NET or C#, or to make interlanguage debugging possible. An example of a CLS rule is that method calls need not support a variable number of arguments, even though such a construct can be expressed in MSIL.

CLS compliance applies only to publicly visible features. A class, for example, can have a private member that is non-CLS compliant and still be a base class for a class in another .NET language. For example, C# code should not define public and protected class names that differ only by case-sensitivity, since languages such as VB.NET are not case-sensitive. Private fields could have case-sensitive names.

Microsoft itself is providing several CLS-compliant languages: C#, Visual Basic.NET, and C++ with Managed Extensions. Third parties are providing additional languages (there are over a dozen so far). ActiveState is implementing Perl and Python. Fujitsu is implementing COBOL.

## Managed Code

In the serialization example a second instance of the Customer object was assigned to the same variable (**cust**) as the first instance without freeing it. None of the allocated storage in the example was ever deallocated. .NET uses automatic garbage collection to reclaim memory. When memory allocated on the heap becomes orphaned, or passes out of scope, it is placed on a list of memory locations to be freed. Periodically, the system runs a garbage collection thread that returns the memory to the heap.

By having automatic memory management the system has eliminated memory leakage, which is one of the most common programming errors. In most cases, memory allocation is much faster with garbage collection than with classic heap allocation schemes. Note that variables such as **cust** and **list** are object references, not the objects themselves. This makes the garbage collection possible.

Garbage collection is one of several services provided by the *Common Language Runtime* (CLR) to .NET programs.[7] Data that is under the control of the CLR garbage collection process is called managed data. Managed code is code that can use the services of the CLR. .NET compilers that produce MSIL can produce managed code.

Managed code is not automatically type safe. C++ provides the classic example. You can use the __gc attribute to make a class garbage collected. The C++ compiler will prevent such classes from using pointer arithmetic. Nonetheless, C++ cannot be reliably verified.[8]

Code is typically verified for type safety before compilation. This step is optional and can be skipped for trusted code. One of the most significant differences between verified and unverified code is that verified code cannot

---

[7] Technically, metadata, the CTS, the CLS, and the Virtual Execution System (VES) are also part of the CLR. We are using CLR here in the sense that it is commonly used. The VES loads and runs .NET programs and supports late binding. For more details refer to the Common Language Infrastructure (CLI) Partition I: Concepts and Architecture document submitted to ECMA. This document is loaded with the .NET Framework SDK.

[8] The most immediate reason for this is that the C Runtime Library (CRT) that is the start-up code for C++ programs was not converted to run under .NET because of time constraints. Even if this were to be done, however, there are two other obstacles to verifying C++ code. First, to ensure that the verification process can complete in a reasonable amount of time, the CLR language specifications require certain IL language patterns to be used and the managed C++ compiler would have to be changed to accommodate this. Second, after disallowing the C++ constructs that inhibit verification (like taking the address of a variable on the stack, or pointer arithmetic), you would wind up with a close approximation to the C# language.

use pointers.[9] Code that used pointers could subvert the Common Type System and access any memory location.

Type safe code cannot be subverted. A buffer overwrite is not able to corrupt other data structures or programs. Methods can only start and end at well-defined entry and exit points. Security policy can be applied to type safe code.[10] For example, access to certain files or user interface features can be allowed or denied. You can prevent the execution of code from unknown sources. You can prevent access to unmanaged code to prevent subversion of .NET security. Type safety also allows paths of execution of .NET code to be isolated from one another.[11]

## Assemblies

Another function of the CLR is to load and run .NET programs.

.NET programs are deployed as assemblies. An *assembly* is one or more EXEs or DLLs with associated metadata information. The metadata about the entire assembly is stored in the assembly's manifest. The manifest contains, for example, a list of the assemblies upon which this assembly is dependent.

In our Serialize example there is only file in the assembly, **serialize.exe**. That file contains the metadata as well as the code. Since the manifest is stored in the assembly and not in a separate file (like a type library or registry), the manifest cannot get out of sync with the assembly. Figure 2–2 shows the metadata in the manifest for this example.[12] Note the **assembly extern** statements that indicate the dependencies on the Framework assemblies **mscorlib** and **System.Runtime.Formatters.SOAP**. These statements also indicate the version of those assemblies that serialize.exe depends on.

Assemblies can be versioned, and the version is part of the name for the assembly. To version an assembly it needs a unique name. Public/private encryption keys are used to generate a unique (or strong) name.

Assemblies can be deployed either privately or publicly. For private deployment all the assemblies that an application needs are copied to the same directory as the application. If an assembly is to be publicly shared, an entry is made in the *Global Assembly Cache* (GAC) so that other assemblies can locate it. For assemblies put in the GAC a strong name is required. Since the version is part of the assembly name, multiple versions can be deployed

---

[9] It would not be correct to say that code written in MSIL is managed code. The CTS permits MSIL to have unmanaged pointers in order to work with unmanaged data in legacy code. The reverse is not true; unmanaged code cannot access managed data. The CLS prohibits unmanaged pointers.

[10] This is discussed in more detail in Chapter 12.

[11] See the discussion of Application Domains in Chapter 8.

[12] Open **serialize.exe** in ILDASM and double-click on the MANIFEST item.

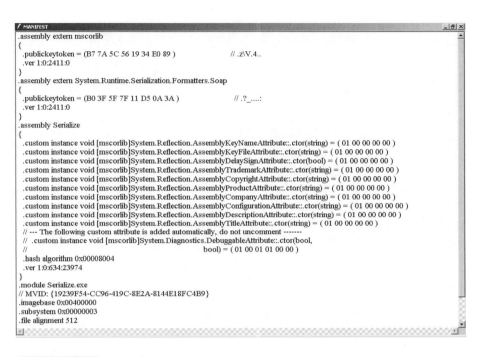

**Figure 2–2**     *Manifest for the Serialize assembly.*

side by side on the same machine without interfering with each other. Whether you use public or private deployment there is no more "DLL Hell."[13]

Assembly deployment with language interoperability makes component development almost effortless.

## JIT Compilation

Before executing on the target machine, MSIL has to be translated into the machine's native code. This can either be done before the application is called, or at runtime. At runtime, the translation is done by a just-in-time (JIT) compiler. The Native Image Generator (Ngen.exe) translates MSIL into native code so that it is already translated when the program is started.

The advantage of pretranslation is that optimizations can be performed. Optimizations are generally impractical with JIT because the time it takes to do the optimization can be longer than it takes to compile the code. Start-up time is also faster with pretranslation because no translation has to be done when the application starts.

---

[13] This is discussed in much more detail in Chapter 7.

The advantage of JIT is that it knows what the execution environment is when the program is run and can make better assumptions, such as register assignments, when it generates the code. Only the code that is actually executed is translated, code that never gets executed is never translated.

In the first release of .NET, the Native Image Generator and the JIT compiler use the same compiler. No optimizations are done for Ngen, its only current advantage is faster start-up. For this reason we do not discuss Ngen in this book.

## Performance

You may like the safety and ease-of-use features of managed code but you might be concerned about performance. Early assembly language programmers had similar concerns when high-level languages came out.

The CLR is designed with high performance in mind. With JIT compilation, the first time a method is encountered, the CLR performs verifications and then compiles the method into native code (which will contain safety features, such as array bounds checking). The next time the method is encountered, the native code executes directly. Memory management is designed for high performance. Allocation is almost instantaneous, just taking the next available storage from the managed heap. Deallocation is done by the garbage collector, which has an efficient multiple-generation algorithm.

You do pay a penalty when security checks have to be made that require a stack walk as we will explain in the Security chapter.

Web pages use compiled code, not interpreted code. As a result ASP.NET is much faster than ASP.

For 98% of the code that programmers write, any small loss in performance is far outweighed by the gains in reliability and ease of development. High performance server applications might have to use technologies such as ATL Server and C++.

## Summary

.NET solves the problems that have plagued Windows development in the past. There is one development paradigm for all languages. Design and programming language choices are no longer in conflict. Deployment is more rational and includes a versioning strategy. While we will talk more about it in later chapters, metadata, attribute-based security, code verification, and type-safe assembly isolation make developing secure applications much easier. The plumbing code for fundamental system services is provided, yet you can extend or replace it if you must.

The Common Language Runtime provides a solid base for developing applications of the future. The CLR is the foundation whose elements are the Common Type System, metadata, the Common Language Specification, and the Virtual Execution System (VES) that executes managed code.[14] As we shall see in future chapters, .NET makes it easier to develop Internet applications for both service providers and customer-based solutions. With the unified development platform .NET provides, it will be much easier than in the past for Microsoft or others to provide extensions.

All this is made possible by putting old technologies together in the CLR creatively: intermediate languages, type-safe verification, and of course, metadata. As you will see, metadata is used in many features in .NET.

We shall expand on these topics in the course of the book. We next cover the C# language. Depending on your knowledge of C#, you might be able to skim Chapters 3, 4, and 5. Chapter 4 introduces the Acme Travel Agency case study, which is used throughout the book. Chapter 5 covers important topics about the interaction of C# and the .NET Framework.

---

[14] The Base Class Libraries classes (BCL) are also part of the CLR.

# C# Overview for Sophisticated Programmers

*I*n this chapter we quickly cover the essentials of the C# language, which should be quite easy for you to learn if you have experience with C++ or Java. A "hello, world" program introduces the basic structure of C# programs. We then cover variables, operators, control structures, formatting, methods, and input/output. Classes are fundamental in C#, and we examine them in some detail. Besides the standard features, C# adds some convenience features, such as properties. We cover the essentials of data types in C#, which correspond to types in the Common Type System. We discuss the fundamental distinction between value and reference types and see how to convert between them using boxing and unboxing operations.

C# has a **string** type, and the **StringBuilder** class can be used for dynamically changing strings. We examine arrays in C# and some operations provided by the **System.Array** class. We then cover some additional topics concerning methods, including parameter passing, variable length parameter lists, method overloading, and operator overloading. We discuss exception handling in C# in some detail, including the use of user-defined exception classes and structured exception handling.

We conclude the chapter by looking at how you can have "unsafe" sections of C# code, which can be used to work with pointers for efficiency or for interoperating with legacy code.

## Hello World in C#

Whenever learning a new programming language, a good first step is to write and run a simple program that will display a single line of text. Such a program demonstrates the basic structure of the language, including output.

Here is "Hello, World" in C#. (See the **Hello** directory for this chapter.)

```
// Hello.cs

using System;

class Hello
{
    public static int Main(string[] args)
    {
        Console.WriteLine("Hello, World");
        return 0;

    }
}
```

## Compiling and Running (Command Line)

You can learn how to use the Microsoft Visual Studio.NET IDE (integrated development environment) in Appendix A. You can also use the command-line tools of the .NET Framework SDK. Be sure to get the environment variables set up properly, as described in the sidebar. To compile this program at the command line, enter the command

```
>csc Hello.cs
```

An executable file **Hello.exe** will be generated. To execute your program, type at the command line:

```
>Hello
```

The program will now execute, and you should see displayed the greeting:

```
Hello, World
```

### Setting Environment Variables

In order to run command-line tools such as the C# compiler using a simple name such as **csc** rather than a complete path, we must set certain environment variables. To do so we can use a batch file, **corvars.bat**, which can be found in the **bin** directory of the Framework SDK.

I experienced different behavior in different beta versions of the .NET Framework SDK. In one version the environment variables were set up automatically as part of the install, and in another version I had to use the **corvars.bat** file.

If you have Visual Studio.NET installed, you can ensure that the environment variables are set up by starting your command prompt session from Start | Programs | Microsoft Visual Studio.NET 7.0 | Microsoft Visual Studio Tools | Microsoft Visual Studio.NET Command Prompt.

## Program Structure

```
// Hello.cs

class Hello

{
...
}
```

Every C# program has at least one *class*. A class is the foundation of C#'s support of object-oriented programming. A class encapsulates data (represented by *variables*) and behavior (represented by *methods*). All of the code defining the class (its variables and methods) will be contained between the curly braces. We will discuss classes in detail later.

Note the comment at the beginning of the program. A line beginning with a double slash is present only for documentation purposes and is ignored by the compiler. C# files have the extension **.cs**.

```
// Hello.cs

...
```

An alternate form of comment is to use an opening /* and a closing */.

```
/* This is a comment
   that may be continued over
   several lines */
```

There is a distinguished class, which has a method whose name must be **Main**. The method should be **public** and **static**. An **int** exit code can be returned to the operating system. Note that in C# the file name need not be the same as the name of the class containing the **Main** method.

```
// Hello.cs

using System;

class Hello
{
    public static int Main(string[] args)
    {
        ...
        return 0;
    }
}
```

Use **void** if you do not return an exit code.

```
public static void Main(string[] args)
```

Command-line arguments are passed as an array of strings. The runtime will call this **Main** method—it is the entry point for the program. All the code of the **Main** method will be between the curly braces.

```
// Hello.cs

using System;

class Hello
{
    public static int Main(string[] args)
    {
        Console.WriteLine("Hello, World");
        return 0;
    }
}
```

Every method in C# has one or more *statements*. A statement is terminated by a semicolon. A statement may be spread out over several lines.

The **Console** class provides support for standard output and standard input. The method **WriteLine** displays a string, followed by a new line.

## Namespaces

Much standard functionality in C# is provided through many classes in the .NET Framework. Related classes are grouped into *namespaces*. Many useful classes, such as **Console**, are in the **System** namespace. The fully qualified name of a class is specified by the namespace followed by a dot followed by a class name.

```
System.Console
```

A **using** statement allows a class to be referred to by its class name alone.

```
// Hello.cs

using System;

class Hello
{
    public static int Main(string[] args)
    {
        Console.WriteLine("Hello, World");
        return 0;
    }
}
```

## Performing Calculations in C#

Our "Hello, World" program illustrated the basic structure of a C# program, but we will need a slightly more elaborate example to show the use of other basic programming constructs, such as variables, expressions, and control structures. Our next example is a simple calculator for an IRA account. We calculate the accumulation of deposits to an IRA of $2000.00 a year at 6% interest for 10 years, assuming that each deposit is made at the end of the year. Our calculation is performed two ways:

- In a loop, year by year, accumulating a total as we go
- Using a formula

The example program is in the folder **Ira\Step1.**

```
// Ira.cs - Step 1

using System;

class Ira
{
   public static int Main(string[] args)
   {
      int years = 10;
      decimal rate = 0.06m;
      decimal amount = 2000M;
      decimal interest;
      decimal total = 0m;
      Console.WriteLine("{0,4} {1,12} {2,12} {3,12}",
         "Year", "Amount", "Interest", "Total");
      for (int i = 1; i <= years; i++)
      {
         interest = total * rate;
         total += amount + interest;
         Console.WriteLine(
            "{0, -4} {1, 12:C} {2, 12:C} {3, 12:C}",
            i, amount, interest, total);
      }
      Console.WriteLine("\nTotal using formula = {0}",
         IraTotal(years, (double) rate, (double) amount));
      return 0;
   }
   public static double IraTotal(int years, double rate,
      double amount)
   {
      double total =
         amount * (Math.Pow(1 + rate, years) - 1) / rate;
      long total_in_cents = (long) Math.Round(total * 100);
      total = total_in_cents /100.0;
```

```
        return total;
    }
}
```

If you compile and run it, you will see this output:

```
Year        Amount      Interest        Total
1        $2,000.00        $0.00    $2,000.00
2        $2,000.00      $120.00    $4,120.00
3        $2,000.00      $247.20    $6,367.20
4        $2,000.00      $382.03    $8,749.23
5        $2,000.00      $524.95   $11,274.19
6        $2,000.00      $676.45   $13,950.64
7        $2,000.00      $837.04   $16,787.68
8        $2,000.00    $1,007.26   $19,794.94
9        $2,000.00    $1,187.70   $22,982.63
10       $2,000.00    $1,378.96   $26,361.59

Total using formula = 26361.59
```

## Variables

In C# variables are of a specific data type. Some common types are **int** for integers and **double** for floating-point numbers. C# has the **decimal** data type, which has a high degree of precision, suitable for monetary calculations.

You must declare and initialize variables before you can use them.

```
int years = 10;    // reserves space and assigns
                   // an initial value
decimal interest;  // reserves space but does
                   // not initialize it to any value
```

If an initial value is not specified in the declaration, the variable must be initialized in code before it can be used. We will discuss initialization later in the chapter.

Variables must be either local within a method or members of a class. There are no global variables in C#.

## Literals

A *literal* is used when you explicitly write a value for a variable in a program. An integer literal is represented by either an ordinary decimal integer or a hexadecimal integer. A floating-point or decimal literal is represented by a number with a decimal point or by exponential notation. You may influence the type[1] that is used for storing a literal by a suffix. The suffix **f** or **F**

---

[1] We discuss C# types, such as **float**, **double**, and **decimal**, later in the chapter.

indicates single precision floating point. The suffix **d** or **D** indicates double precision floating point. The suffix **m** or **M** indicates decimal (think money).

```
decimal rate = 0.06m;
decimal amount = 2000M;
```

There are two forms for string literals. Escape sequences are not processed for string literals that are prefixed with **@**.

```
string file1 ="c:\\test1.txt";
string file2 = @"c:\test2.txt";
```

## C# Operators and Expressions

You can combine variables and literals via operators to form expressions. The C# operators are similar to those in C and C++, having similar precedence and associativity rules. There are three kinds of operators,

- *Unary* operators take one operand and use prefix notation (e.g., **−−a**) or postfix notation (e.g., **a++**).
- **Binary** operators take two operands and use infix notation (e.g., **a + b**).
- The one *ternary* operator **?:** takes three operands and uses infix notation (e.g., **expr ? x : y**).

Operators are applied in the precedence order shown in Table 3–1. For operators of the same precedence, order is determined by associativity.

- The assignment operator is right-associative (operations are performed from right to left).
- All other binary operators are left-associative (operations are performed from left to right).

Precedence and associativity can be controlled by parentheses; what is done first is shown as the primary operator **(x)** in the precedence table. C# has **checked** and **unchecked** operators, which will be discussed later.

| **Table 3–1** | *Operator Precedence in C#* |

| Category | Operators |
|----------|-----------|
| Primary | `(x)  x.y  f(x)  a[x]  x++  x–  new  typeof` `sizeof  checked  unchecked` |
| Unary | `+  -  !  ~  ++x  --x  (T)x` |
| Multiplicative | `*  /  %` |
| Additive | `+  -` |
| Shift | `<<  >>` |
| Relational | `<  >  <=  >=  is  as` |
| Equality | `==  !=` |
| Logical AND | `&` |
| Logical XOR | `^` |
| Logical OR | `|` |
| Conditional AND | `&&` |
| Conditional OR | `||` |
| Conditional | `?:` |
| Assignment | `=  *=  /=  %=  +=  -=  <<=  >>=  &=  ^=` `|=` |

## Output and Formatting

The **Console** class in the **System** namespace supports two simple methods for performing output:

- **WriteLine** writes out a string followed by a new line.
- **Write** writes out just the string without the new line.

You can write out other data types by relying on the **ToString** method of **System.Object**, which will provide a string representation of any data type. We will discuss the root class **System.Object** in Chapter 5, where you will also see how to override **ToString** for your own custom data type. You can use the string concatenation operator **+** to build up an output string.

```
int x = 24;
int y = 5;
int z = x * y;
Console.Write("Product of " + x + " and " + y);
Console.WriteLine(" is " + z);
```

The output is all on one line:

```
Product of 24 and 5 is 120
```

## PLACEHOLDERS

A more convenient way to build up an output string is to use *placeholders* {0}, {1}, and so on. An equivalent way to do the output shown above is

```
Console.WriteLine("Product of {0} and {1} is {2}", x,y,z);
```

The program **OutputDemo** illustrates the output operations just discussed.

We will generally use placeholders for our output from now on. Placeholders can be combined with formatting characters to control output format.

## FORMAT STRINGS

C# has extensive formatting capabilities, which you can control through placeholders and format strings.

- Simple placeholders: {n}, where n is 0, 1, 2, . . . , indicating which variable to insert
- Control width: {n,w}, where w is width (positive for right-justified and negative for left-justified) of the inserted variable
- Format string: {n:S}, where S is a format string indicating how to display the variable
- Width and format string: {n,w:S}

A format string consists of a format character followed by an optional precision specifier. Table 3–2 shows the available format characters.

**Table 3–2**     *C# Format Characters*

| Format Character | Meaning |
|---|---|
| C | Currency (locale specific) |
| D | Decimal integer |
| E | Exponential (scientific) |
| F | Fixed point |
| G | General (E or F) |
| N | Number with embedded commas |
| X | Hexadecimal |

## SAMPLE FORMATTING CODE

The program **FormatDemo** illustrates formatting. Our sample program **Ira\Step1** provides another example. The header uses width specifiers, and the output inside the loop uses width specifiers and the currency format character.

```
. . .
Console.WriteLine("{0,4} {1,12} {2,12} {3,12}",
   "Year", "Amount", "Interest", "Total");
for (int i = 1; i <= years; i++)
{
   interest = total * rate;
   total += amount + interest;
   Console.WriteLine(
      "{0, -4} {1, 12:C} {2, 12:C} {3, 12:C}",
      i, amount, interest, total);
}
. . .
```

## Control Structures

The preceding code fragment illustrates a **for** loop. The C# control structures include the familiar control structures of the C family of languages,

- if
- while
- do
- for
- switch
- break
- continue
- return
- goto

These all have standard semantics, except for *switch*, which is less error-prone in C#. There are several other control statements in C#:

- There is a **foreach** loop, which we will discuss later in connection with arrays and collections.
- The **throw** statement is used with exceptions. We will discuss exceptions later in this chapter.
- The **lock** statement can be used to enforce synchronization in multi-threading situations. We will discuss multithreading in Chapter 8.

### SWITCH STATEMENT

In C#, after a particular case statement is executed, control does not automatically continue to the next statement. You must explicitly specify the next statement, typically by a **break** or **goto** *label*. (As in C and C++, you may call for identical handling of several cases by having empty statements for all the case labels except the last one.) In C# you may also switch on a **string** data type. The program **SwitchDemo** illustrates use of the **switch** statement in C#.

```
   ...
   switch(scores[i])
   {
      case 1:
         Console.Write("Very ");
         goto case 2;        // cannot fall through
      case 2:
         Console.WriteLine("Low");
         break;
      case 3:
         Console.WriteLine("Medium");
         break;
      case 4:
      case 5:
         Console.WriteLine("High");
         break;
      default:
         Console.WriteLine("Special Case");
         break;
   }
   ...
```

## Methods

Our **Ira\Step1** example program has a method **IraTotal** for computing the total IRA accumulation by use of a formula. In C# *every* function is a method of some class; there are no freestanding functions. If the method does not refer to any instance variables of the class, the method can be *static*. We will discuss instance data of a class later in this chapter. Since the method is accessed only from within the class, it is designated as *private*.

Note the use of the **Pow** and **Round** methods of the **Math** class, which is another class in the **System** namespace. These methods are static methods. To call a static method from outside the class in which it is defined, place the name of the class followed by a period before the method name. In C# you cannot employ the alternative C++ style of using an instance name to qualify a static method.

```
...
private static double IraTotal(int years, double rate,
   double amount)
{
   double total =
      amount * (Math.Pow(1 + rate, years) - 1) / rate;
      long total_in_cents = (long) Math.Round(total * 100);
   total = total_in_cents /100.0;
   return total;
}
...
```

## Console Input in C#

Our first **Ira** program is not too useful, because the data are hardcoded. To perform the calculation for different data, you would have to edit the source file and recompile. What we really want to do is allow the user of the program to enter the data at runtime.

An easy, uniform way to do input for various data types is to read the data as a string and then convert to the desired data type. Use the **ReadLine** method of the **System.Console** class to read in a string. Use the **ToXxxx** methods of the **System.Convert** class to convert the data to the type you need.

```
Console.Write("amount: ");
string data = Console.ReadLine();
amount = Convert.ToDecimal(data);
```

Although console input in C# is fairly simple, we can make it even easier using object-oriented programming. We can encapsulate the details of input in an easy-to-use wrapper class, **InputWrapper** (which is not part of the .NET Framework class library).

### USING THE INPUTWRAPPER CLASS

In C# you instantiate a class by using the **new** keyword.

```
InputWrapper iw = new InputWrapper();
```

This code creates the object instance **iw** of the **InputWrapper** class.

The **InputWrapper** class wraps interactive input for several basic data types. The supported data types are **int**, **double**, **decimal**, and **string**. Methods **getInt**, **getDouble**, **getDecimal**, and **getString** are provided to read those types from the command line. A prompt string is passed as an input parameter. The directory **InputWrapper** contains the files **InputWrapper.cs**, which implements the class, and **TestInputWrapper.cs**, which tests the class. (For convenience, we provide the file **InputWrapper.cs** in each project where we use it.)

You can use the **InputWrapper** class without knowing its implementation. With such encapsulation, complex functionality can be hidden by an easy-to-use interface. (A listing of the **InputWrapper** class is in the next section.)

Here is the code for **Ira\Step2**. We read in the deposit amount, the interest rate, and the number of years, and we compute the IRA accumulation year by year. The first input is done directly, and then we use the **InputWrapper** class. The bolded code illustrates how to use the **InputWrapper** class. Instantiate an **InputWrapper** object **iw** by using **new**. Prompt for and obtain input data by calling the appropriate **getXXX** method.

```csharp
// Ira.cs - Step 2

using System;

class Ira
{
    public static int Main(string[] args)
    {
        InputWrapper iw = new InputWrapper();
        decimal amount;    // annual deposit amount
        decimal rate;      // interest rate
        int years;         // number of years
        decimal total;     // total accumulation
        decimal interest;  // interest in a year
        Console.Write("amount: ");
        string data = Console.ReadLine();
        amount = Convert.ToDecimal(data);
        rate = iw.getDecimal("rate: ");
        years = iw.getInt("years: ");
        total = 0m;
        Console.WriteLine("{0,4} {1,12} {2,12} {3,12}",
            "Year", "Amount", "Interest", "Total");
        for (int i = 1; i <= years; i++)
        {
            interest = total * rate;
            total += amount + interest;
            Console.WriteLine(
                "{0, -4} {1, 12:C} {2, 12:C} {3, 12:C}",
                i, amount, interest, total);
        }
        Console.WriteLine("\nTotal using formula = {0}",
            IraTotal(years, (double) rate, (double) amount));
        return 0;
    }
    private static double IraTotal(int years, double rate,
        double amount)
    {
        double total =
            amount * (Math.Pow(1 + rate, years) - 1) / rate;
        long total_in_cents = (long) Math.Round(total * 100);
        total = total_in_cents /100.0;
        return total;
    }
}
```

## COMPILING MULTIPLE FILES

The program in **Ira\Step2** is our first example of the common situation of a program with multiple files (in this case, just two: **Ira.cs** and **InputWrapper.cs**). It is easy to compile multiple files at the command line.

```
> csc /out:Ira.exe *.cs
```

This will compile all the files in the current directory. You should use the **/out** option to specify the name of the output file.

If multiple classes contain a **Main** method, you can use the **/main** command-line option to specify which class contains the **Main** method that you want to use as the entry point into the program.

```
>csc /main:Ira /out:Ira.exe *.cs
```

## INPUTWRAPPER CLASS IMPLEMENTATION

The **InputWrapper** class is implemented in the file **InputWrapper.cs**. You should find the code reasonably intuitive, given what you already know about classes.

```
// InputWrapper.cs
//
// Class to wrap simple stream input
// Datatype supported:
//      int
//      double
//      decimal
//      string

using System;

class InputWrapper
{
   public int getInt(string prompt)
   {
      Console.Write(prompt);
      string buf = Console.ReadLine();
      return Convert.ToInt32(buf);
   }
   public double getDouble(string prompt)
   {
      Console.Write(prompt);
      string buf = Console.ReadLine();
      return Convert.ToDouble(buf);
   }
   public decimal getDecimal(string prompt)
   {
      Console.Write(prompt);
      string buf = Console.ReadLine();
```

```
      return Convert.ToDecimal(buf);
   }
   public string getString(string prompt)
   {
      Console.Write(prompt);
      string buf = Console.ReadLine();
      return buf;
   }
}
```

Note that, unlike the method **IraTotal**, the methods of the **InputWrapper** class are used outside of the class so they are marked as *public*.

If bad input data is presented, an *exception* will be thrown. Exceptions are discussed later in this chapter.

# Classes

In this section we carefully examine the C# *class*, which is fundamental to programming in C#. For illustration we introduce two classes, **Customer** and **Hotel**, which will be elaborated in a case study that is used throughout the book. We will introduce the case study itself in Chapter 4.

If you are a Java programmer, you will find the C# class to be quite familiar, and you should be able to skim this section. C++ programmers must read much more carefully. C# differs from C++ with respect to object instantiation, assignment, and destruction. Our pace is somewhat more leisurely in this section, because classes are so fundamental to programming in C#.

## Classes as Structured Data

C# defines primitive data types that are built into the language. Data types, such as **int** and **decimal**, can be used to represent simple data. C# provides the *class* mechanism to represent more complex forms of data. Through a class, you can build up structured data out of simpler elements, which are called data members, or *fields*. (See **TestCustomer\Step1**.)

```
// Customer.cs - Step 1

public class Customer
{
   public int CustomerId;
   public string FirstName;
   public string LastName;
   public string EmailAddress;
   public Customer(string first, string last, string email)
   {
```

```
        FirstName = first;
        LastName = last;
        EmailAddress = email;
    }
}
```

**Customer** is now a new data type. A customer has a **CustomerId**, a **FirstName**, a **LastName**, and an **EmailAddress**.

## CLASSES AND OBJECTS

A class represents a "kind of," or type of, data. It is analogous to the built-in types like **int** and **decimal**. A class can be thought of as a template from which individual instances can be created. An instance of a class is called an object. Just as you can have several individual integers that are instances of **int**, you can have several customers that are instances of **Customer**. The fields, such as **CustomerId** and **FirstName** in our example, are sometimes also called *instance variables*.

## REFERENCES

There is a fundamental distinction between the primitive data types and the extended data types that can be created using classes. When you declare a variable of a primitive data, you are allocating memory and creating the instance.

```
int x;   // 4 bytes of memory have been allocated
```

When you declare a variable of a class type (an *object reference*), you are only obtaining memory for a *reference* to an object of the class type. No memory is allocated for the object itself, which may be quite large. This behavior is very different from that of C++, where declaring an object in this way causes an instance to be created, using the default constructor. The behavior is identical to what happens in Java.

```
Customer cust; // cust is a reference to a Customer object
               // The object itself does not yet exist
```

## CONSTRUCTORS

Through a constructor, you can initialize individual objects in any way you wish. Besides initializing instance data, you can perform other appropriate initializations (e.g., open a file).

A constructor is like a special method that is automatically called when an object is created via the **new** keyword. A constructor

- has no return type
- has the same name as the class
- should usually have **public** access
- may take parameters, which are passed when invoking **new**

In the calling program, you use **new** to instantiate object instances, and you pass desired values as parameters.

## DEFAULT CONSTRUCTOR

If you do not define a constructor in your class, C# will implicitly create one for you. It is called the *default constructor* and takes no arguments. The default constructor will assign instance data, using any assignments in the class definition. Fields without an initializer are assigned default values (0 for numerical data types, empty string for **string**, and so on). The default constructor is called when an object instance is created with **new** and no parameters. If you provide code for any constructor in your class, you must explicitly define a default constructor with no arguments, if you want one.

## INSTANTIATING AND USING AN OBJECT

You instantiate an object by the **new** operator, which will cause a constructor to be invoked.

```
cust = new Customer("Rocket",
                    "Squirrel",
                    "rocky@frosbitefalls.com");
// Customer object now exists and cust is a reference to it
```

Once an object exists, you work with it, including accessing its fields and methods. Our simple **Customer** class at this point has no methods, only four fields. You access fields and methods using a dot.

```
cust.CustomerId = 1; // all fields have now been assigned
```

**TestCustomer\Step0** provides a simple test program to exercise the **Customer** class. Note that an unassigned field of a class receives a default value, such as 0, when an object is instantiated.

## ASSIGNING OBJECT REFERENCES

**TestCustomer\Step1** provides a more complete test program to exercise the **Customer** class. Two object instances are created, an assignment is made of one object reference to another, and a field is assigned a value.

```
// TestCustomer.cs

using System;

public class TestCustomer
{
    public static void Main()
    {
        Customer cust1, cust2;
        cust1 = new Customer("Rocket",
```

```
                                   "Squirrel",
                                   "rocky@frosbitefalls.com");
        cust1.CustomerId = 1;
        cust2 = new Customer("Bullwinkle",
                             "Moose",
                             "moose@wossamotta.edu");
        cust2.CustomerId = 2;
        ShowCustomer("cust1", cust1);
        ShowCustomer("cust2", cust2);
        cust1 = cust2;
        cust1.EmailAddress = "bob@podunk.edu";
        ShowCustomer("cust1", cust1);
        ShowCustomer("cust2", cust2);
    }
    private static void ShowCustomer(string label,
                                     Customer cust)
    {
        Console.WriteLine("---- {0} ----", label);
        Console.WriteLine("CustomerId = {0}",
                          cust.CustomerId);
        Console.WriteLine("FirstName = {0}", cust.FirstName);
        Console.WriteLine("LastName = {0}", cust.LastName);
        Console.WriteLine("EmailAddress = {0}",
                          cust.EmailAddress);
    }
}
```

Figure 3–1 shows the object references **cust1** and **cust2** and the data they refer to after the objects have been instantiated and the **CustomerId** field has been assigned.

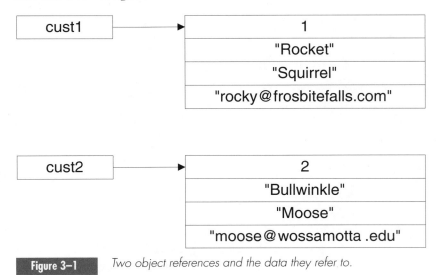

**Figure 3–1**    *Two object references and the data they refer to.*

When you assign an object variable, you are assigning only the reference; *there is no copying of data.*[2] Figure 3–2 shows both object references and their data after the assignment:

```
cust1 = cust2; // cust1 and cust2 now refer to same object
```

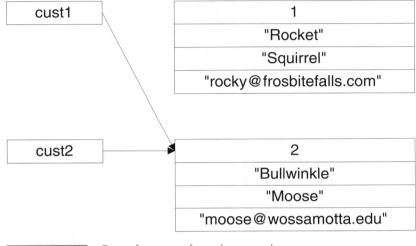

 **Figure 3–2**    *Two references refer to the same data.*

Now when you assign a new value a field of one object,

```
cust1.EmailAddress = "bob@podunk.edu";
```

you will see the same data through both object references. Here is the output from running **TestCustomer\Step1**.

```
---- cust1 ----
CustomerId = 1
FirstName = Rocket
LastName = Squirrel
EmailAddress = rocky@frosbitefalls.com
---- cust2 ----
CustomerId = 2
FirstName = Bullwinkle
LastName = Moose
EmailAddress = moose@wossamotta.edu
---- cust1 ----
CustomerId = 2
FirstName = Bullwinkle
LastName = Moose
EmailAddress = bob@podunk.edu
```

---

[2] C and C++ programmers will recognize assignment of references as similar to assignment of pointers.

```
---- cust2 ----
CustomerId = 2
FirstName = Bullwinkle
LastName = Moose
EmailAddress = bob@podunk.edu
```

### GARBAGE COLLECTION

Through the assignment of a reference, an object may become orphaned. Objects may also be orphaned when they pass out of scope. Such an orphan object (or "garbage") takes up memory in the computer, which can now never be referenced. In Figure 3–2 the customer with **CustomerId** of 1 is now garbage.

The Common Language Runtime automatically reclaims the memory of unreferenced objects. This process is known as *garbage collection*. Garbage collection takes up some execution time, but it is a great convenience for programmers, helping to avoid a common program error known as a *memory leak*. Garbage collection is discussed in more detail in Chapter 8.

## Methods

Typically, a class will specify *behavior* as well as data. A class *encapsulates* data and behavior in a single entity. A method specifies the behavior and consists of

- An access specifier, typically **public** or **private**
- A return type (can be **void** if the method does not return data)
- A method name, which can be any legal C# identifier
- A parameter list, enclosed by parentheses, which specifies data that is passed to the method (can be empty if no data is passed)
- A method body, enclosed by curly braces, which contains the C# code that the method will execute

```
public void RaisePrice(decimal amount)
{
   rate += amount;
}
```

In this example the return type is **void** (no data is passed back), the method name is **RaisePrice**, the parameter list consists of a single parameter of type **decimal**, and the body contains one line of code that increments the member variable **rate** by the value that is passed in.

**RaisePrice** is a method in the **Hotel** class. The initial version of the **Hotel** class with a simple test program is in the folder **TestHotel\Step1**.

## PUBLIC AND PRIVATE

Fields and methods of a C# class can be specified as **public** or **private**. Normally, you declare fields as **private**. A private field can be accessed only from within the class, not from outside.

```
public class Hotel
{
    private string city;
    private string name;
    private int number = 50;     // legal in C#
    private decimal rate;
    . . .
```

Note that in C# you can initialize fields when they are declared. This kind of initialization is not legal in C++.

Methods may be declared as either **public** or **private**. Public methods are called from outside the class and are used to perform calculations and to manipulate the private data. You may also provide public "accessor" methods to provide access to private fields.

```
    . . .
    public decimal GetRate()
    {
        return rate;
    }
    public void SetRate(decimal val)
    {
        rate = val;
    }
    . . .
```

You may also have private methods, which can be thought of as "helper functions" for use within the class. Rather than duplicating code in several places, you may create a private method, which will be called wherever it is needed. An example is the **ShowHotel** method in **TestHotel.cs**.

## THIS

Sometimes it is convenient within code for a method to be able to access the current object reference. C#, like C++, defines a keyword **this**, which is a special variable that always refers to the current object instance. With **this** you can then refer to the instance variables. The **Hotel** class has a constructor to initialize its instance data with values passed as parameters. We can make use of the same names for parameters and fields and remove ambiguity by using the **this** variable. Here is the code for the constructor:

```
    public Hotel(string city, string name, int number,
            decimal rate)
```

```
   {
      this.city = city;
      this.name = name;
      this.number = number;
      this.rate = rate;
   }
```

## SAMPLE PROGRAM

The program **TestHotel\Step1** illustrates all the features we have discussed so far. Here is the class definition:

```
// Hotel.cs - Step 1

public class Hotel
{
   private string city;
   private string name;
   private int number = 50;    // legal in C#
   private decimal rate;
   public Hotel(string city, string name, int number,
               decimal rate)
   {
      this.city = city;
      this.name = name;
      this.number = number;
      this.rate = rate;
   }
   public Hotel()
   {
   }
   public string GetCity()
   {
      return city;
   }
   public string GetName()
   {
      return name;
   }
   public int GetNumber()
   {
      return number;
   }
   public void SetNumber(int val)
   {
      number = val;
   }
   public decimal GetRate()
   {
      return rate;
```

```
    }
    public void SetRate(decimal val)
    {
        rate = val;
    }
    public void RaisePrice(decimal amount)
    {
        rate += amount;
    }
}
```

Here is the test program:

```
// Test.cs - Step 1

using System;

public class TestHotel
{
    public static void Main()
    {
        Hotel generic = new Hotel();
        ShowHotel(generic);
        Hotel ritz = new Hotel("Atlanta", "Ritz", 100, 95m);
        ShowHotel(ritz);
        ritz.RaisePrice(50m);
        ritz.SetNumber(125);
        ShowHotel(ritz);
    }
    private static void ShowHotel(Hotel hotel)
    {
        Console.WriteLine(
            "{0} {1}: number = {2}, rate = {3:C}",
            hotel.GetCity(), hotel.GetName(),
            hotel.GetNumber(), hotel.GetRate());
    }
}
```

Here is the output:

```
: number = 50, rate = $0.00
Atlanta Ritz: number = 100, rate = $95.00
Atlanta Ritz: number = 125, rate = $145.00
```

## Properties

The encapsulation principle leads us to typically store data in private fields and to provide access to this data through public accessor methods that allow us to set and get values. For example, in the **Hotel** class we provided a method **GetCity** to access the private field **city**. You don't need any special syntax; you can simply provide methods and call these methods what you want, typically **GetXXX** and **SetXXX**.

C# provides a special *property* syntax that simplifies user code. You can access a private field as if it were a public member. Here is an example of using a **Number** property of our **Hotel** class.

```
ritz.Number = 125;
Console.WriteLine("There are now {0} rooms", ritz.Number);
```

As you can see, the syntax using the property is a little more concise. Properties were popularized in Visual Basic and are now part of .NET and available in selected other .NET languages, such as C#. The program **TestHotel\Step2,** illustrates implementing and using several properties, **City**, **Name**, **Number**, and **Rate**. The first two properties are read-only (only **get** defined), and the other properties are read/write (both **get** and **set**). It is also possible to have a write-only property (only **set** defined). Here is the code for the properties **Name** (read-only) and **Number** (read-write) in the second version of the **Hotel** class. Notice the syntax and the C# keyword **value** to indicate the new value of the field.

```
// Hotel.cs - Step 2

public class Hotel
{
    private string city;
    private string name;
    private int number;
    private decimal rate;
    ...
    public string Name
    {
        get
        {
            return name;
        }
    }
    public int Number
    {
        get
        {
            return number;
        }
        set
        {
            number = value;
        }
    }
    ...
```

## Static Fields and Methods

In C# a field normally is assigned on a *per-instance* basis, with a unique value for each object instance of the class. Sometimes it is useful to have a single value associated with the entire class. This type of field is called a **static** field. Like instance data members, static data members can be either **public** or **private**. To access a public static member, you use the dot notation, but in place of an object reference before the dot you use the name of the class.

### STATIC METHODS

A method may also be declared **static**. A static method can be called without instantiating the class. An example we have already seen is the **Main** method in a class, which the runtime system is able to call without instantiating an object. The **Main** method must always be static.

You call a static method by using the dot notation, with the class name in front of the dot. Because you must call a static method without an instance, a static method can use only static data members and not instance data members.

Static methods may be declared **public** or **private**. A private static method, like other private methods, may be used as a helper function within a class, but not called from outside.

### SAMPLE PROGRAM

Our previous **Customer** class relied on the user of the class to assign a **CustomerId** for the customer. A better approach is to encapsulate assigning an id within the class itself, so that a unique id will be automatically generated every time a new **Customer** object is created. It is easy to implement such a scheme by using a static field **nextCustId**, which is used to assign an id. Every time the id is assigned, **nextCustId** is incremented. **TestCustomer\Step2** demonstrates this solution and also illustrates the use of a static method. Here is the code defining the **Customer** class:

```
// Customer.cs - Step 2

public class Customer
{
    public int CustomerId;
    public string FirstName;
    public string LastName;
    public string EmailAddress;
    static private int nextCustId = 1;
    public Customer(string first, string last, string email)
    {
        CustomerId = nextCustId++;
        FirstName = first;
```

```
        LastName = last;
        EmailAddress = email;
    }
    public static int GetNextId()
    {
        return nextCustId;
    }
}
```

Here is the test program:

```
// TestCustomer.cs - Step 2

using System;

public class TestCustomer
{
    public static void Main()
    {
        Console.WriteLine("next id = {0}",
                        Customer.GetNextId());
        Customer cust1, cust2;
        cust1 = new Customer("John", "Doe",
                        "john@rocky.com");
        cust2 = new Customer("Mary", "Smith",
                        "mary@moose.edu");
        ShowCustomer("cust1", cust1);
        ShowCustomer("cust2", cust2);
    }
    private static void ShowCustomer(string label,
                                    Customer cust)
    ...
```

Note that the static method **GetNextId** is accessed through the *class* **Customer** and not through an object reference such as **cust1**. This program also illustrates the fact that **Main** is a static method and is invoked by the runtime without an instance of the **TestCustomer** class being created. Since there is no instance, any method of **TestCustomer** called from within **Main** must also be declared **static**, as illustrated by **ShowCustomer**.

## Static Constructor

Besides having static fields and static methods, a class may also have a *static constructor*. A static constructor is called only once, before any object instances have been created. A static constructor is defined by prefixing the constructor with **static**. A static constructor mut take no parameters and has no access modifier (such as **public** or **private**).

In a language such as C++, where there can be global variables not attached to any class, you may initialize a library through the constructor for a global object. In C# there are no such freestanding global objects, but you can achieve similar initialization through use of a static constructor. As a somewhat whimsical example of a static constructor, consider the **StaticWorld** program, which provides an alternative implementation of "Hello, World."

```
// StaticWorld.cs

public class Hello
{
    static Hello()
    {
        System.Console.Write("Hello, ");
    }
    public static void World()
    {
        System.Console.WriteLine("World");
    }
}

public class World
{
    public static void Main(string[] args)
    {
        Hello.World();
    }
}
```

## Constant and Readonly Fields

If you want to make sure that a variable always has the same value, you can assign the value via an initializer and use the **const** modifier. Such a constant is automatically static, and you will access it from outside the class through the class name.

Another situation may call for a one-time initialization at runtime, and after that the value cannot be changed. You can achieve this effect through a **readonly** field. Such a field may be either an instance member or a static member. In the case of an instance member, it will be assigned in an ordinary constructor. In the case of a static member, it will be assigned in a static constructor.

The program **ConstantHotel** illustrates the use of both **const** and **readonly**. In both cases, you will get a compiler error if you try to modify the value.

```
// ConstantHotel.cs

public class Hotel
{
```

```
   public const decimal rate = 100m;
   public readonly string name;
   public Hotel(string name)
   {
       this.name = name;
   }
}
```

Here is the test program:

```
// TestHotel.cs

using System;

public class TestHotel
{
   public static void Main()
   {
      Console.WriteLine("rate = {0:C}", Hotel.rate);
      //Hotel.rate = 150m;          // illegal
      Hotel hotel = new Hotel("Ritz");
      Console.WriteLine("hotel name = {0}", hotel.name);
      //hotel.name = "Sheraton";    // illegal
   }
}
```

Here is the output:

```
rate = $100.00
hotel name = Ritz
```

## C# Type System

In C# there is a fundamental distinction between *value* types and *reference* types. Value types have storage allocated immediately on the stack when the variable is declared. Reference types have storage allocated on the heap, and the variable is only a reference to the actual data, which can be allocated later.

We have been looking at classes in some detail. A class defines a reference type. In this section we survey the entire C# type system, including simple types such as **int** and **decimal**. In C# a **struct** has many similarities to a **class** but is a value type. Another important kind of value type in C# is an **enum**.

We examine later several other important types, including string, array, interface, and delegate. We will discuss the default values that get assigned to variables when there is not an explicit initialization. We will see that all types in C# are rooted in a fundamental base class called **object**. In C# "everything is an object," and value types are transparently converted to object references as needed through a process known as *boxing*. The inverse process, *unboxing*, returns an object to the value type from which it came.

## Overview of Types in C#

In C# there are three kinds of types:

* Value types
* Reference types
* Pointer types

### VALUE TYPES

Value types directly contain their data. Each variable of a value type has its own copy of the data. Value types typically are allocated on the stack and are automatically destroyed when the variable goes out of scope. Value types include the simple types like **int** and **decimal**, structures, and enumeration types.

### REFERENCE TYPES

Reference types do not contain data directly but only refer to data. Variables of reference types store references to data, called objects. Two different variables can reference the same object. Reference types are allocated on the *managed heap* and eventually get destroyed through a process known as *garbage collection*.

Reference types include **string**, **object**, class types, array types, interfaces, and delegates.

### POINTER TYPES

Pointer types are used only in unsafe code and will be discussed later in this chapter.

## Value Types

In this section we survey all the value types, including the simple types, structures, and enumerations.

### SIMPLE TYPES

The simple data types are general-purpose value data types, including numeric, character, and Boolean.

* The **sbyte** data type is an 8-bit signed integer.
* The **byte** data type is an 8-bit unsigned integer.

- The **short** data type is a 16-bit signed integer.
- The **ushort** data type is a 16-bit unsigned integer.
- The **int** data type is a 32-bit signed integer.
- The **uint** data type is a 32-bit unsigned integer.
- The **long** data type is a 64-bit signed integer.
- The **ulong** data type is a 64-bit unsigned integer.
- The **char** data type is a Unicode character (16 bits).
- The **float** data type is a single-precision floating point.
- The **double** data type is a double-precision floating point.
- The **bool** data type is a Boolean (**true** or **false**).
- The **decimal** data type is a decimal type with 28 significant digits (typically used for financial purposes).

## TYPES IN SYSTEM NAMESPACE

There is an exact correspondence between the simple C# types and types in the **System** namespace. C# reserved words are simply aliases for the corresponding types in the **System** namespace. Table 3–3 shows this correspondence.

**Table 3–3**    *Types in C# and the System Namespace*

| C# Reserved Word | Type in System Namespace |
|---|---|
| sbyte | System.SByte |
| byte | System.Byte |
| short | System.Int16 |
| ushort | System.UInt16 |
| int | System.Int32 |
| uint | System.UInt32 |
| long | System.Int64 |
| ulong | System.UInt64 |
| char | System.Char |
| float | System.Single |
| double | System.Double |
| bool | System.Boolean |
| decimal | System.Decimal |

## STRUCTURES

A **struct** is a value type which can group heterogeneous types together. It can also have constructors and methods. In C++ the concept of **class** and **struct** is very close. In C++ a class has default visibility of **private** and a struct has default visibility of **public**, and that is the *only* difference. There is a more fundamental difference in C#.

In C# the key difference between a class and a struct is that a class is a *reference* type and a struct a *value* type. A class must be instantiated explicitly using **new**. The new instance is created on the heap, and memory is managed by the system through a garbage-collection process. Since a default constructor will be created for a struct if none is defined, a struct declared on the stack will be initialized. You may also use **new**. A new instance of a struct is created on the stack, and the instance will be deallocated when it goes out of scope.

There are different semantics for assignment, whether done explicitly or via call by value mechanism in a method call. For a class, you will get a second object reference, and both object references refer to the same data. For a struct, you will get a completely independent copy of the data in the struct.

A struct is a convenient data structure to use for moving data across a process or machine boundary, and we will use structs in our case study. For example, we will use a struct to represent customer data.

```
public struct CustomerListItem
{
    public int CustomerId;
    public string FirstName;
    public string LastName;
    public string EmailAddress;
}
```

## ENUMERATION TYPES

The final kind of value type is an *enumeration* type. An enumeration type is a distinct type with named constants. Every enumeration type has an underlying type, which is one of the following.

- **byte**
- **short**
- **int**
- **long**

An enumeration type is defined through an **enum** declaration.

```
public enum BookingStatus : byte
{
    HotelNotFound,     // 0 implicitly
    RoomsNotAvailable, // 1 implicitly
```

```
      Ok = 5        // explicit value
}
```

If the type is not specified, **int** is used. By default, the first **enum** member is assigned the value 0, the second member 1, and so on. Constant values can be explicitly assigned.

You can make use of an enumeration type by declaring a variable of the type indicated in the **enum** declaration (e.g., **BookingStatus**). You can refer to the enumerated values by using the dot notation. Here is some illustrative code:

```
BookingStatus status;
status = hotel.ReserveRoom(name, date);
if (status == BookingStatus.HotelNotFound)
   Console.WriteLine("Hotel not found");
...
```

## Reference Types

A variable of a reference type does not directly contain its data but instead provides a *reference* to the data stored in the heap. In C# there are the following kinds of reference types:

- Class
- Array
- Interface
- Delegate

Reference types have a special value **null**, which indicates the absence of an instance.

We have already examined classes in some detail, and we will look at arrays later in this chapter. Interfaces and delegates will be covered in Chapter 5.

### CLASS TYPES

A class type defines a data structure that has fields, methods, constants, and other kinds of members. Class types support *inheritance*. Through inheritance a derived class can extend or specialize a base class. We will discuss inheritance in Chapter 4.

Two classes in the .NET Framework Class Library are so important that they have C# reserved words as aliases for them: **object** and **string**.

### OBJECT

The **object** class type is the ultimate base type for all types in C#. Every C# type derives directly or indirectly from **object**. The **object** keyword in C# is an alias for the predefined **System.Object** class. **System.Object** has methods such as **ToString**, **Equals**, and **Finalize**, which we will study later.

### STRING

The **string** class encapsulates a Unicode character string. The **string** keyword is an alias for the predefined **System.String** class. The string type is a *sealed* class. (A sealed class is one that cannot be used as the base class for any other classes.)

The **string** class inherits directly from the root **object** class. String literals are defined using double quotes. There are useful built-in methods for **string**. For now, note that the **Equals** method can be used to test for equality of strings.

```
string a = "hello";
if (a.Equals("hello"))
      Console.WriteLine("equal");
else
      Console.WriteLine("not equal");
```

There are also overloaded operators:

```
if (a == "hello")
      . . .
```

We will study **string** in detail later in this chapter.

## Default Values

Several kinds of variables are automatically initialized to default values:

- Static variables
- Instance variables of class and struct instances
- Array elements

Local variables are *not* automatically initialized, and you will get a compiler error message if you try to use a local variable that has not been initialized.

The default value of a variable of reference type is **null**.

The default value of a variable of value type is the value assigned in the default constructor. For simple types this value corresponds to a bit pattern of all zeros:

- For integer types, the default value is 0
- For **char**, the default value is '\u0000'
- For **float**, the default value is 0.0f
- For **double**, the default value is 0.0d
- For **decimal**, the default value is 0.0m
- For **bool**, the default value is **false**

For an **enum** type, the default value is 0. For a **struct** type, the default value is obtained by setting all value type fields to their default values, as described above, and all reference type fields to **null**.

## Boxing and Unboxing

One of the strong features of C# is that is has a unified type system. Every type, including the simple built-in types such as **int**, derive from **System.Object**. In C# "everything is an object."

A language such as Smalltalk also has such a feature but pays the price of inefficiency for simple types. Languages such as C++ and Java treat simple built-in types differently from objects, thus obtaining efficiency but at the cost of a unified type system.

C# enjoys the best of both worlds through a process known as *boxing*. Boxing converts a value type such as **int** or a **struct** to an object reference and is done implicitly. *Unboxing* converts a boxed value type (stored on the heap) back to an unboxed simple value (stored on the stack). Unboxing is done through a type cast.

```
int x = 5;
object o = x;          // boxing
x = (int) o;           // unboxing
```

# Strings

Characters and strings are very important data types in practical programming. C# provides a **string** type, which is an alias for the **String** class in the **System** namespace. As a class type, **string** is a reference type. Much string functionality, available in all .NET languages, is provided by the **String** class. The C# compiler provides additional support to make working with strings more concise and intuitive. In this section we will first look at characters and then outline the main features of the **String** class. We will look at string input, at the additional support provided by C#, and at the issues of string equality. The section that follows surveys some of the useful methods of the **String** class. The section after that discusses the **StringBuilder** class.

## Characters

C# provides the primitive data type **char** to represent individual characters. A character literal is represented by a character enclosed in single quotes.

```
char ch1 = 'a';
```

A C# **char** is represented internally as an unsigned two-byte integer. You can cast back and forth between **char** and integer data types.

```
char ch1 = 'a';
int n = (int) ch1;
n++;
ch1 = (char) n;              // ch1 is now 'b'
```

The relational operators **==**, **<**, **>**, and so on apply to **char**.

```
char ch1 = 'a';
char ch2 = 'b'
if (ch1 < ch2)              // expression is true
       ...
```

## ASCII AND UNICODE

Traditionally, a one-byte character code called ASCII has been used to represent characters. ASCII code is simple and compact. But ASCII cannot be employed to represent many different alphabets used throughout the world.

Modern computer systems prefer to use a two-byte character code called Unicode. Most modern (and many ancient) alphabets can be represented by Unicode characters. ASCII is a subset of Unicode, corresponding to the first 255 Unicode character codes. For more information on Unicode, you can visit the Web site *www.unicode.org*. C# uses Unicode to represent characters.

## ESCAPE SEQUENCES

You can represent any Unicode character in a C# program by using the special escape sequence beginning with \u followed by hexadecimal digits.

```
char A = '\u0041'; // 41 (hex) is 65 (dec) or 'A'
```

Special escape sequences are provided for a number of standard nonprinting characters and for characters like quotation marks that would be difficult to represent otherwise. Table 3–4 shows the standard escape sequences in C#.

| Table 3–4 | Escape Characters in C# |

| | Escape Character | Name | Value |
|---|---|---|---|
| \' | Single quote | 0x0027 | |
| \" | Double quote | 0x0022 | |
| \\ | Backslash | 0x005C | |
| \0 | Null | 0x0000 | |
| \a | Alert | 0x0007 | |
| \b | Backspace | 0x0008 | |
| \f | Form feed | 0x000C | |
| \n | New line | 0x000A | |
| \r | Carriage return | 0x000D | |
| \t | Horizontal tab | 0x0009 | |
| \v | Vertical tab | 0x000B | |

## String Class

The **String** class inherits directly from **Object** and is a *sealed* class, which means that you cannot further inherit from **String**. We will discuss inheritance and sealed classes in Chapter 4. When a class is sealed, the compiler can perform certain optimizations to make methods in the class more efficient.

Instances of **String** are *immutable,* which means that once a string object is created, it cannot be changed during its lifetime. Operations that appear to modify a string actually return a new string object. If, for the sake of efficiency, you need to modify a stringlike object directly, you can make use of the **StringBuilder** class, which we will discuss in a later section.

A string has a zero-based index, which can be used to access individual characters in a string. That means that the first character of the string **str** is **str[0]**, the second character is **str[1]**, and so on.

By default, comparison operations on strings are case-sensitive, although there is an overloaded version of the **Compare** method that permits case-insensitive comparisons.

The empty string should be distinguished from **null**. If a string has not been assigned, it will be a null reference. Any string, including the empty string, compares greater than a null reference. Two null references compare equal to each other.

## Language Support

The C# language provides a number of features to make working with strings easier and more intuitive.

## STRING LITERALS AND INITIALIZATION

You can define a **string** literal by enclosing a string of characters in double quotes. Special characters can be represented using an escape sequence, as discussed earlier in the chapter. You may also define a "verbatim" string literal using the **@** symbol. In a verbatim string, escape sequences are not converted but are used exactly as they appear. If you want to represent a double quote inside a verbatim string, use two double quotes.

    The proper way to initialize a string variable with a literal value is to supply the literal after an equals sign. You do not need to use **new** as you do with other data types. Here are some examples of string literals and initializing string variables.

```
string s1 = "bat";
string path1 = "c:\\OI\\NetCs\\Chap3\\Concat";
string path = @"c:\OI\NetCs\Chap3\Concat\";
string greeting = @"""Hello, world""";
```

## CONCATENATION

The **String** class provides a method **Concat** for concatenating strings. In C# you can use the operators **+** and **+=** to perform concatenation. The following program illustrates string literals and concatenation.

```
// Concat.cs

using System;

public class Concat
{
    public static void Main(string[] args)
    {
        string s1 = "bat";
        Console.WriteLine("s1 = {0}", s1);
        string s2 = "man";
        Console.WriteLine("s2 = {0}", s2);
        s1 += s2;
        Console.WriteLine(s1);
        string path1 = "c:\\OI\\NetCs\\Chap3\\Concat";
        Console.WriteLine("path1 = {0}", path1);
        string path = @"c:\OI\NetCs\Chap3\Concat\";
        string file = "Concat.cs";
        path = path + file;
        Console.WriteLine(path);
        string greeting = @"""Hello, world""";
        Console.WriteLine(greeting);
    }
}
```

Here is the output:

```
s1 = bat
s2 = man
batman
path1 = c:\OI\NetCs\Chap3\Concat
c:\OI\NetCs\Chap3\Concat\Concat.cs

"Hello, world"
```

### INDEX

You can extract an individual character from a string using a square bracket and a zero-based index.

```
string s1 = "bat";
char ch = s1[0];    // contains 'b'
```

### RELATIONAL OPERATORS

In general, for reference types, the **==** and **!=** operators check if the *object references* are the same, not whether the contents of the memory locations referred to are the same. However, the **String** class overloads these operators, so that the textual content of the strings is compared. The program **StringRelation** illustrates using these relational operators on strings. The inequality operators, such as **<**, are *not* available for strings; use the **Compare** method.

## String Equality

To fully understand issues of string equality, you should be aware of how the compiler stores strings. When string literals are encountered, they are entered into an internal table of string identities. If a second literal is encountered with the same string data, an object reference will be returned to the existing string in the table; no second copy will be made. As a result of this compiler optimization, the two object references will be the same, as represented in Figure 3-3.

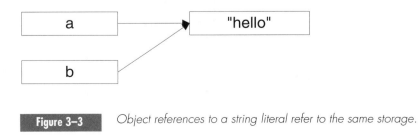

**Figure 3–3**    *Object references to a string literal refer to the same storage.*

You should not be misled by this fact to conclude that two object references to the same string data will always be the same. If the contents of the string get determined at runtime, for example, by the user inputting the data, the compiler has no way of knowing that the second string should have an identical object reference. Hence you will have two distinct object references, which happen to refer to the same data, as illustrated in Figure 3-4.

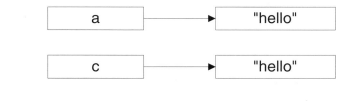

Figure 3–4 *Two distinct object references, which happen to refer to the same data.*

As discussed, when strings are checked for equality, either through the relational operator **==** or through the **Equals** method, a comparison is made of the *contents* of the strings, not of the object references. So in both the previous cases the strings **a** and **b** will check out as equal. You have to be more careful with other reference types, where reference equality is *not* the same as content equality.

## String Comparison

The fundamental way to compare strings for equality is to use the **Equals** method of the **String** class. There are several overloaded versions of this function, including a static version that takes two **string** parameters and a nonstatic version that takes one **string** parameter that is compared with the current instance. These methods perform a case-sensitive comparison of the contents of the strings. A **bool** value of **true** or **false** is returned.

If you wish to perform a case-insensitive comparison, you may use the **Compare** method. This method has several overloaded versions, all of them static. Two strings, s1 and s2, are compared. An integer is returned expressing the lexical relationship between the two strings, as shown in Table 3–5.

**Table 3–5** *Return Values of the Compare Method*

| Relationship | Return Value |
| --- | --- |
| s1 less than s2 | negative integer |
| s1 equal to s2 | 0 |
| s1 greater than s2 | positive integer |

A third parameter allows you to control the case sensitivity of the comparison. If you use only two parameters, a case-sensitive comparison is performed. The third parameter is a **bool**. A value of **false** calls for a case-sensitive comparison, and a value of **true** calls for ignoring case.

The program **StringCompare** illustrates a number of comparisons, using both the **Equal** and **Compare** methods.

## String Input

The **Console** class has methods for inputting characters and strings. The **Read** method reads in a single character (as an **int**). The **ReadLine** method reads in a line of input, terminated by a carriage return, line feed, or combination, and will return a **string**. In general, the **ReadLine** method is the easier to use and synchronizes nicely with **Write** and **WriteLine**. The program **ReadStrings** illustrates reading in a first name, a middle initial, and a last name. All input is done via **ReadLine**. The middle initial as a character is determined by extracting the character at position 0.

Our **InputWrapper** class has a method **getString**, which provides a prompt and reads in a string.

## String Methods and Properties

In this section we will survey a few useful methods and properties of the **String** class. Many of the methods have various overloaded versions. We show a representative version. Consult the online documentation for details on these and other methods. The program **StringMethods** demonstrates all the examples that follow.

### LENGTH

```
public int Length {get;}
```
This property returns the length of a string. Notice the convenient shorthand notation that is used for declaring a property.
```
string str = "hello";
int n = str.Length;                        // 5
```

### TOUPPER

```
public string ToUpper ();
```
This method returns a new string in which all characters of the original string have been converted to uppercase.
```
str = "goodbye";
str = str.ToUpper();                       // GOODBYE
```

### TOLOWER

```
public string ToLower ();
```

This method returns a new string in which all characters of the original string have been converted to lowercase.

```
str = str.ToLower();                    // goodbye
```

### SUBSTRING

```
public string Substring(int startIndex, int length);
```

This method returns a substring that starts from a specified index position in the value and continues for a specified length. Remember that in C# the index of the first character in a string is 0.

```
string sub = str.Substring(4,3);        // bye
```

### INDEXOF

```
public int IndexOf(string value);
```

This method returns the index of the first occurrence of the specified string. If the string is not found, –1 is returned.

```
str = "goodbye";
int n1 = str.IndexOf("bye");    // 4
int n2 = str.IndexOf("boo");    // -1
```

## StringBuilder Class

As we have discussed, instances of the **String** class are immutable. As a result, when you manipulate instances of **String**, you are frequently obtaining new **String** instances. Depending on your applications, creating all these instances may be expensive. The .NET library provides a special class **StringBuilder** (located in the **System.Text** namespace) in which you may directly manipulate the underlying string without creating a new instance. When you are done, you can create a **String** instance out of an instance of **StringBuilder** by using the **ToString** method.

A **StringBuilder** instance has a capacity and a maximum capacity. These capacities can be specified in a constructor when the instance is created. By default, an empty **StringBuilder** instance starts out with a capacity of 16. As the stored string expands, the capacity will be increased automatically. The program **StringBuilderDemo** provides a simple demonstration of using the **StringBuilder** class. It shows the starting capacity and the capacity after strings are appended. At the end, a **String** is returned.

```
// StringBuilderDemo.cs

using System;
```

```
using System.Text;

public class StringBuilderDemo
{
   public static void Main(string[] args)
   {
      StringBuilder build = new StringBuilder();
      Console.WriteLine("capacity = {0}", build.Capacity);
      build.Append("This is the first sentence.\n");
      Console.WriteLine("capacity = {0}", build.Capacity);
      build.Append("This is the second sentence.\n");
      Console.WriteLine("capacity = {0}", build.Capacity);
      build.Append("This is the last sentence.\n");
      Console.WriteLine("capacity = {0}", build.Capacity);
      string str = build.ToString();
      Console.Write(str);
   }
}
```

Here is the output:

```
capacity = 16
capacity = 34
capacity = 70
capacity = 142
This is the first sentence.
This is the second sentence.
This is the last sentence.
```

# Arrays and Indexers

Arrays are another important data type in practical programming. In C# arrays are objects. They are a reference data type. They are based on the class **System.Array** and so inherit the properties and methods of this class. After examining one-dimensional arrays, we examine two higher-dimensional varieties. A "jagged" array is an array of arrays, and each row can have a different number of elements. In "rectangular" arrays, all rows have the same number of elements. Arrays are a special kind of collection, which means that the **foreach** loop can be used in C# for iterating through array elements.

We conclude the section with a discussion of indexers, which provides a way to access encapsulated data in a class with an array notation.

## Arrays

An array is a collection of elements with the following characteristics.

- All array elements must be of the same type. The element type of an array can be any type, including an array type. An array of arrays is often referred to as a *jagged* array.
- An array may have one or more dimensions. For example, a two-dimensional array can be visualized as a table of values. The number of dimensions is known as the array's *rank*.
- Array elements are accessed using one or more computed integer values, each known as an *index*. A one-dimensional array has one index.
- In C# an array index starts at 0, as in other C family languages.
- The elements of an array are created when the array object is created. The elements are automatically destroyed when there are no longer any references to the array object.

## ONE-DIMENSIONAL ARRAYS

An array is declared using square brackets [] after the type, not after the variable.

```
int [] a;                 // declares an array of int
```

Note that the size of the array is not part of its type. The variable declared is a *reference* to the array.

You create the array elements and establish the size of the array using the **new** operator.

```
a = new int[10];   // creates 10 array elements
```

The new array elements start out with the appropriate default values for the type (0 for **int**).

You may both declare and initialize array elements using curly brackets, as in C/C++.

```
int a[] = {2, 3, 5, 7, 11};
```

You can indicate you are done with the array elements by assigning the array reference to **null**.

```
a = null;
```

The garbage collector is now free to deallocate the elements.

## System.Array

Arrays are objects. **System.Array** is the abstract base class for all array types. Accordingly, you can use the properties and methods of **System.Array** for any array. Here are some examples:

- **Length** is a property that returns the number of elements currently in the array.
- **Sort** is a static method that will sort the elements of an array.
- **BinarySearch** is a static method that will search for an element in a sorted array, using a binary search algorithm.

```
int [] array = {5, 2, 11, 7, 3};
Array.Sort(a);              // sorts the array
for (int i = 0; i < a.Length; i++)
    Console.Write("{0} ", a[i]);
Console.WriteLine();
int target = 5;
int index = Array.BinarySearch(a, target);
if (index < 0)
    Console.WriteLine("{0} not found", target);
else
    Console.WriteLine("{0} found at {1}", target, index);
```

A complete program containing the code shown above can be found in **ArrayMethods**. Here is the output:

```
2 3 5 7 11
5 found at 2
```

## Sample Program

The program **ArrayDemo** is an interactive test program for arrays. A small array is created initially, and you can create new arrays. You can populate an array either with a sequence of square numbers or with random numbers. You can sort the array, reverse the array, and perform a binary search (which assumes that the array is sorted in ascending order). You can destroy the array by assigning the array reference to **null**.

## Interfaces for System.Array

If you look at the documentation for methods of **System.Array**, you will see many references to various *interfaces,* such as **IComparable**. By using such interfaces you can control the behavior of methods of **System.Array**. For example, if you want to sort an array of objects of a class that you define, you must implement the interface **IComparable** in your class so that the **Sort** method knows how to compare elements to carry out the sort. The .NET Framework provides an implementation of **IComparable** for all the primitive types. We will come back to this point after we discuss interfaces in Chapter 5.

## Random-Number Generation

The **ArrayDemo** program contains the following code for populating an array with random integers between 0 and 100.

```
Random rand = new Random();
for (int i = 0; i < size; i++)
{
    array[i] = rand.Next(100);
}
```

The .NET Framework provides a useful class, **Random**, in the **System** namespace that can be used for generating pseudorandom numbers for simulations.

### CONSTRUCTORS

There are two constructors:

```
Random();          // uses default seed
Random(int seed);  // seed is specified
```

The default seed is based on date and time, resulting in a different stream of random numbers each time. By specifying a seed, you can produce a deterministic stream.

### NEXT METHODS

There are three overloaded **Next** methods that return a random **int**.

```
int Next();
int Next(int maxValue);
int Next(int minValue, int maxValue);
```

The first method returns an integer greater than or equal to zero and less than **Int32.MaxValue**. The second method returns an integer greater than or equal to zero and less than **maxValue**. The third method returns an integer greater than or equal to **minValue** and less than or equal to **maxValue**.

### NEXTDOUBLE METHOD

The **NextDouble** method produces a random double between 0 and 1.

```
double NextDouble();
```

The return value **r** is in the range: $0 <= r < 1$.

## Jagged Arrays

You can declare an array of arrays, or a "jagged" array. Each row can have a different number of elements.

```
int [][] binomial;
```

You then create the array of rows, specifying how many rows there are (each row is itself an array).

```
binomial = new int [rows][];
```

Next you create the individual rows.

```
binomial[i] = new int [i+1];
```

Finally you can assign individual array elements.

```
binomial[0][0] = 1;
```

The example program **Pascal** creates and prints Pascal's triangle using a two-dimensional jagged array. Higher-dimensional jagged arrays can be created following the same principles.

## Rectangular Arrays

C# also permits you to define rectangular arrays, where all rows have the same number of elements. First you declare the array.

```
int [,] MultTable;
```

Then you create all the array elements, specifying the number of rows and columns.

```
MultTable = new int[rows, columns];
```

Finally you can assign individual array elements.

```
MultTable[i,j] = i * j;
```

The example program **RectangularArray** creates and prints out a multiplication table.

Higher-dimensional rectangular arrays can be created following the same principles.

## Arrays as Collections

The class **System.Array** supports the **IEnumerable** interface. Hence arrays can be treated as *collections*, a topic we will discuss in Chapter 5. This means that a **foreach** loop can be used to iterate through the elements of an array.

The **Pascal** example code contains nested **foreach** loops to display the jagged array. The outer loop iterates through all the rows, and the inner loop iterates through all the elements within a row.

```
// Pascal.cs
...
Console.WriteLine(
   "Pascal triangle via nested foreach loop");
foreach (int[] row in binomial)
{
   foreach (int x in row)
   {
      Console.Write("{0} ", x);
   }
   Console.WriteLine();
 }
```

## Indexers

C# provides various ways to help the user of a class access encapsulated data. Earlier in the chapter we saw how *properties* can provide access to a single piece of data associated with a class, making it appear like a public field. In this section we will see how *indexers* provide a similar capability for accessing a group of data items, using an array index notation. Indexers can be provided when there is a private array or other collection.

The program **TestHotel\Step3** provides an illustration. This version of the **Hotel** class adds the capability to make hotel reservations, and the private array **reservations** stores a list of reservations in the form of **ReservationListItem** structure instances. The **Hotel** class provides the read-only property **NumberReservations** for the number of reservations in this list, and it provides a read-write indexer for access to the elements in this list. Note use of the keywords **this** and **value** in the indexer, which has a general syntax similar to that of properties.

```
// Hotel.cs - Step 3

using System;

public struct ReservationListItem
{
   public int CustomerId;
   public int ReservationId;
   public string HotelName;
   public string City;
   public DateTime ArrivalDate;
   public DateTime DepartureDate;
   public int NumberDays;
}

...

public class Hotel
{
   private string city;
   private string name;
   private int number;
   private decimal rate;
   private const int MAXDAY = 366;
   private int[] numGuests;
   private int nextReservation = 0;
   private int nextReservationId = 1;
   private const int MAXRESERVATIONS = 100;
   private ReservationListItem[] reservations;
   ...
   public int NumberReservations
   {
      get
      {
         return nextReservation;
      }
   }
   public ReservationListItem this[int index]
```

```
{
    get
    {
        return reservations[index];
    }
    set
    {
        reservations[index] = value;
    }
}
```

The test program **TestHotel.cs** illustrates reading and writing individual array elements using the index notation.

```
// Change the CustomerId of first reservation
ReservationListItem item = ritz[0];
item.CustomerId = 99;
ritz[0] = item;
ShowReservations(ritz);
```

# More about Methods

In this section we look at several other topics pertaining to methods in C#:

- Parameter passing
- Variable-length parameter lists
- Method overloading
- Operator overloading

## Parameter Passing

Programming languages have different mechanisms for passing parameters. In the C family of languages the standard is "call by value." This means that the actual data values themselves are passed to the method. Typically, these values are pushed onto the stack, and the called function obtains its own independent copy of the values. Any changes made to these values will not be propagated back to the calling program. C# provides this mechanism of parameter passing as the default, but C# also supports "reference" parameters and "output" parameters.

Some terminology will help us in the following discussion. Storage is allocated on the stack for method parameters. This storage area is known as the *activation record*. It is popped when the method is no longer active. The *formal parameters* of a method are the parameters as seen within the method. They are provided storage in the activation record. The *actual parameters* of a method are the expressions between commas in the parameter list of the method call.

```
int sum = SimpleMath.Add(5, 7);        // actual parameters
                                       //are 5 and 7
...
public static int Add(int x, int y)
{                                      // formal parameters
                                       //are x and y
   ...
}
```

## Value Parameters

Parameter passing is the process of initializing the storage of the formal parameters by the actual parameters. The default method of parameter passing in C# is *call-by-value,* in which the values of the actual parameters are copied into the storage of the formal parameters. Call-by-value is "safe," because the method never directly accesses the actual parameters, only its own local copies. But there are drawbacks to call-by-value:

- There is no direct way to modify the value of an argument. You may use the return type of the method, but that allows you to pass only one value back to the calling program.
- There is overhead in copying a large object.

The overhead in copying a large object is borne when you pass a struct instance. If you pass a class instance, or an instance of any other reference type, you are passing only a reference and not the actual data itself. This may sound like "call-by-reference," but what you are actually doing is passing a reference by value.

## Reference Parameters

Consider a situation in which you want to pass more than one value back to the calling program. C# provides a clean solution through *reference parameters.* You declare a reference parameter with the **ref** keyword, which is placed before both the formal parameter and the actual parameter. A reference parameter does not result in any copying of a value. Instead, the formal parameter and the actual parameter refer to the same storage location. Thus, changing the formal parameter will result in the actual parameter changing, as both are referring to exactly the same storage location.

The program **ReferenceMath** illustrates using **ref** parameters. There is a single method, **Calculate**, which passes back two values as reference parameters.

```
// ReferenceMath.cs

public class ReferenceMath
{
```

```
    public static void Calculate(int x, int y,
                                 ref int sum, ref int prod)
    {
       sum = x + y;
       prod = x * y;
    }
}
```

Notice the use of the **ref** keyword in front of the third and fourth parameters. Here is the test program:

```
// TestReferenceMath.cs

using System;

public class TestReferenceMath
{
    public static void Main(string[] args)
    {
        int sum = 0, product = 0;
        MultipleMath.Calculate(5, 7, ref sum, ref product);
        Console.WriteLine("sum = {0}", sum);
        Console.WriteLine("product = {0}", product);
    }
}
```

Again we need to have the **ref** keyword in front of the parameters. It is also necessary to initialize the variables before using them as reference parameters.

## Output Parameters

A reference parameter is really designed for two-way communication between the calling program and the called program, both passing data in and getting data out. Thus there is a requirement that reference parameters be initialized before their use. In the case we have just looked at, where we are only obtaining output, initializing the variables only for them to be assigned new values is rather pointless. C# provides for this case with *output parameters*. Use the keyword **out** wherever you would use the keyword **ref**. Then you do not have to initialize the variable before use. Within the method you must be sure to assign the **out** parameter, and you could not use it before such an assignment. The program **OutputMath** illustrates the use of output parameters.

## Method Overloading

In a traditional programming language such as C, you need to create unique names for all your methods. If methods do basically the same thing but apply only to different data types, it becomes tedious to create unique names. For example, suppose you have a **FindMax** method that can find the maximum of two **int** or two **long** or two **string.** If we need to come up with a unique name for each method, we would have to create method names such as **FindMaxInt**, **FindMaxLong**, and **FindMaxString**.

In C#, as in other object-oriented languages such as C++ and Java, you may *overload* method names. That is, different methods can have different names, if they have different *signatures*. Two methods have the same signature if they have the same number of parameters, the parameters have the same data types, and the parameters have the same modifiers (none, **ref**, or **out**). The return type does not contribute to defining the signature of a method.

At runtime the compiler will resolve a given invocation of the method by trying to match up the actual parameters with formal parameters. A match occurs if the parameters match exactly or if they can match through an implicit conversion. For the exact matching rules, consult the *C# Language Specification.*

The program **OverloadDemo** illustrates method overloading. The method **FindMax** is overloaded to take either **long** or **string** parameters. The method is invoked three times, for **int**, **long**, and **string** parameters. There is an exact match for the case of **long** and **string**. The call with **int** actual parameters can resolve to the **long** version, because there is an implicit conversion of **int** into **long**.

## MODIFIERS AS PART OF THE SIGNATURE

It is important to understand that if methods have identical types for their formal parameters, but differ in a modifier (none, **ref**, or **out**), then the methods have different signatures. The program **OverloadHotel** provides an illustration. We have two **RaisePrice** methods. In the first, the hotel is passed as a value parameter. In the second, the hotel is passed as a reference parameter. These methods have different signatures.

```
// HotelTest.cs

using System;

public class HotelDemo
{
   public static void Main()
   {
      Hotel ritz = new Hotel("Boston", "Ritz", 100,
                             200.00m);
      Hotel flop = new Hotel("Podunk", "Flop", 50, 20.00m);
      // The Ritz before and after
      Console.WriteLine("Before price hike");
      ritz.Show();
      RaisePrice(ritz, 50.00m);
```

```
            Console.WriteLine("After price hike");
            ritz.Show();
            // The Flop before and after -- use ref version
            Console.WriteLine("Before price hike");
            flop.Show();
            RaisePrice(ref flop, 50.00m);
            Console.WriteLine("After price hike");
            flop.Show();
        }
        private static void RaisePrice(Hotel hotel,
                                      decimal delta)
        {
            hotel.cost += delta;
            Console.WriteLine("new cost = {0:C}", hotel.cost);
        }
        private static void RaisePrice(ref Hotel hotel,
                                      decimal delta)
        {
            hotel.cost += delta;
            Console.WriteLine("new cost = {0:C}", hotel.cost);
        }
    }
```

## Variable-Length Parameter Lists

Our **FindMax** methods in the previous section were very specific with respect to the number of parameters—there were always exactly two parameters. Sometimes you may want to be able to work with a variable number of parameters—for example, to find the maximum of two, three, four, or more numbers. C# provides a **params** keyword, which you can use to indicate that an array of parameters is provided. Sometimes you may want to provide both a general version of your method that takes a variable number of parameters and also one or more special versions that take an exact number of parameters. The special version will be called in preference, if there is an exact match. The special versions are more efficient. The program **VariableMax** illustrates a general **FindMax** method that takes a variable number of parameters. There is also a special version that takes two parameters. Each method prints out a line identifying itself, so you can see which method takes precedence. Here is the program:

```
// VariableMax.cs

using System;

public class VariableMax
{
    public static void Main()
    {
```

```
        Console.WriteLine("max of {0}, {1} = {2}",
                        5,7,FindMax(5,7));
        Console.WriteLine("max of {0}, {1}, {2} = {3}",
                        500,5,7,FindMax(500,5,7));
        Console.WriteLine("max of {0}, {1}, {2}, {3} = {4}",
                        500,5,7,80,FindMax(500,5,7,80));
    }
    static int FindMax(int a, int b)
    {
        Console.WriteLine("FindMax with Two Parameters");
        return a < b ? b : a;
    }
    static int FindMax(params int[] args)
    {
        Console.WriteLine(
            "FindMax with Variable Number of Parameters");
        int imax = Int32.MinValue;
        for (int i = 0; i < args.Length; i++)
        {
            if (args[i] > imax)
                imax = args[i];
        }
        return imax;
    }
}
```

Here is the output:

```
FindMax with Two Parameters
max of 5, 7 = 7
FindMax with Variable Number of Parameters
max of 500, 5, 7 = 500
FindMax with Variable Number of Parameters
max of 500, 5, 7, 80 = 500
```

## Operator Overloading

C#, like C++ but unlike Java, supports *operator overloading*. The idea is that certain method invocations can be implemented more concisely using operators rather than method calls. Suppose we have a class **Matrix** that has static methods to add and multiply matrices. Using methods, we could write a matrix expression like this:

```
Matrix a, b, c, d;
// code to initialize the object references
d = Matrix.Multiply(a, (Matrix.Add(b, c));
```

If we overload the operators + and *, we can write this code more succinctly:

```
d = a * (b + c);
```

You cannot create a brand new operator, but you can overload many of the existing C# operators to be an alias for a static method. For example, given the static method **Add** in the **Matrix** class:

```
class Matrix
{
...
    public static Matrix Add(Matrix x, Matrix y)
    {
```

you can write instead:

```
    public static Matrix operator+(Matrix x, Matrix y)
```

All of the rest of the class implementation code stays the same, and you can then use operator notation in client code. Operator declarations, such as **operator+** shown above, must obey the following rules:

- Operators must be **public** and **static** and may not have any other modifiers.
- Operators take only value parameters and not reference or output parameters.
- Operators must have a signature that differs from the signatures of all other operators in the class.

The program **OperatorOverloadDemo** provides a simple example of operator overloading. The **+** operator is overloaded in the **HotelList** class to add a hotel to an array of hotels. In C# if you overload a binary operator such as **+,** the corresponding compound assignment operator **+=** will be overloaded for you automatically by the compiler. Thus, in our test program, we add the hotel objects **ritz** and **sheraton** to the list of hotels using the **+** and **+=** operators.

```
// OperatorOverloadDemo.cs

using System;

public class OperatorOverloadDemo
{
    public static void Main()
    {
        HotelList list = new HotelList();
        Hotel ritz = new Hotel("Atlanta", "Ritz");
        Hotel sheraton = new Hotel("Boston", "Sheraton");
        list = list + ritz;
        list += sheraton;
        list.ShowHotels();
    }
}
```

# Exceptions

An inevitable part of programming is dealing with error conditions of various sorts. This section introduces the exception-handling mechanism of C#, beginning with a discussion of the fundamentals of error processing and various alternatives that are available. We then carefully go through the C# exception mechanism, which includes a **try** block, **catch** handlers, and a **finally** block. You can raise exceptions by means of a **throw** statement. The .NET class library provides an **Exception** class, which you can use to pass information about an exception that occurred. To further specify your exception and to pass additional information, you can derive your own class from **Exception**. When handling an exception you may want to throw a new exception. In such a case you can use the "inner exception" feature of the **Exception** class to pass the original exception on with your new exception.

## Exception Fundamentals

The traditional way to deal with runtime errors is to have the functions you call return a status code. The status code may have a particular value for a good return and other values to denote various error conditions. The calling function checks this status code, and if an error was encountered, it performs appropriate error handling. This function in return may pass an error code to its calling function, and so on up the call stack.

Although straightforward, this mechanism has a number of drawbacks. The basic disadvantage is lack of robustness. The called function may have impeccable error-checking code and return appropriate error information, but all this information is useless if the calling function does not make use of it. The program may continue operation as if nothing were amiss and some time later crash for some mysterious reason. Also, status codes are nonstandard. A 0 may indicate success in one case but failure in another. And the caller and callee have to agree on return codes and their meaning.

Another disadvantage is that every function in the call stack must participate in the process, or the chain of error information will be broken. Also, unusual flow control can leave memory hanging without being deallocated.

Furthermore, in languages such as C# that have constructors and overloaded operators, there isn't a return value for some operations.

### .NET EXCEPTION HANDLING

C# provides an *exception* mechanism that can be used for reporting and handling errors. An error is reported by "throwing" an exception. The error is handled by "catching" the exception. This mechanism is similar in concept to that for exceptions in C++ and Java.

Exceptions are implemented in .NET by the Common Language Runtime, so exceptions can be thrown in one .NET language and caught in another. The exception mechanism involves the following elements:

- Code that might encounter an exception should be enclosed in a **try** block.
- Exceptions are caught in a **catch** block.
- An Exception object is passed as a parameter to **catch**. The data type of the Exception object is **System.Exception** or a derived type.
- You may have multiple **catch** blocks. A match is made based on the data type of the Exception object.
- An optional **finally** clause contains code that will be executed whether or not an exception is encountered.
- In the called method, an exception is raised through a **throw** statement.

### EXCEPTION FLOW OF CONTROL

The general structure of code which might encounter an exception is shown below:

```
try
{
    // code that might cause an exception to be thrown
}
catch (ExceptionClass1 e)
{
    // code to handle this type of exception
}
catch (ExceptionClass2 e)
{
    // code to handle this other type of exception
}
// possibly more catch handlers
// optional finally clause (discussed later)
// statements after try ... catch
finally
{

  // cleanup code that is executed whether or not
  // an exception is caught or if catch handler itself
  // throws an exception
}
```

Each catch handler has a parameter specifying the data type of exception that it can handle. The exception data type can be **System.Exception** or a class ultimately derived from it. If an exception is thrown, the *first* catch handler that matches the exception data type is executed, and then control passes to the statement just after the catch block(s). If no handler is found, the exception is thrown to the next higher "context" (e.g., the function that called the current one). If no exception is thrown inside the try block, all the catch handlers are skipped.

## CONTEXT AND STACK UNWINDING

As the flow of control of a program passes into nested blocks, local variables are pushed onto the stack and a new "context" is entered. Likewise a new context is entered on a method call, which also pushes a return address onto the stack.

If an exception is not handled in the current context, it is passed to successively higher contexts until it is finally handled (or else is "uncaught" and is handled by a default system handler).

When the higher context is entered, C# adjusts the stack properly, a process known as stack unwinding. In C# exception handling, stack unwinding involves both setting the program counter and cleaning up variables (popping stack variables and marking heap variables as free, so that the garbage collector can deallocate them).

## EXAMPLE PROGRAM

Now let's look at some code that illustrates the principles we have discussed so far. We will use a simplified version of our **Hotel** class. This hotel accepts reservations for only a single date. There is a property **Capacity** and there are methods **MakeReservation** and **CancelReservation**. A reservation has an id, a customer name, and the number of rooms requested. (In this example we have added a feature. Previously, a customer could reserve only a single room. We are now allowing multiple room requests. This is to simplify exercising our program to bump against the exception condition of exceeding the capacity of the hotel.) There is a property, **NumberReservations**, and an indexer to allow the calling program to access the reservation list.

There are several possible exceptions:

- User does not request a positive number of rooms.
- Room request exceeds the capacity of the hotel.
- Index out of range when attempting to store reservation in array of reservations.

The first two exceptions are thrown explicitly by our **Hotel** class, and the index out-of-range exception is thrown by the .NET library.

Our example program is in the directory **HotelException\Step1**.

```
// HotelException.cs - Step 1

using System;

public struct ReservationListItem
```

```csharp
{
    public int ReservationId;
    public string CustomerName;
    public int NumberRooms;
}

public class Hotel
{
    private int capacity;
    private int numGuests;
    private int nextReservation = 0;
    private int nextReservationId = 1;
    private const int MAXRESERVATIONS = 3;
    private ReservationListItem[] reservations;
    public Hotel(int capacity)
    {
        this.capacity = capacity;
        reservations =
            new ReservationListItem[MAXRESERVATIONS];
    }
    public int MakeReservation(string cust, int rooms)
    {
        // Requested number of rooms should be positive
        if (rooms <= 0)
            throw new Exception(
                "Please request a positive number of rooms");
        // Check if rooms are available
        if (numGuests + rooms > capacity)
            throw new Exception("Rooms not available");
        // Reserve the room for requested dates
        numGuests += rooms;
        // Fill in information for reservation
        ReservationListItem item;
        item.ReservationId = nextReservationId++;
        item.CustomerName = cust;
        item.NumberRooms = rooms;
        // Add reservation to reservation list and return
        // reservation id
        reservations[nextReservation++] = item;
        return item.ReservationId;
    }
    ...
```

The next code fragment is the test program. Notice that we place the entire body of the command-processing loop inside a try block. The catch handler prints an error message that is passed within the exception object. Then, after either normal processing or displaying an error message, a new command is read in. This simple scheme provides reasonable error processing, as a bad command will not be acted upon, and the user will have an opportunity to enter a new command.

```csharp
// Test.cs

using System;

public class TestHotel
{
    public static void Main()
    {
        InputWrapper iw = new InputWrapper();
        Hotel hotel = new Hotel(10);
        ShowHotel(hotel);
        string cmd;
        Console.WriteLine("Enter command, quit to exit");
        cmd = iw.getString("H> ");
        while (! cmd.Equals("quit"))
        {
            try
            {
                if (cmd.Equals("new"))
                {
                    int capacity = iw.getInt("capacity: ");
                    hotel = new Hotel(capacity);
                    ShowHotel(hotel);
                }
                else if (cmd.Equals("book"))
                {
                    string customer =
                        iw.getString("customer name: ");
                    int rooms = iw.getInt("number of rooms: ");
                    int id =
                        hotel.MakeReservation(customer, rooms);
                    Console.WriteLine(
                        "Reservation has been booked");
                    Console.WriteLine(
                        "ReservationId = {0}", id);
                }
                else if (cmd.Equals("cancel"))
                {
                    int id = iw.getInt("reservation id: ");
                    hotel.CancelReservation(id);
                }
                else if (cmd.Equals("show"))
                    ShowReservations(hotel);
                else
                    hotelHelp();
            }
            catch (Exception e)
            {
                Console.WriteLine("Exception: {0}", e.Message);
            }
```

```
          cmd = iw.getString("H> ");
      }
   }
```

Here is a transcript of a sample run. We try several kinds of errors.

```
The hotel has 10 rooms
Enter command, quit to exit
H> book
customer name: bob
number of rooms: xxx
Exception: Input string was not in a correct format.
H> book
customer name: bob
number of rooms: -5
Exception: Please request a positive number of rooms
H> book
customer name: bob
number of rooms: 5
Reservation has been booked
ReservationId = 1
H> book
customer name: mary
number of rooms: 6
Exception: Rooms not available
H> book
customer name: mary
number of rooms: 3
Reservation has been booked
ReservationId = 2
H> book
customer name: david
number of rooms: 1
Reservation has been booked
ReservationId = 3
H> show
1       bob             5
2       mary            3
3       david           1
H> book
customer name: ellen
number of rooms: 1
Exception: Exception of type
System.IndexOutOfRangeException was thrown.
H>
```

Notice that we threw two of the exceptions ourselves. A third (entering "xxx" for the number of rooms) was caught by the .NET library inside our **InputWrapper** class. A fourth (index out of range) was also caught by .NET, inside the **Hotel** class. Our catch handler deals with all these different exceptions in a simple, uniform manner.

## SYSTEM.EXCEPTION

The **System.Exception** class provides a number of useful methods and properties for obtaining information about an exception.

- **Message** returns a text string providing information about the exception. This message is set when the exception object is constructed. If no message is specified, a generic message will be provided indicating the type of the exception. The **Message** property is read-only. (Hence, if you want to specify your own message, you must construct a new exception object, as done in the example above.)
- **StackTrace** returns a text string providing a stack trace at the place where the exception arose.
- **InnerException** holds a reference to another exception. When you throw a new exception, it is desirable not to lose the information about the original exception. The original exception can be passed as a parameter when constructing the new exception. The original exception object is then available through the **InnerException** property of the new exception. (We will provide an example of using inner exceptions later in this chapter.)

# User-Defined Exception Classes

You can do basic exception handling using only the base **Exception** class, as previously illustrated. In order to obtain finer-grained control over exceptions, it is frequently useful to define your own exception class, derived from **Exception**. You can then have a more specific catch handler that looks specifically for your exception type. You can also define other members in your derived exception class, so that you can pass additional information to the catch handler.

We will illustrate by enhancing the **MakeReservation** method of our **Hotel** class. We want to distinguish between the two types of exceptions we throw. The one type is essentially bad input data (a nonpositive value). We will continue to handle this exception in the same manner as before (that is, bad input data gives rise to a format exception, thrown by .NET library code). We will define a new exception class **RoomException** to cover the case where the hotel does not have enough rooms to fulfill the request. (In this case we want to allow the user an opportunity to submit another reservation request with fewer rooms.) Our example program is **HotelException\Step2**. Here is the definition of our new exception class. This class is defined using inheritance, which we will discuss in Chapter 4, where we will explain the "base(message)" syntax.

```
public class RoomException : Exception
{
```

```
      private int available;
      public RoomException(string message, int available)
         : base(message)
      {
         this.available = available;
      }
      public int Available
      {
         get
         {
            return available;
         }
      }
}
```

Note that we define a property **Available** that can be used to retrieve the information about how many rooms are available. The constructor of our exception class takes two parameters. The first is an error message string, and the second is the number of rooms available. We pass the message string to the constructor of the base class. We must also modify the code of the **Hotel** class to throw our new type of exception when too many rooms are requested.

```
// HotelException.cs - Step 2

...
public class Hotel
{
...
   public int MakeReservation(string cust, int rooms)
   {
      // Requested number of rooms should be positive
      if (rooms <= 0)
         throw new Exception(
            "Please request a positive number of rooms");
      // Check if rooms are available
      int available = capacity - numGuests;
      if (rooms > available)
         throw new RoomException(
            "Rooms not available", available);
      ...
```

Finally we modify the code in our test program that processes the "book" command. We place the call to **MakeReservation** inside another **try** block, and we provide a catch handler for a **RoomException**. In this catch handler we allow the user an opportunity to request fewer rooms. Here is the code:

```
...
else if (cmd.Equals("book"))
```

```
{
   string customer = iw.getString("customer name: ");
   int rooms = iw.getInt("number of rooms: ");
   int id;
   try
   {
      id = hotel.MakeReservation(customer, rooms);
   }
   catch (RoomException e)
   {
      Console.WriteLine("Exception: {0}", e.Message);
      Console.WriteLine(
         "{0} rooms are available", e.Available);
      // try again
      rooms = iw.getInt("number of rooms: ");
      id = hotel.MakeReservation(customer, rooms);
   }
   Console.WriteLine("Reservation has been booked");
   Console.WriteLine("ReservationId = {0}", id);
   ...
```

Here is a transcript of a sample run of our program:

```
The hotel has 10 rooms
Enter command, quit to exit
H> book
customer name: bob
number of rooms: 11
Exception: Rooms not available
10 rooms are available
number of rooms: 5
Reservation has been booked
ReservationId = 1
```

## Structured Exception Handling

One of the principles of structured programming is that a block of code should have a single entry point and a single exit point. The single exit point is convenient, because you can consolidate cleanup code in one place. The **goto** statement is usually bad, because it facilitates breaking this principle. But there are other ways to violate the principle of a single exit point, such as multiple **return** statements from a method.

Multiple return statements may not be too bad, because these may be encountered during normal, anticipated flow of control. But exceptions can cause a particular difficulty, since they interrupt the normal flow of control. In a common scenario you can have at least *three* ways of exiting a method:

- No exception is encountered, and any catch handlers are skipped.
- An exception is caught, and control passes to a catch handler and then to the code after the catch handlers.

- An exception is caught, and the catch handler itself throws another exception. Then code after the catch handler will be bypassed.

The first two cases do not present a problem, as control passes to the code after the catch handlers. But the third case is a source of difficulty.

## FINALLY BLOCK

The structured exception handling mechanism in C# resolves this problem with a **finally** block. The **finally** block is optional, but if present must appear immediately after the **catch** handlers. It is guaranteed, in all three cases described above, that the code in the **finally** block will *always* execute before the method is exited.

We illustrate use of **finally** in the "cancel" command of our **Hotel** example. See the directory **HotelException\Step3**. There are several ways to exit this block of code, and the user might become confused about whether a cancellation was actually made or not. We insert a **finally** block which will *always* display all the reservations. Here is the code:

```
else if (cmd.Equals("cancel"))
{
   int id;
   id = iw.getInt("reservation id: ");
   try
   {
      hotel.CancelReservation(id);
   }
   catch (Exception e)
   {
      Console.WriteLine("Exception: {0}", e.Message);
      id = iw.getInt("reservation id: ");
      hotel.CancelReservation(id);
   }
   finally
   {
      ShowReservations(hotel);
   }
}
```

It is instructive to compare the "book" and "cancel" commands. In the "book" command there is code after the catch handler. This code will be executed if the catch handler is skipped (no exception). The code will also be executed if the catch handler exits normally (user enters a small enough number of rooms). But if an exception is thrown inside the catch handler, this code will be skipped. In the case of "cancel," there is a **finally** block. The code inside the **finally** block will always be executed, even if the catch handler throws an exception (user enters an invalid id a second time).

## Inner Exceptions

In general it is wise to handle exceptions, at least at some level, near their source, because you have the most information available about the context in which the exception occurred. A common pattern is to create a new exception object that captures more detailed information and throw this onto the calling program. So that information is not lost about the original exception, you may pass the original exception as a parameter when constructing the new exception. Then the calling program can gain access to both exceptions through the **InnerException** property of the exception object.

The program **HotelException\Step3** also illustrates using inner exceptions. In the **MakeReservation** method we explicitly check for an **IndexOutOfRangeException**. We throw a new exception, which we construct by passing the original exception as a parameter.

```
// Add reservation to reservation list and return
// reservation id
try
{
   reservations[nextReservation++] = item;
}
catch (IndexOutOfRangeException e)
{
   throw new Exception(
      "Reservation table size exceeded", e);
}
```

In the test program we make use of the **InnerException** property.

```
catch (Exception e)
{
   Console.WriteLine("Exception: {0}", e.Message);
   if (e.InnerException != null)
   {
      Console.WriteLine(
         "InnerException: {0}", e.InnerException.Message);
   }
}
```

## Multiple Catch Handlers

You may have several catch handlers for the same **try** block. Each catches a different type of exception. The first catch handler that matches the exception object will be executed.

The program **HotelException\Step3** also illustrates using multiple catch handlers. In the test program we have handlers for both **FormatException** and **Exception**. Note that you do not have to instantiate an exception object instance in the **catch** statement if you do not use it. The **catch** statement can be used without any parameters if you want to catch any exception and do not care about the exception object.

```
catch (FormatException)
{
   Console.WriteLine(
      "Please enter your data in correct format");
}
catch (Exception e)
{
   Console.WriteLine("Exception: {0}", e.Message);
   if (e.InnerException != null)
   {
      Console.WriteLine(
         "InnerException: {0}", e.InnerException.Message);
   }
}
```

Here is a sample run of the program. When we use an incorrect format, the first catch handler is invoked. When we use the correct format, but an illegal negative value for the number of rooms, we don't get a match for the first catch handler, but we do get a match for the second, since we are using the base **Exception** class.

```
The hotel has 10 rooms
Enter command, quit to exit
H> book
customer name: bob
number of rooms: xxx
Please enter your data in correct format
H> book
customer name: bob
number of rooms: -1
Exception: Please request a positive number of rooms
H>
```

# Unsafe Code

The mainstream use of C# is to write *managed code*, which runs on the Common Language Runtime. As we shall see in Chapter 14, it is quite possible for a C# program to call *unmanaged code*, such as a legacy COM component, which runs directly on the operating system. This facility is important, because a tremendous amount of legacy code exists, which is all unmanaged.

There is overhead in transitioning from a managed environment to an unmanaged one and back again. C# provides another facility, called *unsafe code*, which allows you to bypass the .NET memory management and get at memory directly, while still running on the CLR. In particular, in unsafe code you can work with *pointers*, which we will discuss later in this section.

## Unsafe Blocks

The most circumspect use of unsafe code is within a block, which is specified using the C# keyword **unsafe**. The program **UnsafeBlock** illustrates using the **sizeof** operator to determine the size in bytes of various data types. You will get a compiler error if you try to use the **sizeof** operator outside of unsafe code.

```
// UnsafeBlock.cs

using System;

struct Account
{
   private int id;
   private decimal balance;
}

public class UnsafeBlock
{
   public static void Main()
   {
      unsafe
      {
         Console.WriteLine("size of int = {0}",
                           sizeof(int));
         Console.WriteLine("size of decimal = {0}",
                           sizeof(decimal));
         Console.WriteLine("size of Account = {0}",
                           sizeof(Account));
      }
   }
}
```

To compile this program at the command line, open up a DOS window and navigate to the directory **c:\OI\NetCs\Chap3\UnsafeBlock**. You can then enter the following command to compile using the **/unsafe** compiler option.

```
csc /unsafe UnsafeBlock.cs
```

(You may ignore the warning messages, as our program does not attempt to use fields of **Account**. It applies only the **sizeof** operator.) To run the program, type **unsafeblock** at the command line, obtaining the output shown below:

```
C:\OI\NetCs\Chap3\UnsafeBlock>unsafeblock
size of int = 4
size of decimal = 16
size of Account = 20
```

To set the unsafe option in Visual Studio, perform the following steps:

1. Right-click over the project in the Solution Explorer and choose Properties.
2. In the Property Pages window that comes up, click on Configuration Properties and then on Build.
3. In the dropdown for Allow unsafe code blocks choose True. See Figure 3–5.
4. Click OK. You can now compile your project in unsafe mode.

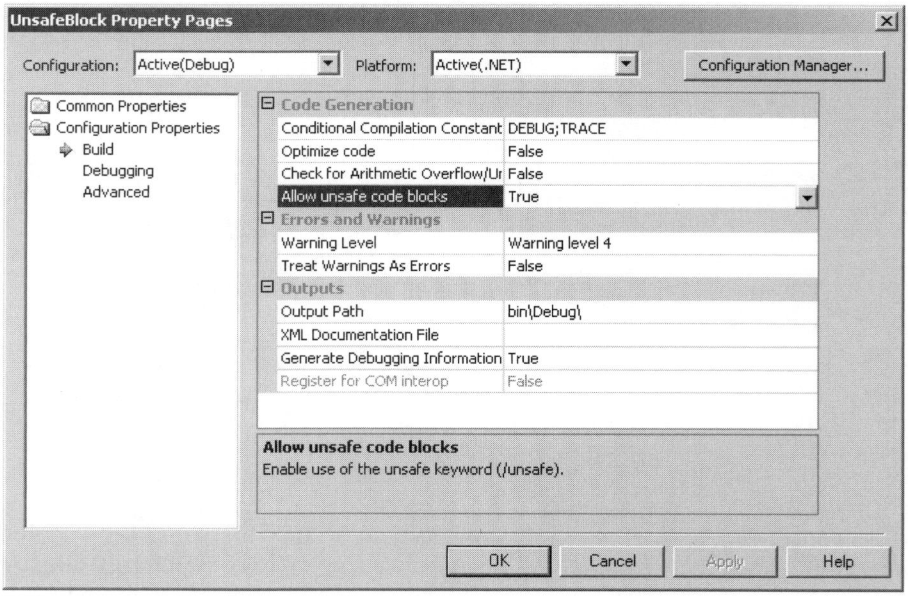

**Figure 3–5**    *Configuring a project for unsafe mode in Visual Studio.*

## Pointers

Earlier in this chapter we saw that C# has three kinds of data types:

- Value types, which directly contain their data
- Reference types, which refer to data contained somewhere else
- Pointer types

Pointer types can be used only in unsafe code. A pointer is an *address* of an actual memory location. A pointer variable is declared using an asterisk after the data type. To refer to the data a pointer is pointing to, use the *dereferencing* operator, which is an asterisk before the variable. To obtain a pointer from a memory location, apply the *address of* operator, which is an ampersand in front of the variable. Here are some examples.

```
int* p;          // p is a pointer to an int
int a = 5;       // a is an int, with 5 stored
p = &a;          // p now points to a
*p = 12;         // 12 is now stored in location pointed
                 // to by p. So a now has 12 stored
```

Pointers were widely used in the C programming language, because functions in C pass data only by value. Thus, if you want a function to return data, you must pass a pointer rather than the data itself. The program **UnsafePointer** illustrates a **Swap** method, which is used to interchange two integer variables. Since the program is written in C#, we can pass data by reference. We illustrate with two overloaded versions of the **Swap** method, one using **ref** parameters and the other using pointers. Rather than using an **unsafe** block, this program uses **unsafe** methods, which are defined by including **unsafe** among the modifiers of the method. Both the **Main** method and the one **Swap** method are unsafe.

```
// UnsafePointer.cs

using System;

public class UnsafePointer
{
    public static unsafe void Main()
    {
        int x = 55;
        int y = 777;
        Show("Before swap", x, y);
        Swap(ref x, ref y);
        Show("After swap", x, y);
        Swap(&x, &y);
        Show("After unsafe swap", x, y);
    }
    private static void Show(string s, int x, int y)
    {
```

```
   Console.WriteLine("{0}: x = {1}, y = {2}", s, x, y);
}
private static void Swap(ref int x, ref int y)
{
   int temp = x;
   x = y;
   y = temp;
}
private static unsafe void Swap(int* px, int* py)
{
   int temp = *px;
   *px = *py;
   *py = temp;
}
}
```

Again you should compile the program using the **unsafe** option, either at the command line or in the Visual Studio project. Here is the output. The first swap interchanges the values. The second swap brings the values back to their original state.

```
Before swap: x = 55, y = 777
After swap: x = 777, y = 55
After unsafe swap: x = 55, y = 777
```

## Fixed Memory

When working with pointers there is a pitfall. Suppose you have obtained a pointer to a region of memory that contains data you are working on. Since you have a pointer, you are accessing memory directly. But suppose the garbage collector collects garbage and moves data about in memory. Then your object may now reside at a different location, and your pointer may no longer be valid.

To deal with such a situation, C# provides the keyword **fixed**, which declares that the memory in question is "pinned" and cannot be moved by the garbage collector. Note that you should use **fixed** only for temporary, local variables, and you should keep the scope as circumscribed as possible. If too much memory is pinned, the CLR memory-management system cannot manage memory efficiently.

The program **UnsafeAccount** illustrates working with **fixed** memory. This program declares an array of five **Account** objects and then assigns them all the same value. The attempt to determine the size of this array is commented out, because you cannot apply the **sizeof** operator to a managed type such as **Account[]**.

It also illustrates the arrow operator for dereferencing a field in a struct, when you have a pointer to the struct. For example, if **p** is a pointer to an instance of the struct **Account** shown below, the code that follows afterward will assign values to the account object pointed to by **p**.

```
p->id = 101;              // assign the id field
p->balance = 50.00m;      // assign the balance field
```

Here is the code.

```
// UnsafeAccount.cs

using System;

struct Account
{
   public int id;
   public decimal balance;
   public Account(int id, decimal balance)
   {
      this.id = id;
      this.balance = balance;
   }
}

public class UnsafeAccount
{
   public static unsafe void Main()
   {
      int id = 101;
      decimal balance = 50.55m;
      Account acc = new Account(id, balance);
      ShowAccount(&acc);
      Account[] array = new Account[5];
      //Console.WriteLine("size of Account[] = {0}",
      //                  sizeof(Account[]));
      ShowArray(array);
      fixed (Account* pStart = array)
      {
         Account* pAcc = pStart;
         for (int i = 0; i< array.Length; i++)
            *pAcc++ = acc;
      }
      ShowArray(array);
   }
   private static unsafe void ShowAccount(Account* pAcc)
   {
      Console.WriteLine("id = {0}, balance = {1:C}",
                        pAcc->id, pAcc->balance);
   }
   private static void ShowAccount(Account acc)
   {
      Console.WriteLine("id = {0}, balance = {1:C}",
```

```
                              acc.id, acc.balance);
    }
    private static void ShowArray(Account[] array)
    {
        for (int i = 0; i < 5; i++)
        {
            ShowAccount(array[i]);
        }
    }
}
```

## Summary

In this chapter we have covered the essentials of the C# language, which should equip you to start writing nontrivial programs in C#. We surveyed variables, operators, control structures, formatting, methods, and input/output. We examined classes in detail, and we looked at some convenience features, such as properties. We covered the essentials of data types in C#, which map to the Common Type System. We discussed the fundamental distinction between value and reference types, and saw how to convert between them using boxing and unboxing operations. We examined some standard types, such as **string**, **StringBuilder**, and **Array**. We covered some additional topics concerning methods, including parameter passing, variable length parameter lists, method overloading, and operator overloading. We discussed exception handling in C# in some detail, including the use of user defined exception classes and structured exception handling. We concluded the chapter by looking at how you can have "unsafe" sections of C# code, which can be used to work with pointers for efficiency or for interoperating with legacy code.

A number of examples pertained to a hotel reservation system. In the next chapter we will study object-oriented programming in C#, and we will extend our hotel reservation example to a case study, which will be continued throughout the rest of the book.

# Object-Oriented Programming in C#

*I*n this chapter we study in detail the object-oriented aspects of C#, with an emphasis on inheritance. First we review the fundamentals of object-oriented programming. Next, the Acme Travel Agency case study is introduced. This case study is developed throughout the entire book, as we explain more about .NET. We consider some abstractions that will enable us to implement a reservation system for a variety of resources, and we provide an implementation of a hotel reservation system. The abstract base classes we define provide reusable code that enables us to easily implement other kinds of reservation systems. The key is finding the right abstractions.

We will see how C# language features facilitate object-oriented programming. Certain details of C#, such as use of access control (public, private, and protected) and properties can help express abstractions in a way that is safe and easy to use. We will then look at other object-oriented features of C#, such as virtual methods, method hiding, method overriding, and polymorphism. A problem in languages supporting inheritance is the fragile base class problem, and we will see how C# helps in avoiding this pitfall.

This chapter is very much driven by our case study. We introduce object-oriented features of C# as we elaborate the case study. At the end of the chapter we cover additional concepts not illustrated by the case study.

## Review of Object-Oriented Concepts

In this preliminary section we review the fundamentals of object-oriented programming. If you are an experienced C++ or Java programmer, you may skim through this section as a refresher and begin your careful reading with the next section, where we introduce the case study.

# Objects

Objects have both a real-world and a software meaning. The object model describes a relationship between them.

## OBJECTS IN THE REAL WORLD

The term *object* has an intuitive real-world meaning. There are concrete, tangible objects, such as a ball, an automobile, and an airplane. There are also more abstract objects that have a definite intellectual meaning, such as a committee, a patent, or an insurance contract.

Objects have both attributes (or characteristics) and operations that can be performed upon them. A ball has a size, a weight, a color, and so on. Operations may be performed on the ball, such as throw, catch, and drop.

There can be various types of relationships among classes of objects. One, for example, is a specialization relationship, such as an automobile is a special kind of vehicle. Another is a whole/part relationship, such as an automobile consists of an engine, a chassis, wheels, and other parts.

## OBJECT MODELS

Objects can also be used in programs. Objects are useful in programming because you can set up a software model of a real-world system. Software objects abstract the parts of objects in the real world that are relevant to the problem being solved. The model can then be implemented as software using a programming language. A software system implemented in this way tends to be more faithful to the real system, and it can be changed more readily when the real system is changed.

There are formal languages for describing object models. The most popular language is UML (Unified Modeling Language), which is a synthesis of several earlier modeling languages. Formal modeling languages are beyond the scope of this book, but we will find that informal models are useful.

## REUSABLE SOFTWARE COMPONENTS

Another advantage of objects in software is that they can facilitate reusable software components. Hardware has long enjoyed significant benefits from reusable hardware components. For example, computers can be created from power supplies, printed circuit boards, and other components. Printed circuit boards in turn can be created from chips. The same chip can be reused in many different computers, and new hardware designs do not have to be done from scratch.

With appropriate software technology, similar reuse is feasible in software systems. Objects provide the foundation for software reuse.

## OBJECTS IN SOFTWARE

An *object* is a software entity containing data (*state*) and related functions (*behavior*) as a self-contained module. For example, a **HotelBroker** may contain a list of hotels (the state) and provide operations to add a hotel and make a reservation (behavior).

## ABSTRACTION

An *abstraction* captures the essential features of a real-world object, suppressing unnecessary details. All instances of an abstraction share these common features. Abstraction helps us deal with complexity. For example, consider the problem of booking a reservation. There are many different kinds of things you might want to reserve, such as a hotel, an airplane flight, or a conference room. Such "reservables" have many differences, but they have certain essentials in common., such as a capacity.

## ENCAPSULATION

The implementation of an abstraction should be hidden from the rest of the system, or *encapsulated*. For example, the list of hotels may be contained in several different kinds of data structures, such as an array, a collection, or a database. The rest of the system should not need to know the details of the representation.

# Classes

A *class* groups all objects with common behavior and common structure. A class allows creation of new objects of the same type. An object is an instance of some class. We refer to the process of creating an individual object as *instantiation.*

Classes can be related in various ways, such as by *inheritance* and by *containment.*

## INHERITANCE

Inheritance is a key feature of the object-oriented programming paradigm. You abstract out common features of your classes and put them in a high-level base class. You can add or change features in more specialized derived classes, which "inherit" the standard behavior from the base class. Inheritance facilitates code reuse and extensibility.

Consider **Reservable** as a base class, with derived classes **Hotel** and **Flight**. All reservables share some characteristics, such as a capacity. Different kinds of reservables differ in other respects. For example, a hotel has a city and a name, while a flight has an origin and a destination. Figure 4–1 illustrates the relationship among these different kinds of reservables.

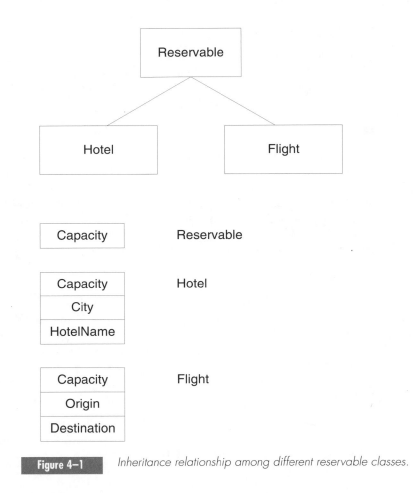

**Figure 4–1** *Inheritance relationship among different reservable classes.*

## ABSTRACT CLASSES

Sometimes a class is not meant to be instantiated, but only to provide a template for derived classes. The **Reservable** class is an example—it is too abstract to actually instantiate. Only specific kinds of reservable classes, such as **Hotel** and **Flight,** may actually be instantiated. We call a class such as **Reservable** that cannot be instantiated an *abstract* class. A class that can be instantiated is called a *concrete* class.

## RELATIONSHIPS AMONG CLASSES

Classes may be related to each other in various ways.

- The inheritance (IS-A) relationship specifies how one class is a special case of another class. A **Hotel** (subclass or derived class) is a special kind of **Reservable** (superclass or base class).

- The composition (HAS-A) relationship specifies how one class (the whole) is made up of other classes (the parts). A **HotelBroker** (whole) has a list of **Hotel** objects.
- A weaker kind of relationship (USES-A) can be identified when one class merely makes use of some other class when carrying out its responsibilities.

## Polymorphism

Consider the problem of generating a payroll for various categories of employees. Different kinds of employees may have pay calculated in a different manner. A salaried employee receives a fixed salary. A wage employee is paid according to the number of hours worked. A sales employee is paid according to the commissions earned on sales that were made.

A traditional approach is to maintain a type field in an employee structure and to perform processing in a switch statement, with cases for each type. Such use of switch statements is error prone and requires much maintenance when adding a new employee type.

An alternative is to localize the intelligence to calculate pay in each employee class, which will support its own **GetPay** method. Generic payroll code can then be written that will handle different types of employees and will not have to be modified to support an additional employee type. Provide a **GetPay** method in the base class and an override of this method in each derived class. Call **GetPay** through an object reference to a general **Employee** object. Depending on the actual employee class referred to, the appropriate **GetPay** method will be called.

The ability for the same method call to result in different behavior depending on the object through which the method is invoked is referred to as *polymorphism*. Polymorphism can greatly simplify complex systems and is an important part of the object-oriented paradigm.

You should not try to coerce your design so that you can take advantage of polymorphism. We will see in our Acme Travel Agency case study that we have three different abstract base classes, but we do not need polymorphism to achieve quite general behavior. On the other hand, the .NET Framework classes use polymorphism heavily, as we shall see beginning in Chapter 5. Later in this chapter we will provide a small example of polymorphism using an employee class hierarchy, as outlined above.

## Acme Travel Agency Case Study: Design

The Acme Travel Agency provides various services, including the booking of hotel, plane, and car rental reservations. We will use this simple theme of booking reservations to illustrate various features of .NET throughout the book. In this chapter we design the architecture of a general system for booking different kinds of reservations. We illustrate the reservation system with an implementation of a hotel broker system that supports the following basic features:

- Add a hotel to the list of hotels
- Show all the hotels
- Show all the hotels in a particular city
- Reserve a hotel room for a range of dates
- Show all the reservations
- Show all the reservations for a particular customer

The system also maintains a list of customers. Customers may register by giving their name and email address, and they will be assigned a customer ID. The following features are supported in the basic customer management subsystem:

- Register as a customer
- Change the email address of a customer
- Show a single customer or all the customers

In this chapter various lists, such as hotels, reservations, and customers, will be maintained as arrays. In the next chapter we will use .NET collections in place of arrays, and we will implement more features, such as the ability to delete a hotel, cancel a reservation, and the like. In later chapters we will extend the case study in various ways, such as providing a graphical user interface, storing all data in a database, deploying as a Web application, and so on.

The code for our case study is in the **CaseStudy** folder for this chapter.

## Designing the Abstractions

Bearing in mind that eventually we want to implement not only a hotel reservation system, but also a system for other kinds of reservations, including plane and car rental, it behooves us at the beginning to look for appropriate abstractions. The more functionality we are able to put in base classes, the less work we will have to do in order to implement a particular kind of reservation system. On the other hand, having more functionality in the base classes can reduce the range of problems to which they are applicable. Good design is a balancing act.

Another attribute of good abstractions is that they will survive major changes in implementation. As we shall see later in this book, our C# abstractions of the hotel reservation system remain intact as we implement the system on an SQL Server database.

These abstractions will be represented in C# by abstract classes, defined in the file **Broker.cs** in the **CaseStudy** folder for this chapter.

## RESERVABLE

Our first abstraction is the thing we are looking to reserve. We will denote this abstraction as simply **Reservable**. The basic issue in reservations is resource usage. There are a limited number of reservable resources. Hence the key attribute of a **Reservable** is **capacity**. For example, a hotel may have 100 rooms. A flight may have 250 seats. We will also want a unique identifier for a **Reservable**, which we will denote by **unitid**. (The shorter name **unitid** is used in preference to the longer, more awkward name **reservableid**. Later we will see other uses of the terminology "unit." For example, the method to add a reservable is called **AddUnit**.)

For our applications we are going to introduce an additional attribute, **cost**. There is a room rate for a hotel, a ticket cost for a flight, and so on. Note that this attribute may not be applicable to all things that are being reserved. For example, a conference room within a company may not have a cost assigned to it. However, our applications are for commercial customers, so we choose to include **cost** in our model.

### Simplifications

Because our case study is designed to illustrate concepts in C# and .NET, we will choose many simplifications in our design, so that we do not become bogged down in too detailed coding. For example, in real life a hotel has several different kinds of rooms, each having a different rate. Similarly, an airplane flight will have different classes of seats. Here the situation in real life is even more complicated, because the price of a seat may vary wildly depending on when the reservation was made, travel restrictions, and so on. To make life simple for us, we are assuming that each instance of a particular reservable will have the same cost.

In C# we will represent a **Reservable** by an *abstract class*.

```
public abstract class Reservable
{
    static private int nextid = 0;
    protected int unitid;
    internal protected int capacity;
    internal protected decimal cost;
    public Reservable(int capacity, decimal cost)
    {
        this.capacity = capacity;
        this.cost = cost;
        unitid = nextid++;
    }
}
```

A constructor allows us to specify the **capacity** and **cost** when the object is created. The **unitid** is autogenerated by a static variable. This id starts out at 0, because it is also going to be used in our implementation as an index in a two-dimensional array to track the number of customers having a reservation at a given reservable on a given date.

We will discuss the role of the **private**, **internal**, and **protected** access control specifiers later.

## RESERVATION

When a customer books a reservation of a reservable, a record of the reservation will be made. The **Reservation** class holds the information that will be stored.

```
public abstract class Reservation
{
   public int ReservationId;
   public int UnitId;
   public DateTime Date;
   public int NumberDays;
   static private int nextReservationId = 1;
   public Reservation()
   {
      ReservationId = nextReservationId++;
   }
}
```

The **ReservationId** is autogenerated. The **UnitId** identifies the reservable that was booked. **Date** is the starting date of the reservation, and **NumberDays** specifies the number of days for which the reservation was made.

## BROKER

Our third abstraction, **Broker**, models a broker of any kind of reservable, and is also represented by an abstract class. It maintains a list of reservables, represented by the array **units**, and a list of reservations, represented by the array **reservations**. The two-dimensional array **numCust** keeps track of the number of customers having a reservation at a given reservable on a given day.

```
public abstract class Broker
{
   private int MaxDay;
   private const int MAXRESERVATION = 10;
   private static int nextReservation = 0;
   private static int nextUnit = 0;
   private int[,] numCust;
   protected Reservation[] reservations;
```

```
protected Reservable[] units;
public Broker(int MaxDay, int MaxUnit)
{
    this.MaxDay = MaxDay;
    numCust = new int[MaxDay, MaxUnit];
    units = new Reservable[MaxUnit];
    reservations = new Reservation[MAXRESERVATION];
}
...
```

## RESERVATIONRESULT

A simple structure is used for returning the result from making a reservation.

```
public struct ReservationResult
{
    public int ReservationId;
    public decimal ReservationCost;
    public decimal Rate;
    public string Comment;
}
```

The **Rate** is the cost for one day, and **ReservationCost** is the total cost, which is equal to the number of days multiplied by the cost for one day. The **ReservationId** is returned as –1 if there was a problem, and an explanation of the problem is provided in the **Comment** field. This structure is created so that result information can be passed in distributed scenarios, such as Web Services, where you cannot throw exceptions.

## Base Class Logic

The base class **Broker** not only represents the abstraction of a broker of any kind of reservable. It also contains general logic for booking reservations and maintaining a list of reservations. Our ability to capture this logic abstractly gives the power to this base class and will make implementing reservations in a derived class relatively simple.

### RESERVE

The core method of the **Broker** class is **Reserve**.

```
protected ReservationResult Reserve(Reservation res)
{
    int unitid = res.UnitId;
    DateTime dt = res.Date;
    int numDays = res.NumberDays;
    ReservationResult result = new ReservationResult();
    // Check if dates are within supported range
    int day = dt.DayOfYear - 1;
```

```
    if (day + numDays > MaxDay)
    {
        result.ReservationId = -1;
        result.Comment = "Dates out of range";
        return result;
    }
    // Check if rooms are available for all dates
    for (int i = day; i < day + numDays; i++)
    {
        if (numCust[i, unitid] >= units[unitid].capacity)
        {
            result.ReservationId = -1;
            result.Comment = "Room not available";
            return result;
        }
    }
    // Reserve a room for requested dates
    for (int i = day; i < day + numDays; i++)
        numCust[i, unitid] += 1;
    // Add reservation to reservation list and
    // return result
    AddReservation(res);
    result.ReservationId = res.ReservationId;
    result.ReservationCost = units[unitid].cost * numDays;
    result.Rate = units[unitid].cost;
    result.Comment = "OK";
    return result;
}
```

The **Reserve** method is designed to implement booking several different kinds of reservations. Thus the **Reservation** object, which will be stored in the list of reservations, is created in a more specialized class derived from **Broker** and is passed as a parameter to **Reserve**. For example, a **HotelBroker** will book a **HotelReservation**, and so on. The **UnitId**, **Date**, and **NumberDays** fields are extracted from the **Reservation** object, and a **ReservationResult** object is created to be returned.

```
protected ReservationResult Reserve(Reservation res)
{
    int unitid = res.UnitId;
    DateTime dt = res.Date;
    int numDays = res.NumberDays;
    ReservationResult result = new ReservationResult();
    ...
```

Next we check that all the dates requested for the reservation are within the supported range (which for simplicity we are taking as a single year). We make use of the **DateTime** structure from the **System** namespace. We return an error if a date lies out of range.

```
// Check if dates are within supported range
int day = dt.DayOfYear - 1;
if (day + numDays > MaxDay)
{
   result.ReservationId = -1;
   result.Comment = "Dates out of range";
   return result;
}
...
```

Now we check that space is available for each date, using the **numCust** array that tracks how many customers currently have reservations for each day and comparing against the capacity. The first dimension of this two-dimensional array indexes on days, and the second dimension indexes on the unit id. (Note that for simplicity we have given our fields and methods names suitable for our initial application, a **HotelBroker**.)

```
// Check if rooms are available for all dates
for (int i = day; i < day + numDays; i++)
{
   if (numCust[i, unitid] >= units[unitid].capacity)
   {
      result.ReservationId = -1;
      result.Comment = "Room not available";
      return result;
   }
}
...
```

Next we actually reserve the unit for the requested days, which is implemented by incrementing the customer count in **numCust** for each day.

```
// Reserve a room for requested dates
for (int i = day; i < day + numDays; i++)
   numCust[i, unitid] += 1;
...
```

Finally, we add the reservation to the list of reservations and return the result.

```
// Add reservation to reservation list and
// return result
AddReservation(res);
result.ReservationId = res.ReservationId;
result.ReservationCost =
   units[unitid].cost * numDays;
result.Rate = units[unitid].cost;
result.Comment = "OK";
return result;
}
```

### LISTS OF RESERVATIONS AND RESERVABLES

The **Broker** class also maintains lists of reservations and reservables. For our simple array implementation we only implement **Add** methods. In a later version we will provide logic to remove elements from lists.

```
private void AddReservation(Reservation res)
{
    reservations[nextReservation++] = res;
}
protected void AddUnit(Reservable unit)
{
    units[nextUnit++] = unit;
}
```

## Designing the Encapsulation

In our current implementation of **Broker** all lists are represented by arrays. Since this implementation may not (and in fact will not) be preserved in later versions, we do not want to expose the arrays themselves or the subscripts that are used for manipulating the arrays. We provide public properties **NumberUnits** and **NumberReservations** to provide read-only access to the private variables **nextUnit** and **nextReservation**.

```
public int NumberUnits
{
    get
    {
        return nextUnit;
    }
}
public int NumberReservations
{
    get
    {
        return nextReservation;
    }
}
```

In our **Reservation** class the simple fields **ReservationId**, **UnitId**, **Date**, and **NumberDays** are not likely to undergo a change in representation, so we do not encapsulate them. Later, if necessary, we could change some of these to properties, without breaking client code. For now, and likely forever, we simply use public fields.

```
public abstract class Reservation
{
    public int ReservationId;
    public int UnitId;
```

```
public DateTime Date;
public int NumberDays;
...
```

# Inheritance in C#

C# supports a single inheritance model. Thus a class may derive from a single base class, and not from more than one. (In fact, as we saw in the previous chapter, every class in C# ultimately derives from the root class **System.Object**. In C# we may use the alias **object** for this root class.) This single inheritance model is simple and avoids the complexities and ambiguities associated with multiple inheritance in C++. Although a C# class can inherit only from a single base *class*, it may inherit from several *interfaces*, a topic we will discuss in the next chapter.

In this section we discuss inheritance in connection with a further elaboration of our hotel reservation case study. In the following section we will cover additional features of inheritance in C#, illustrated by an employee class hierarchy.

## Inheritance Fundamentals

With inheritance, you factor the abstractions in your object model, and put the more reusable abstractions in a high-level base class. You can add or change features in more specialized derived classes, which "inherit" the standard behavior from the base class. Inheritance facilitates code reuse and extensibility. A derived class can also provide a more appropriate interface to existing members of the base class.

Consider **Reservable** as a base class, with derived classes such as **Hotel**. All reservables share some characteristics, such as an id, a capacity, and a cost. Different kinds of reservables differ in other respects. For example, a hotel has a **City** and a **HotelName**.

### C# INHERITANCE SYNTAX

You implement inheritance in C# by specifying the derived class in the **class** statement with a colon followed by the base class. The file **HotelBroker.cs** in the **CaseStudy** folder illustrates deriving a new class **Hotel** from the class **Reservable**.

```
// HotelBroker.cs

namespace OI.NetCs.Acme[1]
```

---

[1] We discuss creating a namespace with the **namespace** directive later in the chapter.

```
{
   using System;

   public class Hotel : Reservable
   {
      public string City;
      public string HotelName;

      public Hotel(string city, string name,
                   int number, decimal cost)
         : base(number, cost)
      {
         City = city;
         HotelName = name;
      }
      public int HotelId
      {
         get
         {
            return unitid;
         }
      }
      public int NumberRooms
      {
         get
         {
            return capacity;
         }
      }
      public decimal Rate
      {
         get
         {
            return cost;
         }
      }
   }
}
```

The class **Hotel** automatically has all the members of **Reservable**, and in addition has the fields **City** and **HotelName**.

## CHANGING THE INTERFACE TO EXISTING MEMBERS

The base class **Reservable** has members **unitid**, **capacity**, and **cost**, which are designed for internal use and are not intended to be exposed as such to the outside world. In the **Hotel** class we provide public properties **HotelId**,

**NumberRooms**, and **Rate** to give clients read-only access to these fields. When we implement a property in this way, we can choose a name that is meaningful, such as **NumberRooms**, in place of a more abstract name, such as **capacity**, used in the base class.

### INVOKING BASE CLASS CONSTRUCTORS

If your derived class has a constructor with parameters, you may wish to pass some of these parameters along to a base class constructor. In C# you can conveniently invoke a base class constructor by using a colon, followed by the **base** keyword and a parameter list.

```
public Hotel(string city, string name,
             int number, decimal cost)
   : base(number, cost)
{
   City = city;
   HotelName = name;
}
```

Note that the syntax allows you to explicitly invoke a constructor only of an immediate base class. There is no notation that allows you to directly invoke a constructor higher up the inheritance hierarchy.

# Access Control

C# has two means for controlling accessibility of class members. Access can be controlled at both the class level and the member level.

## Class Accessibility

An access modifier can be placed in front of the **class** keyword to control who can get at the class at all. Access can be further restricted by member accessibility, discussed in the next subsection.

### PUBLIC

The most common access modifier of a class is **public**, which makes the class available to everyone. Whenever we are implementing a class that anyone can use, we want to make it **public**.

### INTERNAL

The **internal** modifier makes a class available within the current *assembly,* which can be thought of as a logical EXE or DLL. (Assemblies were introduced in Chapter 2 and will be discussed in more detail in Chapter 7.) All of our projects so far have built a single assembly, with both the client test pro-gram and the class(es) in this assembly. That means that if we had used **internal** for the class modifier, the programs would have still worked. But later, if we put our classes into a DLL and tried to access them from a client program in a separate EXE, any **internal** classes would not be accessible. So using **public** for class accessibility is generally a good idea.

A common use of the **internal** modifier is for helper classes that are intended to be used only within the current assembly, and not generally.

Note that if you omit the access modifier in front of a class, **internal** will be the default used by the compiler.

## Member Accessibility

Access to individual class members can be controlled by placing an access modifier such as **public** or **private** in front of the member. Member access can only further restrict access to a class, not widen it. Thus if you have a class with **internal** accessibility, making a member **public** will not make it accessible from outside the assembly.

### PUBLIC

A **public** member can be accessed from outside the class.

### PRIVATE

A **private** member can be accessed only from within the class (but not from derived classes).

### PROTECTED

Inheritance introduces a third kind of accessibility, **protected**. A protected member can be accessed from within the class and from within any derived classes.

### INTERNAL

An **internal** member can be accessed from within classes in the same assembly but not from classes outside the assembly.

### INTERNAL PROTECTED

An **internal protected** member can be accessed from within the assembly and from outside the assembly by a derived class.

## Access Control in the Case Study

The **Reservable** class in the file **broker.cs** illustrates most of the member access-control options that we have been discussing.

```
public abstract class Reservable
{
    static private int nextid = 0;
    protected int unitid;
    internal protected int capacity;
    internal protected decimal cost;
    public Reservable(int capacity, decimal cost)
    {
        this.capacity = capacity;
        this.cost = cost;
        unitid = nextid++;
    }
}
```

The static member **nextid** is strictly **private**, because it is used for autogenerating an id and has no use outside the class. The member **unitid** is **protected** because it is used in derived classes, such as **Hotel**, but not elsewhere. The members **capacity** and **cost** are used both in derived classes (such as **Hotel**) and in the class **Broker**, which is not a derived class but is in the same assembly. The **internal protected** access-control specification is ideal for this case. Note that if we had used just **internal**, the program would have still compiled. But since later we may wish to implement derived classes in other assemblies, **internal protected** is more appropriate. Finally, the constructor is **public**.

## Acme Travel Agency Case Study: Implementation

With the abstractions **Reservable, Reservation**, and **Broker** already in place, it now becomes very easy to implement a reservation system for a particular kind of reservable, such as a **Hotel**. Figure 4–2 illustrates our inheritance

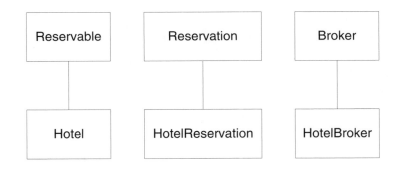

**Figure 4–2**    *Class hierarchy for Acme hotel reservation system.*

hierarchy. **Hotel** derives from **Reservable**, **HotelReservation** derives from **Reservation**, and **HotelBroker** derives from **Broker**.

In this section we will examine key pieces of the implementation of the case study, which is in the **CaseStudy** folder for this chapter.

## Running the Case Study

Before proceeding with our code walkthrough, it would be a good idea to build and run the case study. The program **TestBroker.exe** is a console application. By typing "help" at the command prompt, you can obtain a list of commands:

```
Enter command, quit to exit
H> help
The following commands are available:
        hotels    shows all hotels in a city
        all       shows all hotels
        cities    shows all cities
        add       adds a hotel
        book      book a reservation
        bookings  show all bookings
        register  register a customer
        email     change email address
        show      show customers
        quit      exit the program
H>
```

Experiment with this program until you have a clear understanding of its various features.

## HotelReservation

**HotelReservation** is a simple class derived from **Reservation**. The code is in the file **hotelbroker.cs**. It adds some additional public fields and provides the property **ArrivalDate** as a more meaningful wrapper around the generic **Date** field of the base class.

```
public class HotelReservation : Reservation
{
   public int CustomerId;
   public string HotelName;
   public string City;
   public DateTime DepartureDate;
   public DateTime ArrivalDate
   {
      get
      {
         return Date;
```

```
      }
      set
      {
         Date = value;
      }
   }
}
```

## HotelBroker

The heart of the implementation is the **HotelBroker** class, derived from **Broker**. The code is also in the file **hotelbroker.cs**.

```
public class HotelBroker : Broker
{
   private const int MAXDAY = 366;
   private const int MAXUNIT = 10;
   private const int MAXCITY = 5;
   static private int nextCity = 0;
   private string[] cities;
   public HotelBroker() : base(MAXDAY, MAXUNIT)
   {
      cities = new String[MAXCITY];
      AddHotel("Atlanta", "Dixie", 100, 115.00M);
      AddHotel("Atlanta", "Marriott", 500,
         70.00M);
      AddHotel("Boston", "Sheraton", 250,
         95.00M);
   }
   ...
```

There are constants for various array definitions and a new array to hold the cities. The constructor passes some array definitions to the base class, initializes the **cities** array, and adds some starter hotels as test data.

The next part of the code defines a **NumberCity** property and provides a method to add a hotel.

```
public int NumberCity
{
   get
   {
      return nextCity;
   }
}
public string AddHotel(string city, string name,
                       int number, decimal cost)
{
   if (FindId(city, name) != -1)
      return "Hotel is already on the list";
```

```
    Hotel hotel = new Hotel(city, name, number, cost);
    AddUnit(hotel);
    AddCity(city);
    return "OK";
}
...
```

Private helper functions are provided to find the id of a hotel and to add a city to the list of cities. A city can be added only if it is not already on the list; duplicates are not permitted.

```
private int FindId(string city, string name)
{
    for (int i = 0; i < NumberUnits; i++)
    {
        Hotel hotel = (Hotel) units[i];
        if ((hotel.City == city)
            && (hotel.HotelName == name))
            return hotel.Id;
    }
    return -1;
}
private void AddCity(string city)
{
    // check if city already on list, add if not
    if (!Contains(city))
        cities[nextCity++] = city;
}
private bool Contains(string city)
{
    for (int i = 0; i < NumberCity; i++)
    {
        if (cities[i] == city)
            return true;
    }
    return false;
}
```

Methods are provided to show all the hotels, all the hotels in a given city, and to show the cities. You may wish to examine this code for a review of formatting in C#.

We finally come to the key method **Reserve**, which is used to book a hotel reservation.

```
public ReservationResult Reserve(int customerId,
    string city, string name, DateTime dt, int numDays)
{
    int id = FindId(city, name);
    if (id == -1)
    {
```

```
      ReservationResult result =
         new ReservationResult();
      result.ReservationId = -1;
      result.Comment = "Hotel not found";
      return result;
   }
   HotelReservation res = new HotelReservation();
   res.UnitId = id;
   res.CustomerId = customerId;
   res.HotelName = name;
   res.City = city;
   res.ArrivalDate = dt;
   res.DepartureDate = dt + new TimeSpan(numDays, 0, 0, 0);
   res.NumberDays = numDays;
   return Reserve(res);
}
```

The code in this class is very simple, because it relies upon logic in the base class **Broker**. An error is returned if the hotel cannot be found on the list of hotels. Then a **HotelReservation** object is created, which is passed to the **Reserve** method of the base class. We create the reservation object in the derived class, because we are interested in all the fields of the derived **HotelReservation** class, not just the fields of the base **Reservation** class. We have previously used the **DateTime** structure, and we now use the **TimeSpan** structure in calculating the departure date by adding the number of days of the stay to the arrival date. This calculation relies on the fact that the **+** operator is overloaded in the **DateTime** structure.

## Customers

No reservation system can exist without modeling the customers that use it. The **Customers** class in the file **customer.cs** maintains a list of **Customer** objects. Again we use an array as our representation. This code has very similar structure to code dealing with hotels, and so we show it only in outline form, giving the data structures and the declarations of the public methods and properties.

```
// Customer.cs

namespace OI.NetCs.Acme
{
   using System;

   public class Customer
   {
      public int CustomerId;
      public string FirstName;
      public string LastName;
```

```
    public string EmailAddress;
    static private int nextCustId = 1;
    public Customer(string first, string last,
                    string email)
  {
    CustomerId = nextCustId++;
    FirstName = first;
    LastName = last;
    EmailAddress = email;
  }
}

public class Customers
{
  private Customer[] customers;
  static private int nextCust = 0;
  public Customers(int MaxCust)
  {
    customers = new Customer[MaxCust];
    RegisterCustomer("Rocket","Squirrel",
                     "rocky@frosbitefalls.com");
    RegisterCustomer("Bullwinkle", "Moose",
                     "moose@wossamotta.edu");
  }
  public int NumberCustomers
  ...
  public int RegisterCustomer(string firstName,
     string lastName, string emailAddress)
  ...
  public void ShowCustomers(int customerId)
  ...
  public void ChangeEmailAddress(int id,
     string emailAddress)
  ...
```

## Namespace

All case study code is in the namespace **OI.NetCs.Acme**. All of the files
defining classes begin with a **namespace** directive. There is a corresponding
**using** directive, which you will see in the file **TestHotel.cs**.

```
// Customer.cs

namespace OI.NetCs.Acme
{
...
```

## TestHotel

The **TestHotel** class in the file **TestHotel.cs** contains an interactive program to exercise the hotel and customer classes, supporting the commands shown previously where we suggested running the case study. There is a command loop to read in a command and then exercise it. There is a big **try** block around all the commands with a **catch** handler afterward. Note the **using** statement to gain access to the namespace.

```csharp
// TestHotel.cs

using System;
using OI.NetCs.Acme;

public class TestHotel
{
    public static void Main()
    {
        const int MAXCUST = 10;
        HotelBroker hotelBroker = new HotelBroker();
        Customers customers = new Customers(MAXCUST);
        InputWrapper iw = new InputWrapper();
        string cmd;
        Console.WriteLine("Enter command, quit to exit");
        cmd = iw.getString("H> ");
        while (! cmd.Equals("quit"))
        {
            try
            {
                if (cmd.Equals("hotels"))
                {
                    string city = iw.getString("city:");
                    hotelBroker.ShowHotels(city);
                }
                else if (cmd.Equals("all"))
                    hotelBroker.ShowHotels();
                ...
                else
                    hotelhelp();
            }
            catch (Exception e)
            {
                Console.WriteLine(
                    "Exception: {0}", e.Message);
            }
            cmd = iw.getString("H> ");
        }
    }
    private static void hotelhelp()
    {
        Console.WriteLine(
```

```
                "The following commands are available:");
            ...
        }
    }
```

# More about Inheritance

Our case study has illustrated many important features of object-oriented programming, but there is more to the story. Methods in a derived class may *hide* the corresponding method in the base class, possibly making use of the base class method in their implementation. Alternatively, the base class may have *virtual methods*, which are not bound to an object at compile time but are bound dynamically at runtime. A derived class may *override* a virtual method. This dynamic behavior enables *polymorphic* code, which is general code that applies to classes in a hierarchy, and the specific class that determines the behavior is determined at runtime.

C# provides keywords **virtual** and **override** that precisely specify in base and derived classes, respectively, that the programmer is depending on dynamic binding. By providing a mechanism to specify polymorphic behavior in the language, C# helps programs deal with an issue known as the *fragile base class problem,* which can result in unexpected behavior in a program when a base class in a library is modified but the program itself is unchanged.

## Employee Class Hierarchy

In this section we will use a much simpler class hierarchy to illustrate the important concepts. The base class is **Employee**, which has a public field **Name**. There are two derived classes. The **SalaryEmployee** class has a **salary** field. The **WageEmployee** class has fields for an hourly **rate** of pay and for the number of **hours** worked. Figure 4–3 illustrates this simple class hierarchy.

## Method Hiding

A derived class inherits the methods of its base class, and these inherited methods are automatically available "as is." Sometimes we may want the derived class to do something a little different for some of the methods of the base class. In this case we will put code for these changed methods in the derived class, and we say the derived class "hides" the corresponding methods in the base class. Note that hiding a method requires that the signatures match exactly. (As we discussed in Chapter 3, methods have the same signature if they have the same number of parameters, and these parameters

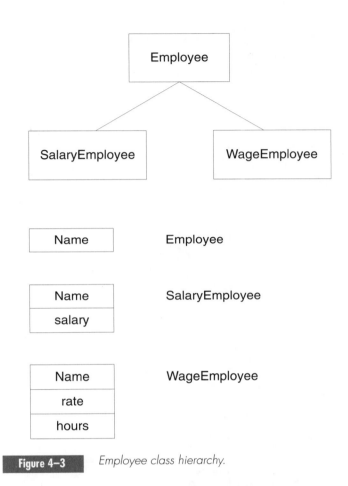

Employee

SalaryEmployee          WageEmployee

Name          Employee

Name          SalaryEmployee
salary

Name          WageEmployee
rate
hours

**Figure 4–3**     *Employee class hierarchy.*

have the same types and modifiers, such as **ref** or **out**. The return type does not contribute to defining the signature of a method.)

In C#, if you declare a method in a derived class that has the same signature as a method in the base class, you will get a compiler warning message. In such a circumstance, there are two things you may wish to do. The first is to *hide* the base class method, which is what we discuss in this section. The second is to *override* the base class method, which we will discuss in the next section.

To hide a base class method, place the keyword **new** in front of the method in the derived class. When you hide a method of the base class, you may want to call the base class method within your implementation of the new method. You can do this by using the keyword **base**, followed by a period, followed by the method name and actual parameters.

The example program **HideEmployee** illustrates method hiding. This program has the **Employee** base class and the **SalaryEmployee** derived class. Each class has a **Show** method. The derived class's **Show** method hides the **Show** method of the base class. But the derived class can call the base class **Show** method through the **base** keyword. Here is the code:

```
// Employee.cs

using System;

public class Employee
{
    public string Name;
    public Employee(string name)
    {
        Name = name;
    }
    public void Show()
    {
        Console.WriteLine("name = {0}", Name);
    }
}

public class SalaryEmployee : Employee
{
    private decimal salary;
    public SalaryEmployee(string name,
                          decimal salary)
        : base(name)
    {
        this.salary = salary;
    }
    new public void Show()
    {
        base.Show();
        Console.WriteLine(
            "salary = {0:C}", salary);
    }
}
```

If you delete the **new** in the derived class **Show** method, you will get a compiler warning message:

```
warning CS0108: The keyword new is required on
'SalaryEmployee.Show()' because it hides
inherited member 'Employee.Show()'
```

## Static Binding

In C# the normal way methods are tied to classes is through *static binding*. That means the object reference type is used at compile time to determine the class whose method is called. The **HideEmployee** program we just looked at illustrates static binding, using a simple **Employee** class and a derived **SalaryEmployee** class. Here is the test program:

```
// TestEmployee.cs

using System;

public class TestEmployee
{
   public static void Main(string[] args)
   {
      Employee emp = new Employee("Ellen");
      SalaryEmployee sal =
         new SalaryEmployee("Sally", 100m);
      emp.Show();
      sal.Show();
      //sal = emp;
      emp = sal;
      emp.Show();
   }
}
```

In this program **emp** is an object reference of type **Employee**. Calling **Show** through this object reference will *always* result in **Employee.Show** being called, no matter what kind of object **emp** may actually be referring to. Here is the output. Notice that the second time we call **Show** through **emp** we are still getting the **Employee** version of **Show** (only the name is displayed).

```
name = Ellen
name = Sally
salary = $100.00
name = Sally
Press any key to continue
```

## TYPE CONVERSIONS IN INHERITANCE

This program also illustrates another feature of inheritance, type conversions. After the objects **emp** and **sal** have been instantiated, the object references will be referring to different objects, one of type **Employee** and the other of type **SalaryEmployee**. Note that the **SalaryEmployee** object has an additional field, **salary**.

The test program tries two type conversions:

```
      //sal = emp;
      emp = sal;
```

The first assignment is illegal (as you can verify by uncommenting and trying to compile). Suppose the assignment were allowed. Then you would have an object reference of type **SalaryEmployee** referring to an **Employee** object. If the conversion "down the hierarchy" (from a base class to a derived class) were allowed, the program would be open to a bad failure at runtime. What would happen if the code tried to access a nonexistent member, such as **sal** accessing the member **salary?**

The opposite assignment:

```
emp = sal;
```

is perfectly legal. We are converting "up the hierarchy." This is okay because of the IS-A relationship of inheritance. A salary employee "is" an employee. It is a special kind of employee. Everything that applies to an employee also applies to a salary employee. There is no "extra field" in the **Employee** class that is not also present in the **SalaryEmployee** class.

## Virtual Methods

In C# you can specify that a method in C# will be bound *dynamically*. Only at runtime will it be determined whether the base or derived class's method will be called. The program **VirtualEmployee** illustrates this behavior. The file **VirtualEmployee.cs** contains class definitions for a base class and a derived class, as before. But this time the **Show** method is declared as **virtual** in the base class. In the derived class the **Show** method is declared **override** (in place of **new** that we used before with method hiding). Now the **Show** method in the derived class does not hide the base class method but *overrides* it.

```
// VirtualEmployee.cs

using System;

public class Employee
{
   public string Name;
   public Employee(string name)
   {
      Name = name;
   }
   virtual public void Show()
   {
      Console.WriteLine("name = {0}", Name);
   }
}

public class SalaryEmployee : Employee
{
   private decimal salary;
   public SalaryEmployee(string name,
                         decimal salary)
```

```
        : base(name)
   {
      this.salary = salary;
   }
   override public void Show()
   {
      base.Show();
      Console.WriteLine(
         "salary = {0:C}", salary);
   }
}
```

We use the same test program. Here is the output. Now, the second time we call **Show** through **sal**, we will be getting the **SalaryEmployee.Show** method, showing the salary as well as the name.

```
name = Ellen
name = Sally
salary = $100.00
name = Sally
salary = $100.00
Press any key to continue
```

## VIRTUAL METHODS AND EFFICIENCY

Virtual method invocation (dynamic binding) is slightly less efficient than calling an ordinary nonvirtual method (static binding). With a virtual method call, there is some overhead at runtime associated with determining which class's method will be invoked. C# allows you to specify in a base class whether you want the flexibility of a virtual method or the slightly greater efficiency of a nonvirtual method. You simply decide whether or not to use the keyword **virtual**. (In some languages all methods are virtual, and you don't have this choice.)

## METHOD OVERRIDING

The **override** keyword in C# is very useful for making programs clearer. In some languages, such as C++, there is no special notation for overriding a method in a derived class. You simply declare a method with the same signature as a method in the base class. If the base class method is virtual, the behavior is to override. If the base class method is not virtual, the behavior is to hide. In C# this behavior is made explicit.

## The Fragile Base Class Problem

One subtle pitfall in object-oriented programming is the fragile base class problem. Suppose the **override** keyword syntax did not exist. Suppose further that you derive a class from a third-party class library, and you have a method in the derived class that does not hide or override any method in the base class.

Now a new version of the class library comes out, and the base class has a new virtual method whose signature happens to match one of the methods in your class. Now you can be in trouble! Classes that derive from your class may now behave in unexpected ways. Code that was "expected" to call the new method in the class library—or in code in a derived class that deliberately overrides this method—may now call your method that has nothing whatever to do with the method in the class library.

This situation is rare, but if it occurs it can be extremely vicious. Fortunately, C# helps you avoid such situations by requiring you to use the **override** keyword if you are indeed going to perform an override. If you do not specify either **override** or **new** and a method in your derived class has the same signature as a method in a base class, you will get a compiler error or warning. Thus, if you build against a new version of the class library that introduces an accidental signature match with one of your methods, you will get warned by the compiler.

### COM and the Fragile Base Class Problem

There is no inheritance in Microsoft's Component Object Model (COM). Microsoft used the fragile base class problem as a rationale for not providing inheritance. The issue is much more important for binary components, such as COM objects, than for traditional class libraries distributed in source code, because if the problem arises and you have no source for the library, your options are limited. The real killer is for the problem not to reveal itself in the development lab, but to crop up only in the field after the application has been deployed.

Microsoft .NET has similar aims to COM in providing binary components in multiple languages. The C# **override** concept uses a corresponding feature of .NET, so .NET is able to effectively utilize inheritance with less vulnerability than COM would have had.

## Polymorphism

Virtual functions make it easy to write polymorphic code in C#. Our employee example illustrates the concept of polymorphic code. Imagine a large system with a great many different kinds of employees. How will you write and maintain code that deals with all these different employee types?

A traditional approach is to have a "type field" in an employee structure. Then code that manipulates an employee can key off this type field to determine the correct processing to perform, perhaps using a **switch** statement. Although straightforward, this approach can be quite tedious and error-prone. Introducing a new kind of employee can require substantial maintenance.

Polymorphism can offer a cleaner solution. You organize the different kinds of employees in a class hierarchy, and you structure your program so that you write general-purpose methods that act upon an object reference whose type is that of the base class. Your code calls virtual methods of the base class. The call will be automatically dispatched to the appropriate class, depending on what kind of employee is actually being referenced.

You trade off some slight degradation in runtime performance for more reliable code development.

The program **PolyEmployee\Step1** provides an illustration. The **GetPay** method is virtual, and methods in the derived class will override it. Here is the code for the base class:

```
// Employee.cs

public class Employee
{
      public string Name;
      public Employee(string name)
      {
           Name = name;
      }
      virtual public decimal GetPay()
      {
           return 1.0m;
      }
}
```

Methods in the derived classes override the virtual method in the base class. Here is the code for **SalaryEmployee**:

```
// SalaryEmployee.cs

public class SalaryEmployee : Employee
{
   private decimal salary;
   public SalaryEmployee(string name, decimal salary)
           : base(name)
   {
        this.salary = salary;
   }
   override public decimal GetPay()
   {
```

```
        return salary;
    }
}
```

The **WageEmployee** class provides its own override of **GetPay**, where pay is calculated differently.

```
// WageEmployee.cs

using System;

public class WageEmployee : Employee
{
    private decimal rate;
    private double hours;
    public WageEmployee(string name, decimal rate,
                        double hours)
        : base(name)
    {
        this.rate = rate;
        this.hours = hours;
    }
    override public decimal GetPay()
    {
        return rate * Convert.ToDecimal(hours);
    }
}
```

The payoff comes in the client program, which can now call **GetPay** polymorphically. Here is the code for the test program:

```
// TestPoly.cs

using System;

public class TestPoly
{
    private static Employee[] employees;
    private const int MAXEMPLOYEE = 10;
    private static int nextEmp = 0;
    public static void Main(string[] args)
    {
        employees = new Employee[MAXEMPLOYEE];
        AddSalaryEmployee("Amy", 500.00m);
        AddWageEmployee("Bob", 15.00m, 40);
        AddSalaryEmployee("Charlie", 900.00m);
        PayReport();
    }
    private static void AddSalaryEmployee(
        string name, decimal salary)
    {
```

```
        employees[nextEmp++] =
            new SalaryEmployee(name, salary);
    }
    private static void AddWageEmployee(
        string name, decimal rate, double hours)
    {
        employees[nextEmp++] =
            new WageEmployee(name, rate, hours);
    }
    private static void PayReport()
    {
        for (int i = 0; i < nextEmp; i++)
        {
            Employee emp = employees[i];
            string name = emp.Name.PadRight(10);
            string pay = string.Format("{0:C}",
emp.GetPay());
            string str = name + pay;
            Console.WriteLine(str);
        }
    }
}
```

Here is the output:

```
Amy         $500.00
Bob         $600.00
Charlie     $900.00
```

## Abstract Classes

Sometimes it does not make sense to instantiate a base class. Instead, the base class is used to define a standard template to be followed by the various derived classes. Such a base class is said to be *abstract,* and it cannot be instantiated. In C# you can designate a base class as abstract by using the keyword **abstract**. The compiler will then flag an error if you try to instantiate the class.

An abstract class may have abstract methods, which are not implemented in the class but only in derived classes. The purpose of an abstract method is to provide a template for polymorphism. The method is called through an object reference to the abstract class, but at runtime the object reference will actually be referring to one of the concrete derived classes. The keyword **abstract** is also used to declare abstract methods. In place of curly brackets and implementation code, you simply provide a semicolon after the declaration of the abstract method.

An abstract class can be used to provide a cleaner solution of our polymorhphic payroll example. In the Step 1 solution we discussed previously,

there was a virtual function **GetPay** in the base class which returned an arbitrary amount of $1.00. We know that this method is going to be overridden,
and in fact the **Employee** class will itself never be instantiated. Hence we
make **Employee** an abstract class and **GetPay** an abstract method. This solution is illustrated in **PolyEmployee\Step2**.

```
// Employee.cs

using System;

abstract public class Employee
{
   public string Name;
   public Employee(string name)
   {
      Name = name;
   }
   abstract public decimal GetPay();
}
```

## Sealed Classes

At the opposite end of the spectrum from abstract classes are *sealed* classes.
While you *must* derive from an abstract class, you *cannot* derive from a
sealed class. A sealed class provides functionality that you can use as is, but
you cannot derive from the class and hide or override some of the methods.
An example in the .NET Framework class library of a sealed class
is **System.String**.

Marking a class as sealed protects against unwarranted class deriva-
tions. It can also make the code a little more efficient, because any virtual
functions inherited by the sealed class are automatically treated by the compiler as nonvirtual.

In C# you use the **sealed** keyword to mark a class as sealed.

## Heterogeneous Collections

A class hierarchy can be used to implement heterogeneous collections that
can be treated polymorphically. For example, you can create an array whose
type is that of a base class. Then you can store within this array object references whose type is the base class, but which actually may refer to instances
of various derived classes in the hierarchy. You may then iterate through the
array and call a virtual method. The appropriate method will be called for
each object in the array.

The program **PolyEmployee** example illustrates a heterogeneous array
of three employees, which are a mixture of salary and wage employees.

# Summary

In this chapter we studied, in detail, the object-oriented aspects of C#, with an emphasis on inheritance. After a review of the fundamentals of object-oriented programming, we introduced the Acme Travel Agency case study, which runs as a strand throughout the entire book. We examined the suitable abstractions that enable us to implement a reservation system for a variety of resources that must be reserved, and we provided an implementation of a hotel reservation system. The abstract base classes we defined provide reusable code that can enable us to easily implement other kinds of reservation systems. The key is finding the right abstractions.

We saw how C# language features facilitate object-oriented programming. Certain details of C#, such as use of access control (public, private and protected) and properties can help express abstractions in a way that is safe and easy to use.

We concluded the chapter by looking at other object-oriented features of C#, such as virtual methods, method hiding, method overriding, and polymorphism. A pitfall in languages supporting inheritance is the fragile base class problem, and we have seen how C# helps in avoiding this pitfall.

# C# in the .NET Framework

$C$# as a language is elegant and powerful. To fully use its capabilities you need to understand how it works within the .NET Framework. We begin with the root class **object**. Collections are examined next, including the methods of the **object** class that should be overridden to tap into the functionality provided by the .NET Framework. We then introduce interfaces, which allow you to rigorously define a contract for a class or struct to implement. In C# a class can implement multiple interfaces, even though it can inherit from only one class. Interfaces allow for dynamic programming; you can query a class at runtime to see whether it supports a particular interface.

The interfaces supporting collections are examined in detail. We investigate issues involved in copying objects, such as shallow copy and deep copy. Instead of using copy constructors as in C++, in C# you implement the **ICloneable** interface. We explore generic interfaces in the .NET Framework programming model and compare the .NET and COM component models. A further illustration of generic interfaces is provided by sorting in different orders with the **IComparable** interface. The examples offer insight into the workings of frameworks, which are more than class libraries. In a framework, you call the framework, and the framework calls you. Your code can be viewed as the middle layer of a sandwich. This key insight can help you grasp what makes .NET programming "tick." While callback functions have been used for years in programming, C# uses this concept in delegates and events. Two simple and intuitive examples are presented: a stock market simulation and an online chat room. The chapter concludes with a discussion of attributes, which are pervasive in the .NET Framework.

# System.Object

As we have already seen, every type in C#, whether it is a value type or a reference type, ultimately inherits from the root class **System.Object**. C# provides **object** as a keyword alias for this root class. The class **ValueType** inherits directly from **object. ValueType** is the root for all value types, such as structures and simple types like **int** and **decimal**.

## Public Instance Methods of object

There are four public instance methods of **object**, three of which are virtual and frequently overridden by classes.

### EQUALS

```
public virtual bool Equals(object obj);
```

This method compares an object with the object passed as a parameter and returns **true** if they are equal. **object** implements this method to test for reference equality. **ValueType** overrides the method to test for content equality. Many classes override the method to make equality behave appropriately for the particular class.

### TOSTRING

```
public virtual string ToString();
```

This method returns a human-readable string representation of the object. The default implementation returns the type name. Derived classes frequently override this method to return a meaningful string representation of the particular object.

### GETHASHCODE

```
public virtual int GetHashCode();
```

This method returns a hash value for an object, suitable for use in hashing algorithms and hash tables. You should normally override this method if you override **ToString**. (The C# compiler will give you a warning message if you override one and not the other.)

### GETTYPE

```
public Type GetType();
```

This method returns type information for the object. This type information can be used to get the associated metadata through *reflection*, a topic we discuss in Chapter 8.

## Protected Instance Methods

There are two protected instance methods, which can be used only within derived classes.

### MEMBERWISECLONE

```
protected object MemberwiseClone();
```

This method creates a shallow copy of the object. To perform a deep copy, you should implement the **ICloneable** interface We will discuss shallow and deep copy later in this chapter.

### FINALIZE

```
~Object();
```

This method allows an object to free resources and perform other cleanup operations before it is reclaimed by garbage collection. In C# the **Finalize** method is represented by "destructor" notation like that used in C++. But note that the semantics are totally different. In C++, destructors are invoked in a deterministic manner, which the programmer can depend upon. In C#, finalization is nondeterministic, dependent upon the garbage collector. We discuss finalization in Chapter 8.

## Generic Interfaces and Standard Behavior

If you are used to a language like Smalltalk, the set of behaviors specified in **object** may seem quite limited. Smalltalk, which introduced the concept of a class hierarchy rooted in a common base class, has a very rich set of methods defined in its **Object** class. I counted 38 methods![1] These additional methods support features such as comparing objects and copying objects. The .NET Framework class library has similar methods, and many more. But rather than putting them all in a common root class, .NET defines a number of standard *interfaces*, which classes can optionally support. This kind of organization, which is also present in Microsoft's Component Object Model (COM) and in Java, is very flexible. We will study interfaces later in this chapter, and we will discuss some of the generic interfaces of the .NET Framework.

---

[1] The methods of Smalltalk's **Object** class are described in Chapters 6 and 14 of *Smalltalk-80: The Language and its Implementation,* by Adele Goldberg and David Robson.

## Using object Methods in the Customer Class

As a simple illustration of **object** methods, let's look at our **Customer** class before and after overriding the **Equals**, **ToString**, and **GetHashCode** methods.

### DEFAULT METHODS OF OBJECT

If our class does not provide any overrides of the virtual instance methods of **object**, our class will inherit the standard behavior. This behavior is demonstrated in **CustomerObject\Step1**.

```
// Customer.cs

public class Customer
{
   public int CustomerId;
   public string FirstName;
   public string LastName;
   public string EmailAddress;
   public Customer(int id, string first, string last,
                   string email)
   {
      CustomerId = id;
      FirstName = first;
      LastName = last;
      EmailAddress = email;
   }
}
```

Here is the test program:

```
// TestCustomer.cs

using System;

public class TestCustomer
{
   public static void Main()
   {
      Customer cust1, cust2;
      cust1 = new Customer(99, "John", "Doe",
                           "john@rocky.com");
      cust2 = new Customer(99, "John", "Doe",
                           "john@rocky.com");
      ShowCustomerObject("cust1", cust1);
      ShowCustomerObject("cust2", cust2);
      CompareCustomerObjects(cust1, cust2);
```

```
   }
   private static void ShowCustomerObject(string label,
                                          Customer cust)
   {
      Console.WriteLine("---- {0} ----", label);
      Console.WriteLine("ToString() = {0}",
                        cust.ToString());
      Console.WriteLine("GetHashCode() = {0}",
                        cust.GetHashCode());
      Console.WriteLine("GetType() = {0}",
          cust.GetType());
   }
   private static void CompareCustomerObjects(
      Customer cust1, Customer cust2)
   {
      Console.WriteLine("Equals() = {0}",
                        cust1.Equals(cust2));
   }
}
```

Run the test program and you will see this output:

```
---- cust1 ----
ToString() = Customer
GetHashCode() = 4
GetType() = Customer
---- cust2 ----
ToString() = Customer
GetHashCode() = 6
GetType() = Customer
Equals() = False
```

The default implementation is not at all what we want for our **Customer** object. **ToString** returns the name of the class, not information about a particular customer. **Equals** checks for reference equality. In our example, we have two different references to **Customer** objects with the same content, and **Equals** return **false**.

## OVERRIDING METHODS OF OBJECT

The version of the project in **CustomerObject\Step2** demonstrates overriding these virtual methods. Our override of **Equals** tests for content equality.

```
// Customer.cs

public class Customer
{
   public int CustomerId;
   public string FirstName;
   public string LastName;
```

```
      public string EmailAddress;
      public Customer(int id, string first, string last,
                   string email)
      {
         CustomerId = id;
         FirstName = first;
         LastName = last;
         EmailAddress = email;
      }
      public override bool Equals(object obj)
      {
         Customer cust = (Customer) obj;
         return (cust.CustomerId == CustomerId);
      }
      public override int GetHashCode()
      {
         return CustomerId;
      }
      public override string ToString()
      {
         return FirstName + " " + LastName ;
      }
}
```

The test program is identical. Here is the new output:

```
---- cust1 ----
ToString() = John Doe
GetHashCode() = 99
GetType() = Customer
---- cust2 ----
ToString() = John Doe
GetHashCode() = 99
GetType() = Customer
Equals() = True
```

# Collections

The .NET Framework class library provides an extensive set of classes for working with collections of objects. These classes are all in the **System.Collections** namespace and implement a number of different kinds of collections, including lists, queues, stacks, arrays, and hashtables. The collections contain **object** instances. Since all types derive ultimately from **object**, any built-in or user-defined type may be stored in a collection.

In this section we will look at a representative class in this namespace, **ArrayList**, and see how to use array lists in our programs.

## ArrayList Example

To get our bearings, let's begin with a simple example of using the **ArrayList** class. An array list, as the name suggests, is a list of items stored like an array. An array list can be dynamically sized and will grow as necessary to accommodate new elements being added.

Collection classes are made up of instances of type **object**. We will create and manipulate a collection of **Customer** objects. We could just as easily create a collection of any other built-in or user-defined type. If our type were a value type, such as **int**, the instance would be boxed before being stored in the collection. When the object is extracted from the collection, it will be unboxed back to **int**.

Our example program is **CustomerCollection**. It initializes a list of customers and then lets the user show the customers, register a new customer, unregister a customer, and change an email address. A simple "help" method displays the commands that are available:

```
Enter command, quit to exit
H> help
The following commands are available:
        register    register a customer
        unregister  unregister a customer
        email       change email address
        show        show customers
        quit        exit the program
```

Before examining the code it would be a good idea to run the program to register a new customer, show the customers, change an email address, unregister a customer, and show the customers again. Here is a sample run of the program:

```
H> show
id (-1 for all): -1
    1    Rocket       Squirrel    rocky@frosbitefalls.com
    2    Bullwinkle   Moose       moose@wossamotta.edu
H> register
first name: Bob
last name: Oberg
email address: oberg@objectinnovations.com
id = 3
H> email
customer id: 1
email address: rocky@objectinnovations.com
H> unregister
id: 2
H> show
id (-1 for all): -1
```

```
    1    Rocket         Squirrel
rocky@objectinnovations.com
    3    Bob            Oberg
oberg@objectinnovations.com
```

## CUSTOMERS CLASS

All the code for this project is in the folder **CustomerCollection**. The file **customer.cs** has code for the **Customer** and **Customers** classes. The code for **Customer** is almost identical to what we looked at previously. The only addition is a special constructor that instantiates a **Customer** object with a specified id. We use this constructor in the **Customers** class when we remove an element and when we check if an element is present in the collection.

```
public class Customer
{
...
    public Customer(int id)
    {
        CustomerId = id;
        FirstName = "";
        LastName = "";
        EmailAddress = "";
    }
...
}
```

The **Customers** class contains a list of customers, represented by an **ArrayList**.

```
public class Customers
{
    private ArrayList customers;
    public Customers()
    {
        customers = new ArrayList();
        RegisterCustomer("Rocket", "Squirrel",
                    "rocky@frosbitefalls.com");
        RegisterCustomer("Bullwinkle", "Moose",
                    "moose@wossamotta.edu");
    }
    public int RegisterCustomer(string firstName,
        string lastName, string emailAddress)
    {
        Customer cust = new Customer(firstName, lastName,
                                emailAddress);
        customers.Add(cust);
        return cust.CustomerId;
```

```
    }
    public void UnregisterCustomer(int id)
    {
        Customer cust = new Customer(id);
        customers.Remove(cust);
    }
    public void ChangeEmailAddress(int id,
                                  string emailAddress)
    {
        foreach (Customer cust in customers)
        {
            if (cust.CustomerId == id)
            {
                cust.EmailAddress = emailAddress;
                return;
            }
        }
        throw new Exception("id " + id + " not found");
    }
    public void ShowCustomers(int id)
    {
        if (!CheckId(id) && id != -1)
            return;
        foreach (Customer cust in customers)
        {
            if (id == -1 || id == cust.CustomerId)
            {
                string sid =
                    cust.CustomerId.ToString().PadLeft(4);
                string first = cust.FirstName.PadRight(12);
                string last = cust.LastName.PadRight(12);
                string email = cust.EmailAddress.PadRight(20);
                string str = sid + "   " + first + "    " +
                    last + "    " + email;
                Console.WriteLine(str);
            }
        }
    }
    private bool CheckId(int id)
    {
        Customer cust = new Customer(id);
        return customers.Contains(cust);
    }
}
```

The lines in the listing in bold show the places where we are using collection class features. In Chapter 3 we have already used **foreach** with arrays. The reason **foreach** can be used with arrays is that the **Array** class, like **ArrayList**, implements the **IEnumerable** interface that supports **foreach** syntax. We will discuss **IEnumerable** and the other collection interfaces later in this chapter.

The **Add** and **Remove** methods, as their names suggest, are used for adding and removing elements from a collection. The **Remove** method searches for an object in the collection that **Equals** the object passed as a parameter. Our special constructor creates an object having the id of the element we want to remove. Since we provided an override of the **Equals** method that bases equality on **CustomerId**, the proper element will be removed.

Similarly, the **Contains** method used in our **CheckId** helper method also relies on the override of the **Equals** method.

Compare the code in this program with the use of arrays in the code in the previous chapter's case study. The collection code is much simpler. Using collections makes it easy to remove elements as well as add them. Using arrays, you would have to write special code to move array elements to fill in the space where an element was deleted. Also, collections are not declared to have a specific size, but can grow as required.

# Interfaces

*Interface* is a very fundamental concept in computer programming. A large system is inevitably decomposed into parts, and it is critical to precisely specify the interfaces between these parts. Interfaces should be quite stable, as changing an interface affects multiple parts of the system. In C# **interface** is a keyword and has a very precise meaning. An interface is a reference type, similar to an abstract class, that *specifies* behavior as a set of methods, properties, indexers, and events.[2] An interface is a contract. When a class or struct implements an interface, it must adhere to the contract.

Interfaces are a useful way to partition functionality. You should first specify interfaces and then design appropriate classes to implement the interfaces. While a class in C# can inherit from only one other class, it can implement multiple interfaces.

Interfaces facilitate dynamic programs—you can query a class at runtime to see whether it supports a particular interface, and take action accordingly. Interfaces in C# and .NET are conceptually very similar to interfaces in Microsoft's Component Object Model, but as we will see, they are *much* easier to work with.

In this section we will study the fundamentals of interfaces and provide illustrations using some small sample programs. Then we will restructure our Acme case study to take advantage of interfaces and explore their use in

---

[2] We discuss events later in this chapter.

detail. After that we will examine several important generic interfaces in the .NET library, which will help us gain an understanding of how C# and the .NET library support each other to help us develop powerful and useful programs.

## Interface Fundamentals

Object-oriented programming is a useful paradigm for helping to design and implement large systems. Using classes helps us to achieve abstraction and encapsulation. Classes are a natural decomposition of a large system into manageable parts. Inheritance adds another tool for structuring our system, enabling us to factor out common parts into base classes, helping us to accomplish greater code reuse.

The main purpose of an interface is to specify a *contract* independently of implementation. It is important to understand that conceptually the *interfaces come first.*

### INTERFACES IN C#

In C# **interface** is a keyword, and you define an interface in a manner similar to defining a class. Like classes, interfaces are reference types. The big difference is that there is no implementation code in an interface; it is pure specification. Also note that an interface can have properties as well as methods (it could also have other members, such as indexers). As a naming convention, interface names usually begin with a capital I.

The **IAccount** interface specifies operations to be performed on a bank account.

```
interface IAccount
{
   void Deposit(decimal amount);
   void Withdraw(decimal amount);
   decimal Balance {get;}
   void Show();
}
```

This interface illustrates the syntax for declaring the read-only **Balance** property—you specify the data type, the property name, and in curly brackets which of **set** and **get** apply (only **get** in this case, because the property is read-only).

### IMPLEMENTING AN INTERFACE

In C# you specify that a class or struct implements an interface by using the colon notation that is employed for class inheritance. A class can also inherit both from a class and from an interface. In this case the base class should appear first in the derivation list after the colon.

```
public class AccountC : Account, IAccount
{
   public void Show()³
   {
      Console.WriteLine("balance = {0}", Balance);
   }
}
```

In our example the class **AccountC** inherits from the class **Account**, and it implements the interface **IAccount**. The methods of the interface must all be implemented by **Account**, either directly or in one of the base classes in its inheritance hierarchy.

We will examine a full-blown example of interfaces with the reservation-broker inheritance hierarchy later in the chapter, when we implement Step 2 of the case study.

As a small example, consider the program **InterfaceDemo**. The interface **IAccount** is defined, and two different classes, **AccountC** and **AccountW**, implement the interface. These implementations differ only in the **Show** method. The **AccountC** implementation performs console output to display the account balance, and **AccountW** uses a Windows message box.⁴ The **Deposit** and **Withdraw** methods and the **Balance** property are all implemented in the **Account** base class.

```
// Account.cs

using System;
using System.Windows.Forms;

interface IAccount
{
   void Deposit(decimal amount);
   void Withdraw(decimal amount);
   decimal Balance {get;}
   void Show();
}

public class Account
{
   private decimal balance;
   public Account()
```

---

³ Note that we do not need the **override** keyword when our class implements the **Show** method of the **IAccount** interface. Unlike overriding a virtual method in a class, we are implementing a method which was only specified but not implemented in the interface definition.

⁴ We will discuss Windows programming in Chapter 6. The example program has all needed references to libraries, and all you need to do to display a message box is to call the **Show** method of the **MessageBox** class.

```
   {
      balance = 100;
   }
   public void Deposit(decimal amount)
   {
      balance += amount;
   }
   public void Withdraw(decimal amount)
   {
      balance -= amount;
   }
   public decimal Balance
   {
      get
      {
         return balance;
      }
   }
}

public class AccountC : Account, IAccount
{
   public void Show()
   {
      Console.WriteLine("balance = {0}", Balance);
   }
}

public class AccountW : Account, IAccount
{
   public void Show()
   {
      MessageBox.Show("balance = " + Balance);
   }
}
```

## USING AN INTERFACE

You may call methods of an interface through an object reference to the class, or you may obtain an interface reference and call the methods through this interface reference.[5] The test program in the file **InterfaceDemo.cs** demonstrates both. We obtain the interface reference **iacc** by an implicit cast when we do the assignment to the object reference **acc** or **accw**. Note the

---

[5] As we will see later in the chapter when we discuss "explicit interface implementation," you can force a client program to use an interface reference and not a class reference.

polymorphic behavior of the call to **Show**, using console or Windows output depending on which object is being used.

```csharp
// InterfaceDemo.cs

using System;

class InterfaceDemo
{
    public static void Main()
    {
        // Use an object reference
        AccountC acc = new AccountC();
        acc.Deposit(25);
        acc.Show();
        // Use an interface reference
        IAccount iacc = acc;
        iacc.Withdraw(50);
        iacc.Show();
        // Use interface reference for another class
        // that implements IAccount
        AccountW accw = new AccountW();
        iacc = accw;
        iacc.Show();
    }
}
```

## Multiple Interfaces

Our first example illustrated two classes providing different implementations of the same interface. Another common scenario is for a class to implement multiple interfaces, and in C# it is easy to test at runtime which interfaces are implemented by a class.

Our example program is **MultipleInterfaces**, which also illustrates interface inheritance. The interfaces **IBasicAccount**, **IDisplay**, and **IAccount** are defined in the file **AccountDefs.cs**.

```csharp
// AccountDefs.cs

interface IBasicAccount
{
    void Deposit(decimal amount);
    void Withdraw(decimal amount);
    decimal Balance {get;}
}

interface IDisplay
{
    void Show();
```

```
}

interface IAccount : IBasicAccount, IDisplay
{
}
```

## INTERFACE INHERITANCE

Interfaces can inherit from other interfaces. Unlike classes in C#, for which there is only single inheritance, there can be multiple inheritance of interfaces. In our example, the interface **IAccount** is declared by inheriting from the two smaller interfaces, **IBasicAccount** and **IDisplay**. The advantage of factoring the original interface into two smaller interfaces is an increase in flexibility. For example, a class implementing **IBasicAccount** may run on a server, where it would not be appropriate to implement **IDisplay**.

When declaring a new interface using interface inheritance, you can also introduce additional methods, as illustrated for **IAccount2**.

```
interface IAccount2 : IBasicAccount, IDisplay
{
    void NewMethod();
}
```

## IMPLEMENTING MULTIPLE INTERFACES

A class implements multiple interfaces by mentioning each interface in its inheritance list and by providing code for the methods of each interface. A method may be implemented through inheritance from a base class. The file **Account.cs** in the **MultipleInterfaces** project illustrates two classes. **BasicAccount** implements only the interface **IBasicAccount**, and **Account** implements the two interfaces, **IBasicAccount** and **IDisplay**.

```
// Account.cs

using System;

public class BasicAccount : IBasicAccount
{
    private decimal balance;
    public BasicAccount()
    {
        balance = 100;
    }
    public void Deposit(decimal amount)
    {
        balance += amount;
    }
```

```
    public void Withdraw(decimal amount)
    {
        balance -= amount;
    }
    public decimal Balance
    {
        get
        {
            return balance;
        }
    }
}

public class Account : BasicAccount, IBasicAccount,
IDisplay
{
    public void Show()
    {
        Console.WriteLine("balance = {0}", Balance);
    }
}
```

## USING MULTIPLE INTERFACES

The test program **MultipleInterfaces.cs** illustrates using (or trying to use) the two interfaces with an **Account** object and a **BasicAccount** object. Both interfaces can be used with **Account**, but we cannot use the **IDisplay** interface with **BasicAccount**. If we attempted to do an implicit cast from **BasicAccount** to **IDisplay**, the compiler would flag an error message. In our code we perform an explicit cast within a **try** block. The code compiles, but we get a runtime **InvalidCast** exception, which we catch. The program also illustrates that we can sometimes take a reasonable, alternative course of action if the desired interface is not available. In our case, we are able to perform the output ourselves, making use of the **Balance** property of the **IBasicAccount** interface.

```
// MultipleInterfaces.cs

using System;

class MultipleInterfaces
{
    public static void Main()
    {
        IBasicAccount iacc;
        IDisplay idisp;
        // Use an Account object, which has full functionality
        Account acc = new Account();
```

```
        iacc = acc;
        idisp = acc;
        iacc.Deposit(25);
        idisp.Show();
        // Use BasicAccount object, with reduced functionality
        BasicAccount bacc = new BasicAccount();
        iacc = bacc;
        iacc.Withdraw(50);
        try
        {
            idisp = (IDisplay) bacc;
            idisp.Show();
        }
        catch (InvalidCastException e)
        {
            Console.WriteLine("IDisplay is not supported");
            Console.WriteLine(e.Message);
            // Display the balance another way
            Console.WriteLine("balance = {0}", iacc.Balance);
        }
    }
}
```

Here is the output from running the program:

```
balance = 125
IDisplay is not supported
Exception of type System.InvalidCastException was thrown.
balance = 50
```

## Dynamic Use of Interfaces

A powerful feature of interfaces is their use in dynamic scenarios, allowing us to write general code that can test whether an interface is supported by a class. If the interface is supported, our code can take advantage of it; otherwise our program can ignore the interface. We could in fact implement such dynamic behavior through exception handling, as illustrated previously. Although entirely feasible, this approach is very cumbersome and would lead to programs that are hard to read. C# provides two operators, **as** and **is**, that facilitate working with interfaces at runtime.

As an example, consider the program **DynamicInterfaces**, which uses the interface definitions and class implementations from our previous example. The test program illustrates using each of the C# **as** and **is** operators to check whether the **IDisplay** interface is supported.

```
// DynamicInterfaces.cs

using System;
```

```
class DynamicInterfaces
{
    public static void Main()
    {
        IBasicAccount iacc;
        IDisplay idisp;
        BasicAccount bacc = new BasicAccount();
        iacc = bacc;
        iacc.Withdraw(50);
        // Check IDisplay via C# "as" operator
        idisp = bacc as IDisplay;
        if (idisp != null)
            idisp.Show();
        else
        {
            Console.WriteLine("IDisplay is not supported");
            // Display the balance another way
            Console.WriteLine("balance = {0}", iacc.Balance);
        }
        // Check IDisplay via C# "is" operator
        if (bacc is IDisplay)
        {
            idisp = (IDisplay) bacc;
            idisp.Show();
        }
        else
        {
            Console.WriteLine("IDisplay is not supported");
            // Display the balance another way
            Console.WriteLine("balance = {0}", iacc.Balance);
        }
    }
}
```

Here is the output from running the test program:

```
IDisplay is not supported
balance = 50
IDisplay is not supported
balance = 50
```

## AS OPERATOR[6]

The **as** operator is used to convert one reference type to another reference type. A common application is to convert an object reference or an interface

---

[6] The C# **as** operator is similar to **dynamic_cast** in C++.

reference to another interface reference. Unlike performing the conversion by a cast operation, the **as** operator never throws an exception. If the conversion fails, the result value is **null**.

```
idisp = bacc as IDisplay;
if (idisp != null)
    // idisp is a valid interface reference
```

The **as** operator can also be used to explicitly convert a value type to a reference type by a boxing operation. Again, **null** is returned if the conversion fails.

## IS OPERATOR[7]

The **is** operator dynamically checks if the runtime type of an object is compatible with a given type. The result is a boolean value. The **is** operator can be used to check if an object refers to a class supporting a given interface, as illustrated in our **DynamicInterfaces** program.

```
if (bacc is IDisplay)
{
    idisp = (IDisplay) bacc;
    idisp.Show();
}
```

The **is** operator is not the most efficient solution, as a check of the type is made *twice*. The first time is when the **is** operator is invoked. But the check is made all over again when the cast operation is performed, because the runtime will throw an exception if the interface is not supported. For this situation, **as** is more efficient, since you obtain the interface reference directly.

The **is** operator is useful if you want to check whether an interface is supported but you don't need to directly call a method of the interface. Later in the chapter we will see an example of this situation, when we discuss the **IComparable** interface. If the elements of a collection support **IComparable**, you will be able to call a **Sort** method on the collection. The **Sort** method calls the **CompareTo** method of **IComparable**, although your own code does not.

---

[7] The C# **is** operator is similar to **type_id** in C++.

## Interfaces in C# and COM

There are many similarities between .NET and COM. In both, the concept of interface plays a fundamental role. Interfaces are useful for specifying contracts. Interfaces support a very dynamic style of programming.

In COM you must yourself provide a very elaborate infrastructure in order to implement a COM component. You must implement a class factory for the creation of COM objects. You must implement the **QueryInterface** method of **IUnknown** for the dynamic checking of interfaces. You must implement **AddRef** and **Release** for proper memory management.

With C# (and other .NET languages) the Common Language Runtime does all this for you automatically. You create an object via **new**. You check for an interface via **is** or **as** and obtain the interface by a cast. The garbage collector takes care of memory management for you.

## Explicit Interface Implementation

When working with interfaces, an ambiguity can arise if a class implements two interfaces and each has a method with the same name and signature. As an example, consider the following versions of the interfaces **IAccount** and **IStatement**. Each interface contains the method **Show**.

```
interface IAccount
{
    void Deposit(decimal amount);
    void Withdraw(decimal amount);
    decimal Balance {get;}
    void Show();
}

interface IStatement
{
    int Transactions {get;}
    void Show();
}
```

How can the class specify implementations of these methods? The answer is to use the interface name to qualify the method, as illustrated in the program **Ambiguous**. The **IAccount** version **IAccount.Show** will display only the balance, and **IStatement.Show** will display both the number of transactions and the balance.

```
// Account.cs (project "Ambiguous")
```

. . .

```
public class Account : IAccount, IStatement
{
    private decimal balance;
    int numXact = 0;
    public Account(decimal balance)
    {
        this.balance = balance;
    }
    public void Deposit(decimal amount)
    {
        balance += amount;
        ++numXact;
    }
    public void Withdraw(decimal amount)
    {
        balance -= amount;
        ++numXact;
    }
    public decimal Balance
    {
        get
        {
            return balance;
        }
    }
    void IAccount.Show()
    {
        Console.WriteLine("balance = {0}", balance);
    }
    public int Transactions
    {
        get
        {
            return numXact;
        }
    }
    void IStatement.Show()
    {
        Console.WriteLine("{0} transactions, balance = {1}",
                        numXact, balance);
    }
}
```

You will notice that in the definition of the class **Account**, the qualified methods **IAccount.Show** and **IStatement.Show** do not have an access modifier such as **public**. Such qualified methods *cannot be accessed* through a reference to a class instance. They can *only* be accessed through an interface reference of the type explicitly shown in the method definition. The test program shows that we cannot call the **IAccount.Show** method through an **Account** object reference but only through an **IAccount** interface reference.

By obtaining an **IStatement** interface reference, we can call
**IStatement.Show**.

```
// Ambiguous.cs

using System;

public class Ambiguous
{
    public static void Main()
    {
        Account acc = new Account(100);
        // acc.Show(); // illegal - MUST go through an
                       // interface
        IAccount iacc = (IAccount) acc;
        IStatement istat = (IStatement) acc;
        iacc.Show();
        istat.Show();
        iacc.Deposit(25);
        iacc.Withdraw(10);
        iacc.Show();
        istat.Show();
    }
}
```

Even when there is no ambiguity, you may wish to use explicit interface implementation, in order to force client programs to use interfaces to
call the methods specified in the interfaces. This approach makes it very
clear that the client code is programming against specific interfaces and not
against a large amorphous collection of methods of a class. The code will be
easily adaptable to using different classes that implement the same interfaces.

## Acme Travel Agency Case Study: Step 2

We will now apply our knowledge of interfaces to a little restructuring of the
Acme case study. A major benefit of using interfaces is that they raise the
level of abstraction somewhat, helping you to understand the system by
way of the interface contacts, without worrying about how the system
is implemented.

As usual, our case study code is in the **CaseStudy** directory for
this chapter.

### The Contracts

There are two main sets of contracts in the Acme Travel Agency Case Study.
The first specifies operations on customers, and the second, operations
involving hotels.

## CUSTOMER CONTRACT

The **ICustomer** interface shown below specifies the methods to be used by clients in the Acme Travel Agency system.

```
public interface ICustomer
{
    int RegisterCustomer(string firstName, string lastName,
                        string emailAddress);
    void UnregisterCustomer(int id);
    ArrayList GetCustomer(int id);
    void ChangeEmailAddress(int id, string emailAddress);
}
```

The **RegisterCustomer**, **UnregisterCustomer**, and **ChangeEmailAddress** method definitions are exactly the same as the methods we implemented in the **Customers** class. The **GetCustomer** method is new. Previously, we had a **ShowCustomers** method, which displayed a list of customers to the console. This method was strictly temporary. For general use we want to return data and let the client decide what to do with it. The **GetCustomer** method returns information about one or all customers in an array list. If –1 is passed for the id, the list will contain all the registered customers. Otherwise, the list will contain the customer information for the customer with the given id. If no customer has that id, the list will be empty.

## HOTEL CONTRACTS

We next look at the functionality of the class **HotelBroker**. The methods divide fairly naturally into three groups.

- Hotel information, such as the cities where hotels are available and the hotels within a city
- Hotel administration, such as adding or deleting a hotel, or changing the number of rooms and rate of a hotel
- Hotel reservations, such as booking or canceling a reservation or obtaining a list of reservations

Accordingly we create three interfaces for the **HotelBroker**. These interfaces are defined in **AcmeDefinitions.cs**.

```
public interface IHotelInfo
{
    ArrayList GetCities();
    ArrayList GetHotels();
    ArrayList GetHotels(string city);
}

public interface IHotelAdmin
```

```
{
    string AddHotel(string city, string name,
        int numberRooms, decimal rate);
    string DeleteHotel(string city, string name);
    string ChangeRooms(string city, string name,
        int numberRooms, decimal rate);
}

public interface IHotelReservation
{
    ReservationResult MakeReservation(int customerId,
        string city, string hotel, DateTime checkinDate,
        int numberDays);
    void CancelReservation(int id);
    ArrayList FindReservationsForCustomer(int customerId);
}
```

## The Implementation

We examined the Step 1 implementation of the hotel brokerage system in detail in Chapter 4. The Step 2 implementation uses collections in place of arrays, and it passes information to the client rather than displays information directly.

### STRUCTURES

One detail of our implementation concerns the data structures used to pass lists to the client. We use the **ArrayList** class. But what do we store in each array list? We could use **Customer** objects and **Hotel** objects. The problem here is that these classes have implementation-specific data in them, as well as the information fields that the client program cares about. To obtain implementation neutral representations, we introduce several structures.

In **Customers.cs** we define the **CustomerListItem** structure for passing customer information.

```
public struct CustomerListItem
{
    public int CustomerId;
    public string FirstName;
    public string LastName;
    public string EmailAddress;
}
```

In **AcmeDefinitions.cs** we define structures for hotels, reservations, and reservation results.

```
public struct HotelListItem
{
```

```
    public string City;
    public string HotelName;
    public int NumberRooms;
    public decimal Rate;
}

public struct ReservationListItem
{
    public int CustomerId;
    public int ReservationId;
    public string HotelName;
    public string City;
    public DateTime ArrivalDate;
    public DateTime DepartureDate;
    public int NumberDays;
}

public struct ReservationResult
{
    public int ReservationId;
    public decimal ReservationCost;
    public decimal Rate;
    public string Comment;
}
```

The **ReservationResult** returns a **ReservationId** of –1 if there is a problem, giving an explanation of the problem in the **Comment** field. Otherwise "OK" is returned in the **Comment** field.

We invite you to examine the code in the **CaseStudy** folder and to build and run the program.

# Generic Interfaces in .NET

The .NET Framework exposes much standard functionality through generic interfaces, which are implemented in various combinations by classes in the Framework itself, and which can also be implemented by your own classes in order to tap into standard functionality defined by the Framework. In this section we will look at several categories of operations that are supported by these standard, generic interfaces,

- Collections
- Copying objects
- Comparing objects

Our survey of generic interfaces is by no means exhaustive, but our sampling should give you a good understanding of how generic interfaces work in the .NET Framework.

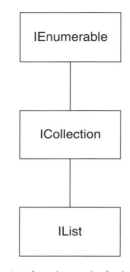

**Figure 5–1**    *Interface hierarchy for lists.*

## Collection Interfaces

Now that we understand the concept of interfaces, we are equipped to take a closer look at collections, and in particular the **ArrayList** class that we have used so heavily in the case study. If we look at the definition of **ArrayList**, we see that it implements four standard interfaces.

```
public class ArrayList : IEnumerable, ICollection,
                         IList, ICloneable
```

The first three interfaces form a simple interface hierarchy, as shown in Figure 5–1. As you go down the hierarchy, additional methods are added, until **IList** specifies a fully featured list.

The fourth interface, **ICloneable**, is independent and is used to support deep copying. As a simple illustration of the collection interfaces we provide the program **StringList**. Here is the **Main** method. We'll look at the individual helper methods as we examine the various collection interfaces.

```
// StringList.cs

using System;
using System.Collections;

public class StringList
{
   private static ArrayList list;
   public static void Main()
   {
```

```
        // Initialize strings and show starting state
        list = new ArrayList(4);
        ShowCount();
        AddString("Amy");
        AddString("Bob");
        AddString("Charlie");
        ShowEnum(list);        // enumerator
        ShowCount();
        // Add two more strings and show state again
        AddString("David");
        AddString("Ellen");
        ShowList(list);        // foreach
        ShowCount();
        // Remove two strings from list and show state
        RemoveString("David");
        RemoveAt(0);
        ShowArray(list);       // index notation
        ShowCount();
        // Try to remove two strings not in list
        RemoveString("Amy");
        RemoveAt(3);
    }
    ...
```

Here is the output:

```
list.Count = 0
list.Capacity = 4
Amy
Bob
Charlie
list.Count = 3
list.Capacity = 4
array[0] = Amy
array[1] = Bob
array[2] = Charlie
array[3] = David
array[4] = Ellen
list.Count = 5
list.Capacity = 8
Bob
Charlie
Ellen
list.Count = 3
list.Capacity = 8
List does not contain Amy
No element at index 3
```

## INTERFACE DOCUMENTATION

Interfaces are documented in the online .NET Framework SDK Documentation. Figure 5–2 illustrates the documentation of the

**IEnumerable** interface. The right-hand pane has a language filter button ▼, which we have used to show only C# versions. If you are using the interface in one of the .NET Framework classes that implement the interface, you do not need to implement any of the methods yourself. If you are creating your own class that supports an interface, you must provide implementations of all the methods of the interface. In either case, the documentation describes the methods for you.

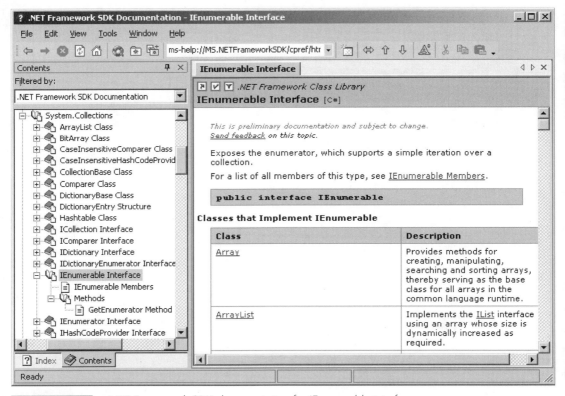

**Figure 5–2**    *NET Framework SDK documentation for IEnumerable interface.*

### IENUMERABLE AND IENUMERATOR

The basic interface that must be supported by collection classes is **IEnumerable**, which has a single method, **GetEnumerator**.

```
interface IEnumerable
{
    IEnumerator GetEnumerator();
}
```

**GetEnumerator** returns an interface reference to **IEnumerator**, which is the interface used for iterating through a collection. This interface has the property **Current** and the methods **MoveNext** and **Reset**.

```
interface IEnumerator
{
   object Current {get;}
   bool MoveNext();
   void Reset();
}
```

The enumerator is initially positioned *before* the first element in the collection, and it must be advanced before it is used. The **ShowEnum** method (in the **StringList** example) illustrates using an enumerator to iterate through a list.

```
private static void ShowEnum(ArrayList array)
{
   IEnumerator iter = array.GetEnumerator();
   bool more = iter.MoveNext();
   while (more)
   {
      string str = (string) iter.Current;
      Console.WriteLine(str);
      more = iter.MoveNext();
   }
}
```

This pattern of using an enumerator to iterate through a list is so common that C# provides a special kind of loop, **foreach**, that can be used for iterating through the elements of *any* collection. Here is the comparable code using **foreach**.

```
private static void ShowList(ArrayList array)
{
   foreach (string str in array)
   {
      Console.WriteLine(str);
   }
}
```

## ICOLLECTION

The **ICollection** interface is derived from **IEnumerable** and adds a **Count** property and a **CopyTo** method.

```
interface ICollection : IEnumerable
{
   int Count {get;}
   bool IsSynchronized {get;}
```

```
   object SyncRoot {get;}
   void CopyTo(Array array, int index);
}
```

There are also synchronization properties that can help you deal with thread safety issues. "Is it thread safe?" is a question frequently asked about library code. The short answer to this question for the .NET Framework class library is "No." This does not mean that the designers of the Framework did not think about thread safety issues. On the contrary, there are many mechanisms to help you write thread-safe code when you need to. The reason that collections are not automatically thread safe is that your code should not have to pay the performance penalty to enforce synchronization when it is not running in a multithreading scenario. If you do need thread safety, you may use the thread-safety properties to easily implement. We discuss the .NET mechanisms for thread synchronization in Chapter 8.

Our **StringList** program illustrates use of the **Count** property of **ICollection**.

```
private static void ShowCount()
{
   Console.WriteLine("list.Count = {0}", list.Count);
   Console.WriteLine("list.Capacity = {0}",
list.Capacity);
}
```

## ILIST

The **IList** interface is derived from **ICollection** and provides methods for adding an item to a list, removing an item, and so on. An indexer is provided that enables array notation to be used. (We discussed indexers in Chapter 3.)

```
interface IList : ICollection
{
   object this[int index] {get; set;}
   int Add(object value);
   void Clear();
   bool Contains(object value);
   int IndexOf(object value);
   void Insert(int index, object value);
   void Remove(object value);
   void RemoveAt(int index);
}
```

Our **StringList** sample code illustrates using the indexer and the **Add**, **Contains**, **Remove**, and **RemoveAt** methods.

```
private static void ShowArray(ArrayList array)
{
   for (int i = 0; i < array.Count; i++)
```

```
    {
        Console.WriteLine("array[{0}] = {1}", i, array[i]);
    }
}
private static void AddString(string str)
{
    if (list.Contains(str))
        throw new Exception("list contains " + str);
    list.Add(str);
}
private static void RemoveString(string str)
{
    if (list.Contains(str))
        list.Remove(str);
    else
        Console.WriteLine("List does not contain {0}", str);
}
private static void RemoveAt(int index)
{
    try
    {
        list.RemoveAt(index);
    }
    catch (ArgumentOutOfRangeException)
    {
        Console.WriteLine("No element at index {0}", index);
    }
}
```

## Copy Semantics and ICloneable

Sometimes you have to make a copy of an object. When you copy objects that contain objects and object references, you have to be aware of. the copy semantics of C#. We will compare reference copy, shallow memberwise copy, and deep copy. We will see that by implementing the **ICloneable** interface in your class, you can make a deep copy.

Recall that C# has value types and reference types. A value type contains all its own data, while a reference type refers to data stored somewhere else. If a reference variable gets copied to another reference variable, both will refer to the same object. If the object referenced by the second variable is changed, the first variable will also reflect the new value. Sometimes you want this behavior, but sometimes you do not.

### SHALLOW COPY AND DEEP COPY

A struct in C# automatically implements a "memberwise" copy, sometimes known as a "shallow copy." The **object** root class has a protected method,

**MemberwiseClone**, which will perform a memberwise copy of members of a class.

If one or more members of a class are of a reference type, this memberwise copy may not be good enough. The result will be two references to the same data, not two independent copies of the data. To actually copy the data itself and not merely the references, you will need to perform a "deep copy." Deep copy can be provided at either the language level or the library level. In C++ deep copy is provided at the language level through a *copy constructor*. In C# deep copy is provided by the .NET Framework through a special interface, **ICloneable**, which you can implement in your classes in order to enable them to perform deep copy.

## EXAMPLE PROGRAM

We will illustrate all these ideas in the program **CopyDemo**. This program makes a copy of a **Course** instance. The **Course** class consists of a title and a collection of students.

```
// Course.cs

using System;
using System.Collections;

public class Course : ICloneable
{
   public string Title;
   public ArrayList Roster;
   public Course(string title)
   {
      Title = title;
      Roster = new ArrayList();
   }
   public void AddStudent(string name)
   {
      Roster.Add(name);
   }
   public void Show(string caption)
   {
      Console.WriteLine("-----{0}-----", caption);
      Console.WriteLine("Course : {0} with {1} students",
         Title, Roster.Count);
      foreach (string name in Roster)
      {
         Console.WriteLine(name);
      }
   }
   public Course ShallowCopy()
   {
```

```
            return (Course) this.MemberwiseClone();
         }
         public object Clone()
         {
            Course course = new Course(Title);
            course.Roster = (ArrayList) Roster.Clone();
            return course;
         }
}
```

The test program constructs a **Course** instance **c1** and then makes a copy **c2** by various methods.

## REFERENCE COPY BY ASSIGNMENT

The first way the copy is performed is by the straight assignment **c2 = c1**. Now we get two references to the same object, and if we make any change through the first reference, we will see the same change through the second reference. The first part of the test program illustrates such an assignment.

```
// CopyDemo.cs

using System;
using System.Collections;

public class CopyDemo
{
   private static Course c1, c2;
   public static void Main()
   {
      Console.WriteLine("Copy is done via c2 = c1");
      InitializeCourse();
      c1.Show("original");
      c2 = c1;
      c2.Title = ".NET Programming";
      c2.AddStudent("Charlie");
      c2.Show("copy with changed title and new student");
      c1.Show("original");

      ...
   }
   private static void InitializeCourse()
   {
      c1 = new Course("Intro to C#");
      c1.AddStudent("John");
      c1.AddStudent("Mary");
   }
}
```

We initialize with the title "Intro to C#" and two students. We make the assignment **c2 = c1** and then change the title and add another student for **c2**. We then show both **c1** and **c2**, and we see that both reflect both of these changes. Here is the output from this first part of the program:

```
Copy is done via c2 = c1
-----original-----
Course : Intro to C# with 2 students
John
Mary
-----copy-----
Course : Intro to C# with 2 students
John
Mary
-----copy with changed title and new student-----
Course : .NET Programming with 3 students
John
Mary
Charlie
-----original-----
Course : .NET Programming with 3 students
John
Mary
Charlie
```

## MEMBERWISE CLONE

Next we will illustrate doing a memberwise copy, which can be accomplished using the **MemberwiseClone** method of **object**. Since this method is **protected**, we cannot call it directly from outside our **Course** class. Instead, in **Course** we define a method, **ShallowCopy**, which is implemented using **MemberwiseClone**.

```
// Course.cs

using System;
using System.Collections;

public class Course : ICloneable
{
   ...
   public Course ShallowCopy()
   {
      return (Course) this.MemberwiseClone();
   }
   ...
}
```

Here is the second part of the test program, which calls the **ShallowCopy** method. Again we change the title and a student in the second copy.

```
// CopyDemo.cs

using System;
using System.Collections;

public class CopyDemo
{
    ...
    Console.WriteLine(
        "\nCopy is done via c2 = c1.ShallowCopy()");
    InitializeCourse();
    c2 = c1.ShallowCopy();
    c2.Title = ".NET Programming";
    c2.AddStudent("Charlie");
    c2.Show("copy with changed title and new student");
    c1.Show("original");
    ...
```

Here is the output of this second part of the program. Now the **Title** field has its own independent copy, but the **Roster** collection is just copied by reference, so each copy refers to the same collection of students.

```
Copy is done via c2 = c1.ShallowCopy()
-----copy with changed title and new student-----
Course : .NET Programming with 3 students
John
Mary
Charlie
-----original-----
Course : Intro to C# with 3 students
John
Mary
Charlie
```

## USING ICLONEABLE

The final version of copy relies on the fact that our **Course** class supports the **ICloneable** interface and implements the **Clone** method. To clone the **Roster** collection we use the fact that **ArrayList** also implements the **ICloneable** interface, as discussed earlier in the chapter. Note that the **Clone** method returns an **object**, so we must cast to **ArrayList** before assigning to the **Roster** field.

```
// Course.cs

using System;
```

```
using System.Collections;

public class Course : ICloneable
{
    ...
    public object Clone()
    {
        Course course = new Course(Title);
        course.Roster = (ArrayList) Roster.Clone();
        return course;
    }
}
```

Here is the third part of the test program, which calls the **Clone** method. Again we change the title and a student in the second copy.

```
// CopyDemo.cs

using System;
using System.Collections;

public class CopyDemo
{
        ...
        Console.WriteLine(
            "\nCopy is done via c2 = c1.Clone()");
        InitializeCourse();
        c2 = (Course) c1.Clone();
        c2.Title = ".NET Programming";
        c2.AddStudent("Charlie");
        c2.Show("copy with changed title and new student");
        c1.Show("original");
        ...
```

Here is the output from the third part of the program. Now we have completely independent instances of **Course**. Each has its own title and set of students.

```
Copy is done via c2 = c1.Clone()
-----copy with changed title and new student-----
Course : .NET Programming with 3 students
John
Mary
Charlie
-----original-----
Course : Intro to C# with 2 students
John
Mary
```

## Comparing Objects

We have quite exhaustively studied *copying* objects. We now examine *comparing* objects. To compare objects, the .NET Framework uses the interface **IComparable**. In this section we use the interface **IComparable** to sort an array.

### SORTING AN ARRAY

The **System.Array** class provides a static method, **Sort**, that can be used for sorting an array. The program **ArrayName** illustrates applying this **Sort** method to an array of **Name** objects, where the **Name** class simply encapsulates a **string** through a read-only property **Text**. Here is the main program.

```
// ArrayName.cs
...

public class ArrayName
{
    public static void Main(string[] args)
    {
        Name[] array = new Name[10];
        array[0] = new Name("Michael");
        array[1] = new Name("Charlie");
        array[2] = new Name("Peter");
        array[3] = new Name("Dana");
        array[4] = new Name("Bob");
        if (array[0] is IComparable)
            Array.Sort(array);
        else
            Console.WriteLine(
                "Name does not implement IComparable");
        foreach (Name name in array)
        {
            if (name != null)
                Console.WriteLine(name);
        }
    }
}
```

### IMPLEMENTING ICOMPARABLE

In order for the **Sort** method to function, there must be a way of comparing the objects that are being sorted. This comparison is achieved through the **CompareTo** method of the interface **IComparable**. Thus to sort an array of a type you define, you must implement **IComparable** for your type.

```
public interface IComparable
{
        int CompareTo(object object);
}
```

Here is the implementation of the **Name** class, with its implementation of **IComparable**.

```
public class Name : IComparable
{
    private string text;
    public Name(string text)
    {
        this.text = text;
    }
    public string Text
    {
        get
        {
            return text;
        }
    }
    public int CompareTo(object obj)
    {
        string s1 = this.Text;
        string s2 = ((Name) obj).Text;
        return String.Compare(s1, s2);
    }
}
```

## Understanding Frameworks

Our example offers some insight into the workings of frameworks. A framework is *more* than a library. In a typical library, you are concerned with your code calling library functions. In a framework, you call into the framework *and the framework might call you.* Your program can be viewed as the middle layer of a sandwich.

- Your code calls the bottom layer.
- The top layer calls your code.

The .NET Framework is an excellent example of such an architecture. There is rich functionality that you can call directly. There are many interfaces, which you can optionally implement to make your program behave appropriately when called by the framework, often on behalf of other objects.

## Delegates

Interfaces facilitate writing code so that your program can be *called into* by some other code. This style of programming has been available for a long time, under the guise of "callback" functions. In this section we examine *del-*

*egates* in C#, which can be thought of as type-safe and object-oriented call-back functions. Delegates are the foundation for a design pattern, known as *events*, which we'll look at in the next section.

A *callback function* is one which your program specifies and "registers" in some way, and which then gets called by another program. In C and C++ callback functions are implemented by function pointers.

In C# you can encapsulate a reference to a method inside a delegate object. A delegate can refer to either a static method or an instance method. When a delegate refers to an instance method, it stores both an object instance and an entry point to the instance method. The instance method can then be called through this object instance. When a delegate object refers to a static method, it stores just the entry point of this static method.

You can pass this delegate object to other code, which can then call your method. The code that calls your delegate method does not have to know at compile time which method is being called.

In C# a delegate is considered a reference type that is similar to a class type. A new delegate instance is created just like any other class instance, using the **new** operator. In fact, C# delegates are implemented by the .NET Framework class library as a class, derived ultimately from **System.Delegate**.

Delegates are object oriented and type safe, and they enjoy the safety of the managed code execution environment.

## Declaring a Delegate

You declare a delegate in C# using a special notation with the keyword **dele-gate** and the signature of the encapsulated method. A naming convention suggests that your name should end with "Callback."

We illustrate delegates in the sample program **DelegateAccount.** Here is an example of a delegate declaration from the file **DelegateAccount.cs**.

```
public delegate void NotifyCallback(decimal balance);
```

## Defining a Method

When you instantiate a delegate, you will need to specify a method, which must match the signature in the delegate declaration. The method may be either a static method or an instance method. Here are some examples of methods that can be hooked to the **NotifyCallback** delegate:

```
private static void NotifyCustomer(decimal balance)
{
   Console.WriteLine("Dear customer,");
   Console.WriteLine(
      "   Account overdrawn, balance = {0}", balance);
}
private static void NotifyBank(decimal balance)
```

```
    {
        Console.WriteLine("Dear bank,");
        Console.WriteLine(
            "   Account overdrawn, balance = {0}", balance);
    }
    private void NotifyInstance(decimal balance)
    {
        Console.WriteLine("Dear instance,");
        Console.WriteLine(
            "   Account overdrawn, balance = {0}", balance);
    }
```

## Creating a Delegate Object

You instantiate a delegate object with the **new** operator, just as you would
with any other class. The following code illustrates creating two delegate
objects. The first one is hooked to a static method, and the second to
an instance method. The second delegate object internally will store both
a method entry point and an object instance that is used for invoking
the method.

```
NotifyCallback custDlg =
    new NotifyCallback(NotifyCustomer);
...
DelegateAccount da = new DelegateAccount();
NotifyCallback instDlg =
    new NotifyCallback(da.NotifyInstance);
```

## Calling a Delegate

You "call" a delegate just as you would a method. The delegate object is not
a method, but it has an encapsulated method. The delegate object "delegates" the call to this encapsulated method, hence the name "delegate." In
the following code the delegate object **notifyDlg** is called whenever a negative balance occurs on a withdrawal. In this example the **notifyDlg** delegate
object is initialized in the method **SetDelegate**.

```
    private NotifyCallback notifyDlg;
    ...
    public void SetDelegate(NotifyCallback dlg)
    {
        notifyDlg = dlg;
    }
    ...
    public void Withdraw(decimal amount)
    {
        balance -= amount;
        if (balance < 0)
```

```
        notifyDlg(balance);
}
```

## Combining Delegate Objects

A powerful feature of delegates is that you can combine them. Delegates are "multicast," in which they have an invocation list of methods. When such a delegate is called, all the methods on the invocation list will be called in the order they appear in the invocation list. The **+** operator can be used to combine the invocation methods of two delegate objects. The **−** operator can be used to remove methods.

```
NotifyCallback custDlg =
    new NotifyCallback(NotifyCustomer);
NotifyCallback bankDlg = new NotifyCallback(NotifyBank);
NotifyCallback currDlg = custDlg + bankDlg;
```

In this example we construct two delegate objects, each with an associated method. We then create a new delegate object whose invocation list will consist of both the methods **NotifyCustomer** and **NotifyBank**. When **currDlg** is called, these two methods will be invoked. Later on in the code we may remove a method.

```
currDlg -= bankDlg;
```

Now **NotifyBank** has been removed from the delegate, and the next time **currDlg** is called, only **NotifyCustomer** will be invoked.

## Complete Example

The program **DelegateAccount** illustrates using delegates in our bank account scenario. The file **DelegateAccount.cs** declares the delegate **NotifyCallback**. The class **DelegateAccount** contains methods matching the signature of the delegate. The **Main** method instantiates delegate objects and combines them in various ways. The delegate objects are passed to the **Account** class, which uses its encapsulated delegate object to invoke suitable notifications when the account is overdrawn.

Observe how this structure is dynamic and loosely coupled. The **Account** class does not know or care which notification methods will be invoked in the case of an overdraft. It simply calls the delegate, which in turn calls all the methods on its invocation list. These methods can be adjusted at runtime.

Here is the code for the **Account** class:

```
// Account.cs

public class Account
{
```

```
      private decimal balance;
      private NotifyCallback notifyDlg;
      public Account(decimal bal, NotifyCallback dlg)
      {
         balance = bal;
         notifyDlg = dlg;
      }
      public void SetDelegate(NotifyCallback dlg)
      {
         notifyDlg = dlg;
      }
      public void Deposit(decimal amount)
      {
         balance += amount;
      }
      public void Withdraw(decimal amount)
      {
         balance -= amount;
         if (balance < 0)
            notifyDlg(balance);
      }
      public decimal Balance
      {
         get
         {
            return balance;
         }
      }
   }
```

Here is the code declaring and testing the delegate:

```
// DelegateAccount.cs

using System;

public delegate void NotifyCallback(decimal balance);

public class DelegateAccount
{
   public static void Main(string[] args)
   {
      NotifyCallback custDlg =
         new NotifyCallback(NotifyCustomer);
      NotifyCallback bankDlg =
         new NotifyCallback(NotifyBank);
      NotifyCallback currDlg = custDlg + bankDlg;
      Account acc = new Account(100, currDlg);
      Console.WriteLine("balance = {0}", acc.Balance);
      acc.Withdraw(125);
      Console.WriteLine("balance = {0}", acc.Balance);
```

```
        acc.Deposit(200);
        acc.Withdraw(125);
        Console.WriteLine("balance = {0}", acc.Balance);
        currDlg -= bankDlg;
        acc.SetDelegate(currDlg);
        acc.Withdraw(125);
        DelegateAccount da = new DelegateAccount();
        NotifyCallback instDlg =
            new NotifyCallback(da.NotifyInstance);
        currDlg += instDlg;
        acc.SetDelegate(currDlg);
        acc.Withdraw(125);
    }
    private static void NotifyCustomer(decimal balance)
    {
        Console.WriteLine("Dear customer,");
        Console.WriteLine(
            "   Account overdrawn, balance = {0}", balance);
    }
    private static void NotifyBank(decimal balance)
    {
        Console.WriteLine("Dear bank,");
        Console.WriteLine(
            "   Account overdrawn, balance = {0}", balance);
    }
    private void NotifyInstance(decimal balance)
    {
        Console.WriteLine("Dear instance,");
        Console.WriteLine(
            "   Account overdrawn, balance = {0}", balance);
    }
}
```

Here is the output from running the program. Notice which notification methods get invoked, depending upon the operations that have been performed on the current delegate object.

```
balance = 100
Dear customer,
    Account overdrawn, balance = -25
Dear bank,
    Account overdrawn, balance = -25
balance = -25
balance = 50
Dear customer,
    Account overdrawn, balance = -75
Dear customer,
    Account overdrawn, balance = -200
Dear instance,
    Account overdrawn, balance = -200
```

## Stock Market Simulation

As a further illustration of the use of delegates, consider the simple stock-market simulation, implemented in the directory **StockMarket**. The simulation consists of two modules:

- The **Admin** module provides a user interface for configuring and running the simulation. It also implements operations called by the simulation engine.
- The **Engine** module is the simulation engine. It maintains an internal clock and invokes randomly generated operations, based on the configuration parameters passed to it.

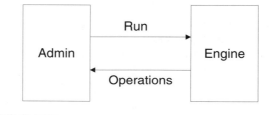

**Figure 5–3** *Architecture of stock-market simulation.*

Figure 5–3 shows the high-level architecture of the simulation. The following operations are available:

- PrintTick: shows each clock tick.
- PrintTrade: shows each trade.

The following configuration parameters can be specified:

- Ticks on/off
- Trades on/off
- Count of how many ticks to run the simulation

### RUNNING THE SIMULATION

Build and run the example program in **StockMarket**. Start with the default configuration: Ticks are OFF, Trades are ON, Run count is 100. (Note that the results are random and will be different each time you run the program.)

```
Ticks are OFF
Trades are ON
Run count = 100
Enter command, quit to exit
: run
    2   ACME     23    600
   27   MSFT     63    400
   27   IBM     114    600
```

```
38   MSFT    69    400
53   MSFT    75    900
62   INTC    27    800
64   MSFT    82    200
68   MSFT    90    300
81   MSFT    81    600
83   INTC    30    800
91   MSFT    73    700
99   IBM    119    400
:
```

The available commands are listed when you type "help" at the colon prompt. The commands are:

```
count      set run count
ticks      toggle ticks
trades     toggle trades
config     show configuration
run        run the simulation
quit       exit the program
```

The output shows clock tick, stock, price, volume.

### DELEGATE CODE

Two delegates are declared in the **Admin.cs** file.

```
public delegate void TickCallback(int ticks);
public delegate void TradeCallback(int ticks, string stock,
                                   int price, int volume);
```

As we saw in the previous section, a delegate is similar to a class, and a delegate object is instantiated by **new**.

```
TickCallback tickDlg = new TickCallback(PrintTick);
TradeCallback tradeDlg = new TradeCallback(PrintTrade);
```

A method is passed as the parameter to the delegate constructor. The method signature must match that of the delegate.

```
public static void PrintTick(int ticks)
{
   Console.Write("{0} ", ticks);
   if (++printcount == LINECOUNT)
   {
      Console.WriteLine();
      printcount = 0;
   }
}
```

## PASSING THE DELEGATES TO THE ENGINE

The **Admin** class passes the delegates to the **Engine** class in the constructor of the **Engine** class.

```
Engine engine = new Engine(tickDlg, tradeDlg);
```

## RANDOM-NUMBER GENERATION

The heart of the simulation is the **Run** method of the **Engine** class. At the core of the **Run** method is assigning simulated data based on random numbers. We use the **System.Random** class, which we discussed in Chapter 3.

```
double r = rangen.NextDouble();
if (r < tradeProb[i])
{
   int delta = (int) (price[i] * volatility[i]);
   if (rangen.NextDouble() < .5)
   {
      delta = -delta;
   }
   price[i] += delta;
   int volume = rangen.Next(minVolume, maxVolume) * 100;
   tradeOp(tick, stocks[i], price[i], volume);
}
```

## USING THE DELEGATES

In the **Engine** class, delegate references are declared:

```
TickCallback tickOp;
TradeCallback tradeOp;
```

The delegate references are initialized in the **Engine** constructor:

```
public Engine(TickCallback tickOp, TradeCallback tradeOp)
{
   this.tickOp = tickOp;
   this.tradeOp = tradeOp;
}
```

The method that is wrapped by the delegate object can then be called through the delegate reference:

```
if (showTicks)
   tickOp(tick);
```

# Events

Delegates are the foundation for a design pattern known as *events.* Conceptually, servers implement *incoming* interfaces, which are called by clients. In a diagram, such an interface may be shown with a small bubble (a notation used in COM). Sometimes a client may wish to receive notifications from a server when certain "events" occur. In such a case the server will specify an *outgoing* interface. The server defines the interface and the client implements it. In a diagram, such an interface may be shown with an arrow (again, a notation used in COM). Figure 5–4 illustrates a server with one incoming and one outgoing interface. In the case of the outgoing interface, the client will implement an incoming interface, which the server will call.

A good example of a programming situation with events is a graphical user interface. An event is some external action, typically triggered by the user, to which the program must respond. Events include user actions such as clicking a mouse button or pressing a key on the keyboard. A GUI program must contain *event handlers* to respond to or "handle" these events. We will see many examples of GUI event handling in Chapter 6, where we discuss Windows Forms.

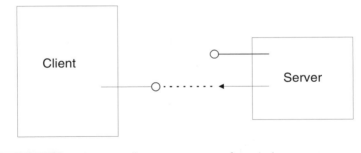

**Figure 5–4**    *A server with an incoming interface and an outgoing interface.*

## Events in C# and .NET

The .NET Framework provides an easy-to-use implementation of the event paradigm built on delegates. C# simplifies working with .NET events by providing the keyword **event** and operators to hook up event handlers to events and to remove them. The Framework also defines a base class **EventArgs** to be used for passing arguments to event handlers. There are a number of derived classes defined by the Framework for specific types of events, such as **MouseEventArgs**, **ListChangedEventArgs**, and so forth. These derived classes define data members to hold appropriate argument information.

An event handler is a delegate with a specific signature,

```
public delegate void EventHandler(
   object sender,
   EventArgs e);
```

The first argument represents the source of the event, and the second argument contains data associated with the event.

We will examine this event architecture through salient code from the example program **EventDemo**, which illustrates a chat room.

## Server-Side Event Code

We begin with server-side code, in **ChatServer.cs**. The .NET event architecture uses delegates of a specific signature:

```
public delegate void JoinHandler(object sender,
                                  ChatEventArg e);
```

The first parameter specifies the object that sent the event notification. The second parameter is used to pass data along with the notification. Typically, you will derive a class from **EventArg** to hold your specific data.

```
public class ChatEventArg : EventArgs
{
   public string Name;
   public ChatEventArg(string name)
   {
      Name = name;
   }
}
```

A delegate object reference is declared using the keyword **event**.

```
public event JoinHandler Join;
```

A helper method is typically provided to facilitate calling the delegate object(s) that have been hooked up to the event.

```
protected void OnJoin(ChatEventArg e)
{
   if (Join != null)
   {
      Join(this, e);
   }
}
```

A test for **null** is made in case no delegate objects have been hooked up to the event. Typically, access is specified as **protected**, so that a derived class has access to this helper method. You can then "fire" the event by calling the helper method.

```
public void JoinChat(string name)
{
    members.Add(name);
    OnJoin(new ChatEventArg(name));
}
```

## Client-Side Event Code

The client provides event handler functions.

```
public static void OnJoinChat(object sender,
    ChatEventArg e)
{
    Console.WriteLine(
        "sender = {0}, {1} has joined the chat",
        sender, e.Name);
}
```

The client hooks the handler to the event, using the **+=** operator.

```
ChatServer chat = new ChatServer("OI Chat Room");
// Register to receive event notifications from the server
chat.Join += new JoinHandler(OnJoinChat);
```

The event starts out as **null**, and event handlers get added through **+=**. All of the registered handlers will get invoked when the event delegate is called. You may unregister a handler through **—=**.

## Chat Room Example

The chat room example in **EventDemo** illustrates the complete architecture on both the server and client sides. The server provides the following methods:

- JoinChat
- QuitChat
- ShowMembers

Whenever a new member joins or quits, the server sends a notification to the client. The event handlers print out an appropriate message. Here is the output from running the program:

```
sender = OI Chat Room, Michael has joined the chat
sender = OI Chat Room, Bob has joined the chat
sender = OI Chat Room, Sam has joined the chat
--- After 3 have joined---
Michael
Bob
Sam
sender = OI Chat Room, Bob has quit the chat
```

```
--- After 1 has quit---
Michael
Sam
```

## CLIENT CODE

The client program provides event handlers. It instantiates a server object and then hooks up its event handlers to the events. The client then calls methods on the server. These calls will trigger the server, firing events back to the client, which get handled by the event handlers.

```
// ChatClient.cs

using System;

class ChatClient
{
    public static void OnJoinChat(object sender,
                                  ChatEventArg e)
    {
        Console.WriteLine(
            "sender = {0}, {1} has joined the chat",
            sender, e.Name);
    }
    public static void OnQuitChat(object sender,
                                  ChatEventArg e)
    {
        Console.WriteLine(
            "sender = {0}, {1} has quit the chat",
            sender, e.Name);
    }
    public static void Main()
    {
        ChatServer chat = new ChatServer("OI Chat Room");
        // Register to receive event notifications from the
        // server
        chat.Join += new JoinHandler(OnJoinChat);
        chat.Quit += new QuitHandler(OnQuitChat);
        // Call methods on the server
        chat.JoinChat("Michael");
        chat.JoinChat("Bob");
        chat.JoinChat("Sam");
        chat.ShowMembers("After 3 have joined");
        chat.QuitChat("Bob");
        chat.ShowMembers("After 1 has quit");
    }
}
```

## SERVER CODE

The server provides code to store in a collection the names of people who have joined the chat. When a person quits the chat, the name is removed from the collection. Joining and quitting the chat triggers firing an event back to the client. The server also contains the "plumbing" code for setting up the events, including declaration of the delegates, the events, and the event arguments. There are also helper methods for firing the events.

```csharp
// ChatServer.cs

using System;
using System.Collections;

public class ChatEventArg : EventArgs
{
   public string Name;
   public ChatEventArg(string name)
   {
      Name = name;
   }
}

public delegate void JoinHandler(object sender,
                                 ChatEventArg e);
public delegate void QuitHandler(object sender,
                                 ChatEventArg e);

public class ChatServer
{
   private ArrayList members = new ArrayList();
   private string chatName;
   public event JoinHandler Join;
   public event QuitHandler Quit;
   public ChatServer(string chatName)
   {
      this.chatName = chatName;
   }
   override public string ToString()
   {
      return chatName;
   }
   protected void OnJoin(ChatEventArg e)
   {
      if (Join != null)
      {
         Join(this, e);
      }
   }
   protected void OnQuit(ChatEventArg e)
```

```
    {
        if (Quit != null)
        {
            Quit(this, e);
        }
    }
    public void JoinChat(string name)
    {
        members.Add(name);
        OnJoin(new ChatEventArg(name));
    }
    public void QuitChat(string name)
    {
        members.Remove(name);
        OnQuit(new ChatEventArg(name));
    }
    public void ShowMembers(string msg)
    {
        Console.WriteLine("--- " + msg + "---");
        foreach (string member in members)
        {
            Console.WriteLine(member);
        }
    }
}
```

It may appear that there is a fair amount of such "plumbing" code, but it is *much* simpler than the previous connection-point mechanism used by COM for events. Also, in certain areas various wizards and other tools (such as the Forms designers) will generate the infrastructure for you automatically. We will see how easy it is to work with events in Windows programming in Chapter 6.

## Attributes

A modern approach to implementing complex code is to let the system do it for you. There must be a way for the programmer to inform the system of what is desired. In the .NET Framework such cues can be given to the system by means of *attributes*.

Microsoft introduced attribute-based programming in Microsoft Transaction Server. The concept was that MTS, not the programmer, would implement complex tasks such as distributed transactions. The programmer would "declare" the transaction requirements for a COM class, and MTS would implement it. This use of attributes was greatly extended in the next generation of MTS, known as COM+. In MTS and COM+ attributes are stored in a separate repository, distinct from the program itself.

Attributes are also used in Interface Definition Language (IDL), which gives a precise specification of COM interfaces, including the methods and signatures. Part of the function of IDL is to make it possible for a tool to generate proxies and stubs for remoting a method call across a process boundary or even across a network. When parameters are passed remotely, it is necessary to give more information than when they are passed within the same process. For example, within a process, you can simply pass a reference to an array. But in passing an array across a process boundary, you must inform the tool of the size of the array. This information is communicated in IDL by means of attributes, which are specified using a square-bracket notation. Here is an example of IDL that shows the use of attributes.

```
[
    object,
    uuid(AAA19CDE-C091-47BF-8C96-C80A00989796),
    dual,
    pointer_default(unique)
]
interface IAccount : IDispatch
{
    [id(1)] HRESULT Deposit([in] long id, [in] long
amount);
    [id(2)] HRESULT Withdraw([in] long id, [in] long
amount);
    [id(3)] HRESULT GetBalance([in] long id,
            [out] long *pBal);
    [id(4)] HRESULT GetAllBalances([in, out] long* pCount,
            [out, size_is(*pCount)] long balances[]);
};
```

If you are experienced with COM, such IDL will be familiar to you. If not, just notice the general structure of how attributes are used. Attributes such as **object** and **uuid** are applied to the interface, the **id** attribute is applied to methods, and the attributes **in**, **out**, and **size_is** are applied to parameters.

A problem with attributes in both MTS/COM+ and IDL is that they are separate from the program source code. When the source code is modified, the attribute information may get out of sync with the code.

## Attributes in .NET

In .NET, attributes are declared with square brackets, as in IDL. But unlike IDL, the attributes are part of the program source code. When compiled into intermediate language, the attributes become part of the metadata. There are some predefined attributes in C#, there are many attributes associated with various .NET classes, and there is a mechanism to create custom attributes for your own classes. In this section we look at the general characteristics of how attributes are used, beginning with a simple example of using one of the predefined attributes in C#. In later chapters attributes associated with specific .NET classes will be used extensively, and in Chapter 8, after we've discussed Reflection, we will see how to create and use custom attributes.

The **AttributeDemo** program provides a simple example of using the predefined C# attribute **Conditional**, which is used to mark a method to be executed only if a preprocessor symbol is defined.

```
// AttributeDemo.cs

#define LINUX

using System;
using System.Diagnostics;

public class AttributeDemo
{
   public static void Main(string[] args)
   {
      Notice();
      MultiNotice();
      Console.WriteLine("Goodbye");
   }
   [ConditionalAttribute("UNIX")]
   private static void Notice()
   {
      Console.WriteLine("Notice: Unix version");
   }
   [Conditional("UNIX")] [Conditional("LINUX")]
   private static void MultiNotice()
   {
      Console.WriteLine("Notice: Some version of Unix");
   }
}
```

**Conditional** is one of three predefined attributes in C#.[8] Its full name is **ConditionalAttribute**, but C# has the convenience feature that when an attribute's name ends with the **Attribute** suffix, you may drop the suffix. **Conditional** is used to mark a method with a symbol. If that symbol is defined by the preprocessor, calls to the method will be included, otherwise calls will be omitted. The **Conditional** attribute is *multiuse*, which means that it may be used several times in front of a method. For example, in the code above the **MultiNotice** method is conditioned on either "UNIX" or

---

[8] The other two predefined attributes in C# are **Obsolete and AttributeUsage**. **Obsolete** is used to mark a program entity that should not be used, causing the compiler to issue a warning or error message if it is used. We will discuss **AttributeUsage** in Chapter 8 in connection with custom attributes.

"LINUX," and calls to this method will be included if either symbol is defined. The preprocessor **#define** directive[9] defines the symbol "LINUX." The "UNIX" symbol is not defined (unless done via a compiler option, which we'll look at shortly). The **Conditional** attribute requires the namespace **System.Diagnostics**. (We will discuss .NET diagnostic support in detail in Chapter 13.)

Running the program produces the following output:

```
Notice: Some version of Unix
Goodbye
```

The call to **Notice** is omitted, but the call to **MultiNotice** is included. You may experiment with this program by defining no symbols, defining "UNIX," etc.

### PREPROCESSOR SYMBOLS USING COMPILER OPTION

Besides using a **#define** preprocessor directive in your source code, you can also define preprocessor symbols using the **/define** command-line option of the C# compiler. For example, you can define the symbol "UNIX" using the following command:

```
csc /define:UNIX AttributeDemo.cs
```

---

[9] C#, unlike C and C++, does not allow use of preprocessor directives to define macros.

You can also specify preprocessor directives in Visual Studio. In Solution Explorer right-click on the solution. From the context menu choose Properties. Select Build from Configuration Properties, and enter your desired string in the Conditional Compilation Constant section, as illustrated in Figure 5–5.

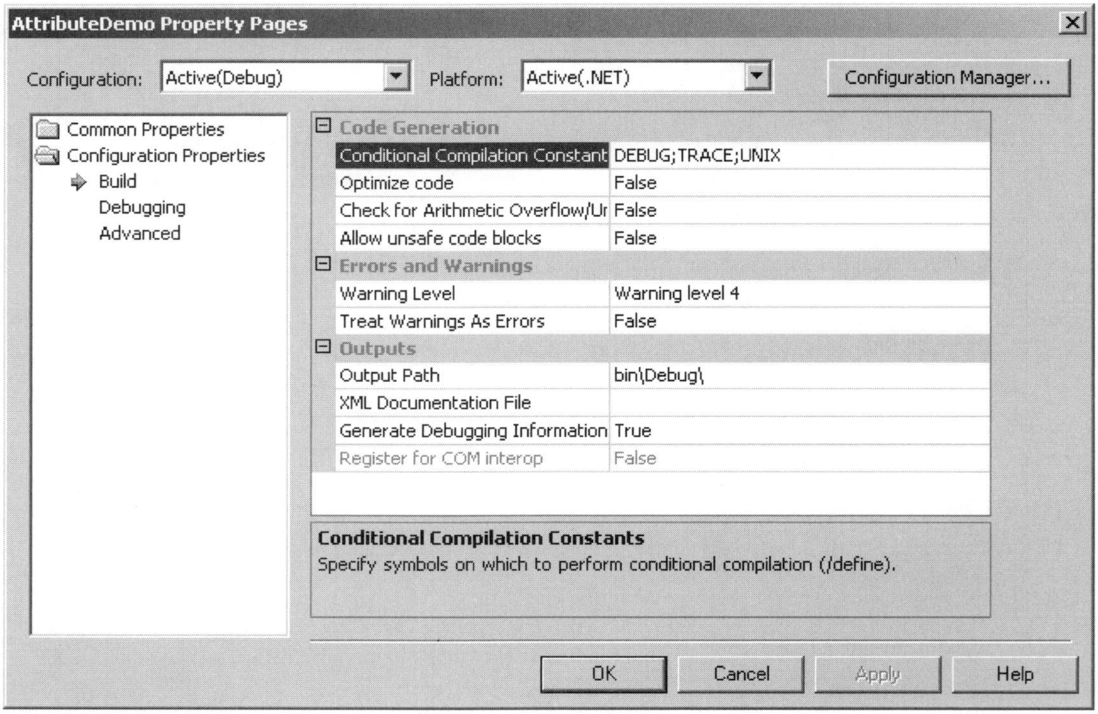

**AttributeDemo Property Pages**                                                          ✕

Configuration: [Active(Debug)      ▼]    Platform: [Active(.NET)      ▼]      [Configuration Manager...]

- Common Properties
- Configuration Properties
  - ➡ Build
    - Debugging
    - Advanced

| ⊟ **Code Generation** | |
| Conditional Compilation Constant | DEBUG;TRACE;UNIX |
| Optimize code | False |
| Check for Arithmetic Overflow/Un | False |
| Allow unsafe code blocks | False |
| ⊟ **Errors and Warnings** | |
| Warning Level | Warning level 4 |
| Treat Warnings As Errors | False |
| ⊟ **Outputs** | |
| Output Path | bin\Debug\ |
| XML Documentation File | |
| Generate Debugging Information | True |
| Register for COM interop | False |

**Conditional Compilation Constants**
Specify symbols on which to perform conditional compilation (/define).

[ OK ]     [ Cancel ]     [ Apply ]     [ Help ]

**Figure 5–5**     *Specifying a preprocessor symbol in Visual Studio.*

## USING ATTRIBUTES

The example program demonstrated an attribute with a single **string** parameter. Attributes can take multiple parameters, and there can also be named parameters. Named parameters are useful when there are many different parameters, and in a particular case you may use only some of them. Named parameters can appear in any order.

As an example, the **DllImport** attribute takes a single positional parameter (the name of the DLL) and several positional parameters. Here is an example of using the **DllImport** attribute, with named parameters **CharSet** and **CallingConvention**:

```
[DllImport("KERNEL32.DLL", CharSet=CharSet.Unicode,
CallingConvention=CallingConvention.StdCall)]
```

We will see examples of the use of **DllImport** in Chapter 14, when we discuss the Platform Invocation Service (or PInvoke), which enables you to call unmanaged code through functions implemented in a DLL.

### ATTRIBUTE TARGETS

An attribute may be applicable to different kinds of entities. In the COM IDL example we saw examples of attributes for interfaces, methods, and parameters. In .NET attributes may be applied to many different kinds of entities, including

- assembly
- module
- class
- struct
- interface
- method
- parameter

and many more. The specification of legal entities to which an attribute may be applied is part of the definition of an attribute, and you will get a compiler error message if you attempt to use an attribute on the wrong kind of entity. When we discuss custom attributes in Chapter 8, we will see how to specify the legal attribute targets for our own attributes.

# Summary

This chapter explored several important interactions between C# and the .NET Framework, beginning with the root class **object**. We examined collections, including the methods of the **object** class that should be overridden to tap into the functionality provided by the .NET Framework. We introduced interfaces, which allow you to rigorously define a contract for a class to implement. While a class in C# can inherit from only one other class, it can implement multiple interfaces. Another benefit of interfaces is that they facilitate very dynamic programs. C# provides convenient facilities to query a class at runtime to see whether it supports a particular interface.

The interfaces supporting collections were examined in detail, and copy semantics were explored. While C++ relies on a language feature of a copy constructor, in C# you provide the capability by implementing a special interface, **ICloneable**. This led to an exploration of the role of generic interfaces in the .NET Framework programming model and to a comparison of the .NET and COM component models. A further illustration of programming with generic interfaces was provided by sorting in different orders with the **IComparable** interface. The examples offered insight into the workings of frameworks, which are more than class libraries. In a framework, you call the framework, and the framework calls you. Your code can be viewed as the middle layer of a sandwich. This key insight can help you grasp what makes .NET programming "tick."

This behavior of being called into has been around for a long time in the form of callback functions. The chapter included a careful examination of delegates and events. Two simple and intuitive examples were presented: a stock market simulation and an online chat room.

Finally, we covered attributes, which can be used to modify the behavior of entities of our program according to our specifications.

This chapter concludes our exploration of the C# programming language. In the next chapter we begin our detailed examination of the .NET Framework with a study of user interface programming using Windows Forms.

# User Interface Programming

*A* fundamental feature of modern user interaction with a computer is a graphical user interface or GUI. In this chapter we learn how to implement a GUI using the Windows Forms classes of the .NET Framework. Practical Windows programming involves extensive use of tools and wizards that greatly streamline the process. But all this automation can obscure the fundamentals of what is going on. Hence we begin with the basics, employing the .NET Framework SDK to create simple Windows applications from scratch, without use of any special tools. We describe the fundamentals of drawing in Windows Forms, using a font and a brush. We explain the principles of event handling in Windows Forms and implement handlers for mouse events. We implement menus in Windows Forms and corresponding event handlers. Controls are introduced.

At this point we switch over to using Visual Studio.NET, which makes it easy to create a starter project, draw controls using a Forms Designer, create menus, add event handlers, and perform other useful tasks. Dialog boxes are covered, and the listbox control is introduced. We illustrate GUI programming by constructing a GUI for our Acme Travel Agency case study.

## Windows Forms Hierarchy

Windows Forms is that part of the .NET Framework that supports building traditional GUI applications on the Windows platform. Windows Forms provides a large set of classes that make it easy to create sophisticated user interfaces. These classes are available to all .NET languages.

Your application will typically have a main window implemented by deriving from the **Form** class. Figure 6–1 illustrates how your class derives from the Windows Forms hierarchy.

191

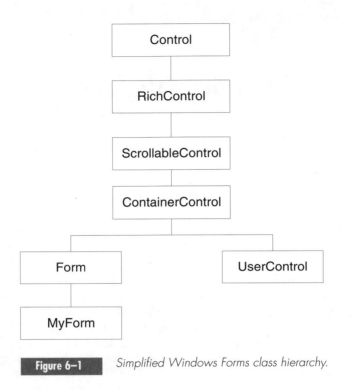

| Figure 6–1 |    *Simplified Windows Forms class hierarchy.*

## Simple Forms Using .NET SDK

To gain insight into the fundamentals of Windows Forms it will be helpful to build a simple application using only the .NET Framework SDK. See the program **SimpleForm** with several progressive steps. None of these steps has a Visual Studio project. There is a simple batch file **build.bat** that you should run at the command prompt.

### Step 0: A Simple Form

Here is a bare-bones Windows application. It is Step 0 of the example **SimpleForm**.

```
using System;
using System.Windows.Forms;

public class Form1: Form
{
   public Form1()
   {
      Size = new System.Drawing.Size(300,200);
      Text = "Simple Form - Step 0";
```

```
    }
    public static void Main(string[] args)
    {
        Application.Run(new Form1());
    }
}
```

Our **Form1** class inherits from **System.Windows.Forms**. The class **System.Application** has static methods, such as **Run** and **Exit**, to control an application. The **Main** method instantiates a new form and runs it as the main window.

The constructor of the form does initializations: The **Size** field sets the size of the new form in pixels. The **Text** field specifies the caption to be shown in the title bar of the new form.

The key to Windows Forms programming is the **Form** base class. This class contains a great deal of functionality, which is inherited by form classes that we design.

You can build the application at the command line using the batch file **build.bat**. To run the batch file, open up a DOS window and navigate to the **SimpleForm\Step0** directory and type **build**. Remember that you must have the environment variables set up properly, which you can ensure by running the Visual Studio.NET Command Prompt.

```
csc /target:winexe /r:System.dll /r:System.Drawing.dll
/r:System.Windows.Forms.dll SimpleForm.cs
```

The target is a Windows executable, and there are references to the required .NET libraries, **System.dll**, **System.Drawing.dll**, and **System.Windows.Forms.dll**.

After you have built the application using the batch file, you can run it by typing **SimpleForm** at the command line. You can also double-click on the file **SimpleForm.exe** in Windows Explorer. Figure 6–2 shows this simple application. Although trivial, it already has a great deal of functionality, which is inherited from the **Form** base class. You can drag the window around, resize it, minimize it, maximize it, open the system menu (click in top left of the window), and so forth.

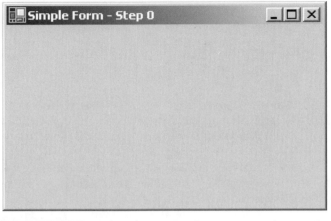

**Figure 6–2** *A bare-bones Windows Forms application (Step 0).*

## WINDOWS MESSAGES

Visual Studio.NET supplies a tool called Spy++, which can be used to "spy" on windows, gaining some inkling of things taking place under the hood. Spy++ can be started from the Visual Studio Tools menu. With the Step 0 version of **SimpleForm.exe** running, start Spy++. Bring up the Find Window dialog from the menu Spy | Find Window. Click on the Messages radio button. See Figure 6–3.

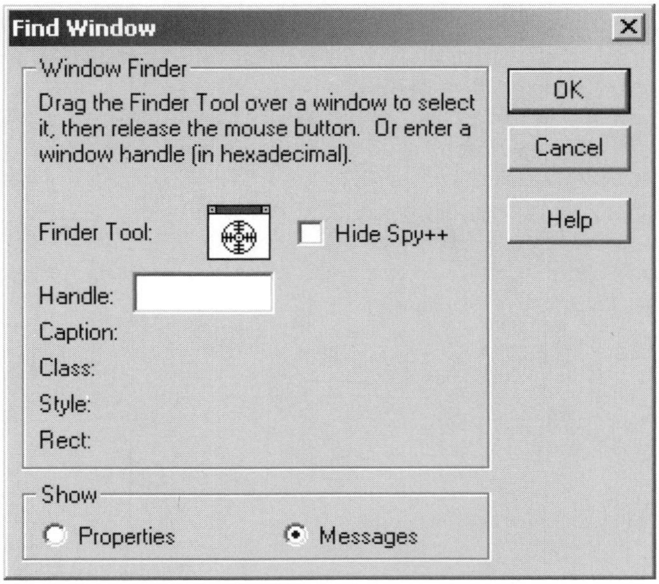

**Figure 6–3** *The Finder Tool lets you select a window to spy upon.*

Using the left mouse button, drag the Finder Tool over the window of the **SimpleForm** application and release the button. Now. as you interact with the **SimpleForm** window, you will see *windows messages* displayed in a window of Spy++, as illustrated in Figure 6–4.

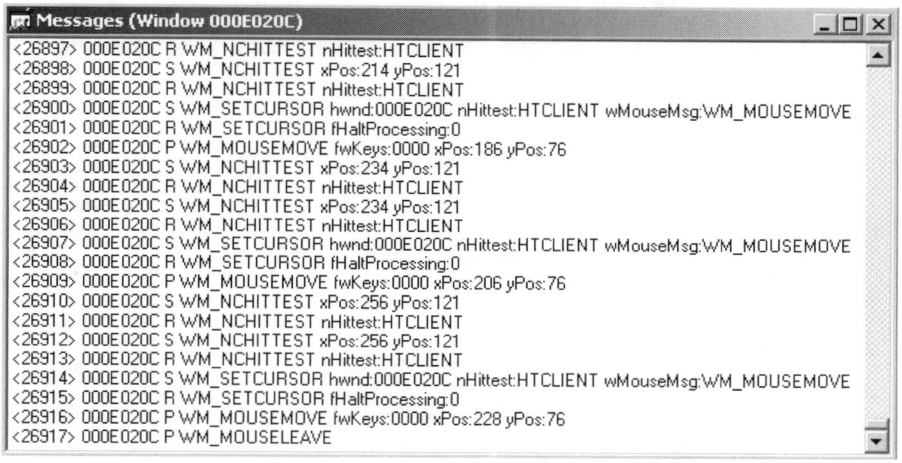

```
Messages (Window 000E020C)                                                    _ □ ×
<26897> 000E020C R WM_NCHITTEST nHittest:HTCLIENT
<26898> 000E020C S WM_NCHITTEST xPos:214 yPos:121
<26899> 000E020C R WM_NCHITTEST nHittest:HTCLIENT
<26900> 000E020C S WM_SETCURSOR hwnd:000E020C nHittest:HTCLIENT wMouseMsg:WM_MOUSEMOVE
<26901> 000E020C S WM_SETCURSOR fHaltProcessing:0
<26902> 000E020C P WM_MOUSEMOVE fwKeys:0000 xPos:186 yPos:76
<26903> 000E020C S WM_NCHITTEST xPos:234 yPos:121
<26904> 000E020C R WM_NCHITTEST nHittest:HTCLIENT
<26905> 000E020C S WM_NCHITTEST xPos:234 yPos:121
<26906> 000E020C R WM_NCHITTEST nHittest:HTCLIENT
<26907> 000E020C S WM_SETCURSOR hwnd:000E020C nHittest:HTCLIENT wMouseMsg:WM_MOUSEMOVE
<26908> 000E020C R WM_SETCURSOR fHaltProcessing:0
<26909> 000E020C P WM_MOUSEMOVE fwKeys:0000 xPos:206 yPos:76
<26910> 000E020C S WM_NCHITTEST xPos:256 yPos:121
<26911> 000E020C R WM_NCHITTEST nHittest:HTCLIENT
<26912> 000E020C S WM_NCHITTEST xPos:256 yPos:121
<26913> 000E020C R WM_NCHITTEST nHittest:HTCLIENT
<26914> 000E020C S WM_SETCURSOR hwnd:000E020C nHittest:HTCLIENT wMouseMsg:WM_MOUSEMOVE
<26915> 000E020C R WM_SETCURSOR fHaltProcessing:0
<26916> 000E020C P WM_MOUSEMOVE fwKeys:0000 xPos:228 yPos:76
<26917> 000E020C P WM_MOUSELEAVE
```

**Figure 6–4**    *The Finder Tool lets you select a window to spy upon.*

Windows applications are structured to handle events. The Windows operating system sends messages to applications in response to user actions such as clicking a mouse button, selecting a menu, typing at the keyboard, and so on. A Windows application must be structured so that it can respond to such messages.

The nice thing about Windows programming using the .NET Framework classes is that you program at a much higher level of abstraction. We have already seen how simple the Step 0 application is. In the next several sections we will progressively implement some basic features, illustrating the fundamentals of GUI programming using the Windows Forms classes.

## Step 1: Drawing Text on a Form

Step 1 illustrates drawing text on a form. Figure 6–5 shows a run of the application.

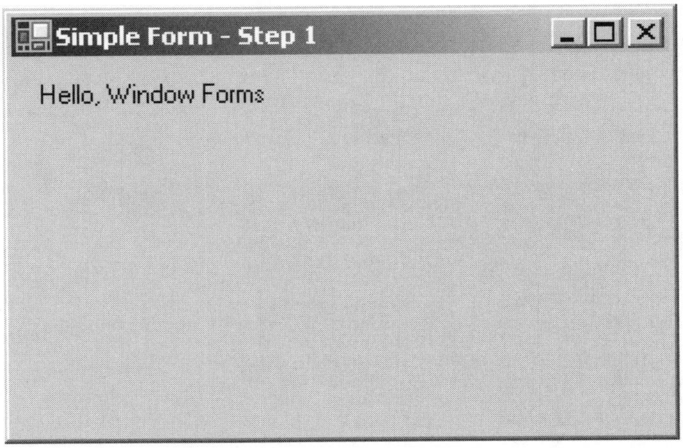

**Figure 6–5**    *Drawing text on a simple form (Step 1).*

Performing output in Windows programs is very different from outputting in console applications, where we simply use methods such as **Console.WriteLine**. Drawing output in a window is referred to as "painting." Painting is done in response to a special kind of message, a "paint" message WM_PAINT. This "on-demand" style of painting ensures that the output of a window will be shown correctly even if the window is covered up and uncovered again.

Another difference in output in Windows programs is that you have to specify details, such as the coordinates at which it is drawn, a "brush" to draw with, a font for text, and so forth. Here is the code for Step 1.

```
// SimpleForm.cs - Step 1

using System;
using System.Windows.Forms;
using System.Drawing;

public class Form1: Form
{
   private float x, y;
   private Brush stdBrush;
   public Form1()
   {
      Size = new System.Drawing.Size(300,200);
      Text = "Simple Form - Step 1";
      x = y = 10;
      stdBrush = new SolidBrush(Color.Black);
   }
   protected override void OnPaint(PaintEventArgs e)
```

```
    {
        e.Graphics.DrawString("Hello, Window Forms",
                              Font, stdBrush, x, y);
    }
}
...
```

To draw in Windows Forms, you must override the virtual method **OnPaint**. The class **PaintEventArgs** has a **Graphics** object as a read-only property. The **Graphics** class, part of the **System.Drawing** namespace, has methods for drawing.

The **DrawString** method has parameters for:

- The string to be drawn
- The font (**Font** is a property of **Form** that gives the default font for the form)
- The brush to be used
- The pixel coordinates (as **float** numbers)

A black **SolidBrush** is constructed as our standard brush.

## Windows Forms Event Handling

GUI applications are event-driven: The application executes code in response to user events, such as clicking the mouse, choosing a menu item, and so on. Each form or control has a predefined set of events. For example, every form has a **MouseDown** event.

Windows Forms employs the .NET event model,[1] which uses delegates to bind events to the methods that handle them. The Windows Forms classes use multicast delegates. A multicast delegate maintains a list of the methods it is bound to. When an event occurs in an application, the control raises the event by calling the delegate for that event. The delegate then calls all the methods it is bound to.

C# provides the overloaded += operator for adding a delegate to an event. The following code adds the **Form1_MouseDown** method to the **MouseDown** event.

```
MouseDown += new MouseEventHandler (Form1_MouseDown);
```

We will see this code in context shortly.

---

[1] You may wish to review the discussion of delegates and events in Chapter 5.

## Events Documentation

You can find all the events associated with a class in the .NET Framework Reference. The screen shot in Figure 6–6 shows the predefined events associated with the **Form** class.

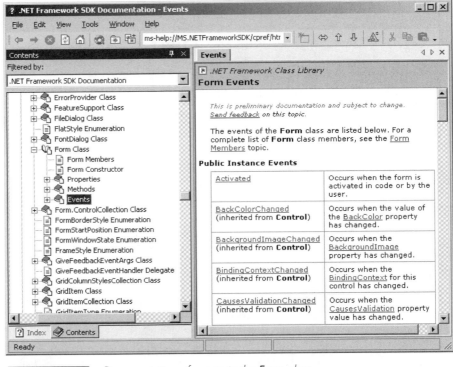

**Figure 6–6**    *Documentation of events in the **Form** class.*

## MouseDown Event

One of the predefined events in the **Control** class, from which the **Form** class derives, is **MouseDown**.

```
public event MouseEventHandler MouseDown;
```

Here is the declaration of **MouseEventHandler**:

```
public delegate void MouseEventHandler(
    object sender,
    MouseEventArgs e
);
```

The event handler receives a **MouseEventArgs** (derived from **EventArgs**), which has read-only properties to provide information specific to this event:

- **Button** specifies which button (left, right, or the like) was pressed.
- **Clicks** indicates how many times the button was pressed and released.
- **Delta** provides a count of rotations of a mouse wheel.
- **X** and **Y** provide the coordinates where the mouse button was pressed.

## Step 2: Handling a Mouse Event

In Step 2 a mouse click (any button) will reposition the location of the greeting string. Figure 6–7 shows the string relocated after we have clicked the mouse.

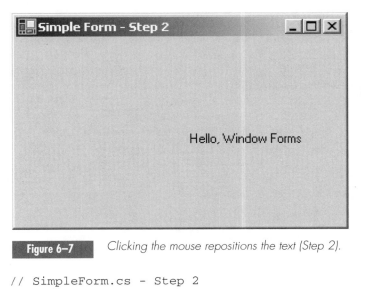

**Figure 6–7**  *Clicking the mouse repositions the text (Step 2).*

```
// SimpleForm.cs - Step 2

using System;
using System.Windows.Forms;
using System.Drawing;

public class Form1: Form
{
   private void InitializeComponent()
   {
      MouseDown += new MouseEventHandler (Form1_MouseDown);
   }

   private float x, y;
```

```
private Brush stdBrush;
public Form1()
{
   InitializeComponent();
   Size = new System.Drawing.Size(300,200);
   Text = "Simple Form - Step 2";
   x = y = 10;
   stdBrush = new SolidBrush(Color.Black);
}
protected void Form1_MouseDown (object sender,
                                   MouseEventArgs e)
{
   x = e.X;
   y = e.Y;
   Invalidate();
}
...
```

As part of its initialization, our program registers the **Form1_MouseDown** method with the **MouseDown** event. This method sets the **x** and **y** coordinates of our text to the location where the mouse was clicked. To understand the role of **Invalidate**, comment out the code and build again. Click the mouse to relocate the greeting string. What happens? The string is not relocated. Now cover the **SimpleForm** window with some other window and then uncover it. Now you should see the string relocated.

The **Invalidate** method is defined in the **Control** base class. There are several overloaded versions of this method. Each invalidates some region of the control and causes a paint message to be sent to the control. The method with no parameters causes the entire control to be invalidated. To minimize the amount of redrawing done, a more sophisticated application might invalidate just a rectangle.

## Step 2M: Multiple Event Handlers

Step 2M illustrates tying two different event handlers to the **MouseDown** event. The second handler merely displays a message box.[2]

```
// SimpleForm.cs - Step 2M
...

public class Form1: Form
{
   private void InitializeComponent()
   {
      MouseDown += new MouseEventHandler (Form1_MouseDown);
```

---

[2] A message box is a special kind of dialog box and will be discussed later in this chapter.

```
        MouseDown += new MouseEventHandler (ShowClick);
    }
    ...
protected void Form1_MouseDown (object sender,
                                MouseEventArgs e)
    {
        x = e.X;
        y = e.Y;
        Invalidate();
    }
protected void ShowClick(object sender,
                         MouseEventArgs e)
    {
        MessageBox.Show("Mouse clicked!!!");
    }
    ...
}
```

## Step 3: MouseDown and KeyPress Events

Step 3 of our demonstration illustrates handling an additional event, **KeyPress**, and also distinguishing between left and right buttons in **MouseDown**.

### HANDLING LEFT AND RIGHT BUTTONS

We can distinguish between left and right buttons by using the **Button** property of the **MouseEventArgs** parameter. Right button down is used for clearing the message string, which is now stored in a **StringBuilder** data member **str**.

```
protected void Form1_MouseDown (object sender,
                                MouseEventArgs e)
{
    if (e.Button == MouseButtons.Left)
    {
        x = e.X;
        y = e.Y;
    }
    else if (e.Button == MouseButtons.Right)
    {
        str = new StringBuilder();
    }
    Invalidate();
}
```

## KEYPRESS EVENT

Step 3 also illustrates handling a **KeyPress** event. Every time the user presses a key, the corresponding character is appended to the greeting string. Note use of the **StringBuilder** class, which is more efficient in this context than **string**. **String** is immutable, and hence **string** objects would be continually created and destroyed while we appended characters.

```
private StringBuilder str;
...
protected void Form1_KeyPress (object sender,
                                    KeyPressEventArgs e)
{
   str.Append(e.KeyChar);
   Invalidate();
}
```

As with Step 2 we call **Invalidate** to force a repaint after we have made a change in the data to be displayed. Figure 6–8 illustrates our **SimpleForm** window after the starting text has been cleared and some new text typed in.

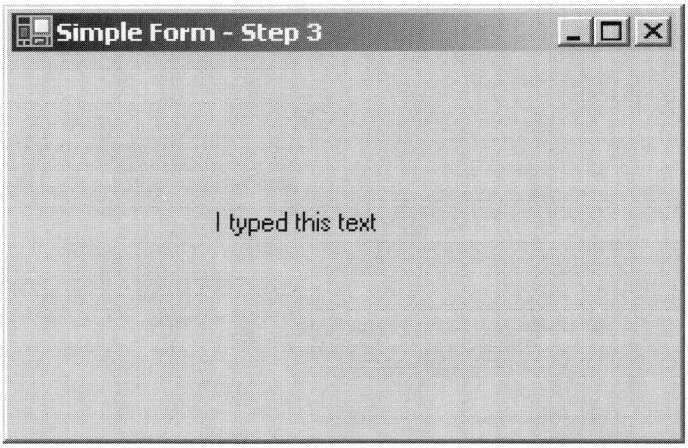

**Figure 6–8**    *Exercising mouse and key press events (Step 3).*

# Menus

As a user of Windows applications you should be acquainted with menus, which provide a simple mechanism for choosing commands. In .NET menus are implemented in code. There is no separate resource file.

## Step 4: A Menu to Exit the Program

Step 4 of our **SimpleForm** program illustrates adding a simple menu. File |
Exit is used to exit the program. See Figure 6–9.

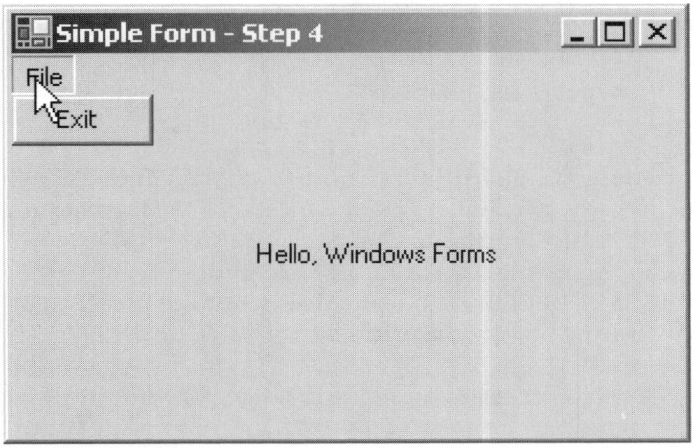

**Figure 6–9**　*A File | Exit menu is added to our form (Step 4).*

## Menu Code

```
// SimpleForm.cs - Step 4
. . .
private MenuItem menuExit;
private MenuItem menuFile;
private MainMenu mainMenu1;
public Form1()
{
   InitializeComponent();
   Size = new System.Drawing.Size(300,200);
   Text = "Simple Form - Step 4";
   x = y = 10;
   stdBrush = new SolidBrush(Color.Black);
   str = new StringBuilder("Hello, Windows Forms");
}
private void InitializeComponent()
{
     mainMenu1 = new MainMenu ();
     menuFile = new MenuItem ();
     menuExit = new MenuItem ();
     // mainMenu1
     mainMenu1.MenuItems.Add(menuFile);
     // menuFile
```

```
menuFile.Index = 0;
menuFile.MenuItems.Add(menuExit);
menuFile.Text = "File";
// menuExit
menuExit.Index = 0;
menuExit.Text = "Exit";
menuExit.Click += new EventHandler(menuExit_Click);

Menu = mainMenu1;
...
```

The code in **InitializeComponent** builds up the hierarchical menu structure, represented by an instance of the **MainMenu** class. A menu is composed of **MenuItem** objects that represent the individual menu commands in the menu structure. Each **MenuItem** can be a command for your application or a parent menu for other submenu items. You bind the **MainMenu** to the Form that will display it by assigning the **MainMenu** to the **Menu** property of the Form.

When we discuss the Forms Designer later in the chapter, we will see that it is easy to create a menu by dragging a **MainMenu** control from the toolbox to the form. The Forms Designer will take care of generating appropriate boilerplate code.

## Menu Event Code

A delegate is hooked to the event, as with other Windows Forms events. Clicking on a menu item causes the corresponding command to be executed.

```
private void InitializeComponent()
{
  ...
    menuExit.Click +=
     new EventHandler(this.menuExit_Click);
  ...
}

private void menuExit_Click(object sender,
                            EventArgs e)
{
  Application.Exit();
}
  ...
```

# Controls

In the program we have just discussed, **mainMenu1** is an example of a *control*. It is an instance of the **MainMenu** class. A control is an object that is contained within a form and is used to add functionality to the form. A control can perform many tasks automatically on behalf of its parent form. It simplifies programming, as you do not have to be concerned with painting, invalidating, working with graphics elements, and so forth. The simple menu that we just illustrated would have required a substantial amount of code if we had to implement it from scratch. Controls provide rich reusable code—a big benefit from programming with objects.

## Step 5: Using a TextBox Control

Step 5 of our **SimpleForm** application illustrates using a **TextBox** control to display our greeting text. As with earlier versions of the application, you can reposition the greeting by clicking the left mouse button, and you can clear the greeting by clicking the right mouse button. You can also type in your own greeting text. Now you have full editing capability. You can insert characters wherever you wish in the control, cut and paste (Ctrl+X and Ctrl+V), and so forth. All of this editing capability is provided by the **TextBox** control. Figure 6–10 illustrates the application after the greeting has been repositioned and we have typed in some text of our own.

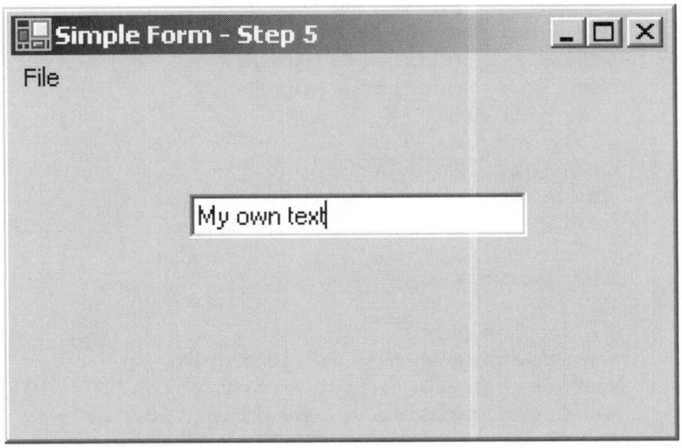

**Figure 6–10**    *The greeting text is now displayed using a control (Step 5).*

Here is the new version of our program. Note that it has both greater simplicity and more functionality. We no longer need member variables for the coordinates or text of the greeting string (this information is now stored in the **TextBox** control **txtGreeting)**. We do not need **OnPaint** any longer, either, because the text box knows how to paint itself. We can then also get rid of the brush. We don't need to handle **KeyPress** events, because this functionality is handled (in a much more full-blown way) by the **TextBox** control.

```csharp
// SimpleForm.cs - Step 5
...

public class Form1: Form
{
    private TextBox txtGreeting;
    private MenuItem menuExit;
    private MenuItem menuFile;
    private MainMenu mainMenu1;
    public Form1()
    {
        InitializeComponent();
        Size = new System.Drawing.Size(300,200);
        Text = "Simple Form - Step 5";
    }
    private void InitializeComponent()
    {
        mainMenu1 = new MainMenu ();
        menuFile = new MenuItem ();
        menuExit = new MenuItem ();
        // mainMenu1
        mainMenu1.MenuItems.Add(menuFile);
        // menuFile
        menuFile.Index = 0;
        menuFile.MenuItems.Add(menuExit);
        menuFile.Text = "File";
        // menuExit
        menuExit.Index = 0;
        menuExit.Text = "Exit";
        menuExit.Click += new EventHandler(menuExit_Click);

        Menu = mainMenu1;

        // txtGreeting
        txtGreeting = new TextBox();
        txtGreeting.Location = new Point(10, 10);
        txtGreeting.Size = new Size(150, 20);
        txtGreeting.Text = "Hello, Windows Forms";

        Controls.Add(txtGreeting);

        this.MouseDown +=
            new MouseEventHandler (Form1_MouseDown);
    }
```

```
protected void Form1_MouseDown (object sender,
                                MouseEventArgs e)
{
    if (e.Button == MouseButtons.Left)
    {
        txtGreeting.Location = new Point(e.X, e.Y);
    }
    else if (e.Button == MouseButtons.Right)
    {
        txtGreeting.Text = "";
    }
}
private void menuExit_Click(object sender, EventArgs e)
{
    Application.Exit();
}
public static void Main(string[] args)
{
    Application.Run(new Form1());
}
}
```

Using the **TextBox** control is very easy. As part of the initialization we instantiate it and assign the **Location, Size,** and **Text** properties. We add our new control to the **Controls** collection of our form. In the mouse event handler we reposition the control by assigning the **Location** property. We clear the text by assigning the **Text** property.

# Visual Studio.NET and Forms

Although it is perfectly feasible to create Windows Forms applications using only the command-line tools of the .NET Framework SDK, in practice it much easier to use Visual Studio.NET. You can get started by creating a Windows Application project, which provides starter code and sets up references to the required .NET libraries. You can then use the Forms Designer to drag and drop controls from a toolbox onto your forms. The Forms Designer inserts all the needed boilerplate code to make your controls work within your forms. There is a Properties window which makes it easy to set properties of your controls at design time. You can, of course, also set properties at runtime, which is what we did with our **txtGreeting** text box in the code shown previously.

The same Forms Designer can be used in all .NET languages. A similar Designer is available for visually drawing Web Forms, which we will discuss in Chapter 10 on ASP.NET.

## Windows Forms Demonstration

The best way to become acquainted with using Visual Studio.NET to create Windows applications is to build a small application from scratch yourself. Our demonstration creates a Windows application to make deposits and withdrawals from a bank account. Do all your work in the **Demos** directory for this chapter.

1. Create a new C# project **BankGui** of type Windows Application in the **Demos** folder. See Figure 6–11.

*Creating a new Windows Application project.*

2. Open up the Toolbox by dragging the mouse over the vertical Toolbox tab on the left side of the main Visual Studio window. If the Toolbox tab does not show, you can open it from the menu View | Toolbox. You can make the Toolbox stay open by clicking on the "push-pin" next to the X on the title bar of the Toolbox. (The little yellow box will say "Auto Hide" when you pause the mouse over the push-pin.)

3. From the Toolbox, drag two labels, two textboxes, and two buttons to the form. See Figure 6–12.

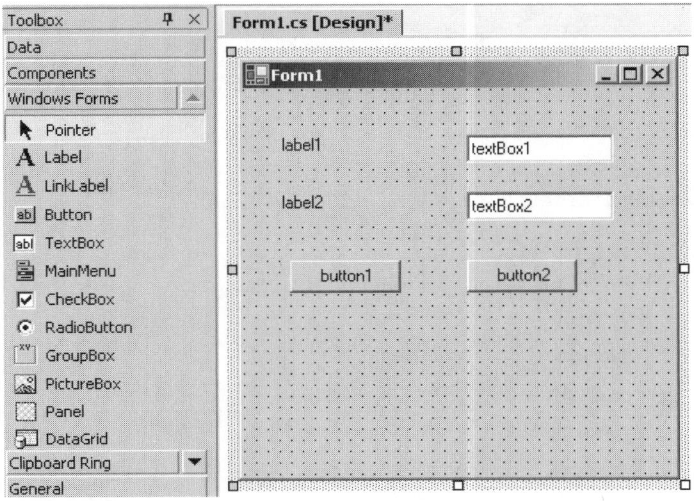

**Figure 6–12**    *Dragging controls from the Toolbox onto a form.*

4. Click on **label1** in the Forms Designer. This will select that control in the Properties window, just beneath the Solution Explorer. You can use the Properties window to make changes to properties of controls. Change the Text property to **Amount**. After you type the desired value, hit the carriage return. You will then see the new text shown on the form. Figure 6–13 shows the Properties window after you have changed the Text property of the first label.

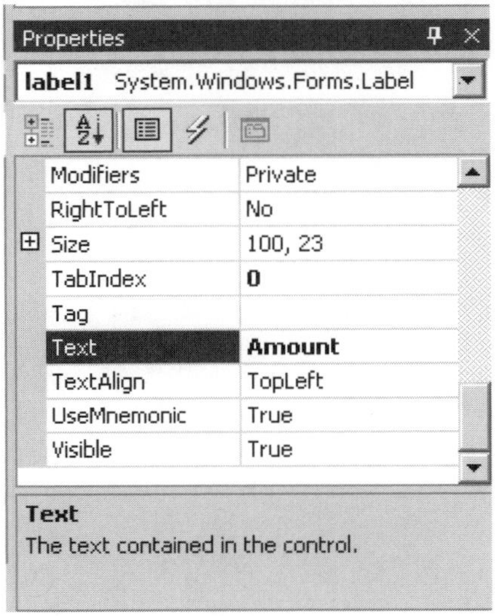

**Figure 6–13**    *Changing property values in the Properties window.*

5. Similarly, change the text of **label2** to **Balance**.

6. Enter property values for the textboxes and buttons, as shown in Table 6–1.

| Table 6–1 | Property Values for Textboxes and Buttons |
|-----------|---------------------------|
| **Name** | **Text** |
| txtAmount | (blank) |
| txtBalance | (blank) |
| cmdDeposit | Deposit |
| cmdWithdraw | Withdraw |

1. Resize the form by dragging the sizing handles on the middle of each side. Reposition the controls as desired by dragging with the mouse, and resize the controls with the mouse, if you wish. When you are satisfied with the appearance of your form, save the project. Your form should now look similar to Figure 6–14.

| Figure 6–14 | Form for BankGui application. |

2. Add event handlers for the buttons by double-clicking on each button.

3. Add the following code:

```
public class Form1 : System.Windows.Forms.Form
{
```

```
...
    public Form1()
    {
        //
        // Required for Windows Form Designer support
        //
        InitializeComponent();

        //
        // TODO: Add any constructor code after
        // InitializeComponent call
        //
        txtAmount.Text = "25";
        txtBalance.Text = "100";
    }
...
    /// <summary>
    /// The main entry point for the application.
    /// </summary>
    [STAThread]
    static void Main()
    {
        Application.Run(new Form1());
    }

    private void cmdDeposit_Click(object sender,
                                  System.EventArgs e)
    {
        int amount = Convert.ToInt32(txtAmount.Text);
        int balance = Convert.ToInt32(txtBalance.Text);
        balance += amount;
        txtBalance.Text = Convert.ToString(balance);
    }

    private void cmdWithdraw_Click(object sender,
                                   System.EventArgs e)
    {
        int amount = Convert.ToInt32(txtAmount.Text);
        int balance = Convert.ToInt32(txtBalance.Text);
        balance -= amount;
        txtBalance.Text = Convert.ToString(balance);
    }
```

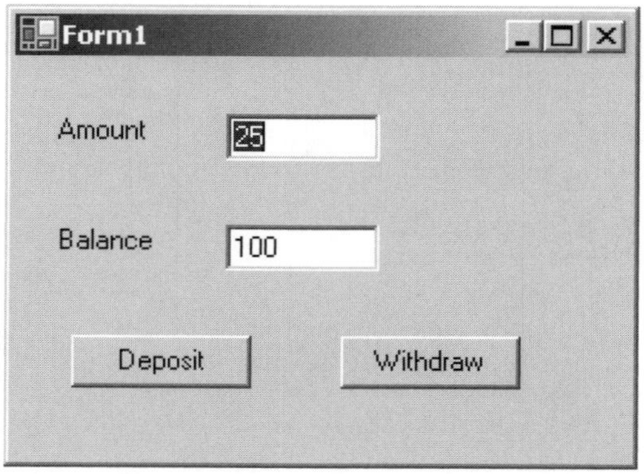

**Figure 6–15**  *The BankGui Windows application.*

4. Build and run the application. It should behave like a standard Windows application. You should be able to make deposits and withdrawals. Figure 6–15 illustrates the running application.

## Design Window and Code Window

The most important thing to understand about navigating Windows Forms projects in Visual Studio is switching between the Design window, where you work with controls on a form, and the Code window, where you work with source code. We can illustrate these two windows from the **Demos\VsForm** project, where we have provided starter code corresponding to **VsForm\Step1** in the main directory for this chapter. The starter project simply displays a fixed greeting string. The state of the project at various points in the demonstration is captured in other numbered steps.

If you double-click on **VsForm.sln** (**Demos** directory) in the Solution Explorer, you will bring up the Design window, as shown in Figure 6–16.

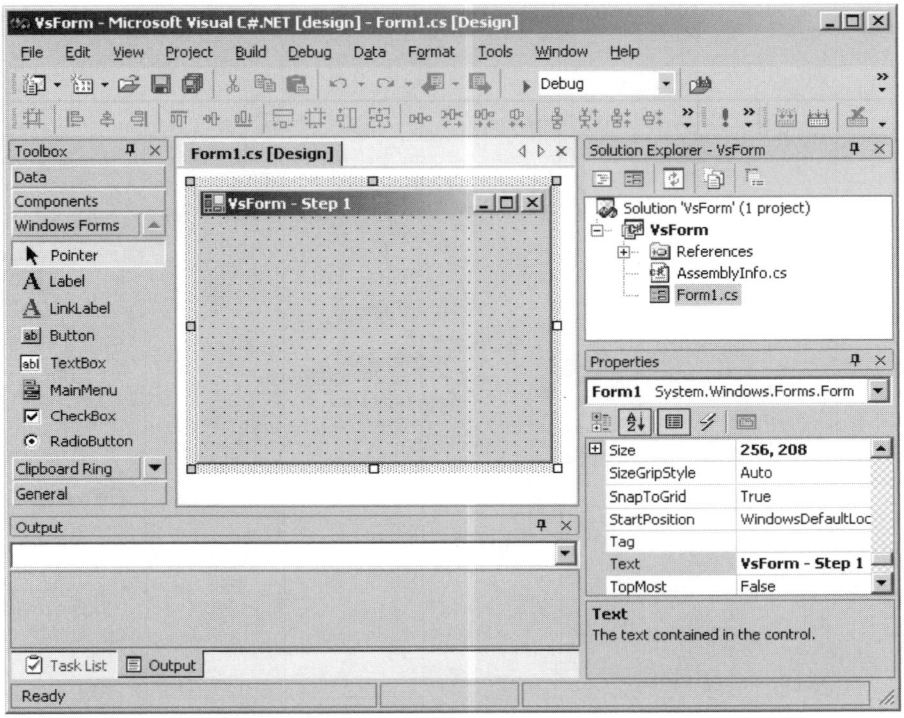

**Figure 6–16**    *The Design window in a Windows Forms project.*

To bring up the Code window, click on the "View Code"  ▣  toolbar button in the Solution Explorer. This will open up the source code, and you will see horizontal tabs at the top of the principal window area, allowing you to select among the open windows. Now the Design window and the Code window for this one form are open. You may also go back to the Design window by clicking on the "View Designer"  ▣  toolbar button. Figure 6–17 shows the open Code window.

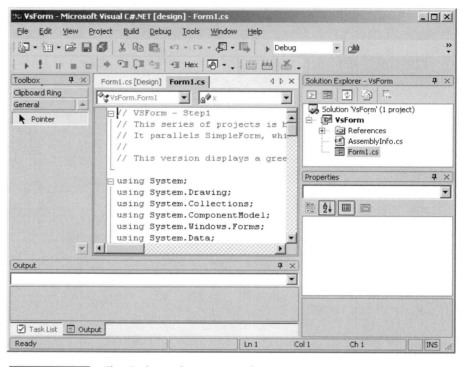

**Figure 6–17** *The Code window in a Windows Forms project.*

## Adding an Event

1. Build and run the starter program. This is a completely static application—it merely displays a greeting at a fixed location.

2. Open up the Design window of the form and click on the Events button ⚡ of the Properties window.

3. Find the **MouseDown** event. See Figure 6–18.

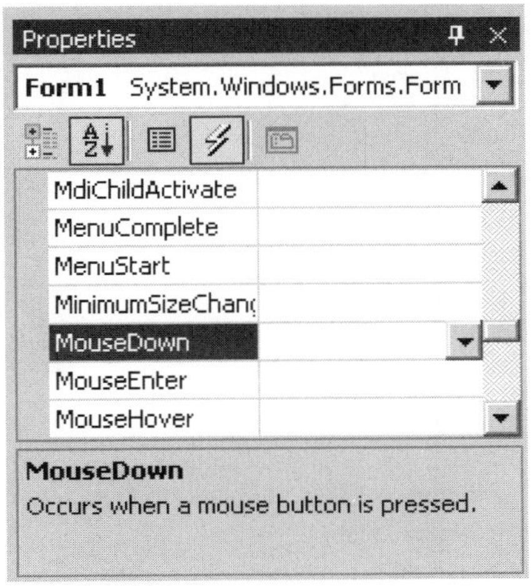

**Figure 6–18**     *Adding an event by using the Events button.*

4. Double-click. This will automatically generate code to register a delegate for the event and provide a skeleton for a method tied to the delegate.[3]

```
private void InitializeComponent()
{
...
  this.MouseDown +=
     new System.WinForms.MouseEventHandler
          (this.Form1_MouseDown);
}

  protected void Form1_MouseDown (object sender,
    System.WinForms.MouseEventArgs e)
  {

  }
  ...
```

## Code for Event Handler

5. Add the highlighted code to the mouse down event handler to set the coordinates of the greeting message. Don't forget to call **Invalidate**!

```
protected void Form1_MouseDown (object sender,
     System.WinForms.MouseEventArgs e)
```

---

[3] If you cannot see this Windows Form Designer generated code, click on the little "+" on the extreme left of the editor window to open up the hidden "region."

```
{
    x = e.X;
    y = e.Y;
    Invalidate();
}
```

6. Build and run. You should now be able to relocate the greeting by clicking the mouse button (either button will work). The project now corresponds to **VsForm\Step2**.

## Using the Menu Control

1. Open up the Toolbox if not already open (click on the Toolbox vertical tab) and drag the **MainMenu** control 🖳 MainMenu onto the form.

2. Type "File" and "Exit," creating a popup menu File with a menu item Exit. See Figure 6–19.

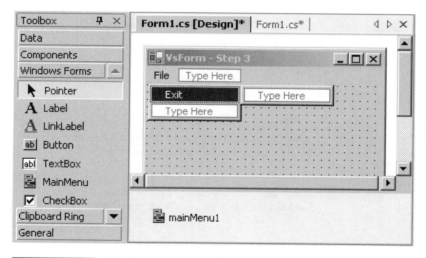

**Figure 6–19**    *Use the Menu Control to add a menu to a form.*

3. In the Properties window change the names of your two menu items to "menuFile" and "menuExit."

4. Double-click on "Exit" to add code for a File | Exit event handler.

5. Add code to the handler to exit the application.

```
protected void menuExit_Click (object sender,
  System.EventArgs e)
{
```

```
       Application.Exit();
}
```

6. Build and run. Your menu should be operational. The project now corresponds to **VsForm\Step3**.

## Closing a Form

As an interesting modification to our program, let us arrange it so that whenever the user attempts to close the application, the user will be queried on whether to really close. There are several ways a window can be closed:

- From the "X" at top right of the window
- From the system menu at the top left of the window
- By the keyboard Alt + F4
- In our application, by File | Exit

When a form is about to close, the **Closing** event is raised. You may stop the closing by setting the **Cancel** property in the handler for this event. (First add a handler for the event **Closing** in the usual way.) Just type in the **MessageBox** code as shown.

```
protected void Form1_Closing (object sender,
       System.ComponentModel.CancelEventArgs e)
{
       DialogResult status = MessageBox.Show(
        "Do you want to close",
          "Simple Form (VS)", MessageBoxButtons.YesNo);
       if (status == DialogResult.No)
       {
             e.Cancel = true;
       }
}
```

To tap into this behavior, in your handler for File | Exit you should not exit the application but instead close the main window by calling the **Close** method:

```
protected void menuExit_Click (object sender,
       System.EventArgs e)
{
       //Application.Exit();
       Close();
}
```

The project now corresponds to **VSForm\Step4**. Run your program and try closing in various ways. You should always see the dialog box shown in Figure 6–20.

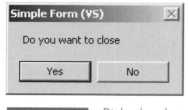

**Figure 6–20** *Dialog box that queries the user whether or not to close.*

# Dialog Boxes

Dialog boxes provide a more elaborate way for a user to interact with a Windows application. A dialog box can provide a number of controls to facilitate data input. The code in the previous section illustrated use of a simple message box dialog that allowed the user to answer a yes or no question. This kind of dialog can be created using the **MessageBox** class. You can implement more general dialog boxes by creating forms for them.

We will illustrate a number of dialogs through a graphical user interface to our Acme Travel Agency case study. As usual, the case study code is in the **CaseStudy** folder for this chapter. Let's begin by examining a simple dialog that is used for adding a new hotel to our list of hotels. Build and run the case study. In the main form click the "Add..." button.[4] The "New Hotel" dialog is brought up, as illustrated in Figure 6–21.

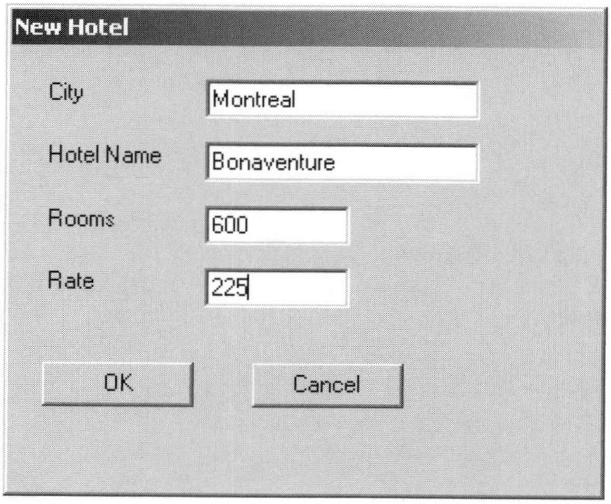

**Figure 6–21** *Dialog box for adding a new hotel.*

---

[4] The three dots are a Windows UI style that indicates the program will not carry out the action immediately but will prompt the user for additional input, typically through a dialog box.

The user can now enter data. Clicking the OK button will cause the information to be accepted. Clicking the Cancel button will cause the new data to be ignored. This dialog box (like the message box in the previous section) is a *modal* dialog, which means that the user cannot work elsewhere in the application until the dialog is closed. If you try do something else on the main form while the "New Hotel" dialog is open—for example, click another button—you will hear a beep. The other kind of dialog is *modeless*, which will allow the user to work elsewhere in the application while the dialog is open.

Dialog boxes normally have special characteristics as forms. For example, they typically do not have a system menu, they have no minimize or maximize buttons, and they have a border that does not permit them to be resized. You can examine these features with the "New Hotel" dialog.

Continuing the demonstration, enter some data for a new hotel and click OK. You will now be brought back to the main form, and your new hotel will be shown in the list of hotels, as illustrated in Figure 6–22. The main form also illustrates some additional GUI features, such as a list box for displaying a list of hotels and a multiline text box that can display text that is too long to fit on one line.

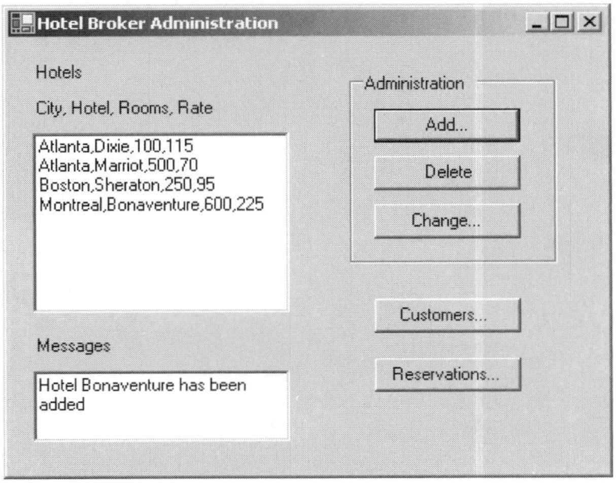

**Figure 6–22**   *Main form for hotel administration.*

## .NET Dialog Documentation

Dialogs are explained clearly in the Documentation in the .NET Framework. Look in "Dialog Boxes in Windows Forms" under "Introduction to Windows

Forms." It is noteworthy that the principles of dialog boxes are the same in all .NET languages. This is in sharp contrast to the days before .NET, where, for example, dialogs in Visual Basic and in Microsoft Foundation Classes were totally different. Figure 6–23 shows the entry point to this documentation.

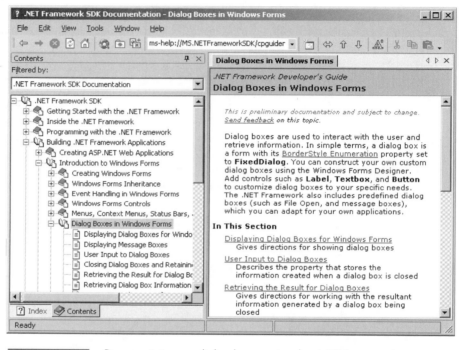

*Documentation on dialog boxes using the .NET Framework.*

## Dialog Box Demonstration

We will demonstrate the implementation details of a dialog box by creating a dialog to change hotel information in a simplified version of our case study. Do your work in the folder **Demo\HotelAdmin**. The starter code is backed up in the folder **HotelAdmin\Step1** in the main folder for this chapter. The completed program is in **HotelAdmin\Step3**. You may run either the case study or the Step 3 solution to see what the completed dialog should look like. In the main form select a hotel by clicking in the list box of hotels. Then click on the "Change..." button. This brings up the "Change Hotel Information" dialog, as illustrated in Figure 6–24. Notice that the City and Hotel Name are grayed out. These items are read-only and cannot be changed. The user can enter new information for the Rooms and Rate.

## CREATING A MODAL DIALOG

The first part of our demonstration illustrates how to create a modal dialog box. We show how to set properties appropriately for the dialog and how to return a dialog result through use of OK and Cancel buttons.

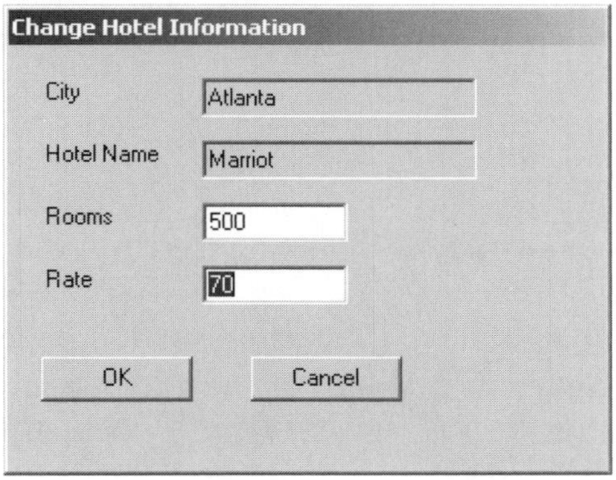

**Figure 6–24**   *Dialog for changing hotel information.*

1. Build and run the starter application. The "Add..." and "Delete" buttons work, but there is only a stub for "Change...", which brings up an empty form. This form is ordinary, with system menu, minimize and maximize buttons, resizability, and so on.

2. Open up **ChangeHotelDialog.cs** in Design mode. In the Properties window, change the **FormBorderStyle** property to **FixedDialog**.

3. Set the **ControlBox**, **MinimizeBox**, and **MaximizeBox** properties to **False**. If you like, you may build and run the application at this point. The dialog now is not resizable, and there is no system menu and no "X" in top right to close the window.[5]

4. The next job is to enter labels and text boxes for the hotel information, plus OK and Cancel buttons. You may practice using the Toolbox to add these controls. Alternatively, you may copy and paste from **NewHotelDialog.cs** (open both files in Design mode).

5. If you used copy and paste, the controls will have proper **Name** and **Text** properties. Otherwise, assign values as shown in Table 6–2.

---

[5] You may use Alt+F4 to close the window.

| Table 6-2 | *Property Values for Textboxes and Buttons for ChangeHotelDialog.cs* |
|-----------|------------------|

| Name | Text |
|------|------|
| txtCity | (blank) |
| txtHotelName | (blank) |
| txtNumberRooms | (blank) |
| txtRate | (blank) |
| cmdOK | OK |
| cmdCancel | Cancel |

6. Change the **ReadOnly** property of **txtCity** and **txtHotelName** to **true**.

7. Resize the form to better fit the controls we have added.

8. Set the **DialogResult** property of the OK button to OK. Similarly set the property of the Cancel button to Cancel. Save **ChangeHotelDialog.cs**.

9. In **MainAdminForm.cs**, add temporary code to the **cmdChange_Click** handler to display "OK" or "Cancel" in the Messages text box, depending on whether the dialog was closed by clicking OK or Cancel. Notice that a dialog is brought up by the method **ShowDialog** in place of **Show**, which is used for ordinary forms. **ShowDialog** returns a result as an **enum** of type **DialogResult**.

```
private void cmdChange_Click(object sender,
                            System.EventArgs e)
{
    ChangeHotelDialog dlg = new ChangeHotelDialog();
    DialogResult status = dlg.ShowDialog();
    if (status == DialogResult.OK)
    {
        txtMessages.Text = "OK";
    }
    else
    {
        txtMessages.Text = "Cancel";
    }
}
```

10. Build and test. You should now be able to bring up the dialog from the menu, and either the OK or Cancel button will close the dialog, and a corresponding message will be displayed. You can verify that the dialog is modal by trying to click elsewhere in the application. The program is now at Step 2.

## PASSING INFORMATION BETWEEN PARENT FORM AND A DIALOG

The second part of our demonstration shows how to pass information to a dialog and how to retrieve information from a dialog. The .NET Framework classes do not provide a built-in mechanism for this purpose, but there is a design pattern you can follow. You create a property in the dialog class for each piece of information you wish to pass between the parent form and the dialog.

In our example we implement write-only[6] properties for **City** and **HotelName** and read-write properties for **Rate** and **NumberRooms**.

1. Add code to **ChangeHotelDialog.cs** to implement these properties.

```
public string City
{
    set
    {
        txtCity.Text = value;
    }
}
public string HotelName
{
    set
    {
        txtHotelName.Text = value;
    }
}
public int NumberRooms
{
    get
    {
        return Convert.ToInt32(txtNumberRooms.Text);
    }
    set
    {

    }
}
public decimal Rate
{
    get
    {
        return Convert.ToDecimal(txtRate.Text);
    }
    set
    {
```

---

[6] The properties are write-only from the perspective of the dialog class, because we pass information a dialog instance. The corresponding controls are read-only, because the user is not allowed to enter new information.

```
        txtRate.Text = value.ToString();
   }
}
```

2. Now add code to the main form **MainAdminForm.cs** to set these
   properties prior to bringing up the dialog and to use the properties if
   the dialog box closes via an OK. Comment out or delete your previous
   test code that displays "OK" or "Cancel" in the Messages box.

```
private void cmdChange_Click(object sender,
                            System.EventArgs e)
{
    ChangeHotelDialog dlg = new ChangeHotelDialog();
    if (currHotel.HotelName != "")
    {
        dlg.City = currHotel.City;
        dlg.HotelName = currHotel.HotelName;
        dlg.NumberRooms = currHotel.NumberRooms;
        dlg.Rate = currHotel.Rate;
    }
    else
    {
        MessageBox.Show("Please select a hotel",
            "Hotel Broker Administration",
            MessageBoxButtons.OK,
            MessageBoxIcon.Exclamation
            );
        return;
    }
    DialogResult status = dlg.ShowDialog();
    if (status == DialogResult.OK)
    {
        string comment = hotelBroker.ChangeRooms(
            currHotel.City,
            currHotel.HotelName,
            dlg.NumberRooms,
            dlg.Rate);
        if (comment == "OK")
        {
            ShowHotelList(hotelBroker.GetHotels());
            txtMessages.Text = "Hotel " + currHotel.HotelName
                + " has been changed";
        }
        else
            txtMessages.Text = comment;
    }
}
```

The structure **currHotel** holds the fields of the hotel that is currently selected in the list box. In the next section we will see how to extract information from a list box and how to populate a list box.

   3. Build and test. Your dialog should now be fully operational. Your project should now correspond to **HotelAdmin\Step3**.

# ListBox Control

The .NET Framework provides a number of controls that you can use to display lists of items to the user. These controls also allow the user to select an item from the list, typically by clicking on the item to be selected. In this section we examine the **ListBox** control.

Our example program is **HotelAdmin\Step3**. The main form in **MainAdminForm.cs** contains the listbox **listHotels**, which maintains a list of hotels. Each hotel is represented by a string with values separated by commas.

## Populating a ListBox

When the **HotelAdmin** program starts up, it populates the listbox **listHotels** with a list of hotels as part of the initialization in the **MainAdminForm** constructor.

```
public MainAdminForm()
{
    //
    // Required for Windows Form Designer support
    //
    InitializeComponent();

    //
    // TODO: Add any constructor code after
    // InitializeComponent call
    //
    hotelBroker = new HotelBroker();
    ShowHotelList(hotelBroker.GetHotels());
}
```

The **ShowHotelList** method displays an array list of hotels in a listbox. This array list is obtained by calling **HotelBroker.GetHotels**. Here is the code for **ShowHotelList**.

```
private void ShowHotelList(ArrayList array)
{
    listHotels.Items.Clear();
    if (array == null)
```

```
   {
      return;
   }
   for each(HotelListItem hotel in array)
   {
      string city = hotel.City.Trim();
      string name = hotel.HotelName.Trim();
      string rooms = hotel.NumberRooms.ToString();
      string rate = hotel.Rate.ToString();
      string str = city + "," + name + ","
                 + rooms + "," + rate;
      listHotels.Items.Add(str);
   }
}
```

A **ListBox** has a property **Items** which maintains a collection of object references. We first call **Items.Clear** to clear out the listbox of items currently being displayed. We then loop through the hotels in the array list and build up a string consisting of the fields of the hotel structure, separated by commas. This string is added to the listbox by calling **Items.Add**.

## Selecting an Item From a ListBox

An item in a listbox is selected by clicking on the item, generating a **SelectedIndexChanged** event. You can access the selected item through the **SelectedIndex** and **SelectedItem** properties. If no item is selected, **SelectedIndex** is −1. Here is the code for the event handler for **SelectedIndexChanged**.

```
private void listHotels_SelectedIndexChanged(object sender,
   System.EventArgs e)
{
   if (listHotels.SelectedIndex != -1)
   {
      string selected = (string) listHotels.SelectedItem;
      char[] sep = new char[] {','};
      string[] fields;
      fields = selected.Split(sep);
      currHotel = new HotelListItem();
      currHotel.City = fields[0];
      currHotel.HotelName = fields[1];
      currHotel.NumberRooms = Convert.ToInt32(fields[2]);
      currHotel.Rate = Convert.ToDecimal(fields[3]);
   }
   else
   {
      currHotel.HotelName = "";
   }
}
```

Since the items in a listbox are stored as object references, we cast the selected item to a **string**. We use **String.Split** to extract the fields that are separated by commas and store them in the **fields** string array. The values are then moved from the array and stored in **currHotel**. In the previous section we saw **currHotel** used to initialize the "New Hotel" and "Change Hotel Information" dialog boxes.

## Acme Travel Agency Case Study—Step 3

The Acme Travel Agency case study was introduced in Chapter 4, where we used arrays as our data structures for storing lists of hotels, customers, and reservations. In Chapter 5 we changed the implementation to use collections in place of arrays. We also specified a number of interfaces, and we passed lists as **ArrayList** object references. We provided a command-line user interface. In the **CaseStudy** folder of the present chapter we provide a graphical user interface, implemented by using Windows Forms.

We have already looked at the main window (see Figure 6–22), which is the same as in the simplified **HotelAdmin**[7] program we used to illustrate dialog boxes. The "Add..." button lets us add a new hotel (Figure 6–21), and the "Change..." button (Figure 6–24) lets us change the number of rooms and the rate of a hotel. The "Delete" button will delete the currently selected hotel.

The "Customers..." button brings up a "Customer Management" form, which shows a list of currently registered customers. You may select a customer by clicking in the listbox. Figure 6–25 shows this form after selecting a customer.

The Id of the selected customer is shown in a textbox. You may unregister this customer by clicking "Unregister." You may change the email address of this customer by clicking "Change Email," which will bring up a dialog box. You may display the information for just this one customer by clicking "One Customer." The "All Customers" button will again show all the customers in the listbox. The "Register" button lets you add a new customer.

---

[7] The **HotelAdmin** program provides only empty forms as stubs for the "Customers…" and "Reservations…" buttons.

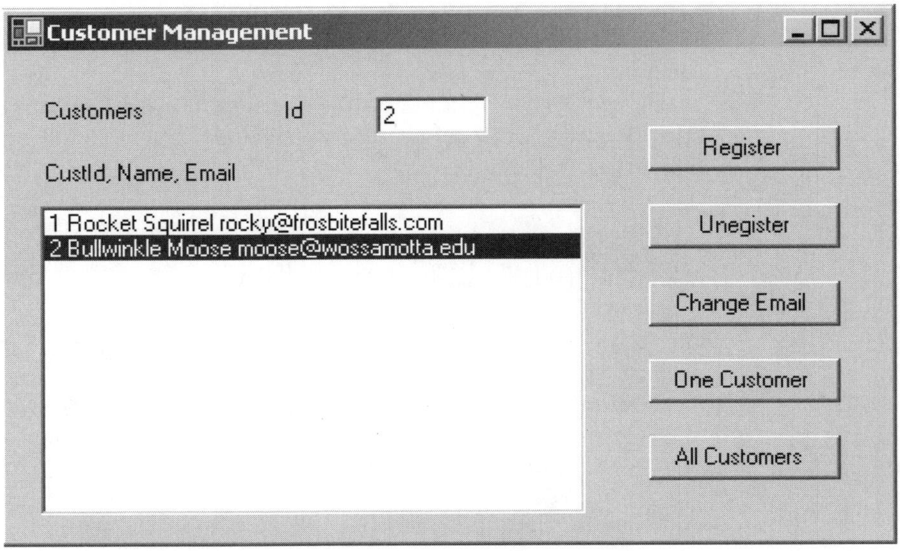

**Figure 6–25**
*Customer Management form.*

The third major form of our user interface is "Hotel Reservations," which is brought up from the main administration form by clicking "Reservations...." To make a reservation, enter the Customer Id, Checkin Date, and Number of Days. You may specify the City and Hotel Name by selecting a hotel from the listbox. To make the reservation, you then simply click the "Make Reservation" button. To show all the reservations for a customer with a particular Customer Id,[8] click "Show Reservations." Figure 6–26 shows this form after the customer whose Id is 1 has made a reservation and we have shown the reservations for this customer.

---

[8] A Customer Id of –1 will show the reservations for all customers.

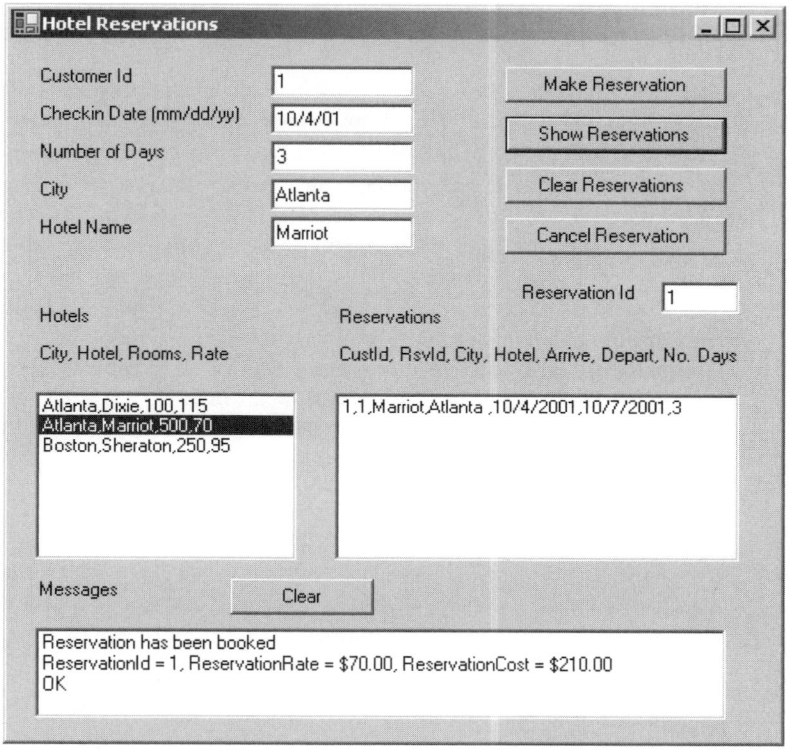

Figure 6–26 *Hotel Reservations form.*

You may clear the reservations listbox by clicking the "Clear Reservations" button. The "Cancel Reservation" will cancel the reservation with a particular Reservation Id, which may either be typed in or selected by clicking in the Reservations listbox.

The Acme Travel Agency case study is used extensively in the following chapters, so you may wish to experiment with it at this point. The graphical user interface makes exercising the case study much easier than our previous command-line interface. On the other hand, the command-line interface and a simple global **try** block around the whole command loop made it easy to check for all exceptions. Such an approach is not feasible for a GUI program. In an industrial-strength application you should check for exceptions wherever they may occur. Our case study is simplified for instructional purposes, and we have not attempted to be thorough in catching exceptions. Another simplification we made is not checking that a Customer Id used in making a reservation corresponds to a real, registered customer. The database implementation in Chapter 9 does provide such a check.

## Summary

In this chapter we learned how to implement a GUI using the Windows Forms classes of the .NET Framework. We began with first principles, using the .NET Framework SDK to create simple Windows applications from scratch, without use of any special tools. Drawing is done in an override of **OnPaint** using a font and a brush. The .NET event mechanism is used to handle user interaction such as mouse events and pressing keys. Controls simplify Windows programming. A menu control makes it easy to add menus to a Windows program. Visual Studio.NET greatly simplifies Windows programming. The Forms Designer lets you drag controls from the Toolbox onto your forms, and you can set properties of the controls at  design time. You can also easily add event handlers. Dialog boxes are a special kind of form, and you can pass information between a parent form and a dialog through use of properties in the dialog. The listbox control makes it easy to display lists of information.

We concluded the chapter by presenting a graphical user interface for our Acme Travel Agency Case Study.

# Assemblies and Deployment

*D*eployment makes the programmer's hard work available to the customer. .NET assemblies make deployment much simpler and much more reliable than current Windows deployment. Private assembly deployment is as simple as copying the component assembly into the same directory as the client program. Alternatively, shared assembly deployment places the component with a unique name (known as a strong name) in the global assembly cache, which makes it available for general use.

This chapter begins with a look at assemblies, which are the fundamental unit of deployment in .NET. Private assembly deployment and shared assembly deployment are described next. Versioning and digital signing of assemblies are discussed in the context of shared deployment. Finally, the Visual Studio.NET deployment and setup wizards are introduced. Throughout our discussion we illustrate a number of useful tools that are part of the .NET Framework SDK.

## Assemblies

In .NET, Assemblies are components. Assemblies, which may be composed of one or more DLL or EXE files, are the unit of deployment. You do not deploy individual DLLs or EXEs. Security evidence and versioning are based on the assembly. Assemblies contain Microsoft Intermediate Language (MSIL) instructions, resource data, and metadata. Since metadata describes the content of the assembly, the assembly does not require any external description, such as in the system registry. .NET components are much simpler and less error prone to install and uninstall than traditional COM components, which had extensive registry entries.

A digital signature is required before an assembly can be deployed in the global assembly cache. Digitally signed assemblies provide cryptographically generated verification information that can be used by the CLR to enforce crucial dependency rules when locating and loading assemblies. This is distinct from the security verification that is done to make sure that code is type safe.

The identity of an unsigned assembly is defined simply as a human-readable name, along with a version number. The identity of a digitally signed assembly is defined by a unique cryptographic key pair. Optionally, an assembly's identity may also include a culture code for supporting culturally specific character sets and string formats.

An assembly's version can be checked, so that the CLR can insure that the same assembly version with which the client was built and tested is loaded. This eliminates the infamous "DLL Hell" problem, where Windows applications could easily break when an older version was replaced with a newer version (or vice versa). A digitally signed assembly can be used to verify that the assembly contents were not altered after it was digitally signed. Not only will you not accidentally use the wrong version, but you will not be tricked into using a maliciously tampered component that could do serious harm.

Although there is often a one-to-one correspondence between namespace and assembly, an assembly may contain multiple namespaces, and one namespace may be distributed among multiple assemblies. While there is often a one-to-one correspondence between assembly and binary code file (i.e., DLL or EXE), one assembly can span multiple binary code files. An assembly is the unit of deployment; an application is the unit of configuration.

## Contents of an Assembly

For our next step of the case study, we split our Hotel Administrator's program into three assemblies. The example **CaseStudy** directory for this chapter has an **AcmeGui** application program (EXE), and two component (DLL) assemblies: **Customer** and **Hotel**. The code associated with the customer and hotel classes has been moved to the appropriate assemblies. When we discuss configuration later in the chapter, it is the **AcmeGui** application that will be configured.

We will use the **Customer** and **Hotel** assemblies to understand the issues associated with deployment. All public members of the **Customer** and **Hotel** assembly will be visible to code outside of their respective assemblies. Members marked as internal can be used only within the assembly.

If you look at Figure 7–1, you will see that the Solution Explorer shows that the **AcmeGui** project has references to the **Customer** and **Hotel** dynamic link libraries. These references enable the compiler to find the **Hotel** and **Customer** types used by **AcmeGui** and then build the application. They do not dictate where the DLLs have to be when the project is deployed; we will explain how this works when we discuss deployment. You will also notice references made to system assemblies such as **System.dll**. Looking at the properties for the reference will show you where the assembly is located.[1]

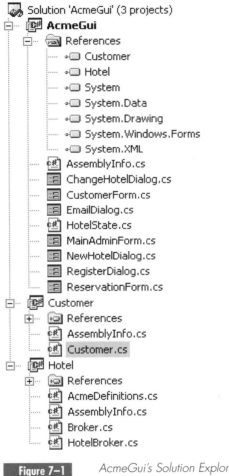

Solution 'AcmeGui' (3 projects)
- AcmeGui
  - References
    - Customer
    - Hotel
    - System
    - System.Data
    - System.Drawing
    - System.Windows.Forms
    - System.XML
  - AssemblyInfo.cs
  - ChangeHotelDialog.cs
  - CustomerForm.cs
  - EmailDialog.cs
  - HotelState.cs
  - MainAdminForm.cs
  - NewHotelDialog.cs
  - RegisterDialog.cs
  - ReservationForm.cs
- Customer
  - References
  - AssemblyInfo.cs
  - Customer.cs
- Hotel
  - References
  - AcmeDefinitions.cs
  - AssemblyInfo.cs
  - Broker.cs
  - HotelBroker.cs

**Figure 7–1**    *AcmeGui's Solution Explorer showing references.*

Creating a DLL is simple. Just select "Class Library" from the New Project Wizard in Visual Studio.NET, specify a location and name, and then start coding. To setup a reference to another DLL from your project you use the Add Reference menu item from the Visual Studio.NET Project menu. Navigate to the DLL you want, select it with the Select button, then click the OK button.[2]

---

[1] Select the assembly in the Solution Explorer, right-mouse click, select Properties in the context menu.

[2] It is straightforward to go from the monolithic program we had in the previous chapter to the componentized one we have now.

Every Assembly has a Manifest that describes the metadata information associated with the Assembly. A manifest provides the following information about an assembly:

- Assembly identity based on name, version, culture, and—optionally—a digital signature
- Files that contribute to the assembly contents
- Other assemblies on which the assembly is dependent
- Permissions required by the assembly

Every assembly created by Visual Studio has a file, **AssemblyInfo.cs**, containing the following attributes that can be used to set the information associated with an assembly:

```
[assembly: AssemblyTitle("")]
[assembly: AssemblyDescription("")]
[assembly: AssemblyConfiguration("")]
[assembly: AssemblyCompany("")]
[assembly: AssemblyProduct("")]
[assembly: AssemblyCopyright("")]
[assembly: AssemblyTrademark("")]
[assembly: AssemblyCulture("")]
[assembly: AssemblyVersion("1.0.*")]
[assembly: AssemblyDelaySign(false)]
[assembly: AssemblyKeyFile("")]
[assembly: AssemblyKeyName("")]
```

---

*(Footnote 2 continued)*

Create two new Class Library projects in the AcmeGui Solution for Customer and Hotel. In Visual Studio select File | New | Project. In the dialog box that comes up, select Visual C# projects in the left top pane, then select Class Library in the right top pane. Enter the name of the project (Customer or Hotel) and make sure the Add to Solution radio button is selected.

Remove the appropriate files from the AcmeGui project and add them to the appropriate project. In the Solution Explorer, select the file in the AcmeGui project, right-mouse click, select exclude from project. Then in the Solution Explorer select the appropriate project and right-mouse click, select Add, then Add Existing Item, navigate to the appropriate file and select it, and hit the open button. You can select more than one file at a time.

Build the two component projects by selecting their project name in the Solution Explorer and select the build option for the assembly in the Build menu. Since we no longer have a monolithic application, we have to indicate to the compiler how to resolve references to the Customer and Hotel classes. Select the AcmeGui project in the Solution Explorer, right-mouse click, then select Add Reference. Click on the Projects tab and you should see the Customer and Hotel dlls there. Select them both and then hit the select button. You should see both dynamic link libraries in the bottom list. Then click the OK button. Now when you rebuild the solution, the AcmeGui project will compile and run. You can click on the plus button next to References in any project to see what dependencies it has.

To explore how versioning, digital signing, and deployment work, we use the **ILDASM** tool introduced in Chapter 2 to view the appropriate metadata. Visual Studio.NET installs with **ILDASM** on the Tools menu. You can also find it in your **\Program Files\Microsoft.Net\FrameworkSDK\Bin** directory.

Figure 7–2 shows the top level that you see when you open the **Customer.dll** assembly in **ILDASM** and double-click on the **OI.NetCs.Acme** namespace. You see entries for the MANIFEST, the **Customers** and **Customer** classes, the **ICustomer** interface, and the **CustomerListItem** value type. Clicking on the plus (+) button will expand an entry.

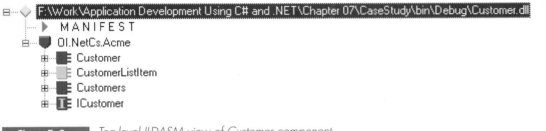

- ◇ F:\Work\Application Development Using C# and .NET\Chapter 07\CaseStudy\bin\Debug\Customer.dll
  - ▶ MANIFEST
  - OI.NetCs.Acme
    - ⊞ E Customer
    - ⊞ E CustomerListItem
    - ⊞ E Customers
    - ⊞ I E ICustomer

**Figure 7–2**    *Top-level ILDASM view of Customer component.*

To view the manifest, double-click the MANIFEST node shown in Figure 7–2; the resulting manifest information is displayed in Figure 7–3. Some of the numbers will vary if you have rebuilt any of the samples, or you have a later version of .NET.

```
.assembly extern mscorlib
{
  .publickeytoken = (B7 7A 5C 56 19 34 E0 89 )                      // .z\U.4..
  .ver 1:0:2411:0
}
.assembly Customer
{
  .custom instance void [mscorlib]System.Reflection.AssemblyKeyNameAttribute::.ctor(string) = ( 01 00 00 00 00 )
  .custom instance void [mscorlib]System.Reflection.AssemblyKeyFileAttribute::.ctor(string) = ( 01 00 00 00 00 )
  .custom instance void [mscorlib]System.Reflection.AssemblyDelaySignAttribute::.ctor(bool) = ( 01 00 00 00 00 )
  .custom instance void [mscorlib]System.Reflection.AssemblyTrademarkAttribute::.ctor(string) = ( 01 00 00 00 00 )
  .custom instance void [mscorlib]System.Reflection.AssemblyCopyrightAttribute::.ctor(string) = ( 01 00 00 00 00 )
  .custom instance void [mscorlib]System.Reflection.AssemblyProductAttribute::.ctor(string) = ( 01 00 00 00 00 )
  .custom instance void [mscorlib]System.Reflection.AssemblyCompanyAttribute::.ctor(string) = ( 01 00 00 00 00 )
  .custom instance void [mscorlib]System.Reflection.AssemblyConfigurationAttribute::.ctor(string) = ( 01 00 00 00 00 )
  .custom instance void [mscorlib]System.Reflection.AssemblyDescriptionAttribute::.ctor(string) = ( 01 00 00 00 00 )
  .custom instance void [mscorlib]System.Reflection.AssemblyTitleAttribute::.ctor(string) = ( 01 00 00 00 00 )
  // --- The following custom attribute is added automatically, do not uncomment ------
  //  .custom instance void [mscorlib]System.Diagnostics.DebuggableAttribute::.ctor(bool,
  //                                                                 bool) = ( 01 00 01 01 00 00 )
  .hash algorithm 0x00008004
  .ver 1:0:592:25677
}
```

**Figure 7–3**    *ILDASM showing manifest of Customer.dll.*

The manifest contains information about the dependencies and contents of the assembly. You can see that the manifest for **Customer** contains, among others, the following external dependency.[3]

---

[3] If you have rebuilt any of the components, you will, of course, see different build and revision numbers.

```
.assembly extern mscorlib
{
  .publickeytoken = (B7 7A 5C 56 19 34 E0 89 )
  .ver 1:0:2411:0
}
```

The **.assembly extern mscorlib** metadata statement indicates that the **Customer** assembly makes use of, and is therefore dependent on, the standard assembly **mccorlib.dll**, which is required by all managed code. When an assembly makes a reference to another assembly, you will see an **.assembly extern** metadata statement. If you open AcmeGui in ILDASM and look at  the manifest, you will see dependencies on the **Customer** and **Hotel** assemblies as well as the **System.Drawing** assembly.

```
.assembly extern Customer
{
    .ver 1:0:592:25677
}
.assembly extern Hotel
{
  .ver 1:0:592:25677
}
.assembly extern System.Drawing
{
  .publickeytoken = (B0 3F 5F 7F 11 D5 0A 3A)
  .ver 1:0:2411:0
}
```

The **System.Drawing** assembly is a shared assembly, which can be seen in the **\WINNT\Assembly** directory using Windows Explorer. **Mscorlib**, which is a shared assembly, is not deployed in the assembly cache. Microsoft made a single exception here: because **mscorlib** is so closely tied with the CLR engine (**mscorwks**[4]), it is installed in the appropriate install directory (**\WINNT\Microsoft.NET\Framework**) for the current .NET version.

In the **System.Drawing** shared assembly, the **.publickeytoken** = (B0 3F 5F 7F 11 D5 0A 3A) metadata statement provides a public key token, which is the lowest 8 bytes of a hash of the public key that matches the corresponding private key owned by the **System.Drawing** assembly's author. This public key token cannot actually be used directly to authenticate the identity of the author of **System.Drawing**. However, the original public key specified in the **System.Drawing** manifest can be used to mathematically verify that the matching private key was actually used to digitally sign the **System.Drawing** assembly. Since Microsoft authored **System.Drawing.dll**, the public key token seen above is Microsoft specific. Of course, the matching private key is a closely guarded corporate secret, and it is believed by

---

[4] Or mscorsvr.dll for servers.

most security experts that such a private key is, in practice, virtually impossible to determine from the public key. However, there is no guarantee that some mathematical genius will not find a back door someday!

## The .publickeytoken declaration

The .publickeytoken declaration provides only the least significant 8 bytes of the SHA1 hash of the producer's public key (which is 128 bytes), which saves some space but can still be used to verify at runtime that the assembly being loaded comes from the same publisher as the one you compiled against. Alternatively, the .publickey declaration could be used, which provides the full public key. This would take up more space but makes it harder for villains to find a private key that matches the full public key.

As we shall see shortly, the **.publickeytoken** statement is present in the client assembly's manifest only if the referenced assembly has been digitally signed, and all assemblies intended for shared deployment must be digitally signed. Microsoft has digitally signed the standard .NET assemblies, such as **mscorlib.dll**, and **System.Windows.Forms.dll** with private keys belonging to them. This is why the public key token for many of those shared assemblies, seen in the **\WINNT\Assembly** directory using Windows Explorer, has the same value repeated. Assemblies authored and digitally signed by other vendors are signed with their own distinct private keys, and they will therefore result in a different public key token in their client assembly's manifests. Later, we will look at how you can create your own private and public key pair and digitally sign your own assemblies for deployment into the global assembly cache.

Nonetheless, while unique, none of these digital keys can identify who the author of a particular module is. A developer of assemblies can use the **signcode** utility to add a digital certificate that will identify the publisher of the assembly.

The **.ver 1:0:2411:0** metadata statement indicates the version of the **System.Drawing** assembly. While these numbers have no intrinsic meaning, the Microsoft suggested format of this version specification is Major:Minor:Build:Revision. Over time, as new versions of this assembly are released, existing clients that were built to use this version will continue using this version, assuming the conventional meaning of major and minor values. Newer client programs will, of course, be able to access newer versions of this assembly as they become available. The old and new versions can be deployed side-by-side in the global assembly cache and be simultaneously available to old and new client programs.

Note that the version **1:0:2411:0** appearing in the client manifest belongs to the current version of the **Acme.Gui** assembly and is unrelated to the "1.0.*" version attribute specified in the **AssemblyInfo.cs** file in the **AcmeGui** source code. We will soon look more closely at the four fields that make up a version number, and how assembly versioning works with the suggested format.

Now let us consider the information about the component itself in its manifest.

**ILDASM** shows the assembly metadata in the **Customer** manifest:

```
.assembly Customer
{
  .custom instance void
      [mscolib]System.Reflection.AssemblyKeyNameAttribute
                   ::.ctor(string) = ( 01 00 00 00 00 )
...
  // --- The following custom attribute is added
                  automatically, do not uncomment -------
  //  .custom instance void
          [mscolib]System.Diagnostics.DebuggableAttribute
                                          ::.ctor(bool,
  //                          bool) = ( 01 00 01 01 00 00 )
  .hash algorithm 0x00008004
  .ver 1:0:592:25677
}
```

## The .assembly Directive

The .assembly directive declares the manifest and specifies to which assembly the current module belongs. In this example, the .assembly directive specifies the name of the assembly to be Customer. It is this name (combined with the version number and optionally a public key) rather than the name of the DLL or EXE file that is used at runtime to resolve the identity of the assembly. Also note that if the assembly is signed, you will see the .publickey defined within the .assembly directive. It also indicates what custom attributes have been added to the metadata.

The **.assembly Customer** metadata statement indicates that the assembly name is **Customer.** Note that this is not the name of a component class within the assembly, but rather the assembly itself. This assembly is not digitally signed, and therefore it does not contain a public key.

In multifile assemblies (discussed in a later section) the manifest stores a hash of each file. The **.hash algorithm 0x00008004** metadata statement indicates that SHA1 is the hash algorithm that is to produce this hash-code value. Many hash-code algorithms exist. Initially, however, only MD5 (0x000803) and SHA1 (0x000804) are supported by .NET.

## Hash Algorithms

A hash algorithm is a mathematical function that takes the original data of arbitrary size as input and generates a hash code, also known as a message digest, which is a fixed-sized binary output. An effective hash function is a one-way function that is highly collision free, with a result that is relatively small and fixed in size. Ideally, a hash function is efficient to calculate as well. A one-way function is a function that has no inverse, so that you cannot effectively reproduce the original data from the hash-code value.[5] The phrase "highly collision free" means that the probability that two distinct original input data samples generate the same hash code is very small, and it is unlikely to calculate two distinct input data samples that result in the same hash-code value. The well-known MD5 and SHA1 hash algorithms are considered to be excellent choices for use in digital signing, and they are both supported by .NET.

## Versioning an Assembly

An assembly manifest contains the version of the assembly as well as the version of each of the assemblies that the assembly depends on. The version number of an assembly is composed of four numerical fields: Major, Minor, Build, and Revision. There are no semantics assigned to any of these fields by the CLR. Microsoft does suggest the following convention:

- Major—a change to this field indicates major incompatible changes.
- Minor—a change to this field indicates minor, but incompatible changes.
- Build number—a change to this field indicates a new backward-compatible release.
- Revision—a change to this field indicates a backward-compatible emergency bug fix.

None of this is enforced by the CLR. You enforce this convention, or any other convention you choose, by testing assemblies for compatibility and specifying the version policy in a configuration file that we will discuss.

In the metadata for the Customer assembly, the **.ver 1:0:592:25677** gives us the assembly's version: Major Version 1, Minor Version 0, Build Number 592, Revision 25677.

The version information for the manifest can be defined in the source code using the assembly attribute **assembly::AssemblyVersion**. This attribute (as with other global attributes) can appear in a source file after a **using** statement but before any namespace or class definitions. The **AssemblyVersionAttribute** class is defined in the **System::Reflection**

---

[5] One-way encryption codes are used to store passwords in a passwords database. When you log in, the password you enter is encrypted and compared with what is stored in the database. If they match, you can log in. The password cannot be reconstructed from the encrypted value stored in the passwords database.

namespace. If this attribute is not used, a default version number of 0.0.0.0 is listed in the assembly manifest, which is generally not desirable.

In a project created with the VisualStudio.NET project wizard, the source file **AssemblyInfo.cs** is automatically generated, with a version of **1.0.***, producing a major version of 1, and a minor version of 0 and automatically generated build and revision values. If you change the **AssemblyVersionAttribute** to, for example, **"1.1.0.0"**, as shown below, the version number displayed in the manifest will be modified accordingly to **1:1:0:0**.

```
//AssemblyInfo.cs
...
[assembly: AssemblyVersion("1.1.0.0")];
```

If you specify any version number at all, you must at a minimum specify the major number. If you specify only the major number, the remaining values will default to zero. If you also specify the minor value, you can omit the remaining fields, which will then default to zero, or you can specify an asterisk, which will provide automatically generated values. The asterisk will cause the build value to equal the number of days since January 1, 2000, and the revision value will be set to the number of seconds since midnight, divided by 2. If you specify major, minor, and build values, and specify an asterisk for the revision value, then only the revision is defaulted to the number of seconds since midnight, divided by 2. If all four fields are explicitly specified, then all four values will be reflected in the manifest. The following examples show valid version specifications.

```
Specified in source        Result in manifest
None                       0:0:0:0
1                          1:0:0:0
1.1                        1:1:0:0
1.1.*                      1:1:464:27461
1.1.43                     1:1:43:0
1.1.43.*                   1:1:43:29832
1.1.43.52                  1:1:43:52
```

If you use the asterisk, then the revision and possibly the build number will automatically change every time you rebuild the component. You must make an explicit change to the major and minor numbers if you wish to have their values changed.

## Strong Names

Before we can discuss version policy, we have to introduce the idea of a strong name. A strong name is guaranteed to be globally unique for any version of any assembly. Strong names are generated by digitally signing the assembly. This ensures that the strong name not only is unique, but can be generated only by an individual that owns a secret private key.

A strong name is made up of a simple text name, a public key, and a hash code that has been encrypted with the matching private key. The hash code is known as a *message digest* and the encrypted hash code is known as a *digital signature*. The digital signature effectively identifies the assembly's author and ensures that the assembly has not been altered. Two assemblies that have the same strong name and version are considered to be identical assemblies. Two assemblies with different strong names are considered to be different. A strong name is also known as a cryptographically strong name, since, unlike a simple text name, a strong name is guaranteed to uniquely identify the assembly based on its contents and its author's private key. A strong name has the following useful properties:

- A strong name guarantees uniqueness based on encryption technology.
- A strong name establishes a unique namespace based on the use of a private key.[6]
- A strong name prevents unauthorized personnel from versioning the assembly.
- A strong name allows the CLR to find the right version of a shared assembly.

## Digital Signatures

Digital signatures are based on public key cryptographic techniques. In the world of cryptography, the two main cryptographic techniques are symmetric ciphers (shared key) and asymmetric ciphers (public key). Symmetric ciphers use one shared secret key for encryption as well as decryption. DES, Triple DES, and RC2 are examples of symmetric-cipher algorithms. Symmetric ciphers can be very efficient and powerful for message privacy between two trusted cooperating individuals, but they are generally unsuitable for digital signatures. Digital signatures are not used for privacy but for identification and authentication. If you shared your symmetric key with everyone who would potentially want to identify or authenticate you, you would inevitably share it with people who would want to impersonate you.

Asymmetric ciphers are used in digital signatures. Asymmetric ciphers, also known as public key ciphers, make use of a public/private key pair. The paired keys are mathematically related and are generated together. It is, however, exceedingly difficult to calculate one key from the other. The public key is typically exposed to everyone who would like to authenticate its owner. On the other hand, the owners keep the matching private signing key secret, so that no one can impersonate them. RSA is an example of a public key cipher system.

---

[6] Do not confuse this namespace with the one used by the compiler to disambiguate class names.

Public key cryptography is based on a very interesting mathematical scheme that allows plain text to be encrypted with one key and decrypted only with the matching key. For example, if a public key is used to encrypt the original data (known as plain text), then only the matching private key is capable of decrypting it. Not even the encrypting key can decrypt it! This scenario is useful for sending secret messages to only the individual who knows the private key.

The opposite scenario is where the individual who owns the private key uses that private key to encrypt the plain text. The resulting cipher text is by no means a secret, since everyone who is interested can obtain the public key to decrypt it. This scenario is useless for secrecy but very effective for authentication purposes. To improve performance, instead of encrypting the original data, a highly characteristic hash code is encrypted instead.

If you use the matching public key to decrypt the encrypted hash code, you can recalculate the hash code on the original data and compare the two values. If they match, you can be certain that the owner of the private key was the digital signer. Of course, the owner of the private key has to make sure to keep the private key secret, otherwise you cannot prove that the data has not been tampered with from the time when it was digitally signed. Figure 7–4 shows how a digital signature works.

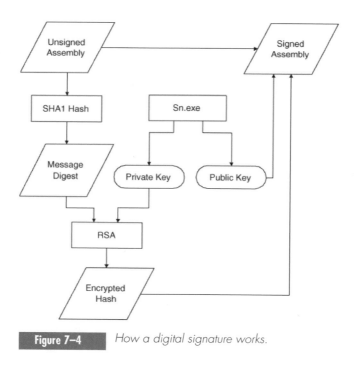

**Figure 7–4**    *How a digital signature works.*

## SHA1 and RSA

To sign the assembly, the producer calculates a SHA1 hash of the assembly (with the bytes reserved for the signature preset to zero) and then encrypts the hash value with a public key using RSA encryption. The public key and the encrypted hash are then stored in the assembly's metadata.

## Digitally Signing an Assembly

The process of digitally signing an assembly involves generating a public/private key pair, calculating a hash code on the assembly, encrypting the hash code with the private key, and writing the encrypted hash code along with the public key into the assembly for all to see. The encrypted hash code and public key together comprise the entire digital signature. The digital signature is written into a reserved area within the assembly that is not included in the hash-code calculation. All these steps are performed with two simple tools—the Strong Name utility (**Sn.exe)** and the Assembly Linker (**Al.exe**). To build and digitally sign an assembly, the following steps are performed.

1. Develop and build the component.
2. Generate a public/private key pair.
3. Calculate a hash code on the contents of the assembly.
4. Encrypt the hash code using the private key.
5. Place the encrypted hash code into the manifest.
6. Place the public key into the manifest.

Step 1 is, of course, usually performed using Visual Studio.NET. Steps 2 through 6 are known as digital signing. Step 2 is accomplished using the Strong Name utility **Sn.exe**. Steps 3 through 6 are accomplished using either Visual Studio.NET or the Assembly Linking utility **Al.exe** (that's "A-el", not "A-one").

To illustrate this process we will develop a version of our **Customer** and **Hotel** assemblies that have strong names. They are located in the **SignedCaseStudy** directory. We generate key pairs for the assemblies using **Sn.exe**, known as the Strong Name utility. This tool generates a cryptographically strong name for the assembly. You generate a public/private key pair and place them into a file named **KeyPair.snk** as shown in the following command (which you can run from the source directory):

```
sn -k KeyPair.snk
```

The resulting **KeyPair.snk** file is a binary file and is not intended to be human readable. If you are curious, you can write these keys into a comma-delimited text file with the following command, then view it using **Notepad.exe**. This is not a required step.

```
sn -o KeyPair.snk KeyPair.txt
```

In the example you will finds these files in the **Customer** and **Hotel** subdirectories.

The next step is to apply the private key to the assembly. For developing and testing it is convenient to do this at compilation time. When you release the assembly, however, you have to use the official private key of the company. For security reasons this key is probably known only to the corporate digital signing authority. The process of creating the strong name cannot be postponed until after the assembly is built, because the public key is part of the assembly's identity. Users of the assembly have to compile against the full identity of the assembly. Delay signing, which splits the process of assigning the strong name into two steps, is designed to solve this problem.

If you just want to apply the digital signature automatically at compile time without delay signing, you simply use the **AssemblyKeyFileAttribute**—which, in the example, is in the file **AssemblyInfo.cs** of the **Customer** project. The **KeyPair.snk** file generated previously with the **Sn.exe** tool is specified in the attribute. The file path has to be relative to the project output directory. Once the **KeyPair.snk** file has been added to the **AssemblyKeyFileAttribute** the code must be recompiled.

```
[assembly: AssemblyKeyFile(".\\Customer\\KeyPair.snk")]
```

Delay signing requires a more complex procedure. When you build the assembly, the public key is supplied to the compiler so that it can be put into the PublicKey field in the assembly's manifest. Space is reserved in the file for the signature, but the signature is not generated. When the actual signature is generated, it is placed in the file with the –R option to the Strong Name utility (**sn.exe**).

To indicate to the compiler that you want to use delay signing, you include **AssemblyDelaySignAttribute** in your source code. You also have to include the public key using the **AssemblyKeyFileAttribute**.

Assuming you have generated the public/private key pair as described previously, you then use the –p option of the Strong Name utility to obtain just the public key without giving out the still secret private key.

```
sn -p KeyPair.snk PublicKey.snk
```

You then add the following two attributes to **AssemblyInfo.cs**:

```
[assembly: AssemblyDelaySign(true)]
[assembly: AssemblyKeyFile(".\\PublicKey.snk")]
```

The assembly still does not have a valid signature. You will not be able to install it into the global assembly cache. You can disable signature verification of a particular assembly by using the –Vr option on the Strong Name utility.

```
sn -Vr Customer.dll
```

Before you ship the assembly you must supply the valid signature. You use the –R option on the Strong Name utility and supply the public/private key pair.

```
sn - R customer.dll KeyPair.snk
```

However you add the key, if you look at the manifest in **ILDASM** you will see that the **.publickey** entry has been added to the assembly's metadata.

The **.publickey** attribute represents the originator's public key that resides in the **KeyPair.snk** file. This is the public key that can be used to decrypt the message digest to retrieve the original hash code. When the assembly is deployed into the global assembly cache, this decrypted hash code is compared with a fresh recalculation of the hash code from the actual assembly contents. This comparison is made to determine if the assembly is legitimate (i.e., identical to the original) or illegitimate (i.e., corrupt or tampered). Of course, when you use **Sn.exe**, it will produce a different key pair, and the public key shown below will be different in your case accordingly.

If you use **ILDASM** to examine the manifest of the **AcmeGui** client program, you will see the following:

```
.assembly extern Customer
{
   .publickeytoken = (8B 0E 61 2D 60 BD E0 CA )
   .ver 1:0:0:0
}
.assembly extern Hotel
{
   .publickeytoken = (CF 0B C2 2F 8E 2C 15 22 )
   .ver 1:0:0:0
}
```

Now that **Customer** and **Hotel** have strong names, references to them have a public key token, which is a hash of the public key that matches the corresponding private key for the assembly. Note that we generated different keys for each assembly. Usually, each company will use the same key pair for all its public components.

Now that we have discussed strong names, we can discuss the two methods of deploying assemblies in .NET, and their associated default version policies. After this discussion we will show how the default policy can be overridden in a configuration file.

## Private Assembly Deployment

For private assembly deployment, the assembly is copied to the same directory as the client program that references it. No registration is needed, and no fancy installation program is required. When the component is removed, no registry cleanup is needed, and no uninstall program is required. Just delete it from the hard drive.[7]

Of course, no self-respecting programmer would ever provide a commercial component that required the end user to manually copy or delete any files in this way, even if it is remarkably simple to do. Users have become accustomed to using a formal installation program, so it should be provided, even if its work is trivial. However, for testing purposes, manually copying and deleting an assembly is an ideal way to quickly and painlessly manage deployment issues for developing, debugging, or testing purposes. Recall that the deployment of COM components was never this simple, requiring at a minimum, a registry script file. Gone are the days where you have to configure the registry on installation, and then later carefully clean out the registry information when you want to discard the component.

To privately deploy our componentized Hotel Administrator case study, create a directory on your hard drive. Copy to that directory the files in the **CaseStudy\bin\Debug** directory, **AcmeGui.exe**, **Customer.dll**, and **Hotel.dll**. Then run **AcmeGui.exe**. It will run. It is really just that simple!

If you view the **AcmeGui** manifest in **ILDASM**, you will see the following dependency entries:

```
.assembly extern Customer
  {
  .ver 1:0:593:19533
}
.assembly extern Hotel
{
  .ver 1:0:593:19532
}
```

Here are the corresponding assembly definitions in the components:

```
.assembly Customer
{
  ...
  .hash algorithm 0x00008004
  .ver 1:0:593:19533
```

---

[7] Of course this process does not put any icons on the desktop or entries on the Start menu.

```
}

.assembly Hotel
{
   ...
   .hash algorithm 0x00008004
   .ver 1:0:593:19532
}
```

From this you can see that the client program was built with **Customer** assembly version 1.0.593.19533 and **Hotel** assembly version 1.0.593.19532. Since neither assembly has a strong name, however, the versions are not checked. If you were to build a **Customer** assembly with a different version, and replace the one that **AcmeGui** was built with, **AcmeGui** would still run. It does not matter whether you change the major build number or the revision number.

If you were to use a version of the **Customer** component with a strong name (even if it had the same version number), you would get the following runtime exception:

```
System.IO.FileLoadException: The located assembly's mani-
fest definition with name 'Customer' does not match the
assembly reference.
```

If the **Customer** assembly has a strong name, even if the version numbers are the same, the assembly names no longer match. If the **AcmeGui** client program was built with an assembly that had a strong name, the CLR will bind only to an assembly that matches exactly with the strong name and version. Even a different revision number will cause the load to fail.

The details on binding failures can be seen in the Assembly Binding Log Viewer (**FUSLOGVW.exe**). The sample log in Figure 7–5 resulted from an attempt to resolve **AcmeGui's** reference to a Customer assembly that had a strong name when it was built with a version of the assembly that did not have a strong name:

```
*** Assembly Binder Log Entry (8/19/2001 @ 6:30:31 PM) ***

Operation Failed.
Bind result: hr = 0x80131040. No description available.
Assembly manager loaded from: F:\WINNT\Microsoft.NET\Framework\v1.0.2914\fusion.dll
Running under executable F:\Work\DeployTest\Unshared\AcmeGui.exe
--- Detailed error log follows...

=== Pre-bind state information ===
LOG: DisplayName = Customer, Version=1.0.593.19533, Culture=neutral, PublicKeyToken=null
 (Fully-specified)
LOG: Appbase = F:\Work\DeployTest\Unshared\
LOG: DEVPATH = NULL
LOG: Initial PrivatePath = NULL
LOG: Dynamic Base = NULL
LOG: Cache Base = NULL
LOG: AppName = NULL
===

LOG: Processing DEVPATH...
LOG: DEVPATH is not set. Falling through to regular bind.
LOG: Policy not being applied to reference at this time (private, custom, partial, or location-based assembly bind).
LOG: Post policy reference: Customer, Version=1.0.593.19533, Culture=neutral, PublicKeyToken=null
LOG: Attempting download of new URL file:///F:/Work/DeployTest/Unshared/Customer.DLL.
LOG: Assembly download successful. Attempting setup of file: F:\Work\DeployTest\Unshared\Customer.DLL
LOG: Entering run-from-source setup phase...
WRN: Assembly name comparison mismatch: PUBLIC KEY TOKEN
ERR: The assembly reference did not match the assembly definition found.
ERR: Failed to complete setup of assembly (hr = 0x80131040). Probing terminated.
```

**Figure 7–5**    *Assembly binding log for customer load failure.*

## Shared Assembly Deployment

The Assembly Cache is a known directory where the CLR looks for shared, side-by-side assemblies. The term "side-by-side" means that multiple versions of the same component may reside within the assembly cache alongside one another. The global assembly cache contains shared assemblies that are globally accessible to all .NET applications on the machine. A download assembly cache is accessible to applications such as Internet Explorer that automatically download assemblies over the network.

### Deploying a Shared Assembly

Before an assembly can be deployed into the global assembly cache, you must digitally sign the assembly as discussed earlier. Developers can place the assembly into the global assembly cache by using either using the Global Assembly Cache Utility **Gacutil.exe** command-line utility, the Windows Explorer with the assembly cache viewer Windows shell extension, or the .NET Admin Tool. Deploying shared assemblies on a user's machine should be done with an installation program.

To illustrate this process we will deploy in the GAC the version of our **Customer** and **Hotel** assemblies that are in the **SignedCaseStudy** directory. To deploy the components into the GAC, you can use the command-line utility, **Gacutil.exe**.

```
Gacutil -i Customer.dll
```

Note that the **-i** option is case sensitive. You should then see the console message "Assembly successfully added to the cache." The effect of this command is that a new global assembly cache node named **Customer** is created in the **\WINNT\Assembly** directory. As can be seen in Figure 7–6, the version number and originator (i.e., public key token) are displayed for the assembly in Windows Explorer. We changed the version of the component to 1.0.0.0 to distinguish it from the unsigned version.

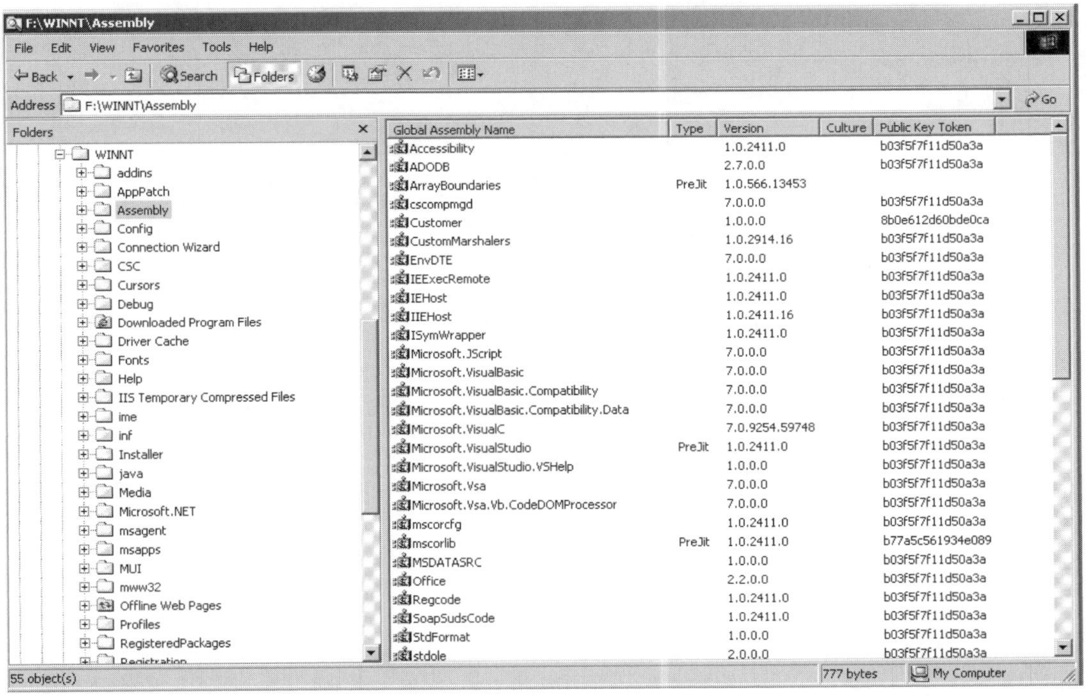

F:\WINNT\Assembly
File Edit View Favorites Tools Help
Back Search Folders
Address F:\WINNT\Assembly
Go
Folders
WINNT
addins
AppPatch
Assembly
Config
Connection Wizard
CSC
Cursors
Debug
Downloaded Program Files
Driver Cache
Fonts
Help
IIS Temporary Compressed Files
ime
inf
Installer
java
Media
Microsoft.NET
msagent
msapps
MUI
mww32
Offline Web Pages
Profiles
RegisteredPackages
Global Assembly Name
Type
Version
Culture
Public Key Token
Accessibility 1.0.2411.0 b03f5f7f11d50a3a
ADODB 2.7.0.0 b03f5f7f11d50a3a
ArrayBoundaries PreJit 1.0.566.13453
cscompmgd 7.0.0.0 b03f5f7f11d50a3a
Customer 1.0.0.0 8b0e612d60bde0ca
CustomMarshalers 1.0.2914.16 b03f5f7f11d50a3a
EnvDTE 7.0.0.0 b03f5f7f11d50a3a
IEExecRemote 1.0.2411.0 b03f5f7f11d50a3a
IEHost 1.0.2411.0 b03f5f7f11d50a3a
IIEHost 1.0.2411.16 b03f5f7f11d50a3a
ISymWrapper 1.0.2411.0 b03f5f7f11d50a3a
Microsoft.JScript 7.0.0.0 b03f5f7f11d50a3a
Microsoft.VisualBasic 7.0.0.0 b03f5f7f11d50a3a
Microsoft.VisualBasic.Compatibility 7.0.0.0 b03f5f7f11d50a3a
Microsoft.VisualBasic.Compatibility.Data 7.0.0.0 b03f5f7f11d50a3a
Microsoft.VisualC 7.0.9254.59748 b03f5f7f11d50a3a
Microsoft.VisualStudio PreJit 1.0.2411.0 b03f5f7f11d50a3a
Microsoft.VisualStudio.VSHelp 1.0.0.0 b03f5f7f11d50a3a
Microsoft.Vsa 7.0.0.0 b03f5f7f11d50a3a
Microsoft.Vsa.Vb.CodeDOMProcessor 7.0.0.0 b03f5f7f11d50a3a
mscorcfg 1.0.2411.0 b03f5f7f11d50a3a
mscorlib PreJit 1.0.2411.0 b77a5c561934e089
MSDATASRC 1.0.0.0 b03f5f7f11d50a3a
Office 2.2.0.0 b03f5f7f11d50a3a
Regcode 1.0.2411.0 b03f5f7f11d50a3a
SoapSudsCode 1.0.2411.0 b03f5f7f11d50a3a
StdFormat 1.0.0.0 b03f5f7f11d50a3a
stdole 2.0.0.0 b03f5f7f11d50a3a
55 object(s)
777 bytes
My Computer


**Figure 7–6** *Windows Explorer showing the global assembly cache.*

You can also can drag and drop a component into the **Assembly** directory to install it in the GAC. Alternatively, you can use the **.NET Admin Tool** to install an assembly into the GAC. The **.NET Admin Tool** is an MMC

snap-in located at **\WINNT\Microsoft.NET\Framework\v1.0.2914\
mscorcfg.msc**.[8] The directory version number will be different in a later
release of the .NET Framework. While it may seem overkill to introduce a
third tool, this MMC snap-in is a very useful utility that simplifies many tasks.
Figure 7–7 shows the top-level window of this tool. To use the tool to add
an assembly to the GAC, just select Assembly Cache in the left pane, right-
mouse click, and select Add. Using the dialog box that pops up to navigate
to the file, select the assembly you want to add, and click the Open button.

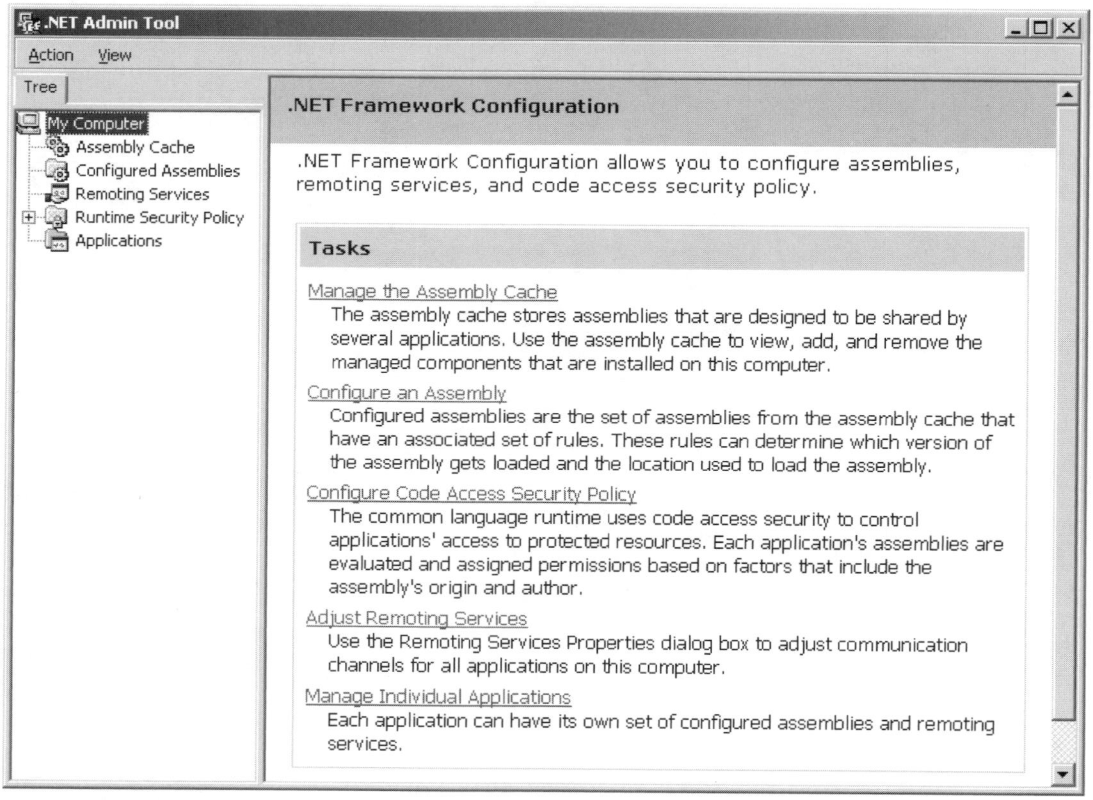

**Figure 7–7**    *.NET Admin Tool supports many .NET administrative functions.*

After you have installed the assemblies in the GAC, copy just the
**AcmeGui** client program in the **SignedCaseStudy** directory to another directory. You can now run it without any assemblies in the same directory.

---

[8] To run a snap-in, you can just double-click on the **.msc** file in Windows Explorer.
Since we are going to use the .NET Admin Tool extensively, you may wish to add the
tool to the Visual Studio Tools menu, which you can do through Tools | External
Tools... . For the command enter **mmc.exe** and for the argument enter the complete
path to **mscorcfg.msc**.

What happens if we remove the version of **Customer** we installed in the GAC and place in the GAC a Customer assembly signed with the same key, but a different version? A **FileNotfoundException** is thrown by the CLR. We would get the same result if we replaced it with a Customer assembly that had the same version, but signed with a different key. The default binding policy for shared assemblies is an exact name match.

## Versioning Shared Components

What happens if you install two versions of the same assembly in the GAC that were signed with the same key? Place a **Customer** assembly with the version 1.1.0.0 in the GAC. Figure 7–8 displays both versions of the **Customer** assembly installed in the Global Assembly Cache with their respective version numbers and identical public key tokens.

| Assembly Name | Version | Locale | Public Key Token |
|---|---|---|---|
| ArrayBoundaries | 1.0.566.13453 | neutral | None |
| Microsoft.VisualStudio | 1.0.2411.0 | neutral | b03f5f7f11d50a3a |
| mscorlib | 1.0.2411.0 | neutral | b77a5c561934e089 |
| System | 1.0.2411.0 | neutral | b77a5c561934e089 |
| System.Design | 1.0.2411.0 | neutral | b03f5f7f11d50a3a |
| System.Drawing | 1.0.2411.0 | neutral | b03f5f7f11d50a3a |
| System.Windows.Forms | 1.0.2411.0 | neutral | b77a5c561934e089 |
| Accessibility | 1.0.2411.0 | neutral | b03f5f7f11d50a3a |
| ADODB | 2.7.0.0 | neutral | b03f5f7f11d50a3a |
| cscompmgd | 7.0.0.0 | neutral | b03f5f7f11d50a3a |
| Customer | 1.0.0.0 | neutral | 8b0e612d60bde0ca |
| Customer | 1.1.0.0 | neutral | 8b0e612d60bde0ca |
| CustomMarshalers | 1.0.2914.16 | neutral | b03f5f7f11d50a3a |
| EnvDTE | 7.0.0.0 | neutral | b03f5f7f11d50a3a |
| Hotel | 1.0.0.0 | neutral | cf0bc22f8e2c1522 |
| IEExecRemote | 1.0.2411.0 | neutral | b03f5f7f11d50a3a |

**Figure 7–8**    *.NET Admin Tool with side-by-side components in the global assembly cache.*

This is called by-side deployment. Both assemblies are available to client programs that require them. Programs can bind to either of them without fear of getting the wrong version.

## Assembly Configuration

The CLR binds to an assembly when either a static or dynamic reference is made to it at runtime. A static reference is defined permanently in the client assembly manifest when it is compiled. A dynamic reference is produced programmatically at runtime, for example, by calling the method **System.Reflection.Assembly.Load**.

You can use a strongly named assembly to force a client to bind to a specific version of an assembly whether you have private or shared deployment.

Suppose you want to allow several backward-compatible assemblies to match? You can use XML configuration file to specify some rules for the CLR to use when it tries to find an assembly that matches. The .NET Admin Tool can be used to create and maintain these files through a graphical interface.

The name of the configuration file client program's name is appended with a **.config** extension. For our **AcmeGui** client the configuration file would be named **AcmeGui.exe.config**. It is placed in the same directory as the client executable.

In addition to an application configuration file, there is an administration configuration file called **Machine.config**. It is found in the **Config** sub-directory under the directory where the .NET runtime is installed (**\WINNT\Microsoft.NET\Framework\v1.0.2914\**, where the version number reflects the current build of .NET). An administration version policy is defined with the same XML tags that an application configuration file uses. However, the administrator configuration file overrides any settings in the application configuration file.

## Resolving an Assembly Reference at Runtime

If the reference has a strong name, the configuration files are examined first to determine the correct assembly version(s) required. If the reference does not have a strong name, any version will satisfy the reference.[9] If the assembly reference has been previously resolved, that previously loaded assembly is used. The assembly cache is checked next and, if the assembly is found there, that assembly is loaded. If the assembly is not found in the assembly cache, the CLR *probes* for the assembly. We will discuss probing after we discuss specifying version policy in the configuration files.

## Specifying the Version Policy in a Configuration File

The **<configuration>** is the top-level tag for .NET configuration files. Assembly binding information is found in the **<runtime>** section. A sample **AcmeGui.exe.config** file might look like this:

```
<?xml version="1.0"?>
<configuration>
  <runtime>
    <assemblyBinding xmlns="urn:schemas-microsoft-
com:asm.v1">
      <dependentAssembly>
        <assemblyIdentity name="Customer"
publicKeyToken="8b0e612d60bde0ca" />
        <bindingRedirect oldVersion="1.0.0.0-1.1.0.0"
newVersion="1.1.0.0" />
```

---

[9] There is also a publishers configuration file that we do not discuss. If you are using Internet Explorer, the configuration files might have to be downloaded from another computer.

```
      </dependentAssembly>
    </assemblyBinding>
  </runtime>
</configuration>
```

Rules defining version policy are found in the **<assemblyBinding>** section. The XML namespace specification is required. Each assembly whose version policy we want to set is placed in its own **<dependentAssembly>** section. The **assemblyIdentity** element has attributes that define the assembly this section refers to. The **name** attribute is required; the **publicKeyToken** and **culture** attributes are optional.[10] The **bindingRedirect** element's attributes define what versions can map to another version. The **oldVersion** attribute can be a range, the **newVersion** attribute can be set only to one version. In the above example, any references to versions 1.0.0.0 to 1.1.0.0 can be resolved by using version 1.1.0.0. In other words, 1.1.0.0 is backward compatible with all those versions. You can specify several **bindingRedirect** elements.

You can use the **.NET Admin Tool** to specify this. To add an application to the tool first select Applications in the left pane. Right-mouse click and select Add from the context menu. Navigate to the application you want to configure. Select it and click the open button. Figure 7–9 shows the **AcmeGui** application added to the admin tool.

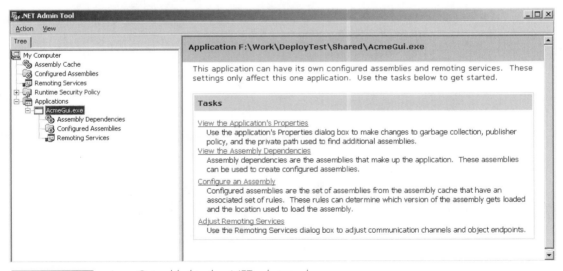

**Figure 7–9**    *AcmeGui added to the .NET admin tool.*

---

[10] You may ask: Why is the publicKeyToken optional? After all, there is no version resolution without it. As we shall see shortly, other policies can be defined that do not require a public key.

To configure the **Customer** assembly, select Configured Assemblies in the left pane, right-mouse click, and select Add from the context menu. In the dialog box that comes up, select the radio button that has the text "Choose an assembly from the list of assemblies this application uses." Then click the "Choose Assembly" button. Select Customer from the list that pops up, and then click the Select button. The Assembly information for the **Customer** assembly should be entered in the "Configure an Assembly" dialog. Click the Finish button on that dialog. Select the "Binding Policy" tab. Figure 7–10 shows what you should see after the binding policy that was in the sample configuration file was recorded.

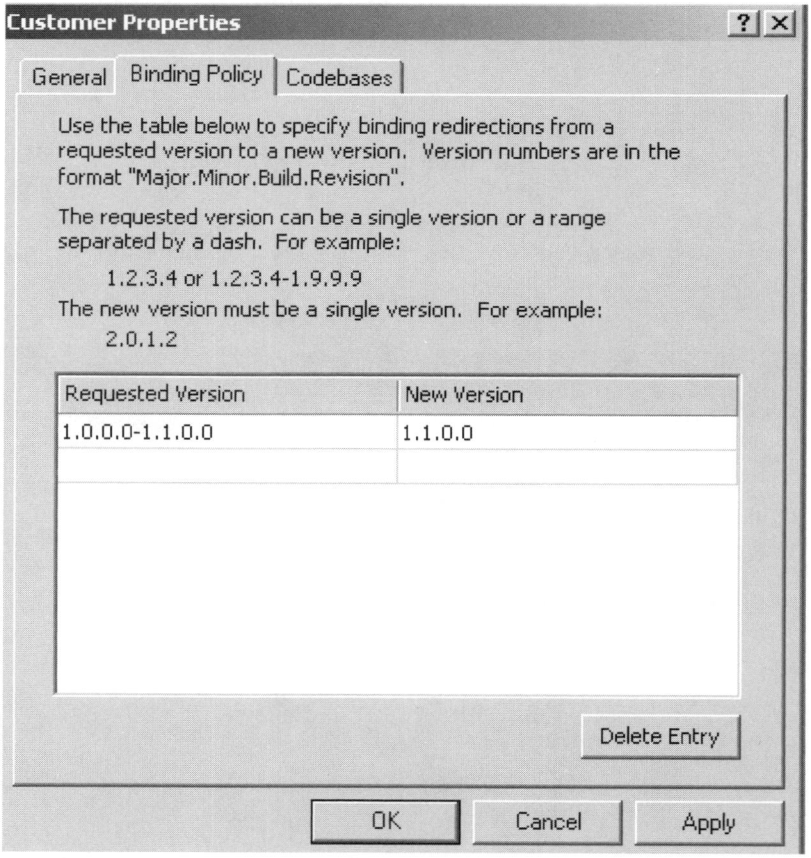

**Figure 7–10**    *Binding policy set for the Customer assembly.*

After you select OK, you can navigate to the directory where the **AcmeGui** executable is, and you will see a configuration file that the tool has created for you. It should resemble our previous example.

## Finding the Assembly's Physical Location

At this point the CLR knows what versions of the assembly will satisfy the reference. The CLR does not yet know where the assembly resides on disk. If the assembly with the right version has been previously loaded because of another reference to that assembly earlier in the program, that assembly is used. If the assembly has a strong name, the assembly cache is checked; if the correct version is found there, that assembly is used.

There are several elements you can specify in the configuration file to tell the CLR where to try and find the assembly.

If the assembly has not yet been found, the runtime checks to see if a codebase has been specified in the configuration file. Under the **<dependentAssembly>** section you can specify a **<codeBase>** element. This element has two attributes, a version and a URI, to check for the assembly. The Codebases tab on the .NET Admin Tool's assembly properties dialog can be used to set them in the configuration file. Examples of this element are:

```
        <codeBase version="1.1.1.1"
href="http://www.abc.com/Customer.dll" />
        <codeBase version="1.1.1.2"
href="file:///c:\AcmeGui\Customer.dll" />
```

To use a Codebase element outside the application's directory or subdirectories, a strong name is required. At this point, whether or not the required assembly is found, the binding process stops. If the assembly is not found, an exception is generated at this point.

If a CodeBase element was not found in the configuration file, the runtime continues to probe for the assembly. At this point all searching is relative to the directory in which the application runs, which is referred to as the *application base*.

The runtime first looks in the application base. It then looks in any subdirectories of the application base that have the same name as the assembly. If a culture is specified in the request, the runtime only looks for the assembly subdirectory under a subdirectory with the name of the culture requested.

Finally, you can specify in the **assemblyBinding** section of the configuration file a privatePath, which is a semicolon-delimited list of subdirectories of the application base to look in.

```
    <probing privatePath="\bin;\assemb" />
```

You can also set the privatePath on the properties tab for the application in the .NET Admin Tool.

## Assembly Location and Visual Studio.NET

Building an assembly within Visual Studio.NET requires a reference to a specific assembly at a specific disk location. The rules just described apply when the application is run, not built.

Within VS.NET you cannot browse to the GAC (**\Winnt\Assembly**) and add a reference. The referenced component must be located somewhere else on disk. One of the properties of a referenced component is the **CopyLocal** property. If set to true, the referenced component is copied to the local project directory. While that copy would be used for the compilation reference, whether it is the one linked to depends on the configuration file settings.

# Multimodule Assemblies

An assembly can be made up of multiple modules. A module is a DLL (or EXE) that contains managed code plus metadata, but not necessarily a manifest. However, an assembly must have one and only one manifest. Hence an assembly can contain multiple modules, but only one of them can have a manifest that provides information on the contents of all the modules in the assembly. The module with the manifest may have just the manifest, or it can contain other code or resources.

The main advantage of breaking an assembly into multiple modules is that each module is contained in a separate DLL file. This allows Web downloads to be performed on demand, on a per-module basis. This can improve performance and memory consumption. Even in a local scenario, the CLR loads classes on the local machine with module granularity, which can improve efficiency. Another reason for constructing an assembly with multiple modules is that you may have written each part of an assembly in a different .NET language. To build an assembly that contains multiple modules, you need to build each module separately, and then combine them with the **Al.exe** utility.

There are two ways to go about creating a multimodule assembly. One way is to create all the modules without any manifest, and then create one additional module that contains only a manifest for the entire assembly, but no actual code. The other technique is to have just one module in the assembly that contains both code and a manifest for the entire assembly, and to have all other modules in the assembly contain only code, with no manifest. We will describe the first alternative, since it is more symmetric and easier to visualize. The second alternative is not described here, however, it is done in a similar way, with the same tools.

Visual Studio.NET does not allow you to do this for C# projects. The **MultiModule** example illustrates the mechanics of how to create a multiple-module assembly. The example directory contains three files. **Add.cs** and **Sub.cs** will be built into separate modules and then combined together in an assembly. **Compute.cs** uses this assembly. **Add.cs** has one class with one method; **Add**. **Sub.cs** has another class that has one method, **Sub**.

```
public class MyCalc
{
        public int Add(int a, int b)
        {
                return a + b;
        }

}
public class MyCalcSub
{
        public int Sub(int a, int b)
        {
                return a - b;
        }

}
```

We create two modules with no assembly manifest by running **build.bat**, which has two commands:

```
csc /target:module /out:add.dll add.cs
csc /target:module /out:sub.dll sub.cs
```

If you look at add.dll in ILDASM, you will see that there is a **.module add.dll** statement but no **.assembly** statement. We now can build an assembly with a manifest using the Assembly Linker tool **Al.exe** by running **link.bat**, which has one command:

```
Al add.dll, sub.dll /out:arith.dll
```

As Figure 7–11 shows, arith.dll contains only a manifest. The manifest shows that the assembly is made up of two separate, distinct files, and the types in those files are listed in the manifest.

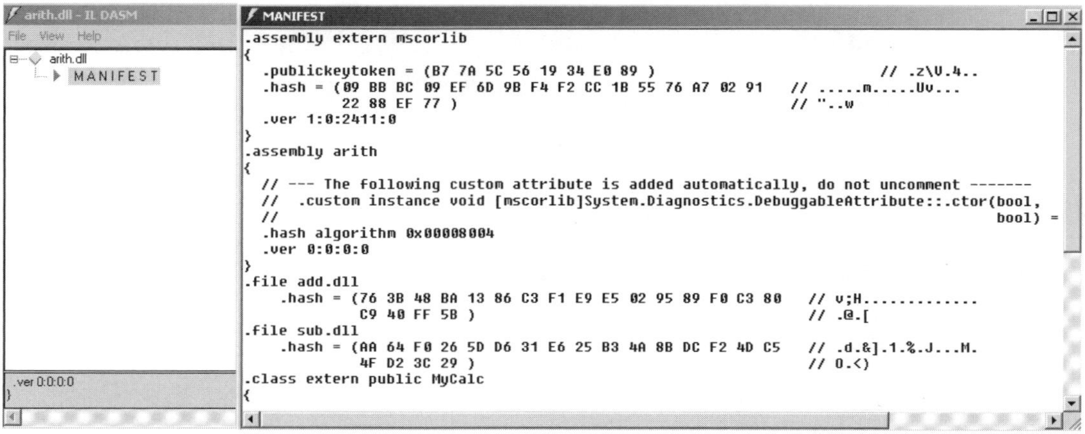
arith.dll - IL DASM
File View Help
arith.dll
MANIFEST
.ver 0:0:0:0
}
MANIFEST
.assembly extern mscorlib
{
.publickeytoken = (B7 7A 5C 56 19 34 E0 89 ) // .z\V.4..
.hash = (09 BB BC 09 EF 6D 9B F4 F2 CC 1B 55 76 A7 02 91 // .....m.....Uv...
22 88 EF 77 ) // "..w
.ver 1:0:2411:0
}
.assembly arith
{
// --- The following custom attribute is added automatically, do not uncomment -------
// .custom instance void [mscorlib]System.Diagnostics.DebuggableAttribute::.ctor(bool,
// bool) =
.hash algorithm 0x00008004
.ver 0:0:0:0
}
.file add.dll
.hash = (76 3B 48 BA 13 86 C3 F1 E9 E5 02 95 89 F0 C3 80 // v;H.............
C9 40 FF 5B ) // .@.[
.file sub.dll
.hash = (AA 64 F0 26 5D D6 31 E6 25 B3 4A 8B DC F2 4D C5 // .d.&].1.%.J...M.
4F D2 3C 29 ) // O.<)
.class extern public MyCalc
{

**Figure 7–11** *Manifest for a multimodule assembly.*

We have a simple client program, **compute.cs**, that uses the types in **arith.dll**.

```
public class Compute
{
        public static void Main(string[] args)
        {
                MyCalc x = new MyCalc();
                int y = x.Add(1, 3);
                Console.WriteLine("y = " + y.ToString());

                MyCalcSub z = new MyCalcSub();
                y = z.Sub(1, 3);
                Console.WriteLine("y = " + y.ToString());

                return;
        }
}
```

We can build it with the command:

```
csc /r:arith.dll compute.cs
```

This will produce compute.exe, which we can run.

## Setup and Deployment Projects

Assemblies may be deployed as regular stand-alone binary code files (i.e., DLL or EXE files), or they may be deployed using CAB, MSI, or MSM files. A CAB file is a cabinet file with the **.cab** file-name extension. A CAB file is used to compress and combine other files into one convenient manageable file. Although CAB files can be used for general purposes, they have traditionally been used for CD-based and Web-based installation purposes. MSI and MSM files are Microsoft Windows Installer files, with the **.msi** and **.msm** file-name extensions. MSI files (and indirectly, MSM files) are used with the **Msiexec.exe** Windows Installer program to deploy stand-alone applications and reusable components.

MSI files are Microsoft Windows Installer installation packages that have the **.msi** file-name extension. MSM files are merge modules that have the **.msm** file-name extension. Windows Installer supports software installation, repair, upgrade, and removal. Windows Installer packages are self-contained database files that provide installation information to the Windows Installer service. An MSM file has an internal structure similar to that of an MSI file, but it is somewhat simplified. Unfortunately, an MSM file cannot be used directly by Windows Installer, since it lacks certain important database tables. Instead, the MSM file must be merged into an MSI file to be used in an actual installation session. However, MSM files are useful for separating out shared installation information into an independent package that can then be merged into many other MSI packages.

Installation may be accomplished using the Windows Installer, Internet Explorer, or simply by manually copying assemblies and associated files. To help the programmer develop setup and deployment solutions, Visual Studio.NET provides several templates and wizards for generating starter setup projects. These tools are available by way of the New Project dialog box under the Setup and Deployment Projects node, as shown in Figure 7–12. As you can see, the following templates are provided for generating starter setup and deployment projects.

- Cab Project
- Setup Project
- Setup Wizard
- Merge Module Project
- Web Setup Project

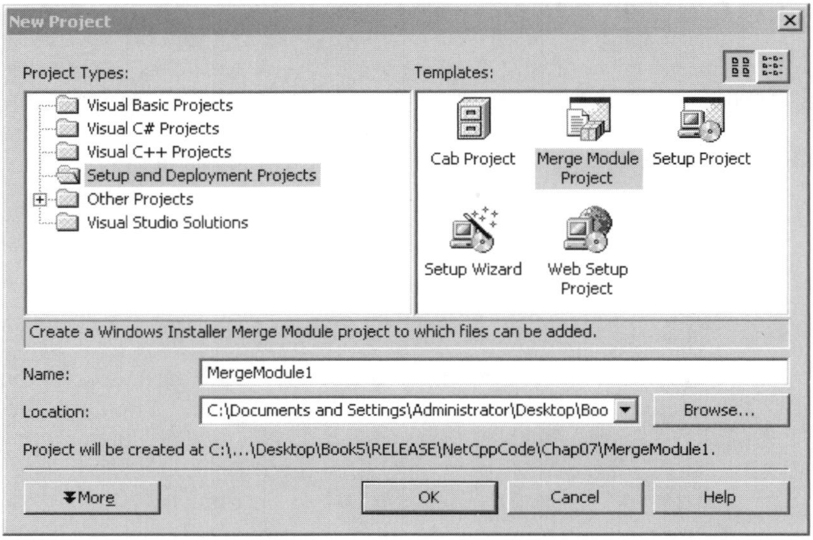

**Figure 7–12**   *Setup and deployment project templates.*

## CAB Project

A CAB project creates a cabinet file containing any number of other files that can be used for traditional deployment purposes. CAB files have been used to package legacy COM components deployed over the Internet, and they have also been used in traditional CD-based installation programs. CAB files may now also be used for packaging managed code. However, for .NET deployment, a CAB file can contain only one assembly, and the CAB file must be assigned the same name as the contained assembly, but with the **.cab** extension. For example, an assembly named **SomeComponent.dll** would have to be contained in a cabinet file named **SomeComponent.cab**.

## Setup Project

The Setup project template creates a Windows Installer **.msi** file for a desktop or distributed application. A Setup project is not intended for deployment of Web-based applications, since a specialized Web Setup project is used for that purpose. A Setup project produces a program that installs an application onto a target machine. You may create Setup projects within the same solution that contains the other projects to be deployed. In a multitier solution, you can create one setup project for each project that is to be deployed to a particular target computer. For example, in a simple three-tier solution, you would probably have three deployment projects. Two simple deployment projects would set up the client and server. A third deployment project would then look after the more complex middle-tier business logic. Additional deployment projects may come into play if the solution was highly complex, or if merge modules were incorporated into the deployment strategy.

To create a Setup project, select File | New, then select Project. In the New Project dialog box, select Setup and Deployment Projects as the Project Type. Finally, select Setup Project as the Template, specify name and location, and then click OK. The result of this is shown in Figure 7–13, showing Solution Explorer and the File System Editor.

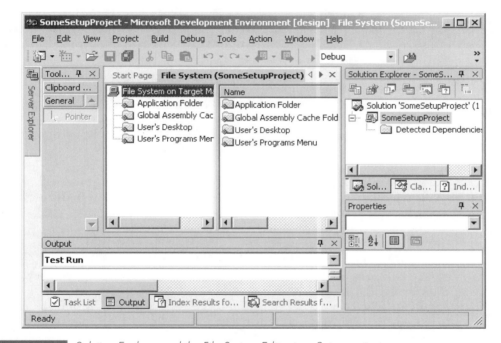

**Figure 7–13** *Solution Explorer and the File System Editor in a Setup project.*

Once the initial Setup project has been created with the Setup Project template, it can be further developed using the File System Editor. The File System Editor allows you to drag and drop, or copy and paste, files to be deployed by the Setup deployment project, and control their destinations on the target machine. Initially, the File System Editor shows an initial list of destination folders that you can deploy into, and you can also add your own folders to this list.

Once you have an MSI file created, you can use Windows Installer, as shown in the following command line:

```
Msiexec /i SomeSetup.msi
```

The Windows Installer program then starts up and displays a series of installation dialogs. After Windows Installer has completed the deployment, you can try running the installed application to verify that the installation was successful. If you run the same command **Msiexec /i SomeSetup.msi**, it will detect that it already exists, so it gives you the choice to either repair the installation or uninstall it.

## Merge Module Project

A Merge Module project packages reusable setup information that can be independently maintained and then merged as a shared installation package into other installation packages. A Merge Module project produces a merge module **.msm** file that can be merged into **.msi** files. This allows you to share common assemblies, associated files, registry values, and setup functionality among multiple applications.

To start the Merge Module Project Wizard, select File | New, then select Project. In the New Project dialog box, select Setup and Deployment Projects as the Project Type. Finally, select Merge Module Project Wizard as the Template, specify name and location, and then click OK.

Typically, an MSI file is intended for use by the end user for installing a complete solution in one simple deployment session. In contrast, an MSM file is typically intended for use by other developers who want to use components that you have developed in their setup projects. Those other developers can merge your MSM file into their own MSI file for deploying your components into their test and development environments, as well as for their ultimate end user. End users should not be provided any MSM files, since they are not directly installable using Windows Installer, and they are not very friendly to work with.

To add an existing merge module project to a Setup project, create or open the Setup project, select File | Add Project, and then select Existing Project. In the Add Existing Project dialog box, browse to the location of the desired merge module project, select the associated **.vdp** deployment project file, and then click Open.

We have just added the merge module project to the solution. We now have to add it to the Setup project itself. Select the Setup project and invoke "Add:Project Output," then select the merge module project in the dialog that appears.

## Web-based Deployment

Web-based deployment uses Internet Explorer on the client to automatically download assemblies packaged as EXE, DLL, or CAB files on demand from a .NET Web server. HTML files can dynamically deploy assemblies as well as configuration files to control the binding process. Web-based deployment results in assemblies being downloaded into the client's assembly download cache on demand.

The Xml **<object>** tag is used to download and install assemblies, using either a relative or an absolute URL. The following shows a relative URL example, where the assembly is located relative to the directory of the containing HTML file on the Web server.

```
<object
   id="SomeComponent"
   classid="./SomeDirectory/MyComponent.dll#SomeClass">
</object>
```

The following shows an absolute URL example, where the assembly is located on a specified Web server.

```
<object
   id="SomeComponent"
classid="http://www.acme.com/MyComponent.dll#SomeClass">
</object>
```

By default, IE creates a separate application domain for each Web site that it encounters. An application domain is a .NET feature that can be thought of as a scalable lightweight process. An application domain efficiently provides fault isolation without the overhead of running multiple processes. Each application domain may optionally have its own configuration file to control binding and security. Also, a configuration file may specify an isolated application domain for individual applications on the same Web server. Each HTML file that specifies the same configuration file will be placed into the same application domain. Application domains are discussed in the next chapter.

## Summary

Deployment is very important, constituting one of the major phases in software development. If it is not done properly, the entire development effort becomes a waste of time and money. Fortunately, with assemblies, which are the fundamental units of .NET deployment, many of the complexities and problems relating to deployment are conveniently solved.

By simply building dynamic link libraries you can have reusable components without all the difficulties associated with building and installing COM components.

Private assembly deployment can be simply copying the assembly to the same directory as the client application. Public assembly deployment involves the creation of a strong name for the assembly, followed by deployment into the global assembly cache. The Strong Name Utility (**Sn.exe**) can be used to create the strong name for an assembly. The Global Assembly

Cache utility **Gacutil.exe**, or the .NET Admin Tool can then be used to deploy the shared assembly into the global assembly cache. It is also possible to combine multiple modules into a single assembly. The Visual Studio.NET CAB and setup wizards are very useful for creating starter setup and deployment projects, which can save a great deal of development time.

# .NET Framework Classes

*I*t is impossible to cover in one chapter or one book all of the .NET Framework classes. The .NET classes cover a large fraction of the Win32 API, as well as much else. While a lot of attention has been focused on changes in Internet-related functionality, the development model for Windows applications has changed as well.

This chapter focuses on classes illustrating the key concepts and patterns that appear throughout the .NET Framework. Over the long run, experienced programmers will find this approach more fruitful than attempting to explain a little about every class that you might need without giving you much insight. Other chapters go into more depth about other parts of the Framework such as Windows Forms, ASP.NET, ADO.NET, security, and Web Services.

We start out by exploring the concept of reflection and metadata. Metadata appears everywhere in .NET and is critical to understanding how the CLR can provide services for your applications. Next we explore file input/output—for several reasons. First, it introduces the important topic of serialization. Second, the **Path** class exemplifies how some Framework classes provide some or all of their functionality through static methods. Third, the formatter classes are used in several places in .NET.

Understanding serialization will give you a concrete idea of how the Framework can handle objects transparently for you. Serialization also appears in a supporting role wherever objects have to be moved or transported. Our discussion of the **ISerializable** interface demonstrates how much easier it is to implement an interface in .NET than with COM.

To develop an understanding of the .NET model for applications, we introduce programming with threads under .NET and several .NET synchronization techniques to handle multithreading issues. The various synchronization techniques illustrate the trade-offs of using attributes supplied by the Framework versus doing it yourself.

To further your understanding of the .NET programming model, we introduce **context** and the use of proxies and stubs. **Application domains** can achieve application isolation with less performance penalty than a Win32 processes.[1]

The asynchronous design pattern appears throughout .NET and is discussed in some detail. We give some examples of remoting because it is a key technology and it summarizes many of the concepts developed in this chapter. The chapter uses several attributes provided by the .NET Framework, and we show how to implement and use custom attributes. We discuss garbage collection, finalization, and the dispose pattern, so that you can understand how to make sure resources are properly freed in your applications.

## Metadata and Reflection

The **Serialization** example in Chapter 2 demonstrates how metadata makes possible many of the services of the Common Language Runtime. Many of the technologies we cover in the rest of the book rely on metadata, although we will not always stop and point this out.

Metadata is information about the assemblies, modules and types that constitute .NET programs. If you have ever had to create IDL to generate a type library so that your C++ COM objects could be called by Visual Basic, or to create proxies and stubs, you will appreciate how useful metadata is and will be grateful that it comes "for free."

Compilers emit metadata, and the CLR, the .NET Framework, or your own programs can use it. Since we want to give you an understanding of how metadata works, we will focus on the use, not the creation, of metadata. Metadata is read using classes in the **System.Reflection** namespace.[2]

When you load an assembly and its associated modules and types, the metadata is loaded along with it. You can then query the assembly to get those associated types. You can also call **GetType** on any CLR type and get its metadata. **GetType** is a method on **System.Object** from which every CLR type inherits. After you get the **Type** associated with an object, you can use the reflection methods to get the related metadata.

The **Reflection** sample program takes the case study's **Customer** assembly and prints out some of the metadata available. You should examine the output and source code as you read the next sections. You should especially

---

[1] Win32 process isolation uses the processor's MMU. .NET's application domain isolation is done in software and requires verifiable code.

[2] There is a lower-level set of unmanaged COM interfaces for accessing metadata but we will not discuss them here. See "Metadata in .NET" by Matt Pietrek in the October 2000 *MSDN Magazine*.

compare the output of the program with the source code in the file **customer.cs**.

The program clearly shows that it is possible to retrieve all of the types in an assembly and reconstruct the structures, interfaces, properties, events, and methods associated with those types.

First we load the assembly into memory and write out its name.

```
Assembly a = Assembly.Load(assemblyName);
Console.WriteLine("Assembly {0} found.", a.FullName);
```

The output for this statement is appropriate for an unsigned assembly:

```
Assembly Customer, Version=1.0.583.29038, Culture=neutral,
PublicKeyToken=null found.
```

One of the properties of the **Assembly** class is the **CodeBase**, discussed in Chapter 7 on Deployment. The security **Evidence** associated with this assembly is another property. The **Evidence** class is discussed in Chapter 12 on Security.

The following code tries to get the entry point for the assembly:

```
MethodInfo entryMethodInfo = a.EntryPoint;
```

Since this is a dynamic linked library (DLL), there is no entry. If it were an executable program we could use the **Invoke** method on the **MethodInfo** class to run the startup code in the assembly.[3]

The sample uses the **Assembly's GetModules** method to find the modules associated with this assembly. In this case we have only one, "customer.dll." We could next find the types associated with the module by using the **GetTypes** method on each **Module** instance returned by **GetModules**. Since there is only one module, we use the Assembly's **GetTypes** method to return an array of the assembly's types. Even if we had several modules, we would use **Assembly.GetTypes** if we did not care about the association of types and modules.

## Type

The abstract class **Type** in the **System** namespace defines .NET types. Since there are no functions outside of classes or global variables in C#,[4] getting all the types in an assembly will allow us to get all the metadata about the code in that assembly. **Type** represents all the types present in .NET: classes, interfaces, values, arrays, and enumerations.

The **Type** class is also returned by the **GetType** method on the **System.Object** class and the static **GetType** method on the **Type** class itself. The latter method can be used with types that can be resolved statically.

---

[3] You can also load and execute the assembly from the AppDomain, as we discuss later in this chapter.

[4] Although they are permitted by the CTS and are legal in managed C++.

One of **Type's** properties is the Assembly to which it belongs. You can get all the types in the containing assembly once you have the **Type** of one object. **Type** is an abstract class; at runtime an instance of **System.RuntimeType** is returned.

If you examine the program's output you will see that each type in the assembly, **CustomerListItem**, **ICustomer**, **Customer**, **Customers** is found and its metadata is printed out. We can find out the standard attributes and the type from which the class derives for each type through the **Attributes** and **BaseType** properties.

The methods associated with the **Type** class enable you to get the associated fields, properties, interfaces, events, and methods. For example, the **Customer** type has no interfaces, properties, or events, four fields, three constructors, and the methods inherited from its **BaseType System.Object**:

```
Interfaces:
Fields:
    CustomerId
    FirstName
    LastName
    EmailAddress
Properties:
Events:
Constructors:
    public .ctor(System.String first, System.String
last, System.String email)
    public .ctor()
    public .ctor(System.Int32 id)
Methods:
    public Int32 GetHashCode()
    public Boolean Equals(System.Object obj)
    public String ToString()
    public Type GetType()
```

The type **Customers** inherits from one interface and has one constructor and four of its own methods in addition to the four it inherited from its **BaseType System.Object**:

```
Interfaces:
    ICustomer
Fields:
Properties:
Events:
Constructors:
    public .ctor()
Methods:
    public Void ChangeEmailAddress(System.Int32 id,
System.String emailAddress)
    public ArrayList GetCustomer(System.Int32 id)
    public Void UnregisterCustomer(System.Int32 id)
```

```
        public Int32 RegisterCustomer(System.String
firstName, System.String lastName, System.String
emailAddress)
        public Int32 GetHashCode()
        public Boolean Equals(System.Object obj)
        public String ToString()
        public Type GetType()
```

These were obtained with the **GetInterfaces**, **GetFields**, **GetProperties**, **GetEvents GetConstructors**, and **GetMethods** methods on the **Type** class. Since an interface is a type, **GetInterfaces** returns an array of **Types** representing the interfaces inherited or implemented by the **Type** queried. Since fields, properties, events, and methods are not types, their accessor methods do not return **Types**. Each of their accessor methods returns an appropriate class: **FieldInfo**, **PropertyInfo**, **EventInfo**, **ConstructorInfo**, and **MethodInfo**. All these classes, as well as the **Type** class, inherit from the **MemberInfo** class that is the abstract base class for member metadata.

Let us examine some of the metadata associated with a class method. Using the reflection methods, we were able to reconstruct the signatures for all the classes and interfaces in the **Customer** assembly. Here is the output for the methods of the **Customers** class:

```
    public Void ChangeEmailAddress(System.Int32 id,
System.String emailAddress)
    public ArrayList GetCustomer(System.Int32 id)
    public Void UnregisterCustomer(System.Int32 id)
    public Int32 RegisterCustomer(System.String firstName,
System.String lastName, System.String emailAddress)
    public Int32 GetHashCode()
    public Boolean Equals(System.Object obj)
    public String ToString()
    public Type GetType()
```

Here is the code from the example that produced the output:

```
for (int j = 0; j < methodInfo.Length; j++)
{
  if (methodInfo[j].IsStatic)
    Console.Write("          static ");
  if (methodInfo[j].IsPublic)
    Console.Write("          public ");
  if (methodInfo[j].IsFamily)
    Console.Write("          protected ");
  if (methodInfo[j].IsAssembly)
    Console.Write("          internal ");
  if (methodInfo[j].IsPrivate)
    Console.Write("          private ");
  Console.Write("{0} ", methodInfo[j].ReturnType.Name);
```

```
   Console.Write("{0}(", methodInfo[j].Name);
   ParameterInfo[] paramInfo =
methodInfo[j].GetParameters();
   long last = paramInfo.Length - 1;
   for (int k = 0; k < paramInfo.Length; k++)
   {
     Console.Write("{0} {1}", paramInfo[k].ParameterType,
       paramInfo[k].Name);
     if (k != last)
       Console.Write(", ");
   }
Console.WriteLine(")");
}
```

Except for the fact that a constructor does not have a return type, the exact same code reconstitutes the calling sequences for the class's constructors.

The **MethodInfo** class has properties that help us determine if the method is static, public, protected, internal, or private as well as the return type and method name. The method parameters are stored in a property array of type **ParameterInfo**.

This example should also make clear that types are assembly relative. The same type name and layout in two different assemblies is treated by the runtime as two separate types. When versioning assemblies, one has to be careful when mixing versioned types, or the same types in two different assemblies.

All this metadata allows the Common Language Runtime and the Framework to provide services to your applications because it can understand the structure of your types.

## Late Binding

Reflection can also be used to implement late binding. In late binding the method to be called is determined during execution rather than compilation. It is one example of how metadata can be used to provide functionality. As the previous example demonstrates, you can extract the signature of a method associated with a type. The **MethodInfo** object has all the needed metadata for a class method. The **DynamicInvocation** sample demonstrates a very simple example of late binding.

We dynamically load an assembly and get the metadata for a method of a particular type:

```
Assembly a = Assembly.Load("Customer");
Type t = a.GetType("OI.NetCs.Acme.Customers");
MethodInfo mi = t.GetMethod("GetCustomer");
```

Using the reflection classes, we could have made this completely dynamic by arbitrarily picking types, methods, and constructors from the **Customer** assembly using the techniques of the last example, but we wanted to keep the **DynamicInvocation** example simple.

The **System** namespace has an **Activator** class that has overloaded **CreateInstance** methods to create an instance of any .NET type using the appropriate constructor. The **Activator** class is discussed in this chapter's section on Remoting. We invoke a constructor with no arguments to create an instance of the **Customers** object.

```
Object customerInstance = Activator.CreateInstance(t);
```

We then build an argument list and use the **Invoke** method of the **MethodInfo** instance to call the **GetCustomer** method.

```
object[] arguments = new Object[1];
int customerId = -1;
arguments[0] = customerId;
object returnType = mi.Invoke(customerInstance,
arguments);
```

Using the reflection methods, we get the type information for each field in a return structure. Note the **GetValue** method that gets the data for a particular field in a structure. This is necessary because we cannot do pointer arithmetic to access an offset into a structure.

```
if (returnType.GetType() ==
Type.GetType("System.Collections.ArrayList"))
{
  System.Collections.ArrayList arrayList =
    (System.Collections.ArrayList)returnType;
  for (int i = 0; i < arrayList.Count; i++)
  {
    Type itemType = arrayList[i].GetType();
    FieldInfo[] fi = itemType.GetFields();
    for (int j = 0; j < fi.Length; j++)
    {
      object fieldValue = fi[j].GetValue(arrayList[i]);
      Console.Write("{0, -10} = {1, -15}", fi[j].Name,
        fieldValue);
    }
  Console.WriteLine();
  }
}
```

This code did not use any specific objects or types from the **Customer** assembly. We did use some knowledge about the assembly to keep the code simple in order to illustrate the main points. It should be clear, however, how to make this completely general.

You can go one step further and use the classes that emit metadata (in **System.Reflection.Emit**). You can dynamically create an assembly and then load and run it.

# Input and Output in .NET

To make a crude generalization, the input/output functions in the .NET Framework can be divided into two broad categories, irrespective of the data storage (disk, memory, and so on) that is being written to, or read from.

Data can be treated as a stream of bytes or characters. We can read a block of bytes from a file to a memory buffer. Data can also be treated as a set of objects. Reading and writing the objects is referred to as deserializing and serializing the objects. We can serialize (write) the list of **Customer** objects to disk. We can then deserialize (read) the list of **Customer** objects back into memory.

The **System.IO** namespace has several classes for reading and writing to various types of storage while treating the data as bytes or characters. Serialization functionality can be found in various places in the .NET framework. The **System.Runtime.Serialization** namespace handles serialization of the Common Type System. The **System.Xml.Serialization** namespace handles XML serialization.

## Streams

**Stream** is an abstract class that is the basis for reading from and writing bytes to some storage such as a file. It supports both synchronous and asynchronous reading and writing. Asynchronous methods are discussed later in this chapter. The **Stream** class has the typical methods that you would expect: **Read**, **Write**, **Seek**, **Flush**, and **Close**.

The **FileStream** class is derived from **Stream** to represent the reading and writing of files as a series of bytes. The **FileStream** constructor builds the actual stream instance. The overridden **Stream** methods implement the reading and writing to the file.

Other classes derived from **Stream** include **MemoryStream**, **BufferedStream**, and **NetworkStream** (in **System.Net.Sockets**).

The **FileStream** example (in the **FileIO** directory, as are all the IO examples) illustrates how to use the **Stream** classes. If the file does not exist, a new file is created and the numbers from 0 to 9 are written to it. If the file already exists, the code starts reading 5 bytes from the end of the file and then writes them out. (You should run the example twice. The first time creates and writes the file, and the second time reads the file.)

```
byte[] data = new Byte[10];
FileStream fs = new FileStream("FileStreamTest.txt",
```

```
      FileMode.OpenOrCreate);
if (fs.Length == 0)
{
  Console.WriteLine("Writing Data...");
  for (short i = 0; i < 10; i++)
    data[i] = (byte)i;
  fs.Write(data, 0, 10);
}
else
{
  fs.Seek(-5, SeekOrigin.End);
  int count = fs.Read(data, 0, 10);
  for (int i = 0; i < count; i++)
  {
    Console.WriteLine(data[i]);
  }
}
fs.Close();
```

## Primitive Datatypes and Streams

The stream derived classes will work if you are reading and writing bytes of data as a block. If you need to read and write the primitive common types (**Boolean**, **String**, **Int32**, and so on) in and out of a stream, use the **BinaryReader** and the **BinaryWriter** classes. The **Binary** example shows how to use these classes. You create the appropriate stream (**FileStream** in the example) and pass it to the **BinaryReader** or **BinaryWriter** constructor. You can then use one of the overloaded **Read** or **Write** methods to read or write a datatype to or from the stream. (Again, you should run the example twice.)

```
FileStream fs = new FileStream("BinaryTest.bin",
FileMode.OpenOrCreate);
if (fs.Length == 0)
{
  Console.WriteLine("Writing Data...");
  BinaryWriter w = new BinaryWriter(fs);
  for (short i = 0; i < 10; i++)
    w.Write(i);
  w.Close();
}
else
{
  BinaryReader r = new BinaryReader(fs);
  for (int i = 0; i < 10; i++)
    Console.WriteLine(r.ReadInt16());
  r.Close();
}
fs.Close();
```

## TextReader and TextWriter

The **TextReader** and **TextWriter** abstract classes treat the data as a sequential stream of characters (i.e., as text). **TextReader** has methods such as **Close**, **Peek**, **Read**, **ReadBlock**, **ReadLine**, and **ReadToEnd**. **TextWriter** has methods such as **Close**, **Flush**, **Write**, and **WriteLine**. The overloaded **Read** methods read characters from the stream. The overloaded **Write** and **WriteLine** methods write various types to the stream. If an object is written to the stream, the object's **ToString** method is used.

   **StringReader** and **StringWriter** are derived from **TextReader** and **TextWriter**. These classes read and write characters from a string. The **StringWriter's** constructor uses a **StringBuilder** object. The **StringBuilder** class was discussed in Chapter 3. **StreamReader** and **StreamWriter** are also derived from **TextReader** and **TextWriter**. They read and write text to and from a **Stream** object. As with the **BinaryReader** and **BinaryWriter** class you create a stream and pass it to the constructor. Hence, these classes can use any **Stream** derived class data storage. The **Text** example uses the **StreamWriter** and **StreamReader** classes.

```
FileStream fs = new FileStream("TextTest.txt",
FileMode.OpenOrCreate);
if (fs.Length == 0)
{
  Console.WriteLine("Writing Data...");
  StreamWriter sw = new StreamWriter(fs);
  sw.Write(100);
  sw.WriteLine(" One Hundred");
  sw.WriteLine("End of File");
  sw.Close();
}
else
{
  string text;
  StreamReader sr = new StreamReader(fs);
  text = sr.ReadLine();
  while (text != null)
  {
    Console.WriteLine(text);
    text = sr.ReadLine();
  }
  sr.Close();
}
fs.Close();
```

## File Manipulation

The framework has two classes that are very useful for working with files.

If you need to manipulate the file in addition to reading and writing to it, the **File** class provides the basic functionality. Since the **File** class has only static members, you have to provide the name of the file as an argument. The **FileInfo** class has a constructor that creates an object that represents a file. You then use the methods to manipulate that particular file.

The **File** class methods always perform a security check. If you are going to continually access a particular file, you may want to use the **FileInfo** class, because the security check is made only once in the constructor. Security is discussed in more detail in Chapter 12.

### FILE CLASS

The **File** class has methods for creating and opening files that return **FileStream**, **StreamWriter**, or **StreamReader** objects that do the actual reading and writing. The overloaded **Create** methods return a **FileStream** object. The **CreateText** method returns a **StreamWriter.** The overloaded **Open** method can either create a new file or open an existing one for reading or writing, depending on the method parameters. The object returned is a **FileStream** object. The **OpenText** method returns a **StreamReader**. The **OpenRead** method returns a **FileStream** object. The **OpenWrite** method returns a **FileStream**.

The **File** class also has methods for copying, deleting, and moving files. You can test for the existence of a file. File attributes can be read or modified, such as:

- creation time
- last access time
- last write time
- archive, hidden, normal, system, or temporary
- compressed, encrypted
- read-only
- whether the file is a directory

### PATH CLASS

Many of the file names needed for input arguments have to be full paths. Or you might only want to manipulate parts of the path. The **Path** class has static methods that make this easier. The **Path** class has static fields that indicate various platform-specific aspects of pathnames such as the separator characters for directories, paths, and volumes, and the illegal characters for pathnames.

Its static methods let you change the extension of a file, or find the directory where temporary files reside. The **GetFullPath** method is particularly useful. You can pass it a relative path such as ".\foo.txt" and it will return the full path of the file. This is very useful for the **File** or security classes that require the full file path.

### FILEINFO CLASS

The **FileInfo** constructor creates an object that represents a disk file. The constructor takes one argument, a string representing the name of the file. The class has properties that represent file properties such as the creation time, full pathname, and size of the file. It has creation and open methods that are analogous to the **File** class methods but operate on this file instance and therefore do not need a file-name parameter. The **FileInfo** class also has methods to move and copy the file.

### FILE EXAMPLE

The **File** example illustrates the use of the **File** and **FileInfo** classes.

The static **Delete** method of the **File** class is used to remove a previous version of a file if it is present. The static **CreateText** method creates a new file and returns a **StreamWriter** instance which is used to write some text to the file. The stream is then closed. The static **Move** method then renames the file.

A **FileInfo** instance is constructed to represent this renamed file. The complete file name, size, and creation date for the file are written to the console. The file is opened as text and a **StreamReader** instance is used to read and write out the contents of the file.

```
File.Delete("file2.txt");
  StreamWriter sw = File.CreateText("file.txt");
sw.WriteLine("The time has come the Walrus said, to talk
of many things");
sw.WriteLine("Of shoes, and ships, and sealing wax, of
cabbages and kings");
sw.WriteLine("And why the sea is boiling hot, and whether
pigs have wings.");
sw.Close();

File.Move("file.txt", "file2.txt");
FileInfo fileInfo = new FileInfo("file2.txt");
Console.WriteLine("File {0} is {1} bytes in length and was
created on {2}", fileInfo.FullName, fileInfo.Length,
fileInfo.CreationTime);
Console.WriteLine("");

StreamReader sr = fileInfo.OpenText();
String s = sr.ReadLine();
```

```
while (s != null)
{
  Console.WriteLine(s);
  s = sr.ReadLine();
 }
sr.Close();
Console.WriteLine("");
```

# Serialization

Using the **File** and **Stream** classes can be quite cumbersome if you have to save a complicated data structure with linked objects. You have to save the individual fields to disk, remembering which field belongs to which object, and which object instance was linked to another object instance. When restoring the data structure you have to reconstitute that arrangement of fields and object references.

The serialization technology provided by the .NET Framework does this for you. Serialization converts managed data structures to a byte stream. Deserialization converts the byte stream back to managed data structures. Serializing and deserializing can be done on different machines so long as they both host the CLR.

Objects can be serialized without writing special code because, as we have seen, the runtime can query the object's metadata and the serialized stream tags each value with the name of the field to which it applies.

To inform the framework that a class can be serialized, mark the class with the **System.Serializable** attribute. Any field or property that should not be serialized can be marked with the **System.NonSerialized** attribute. For example, fields that represent calculated values need not be serialized. All you have to do is mark the class with the attribute; you need write no other code to save the class's fields. Only instance fields are saved; the static fields of a class are never saved.

The **Serialization** example shows how to apply serialization to the case study's **HotelBroker** class in the **Hotel** assembly. The **Serializable** attribute has been applied to the **HotelBroker** class definition. The **Serializable** attribute has also been applied to all the classes that are used by **HotelBroker** or that **HotelBroker** derives from—**Broker, Hotel, HotelReservation, Reservable**, and **Reservation**—because in order for **HotelBroker** to be serializable, those classes must be as well. If any of those classes were not marked, a runtime exception would be thrown when the framework tried to serialize an object of that type.

```
[Serializable]
public class HotelBroker : Broker, IHotelInfo,
IHotelAdmin, IHotelReservation
```

```
{
private const int MAXDAY = 366;
private const int MAXUNIT = 10;
[NonSerialized] private ArrayList cities;
. . .
[Serializable] public class Hotel : Reservable
. . .
[Serializable] public class HotelReservation : Reservation
. . .
[Serializable] public abstract class Reservable
. . .
[Serializable] public abstract class Reservation
. . .
[Serializable] public abstract class Broker
. . .
```

The cities field has been marked as **NonSerialized**, since the hotel's city is saved with the serialized hotels and therefore can be restored, as the modified **AddCity** method demonstrates. The cities field would be null if the **HotelBroker** class had been deserialized, because the cities field was not saved.[5]

```
private void AddCity(string city)
{
  if (cities == null)
    {
    cities = new ArrayList();
    foreach(Hotel h in units)
      AddCity(h.City);
  }
  if (!cities.Contains(city))
  cities.Add(city);
}
```

## Serialization Objects

Although the framework knows how to save an object marked with the **Serializable** attribute, you still have to specify the format in which the object is saved (i.e., store the data as binary, XML, or some custom format), and the storage medium. To specify the format in which an object is saved, you use an instance of an object that supports the **IFormatter** interface.[6]

The Framework ships with two such classes, **System.Runtime. Serialization.Formatters.Binary.BinaryFormatter** and **System.Runtime. Serialization.Formatters.Soap.SoapFormatter**. The **BinaryFormatter**

---

[5] Of course we could have serialized the cities field and not have to deal with the case where cities could be null, but we wanted to demonstrate the **NonSerialized** attribute.

[6] How does the runtime know whether a class supports the IFormatter interface? Query the metadata!

uses a binary, compact format for serializing and deserializing on platforms that support the Common Language Runtime. The **SoapFormatter** uses the industry-standard SOAP protocol that is discussed in Chapter 11 on Web Services. Since it is an XML-, and therefore text-based protocol, it can be used to communicate with a non-CLR-based platform. The binary format is faster when serializing and deserializing data.

You can, of course, implement your own formatter classes. You might do this if you had to talk to a system with its own legacy byte format.

The **Serialization** example has code to demonstrate saving and restoring both binary and SOAP formats using a **FileStream**. Of course, you could use any **Stream**-based class representing some data medium.

```
private static void Save(HotelBroker broker,
  string formatter)
{
  FileStream s;
  if (formatter == "b")
  {
    s = new FileStream("hotels.bin", FileMode.Create);
    BinaryFormatter b = new BinaryFormatter();
    b.Serialize(s, broker);
  }
  else
  {
    s = new FileStream("hotels.txt", FileMode.Create);
    SoapFormatter sf = new SoapFormatter();
    sf.Serialize(s, broker);
  }
  s.Close();
}
private static void Load(ref HotelBroker broker,
  string formatter)
{
  FileStream s;
  if (formatter == "b")
  {
    s = new FileStream("hotels.bin", FileMode.Open);
    BinaryFormatter b = new BinaryFormatter();
    broker = (HotelBroker) b.Deserialize(s);
  }
  else
  {
    s = new FileStream("hotels.txt", FileMode.Open);
    SoapFormatter sf = new SoapFormatter();
    broker = (HotelBroker)sf.Deserialize(s);
  }
  s.Close();
```

Here is some sample output from the **Serialization** example. First we add a hotel and save it with the SOAP formatter. We then exit the program.

```
Enter command: cities
Atlanta
Boston
Commands: quit, cities, list, add, fetch, save

Enter command: list
City            Name                Rooms       Rate
Atlanta         Dixie               100         115
Atlanta         Marriott            500         70
Boston          Sheraton            250         95
Commands: quit, cities, list, add, fetch, save

Enter command: add
Hotel City: Philadelphia
Hotel Name: Franklin
Number Rooms: 100
Room Rate: 200
Commands: quit, cities, list, add, fetch, save

Enter command: save
Formatter: b(inary), s(oap)s
Commands: quit, cities, list, add, fetch, save

Enter command: cities
Atlanta
Boston
Philadelphia
Commands: quit, cities, list, add, fetch, save

Enter command: list
City            Name                Rooms       Rate
Atlanta         Dixie               100         115
Atlanta         Marriott            500         70
Boston          Sheraton            250         95
Philadelphia    Franklin            100         200
Commands: quit, cities, list, add, fetch, save

Enter command: quit
```

We then run the program again and restore what we saved[7] in the first run.

```
Enter command: cities
Atlanta
Boston
Commands: quit, cities, list, add, fetch, save
```

---

[7] If you look at the **hotels.txt** file you will see a huge file, with a lot of "empty" entries. This stems from the simplistic array data structure we used for reservations, which is a very sparse matrix.

```
Enter command: list
City              Name                    Rooms      Rate
Atlanta           Dixie                   100        115
Atlanta           Marriott                500        70
Boston            Sheraton                250        95
Commands: quit, cities, list, add, fetch, save

Enter command: fetch
Formatter: b(inary), s(oap)s
City              Name                    Rooms      Rate
Atlanta           Dixie                   100        115
Atlanta           Marriott                500        70
Boston            Sheraton                250        95
Philadelphia      Franklin                100        200
Commands: quit, cities, list, add, fetch, save

Enter command: cities
Atlanta
Boston
Philadelphia
```

## ISerializable

Sometimes the serialization provided by the Framework is not satisfactory. You can provide custom serialization for a class by implementing the **ISerializable** interface and adding a constructor to the class. The **ISerializable** interface has one member: **GetObjectData**. This method is used when data is serialized.

The **ISerializable** example demonstrates how this is done. As before, the class has to be marked as **Serializable**.

```
[Serializable]
public class HotelBroker : Broker, IHotelInfo,
IHotelAdmin, IHotelReservation, ISerializable
{
  private const int MAXDAY = 366;
  private const int MAXUNIT = 10;
  private ArrayList cities;
...
```

The **SerializationInfo** class is used to store all the data that needs to be saved. This class's **AddValue** method is overloaded to handle the saving of various types, including **object**.[8] When you save the type you provide a name that is used to recall the object when deserializing the data. The **StreamingContext** class gives you information about the stream being used in the serialization. For example, you can find out if the stream being used is a file or is being remoted to another computer.

```
public void GetObjectData(SerializationInfo info,
  StreamingContext context)
{
  long numberHotels = units.Count;
  info.AddValue("NumberHotels", numberHotels);
  info.AddValue("Hotels", units);
}
```

You also have to implement a special constructor that is used by the framework to recreate the object when it is deserialized. It has the same arguments as does **GetObjectData**. Here you use the various Get methods on **SerializationInfo** to restore the data. Note that since we did not save the cities field, we had to manually restore it. The constructor is private because only the Framework uses it. If you forget to add the constructor, you will get a **SerializationException** when you try to restore the object.

```
private HotelBroker(SerializationInfo info,
  StreamingContext context) : base(MAXDAY, MAXUNIT)
{
  long numberHotels = info.GetInt32("NumberHotels");
  units = (ArrayList)info.GetValue("Hotels",
    typeof(ArrayList));
  if (numberHotels == units.Count)
    Console.WriteLine("All hotels deserialized.");
  else
    Console.WriteLine("Error in deserialization.");

  cities = new ArrayList();
  foreach(Hotel h in units)
    AddCity(h.City);

}
```

In this example we only did custom serialization for the **HotelBroker** object. For all the other objects we still relied on the Framework's

---

[8] Some of the **AddValue** overloads are not CLS compliant when the types being saved are not CLS-compliant types such as unsigned integers. Be careful not to use those types where .NET language interoperability is required. You have to watch for this in other places in the Framework such as the **Convert** class or the **Parse** methods of the various CTS types, or any other place where data is formatted, converted, read, or written out (such as the **TextWriter** classes).

serialization. This example works the same way that the **Serialization** example did. The sample output would look the same.

# .NET Application Model

Serialization gave you a concrete example of the flexible environment the .NET Framework provides for writing code. Now let us take a look at the model in which .NET applications run. The Win32 environment in which a program runs is called its process. This environment consists of

- the address space in which the code and data of the program reside
- one or more threads
- a set of environmental variables that is associated with the program
- a current drive and directory

## Threads

A thread is the actual execution path of a program's code. One or more threads run inside a process to allow for multiple execution paths inside a process. With multiple threads, for example, a program can update the user interface with partial results on one thread as a calculation proceeds on another thread. All threads in the same process share the process environment, so that they can all access process memory.

Threads are scheduled by the operating system; processes and application domains[9] are not scheduled. Threads are given a limited timeslice in which to run, so that they can share the processor with other threads. Higher-priority threads will get to run more often than lower-priority threads. After some time elapses, a thread will get another chance to run. When a thread is restarted, it resumes running from where it was stopped.

Threads maintain a context, which has to be saved and restored when the operating system's scheduler switches from one thread to another. A thread's context includes the machine registers and stack that contain the state of the executing code.

The **System.Threading.Thread** class models an executing thread. The **Thread** object that represents the current executing thread can be found from the static property **System.Threading.Thread.CurrentThread**.

Unless your code runs on a multiprocessor machine, or you are trying to use time while a uniprocessor waits for some event such as an I/O event, using multiple threads does not save any time on your computing tasks. It does, however, allow making the system seem more responsive to tasks requiring user interaction. Using too many threads can decrease performance as contention between the threads for the CPU increases.

---

[9] Application domains are discussed later in this chapter.

To help you understand threads we provide a four-part **Threading** example that uses the **Customer** and **Hotel** assemblies from the case study to make reservations. Let us look first at Step 0. The code is found in the file **Threading.cs**.

.NET threads run as delegates defined by the **System.Threading. ThreadStart** class. The delegate returns void and takes no parameters.

```
public delegate void ThreadStart();
```

The **NewReservation** class has a public member function **MakeReservation** that will define the thread function. Since the thread function takes no parameters, any data that this function uses is assigned to fields in the **NewReservation** instance.

```
ThreadStart threadStart1 = new
    ThreadStart(reserve1.MakeReservation);
```

The thread delegate is created and passed as a parameter to the constructor that creates the **System.Threading.Thread** instance. The **Start** method on the **Thread** instance is invoked to begin the thread's execution. When we discuss the asynchronous programming model, we will show you how to pass parameters to a thread delegate. The program now has two threads—the original one that executed the code to start the program, and the thread we have just created that attempts to make a hotel reservation.

```
public class NewReservation
  {
  . . .
  public void MakeReservation()
  {
    . . .
     Console.WriteLine("Thread {0} starting.",
       Thread.CurrentThread.GetHashCode());
    . . .
     ReservationResult result =
       hotelBroker.MakeReservation(customerId, city, hotel,
       date, numberDays);
     . . .
  }
}
  . . .
  NewReservation reserve1 = new NewReservation(customers,
     hotelBroker);
  reserve1.customerId = 1;
  reserve1.city = "Boston";
  reserve1.hotel = "Presidential";
  reserve1.sdate = "12/12/2001";
```

```
reserve1.numberDays = 3;

ThreadStart threadStart1 = new
    ThreadStart(reserve1.MakeReservation);
Thread thread1 = new Thread(threadStart1);
Console.WriteLine("Thread {0} starting a new thread.",
    Thread.CurrentThread.GetHashCode());
thread1.Start();
```

To cause the original thread to wait until the second thread is done, the **Join** method on the **System.Threading.Thread** instance is called. The original thread now blocks (waits) until the reservation thread is complete. The results of the reservation request are written to the console by the reservation thread.

```
thread1.Join();
Console.WriteLine("Done!");
```

## THREAD SYNCHRONIZATION

An application can create multiple threads. Look at the code in Step 1 of the **Threading** example. Now multiple reservation requests are being made simultaneously.

```
NewReservation reserve1 = new NewReservation(customers,
                         hotelBroker);
. . .
NewReservation reserve2 = new NewReservation(customers,
                         hotelBroker);
. . .
ThreadStart threadStart1 = new
                ThreadStart(reserve1.MakeReservation);
ThreadStart threadStart2 = new
                ThreadStart(reserve2.MakeReservation);

Thread thread1 = new Thread(threadStart1);
Thread thread2 = new Thread(threadStart2);

thread1.Start();
thread2.Start();

thread1.Join();
thread2.Join();
```

The problem with our reservation systems is that there is no guarantee that one thread will not interfere with the work being done with the other thread. Threads run only for a brief period before they are interrupted and another thread is scheduled to run on the processor. They may not be finished with whatever operation they were working on when their timeslice is up.

For example, they might be in the middle of updating a data structure. If another thread tries to use the information in that data structure, or update the data structure, the results of operations will be at best inconsistent and incorrect, and at worst a system crash (i.e., if references to obsolete structures were not yet updated).

Let us look at one of several places in the customer and reservation code where we could have a problem. Examine the code for the **Reserve** method in the file **broker.cs**. First a check is made of the existing bookings for a given hotel for a given date to see if rooms are available. If there are, the booking is made.

```
. . .
// Check if rooms are available for all dates
for (int i = day; i < day + numDays; i++)
{
  if (numCust[i, unitid] >= unit.capacity)
  {
    result.ReservationId = -1;
    result.Comment = "Room not available";
    return result;
  }
}

. . .
// Reserve a room for requested dates
for (int i = day; i < day + numDays; i++)
  numCust[i, unitid] += 1;
. . .
```

This code can produce inconsistent results! One thread could be rescheduled after it finds that the last room is available, but before it gets a chance to make the booking. The other thread could run, find the same available room, and make the booking. When the second thread runs again, starting from where it left off, it will also book the last room at the hotel.

To simulate this occurrence, this step of the threading example puts a **System.Threading.Thread.Sleep** call between the code that checks for availability and the code that makes the booking. The **Sleep(0)** call will cause the thread to stop executing and give up the remainder of its timeslice. We then setup our program so that the two threads try to reserve the only room at a hotel for the same time. Examine the code in the **Main** routine that sets this up:

```
hotelBroker.AddHotel("Boston", "Presidential", 1,
                     (decimal) 10000);
. . .

NewReservation reserve1 = new NewReservation(customers,
                     hotelBroker);
```

```
reserve1.customerId = 1;
reserve1.city = "Boston";
reserve1.hotel = "Presidential";
reserve1.sdate = "12/12/2001";
reserve1.numberDays = 3;

NewReservation reserve2 = new NewReservation(customers,
                         hotelBroker);

reserve2.customerId = 2;
reserve2.city = "Boston";
reserve2.hotel = "Presidential";
reserve2.sdate = "12/13/2001";
reserve2.numberDays = 1;
```

Running the program will give results something like this:

```
Added Boston Presidential Hotel with one room.
Thread 3 starting  new threads.
Thread 5 starting.
Reserving for Customer 1 at the Boston Presidential Hotel
on 12/12/2001 12:00:00 AM for 3 days
Thread 5 entered Broker::Reserve
Thread 5 sleeping in Broker::Reserve
Thread 6 starting.
Reserving for Customer 2 at the Boston Presidential Hotel
on 12/13/2001 12:00:00 AM for 1 days
Thread 6 entered Broker::Reserve
Thread 6 sleeping in Broker::Reserve
Thread 5 left Broker::Reserve
Reservation for Customer 1 has been booked
ReservationId = 1
ReservationRate = 10000
ReservationCost = 30000
Comment = OK
Thread 6 left Broker::Reserve
Reservation for Customer 2 has been booked
ReservationId = 2
ReservationRate = 10000
ReservationCost = 10000
Comment = OK
Done!
```

Both customers get to reserve the last room on December 13! Note how Thread 5 enters the Reserve method and finds the room is available before it gets rescheduled. Thread 6 enters Reserve and also finds the room is available before it gets rescheduled. Thread 5 then books the room, and Thread 6 does as well.

Operating systems provide means for synchronizing the operation of multiple threads, or multiple processes accessing shared resources. The .NET Framework provides several mechanisms to prevent threading conflicts.

Every object in the .NET framework can be used to provide a synchronized section of code (critical section). Only one thread at a time can execute within such a section. If one thread is already executing inside that synchronized code section, any threads that attempt to access that section will block (wait) until the executing thread leaves it.

### SYNCHRONIZATION WITH MONITORS

The **System.Threading.Monitor** class allows you to create a critical section by synchronizing on an object to avoid race conditions or incorrect answers. Step 2 of the **Threading** example demonstrates the use of the **Monitor** class with the **this** pointer of the **HotelBroker** instance.

```
public ReservationResult Reserve(Reservation res)
{
  . . .
  Monitor.Enter(this);
  . . .
  Monitor.Exit(this);
  return result;
}
```

The thread that first calls the **Monitor.Enter(this)** method will be allowed to execute the code of the **Reserve** method because it will acquire the **Monitor** lock based on the **this** pointer. Subsequent threads that try to execute will be forced to wait until the first thread releases the lock with **Monitor.Exit(this)**. At that point they will be able to call **Monitor.Enter(this)** and acquire the lock.

A thread can call **Monitor.Enter** several times, but each call must be balanced by a call to **Monitor.Exit.** If a thread wants to try to acquire a lock, but does not want to block so that it can do some work and try again, it can use the **Monitor.TryEnter** method.

In C# you can use the **lock** keyword in place of **Monitor.Enter/Exit**. With the **lock** keyword, the above fragment would be:

```
public ReservationResult Reserve(Reservation res)
{
  lock(this);
  {
    . . .
  }
  return result;
}
```

Now that we have provided synchronization, the identical case tried in Step 1 does not result in one reservation too many for the hotel. Notice how the second thread cannot enter the Reserve method until the first thread that entered has left.

```
Added Boston Presidential Hotel with one room.
Thread 3 launching 2 threads.
Thread 5 starting.
Reserving for Customer 1 at the Boston Presidential Hotel
on 12/12/2001 12:00:00 AM for 3 days
Thread 5 trying to enter Broker::Reserve
Thread 5 entered Broker::Reserve
Thread 6 starting.
Reserving for Customer 2 at the Boston Presidential Hotel
on 12/13/2001 12:00:00 AM for 1 days
Thread 6 trying to enter Broker::Reserve
Thread 5 left Broker::Reserve
Thread 6 entered Broker::Reserve
Thread 6 left Broker::Reserve
Reservation for Customer 2 could not be booked
Room not available
Reservation for Customer 1 has been booked
ReservationId = 1
ReservationRate = 10000
ReservationCost = 30000
Comment = OK
Done!
```

## NOTIFICATION WITH MONITORS

A thread that has acquired a **Monitor** lock can wait for a signal from another thread that is synchronizing on that same object without leaving the synchronization block. The thread invokes the **Monitor.Wait** method and relinquishes the lock. When notified by another thread, it reacquires the synchronization lock.

A thread that has acquired a **Monitor** lock can send notification to another thread waiting on the same object with the **Pulse** or the **PulseAll** methods. It is important that the receiving thread be waiting when the pulse is sent; otherwise, if the pulse is sent before the wait, the other thread will wait forever and will never see the notification. This is unlike the reset events discussed later in this chapter. If multiple threads are waiting, the **Pulse** method will put only one thread on the ready queue to run. The **PulseAll** will put all of them on the ready queue.

The pulsing thread no longer has the monitor lock but is not blocked from running. Since it is no longer blocked, but does not have the lock, to avoid a deadlock or race condition this thread should try to reacquire the lock (through a **Monitor.Enter** or **Wait**) before doing any potentially damaging work.

The **PulseAll** example illustrates the **Pulse** and **PulseAll** methods. Running the example produces the following output:

```
First thread: 2 started.
Thread: 5 started.
Thread: 6 started.
Thread: 6 waiting.
Thread: 5 waiting.
Thread 6 sleeping.
Done.
Thread 6 awake.
Thread: 6 exited.
Thread 5 sleeping.
Thread 5 awake.
Thread: 5 exited.
```

The class **X** has a field "o" of type object that will be used for a synchronization lock.

The class also has a method **Test** that will be used as a thread delegate. The method acquires the synchronization lock and then waits for a notification. When it gets the notification, it sleeps for half a second and then relinquishes the lock.

The main method creates two threads that use **Test** method of class **X** as their thread delegate and share the same object to use for synchronization. It then sleeps for 2 seconds to allow the threads to issue their wait requests and relinquish their locks. Next it calls **PulseAll** to notify both waiting threads and relinquishes its hold on the locks. Eventually each thread will reacquire the lock, write a message to the console, and relinquish the lock for the last time.

```
class X
{
  object o;

  public X(object o)
  {
    this.o = o;
  }
  public void Test()
  {
    try
      {
        long threadId =Thread.CurrentThread.GetHashCode();
        Console.WriteLine("Thread:{0} started.",threadId);
        Monitor.Enter(o);
        Console.WriteLine("Thread:{0} waiting.",threadId);
        Monitor.Wait(o);
        Console.WriteLine("Thread {0} sleeping",threadId);
        Thread.Sleep(500);
```

```
            Console.WriteLine("Thread {0} awake.", threadId);
            Monitor.Exit(o);
            Console.WriteLine("Thread: {0} exited.",threadId);
        }
    catch(Exception e)
        {
        long threadId =Thread.CurrentThread.GetHashCode();
        Console.WriteLine("Thread: {0} Exception: {1}",
                        threadId, e.Message);
        Monitor.Exit(o);
        }
    }
}

class Class1
{
  static public object o = new object();

  static void Main(string[] args)
  {
    Console.WriteLine("First thread: {0} started.",
                    Thread.CurrentThread.GetHashCode());
    X a = new X(o);
    X b = new X(o);

    ThreadStart ats = new ThreadStart(a.Test);
    ThreadStart bts = new ThreadStart(b.Test);

    Thread at = new Thread(ats);
    Thread bt = new Thread(bts);

    at.Start();
    bt.Start();

    Thread.Sleep(2000);
    Monitor.Enter(o);

    Monitor.PulseAll(o);
    // Monitor.Pulse(o);

    Monitor.Exit(o);

    Console.WriteLine("Done.");
  }
}
```

Comment out the **PulseAll** call, uncomment the **Pulse** call, and only one thread completes because the other thread is never put on the ready queue. Remove the **Sleep(2000)** from the main routine and the other threads block forever, because the pulse occurs before the threads get a chance to call the **Wait** method and hence they will never be notified.

These methods can be used to coordinate several threads' use of synchronization locks.

The **Thread.Sleep** method causes the current thread to stop execution (block) for a given time period. Calling **Thread.Suspend** will cause the thread to block until **Thread.Resume** is called on that same thread. Threads can also block because they are waiting for another thread to finish (**Thread.Join**). This method was used in the **Threading** examples so that the main thread could wait until the reservation requests were completed. Threads can also block because they are waiting on a synchronization lock.

A blocked thread can be awakened by calling **Thread.Interrupt** on the blocked thread. The thread will receive a **ThreadInterruptedException**. If it does not catch this exception, the runtime will catch it and kill the thread.

If, as a last resort, you have to kill a thread outright, call the **Thread.Abort** method on the thread. **Thread.Abort** causes the **ThreadAbortException** to be thrown. This exception cannot be caught, but it will cause all the **finally** blocks to be executed. In addition, **Thread.Abort** does not cause the thread to wake up from a wait.

Since **finally** blocks may take a while to execute, or the thread might be waiting, aborted threads may not terminate immediately. If you need to be sure that the thread has finished, you should wait on the thread's termination using **Thread.Join**.

## SYNCHRONIZATION CLASSES

The .NET Framework has classes that represent the standard Win32 synchronization objects. These classes all derive from the abstract **WaitHandle** class. This class has static methods, **WaitAll** and **WaitAny**, that allow you to wait for all of a set of synchronization objects being signaled or on just one of a set of synchronization objects being signaled. It also has an instance method, **WaitOne**, that allows you to wait for this instance to be signaled. How the object gets signaled depends on the particular type of synchronization object that is derived from **WaitHandle**.

A **Mutex** object is used for interprocess synchronization. **Monitors** and synchronized code sections work only within one process. An **AutoResetEvent** and **ManualResetEvent** are used to signal whether an event has occurred. An **AutoResetEvent** remains signaled until a waiting thread is released. A **ManualResetEvent** remains signaled until its state is set to unsignaled with the **Reset** method. Hence many threads could be signaled by this event. Unlike **Monitors**, code does not have to be waiting for the signal before the pulse is set for the reset events to signal a thread.

The Framework has provided classes to solve some standard threading problems. The **Interlocked** class methods allow atomic operations on shared values such as increment, decrement, comparison, and exchange. **ReaderWriterLock** is used to allow single-writer, multiple-reader access to data structures. The **ThreadPool** class can be used to manage a pool of worker threads.

## AUTOMATIC SYNCHRONIZATION

You can use attributes to synchronize the access to instance methods and fields of a class. Access to static fields and methods is not synchronized. To do this, you derive the class from the class **System.ContextBoundObject** and apply a **Synchronization** attribute to the class. This attribute cannot be applied to an individual method or field.

The attribute is found in **the System.Runtime.Remoting.Contexts** namespace. It describes the synchronization requirements of an instance of the class to which it is applied. You can pass one of four values which are static fields of the **SynchronizationAttribute** class to the **SynchronizatonAttribute** constructor: NOT_SUPPORTED, SUPPORTED, REQUIRED, REQUIRES_NEW. The **Threading** example Step 3 illustrates how to do this.

```
Synchronization(SynchronizationAttribute.REQUIRED)]
public abstract class Broker : ContextBoundObject
{
. . .
```

In order for the CLR to make sure that the thread in which this object runs on is synchronized properly, the CLR has to track the threading requirements of this object. This state is referred to as the *context* of the object. If one object needs to be synchronized, and another does not, they are in two separate contexts. The CLR has to acquire a synchronization lock on behalf of the code when a thread that is executing a method on the object that does not need to be synchronized starts executing a method on an object that does. The CLR knows that this has to be done because it can compare the threading requirements of the first object with the threading requirements of the second object by comparing their contexts.

Objects that share the same state are said to live in the same context. For example, two objects that do not need to be synchronized can share the same context. **ContextBoundObject** and Contexts are discussed in more detail in the section on Contexts.

With this intuitive understanding of contexts we can now explain the meaning of the various Synchronization attributes. NOT_SUPPORTED means that the class cannot support synchronization of its instance methods and fields and therefore must not be created in a synchronized context. REQUIRED means that the class requires synchronization of access to its instance methods and fields. If a thread is already being synchronized, however, it can use the same synchronization lock and live in an existing synchronization context. REQUIRES_NEW means that not only is synchronization required, but access to its instance methods and fields must be with a unique synchronization lock and context. SUPPORTED means that the class does not require synchronization of access to its instance methods and fields, but a new context does not have to be created for it.

You can also pass a Boolean flag to the constructor to indicate if reentrancy is required. If required, call-outs from methods are synchronized. Otherwise, only calls into methods are synchronized.

With this attribute there is no need for **Monitor.Enter** and **Monitor.Exit** in the **Broker::Reserve** method.

Just as in Step 2, this example attempts to make two reservations for the last room in a Hotel. In addition, a third thread attempts to cancel a reservation. Here is the output from running this example:

```
Added Boston Presidential Hotel with one room.
Thread 13 launching 3 threads.
MakeReservation: Thread 28 starting.
Reserving for Customer 1 at the Boston Presidential Hotel
on 12/12/2001 12:00:00 AM for 3 days
Thread 28 entered Reserve.
MakeReservation: Thread 29 starting.
Reserving for Customer 2 at the Boston Presidential Hotel
on 12/13/2001 12:00:00 AM for 1 days
CancelReservation: Thread 30 starting.
Cancelling Reservation 10
Thread 28 left Reserve.
Thread 29 entered Reserve.
Thread 29 left Reserve.
Reservation for Customer 2 could not be booked
Room not available
Thread 30 entered CancelReservation.
Thread 30 left CancelReservation.
Reservation for Customer 1 has been booked
ReservationId = 1
ReservationRate = 10000
ReservationCost = 30000
Comment = OK
Done!
```

As in the previous case the second thread could not enter the **Reserve** method until the thread that entered first finished. Only one reservation is made.

What is different about using the automatic approach is that you get the synchronization in *all* the methods of the class whether you need it or not. Accessing any data in the class is also singly threaded.

Note how only one thread can be in any method of the class; a thread using **CancelReservation** blocks threads from using **MakeReservation**. With a reservation system this is the behavior you want, since you do not want the **MakeReservation** to attempt to use a data structure that might be in the middle of being modified. In situations where a method on the object does not require synchronization, however, you will be synchronized anyway and the interactivity of the application will be reduced.

The other drawback to this approach is that it can increase contention and interfere with scalability since you are not just locking around the specific areas that need synchronizing.

The attribute approach is simpler than using critical sections. You do not have to worry about the details of the getting the synchronization correct. On the other hand, you get behavior that reduces interactivity and scalability. Different applications, or different parts of the same application, will choose the approach that makes the most sense.

## Thread Isolation

An exception generated by one thread will not cause another thread to fail. The **ThreadIsolation** example demonstrates this.

```
class tm
{
public void m()
{
  Console.WriteLine("Thread {0} started",
                    Thread.CurrentThread.GetHashCode());
  Thread.Sleep(1000);
  for(int i = 0; i < 10; i++)
    Console.WriteLine(i);
}
class te
{
  public void tue()
  {
    Console.WriteLine("Thread {0} started",
                      Thread.CurrentThread.GetHashCode());
    Exception e = new Exception("Thread Exception");
    throw e;
  }
}
class ThreadIsolation
{
  static void Main(string[] args)
  {
    tm tt = new tm();
    te tex = new te();
    ThreadStart ts1 = new ThreadStart(tt.m);
    ThreadStart ts2 = new ThreadStart(tex.tue);
    Thread thread1 = new Thread(ts1);
```

```
Thread thread2 = new Thread(ts2);
Console.WriteLine("Thread {0} starting new threads.",
                  Thread.CurrentThread.GetHashCode());
thread1.Start();
thread2.Start();
Console.WriteLine("Thread {0} done.",
                  Thread.CurrentThread.GetHashCode());
    }
}
```

The following output is generated. Note how the second thread can continue to write out the numbers even though the first thread has aborted from the unhandled exception. Note also how the "main" thread that spawned the other two threads can finish without causing the others to terminate.

```
Thread 2 starting new threads.
Thread 2 done.
Thread 5 started
Thread 6 started

Unhandled Exception: System.Exception: Thread Exception
at te.tue() in F:\Work\ThreadIsolation.cs:line 23
0
1
2
3
4
5
6
7
8
9
```

The **AppDomain** class (discussed later in the chapter) allows you to set up a handler to catch an **UnhandledException** event.

## Synchronization of Collections

Some lists, such as **TraceListeners**, are thread safe. When this collection is modified, a copy is modified and the reference is set to the copy. Most collections, like **ArrayList**, are not thread safe. Making them automatically thread safe would decrease the performance of the collection even when thread safety was not an issue.

An **ArrayList** has a static **Synchronized** method to return a thread-safe version of the **ArrayList**. The **IsSynchronized** property allows you to test whether the **ArrayList** you are using is the thread-safe version. The

**SyncRoot** property can return an object that can be used to synchronize access to a collection. This allows other threads that might be using the **ArrayList** to be synchronized with the same object.

# Context

In order for us to understand how the runtime is able to enforce a threading requirement based on an attribute, we have to introduce the concept of context. Step 4 of the **Threading** example is the same code as Step 3, but with some additional output:

```
Is the customer object a proxy? False
Is the bookings object a proxy? True
Added Boston Presidential Hotel with one room.
Thread 13 ContextId 0 launching 3 threads.
MakeReservation: Thread 28 ContextId 0 starting.
Reserving for Customer 1 at the Boston Presidential Hotel
                on 12/12/2001 12:00:00 AM for 3 days
Thread 28 ContextId 1 entered Reserve.
MakeReservation: Thread 29 ContextId 0 starting.
Reserving for Customer 2 at the Boston Presidential Hotel
                on 12/13/2001 12:00:00 AM for 1 days
CancelReservation: Thread 30 ContextId 0 starting.
Cancelling Reservation 10
Thread 28 ContextId 1 left Reserve.
Thread 29 ContextId 1 entered Reserve.
Thread 29 ContextId 1 left Reserve.
Reservation for Customer 2 could not be booked
Room not available
Thread 30 ContextId 1 entered CancelReservation.
Thread 30 ContextId 1 left CancelReservation.
Reservation for Customer 1 has been booked
ReservationId = 1
ReservationRate = 10000
ReservationCost = 30000
Comment = OK
```

In the last step of the **Threading** example we see that when a thread enters a method of the **Broker** class, it has a different ContextId than when it runs outside of the **Broker** class. It runs in a different context.

```
MakeReservation: Thread 28 ContextId 0 starting.
...
    Thread 28 ContextId 1 entered Reserve.
```

Objects derived from **Broker** have different runtime requirements (such as different synchronization requirements) than the other objects in the program, since access to **Broker** objects must be synchronized and access to other objects need not be synchronized. The environment that represents an object's runtime requirements that the CLR needs to be aware of is called a *context*. There are two contexts in the **Threading** Step 3 example—Context 1 where the **Broker** object lives and Context 0 where all other objects live. Every thread in the program runs in Context 1 when executing inside a **Broker** object, Context 0 everywhere else. Contexts are independent of threads.

A context is a collection of one or more objects that have identical runtime requirements. The .NET concept of a context is identical to the COM+ concept of a context.[10] In general you cannot say what the runtime must do to in a given context because it depends on exactly what the runtime requirements are. A context that has transactional requirements requires different action than one that does not. Or a context that has to maintain a REQUIRED synchronization requirement is different from one that has to maintain a REQUIRES_NEW synchronization requirement.

You can get the **Context** class instance that represents the current context from the static property **Thread.CurrentContext**. **ContextId** is a property of that class.

## Proxies and Stubs

How does the runtime enforce the different requirements of different contexts? When an object resides in another context (such as the **HotelBroker** object in the **NewReservation** instance), an object reference to a proxy object is returned instead of a reference to the object itself. The actual object resides in its original, or home, context. The proxy is an object that represents the original object in a different context. The static method **RemotingServices.IsTransparentProxy** determines whether an object reference points to a real object instance or a proxy. Look at the code in the **Threading** Step 4 example main routine:

```
hotelBroker = new HotelBroker();
customers = new Customers();

bool bTrans;
bTrans = RemotingServices.IsTransparentProxy(customers);
Console.WriteLine("Is the customer object a proxy? {0}",
                                                bTrans);

bTrans = RemotingServices.IsTransparentProxy(hotelBroker);
```

---

[10] At this point in time, though, COM+ contexts and .NET contexts are different. For a discussion of contexts in COM+ see *Understanding and Programming COM+* by Robert J. Oberg.

```
Console.WriteLine("Is the bookings object a proxy? {0}",
                                              bTrans);
```

which causes the following output:

```
Is the customer object a proxy? False
Is the bookings object a proxy? True
```

When a program starts up it is given a default context.[11] All objects, like the **Customers** object, that do not have any special requirements are created inside that context (context 0). An object, such as the **HotelBroker** object, that has a different set of requirements (synchronization) is created in a different context (context 1), and a proxy is returned to the creating context (context 0).

Now when you access the **MakeReservation** method in the **HotelBroker** object, you are actually accessing a method on the proxy. The proxy method can apply the synchronization lock and then delegate to the actual **HotelBroker** object's method. When the actual object's method returns, it returns to the proxy. The proxy can then remove the synchronization lock and return to the caller. This technique, where the runtime uses a proxy to intercept method calls to the actual object, is called *interception*.

## ContextBoundObject

The **Broker** class has to derive from the class **ContextBoundObject** so that the runtime knows to setup a different context if one is required. If you remove the derivation of **Broker** from **ContextBoundObject**, you will once again get the unsynchronized access, and both customers will be able to reserve the last room at the hotel, even though the class is still marked with the **Synchronization** attribute. Objects that do not derive from **ContextBoundObject** can run in any context (agile objects).

Since other contexts work with a proxy, or a reference to the actual object, the runtime must translate (marshal) the call from one context to another. Hence, **ContextBoundObject** inherits from **MarshalByRefObject**. **MarshalByRefObject** is the base class for objects that want to be able to be marshaled by reference. Otherwise, as we will discuss in the section on application domains, by default, objects are marshaled by value (i.e., copied).

One advantage of using synchronization techniques such as a **Monitor** is that a **Monitor** can be called from any context. Another potential disadvantage of using automatic synchronization is the performance hit from marshaling and using proxies rather than the actual object.

---

[11] As will be clear in the next section, the sentence should really read, "When a new application domain starts up, it is given a new default context." Contexts are application-domain relative. Two different application domains will have two separate default contexts, each with id 0.

As will be clear when we discuss Application Domains, since the customer object has no dependency on context, it is the actual object, not a proxy. It can be copied to any context within the same application domain.

## Application Isolation

When writing applications it is often necessary to isolate parts of them so that a failure of one part does not cause a failure in another. In Windows, application isolation has been at the process level. In other words, if a process is stopped or crashes, other processes will be unaffected. Unless shared memory is used, one process cannot directly address memory in another process's address space.

For an application to use separate processes to achieve isolation is expensive. To switch from one process to another, the contents of the machine registers must be saved and restored. This includes a thread and process switch. A thread switch requires saving registers, such as the instruction pointer, and loading the information for a new thread, as well as updating the scheduling information for the threads. A process switch includes, accounting information and processor rights that have to be saved for the old process and restored for the new one.

### Application Domain

The .NET Application Domain is a more lightweight unit for application isolation, fault tolerance, and security. Multiple application domains can run in one process. Since the .NET code can be checked for type safety and security, the CLR can guarantee that one App Domain can run without interference from another App Domain in the same process. No process switch is required to achieve application isolation.

Application Domains can have multiple contexts, but a context exists in only one AppDomain. Although a thread runs in one context of one application domain at a time, the **Threading** example Step 3 demonstrates that a thread can execute in more than one context. One or more threads can run in an App Domain at the same time. An object lives in only one context.

Each AppDomain starts with a single thread and one context. Additional threads and contexts are added as needed.

There is no relationship between the number of application domains and threads. A Web server might require an application domain for each hosted application that runs in its process. The number of threads in that process would be far fewer, depending on how much actual concurrency the process can support.

To enforce application isolation, code in one application domain cannot make direct calls into the code (or even reference resources) in another application domain. They must use proxies.

## Application Domains and Assemblies

Applications are built from one or more assemblies, but each assembly is loaded into a particular application domain. Each application domain can be unloaded independently of the others, but you cannot unload an individual assembly from an App Domain. The assembly will be unloaded when the App Domain is unloaded. Unloading an App Domain also frees all resources associated with that App Domain.

Each process has a default application domain that is created when the process is started. This default domain can be unloaded only when the process shuts down.

Applications such as ASP.NET or Internet Explorer critically depend on preventing the various applications that run under it from interfering with each other. By never loading application code into the default domain, they can ensure that a crashing program will not bring down a host.

## AppDomain Class

The **AppDomain** class abstracts application domains. The **AppDomain** sample illustrates the use of application domains.

This class has static methods for creating and unloading application domains:

```
AppDomain domain = AppDmain.CreateDomain("CreatedDomain2",
                                         null, null);

. . .

AppDomain.Unload(domain);
```

While the **CreateDomain** method is overloaded, one signature illustrates application-domain isolation:

```
AppDomain CreateDomain(string Name, Evidence securityInfo,
                       AppDomainSetup info)
```

The **Evidence** parameter is a collection of the security constraints on the application domain. While we will discuss this in greater detail in the Security chapter, the domain's creator can modify this collection to control the permissions that the executing app domain can have. The **AppDomainSetup** parameter specifies setup information about the domain. Among the information specified is the location of the App Domain's configuration file and where private assemblies are loaded. Hence, each App Domain can be configured independently of every other. Code isolation, setup isolation, and control over security combine to ensure that application domains are independent of each other.

## App Domain Events

To help in maintaining application isolation, the AppDomain class allows you to set up event handlers for:

- when a domain unloads
- when the process exits
- when an unhandled exception occurs
- when attempts to resolve assemblies, types, and resources fail

## AppDomain Example

The **AppDomain** example lets us examine various aspects of application domains. If you run the example you will get the output in Figure 8–1.

```
F:\Work\Application Development Using C# and .NET\Chapter 08\AppDomain\bin\Debug\AppDomainTest.exe

At startup, Default AppDomain is AppDomainTest.exe ThreadId: 2 ContextId 0

ExecuteAssembly of TestApp.exe with no arguments in default domain.
        In TestApp Main, AppDomain AppDomainTest.exe ThreadId 2 ContextId 0
        Hello, Application Domain.
Execute Assembly returned: 50 AppDomain: AppDomainTest.exe ThreadId: 2 ContextId 0

Creating instance of serializable Customer object in default domain.
        Customers Constructor: AppDomain AppDomainTest.exe ThreadId 2 ContextId 0
Is handle to new customer object a proxy? : False
Is unwrapped customer object a proxy? : False
Registering a new customer object.
List customer objects.
GetCustomer: AppDomain AppDomainTest.exe ThreadId 2 ContextId 0
1    Rocket      Squirrel      rocky@frosbitefalls.com
2    Bullwinkle  Moose         moose@wossamotta.edu
3    John        Adams         jadams@presidents.org

Creating a new App Domain.
New AppDomain CreatedDomain1 created.
Creating instance of serializable Customer object in new domain.
        Customers Constructor: AppDomain CreatedDomain1 ThreadId 2 ContextId 0
Is handle to new customer object a proxy? : True
Is unwrapped customer object a proxy? : False
List customer objects.
GetCustomer: AppDomain AppDomainTest.exe ThreadId 2 ContextId 0
1    Rocket      Squirrel      rocky@frosbitefalls.com
2    Bullwinkle  Moose         moose@wossamotta.edu

Starting new thread in default AppDomain.
        Created new AppDomain CreatedDomain2 in new Thread Executing ThreadId: 61 ContextId 0
        Executing TestApp.exe with one argument in domain CreatedDomain2
        In TestApp Main, AppDomain CreatedDomain2 ThreadId 61 ContextId 0
        HotelBroker Constructor: AppDomain CreatedDomain2 ThreadId 61 ContextId 1
        HotelBroker MakeReservation: AppDomain CreatedDomain2 ThreadId 61 ContextId 1
        Reservation Id: 1
        Execute Assembly returned: 100 AppDomain: AppDomainTest.exe ThreadId: 61 ContextId 0

Press any key to continue
```

**Figure 8–1**    *Output of AppDomain example.*

First, the name, thread, and context of the default domain are written out.

```
AppDomain currentDomain = AppDomain.CurrentDomain;
Console.WriteLine("At startup, Default AppDomain is {0}
                ThreadId: {1} ContextId {2}\n",
                currentDomain.FriendlyName,
                Thread.CurrentThread.GetHashCode(),
                Thread.CurrentContext.ContextID);
```

We then load and execute an assembly. The code in this assembly just prints out a string and its domain's name, thread, and context. Notice that it executes in the default domain.

```
int val = currentDomain.ExecuteAssembly("TestApp.exe");
```

We then create an instance of the **Customers** type from the **Customer** assembly in the default domain. The **CreateInstance** method of the **AppDomain** class returns an **ObjectHandle** instance. You can pass this **ObjectHandle** between application domains without loading the metadata associated with the wrapped type. When you want to use the object as its actual type instead of as an opaque object instance, you must unwrap it by calling the **Unwrap** method on the **ObjectHandle** instance.

```
ObjectHandle oh = currentDomain.CreateInstance("Customer",
                          "OI.NetCs.Acme.Customers");
. . .
Customers custs = (Customers)oh.Unwrap();
```

We add a new customer and then list all the existing customers. Notice that both the constructor of this type and the methods execute in the same thread and context that the default domain does.

We then create a new domain and create an instance of the same type as before in that new domain.

```
AppDomain domain = AppDmain.CreateDomain("CreatedDomain1",
                          null, null);
. . .
oh = domain.CreateInstance("Customer",
                          "OI.NetCs.Acme.Customers");
. . .
Customers custs2 = (Customers)oh.Unwrap();
```

Note that the constructor call that results from the **CreateInstance** method executes in the new domain and is therefore in a different context from where the **CreateInstance** call was made, but it is executing on the same thread that made the **CreateInstance** call.

When we list the customers in this new object, we get a different list of customers. This is not surprising, since it is a different **Customers** object. Nonetheless, the customer list method executes in the default domain!

Using **RemotingServices.IsTransparentProxy**, we see that the **ObjectHandle** is a proxy to the **Customers** object that lives in the newly created AppDomain. However, when you unwrap the object to get an instance handle, you do not get a proxy, but you get an actual object reference. By default, objects are marshaled by value (copied) from one AppDomain to another.

If the **Customers** object is not serializable, you will get an exception when you try to copy it because the runtime will not know how to make the copy. This exception would be thrown when you do the **Unwrap**, not the **CreateInstance**. The latter returns a reference; the copy is made only when the **ObjectHandle** is unwrapped. If the object cannot be serialized, it cannot be copied from one AppDomain to another.

Next we create a new thread, and that thread creates a new application domain, loads, and executes an assembly. The assembly starts executing at its entry point, the **Main** routine of the **AppDomainTest** class.

```
AppDomain domain = AppDmain.CreateDomain("CreatedDomain2",
                                          null, null);
. . .
string[] args = new String[1];
args[0] = "MakeReservation";
int val = domain.ExecuteAssembly("TestApp.exe", null,
                                                  args);
. . .
AppDomain.Unload(domain);
```

The **Main** routine loads the **Hotel** assembly into the newly created App Domain. It then queries the metadata of the assembly for the **HotelBroker** type information. It uses that type information to create a **HotelBroker** object. The **HotelBroker** class is marked with a synchronization attribute. As a result, the **HotelBroker** constructor and the **MakeReservation** method run in a different context than the default context.

```
Assembly a = AppDomain.CurrentDomain.Load("Hotel");
Type typeHotelBroker =
    a.GetType("OI.NetCs.Acme.HotelBroker");
HotelBroker hotelBroker =
(HotelBroker)Activator.CreateInstance(typeHotelBroker);
DateTime date = DateTime.Parse("12/2/2001");
ReservationResult rr = hotelBroker.MakeReservation(1,
                          "Boston", "Sheraton", date, 3);
Console.WriteLine("\tReservation Id: {0}",
                                      rr.ReservationId);
```

## Marshaling, AppDomains, and Contexts

By default, objects are copied from one App Domain to another (marshal by value). The Remoting section will show how to marshal by reference between App Domains. This ensures that code in one application domain is isolated from another.

Objects are marshaled by reference between contexts. This allows the CLR to enforce the requirements (such as synchronization or transactions) of different objects. This is true whether the client of the object is in the same application domain or not.

Since most objects do not derive from **ContextBoundObject**, they can reside or move from one context to another as required. Threads can cross application domain and context boundaries within the same Win32 process.

# Asynchronous Programming

.NET supports a design pattern for asynchronous programming. This pattern is present in many places in .NET (including I/O operations, as noted earlier, and as we will see in Chapter 11 for Web services). Asynchronous programming provides a way for you to provide a method call without blocking the method caller. From the perspective of the client, the asynchronous model is easier to use than threading. It offers much less control over the synchronization than using synchronization objects, however, and the class designer would probably find threading much easier to use.

## The Asynchronous Design Pattern

This design pattern is composed of two parts, a set of methods and an interface **IAsyncResult**. The methods of the pattern are:

```
IAsyncResult BeginXXX(inputParams, AsyncCallback cb,
                                   Object AsyncObject)
ReturnValue EndXXX(outputParams, IAsyncResult ar);
```

As a design pattern, the XXX represents the actual method being called asynchronously (i.e., **BeginRead/EndRead** for the **System.IO.FileStream** class). The BeginXXX should pass all input parameters of the synchronous version (**in**, **in/out**, and **ref**) as well as the **AsyncCallback** and **AsyncObject** parameters. The EndXXX should have all the output parameters of the synchronous version (**ref** ,**out**, and **in/out**) parameters in its signature. It should return whatever object or value the synchronous version of the method would return. It should also have an **IAsyncResult** parameter. A CancelXXX can be provided if it makes sense.

The **AsyncCallback** is a delegate that represents a callback function.

```
public delegate void AsyncCallback(IAsyncResult ar);
```

The **AsyncObject** is available from **IAsyncResult**. It is provided so that in the callback function you can distinguish which asynchronous read the callback was generated by.

The Framework uses this pattern so that the **FileStream** synchronous **Read**

```
int Read(byte[] array, int offset, int count);
```

becomes in the asynchronous version:

```
IAsyncResult BeginRead(byte[] array, int offset,
            int numBytes, AsyncCallback userCallback,
```

```
                                                   object stateObject);
int EndRead(IAsyncResult asyncResult);
```

Any exception thrown from BeginXXX should be thrown before the asynchronous operation starts. Any exceptions from the asynchronous operation should be thrown from the EndXXX method.

## IAsyncResult

**IAsyncResult** is returned by a BeginXXX method (such as BeginRead). This interface has four elements:

```
interface IAsyncResult
{
    public boolean IsCompleted();
    public boolean CompletedSynchronously;
    public WaitHandle AsyncWaitHandle;
    public Object AsyncState;
}
```

**IsCompleted** is set to true after the server has processed the call. The client can then destroy all resources. If BeginXXX completed synchronously, **CompletedSynchronously** is set to true. Most of the time this is ignored, and **CompletedSynchronously** is set to the default value of false. In general, a client never knows whether the BeginXXX method executed asynchronously or asynchronously. If the asynchronous operation is not yet finished, the EndXXX method will block until it is.

The **AsyncWaitHandle** returns a **WaitHandle** that can be used for synchronization. As discussed previously, this handle can be signaled, so that the client can wait on it. Since you can specify a wait time period, you do not have to block forever if the operation is not yet complete.

The **AsyncState** is the object provided as the last argument in the BeginXXX call. Since it is contained in the **IAsyncResult** passed to the callback function, examining its value would allow you to determine which BeginXXX caused this particular instance of the callback.

## Using Delegates for Asynchronous Programming

Any developer of .NET objects who wants to provide an asynchronous interface should follow this pattern. Nonetheless, there is no need for most developers to develop a custom asynchronous solution for their objects. Delegates provide a very easy way to support asynchronous operations on any method without any action on the class developer's part. Of course, this has to be done with care, because the object was written with certain assumptions about the thread it is running on and its synchronization requirements.

The two **Asynch** examples use the **Customers** object from our case study **Customer** assembly. The first example registers new customers asynchronously and does some processing while waiting for each registration to finish. The second example uses a callback function with the asynchronous processing. In addition to allowing the program to do processing while waiting for the registrations to finish, the callback allows the system to take some asynchronous action for each individual registration.

In the examples, we just print out to the console to show where work could be done. To increase the waiting time to simulate longer processing times we have put calls to **Thread.Sleep()** in **Customers:: RegisterCustomer** as well as in the sample programs. Now let us look at the code within the examples.

Suppose the client wants to call the **RegisterCustomer** method asynchronously. The caller simply declares a delegate with the same signature as the method.

```
public delegate int RegisterCustomerCbk(string firstName,
                 string LastName, string EmailAddress);
```

You then make the actual method the callback function:

```
RegisterCustomerCbk rcc = new
          RegisterCustomerCbk(customers.RegisterCustomer);
```

## BEGIN/END INVOKE

When you declare a delegate, the compiler generates a class with a constructor and three methods: **BeginInvoke**, **EndInvoke**, and **Invoke.** The **BeginInvoke** and **EndInvoke** are type-safe methods that correspond to the BeginXXX and EndXXX methods and allow you to call the delegate asynchronously. The **Invoke** method is what the compiler implicitly uses when you call a delegate.[12] To call **RegisterCustomer** asynchronously just use the **BeginInvoke** and **EndInvoke** methods.

```
RegisterCustomerCbk rcc = new
          RegisterCustomerCbk(customers.RegisterCustomer);

for(int i = 1; i < 5; i++)
{
  firstName = "FirstName" + i.ToString();
  lastName = "SecondName" + (i * 2).ToString();
  emailAddress = i.ToString() + ".biz";

  IAsyncResult ar = rcc.BeginInvoke(firstName, lastName,
                          emailAddress, null, null);
```

---

[12] If you open the executable from the **DelegateAccount** example in Chapter 5 in ILDASM, you can observe this. The **NotifyCallback** class has the **BeginInvoke**, **EndInvoke**, and **Invoke** methods defined. If you look at the **Withdraw** method for **Account**, you will notice that the C# line **notifyDlg(balance)** has been transformed to **instance void NotifyCallback::Invoke(valuetype [mscorlib]System.Decimal).**

```
     while(!ar.IsCompleted)
     {
        Console.WriteLine("Could do some work here while wait-
  ing for customer registration to complete.");
        ar.AsyncWaitHandle.WaitOne(1, false);
     }
     customerId = rcc.EndInvoke(ar);
     Console.WriteLine("    Added CustomerId: " +
                          customerId.ToString());
  }
```

The program waits on the **AsyncWaitHandle** periodically to see if the registration has finished. If it has not, some work could be done in the interim. If **EndInvoke** is called before **RegisterCustomer** is complete, **EndInvoke** will block until **RegisterCustomer** is finished.

## ASYNCHRONOUS CALLBACK

Instead of waiting on a handle, you could pass a callback function to **BeginInvoke** (or a BeginXXX method).

```
RegisterCustomerCbk rcc = new
          RegisterCustomerCbk(customers.RegisterCustomer);
AsyncCallback cb = new AsyncCallback(CustomerCallback);
object objectState;
IAsyncResult ar;

for(int i = 5; i < 10; i++)
{
  firstName = "FirstName" + i.ToString();
  lastName = "SecondName" + (i * 2).ToString();
  emailAddress = i.ToString() + ".biz";
  objectState = i;
  ar = rcc.BeginInvoke(firstName, lastName,
                    emailAddress, cb, objectState);
}

Console.WriteLine
    ("Finished registrations...could some do work here.");
Thread.Sleep(25);
Console.WriteLine(
 "Finished work..waiting to let registrations complete.");
Thread.Sleep(1000);
```

You then get the results in the callback function:

```
public void CustomerCallback(IAsyncResult ar)
{
  int customerId;
```

```
AsyncResult asyncResult = (AsyncResult)ar;
RegisterCustomerCbk rcc =
         (RegisterCustomerCbk)asyncResult.AsyncDelegate;

customerId = rcc.EndInvoke(ar);
   Console.WriteLine("    AsyncState: {0} CustomerId {1}
added.", ar.AsyncState, customerId);
   Console.WriteLine("      Could do processing here.");
 return;
}
```

You could do some work when each customer registration was finished.

## Threading with Parameters

The asynchronous callback runs on a different thread from the one on which **BeginInvoke** was called. If your threading needs are simple and you want to pass parameters to your thread functions, you can use asynchronous delegates to do this. You do not need any reference to the **Threading** namespace. The reference to that namespace in the **AsynchThreading** example is just for the **Thread.Sleep** method needed for demo purposes.

**PrintNumbers** sums the numbers from the starting integer passed to it as an argument to 10 greater than the starting integer. It returns that sum to the caller. **PrintNumbers** can be used for the delegate defined by Print.

```
public delegate int Print(int i);

public class Numbers
{
  public int PrintNumbers(int start)
  {
    int threadId = Thread.CurrentThread.GetHashCode();
    Console.WriteLine("PrintNumbers Id: " +
                                    threadId.ToString());

    int sum = 0;
    for (int i = start; i < start + 10; i++)
    {
      Console.WriteLine(i.ToString());
      Thread.Sleep(500);
      sum += i;
    }

  return sum;
  }
}
```

The **Main** routine then defines two callbacks and invokes them explicitly with different starting integers. It waits until the both of the synchronization handles are signaled. **EndInvoke** is called on both, and the results are written to the console.

```
Numbers n = new Numbers();

Print pfn1 = new Print(n.PrintNumbers);
Print pfn2 = new Print(n.PrintNumbers);

IAsyncResult ar1 = pfn1.BeginInvoke(0, null, null);
IAsyncResult ar2 = pfn2.BeginInvoke(100, null, null);

WaitHandle[] wh = new WaitHandle[2];
wh[0] = ar1.AsyncWaitHandle;
wh[1] = ar2.AsyncWaitHandle;

// make sure everything is done before ending
WaitHandle.WaitAll(wh);

int sum1 = pfn1.EndInvoke(ar1);
int sum2 = pfn2.EndInvoke(ar2);

Console.WriteLine("Sum1 = " + sum1.ToString() +
                            " Sum2 = " + sum2.ToString());
```

Here is the program's output:

```
MainThread Id: 2
PrintNumbers Id: 13
0
PrintNumbers Id: 17
100
1
101
2
102
3
103
4
104
5
105
6
106
7
107
8
108
9
109
Sum1 = 45 Sum2 = 1045
```

# Remoting

While a complete discussion of remoting is beyond the scope of this book, a brief introduction provides a powerful example of how metadata and marshal by reference (MBR) work. Remoting also provides a mechanism for having executable servers.

Unlike remoting in Microsoft's COM technology, it requires a minimal amount of infrastructure programming. The small amount that is required allows programmers either a degree of flexibility or the ability to customize remoting for their particular applications.

The .NET framework provides two ways to provide connections between two applications on different computers. Web Services, discussed in Chapter 11, enable computers that do not host the Common Language Runtime to communicate with computers that do. The remoting technology discussed here builds distributed applications between computers that host the CLR.

## Remoting Overview

The key parts of Remoting are:

- Communication *channels* for transport of messages.
- *Interception* to allow for message generation for communication over the channels.
- *Formatters* to put the messages into a byte stream that is sent over the channel. These are the same formatters that were discussed in the section on serialization.

### INTERCEPTION

Proxies and stubs (referred to in .NET as dispatchers) transform the function calls on the client or server side into messages that are sent over the network. This is called interception, because the proxies and dispatchers intercept a method call to send it to its remote destination. Unlike COM, metadata provides the information so the CLR can generate the proxies and stubs for you.

A *proxy* takes the function call off the stackframe of the caller and transforms it into a message. The message is then sent to its destination. A *dispatcher* takes the message and transforms it into a stackframe so that a call can be made to the object.

For example, assume the **UnregisterCustomer** method from the **Customer** assembly runs in one App Domain and is called from another. It makes no difference whether the App Domains are in the same process or on the same machine.

The proxy would take the integer **id** argument on the stackframe of the client making the call and put it in a message that encoded the call and its argument. On the server side, the dispatcher would take that message and create a function call on the server's stack for the call **UnregisterCustomer (int id)** and make that call into the object. The client and server codes do not know that they are being remoted.

### CHANNELS AND FORMATTERS

The formatter converts the message into a byte stream. The .NET framework comes with two formatters, binary and SOAP (text-based XML discussed in Chapter 11 on Web Services). The byte stream is then sent over a communication channel.

The .NET framework comes with two channels, although you can write your own. The HTTP channel uses the HTTP protocol and is good for communicating over the Internet or through firewalls. The TCP channel uses the TCP (sockets) protocol and is designed for high-speed communication. You have four permutations of formatters and transport: binary over TCP, binary over HTTP, SOAP over HTTP, and SOAP over TCP.

## Remote Objects

Clients obtain a proxy by *activating* a remote object. Remote objects must derive from **MarshalByRefObject**, because you work with a proxy to the object reference, not with the object reference itself. This is the same concept discussed in the section on contexts, where marshal by reference is also used to access context bound objects.

Local objects passed as method parameters from one application domain to another can be passed by value (copied) or by reference.

To be passed by value, they must be serializable. The object is serialized, sent across the transport layer, and recreated on the other side. We have already seen this in the AppDomain example.

To be passed by reference, the class must derive from **MarshalByRefObject**. The Remoting example illustrates pass by reference.

Remote objects can be either server or client activated. Server-activated objects are not created until the first method call on the object. Server-activated objects come in two flavors. **SingleCall** objects are stateless. Each method cause a new object to be created. **Singleton** objects can be used by multiple client activation requests. **Singleton** objects can maintain state. **SingleCall** objects will scale better than **Singleton** objects because they do not retain state and can be load balanced.

Client-activated objects are activated when the client requests them. While they can last for multiple calls and hold state, they cannot store information from different client activations. This is similar to calling **CoCreateInstanceEx** in DCOM.

## Activation

Objects are activated on the client side in one of three ways by using the **Activator** class.

- **Activator.GetObject** is used to get a reference to a server-activated object.

- **Activator.CreateInstance** is used to create a client-activated object. You can pass parameters to the object's constructor using the overloaded **CreateInstance** method that takes an array of objects to be passed to the constructor.

- The C# **new** syntax can be used to create a server- or client-activated object. A configuration file is used to describe how **new** should be used.

## Sample Remotable Object

For our **Remoting** example, we remote our **Customers** object from the **Customer** assembly.

In the remoting example directory there are two solutions. One represents the client program, the other the server program. Each can be built independently of the other. Start the server program first. Notice that it waits for a client request. You can then run the client program, which will run against objects that live inside the server. We will discuss the details of the client and server code and output in the next few sections.

Notice that we had to make only two simple changes to our object. The **Customers** class in the server project had to be made remotable by inheriting from **MarshalByRefObject.**

```
public class Customers : MarshalByRefObject, ICustomer
```

The **CustomerListItem** that was going to be transferred by value had to be made serializable.

```
[Serializable]
public struct CustomerListItem
{
  public int CustomerId;
  public string FirstName;
  public string LastName;
  public string EmailAddress;
}
```

### SAMPLE REMOTING PROGRAM

In the Remoting example the client accesses a server-activated object. The server is the **TcpServerChannel** class that uses using a binary format with the TCP protocol. The channel will use port 8085. The server registers the type being remoted, the endpoint name to refer to this object, and the type of activation. The server then waits for client requests.

```
TcpServerChannel chan = new TcpServerChannel(8085);
ChannelServices.RegisterChannel(chan);
RemotingConfiguration.RegisterWellKnownServiceType(
                typeof(Customers), "AcmeCustomer",
                WellKnownObjectMode.Singleton);
```
. . .

The server has to be started before the client program can access the object.

The client sets up a **TcpClientChannel** object and then connects to the object. In the **Activator.GetObject** method call it specifies the type of the object it wants, and the endpoint where the server is listening to for object requests. If you want to run the client and server on separate machines, substitute the server machine name for localhost in the endpoint. Unlike COM location transparency, the client has to specify a specific endpoint; there is no redirection through an opaque registry entry.

```
TcpClientChannel chan = new TcpClientChannel();
ChannelServices.RegisterChannel(chan);
Customers obj = (Customers)Activator.GetObject(
                typeof(Customers),
                "tcp://localhost:8085/AcmeCustomer");
if (obj == null) System.Console.WriteLine(
                            "Could not locate server");
else
```
. . .

The client then uses the proxy to make calls on the object as if it were a local instance.

```
bool bRet = RemotingServices.IsTransparentProxy(obj);
. . .
ArrayList ar;
ar = obj.GetCustomer(-1);
ShowCustomerArray(ar);

obj.RegisterCustomer("Boris", "Badenough",
                            "boris@no-goodnicks.com");
Console.WriteLine();

ar = obj.GetCustomer(-1);
ShowCustomerArray(ar);
```

To run the program, start the server program in one console window, then run the client program from another console window.

The output depends on what kind of server-activated object is being activated.[13] If the server activation type is **Singleton**, which supports the maintaining state, you get the behavior you would expect from the nonre-moted case. A new customer is added, and you find that new customer in the list when you ask for all the existing customers. As you would expect, the initial activate call results in the **Customers** constructor being called once for each server invocation, no matter how many times the client pro-gram is run.

```
Object reference is a proxy?: True
Client: AppDomain Client.exe Thread 19 Context 0
1    Rocket          Squirrel        rocky@frosbitefalls.com
2    Bullwinkle      Moose           moose@wossamotta.edu

1    Rocket          Squirrel        rocky@frosbitefalls.com
2    Bullwinkle      Moose           moose@wossamotta.edu
3    Boris           Badenough       boris@no-goodnicks.com
```

If the activation type is **SingleCall**, which creates a new object instance for every method call, the results are quite different. Four different objects are created. The first is created by the initial activate request. The second is created by the initial call to **GetCustomer**. The third is created by the **RegisterCustomer** call. The fourth is created by the second call to **GetCustomer**. The last object created never sees the new customer, because no state is saved. Note that the static **nextCustId** member of the **Customer** class is treated as a static with respect to the new object instances of the **Customer** class, just as you would expect. Same client code, different results! Since the object is already activated, if you run the client program a second time for the same server invocation, the **Customers** constructor will be called only three times.

```
Object reference a proxy?: True
Client: AppDomain Client.exe Thread 19 Context 0
3    Rocket          Squirrel        rocky@frosbitefalls.com
4    Bullwinkle      Moose           moose@wossamotta.edu

8    Rocket          Squirrel        rocky@frosbitefalls.com
9    Bullwinkle      Moose           moose@wossamotta.edu
```

Since the client uses a proxy, the object executes inside the server's application domain, but on a different thread than the main server thread.

---

[13] In the example, you can try out both **Singleton** and **SingleCall** activation by com-menting out the appropriate line in the code in **server.cs**.

The object's constructor is not called until the first method call on the object. Notice how in both cases we have remoted an ArrayList of types without any special work aside from making the type serializable. The presence of metadata makes the programmer's work much easier.

## Metadata and Remoting

In order for the client to request an object of a specific type, metadata about the type has to be available to the client. For some applications, a reference can be made to the actual assembly where the object is stored.

For many applications, however, you do not want to give the client access to your source code. For the metadata that the client needs, a reference need only be made to an object without the implementation details.

One way to do this is to build a version of the object that has methods with no implementation. This interface class can then be built into an assembly that can be given to the client. You can throw the **System. NotSupportedException** in the methods if you wish to make sure that it is never used by mistake for the real object.

```
[System.Serializable]
public struct CustomerListItem
{
  public int CustomerId;
  public string FirstName;
  public string LastName;
  public string EmailAddress;
}
. . .
public class Customers : MarshalByRefObject, ICustomer
{
  public int RegisterCustomer(string firstName,
                  string lastName, string emailAddress)
  {
    throw new NotSupportedException();
  }
  public void UnregisterCustomer(int id)
  {
    throw new NotSupportedException();
  }
  public void ChangeEmailAddress(int id,
                                      string emailAddress)
  {
    throw new NotSupportedException();
  }
  public ArrayList GetCustomer(int id)
  {
    throw new NotSupportedException();
  }
}
```

For Web Services you use the SOAPSUDS tool to extract the metadata from the service, and then generate an assembly that has the required metadata. You can then build a proxy DLL and have the client program refer to it. This is conceptually equivalent to the first approach.

The server, of course, has to reference the real object's assembly.

Unlike the COM model, there is no reference counting, interface negotiation, building and registering separate proxies and stubs, worrying about global identifiers, or use of the registry. Because of metadata, all you have to do is inherit from **MarshalByRefObject** to make an object remotable.

## Remoting Configuration Files

You use configuration files to define where the object is activated. The client can then use the **new** operator to create the object. The big advantage here is that as the object location changes (such as a URL or TCP channel), or the formatter you want to use changes, the client does not have to be rebuilt.

Multiple classes can be configured on the client. Configuration files are loaded into the client using the **RemotingConfiguration. Configure** method.

# Custom Attributes

Chapter 5 introduced the concept of attributes, which have already appeared in several examples. In this chapter we used the **Serializable** and **Synchronization** attributes, which are provided by .NET Framework classes. The .NET Framework makes the attribute mechanism entirely extensible, allowing you to define custom attributes, which be added to the class's metadata. This custom metadata is available through reflection and can be used at runtime. To simplify the use of custom attributes, you may declare a base class to do the work of invoking the reflection API to obtain the metadata information.

The example **AttributeCustom** illustrates the custom attribute **InitialDirectory**. **InitialDirectory** controls the initial current directory where the program runs. By default the current directory is the directory containing the program's executable. In the case of a Visual Studio C# project, built in Debug mode, this directory is **bin\Debug**, relative to the project source code directory.

## Using a Custom Attribute

Before we discuss implementing the custom attribute, let us look at how the **InitialDirectory** attribute is used. To be able to control the initial directory for a class, we derive the class from the base class **DirectoryContext**. We may then apply to the class the attribute **InitialDirectory**, which takes a **string** parameter giving a path to what the initial directory should be. The property **DirectoryPath** extracts the path from the metadata. If our class does not have the attribute applied, this path will be the default. Here is the code for our test program.

   When you run this sample on your system, change the directory in the attribute to one that exists on your machine.

```
// AttributeCustom.cs

using System;
using System.IO;

class Normal : DirectoryContext
{
}

[InitialDirectory(@"\OI\NetCs\Chap08")]
class Special : DirectoryContext
{
}

public class AttributeCustom
{
   public static void Main()
   {
      Normal objNormal = new Normal();
      Console.WriteLine("path = {0}",
                        objNormal.DirectoryPath);
      ShowDirectoryContents(objNormal.DirectoryPath);
      Special objSpecial = new Special();
      Console.WriteLine("path = {0}",
                        objSpecial.DirectoryPath);
      ShowDirectoryContents(objSpecial.DirectoryPath);
   }
   private static void ShowDirectoryContents(string path)
   {
      DirectoryInfo dir = new DirectoryInfo(path);
      FileInfo[] files = dir.GetFiles();
      Console.WriteLine("Files:");
      foreach (FileInfo f in files)
         Console.WriteLine("   {0}", f.Name);
```

```
      DirectoryInfo[] dirs = dir.GetDirectories();
      Console.WriteLine("Directories:");
      foreach (DirectoryInfo d in dirs)
         Console.WriteLine("   {0}", d.Name);   }
}
```

Here is the output:

```
path = C:\OI\NetCs\Chap08\AttributeCustom\bin\Debug
Files:
   AttributeDemo.exe
   AttributeDemo.pdb
Directories:
path = c:\OI\NetCs\Chap8
Files:
Directories:
   AppDomain
   Asynch
   AsynchThreading
   AttributeCustom
   DynamicInvocation
   FileIO
   ISerializable
   MarshalByReference
   PulseAll
   Reflection
   Remoting
   Serialization
   Threading
   ThreadIsolation
```

## Defining an Attribute Class

To create a custom attribute, you must define an attribute class, derived from the base class **Attribute**. By convention give your class a name ending in "Attribute." The name of your class without the "Attribute" suffix will be the name of the custom attribute. In our example the class name is **InitialDirectoryAttribute**, so the attribute's name is **InitialDirectory**.

You may provide one or more constructors for your attribute class. The constructors define how to pass positional parameters to the attribute (provide a parameter list, separated by commas). It is also possible to provide "named parameters" for a custom attribute, where the parameter information will be passed using syntax **name = value**.

You may also provide properties to read the parameter information. In our example, we have a property **Path**, which is initialized in the constructor.

```
// DirectoryAttribute.cs

using System;

public class InitialDirectoryAttribute : Attribute
{
    private string path;
    public InitialDirectoryAttribute(string path)
    {
        this.path = path;
    }
    public string Path
    {
        get
        {
            return path;
        }
    }
}
```

## Defining a Base Class

The last step in working with custom attributes is to provide a means to extract the custom attribute information from the metadata using the reflection classes. You can obtain the **Type** of any object by calling the method **GetType**, which is provided in the root class **object**. Using the class's method **GetCustomAttributes** you can read the custom attribute information.

To make the coding of the client program as simple as possible, it is often useful to provide a base class that does the work of reading the custom attribute information.[14] We provide a base class **DirectoryContext**, which is used by a class wishing to take advantage of the **InitialDirectory** attribute. This base class provides the property **DirectoryPath** to return the path information stored in the metadata. Here is the code for the base class:

```
// DirectoryContext.cs

using System;
using System.Reflection;
using System.IO;

public class DirectoryContext
{
    virtual public string DirectoryPath
    {
        get
```

---

[14] With single implementation inheritance there is a cost to providing a base class. If you need to derive from another class such as **ContextBoundObject**, the base class has to derive from that class.

```
    {
        Type t = this.GetType();
        foreach (Attribute a
            in t.GetCustomAttributes(true))
        {
            InitialDirectoryAttribute da =
                a as InitialDirectoryAttribute;
            if (da != null)
            {
                return da.Path;
            }
        }
        return Directory.GetCurrentDirectory();
    }
  }
}
```

We must import the **System.Reflection** namespace because **GetType** returns the current **Type** of the object. **GetCustomAttributes** method can then obtain a collection of **Attribute** objects from the metadata. Since this collection is heterogeneous, consisting of different types, the C# **as** operator is used to test whether a given collection element is of the type **InitialDirectoryAttribute**. If we find such an element, we return the **Path** property. Otherwise, we return the default current directory, obtained from **GetCurrentDirectory**.

## Garbage Collection and Finalization

Memory management is a critical aspect of programming and can be the source of many errors. Whenever a resource is created, memory must be provided for it. And when the resource is no longer needed, the memory should be reclaimed. If the memory is not reclaimed, the amount of memory available is reduced. If such "memory leaks" recur often enough (which can happen in long-running server programs), the program can crash. Another potential bug is to reclaim memory while it is still required by another part of the program.

.NET greatly simplifies the programming of memory management through an automatic *garbage collection* facility. The CLR tracks the use of memory that is allocated on the managed heap, and any memory that is no longer referenced is marked as "garbage." When memory is low, the CLR traverses its data structure of tracked memory and reclaims all the memory marked as garbage. Thus the programmer is relieved of this responsibility.

Although a good foundation for resource management, garbage collection by itself does not address all issues. Memory allocated from the managed heap is not the only kind of resource needed in programs. Other resources, such as file handles and database connections, are not automatically deallocated, and the programmer may need to write explicit code to perform cleanup. The .NET Framework provides a **Finalize** method in the **Object** base class for this purpose. The CLR calls **Finalize** when the memory allocated for an object is reclaimed.

Another concern with garbage collection is performance. Is there a big penalty from the automated garbage collection? The CLR provides a very efficient multigenerational garbage collection algorithm. In this section we examine garbage collection and finalization in the .NET Framework, and we provide several code examples.

## Finalize

**System.Object** has a protected method **Finalize**, which is automatically called by the CLR after an object becomes inaccessible. (As we shall see, finalization for an object may be suppressed by a call to the method **SuppressFinalize** of the **System.GC** class.) Since **Finalize** is protected, it can only be called through the class or a derived class. The default implementation of **Finalize** does nothing. For any cleanup to be performed, a class must override **Finalize**. Also, a class's **Finalize** implementation should call the **Finalize** of its base class.

### C# DESTRUCTOR NOTATION

The C# language provides a special tilde notation **~SomeClass** to represent the overridden **Finalize** method, and this special method is called a *destructor*. The C# destructor automatically calls the base class **Finalize**. Thus the following C# code

```
~SomeClass()
   {
      // perform cleanup
   }
```

generates code that could be expressed

```
protected override void Finalize()
{
   // perform cleanup
   base.Finalize();
}
```

The second code fragment is actually not legal C# syntax, and you must use the destructor notation.

Although C# uses the same notation and terminology for destructor as C++, the two are very different. The C++ destructor is called deterministically when a C++ object goes out of scope or is deleted. The C# destructor is called during the process of garbage collection, a process which is not deterministic, as discussed below.

### LIMITATIONS OF FINALIZATION

Finalization is nondeterministic. **Finalize** for a particular object may run at any time during the garbage collection process, and the order of running finalizers for different objects cannot be predicted. Moreover, under exceptional circumstances a finalizer may not run at all (for example one finalizer goes into an infinite loop, or a process aborts without giving the runtime a chance to clean up).

Also, the thread on which a finalizer runs is not specified.

Another issue with finalization is its effect on performance. There is significantly more overhead associated with managing memory for objects with finalizers, both on the allocation side and on the deallocation side.[15]

Thus you should not implement a finalizer for a class unless you have very good reason for doing do. And if you do provide a finalizer, you should probably provide an alternate, deterministic mechanism for a class to perform necessary cleanup. The .NET Framework provides a **Dispose** design pattern for deterministic cleanup.

## Unmanaged Resources and Dispose

The classic case for a finalizer is a class that contains some unmanaged resource, such as a file handle or a database connection. If they are not released when no longer need, the scalability of your application can be affected. As a simple illustration, consider a class that wraps a file object. We want to make sure that a file that is opened will eventually be closed. The object itself will be destroyed by garbage collection, but the unmanaged file will remain open, unless explicitly closed. Hence we provide a finalizer to close the wrapped file.

But as we discussed, finalization is nondeterministic, so a file for a deleted object might hang around open for a long time. We would like to have a deterministic mechanism for a client program to clean up the wrapper object when it is done with it. The .NET Framework provides the generic **IDisposable** interface for this purpose.

---

[15] Finalization internals and other details of garbage collection are discussed in depth in the two-part article "Garbage Collection" by Jeffrey Richter, *MSDN Magazine*, November and December 2000.

```
public interface IDisposable
{
   void Dispose();
};
```

The design pattern specifies that a client program should call **Dispose** on the object when it is done with it. In the **Dispose** method implementation, the class does the appropriate cleanup. As backup assurance, the class should also implement a finalizer, in case **Dispose** never gets called, perhaps due to an exception being thrown.[16] Since both **Dispose** and **Finalize** perform the cleanup, cleanup code can be placed in **Dispose**, and **Finalize** can be implemented by calling **Dispose**. One detail is that once **Dispose** has been called, the object should not be finalized, because that would involve cleanup being performed twice. The object can be removed from the finalization queue by calling **GC.SuppressFinalize**. Also, it is a good idea for the class to maintain a boolean flag such as **disposedCalled**, so that if **Dispose** is called twice, cleanup will not be performed a second time.

The example program **DisposeDemo** provides an illustration of finalization and the dispose pattern. The class **SimpleLog** implements logging to a file, making use of the **StreamWriter** class (discussed earlier in this chapter).

```
// SimpleLog.cs

using System;
using System.IO;

public class SimpleLog : IDisposable
{
   private StreamWriter writer;          •
   private string name;
   private bool disposeCalled = false;
   public SimpleLog(string fileName)
   {
      name = fileName;
      writer = new StreamWriter(fileName, false);
      writer.AutoFlush = true;
      Console.WriteLine("logfile " + name + " created");
   }
   public void WriteLine(string str)
   {
      writer.WriteLine(str);
      Console.WriteLine(str);
   }
   public void Dispose()
   {
```

---

[16] One of the virtues of the exception handling mechanism is that as the call stack is unwound in handling the exception, local objects go out of scope and so can get marked for finalization. We provide a small demo later in this section.

```
        if(disposeCalled)
            return;
        writer.Close();
        GC.SuppressFinalize(this);
        Console.WriteLine("logfile " + name + " disposed");
        disposeCalled = true;
    }
    ~SimpleLog()
    {
        Console.WriteLine("logfile " + name + " finalized");
        Dispose();
    }
}
```

The class **SimpleLog** supports the **IDisposable** interface, and thus implements **Dispose**. The cleanup code simply closes the **StreamWriter** object. To make sure that a disposed object will not also be finalized, **GC.SuppressFinalize** is called. The finalizer simply delegates to **Dispose**. To help monitor object lifetime, a message is written to the console in the constructor, in **Dispose**, and in the finalizer.[17]

Here is the code for the test program:

```
// DisposeDemo.cs

using System;
using System.Threading;

public class DisposeDemo
{
    public static void Main()
    {
        SimpleLog log = new SimpleLog(@"log1.txt");
        log.WriteLine("First line");
        Pause();
        log.Dispose();
        log.Dispose();
        log = new SimpleLog(@"log2.txt");
        log.WriteLine("Second line");
        Pause();
        log = new SimpleLog(@"log3.txt");
        log.WriteLine("Third line");
        Pause();
        log = null;
        GC.Collect();
        Thread.Sleep(100);
    }
    private static void Pause()
    {
```

---

[17] The **Console.WriteLine** in the finalizer is provided purely for didactic purposes and should not be done in production code, for reasons we shall discuss shortly.

```
        Console.Write("Press enter to continue");
        string str = Console.ReadLine();
    }
}
```

The **SimpleLog** object reference **log** is assigned in turn to three different object instances. The first time, it is properly disposed. The second time, **log** is reassigned to refer to a third object, before the second object is disposed, resulting in the second object becoming "garbage." The **Pause** method provides an easy way to pause the execution of this console application, allowing us to investigate the condition of the files **log1.txt**, **log2.txt**, and **log3.txt** at various points in the execution of the program.

Running the program results in the following output:

```
logfile log1.txt created
First line
Press enter to continue
logfile log1.txt disposed
logfile log2.txt created
Second line
Press enter to continue
logfile log3.txt created
Third line
Press enter to continue
logfile log3.txt finalized
logfile log3.txt disposed
logfile log2.txt finalized
logfile log2.txt disposed
```

After the first pause, the file **log1.txt** has been created, and you can examine its contents in Notepad. If you try to delete the file, you will get a sharing violation, as illustrated in Figure 8–2.

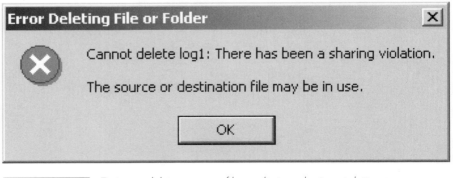

**Figure 8–2**  *Trying to delete an open file results in a sharing violation.*

At the second pause point, **log1.txt** has been disposed, and you will be allowed to delete it. **log2.txt** has been created (and is open). At the third pause point, **log3.txt** has been created. But the object reference to **log2.txt** has been reassigned, and so there is now no way for the client program to dispose of the second object.[18] If **Dispose** were the only mechanism to cleanup the second object, we would be out of luck. Fortunately, the **SimpleObject** class has implemented a finalizer, so the next time garbage is collected, the second object will be disposed of properly. We can see the effect of finalization by running the program through to completion. The second object is indeed finalized, and thence disposed. In fact, as the app domain shuts down, **Finalize** is called on all objects not exempt from finalization, even on objects that are still accessible.

In our code we explicitly make the third object inaccessible by the assignment **log = null**, and we then force a garbage collection by a call to **GC.Collect**. Finally we sleep briefly, to give the garbage collector a chance to run through to completion, before the application domain shuts down. Coding our test program in this way is a workaround for the fact that the order of finalization is nondeterministic. The garbage collector will be called automatically when the program exits and the application domain is shut down. However, at that point, system objects, such as **Console**, are also being closed. Since you cannot rely on the order of finalizations, you may get an exception from the **WriteLine** statement within the finalizer. The explicit call to **GC.Collect** forces a garbage collection while the system objects are still open. If we omitted the last three lines of the **Main** method, we might well get identical output, but we might also take an exception.

We provide similar code at the end of the **Main** methods of our other test programs, so that our print statements in finalizers work properly without randomly throwing exceptions.

## ALTERNATE NAME FOR DISPOSE

The standard name for the method that performs cleanup is **Dispose**. The convention is that once an object is disposed, it is finished. In some cases, the same object instance may be reused, as in the case of a file. A file may be opened, closed, and then opened again. In such a case, an additional cleanup method should be called **Close**. In other cases some other natural name may be used.

---

[18] This example illustrates that it is the client's responsibility to help the scalability of the server by cleaning up objects (using Dispose) before reassigning them. Once an object has been reassigned, there is no way to call Dispose, and the object will hang around for an indeterminate period of time until garbage is collected. Effective memory management involves both the server and client.

Our **SimpleLog** class could plausibly have provided an **Open** method, and then it would have made sense to name our cleanup method **Close**. For simplicity, we did not provide an **Open** method, and so we stuck to the name **Dispose**.

## Garbage Collection and Generations

Using the dispose pattern we can mitigate the issue of nondeterministic finalization, but what about the performance of the garbage collector? It turns out that the overall memory management efficiency of .NET is quite good, thanks to two main points:

- Allocation is *very* fast. Space on the managed heap is always contiguous, so allocating a new object is equivalent to incrementing a pointer. (By contrast, an allocation on an unmanaged heap is relatively slow, because a list of data structures must be walked to find a block that is large enough.)
- The CLR uses *generations* during garbage collecting, reducing the number of objects that are typically checked for being garbage.

### GENERATIONS

As an optimization, every object on the managed heap is assigned to a generation. A new object is in generation 0 and is considered a prime candidate for garbage collection. Older objects are in generation 1. Since such an older object has survived for a while, the odds favor its having a longer lifetime than a generation 0 object. Still older objects are assigned to generation 2 and are considered even more likely to survive a garbage collection. The maximum generation number in the current implementation of .NET is 2, as can be confirmed from the **GC.MaxGeneration** property.

In a normal sweep of the garbage collector, only generation 0 will be examined. It is here that the most likely candidates are for memory to be reclaimed. All surviving generation 0 objects are promoted to generation 1. If not enough memory is reclaimed, a sweep will next be performed on generation 1 objects, and the survivors will be promoted. Then, if necessary, a sweep of generation 2 will be performed, and so on up until **MaxGeneration**.

## Finalization and Stack Unwinding

As mentioned earlier, one of the virtues of the exception handling mechanism is that as the call stack is unwound in handling the exception, local objects go out of scope and so can get marked for finalization. The program **FinalizeStackUnwind** provides a simple illustration. It uses the **SimpleLog** class discussed previously, which implements finalization.

```
// FinalizeStackUnwind.cs

using System;

public class FinalizeStackUnwind
{
   public static void Main()
   {
      try
      {
         SomeMethod();
      }
      catch(Exception e)
      {
         Console.WriteLine(e.Message);
      }
      GC.Collect();
   }
   private static void SomeMethod()
   {
      // local variable
      SimpleLog alpha = new SimpleLog("alpha.txt");
      // force an exception
      throw new Exception("error!!");
   }
}
```

A local variable **alpha** of type **SimpleLog** is allocated in **SomeMethod**. Before the method exits normally, an exception is thrown. The stack unwinding mechanism of exception handling detects that **alpha** is no longer accessible, and so is marked for garbage collection. The call to **GC.Collect** forces a garbage collection, and we see from the output of the program that finalize is indeed called.

```
logfile alpha.txt created
error!!
logfile alpha.txt finalized
logfile alpha.txt disposed
```

## Controlling Garbage Collection with the GC Class

Normally it is the best practice simply to let the garbage collector perform its work behind the scenes. Sometimes, however, it may be advantageous for the program to intervene. The **System** namespace contains the class **GC**, which enables a program to affect the behavior of the garbage collector. We summarize a few of the important methods of the class.

### SUPPRESSFINALIZE

This method requests the system to not call **Finalize** for the specified object. As we saw previously, you should call this method in your implementation of **Dispose**, to prevent a disposed object from also being finalized.[19]

### COLLECT

You can force a garbage collection by calling the **Collect** method. An optional parameter lets you specify which generations should be collected. Use this method sparingly, since normally the CLR has better information on the current state of memory. A possible use would be a case when your program has just released a number of large objects, and you would like to see all this memory reclaimed right away. Another example was provided in the previous section, where a call to **Collect** forced a collection while system objects were still valid.

### MAXGENERATION

This property returns the maximum number of generations that are supported.

### GETGENERATION

This method returns the current generation number of an object.

---

[19] You should be careful in the case of an object that might be "closed" (like a file) and later reopened again. In such a case it might be better not to suppress finalization. Once finalization is suppressed, it can be made eligible for finalization again by calling GC. ReRegisterForFinalize. For a discussion of advanced issues in garbage collection and finalization, refer to the Jeffrey Richter article previously cited.

### GETTOTALMEMORY

This method returns the number of bytes currently allocated. A parameter lets you specify whether the system should perform a garbage collection before returning. If no garbage collection is done, the indicated number of bytes is probably larger than the actual number of bytes actually being used by live objects.

## Sample Program

The program **GarbageCollection** illustrates using these methods of the **GC** class. The example is artificial, simply illustrating object lifetime, and the effect of the various **GC** methods. The class of objects that are allocated is called **Member**. This class has a **string** property called **Name**. Write statements are provided in the constructor, **Dispose**, and in the destructor. A **Committee** class maintains an array list of **Member** instances. The **RemoveMember** method simply removes the member from the array list. The **DisposeMember** method also calls **Dispose** on the member being expunged from the committee. The **ShowGenerations** method displays the generation number of each **Member** object. **GarbageCollection.cs** is a test program to exercise these classes, showing the results of various allocations and deallocations and the use of methods of the **GC** class. The code and output should be quite easy to understand.

All the memory is allocated locally in a method **Demonstrate Generations**. After this method returns and its local memory has become inaccessible, we make an explicit call to **GC.Collect**. This forces the finalizers to be called before the app domain shuts down, and so we avoid a possible random exception of a stream being closed when a **WriteLine** method is called in a finalizer. This is the same point mentioned previously for the earlier examples.

## Summary

This chapter introduced the .NET application model. Through metadata, the framework can understand enough about your application to provide many services that you do not have to implement. On the other hand, we have seen how the framework is structured so that you can substitute your own objects and implementations where needed.

Type safety enables application domains to provide a robust, yet cheap, form of application isolation. Contexts, proxies, and interception allow the runtime to transparently provide services to parts of applications that require them.

Another aspect of the .NET application model is the pervasive use of attributes, which can be easily added to source code and are stored with the metadata. We saw examples of the use of attributes for serialization and for synchronization, and we demonstrated how to implement and use custom attributes.

NET simplifies the programming of memory management through an efficient generational automatic garbage collection facility. Finalization is nondeterministic, but you can support deterministic cleanup by implementing the dispose pattern.

# Programming with ADO.NET

*T*he framework database programming classes are referred to as ADO.NET. ADO.NET introduces the **DataSet** class that works with relational data in a relational manner while you are disconnected from any data source. You need not connect and update or query the database unless you have a specific reason for doing so. You can, of course, work in the traditional connected manner if you choose.

ADO.NET data providers[1] allow you to execute commands directly against the data source. Functionality is exposed directly without intermediary objects such as OLEDB, which stands between ADO and the data source. The .NET **DataAdapter** class models a data source as a set of database commands and a connection to that data source. Differences between data sources are not hidden by generic interfaces. The OLEDB data provider allows for nested transactions with data sources that support that functionality; the SqlServer data provider does not.[2]

.NET Data Providers supply data to a dataset or a data reader. A dataset is a memory-resident, lightweight relational database that is not connected to any database. You can also obtain a dataset from an XML document or create an XML document from a dataset. This allows you to work, if it makes sense, with your data as relational data, or as hierarchical XML data.[3] Data readers model the traditional method of working with a database.

---

[1] .NET Data Providers are what used to be called in the beta literature managed providers. You may still see them referred to by that term.

[2] There is a **Begin** method on the **OleDbTransaction** class; the **SqlTransaction** class does not have such a method.

[3] The many-to-many relations that you can have in a relational database do not automatically map to XML hierarchies. But this is no different from working with the classic object-relational model clash.

The data access classes that currently ship with the framework are found in the namespaces: **System.Data**, **System.Data.SqlClient**, **System.Data.OleDb**, **System.Data.Common**, and **System.Data.SqlTypes**. The Sql and OleDb namespaces reflect the SqlServer and OleDb .NET Data Providers. An ODBC .NET Data Provider has been written, and additional ones will be written in the future.

This chapter changes the implementation of the Customer and Hotel assemblies of the Case Study to use SQL Server. An air travel service that the Acme Travel Agency can use to make air travel reservations is added to illustrate the use of XML.

To make our examples concrete we use SQL Server 2000 and the SQL Server data provider.[4] Nonetheless, much of the basic functionality discussed in this chapter applies to the OleDb data provider as well.

This chapter assumes you have some understanding of database concepts.

---

### Setting Up the Example Databases

This chapter assumes that SQL Server 2000 has been installed using the Local System account, with authentication mode set to Mixed Mode. The user is assumed to be sa, with a blank password.

Several examples in this chapter make use of the Northwind Traders sample database, which is installed along with SQL Server. In addition, there are other example programs that use the HotelBroker and AirlineBroker databases, which are supplied specifically for use with this book.

Some of the example programs make changes to these databases, and other examples assume a freshly installed database. This means that some of the examples will not always work as expected unless you reinstall them again. You can reinstall each of these databases by running the SQL scripts that are provided.

Please refer to the **readme.txt** file in the sample code directory for this chapter for more information about database setup.

---

## .NET Data Providers

The prefix on the database classes and methods indicates the data provider used to access the data source. For example, the OleDb prefix applies to the OleDb data provider. The Sql prefix applies to the SqlServer data provider.

---

[4] If you do not have an SQL Server available you can go to the Microsoft site and download the MSDE, which is a scaled down version of SQL Server. As of this writing MSDE is available for free. Microsoft suggests using MSDE in the future instead of Access. Since we use vanilla functionality you should be able to use the OleDb data provider against the Access version of the Northwind traders by changing the Sql classes to the corresponding OleDb classes. We have not yet tested this scenario, however.

The SqlServer data provider uses the native SQL Server wire protocol. The OleDb data provider goes through the COM interop layer to talk to the various OleDb providers. For example, you could talk to SqlServer through the OleDb data provider to the OLEDB provider for SQL Server. Nonetheless, the performance of going through the SqlServer data provider will be superior. The advantage of the OleDb and the ODBC data providers is that you can work with ADO.NET against most data sources that you work with today.

There are some interfaces that define common functionality, and some base classes that can be used to provide common functionality, but there is no requirement for a data provider to fit a specification that does not correspond to the way the underlying data source works.

For example, the **SqlDataAdapter** class and the **OleDbDataAdapter** class both use the abstract base classes **DbDataAdapter** and **DataAdapter** that are found in the **System.Data.Common** namespace. **SqlTransaction** and the **OleDbTransaction** classes both implement the **IDbTransaction** interface. The **OleDbError** class and the **SqlError** class do not resemble each other at all. Server-side cursors are not in the ADO.NET model because some databases (such as Oracle and DB2) do not have native support for them. Any support for them in the SQL Server data provider would be as an extension.[5]

As Table 9–1 shows, the **Connection**, **Command**, **DataReader**, **DataAdapter**, and **DataParameter** classes of the data providers do have some parallels that are defined by the **IDbConnection**, **IDbCommand**, **IDataReader**, **IDbDataAdapter**, and **IDataParameter** interfaces. Nothing, of course, prevents an implementation of these classes from having additional methods beyond those specified in the interfaces.

**Table 9–1**  Comparison of Parallel Classes in the OleDb and SQL Server Data Providers

| Interface | OleDb | SQL Server |
| --- | --- | --- |
| IDbConnection | OleDbConnection | SqlConnection |
| IDbCommand | OleDbCommand | SqlCommand |
| IDataReader | OleDbDataReader | SqlDataReader |
| IDbDataAdatpter | OleDbDataAdapter | SqlDataAdapter |
| IDbTransaction | OleDbTransaction | SqlTransaction |
| IDataParameter | OleDbDataParameter | SqlDataParameter |

Classes such as the **DataSet** or the **DataTable**, which are independent of any data provider, do not have any prefix.

---

[5] Besides, server-side cursors are rarely appropriate so it is not surprising that databases do not support them. Scrolling through the output is usually the result of a user interaction. Holding state on the server while the user interacts with the data is not the way to build a scalable application.

If database scalability is important, it is important to suppress finalization on any of your classes that do not require it. You will get vastly improved performance because you will reduce the amount of time the finalizer thread runs.

## The Visual Studio.NET Server Explorer

Visual Studio.NET Server Explorer is a very useful tool for working with databases. While not as powerful as the SQL Server Enterprise Manager, it can give you the basic functionality you need when writing or debugging database applications. It will be very useful when we work with the examples in this chapter.

To access the Server Explorer, use the View | Server Explorer menu item. The Server Explorer is a dockable window that can be moved around as required. Figure 9–1 illustrates the Server Explorer.

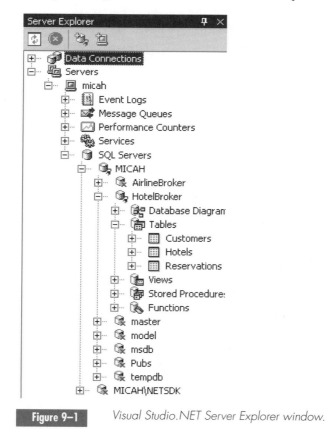

**Figure 9–1**   *Visual Studio.NET Server Explorer window.*

You can find information about all the fields in a table, or look at and edit the data in the tables. You can create or edit stored procedures and design tables. We will use the Server Explorer in the first few examples to show a little bit of how it can be used.

## Data Readers

To make these concepts concrete, let us use some of these classes to access a database. This example is found in this chapter's **Connected** subdirectory.

We will need a connection to the database, a command to issue against the database, and a reader to retrieve the data, so we declare three objects:[6]

```
SqlConnection conn = null;
SqlCommand command = null;
SqlDataReader reader = null;
```

The connection string that is used to connect to the database is set next. You will have to replace the server element with the appropriate value for your machine. You will also have to specify the appropriate user and password for the database.[7] You can also set the connect string as an **SqlConnection** property. A simple select statement will be the command run against the database.

```
String ConnString =
    "server=localhost;uid=sa;pwd=;database=Northwind";
string cmd = "select CustomerId, CompanyName from
                                    Customers";[8]
```

---

[6] The objects are declared outside of the try/catch block so that they can be used in the finally block. They are set to null because their use in the finally block could theoretically occur before they are initialized inside the try block (and so the compiler indicates with a warning).

[7] For Northwind the usual uid=sa;pwd=; will probably work.

[8] Here and several other places long SQL statement strings are broken up and placed on multiple lines to allow for book formatting.

Figure 9–2 shows the tables and stored procedures for the Northwind database.

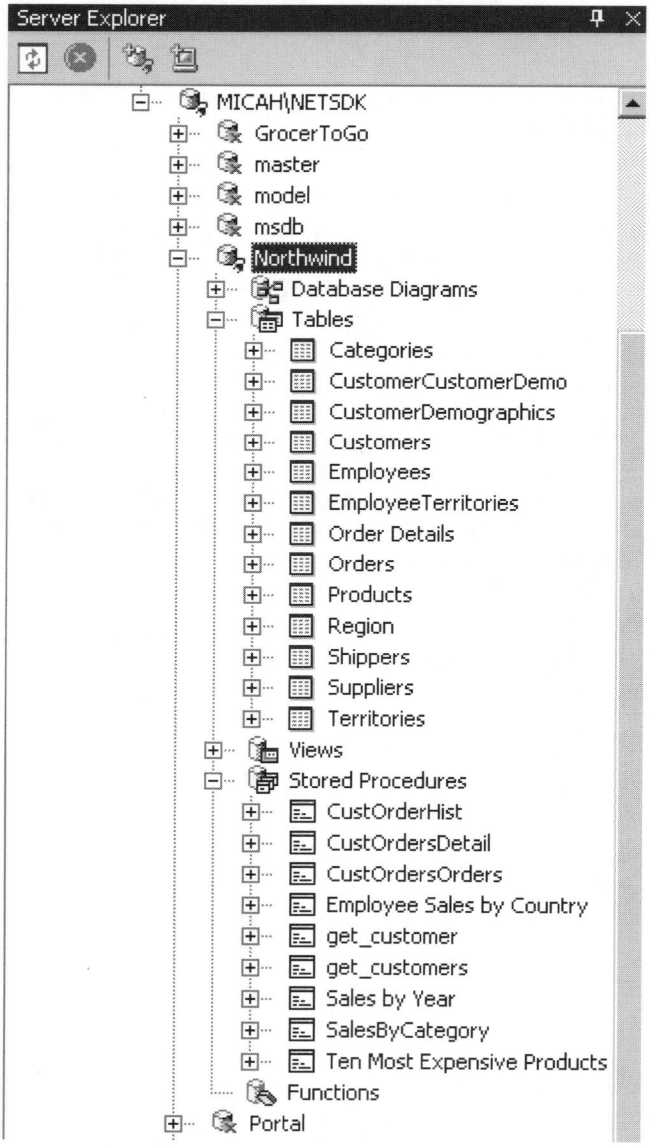

**Figure 9–2**  *Server Explorer showing Northwind database tables and stored procedures.*

We create an **SqlConnection** object and then a create an **SqlCommand** object that is attached to the connection just created. A connection to the database must be opened before any command can be executed.

```
conn = new SqlConnection(ConnString);
command = new SqlCommand(cmd, conn);
conn.Open();
```

When the command is executed using the **ExecuteReader** method on the **SqlCommand** object, an **SqlDataReader** instance is returned. This reader can be used to iterate through the result set. The column names can be used to fetch the data elements from the current result set row.

```
reader = command.ExecuteReader();
if (reader != null)
{
   Console.WriteLine("CustomerId\tCompanyName");
   while (reader.Read())
    Console.WriteLine("{0}\t\t{1}", reader["CustomerId"],
                                    reader["CompanyName"]);
}
```

The reader and the connection are closed in the finally block.

```
if (reader != null) reader.Close();
if (conn.State == ConnectionState.Open) conn.Close();
```

If the connection is not closed explicitly, the finalizer on the **SqlConnection** object will eventually get called and the connection will be closed. Since the garbage collector is not deterministic, there is no way to know when this will happen. Therefore always close your connections. If you do not, you will use more connections than you need (even with connection pooling), and this could interfere with your applications scalability. You could also run out of connections.

Here is the output the program produces:

```
CustomerId      CompanyName
ALFKI           Alfreds Futterkiste
ANATR           Ana Trujillo Emparedados y helados
ANTON           Antonio Moreno Taquería
AROUT           Around the Horn
BERGS           Berglunds snabbköp
BLAUS           Blauer See Delikatessen
BLONP           Blondesddsl père et fils
BOLID           Bólido Comidas preparadas
BONAP           Bon app'
BOTTM           Bottom-Dollar Markets
BSBEV           B's Beverages
...
```

You use the Visual Studio.NET Server Explorer to check the results of the program. Select the Customers table under the Northwind database explorer and right-click to get a context menu. Select "Retrieve Data from Table," and you can retrieve the data associated with the table and compare it with the results of the program. You will see that they are the same. Figure 9–3 shows this.

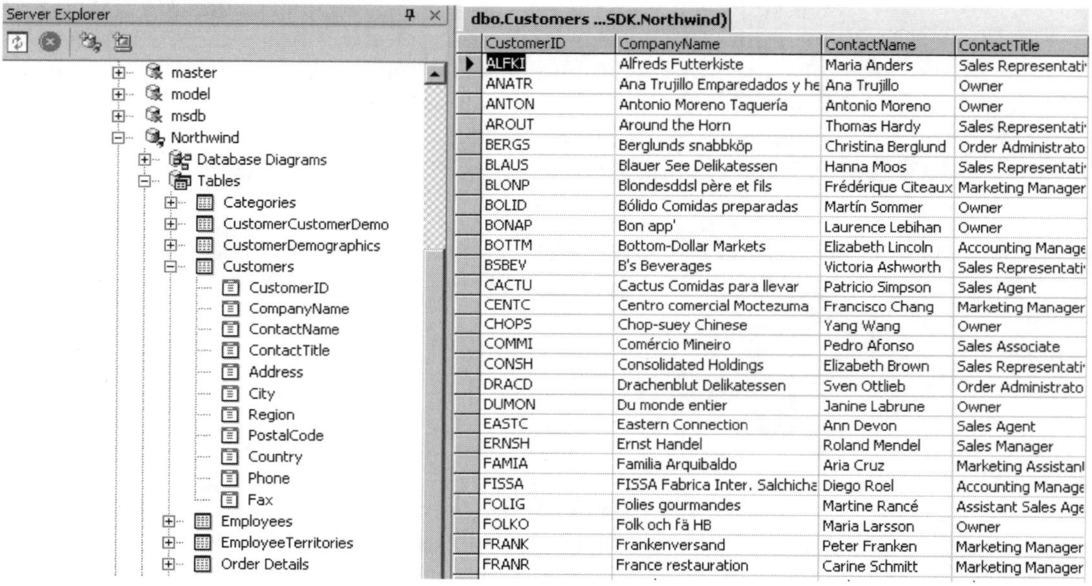

**Figure 9–3**
*Server Explorer showing Customers table, fields, and data.*

## The Connected Database Scenario

This scenario of working with a database is referred to as connected. The program connects to the database, does the work it needs to do, and then disconnects. You can run through the returned data only in the forward direction. This corresponds to the classic ADO forward-only cursor/record-set. In the connected mode you must open and close the database connection explicitly.

Keeping a connection continually open is not the best way to work in an environment where you want to minimize the resources consumed (connections are expensive) to allow for scalability. A **DataSet** allows you to work disconnected from a data source. Nonetheless, as will be discussed later, depending on your concurrency assumptions, using a **DataReader** instead of a **DataSet** might still be the right approach.

As will be discussed later, the **SqlConnection** is used with the **DataAdapter** to establish connections with the database in the same way as illustrated here with the **SqlCommand**. **SqlConnection** also controls database properties such as transactions and isolation levels. A root transaction is issued by invoking the **BeginTransaction** method on the **SqlConnection** class.[9] If in the previous example we connected SQL Server through the **OleDbConnection** class, the connection string would be:

```
"Provider=SQLOLEDB.1;server=localhost;uid=sa;pwd=;
                                database=Northwind";
```

You would have to provide the correct server, user, and password.

While the **SqlCommand** executes a command against a database in the same way whether you use a **DataAdapter** or an **SqlDataReader**, the mechanics of doing so is different. This will become clearer when we discuss the **SqlDataAdapter** class.

You specify the type of **SqlCommand** with the **CommandType** property. For the Sql data provider this can be either Text (the default) or StoredProcedure. The **CommandText** can also be specified as a property. We will soon show how parameters can be applied to database commands.

An **SqlDataReader** instance is returned by the **ExecuteReader** method on an **SqlCommand** instance. If you wanted to program in a way that was independent of a data provider, you could use the **IDataReader** interface instead. You could then invoke methods on the interface instead of an object.

```
IDataReader idr = command.ExecuteReader();
```

Similar techniques can be used with the other data-provider classes that implement interfaces used by multiple data providers. Until the **SqlDataReader** instance is closed, the **SqlCommand** object cannot be used for any purpose other than for executing its **Close** method.

## Executing SQL Statements

The **ExecuteReader** method on the **SqlCommand** returns a **DataReader** instance. Data is returned when the command is a select statement or a stored procedure that returns results. When you know there will be no results returned it is more efficient to use the **ExecuteNonQuery** method. The **SqlCommand.ExecuteReader** method uses the stored procedure **sp_executesql**. Some commands that use "SET" statements may not work properly. Other providers might have different restrictions when their **ExecuteReader** method is used.

---

[9] Since OLEDB allows for nested transactions, nested transactions can be started by invoking the **Begin** method on the **OleDbTransaction** class.

In general, for commands that do not return data, use the **SqlCommand.ExecuteNonQuery** method. The **NonQuery** example shows how this works. For illustrative purposes this example connects to SQL Server through the OleDb data provider.

```
string cmd = "update Customers set CompanyName =
        'Maria Inc' where ContactName = 'Maria Anders'";
...
command = new OleDbCommand(cmd, conn);
int NumberRows = command.ExecuteNonQuery();
```

The number of rows returned should be 1. Figure 9–4 shows the results of the change to the first row.

| **Figure 9–4** | *Rows in Customers table in the Server Explorer showing the changed ContactName. Compare with Figure 9–3 to see the original value of the first row.* |

For insert, update, and delete statements, the number of rows affected is returned. SQL Server returns –1 for all other statements (Native or OLEDB provider). Other providers might return 0 or –1.

To fetch a single value (such as an aggregate computation) use the **ExecuteScalar** method. Against SQL Server 2000 you can use the **SqlCommand.ExecuteXmlReader** to retrieve XML results directly from the server.

## DataReader

When created, the **SqlDataReader** is positioned before the first record returned of the first result set. You must invoke the **Read** method before accessing any data. As the DataReader example demonstrates, the item property can be used to access the individual fields or column values in the current row:

All the fields in a row can be accessed with the **GetValues** method.

```
object[] fields = new object[NumberFields];
...
int NumberFields = reader.GetValues(fields);
```

**GetValue** returns the column value in its native format. You can also access the column values as particular datatypes: **GetBoolean**, **GetDecimal**, **GetString**, etc. The **GetName** method returns the column name of a particular column.

To reinforce what was mentioned earlier, only one record at a time is accessible with a DataReader. Make sure you close the DataReader when you are done with it.

## Multiple Result Sets

The **SqlDataReader** class can handle multiple result sets, as the **DataReader** example demonstrates. Two queries separated by a semicolon represent two SQL statements that will cause two results sets to be generated, one for each statement.

```
string ConnString =
    "server=localhost;uid=sa;pwd=;database=Northwind";
string cmd = "select CustomerId, CompanyName from
              Customers where CustomerId like 'T%';select
              CustomerId, CompanyName from Customers
              where CustomerId like 'W%'";
...
int ResultSetCounter = -1;
int NumberFields = 0;
...
reader = command.ExecuteReader();
if (reader != null)
{
 NumberFields = reader.FieldCount;
 object[] fields = new object[NumberFields];
 Console.WriteLine("Result Set\tCustomerId\tCompanyName");
 do
 {
   ResultSetCounter++;
   while(reader.Read())
   {
```

```
        NumberFields = reader.GetValues(fields);
        Console.Write("\t{0}", ResultSetCounter);
          for (int i = 0; i < NumberFields; i++)
          {
             Console.Write("\t\t{0}", fields[i]);
          }
        Console.Write("\n");
        }
     }while(reader.NextResult());
}
...
```

The **FieldCount** method returns the number of columns in the result set. Since the **GetValues** method returns the native format of the data, an array of objects is passed to it. The **NextResult** method navigates to the next result set.

## Parameters Collection

Sometimes you have to parameterize a SQL statement. You also might have to associate the input and output arguments of a stored procedure with variables in your program.

To do this you build the **SqlCommand** class's **Parameters** property, which is a collection of **SqlParameter** instances. The installation procedure added the **get_customers** stored procedure to the Northwind database to illustrate the use of a simple stored procedure, which takes one input argument that is the company name and returns the customer id for that customer.

```
CREATE PROCEDURE get_customers
(@companyname nvarchar(40), @customerid nchar(5) OUTPUT)
AS
select @customerid = CustomerID from Customers where
  CompanyName = @companyname
RETURN

GO
```

The **StoredProcedure** example shows how to do this.

```
command = new SqlCommand("get_customers", conn);
command.CommandType = CommandType.StoredProcedure;

SqlParameter p = null;
p = new SqlParameter("@companyname", SqlDbType.NVarChar,
                     40);
p.Direction = ParameterDirection.Input;
p.Value = "Ernst Handel";
command.Parameters.Add(p);
```

```
p = new SqlParameter("@customerid", SqlDbType.NChar, 5);
p.Direction = ParameterDirection.Output;
command.Parameters.Add(p);
command.ExecuteNonQuery();
Console.WriteLine("{0} CustomerId = {1}",
                command.Parameters["@companyname"].Value,
                command.Parameters["@customerid"].Value);
```

Each individual **SqlParameter** member of the **Parameters** collection represents one parameter of an SQL statement or stored procedure. As this example illustrates, the parameters need not have any relationship to any particular table or column in the database.

At a minimum you have to specify—either through the constructor or by setting properties—the name and database type of the parameter. If the parameter is of variable length, you have to specify the size.

In this example two parameters are added to the parameters collection. The first represents the input argument to the stored procedure, the second the return value from the stored procedure.

The name of the parameter corresponds to the name of the argument in the stored procedure **get_customers**. The other values to the **SqlParameter** constructor define the data type of the parameter. The first is a variable Unicode string up to 40 characters in length. The second variable is a 5-character fixed-length Unicode string. If this was an OLEDB .NET Data Provider you would bind to the parameters by position since only the SQL Server .NET Data Provider binds parameters by name.

The **Value** property is used to set or get the value of the parameter. It is used to initialize the @companyname parameter for input to the stored procedure. It is also used to obtain the value that the stored procedure set for the @customerid parameter.

Output parameters must be specified as such with the **Direction** property. In this example the @companyname parameter is set as an input parameter with the value **ParameterDirection.Input**. The @customerid parameter is set as an output parameter with the value **ParameterDirection. Output**. Output parameters must be specified, since input parameters are the default. To bind to the return value of a stored procedure use **ParameterDirection.ReturnValue**. For bidirectional parameters use **ParameterDirection.InputOutput**.

You can use the parameter names to access individual parameters in the **SqlCommand** parameters collection.

Parameterized commands work with both **SqlDataReader** and **DataAdapter** classes. When the **DataSet** class is discussed, you will see how to specify the **Source** property of the parameter, which indicates which column in the **DataSet** the parameter represents.

## SqlDataAdapter and the DataSet Class

The **DataSet** class is a memory-resident, lightweight relational database class. It has properties that reflect the tables (**Tables**) and relationships between tables (**Relations**) within the data set. You can control whether corresponding constraints are enforced with the **EnforceConstraints** property. You can name the data set with the **DataSetName** property. You can also set the name of the data set in the **DataSet** constructor.

The **SqlDataAdapter** class is used to get data from the database into the **DataSet**. The constructor of the **HotelBroker** class shows how to use a data adapter class to populate a data set. The code is found in the **Hotel** subdirectory of the **HotelBrokerAdmin** directory of the case study for this chapter.

```
conn = new SqlConnection(connString);
citiesAdapter =  new SqlDataAdapter();
citiesAdapter.SelectCommand = new SqlCommand(
            "select distinct City from Hotels", conn);
citiesDataset = new DataSet();
citiesAdapter.Fill(citiesDataset, "Cities");
```

The **SqlDataAdapter** class has properties associated with it for selecting, inserting, updating, and deleting data from a data source. Here the **SqlCommand** instance is associated with the **SelectCommand** property of the **SqlDataAdapter** instead of being executed independently through one of its own execute methods.

The **Fill** method of the **SqlDataAdapter** is then used to execute the select command and fill the **DataSet** with information to be put in a table whose name is supplied as an argument. If the database connection was closed when the **Fill** method was executed, it will be opened. When finished, the **Fill** method will leave the connection in the same state as it was when it was first called.

At this point the connection to the database could be closed. You now can work with the **DataSet** and its contained data independently of the connection to the database.

**SqlDataAdapter** is implemented with the **SqlDataReader** class, so you can expect better performance with the latter. The **SqlDataReader** might also be more memory efficient depending on how your application is structured. If you do not need the features of the **DataSet**, there is no point incurring the overhead. If you are doing expensive processing you can free up the database connection by using a **DataSet**. You may get better scalability by loading the data into the **DataSet**, freeing the associated database resources, and doing the processing against the **DataSet**.

## Disconnected Mode

This scenario of working with a database is referred to as disconnected. Connected mode represents a tightly coupled, connected environment where state and connections can be maintained. Client-server environments are examples where this is true. ADO and OLEDB were designed for this world. In a connected-mode environment data readers can be used. If necessary, ADO can be used through the COM interop facility. In fact ADO was not rewritten for .NET so that absolute backward compatibility could be maintained, bugs and all.

Connections, however, are expensive to maintain in environments where you want to be able to scale to a large number of users. In this environment there is often no need to hold locks on database tables. This aids scalability because it reduces contention on database tables. The **DataTable** objects in the **DataSet's Tables** collection with their associated constraints can mimic the tables and relationships in the original database. For applications that are implemented completely with .NET, **DataSet** instances can be passed around or remoted to the various parts of an application. For applications that can make optimistic assumptions about concurrency this can produce large gains in scalability and performance. This is true of many types of Internet- or intranet-based applications.

In the disconnected mode, a connection is made in the same way as with the connected mode of operation. Data is retrieved using the data provider's data adapter class. The **SelectCommand** property specifies the SQL statement used to place data into the data set. Unlike the data reader, which is related to a particular database connection, the data set has no relationship to any database, including the one from which the data originally came.

## DataSet Collections

When data is placed into a **DataSet**, the related tables and columns are also retrieved. Each data set has collections that represent all the tables, columns and data rows associated with it.

The **HotelBroker** class in the Case Study has a method called **PrintHotels** that illustrates how to retrieve this information and write it to a Console. The **hotelsDataset** is a data set that has already been filled with the data from the HotelBroker database.

```
DataTable t = hotelsDataset.Tables["Hotels"];
if (t == null)
  return;
foreach(DataColumn c in t.Columns)
  Console.Write("{0, -20}", c.ColumnName);
```

```
Console.WriteLine("");

foreach (DataRow r in t.Rows)
{
  for (int i = 0; i < t.Columns.Count; i++)
    {
      Type type = r[i].GetType();
      if (type.FullName == "System.Int32")
        Console.Write("{0, -20}", r[i]);
      else
      {
        string s = r[i].ToString();
        s = s.Trim();
        Console.Write("{0, -20}", s);
      }
    }
  Console.WriteLine("");
}
Console.WriteLine("");
```

The **Tables** collection includes all the **DataTable** instances in the **DataSet**. In this particular case there is only one, so there is no need to iterate through that collection. The program then iterates through all the columns in the table and sets them up as headers for the data that will be printed out. After the headers have been set up, all the rows in the table are iterated through. For each column in the row, we ascertain its type and print out the value appropriately. The program checks only for the types that are in the Hotels database table. Checking for types instead of printing out the row values as **object** enables us to format the data appropriately.

As we will show later, you can populate the dataset through these collections without having to obtain it from a data source. You can just add tables, columns, and rows to the appropriate collections.

## DataSet Fundamentals

You can also fetch a subset of the data in the **DataSet**. The **Select** method on a **DataTable** uses the same syntax as an SQL statement **where** clause. Column names are used to access the data for a particular row. This example comes for the **HotelBroker** class, where it is used to get the hotels for a particular city.

```
public ArrayList GetHotels(string city)
...
  DataTable t = hotelsDataset.Tables["Hotels"];
  DataRow[] rows = t.Select("City = '" + city + "'");
  HotelListItem hl;
```

```
ArrayList hotels = new ArrayList();
for (int i = 0; i < rows.Length; i++)
{
  hl.HotelName = rows[i]["HotelName"].ToString();
  hl.City = rows[i]["City"].ToString().Trim();
  hl.NumberRooms = (int) rows[i]["NumberRooms"];
  hl.Rate = (decimal) rows[i]["RoomRate"];
  hotels.Add(hl);
}
return hotels;
```

The **AddHotel** method of the **HotelBroker** class demonstrates how to add a new row to a **DataSet**. A new **DataRow** instance is created, and the column names are used to add the data to the columns in the row.

To propagate your new row back to a database, you have to add it to the row collection of the table, and then use the **Update** method on the **SqlDataAdapter** class to do so. It is the data adapter that mediates between the **DataSet** and the database. We will discuss later how to do perform edits on the dataset in order to accept or reject changes before propagating them back to the database.

```
public string AddHotel(string city, string name,
                                    int number, decimal rate)
    ...
DataTable t = hotelsDataset.Tables["Hotels"];
DataRow r = t.NewRow();

r["HotelName"] = name;
r["City"] = city;
r["NumberRooms"] = number;
r["RoomRate"] = rate;
t.Rows.Add(r);

    hotelsAdapter.Update(hotelsDataset, "Hotels");
```

To delete rows from the **DataSet**, you first find the particular row or rows you want to delete and then invoke the **Delete** method on each **DataRow** instance. When the **Update** method on the data adapter is called, it will be deleted from the database.

The **Remove** method removes the **DataRow** from the collection. It is not marked as deleted, since it is no longer in the **DataSet**. When the **Update** method on the data adapter is called, it will not be deleted from the database.

The **DeleteHotel** method in the **HotelBroker** class illustrates deleting rows from a **DataSet**.

```
public string DeleteHotel(string city, string name)
    ...
  t = hotelsDataset.Tables["Hotels"];
```

```
r = t.Select("City = '" + city + "' and HotelName = '"
                                        + name + "'");
...
for (i = 0; i < r.Length; i++)
  r[i].Delete();
...
```

To update a row in a dataset, you just find it and modify the appropriate columns. This example comes from the **ChangeRooms** method in the **HotelBroker** class. When the **Update** method on the data adapter is called, the modification will be propagated back to the database.

```
public string ChangeRooms(string city, string name,
                          int numberRooms, decimal rate)
  ...
  DataTable t = hotelsDataset.Tables["Hotels"];
  DataRow[] r = t.Select(
  "City = '" + city + "' and HotelName = '" + name + "'");
  ...
  for (int i = 0; i < r.Length; i++)
  {
    r[i]["NumberRooms"] = numberRooms;
    r[i]["RoomRate"] = rate;
  }
  ...
```

## Updating the Data Source

How does the **SqlDataAdapter.Update** method propagate changes back to the data source? Changes to the **DataSet** are placed back based on the **InsertCommand**, **UpdateCommand**, and **DeleteCommand** properties of the **SqlDataAdapter** class. Each of these properties takes an **SqlCommand** instance that can be parameterized to relate the variables in the program to the parts of the related SQL statement. The code fragment we use to show this comes from the **HotelBroker** constructor.

A **SqlCommand** instance is created to represent the parameterized SQL statement that will be used when the **SqlDataAdapter.Update** command is invoked to add a new row to the database. At that point, the actual values will be substituted for the parameters.

```
SqlCommand cmd = new SqlCommand("insert Hotels(City,
    HotelName, NumberRooms, RoomRate)
    values(@City, @Name, @NumRooms, @RoomRate)", conn);
```

The parameters have to be associated with the appropriate columns in a **DataRow**. In the **AddHotel** method code fragment discussed previously, columns were referenced by the column names: "HotelName," "City," "NumberRooms," and "RoomRate." Notice how they are related to the SQL statement parameters @Name, @City, @NumRooms, @RoomRate in the **SqlParameter** constructor This last argument sets the **Source** property of the **SqlParameter**. The **Source** property sets the **DataSet** column to which the parameter corresponds. The **Add** method places the parameter in the **Parameters** collection associated with the **SqlCommand** instance.

```
SqlParameter param = new SqlParameter("@City",
                             SqlDbType.Char, 20, "City");
cmd.Parameters.Add(param);

cmd.Parameters.Add(new SqlParameter("@Name",
                    SqlDbType.Char, 20, "HotelName"));
cmd.Parameters.Add(new SqlParameter("@NumRooms",
                    SqlDbType.Int, 4, "NumberRooms"));
cmd.Parameters.Add(new SqlParameter("@RoomRate",
                    SqlDbType.Money, 8, "RoomRate"));
```

Finally the **SqlDataAdapters' InsertCommand** property is set to the **SqlCommand** instance. Now this command will be used whenever the adapter has to insert a new row in the database.

```
hotelsAdapter.InsertCommand = cmd;
```

Similar code appears in the **HotelBroker** constructor for the **UpdateCommand** and **DeleteCommand** properties to be used whenever a row has to be updated or deleted.

```
hotelsAdapter.UpdateCommand = new SqlCommand(
    "update Hotels set NumberRooms = @NumRooms, RoomRate =
      @RoomRate where City = @City and HotelName =
      @Name", conn);
hotelsAdapter.UpdateCommand.Parameters.Add(new
    SqlParameter("@City", SqlDbType.Char, 20, "City"));
hotelsAdapter.UpdateCommand.Parameters.Add(new
    SqlParameter("@Name", SqlDbType.Char, 20,
            "HotelName"));
hotelsAdapter.UpdateCommand.Parameters.Add(new
    SqlParameter("@NumRooms", SqlDbType.Int, 4,
            "NumberRooms"));
hotelsAdapter.UpdateCommand.Parameters.Add(new
    SqlParameter("@RoomRate", SqlDbType.Money, 8,
            "RoomRate"));

hotelsAdapter.DeleteCommand = new SqlCommand(
"delete from Hotels where City = @City and HotelName =
            @Name", conn);
hotelsAdapter.DeleteCommand.Parameters.Add(new
    SqlParameter("@City", SqlDbType.Char, 20, "City"));
hotelsAdapter.DeleteCommand.Parameters.Add(new
    SqlParameter("@Name", SqlDbType.Char, 20,
            "HotelName"));
```

Whatever changes you have made to the rows in the **DataSet** will be propagated to the database when **SqlDataAdapter.Update** is executed. How to accept and reject changes made to the rows before issuing the **SqlDataAdapter.Update** command is discussed in a later section.

## Auto Generated Command Properties

The **SqlCommandBuilder** class can be used to automatically generate any **InsertCommand**, **UpdateCommand**, and **DeleteCommand** properties that have not been defined. Since the **SqlCommandBuilder** needs to derive the necessary information to build those properties dynamically, it requires an extra round trip to the database and more processing at runtime. Therefore, if you know your database layout in the design phase, you should explicitly set the **InsertCommand**, **UpdateCommand**, and **DeleteCommand** properties to avoid the performance hit. If the database layout is not known in advance, and a query is specified by the user, the **SqlCommandBuilder** can be used if the user subsequently wants to update the results.

This technique works for **DataTable** instances that correspond to single tables. If the data in the **DataTable** is generated by a query that uses a join, then the autogeneration mechanism cannot generate the logic to update multiple tables. The **SqlCommandBuilder** uses the **SelectCommand** property to generate the command properties.

A primary key or unique column must exist on the table in the **DataSet**. This column must be returned by the SQL statement set in the **SelectCommand** property. The unique columns are used in a where clause for update and delete.

Column names cannot contain special characters such as spaces, commas, periods, quotation marks, or nonalphanumeric characters. This is true even if the name is delimited by brackets. You can specify a fully qualified table name such as **SchemaName.OwnerName.TableName**.

A simple way to use the **SqlCommandBuilder** class is to pass the **SqlDataAdapter** instance to its constructor. The **SqlCommandBuilder** then registers itself as a listener for **RowUpdating** events. It can then generate the needed **InsertCommand**, **UpdateCommand**, or **DeleteCommand** properties before the row update occurs.

The **CommandBuilder** example demonstrates how to use the **SqlCommandBuilder** class.

## Database Transactions and Updates

When the data adapter updates the data source, it is ***NOT*** done as a single transaction. If you want all the inserts, updates, and deletes done in one transaction, you must handle the transaction programmatically.

The **SqlConnection** object has a **BeginTransaction** method that returns a **SqlTransaction** object. When you invoke the **BeginTransaction** method, you can optionally specify the isolation level. If you know what you are doing, and understand the trade-offs, you can improve the performance and scalability of your application by setting the appropriate isolation level. If you set the isolation level incorrectly or inappropriately, you can have inconsistent or incorrect data results.[10]

The **SqlTransaction** class has **Commit** and **Rollback** methods to commit or abort the transaction. You open the **SqlConnection**, invoke the **BeginTransaction** method, use the **SqlDataAdapter** as normal, and then call **SqlTransaction.Commit** or **SqlTransaction.Rollback** as appropriate. Then close the connection. The **Save** method on **SqlTransaction** can be used to set a savepoint in the transaction.

In order to minimize the database resources you hold, and therefore increase the scalability of your application, you want to minimize the time between calling **BeginTransaction** and the call to **Commit** or **Rollback**.

Here is some code from the **Transactions** example. It uses the AirlineBroker database introduced later in the chapter. Note that we only open the connection right before the **Fill**, and the transaction statements bracket the **Update**.

```
conn = new SqlConnection(ConnString);
da = new SqlDataAdapter();
ds = new DataSet();
da.SelectCommand = new SqlCommand(selectCmd, conn);
da.InsertCommand = new SqlCommand(insertCmd, conn);
...
conn.Open();
da.Fill(ds, "Airlines");
...
trans = conn.BeginTransaction();
da.InsertCommand.Transaction = trans;
da.Update(ds, "Airlines");
trans.Commit();
...
```

To ensure that the SQL Server data provider operates properly, you should use the **Commit** and **Rollback** methods on the **SqlTransaction** object to commit or roll back the transactions started with **SqlConnection.BeginTransaction**. Do not use the SQL Server transaction statements.

---

[10] Discussing isolation levels in detail would remove our focus from .NET to database programming. Any good intermediate to advanced book on database programming would discuss the concept of isolation levels and locking. For specific information about the SQL Server locking mechanism you can read the Microsoft Press *Inside SQL Server* books, among others. Tim Ewald's book *Transactional COM+* has a good chapter on the issue of isolation and its relation to building scalable applications.

If you use stored procedures for your database work, you can certainly issue SQL Server transaction statements inside the stored procedures instead of using the **SqlTransaction** object. Stored procedures can be used to encapsulate transactional changes. The **MakeReservation** stored procedure in the HotelBroker database does just that.

## Optimistic vs. Pessimistic Locking and the DataSet

Transactions help preserve database consistency. When you move money from your savings to your checking account to pay your phone bill, transaction processing ensures that the credit and withdrawal will both happen, or neither will happen. You will not wind up with a situation where the money goes into your checking account but is not withdrawn from the savings (good for you, and bad for the bank) or the reverse (bad for you, but good for the bank). Nothing about that transaction prevents your spouse from using that same money to eat out at a fancy restaurant.[11]

Under an optimistic locking strategy, you assume this will not happen, but you have to be prepared to deal with it when does.[12] A pessimistic locking strategy requires coordination among all the users of a database table so that this never happens. Of course, the fewer locks you hold on database rows to prevent use by more than one user, the more scalable your application will be.

An understanding of how this affects your application applies to both reads and actual updates. For example, suppose your spouse sees that money is available in the checking account and makes plans based on that fact. This could be as much of a problem as the actual withdrawal of money from the joint checking account.

While a discussion of how to solve these problems is beyond the scope of this chapter, it is important to realize that the issue arises because no locks are held on the database records held within a **DataSet**. Just using the **DataSet** with **SqlDataAdapter.Update** assumes an optimistic locking strategy.

Why does this matter? It matters because the performance and scalability of your application depend on it. Why is it so complicated? Because there is no answer that applies to all applications in all situations. If users do not share the same set of data, optimistic concurrency is an excellent assumption. If you have to lock records for a long period of time, this increases the wait to use these resources, thus decreasing performance and scalability.

---

[11] The failure to distinguish between these two leads to the apparently common problem (as related to me by a bank vice president) of people wondering why their checks bounce when their ATM balance said they had enough money to withdraw some cash.

[12] This is the database equivalent of overdraft protection.

You have to understand transaction isolation levels, the database's Lock Manager, the probability of contention for particular rows, and the probability that this contention results in deadlock in your application. You have to understand how much time and resources you can spend reconciling divergent operations, and how much tolerance for inconsistent or incorrect results your application can stand, in order to decide under what circumstances you want to avoid deadlock at all costs, or can deal with the consequences of conflicting operations.[13]

You might have to use the **DataSet** with additional logic to test whether the records in the **DataSet** have been changed since the last time they were fetched or modified. Or you might just decide to use the **SqlDataReader** and refetch the data. It all depends.

For example, when making a reservation in our HotelBroker case study you cannot make an optimistic assumption about the availability of rooms. It is not acceptable to assume an infinite supply of rooms at a hotel and let the reservations clerk deal with what happens when more people show up then there are rooms for.[14] We use the **MakeReservation** stored procedure to check on the availability of a room before we make the reservation.[15]

Sometimes, even without concurrency issues, the **DataSet** cannot be used to add new rows in isolation from the database. Sometimes, as in our HotelBroker application, an arbitrary primary key cannot be used.[16] Many users will be making reservations at the same time. Reservation ids cannot be assigned locally; some central logic on the database has to be employed to issue them.[17] The **MakeReservation** stored procedure does this as well.

The degree of disconnected operation that your application can tolerate has to be understood before you can decide how to use **SqlDataReader** or the **DataSet** in your applications.

---

[13] Tim Ewald's book is worth reading to understand this topic. Philip Bernstein and Eric Newcomer's *Principles of Transaction Processing* is another good reference.

[14] Of course, airlines and hotels overbook. This is a conscious strategy to deal with passengers or guests not making explicit cancellations, not a database concurrency strategy.

[15] In fact, the transaction in **MakeReservation** includes the checking of the availability of the room as well as the actual making of the reservation in order to maintain consistency. It also breaks up what could be one multiple table join into several queries in order to return better error information.

[16] For instance, a GUID. Well, theoretically GUIDs could be used in our case, but when was the last time you got a reservation number from a hotel or airline that was composed of 32 identifiers? Many times a primary key has meaning to an organization—for example, a part number whose subsections indicate various categories.

[17] Of course, if performance were critical, instances of the HotelBroker could be pre-assigned ranges of reservation ids to give out. But this would have to be done by some central authority as well (the database, some singleton object?). But then this raises the issue of state management in the middle tier. This just reinforces my previous point about the dependency of any solution on the specific requirements of your program. It also reinforces the maxim that any programming problem can be solved either by trading memory against time, or adding another level of indirection.

Why bother to use the **DataSet** at all in our HotelBroker application? In fact, the code for the **Customer** object does not use the **DataSet** at all. The **HotelBroker** object does—for two reasons. The first is pedagogical. We wanted to show you how a complete application might use the features of the **DataSet**, rather than just isolated sample programs. Second, in the Web version of the application which is developed in subsequent chapters, it is convenient to cache certain pieces of information. For example, it is probably reasonable to assume that a user can work with their own local copy of reservations. On the other hand, the information about a customer such as their email address can be obtained just once when they log in. There is no need for an elaborate mechanism to cache customer information, so the **Customer** object uses methods on the **SqlCommand** object.

## Working with DataSets

Figure 9–5 depicts the hierarchy of classes that exist within the **DataSet** class. It will be helpful to glance at this diagram over the next few sections that discuss these classes.

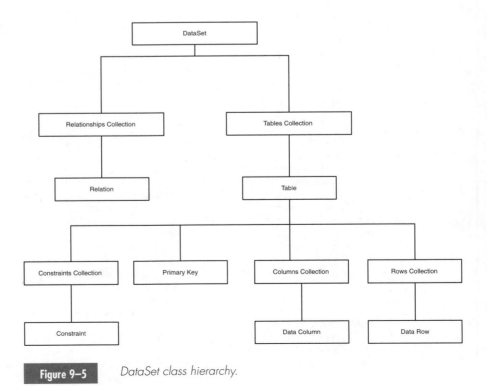

**Figure 9–5**    *DataSet class hierarchy.*

## Multiple Tables in a DataSet

Each **DataSet** has a collection of one or more **DataTable** objects. Each **DataTable** object represents one table.

With a **SelectCommand** that contains a join you can place data from multiple database tables into one **DataTable**. If you want to update the multiple tables, you will have to specify the update commands, because all relationship of the data to the original tables is lost. The **SqlDataAdapter** for the **HotelBroker** object has the following **SelectCommand** property:

```
string cmd = "select CustomerId, HotelName, City,
          ArrivalDate, DepartureDate, ReservationId
          from Reservations, Hotels where
          Reservations.HotelId = Hotels.HotelId";
adapter.SelectCommand = new SqlCommand(cmd, conn);
dataset = new DataSet();
adapter.Fill(dataset, "Reservations");
```

The **DataSet** will only have one **DataTable** called Reservations. The fact that some of the data came from the Hotels table is lost.

You can also load more than one table into a dataset. The **DataSchema** example does just this:

```
adapter.SelectCommand = new SqlCommand(
  "select * from [Order Details] where ProductId = 1",
    conn);
adapter.FillSchema(dataset, SchemaType.Source,
    "Order Details");
adapter.Fill(dataset, "Order Details");

adapter.SelectCommand = new SqlCommand("select * from
    Shippers", conn);
adapter.FillSchema(dataset, SchemaType.Source,
    "Shippers");
adapter.Fill(dataset, "Shippers");
```

There will be two tables, OrderDetails and Shippers, in the **DataSet**. The method **SqlDataAdapter.FillSchema** fills the **DataSet** with the primary key information associated with the tables. The code can now iterate through the tables and print out both the data and the primary keys of the tables. The Columns collection on the **DataTable** enables you to find the **DataColumns** for the **DataTable**.

```
foreach(DataTable t in dataset.Tables)
{
  Console.WriteLine(t.TableName);
  DataColumn[] dc = t.PrimaryKey;
  for (int i = 0; i < dc.Length; i++)
  {
```

```
        Console.WriteLine("\tPrimary Key Field {0} = {1}", i,
                        dc[i].ColumnName);
    }

  Console.Write("\t");
  foreach(DataColumn c in t.Columns)
    Console.Write("{0, -20}", c.ColumnName);
    Console.WriteLine();

  foreach(DataRow r in t.Rows)
  {
    Console.Write("\t");
    foreach(DataColumn c in t.Columns)
      Console.Write("{0, -20}", r[c].ToString().Trim());
    Console.WriteLine();
  }
}
```

The example output shows the tables, primary keys, columns, and data:

```
Order Details
        Primary Key Field 0 = OrderID
        Primary Key Field 1 = ProductID
OrderID     ProductID  UnitPrice Quantity Discount
10285       1          14.4      45       0.2
10294       1          14.4      18       0
...
Shippers
        Primary Key Field 0 = ShipperID
        ShipperID   CompanyName           Phone
        1           Speedy Express        (503) 555-9831
        2           United Package        (503) 555-3199
        3           Federal Shipping      (503) 555-9931
```

## Table Creation without a Data Source

One can use a **DataSet** as a memory-resident relational database not based
on any database. In fact, we will explore various features of the **DataSet** in
the **DataEditing** example by adding the data and relationships directly to the
data set without extracting them from a database.

First we create a new **DataSet** and turn on constraint checking. We
then add four **DataTables** to the **DataSet**: Books, Categories, Authors, and
BookCategories. Even though it is set in the example code for pedagogical
reasons, **EnforceConstraints** by default is true.

```
DataSet ds = new DataSet();
ds.EnforceConstraints = true;

DataTable categories = ds.Tables.Add("Categories");
```

```
DataTable bookcategories = ds.Tables.Add("BookCategories");
DataTable authors = ds.Tables.Add("Authors");
DataTable books = ds.Tables.Add("Books");
```

Each **DataTable** object has a collection of **DataColumn** objects. Each object represents one column of the table. We then add columns to the table definition.

```
Type stringType = System.Type.GetType("System.String");
Type intType = System.Type.GetType("System.Int32");

DataColumn categoryname =
        categories.Columns.Add("Category",stringType);

DataColumn cn = bookcategories.Columns.Add
                          ("CategoryName", stringType);
DataColumn loc =
            bookcategories.Columns.Add(
              "LibraryofCongressNumber", stringType);

DataColumn auid = authors.Columns.Add("AuthorId",
                                        intType);
authors.Columns.Add("AuthorLastName", stringType);
authors.Columns.Add("AuthorFirstName", stringType);

DataColumn ISBN = books.Columns.Add("ISBN", stringType);
DataColumn booksauid = books.Columns.Add("AuthorId",
                                        intType);
books.Columns.Add("Title", stringType);
DataColumn bloc =
  books.Columns.Add("LibraryofCongressNumber", stringType);
```

## Constraints and Relations

Each **DataTable** object has a collection of **DataRow** objects. Each object represents one row of the table. When you add a **DataRow**, it is subject to the constraints on the **DataTable** objects (assuming the **DataSet**'s **EnforceConstraints** property has been set to true).

### PRIMARY KEYS

There are several constraints on a table. The Primary Key constraint is the unique identifier for the table. Other unique constraints force the values in various column(s) to which they are applied to be unique. A Foreign Key constraint forces the values in the column(s) to which it applies to be a primary key in another table in the **DataSet**.

The **DataTable**'s primary key is a property:

```
DataColumn[] bookcategoriesPK = new DataColumn[2];
```

```
bookcategoriesPK[0] = cn;
bookcategoriesPK[1] = loc;
bookcategories.PrimaryKey = bookcategoriesPK;

DataColumn[] authorsPK = new DataColumn[1];
authorsPK[0] = auid;
authors.PrimaryKey = authorsPK;

DataColumn[] booksPK = new DataColumn[1];
booksprimarykey[0] = ISBN;
books.PrimaryKey = booksPK;
```

## CONSTRAINTS

The other constraints on the **Table** are represented by the abstract base class **Constraint** and its derived classes: **UniqueConstraint** and **ForeignKeyConstraint**. The base class enables the constraints to be placed in the table's constraint collection. Primary Keys also appear in the table's constraint collection as a unique constraint with a system-generated name. The **UniqueConstraint.IsPrimaryKey** property can be used to detect primary keys.

We constrain the Category column in the Categories table to be unique. Since the last argument to the **Add** method is false, this is not a primary key of the table. We do not define a primary key for this table, only a unique constraint. In fact, we do not even have to define any constraint on the table. Although that would violate the rules of relational integrity, you are not forced to use the **DataSet** in a relational manner. If you wish you can add a name to the constraint.

```
categories.Constraints.Add("Unique CategoryName
                    Constraint", categoryname, false);
```

Foreign Keys can specify what action should be taken when the primary key on which it is based is changed. Your choices are the standard database choices: **None**, **Cascade**, **SetNull**. You can also use **SetDefault** to set the new value to the **DataColumn's DefaultValue** property. These operations can be specified for both update and delete conditions.

In this example, a foreign key constraint is set so that all author ids in the Books table have to be found in the Authors table. In other words, when a new book row is inserted, it must have an author. We give this constraint a name: "Authors->Books." If the author id is changed, the update rule forces the **DataSet** to change all the author ids in the related rows to the new author id. If the author id is deleted, the **DataSet** will set the deleted author ids in the Book rows to null. If we had set the **DeleteRule** to **Cascade**, a cascading delete would be applied to all those rows in the Books table. The **AcceptRejectRule** applies to editing of the **DataSet**, which we will cover in a future section. This rule dictates what happens when the **AcceptChanges** method is invoked on a **DataSet**, **DataRow**, or **DataTable**. In this case all changes are cascaded. The alternative rule would be to take no action (**None**).

```
DataColumn[] bookauthorFK = new DataColumn[1];
bookauthorFK[0] = booksauid;
ForeignKeyConstraint fk = new
                ForeignKeyConstraint("Authors->Books",
                authorsPK, bookauthorFK);
fk.AcceptRejectRule = AcceptRejectRule.Cascade;
fk.DeleteRule = Rule.SetNull;
fk.UpdateRule = Rule.Cascade;
books.Constraints.Add(fk);
```

### DATA RELATIONS

Besides constraints you can add a relation to the **DataSet**'s **DataRelation** collection. A relation connects two tables so that you can navigate between the parent and the child or the child and the parent. When you add the relation you can optionally create and add the equivalent unique and foreign key constraints to the parent and child tables' constraint collections.[18]

The Categories table is made the parent of the BookCategories table through the Categories and CategoryName columns. In a relation both columns have to be of the same type (string). You can use this relation to navigate by finding all the rows in the child table that have the same value as in the parent table, or finding the row in the parent table that is the parent of a row in the child table. Similarly the Library of Congress number associated with a book has to be found in the Library of Congress field in the BookCategory's Library of Congress field.

```
ds.Relations.Add("Category->BookCategories Relation",
                                        categoryname, cn);
ds.Relations.Add("Book Category LOC->Book LOC Relation",
                                        loc, bloc);
```

## Examining the Schema Information about a DataTable

You can examine the information about a DataTable. Here is how to examine the constraint and key information. A previous example has already shown you how to find the DataColumns for a DataTable. Note the use of the

---

[18] Use the optional boolean **createConstraints** argument when you add a relation to indicate whether the associated constraint should be added. If this argument is not specified, the default is to add the associated constraint.

**IsPrimaryKey** property on the **UniqueConstraint** to detect a primary key.

```
foreach(DataTable t in ds.Tables)
{
  Console.WriteLine(t.TableName);
  Console.WriteLine("\tPrimary Key:");
  for (int i = 0; i < t.PrimaryKey.Length; i++)
  {
    DataColumn c = t.PrimaryKey[i];
    Console.WriteLine("\t\t{0}", c.ColumnName);
  }

  Console.WriteLine("\tConstraints:");
  foreach(Constraint c in t.Constraints)
  {
    string constraintName;
    if (c is ForeignKeyConstraint)
      constraintName = "Foreign Key:" + c.ConstraintName;
    else if (c is UniqueConstraint)
    {
      UniqueConstraint u = (UniqueConstraint)c;
      if (u.IsPrimaryKey)
        constraintName = "Primary Key";
      else
        constraintName = u.ConstraintName;
    }
    else
      constraintName = "Unknown Name";

    Console.WriteLine("\t\t{0, -40}", constraintName);
  }
}
```

This produces the following output. Note how the relations defined as a **DataRelation** appear in the table's constraint collection as a **ForeignKeyConstraint** instance. PrimaryKeys appear in the constraint collection as a **UniqueConstraint** instance. Constraints defined as unique constraints or foreign keys appear as you would expect in the collection.

```
Categories
    Primary Key:
    Constraints:
            Unique CategoryName Constraint
BookCategories
    Primary Key:
            CategoryName
            LibraryofCongressNumber
    Constraints:
            Primary Key
            Foreign Key:Category->BookCategories Relation
            Constraint2
```

```
Authors
    Primary Key:
            AuthorId
    Constraints:
            Primary Key
Books
    Primary Key:
            ISBN
    Constraints:
            Primary Key
            Foreign Key:Authors->Books
            Foreign Key:Book Category LOC->Book LOC Relation
```

Note the BookCategories constraint with the system-generated name. If you examine the code carefully, you will see we never added this constraint. Where did it come from? If you were to look at the columns in that constraint, you would find the Library of Congress field. The system realized that, since the CategoryName is a foreign key in another table, the Library of Congress field should be unique.

You can also examine the relations collection on the **DataSet**. You can examine the parent table and the columns in the parent table involved in the relationship. You can also examine the child table in the relationship and its columns.

```
foreach(DataRelation dr in ds.Relations)
{
  DataTable parentTable = dr.ParentTable;
  DataTable childTable = dr.ChildTable;
  Console.WriteLine("   Relation: {0} ", dr.RelationName);
  Console.WriteLine("        ParentTable: {0, -10}",
                                        parentTable);
  Console.Write("            Columns: ");
  for(int j = 0; j < dr.ParentColumns.Length; j++)
    Console.Write("           {0, -10}",
                        dr.ParentColumns[j].ColumnName);
  Console.WriteLine();
  Console.WriteLine("        ChildTable:  {0, -10}",
                        childTable);
  Console.Write("            Columns: ");
  for(int j = 0; j < dr.ChildColumns.Length; j++)
    Console.Write("           {0, -10}",
                        dr.ChildColumns[j].ColumnName);
  Console.WriteLine();
}
```

Here is the resulting output:

```
Output Relations between tables in the DataSet...
    Relation: Category->BookCategories Relation
        ParentTable: Categories
```

```
         Columns:                    Category
    ChildTable:  BookCategories
         Columns:                    CategoryName
  Relation: Book Category LOC->Book LOC Relation
    ParentTable: BookCategories
         Columns:                    LibraryofCongressNumber
    ChildTable:  Books
         Columns:                    LibraryofCongressNumber
```

## Database Events

Several ADO.NET classes generate events.

The **SqlConnection** class generates the **StateChange** and **InfoMessage** events. The **SqlDataAdapter** generates the **RowUpdated** and **RowUpdating** events. The **DataTable** class generates the **ColumnChanging**, **ColumnChanged**, **RowChanged**, **RowChanging**, **RowDeleted**, and **RowDeleting** events.

For example, the **RowChanged** event occurs after an action has been performed on a row. Continuing with our **DataEditing** example, it defines a handler for the **RowChanged** event in the Books table. Every time a row changes in the Books table, the event handler will run.

```
books.RowChanged+=new
                DataRowChangeEventHandler(Row_Changed);


private static void Row_Changed(object sender,
                    System.Data.DataRowChangeEventArgs e)
{
  DataTable table = (DataTable)sender;
  DataColumn[] primaryKey = table.PrimaryKey;
  string keyName = primaryKey[0].ColumnName;

  Console.WriteLine("Table " + table.TableName + " " +
          e.Action.ToString() + "Row with Primary Key " +
          e.Row[keyName]);

  return;
  }
```

So when the code adds some rows, including some to the Books table:

```
DataRow row
row = categories.NewRow();
row["Category"] = "UnitedStates:PoliticalHistory";
categories.Rows.Add(row);
...

row = authors.NewRow();
```

```
row["AuthorId"] = 1;
row["AuthorLastName"] = "Burns";
row["AuthorFirstName"] = "James M.";
authors.Rows.Add(row);
...
row = books.NewRow();
row["ISBN"] = "0-201-62000-0";
row["Title"] = "The Deadlock of Democracy";
row["AuthorId"] = 1;
row["LibraryofCongressNumber"] = "E183.1";
books.Rows.Add(row);

row = books.NewRow();
row["ISBN"] = "0-201-62000-3";
row["Title"] = "Freedom and Order";
row["AuthorId"] = 2;
row["LibraryofCongressNumber"] = "E183.1";
books.Rows.Add(row);
```

We get one output line for each book added, printed by the event handler:

```
Table Books AddRow with Primary Key 0-201-62000-0
Table Books AddRow with Primary Key 0-201-62000-3
```

If we were to change the ISBN numbers of the two books that were added to the same value, a **ConstraintException** would be thrown. If we changed the **DataSet.EnforceConstraints** property to false, however, no exception would be thrown.

## NAVIGATING RELATIONSHIPS

Using the schema information, we can navigate from parent table to child table and print out the results. This cannot be done with relationships defined as **ForeignKeyConstraint**, only as a **DataRelation** in the relations collection of the **DataSet**.

We previously printed out the schema information associated with the relationships. Now we use this information to print out the parent and child rows in the relationships. By using relationships appropriately, you can walk through the data without using relational queries. This can be quite useful for finding all the books in a certain category, or all order items in an order.

Note the use of the **DataRow** methods **GetChildRows** and **GetParentRows** to do the navigation. For a given relation, first we navigate from parent to children, then from the children to their parent. We also show how you can use different constructs to access the items in the various collections.

```
foreach (DataRelation dr in ds.Relations)
{
```

```
        Console.WriteLine(dr.RelationName);
        DataTable parentTable = dr.ParentTable;
        foreach(DataRow parentRow in parentTable.Rows)
        {
          Console.Write("      Parent Row: ");
          foreach(DataColumn pc in parentTable.Columns)
            Console.Write(" {0} ", parentRow[pc]);
          Console.WriteLine();

          DataRow[] childRows = parentRow.GetChildRows(dr);
          for(int k = 0; k < childRows.Length; k++)
          {
            Console.Write("        Child Row: ");
            foreach(DataColumn cc in childTable.Columns)
              Console.Write(" {0} ", childRows[k][cc]);
            Console.WriteLine();
          }
        }
    Console.WriteLine();

        foreach(DataRow childRow in childTable.Rows)
        {
          Console.Write("      Child Row: ");
          for(int m = 0; m < childTable.Columns.Count; m++)
            Console.Write(" {0} ", childRow[childTable.
                Columns[m].ColumnName].ToString().Trim());
          Console.WriteLine();

          foreach(DataRow pRow in childRow.GetParentRows(dr))
          {
            Console.Write("        Parent Row: ");
            for(int p = 0; p < parentTable.Columns.Count; p++)
              Console.Write(" {0} ", pRow[parentTable.
                  Columns[p].ColumnName].ToString().Trim());
            Console.WriteLine();
          }
        }
      Console.WriteLine();
    }
```

Next let us look at the output that this code produces. Note how we loop through each relation. For each relation we first loop through the parent table and output each row of the parent table with its corresponding child rows. We then loop through the child table and output each row of the child table with its corresponding parent rows.

```
...
Category->BookCategories Relation
  Parent Row:UnitedStates:PoliticalHistory
    Child Row:UnitedStates:PoliticalHistory    E183
  Parent Row:UnitedStates:PoliticalHistory:Opinion
```

```
    Child Row:UnitedStates:PoliticalHistory:Opinion E183.1
    Child Row:UnitedStates:PoliticalHistory:Opinion E183.2
  Parent Row:UnitedStates:PoliticalHistory:Predictions
    Child Row:UnitedStates:PoliticalHistory:Predictions
                                               E183.3

    Child Row:UnitedStates:PoliticalHistory    E183
      Parent Row:UnitedStates:PoliticalHistory
    Child Row:UnitedStates:PoliticalHistory:Opinion  E183.1
      Parent Row:UnitedStates:PoliticalHistory:Opinion
    Child Row:UnitedStates:PoliticalHistory:Opinion E183.2
      Parent Row:UnitedStates:PoliticalHistory:Opinion
    Child Row:UnitedStates:PoliticalHistory:Predictions
                                               E183.3
      Parent Row:UnitedStates:PoliticalHistory:Predictions

Book Category LOC->Book LOC Relation
    Parent Row:UnitedStates:PoliticalHistory    E183
    Parent Row:UnitedStates:PoliticalHistory:Opinion E183.1
      Child Row:0-201-62000-0   1
                   The Deadlock of Democracy   E183.1
      Child Row:0-201-62000-3   2
                   Freedom and Order   E183.1
    Parent Row:UnitedStates:PoliticalHistory:Opinion  E183.2
    Parent Row:UnitedStates:PoliticalHistory:Predictions
                   E183.3

    Child Row:0-201-62000-0   1
                   The Deadlock of Democracy   E183.1
      Parent Row:UnitedStates:PoliticalHistory:Opinion
                                               E183.1
    Child Row:0-201-62000-3   2   Freedom and Order   E183.1
      Parent Row:UnitedStates:PoliticalHistory:Opinion
                   E183.1
```

## DataRow Editing

### BEGINEDIT, ENDEDIT, CANCELEDIT

If you want to make multiple edits to a **DataSet**, and postpone the checking of constraints and events, you can enter a dataset editing mode. You enter this mode by invoking the **BeginEdit** method on the row. You leave it by invoking the **EndEdit** or **CancelEdit** row methods.

In the **DataEditing** example, we violate the foreign-key constraint by adding a row with a nonexistent author id. The foreign-key constraint exception will not be raised until the **EndEdit** method is called.

Since we have called **BeginEdit** in the following code fragment, there is no exception caught.

```
DataRow rowToEdit = books.Rows[0];
rowToEdit.BeginEdit();
try
{
  rowToEdit["AuthorId"] = 21;
    ...
  }
catch(Exception e)
{
  Console.WriteLine("\n" + e.Message +   " while editing a
                                        row.");
  Console.WriteLine();
}
```

However, when we invoke the **EndEdit** method on the row, the exception is raised.

```
try
{
  rowToEdit.EndEdit();
 }
catch(Exception e)
{
  Console.WriteLine();
  Console.WriteLine("\n" + e.Message + " on EndEdit");
  Console.WriteLine();
}
```

The following message is printed out because the illegal value was still present when the editing session was finished.

```
ForeignKeyConstraint Authors->Books requires the child key
     values (21) to exist in the parent table. on EndEdit
```

## DATAROW VERSIONS

Before the row changes have been accepted, both the original and the changed row data are available. The item property[19] of the row can take a **DataRowVersion** to specify which value you want. The version field can be **Original**, **Default**, **Current**, or **Proposed**.

```
Console.WriteLine("BeginEdit called for Book AuthorId.");
rowToEdit.BeginEdit();
rowToEdit["AuthorId"] = 2;
```

---

[19] The item property of the **DataRow** is the indexer for the class.

```
Console.WriteLine("Current Value {0}",
    rowToEdit["AuthorId", DataRowVersion.Current]);
Console.WriteLine("Proposed Value {0}",
    rowToEdit["AuthorId", DataRowVersion.Proposed]);
Console.WriteLine("Default Value {0}",
    rowToEdit["AuthorId", DataRowVersion.Default]);

rowToEdit.EndEdit();

Console.WriteLine("Current Value {0}",
    rowToEdit["AuthorId", DataRowVersion.Current]);
Console.WriteLine("Default Value {0}",
    rowToEdit["AuthorId", DataRowVersion.Default]);

Console.WriteLine("EndEdit called.");
    ...
```

This code caused the following output to be printed out:

```
BeginEdit called for Book AuthorId.
Current Value 1
Proposed Value 2
Default Value 2
...
EndEdit called.
Current Value 2
Default Value 2
```

During editing the **Current** and **Proposed** item values are available. After **CancelEdit**, the **Proposed** value is no longer available. After **EndEdit**, the **Proposed** value becomes the **Current** value, and the **Proposed** value is no longer available.

## DATAROW ROWSTATE PROPERTY

In addition to the **Current** and **Proposed** values of a field, the **DataRow** itself has a property that indicates the state of the particular row. The values can be **Added**, **Deleted**, **Detached**, **Modified**, or **Unchanged**.

A row is in the **Detached** state when it has been created, but has not been added to any **DataRow** collection, or it has been removed from a collection.

The **Default DataRowVersion** of a field returns the appropriate row version depending on the **RowState** property.

## ACCEPTING AND REJECTING CHANGES

Calling **EndEdit** on a **DataRow** does not cause the changes to be made to the row. Calling the **AcceptChanges** or **RejectChanges** method on the **DataSet**, **DataTable**, or **DataRow** ends editing on all the contained rows of the appropriate scope. If **EndEdit** or **CancelEdit** has not been called, these methods do it implicitly for all rows within its scope.

After the **AcceptChanges** method, the **Current** value becomes the **Original** value. If **EndEdit** has not been called the **Proposed** value becomes the new **Current and Original** values. If the **RowState** was **Added**, **Modified**, or **Deleted** it becomes **Unchanged** and the changes are accepted.

After the **RejectChanges** method, the **Proposed** value is deleted. If the **RowState** was **Deleted** or **Modified**, the values revert to their previous values, and the **RowState** becomes **Unchanged**. If the **RowState** was **Added**, the row is removed from the **Rows** collection.

Since the **RowState** after **AcceptChanges** is **Unchanged**, calling the **DataAdapter**'s **Update** method at this point will not cause any changes to made on the data source. Therefore, you should call the **Update** method on the **DataAdapter** to update changes to the data source before calling **AcceptChanges** on any row, table, or **DataSet**.

Here is the code from the case study's **HotelBroker** object's **CancelReservation** method. Note how **AcceptChanges** on the **DataSet** is called if the **SqlDataAdapter.Update** method succeeds. If an exception is thrown, or the update fails, **RejectChanges** is called.

```
public void CancelReservation(int id)
{
 DataTable t = null;
 try
 {
   t = dataset.Tables["Reservations"];
   DataRow[] rc = t.Select("ReservationId = " + id + " ");

   for (int i = 0; i < rc.Length; i++)
     rc[i].Delete();

     int NumberRows = adapter.Update(dataset,
                                 "Reservations");
   if (NumberRows > 0)
    t.AcceptChanges();
   else
    t.RejectChanges();
}
catch(Exception e)
{
  t.RejectChanges();
  throw e;
  }

  return;
}
```

If you do not reject the changes on failure, the rows will still be in the **DataSet**. The next time an update is requested, the update will be rejected again, because the rows are still waiting to be updated. Since the **DataSet** is independent of a database, the fact that an update occurs on the database has nothing to do with accepting or rejecting the changed rows in the **DataSet**.

### DATAROW ERRORS

If there have been any data editing errors on a row, the **HasErrors** property on the **DataSet**, **DataTable**, or **DataRow** will be set to true. To get the error, use the **DataRow**'s **GetColumnError** or the **GetColunmsInError** methods.

## Acme Travel Agency Case Study

At this point we have covered more than enough material for you to understand the database version of the **Customer** and **HotelBroker** objects in the case study. As usual, the code is in the **CaseStudy** directory for this chapter.

Since there will never be any reason for the **Customer** object to hold any state, the **Customer** object methods use **SqlDataReader** to access the database and return the results. Any state that a program might need (i.e., a list of customers) could easily be maintained in the client program and not in a middle-tier object.

The **HotelBroker** and **HotelBookings** objects are a little more complicated. As mentioned earlier, for pedagogical reasons alone these objects would have been implemented using a **DataSet** to show you how that technology would work in an application.

Nonetheless, we will see that with Web applications there might be a reason to keep some state in the middle tier. In that scenario, the **DataSet** can serve as an intelligent cache.

## XML Data Access

As we will discuss in the Web Services chapter, XML has many advantages for describing data that must move between heterogeneous systems and data sources. Since you can validate your XML against an XML schema description, you can pass it in many situations where passing a **DataSet** makes no sense.[20] Since XML is text, it can pass through firewall ports that are normally open, unlike the DCOM or RMI protocols that require special ports to be open.

---

[20] When you remote a **DataSet** it is remoted as XML, nonetheless, if you have to interact with an unmanaged program you can convert the data in the **DataSet** to XML and send it. As discussed in the Web Services chapter, the XML protocol used by remoting and Web Services is not identical.

The thrust of these next sections is not to discuss XML in any great detail. We just want to demonstrate how you can move back and forth between looking at data in XML and looking at data with a **DataSet**.

## XML Schema and Data

XML does not dictate how data is organized or what the meaning of XML documents are. It only describes the rules on how the documents are put together.[21] An XML schema describes the *metadata* of how the data is organized inside an XML document. XML schemas are written in XML.

For example, XML can be used to describe data in a relational database, but an XML schema can be used to describe relationships such as primary and foreign keys. Having the XML schema and the data in one document or text stream is vastly simpler than having to download each table into a dataset and then programmatically set up the relations between the tables.

## XmlDataDocument

Documents can include database output within them. For example, a sales report has an explanation as well as the sales data that was pulled from a data source. The **XmlDataDocument** class can be used to represent data in the form of an XML document.

The **XmlDataDocument** class inherits from **XmlDocument** which represents an XML document for the .NET XML Framework classes. What makes the **XmlDataDocument** particularly interesting is that you can construct an **XmlDataDocument** from a **DataSet** by passing the **DataSet** instance to the **XmlDataDocument** constructor. The **XmlDataDocument** has a read-only **DataSet** property so that you can work with the XML document as relational data if that makes sense.

## DataSet and XML

The **DataSet** has methods, **WriteXml** and **WriteXmlSchema**, that can write out the data and schema associated with the dataset. The XML schema that the **DataSet** writes out is deduced from the current set of tables, columns, constraints, and relations. Unless you explicitly add the constraints to the **DataSet**, such as primary- or foreign-key relationships, they will not be part of the schema.

The **DataSet** also has methods to read XML: **ReadXml** and **ReadXmlSchema**. **ReadXml** can read both the data and the schema into the dataset. If a schema is not present, it will try to infer one from the data. If it cannot infer a schema, it will throw an exception. **ReadXmlSchema** will read in a schema document.

---

[21] Technically speaking, XML documents in the sense that we speak of are defined by the XML Infoset and consist of documents, elements, and attributes.

If there is no schema in an XML document, the **DataSet** extracts elements that would be defined as tables according to a set of rules. The remaining elements, along with the attributes, are then assigned as columns to the tables.

You can use the **ColumnMapping** property of the **DataColumn** class to control whether you want columns written as XML elements or attributes. Elements that are not scalar values become tables; attributes and scalar values are columns. The exact procedure is described in the .NET documentation.

# AirlineBrokers Database

The AirlineBrokers database will be used to study XML data access. This database can be created using the SqlServer Enterprise Manager and the airlinebroker.sql script found in the AcmeDatabaseScripts subdirectory of the case study. The AirlineBrokers database represents another service that the Acme reservation system uses. Acme customers can make airline reservations to the places they wish to go.

The database has several tables:

- Airlines: information about the various airlines in the database
- PlaneType: the various planes that the airlines use
- Flights: information about the various airlines' flights
- Customers: information about customers
- Reservations: information about the customers' reservations

Although in real life the Airline Broker and the Hotel Broker would not have the same Customers table, for simplicity we use the same table structure, and we use the same component to access it.

## DataSet and XML

To illustrate the relationship between the relation model of the **DataSet** and the XML model we will first fetch some information from the database. The **DataSetXml** example uses the same commands and techniques we have studied in this chapter to extract the data.

First the connection, **DataSet**, and the **SqlDataAdapters** for the various tables are created.

```
SqlConnection conn = new SqlConnection(connectString);
DataSet d = new DataSet("AirlineBroker");
SqlDataAdapter  airlinesAdapter = new SqlDataAdapter();
SqlDataAdapter  flightsAdapter = new SqlDataAdapter();
SqlDataAdapter  planetypeAdapter = new SqlDataAdapter();
SqlDataAdapter  customersAdapter = new SqlDataAdapter();
SqlDataAdapter  reservationsAdapter = new SqlDataAdapter();
```

Then the various select commands to fetch the data are created and the dataset is filled with the data from those tables:

```
airlinesAdapter.SelectCommand = new SqlCommand(
                          "select * from Airlines", conn);
airlinesAdapter.Fill(d, "Airlines");

flightsAdapter.SelectCommand = new SqlCommand(
                          "select * from Flights", conn);
flightsAdapter.Fill(d, "Flights");

planetypeAdapter.SelectCommand = new SqlCommand(
                          "select * from PlaneType", conn);
planetypeAdapter.Fill(d, "PlaneType");

customersAdapter.SelectCommand = new SqlCommand(
                          "select * from Customers", conn);
customersAdapter.Fill(d, "Customers");

reservationsAdapter.SelectCommand = new SqlCommand(
                          "select * from Reservations", conn);
reservationsAdapter.Fill(d, "Reservations");
```

We now have the data for the Airlines, Flights, PlaneType, Customers, and Reservations tables in the data set.

Next we have the **DataSet** written out as an XML schema, the schema it infers from the data. Then the **DataSet** writes out the data as XML.

```
d.WriteXmlSchema("Airlines.xsd");
d.WriteXml("Airlines.xml");
```

Here are some of the data that were written to the file Airlines.xml. The main element is Airline Broker, which was the name of the **DataSet**. Elements at the next lower level correspond to the various tables that were added to the database: **Airlines**, **Flights**, **PlaneType**, and **Customers**. There were no reservations in the database. There is one set for each row in the table. The elements under each of these tables correspond to the fields for that particular row.

```
<AirlineBroker>
  <Airlines>
    <Name>America West</Name>
    <Abbreviation>AW</Abbreviation>
    <WebSite>www.americawest.com</WebSite>
    <ReservationNumber>555-555-1212</ReservationNumber>
  </Airlines>
  <Airlines>
    <Name>Delta</Name>
    <Abbreviation>DL</Abbreviation>
    <WebSite>www.delta.com</WebSite>
```

```
        <ReservationNumber>800-456-7890</ReservationNumber>
    </Airlines>
...
    <Flights>
        <Airline>DL</Airline>
        <FlightNumber>987</FlightNumber>
        <StartCity>Atlanta</StartCity>
        <EndCity>New Orleans</EndCity>
        <Departure>2001-10-05T20:15:00.0000000-04:00
                </Departure>
        <Arrival>2001-10-05T22:30:00.0000000-04:00</Arrival>
        <PlaneType>737</PlaneType>
        <FirstCost>1300</FirstCost>
        <BusinessCost>0</BusinessCost>
        <EconomyCost>450</EconomyCost>
    </Flights>
...
    <Flights>
    <PlaneType>
        <PlaneType>737</PlaneType>
        <FirstClass>10</FirstClass>
        <BusinessClass>0</BusinessClass>
        <EconomyClass>200</EconomyClass>
    </PlaneType>
...
    <Customers>
        <LastName>Adams</LastName>
        <FirstName>John</FirstName>
        <EmailAddress>adams@presidents.org</EmailAddress>
        <CustomerId>1</CustomerId>
    </Customers>
</AirlineBroker>
```

From the structure of the data, the **DataSet** deduces a schema that was written to Airlines.xsd. We discuss here an excerpt from that file. There are no relationships or primary keys defined between any of the tables such as **Airlines** and **Flights** as in the database, because none were defined in the **DataSet**. If you look at the actual generated file, you will see that schema information was inferred for **Reservations** even though there were no data in the table.

The schema preamble in the first line, reproduced here, defines the name of the schema as AirlineBroker, and we are using two namespaces in this schema document. One, abbreviated **xsd**, contains the XML Schema standard definitions. The other, abbreviated **msdata**, contains Microsoft definitions.

```
...
<xsd:schema id="AirlineBroker" targetNamespace="" xmlns=""
        xmlns:xsd=http://www.w3.org/2001/XMLSchema
        xmlns:msdata="urn:schemas-microsoft-com:xml-msdata">
```

The next line defines an element called AirlineBroker which has an attribute that indicates this schema came from a **DataSet**. That is a Microsoft defined attribute, not one defined by the W3C Schema namespace. This element AirlineBroker is a complex type. which means it is a structure composed of other types. This structure can have an unlimited number of any (or even none) of the types defined in the rest of the schema.

```
<xsd:element name="AirlineBroker" msdata:IsDataSet="true">
  <xsd:complexType>
  <xsd:choice maxOccurs="unbounded">
```

The Airlines element is defined next. It, too, is a structure, or complex type, whose elements, if present, appear in the structure in the order in which they were defined. Those elements, which correspond to the columns in the database table, are all defined to be strings that are optional. No primary keys were defined, and these strings are certainly not optional in the database, but that was what the **DataSet** deduced from the set of tables, constraints and relationships currently defined in the **DataSet**.

```
<xsd:element name="Airlines">
  <xsd:complexType>
  <xsd:sequence>
    <xsd:element name="Name" type="xsd:string"
                                minOccurs="0" />
    <xsd:element name="Abbreviation"
            type="xsd:string" minOccurs="0" />
    <xsd:element name="WebSite" type="xsd:string"
                                minOccurs="0" />
    <xsd:element name="ReservationNumber"
            type="xsd:string" minOccurs="0" />
  </xsd:sequence>
  </xsd:complexType>
</xsd:element>
```

The table, Flights, is defined similarly to Airlines. In addition to there being no primary key here, there is no foreign key defined for Airline or PlaneType.

```
<xsd:element name="Flights">
  <xsd:complexType>
  <xsd:sequence>
    <xsd:element name="Airline" type="xsd:string"
                                minOccurs="0" />
    <xsd:element name="FlightNumber" type="xsd:int"
                                minOccurs="0" />
    <xsd:element name="StartCity" type="xsd:string"
                                minOccurs="0" />
    <xsd:element name="EndCity" type="xsd:string"
                                minOccurs="0" />
    <xsd:element name="Departure" type="xsd:dateTime"
```

```
                                              minOccurs="0" />
          <xsd:element name="Arrival" type="xsd:dateTime"
                                              minOccurs="0" />
          <xsd:element name="PlaneType" type="xsd:string"
                                              minOccurs="0" />
          <xsd:element name="FirstCost" type="xsd:decimal"
                                              minOccurs="0" />
          <xsd:element name="BusinessCost"
                         type="xsd:decimal" minOccurs="0" />
          <xsd:element name="EconomyCost"
                         type="xsd:decimal" minOccurs="0" />
        </xsd:sequence>
        </xsd:complexType>
      </xsd:element>
...
  </xsd:choice>
  </xsd:complexType>
</xsd:element>
</xsd:schema>
```

We will come back to this schema definition, but for the moment let us continue to work with this example.

## Creating an XML Doc from a Dataset

We create a new XML document from the **DataSet**. Using an XPath query to get the top of the document, we set up an **XmlNodeReader** to read through it. We can then print out the contents of the document to the console. The **XmlNodeReader** class knows how to navigate through the document.

```
XmlDataDocument xmlDataDoc = new XmlDataDocument(d);

XmlNodeReader xmlNodeReader = null;
try
{
  XmlNode node = xmlDataDoc.SelectSingleNode("/");
  xmlNodeReader = new XmlNodeReader (node);
  FormatXml (xmlNodeReader);
}
catch (Exception e)
{
  Console.WriteLine ("Exception: {0}", e.ToString());
}
finally
{
  if (xmlNodeReader != null)
    xmlNodeReader.Close();
}

...
```

```
private static void FormatXml (XmlReader reader)
{
while (reader.Read())
{
  switch (reader.NodeType)
  {
     ...
     case XmlNodeType.Element:
       Format (reader, "Element");
       while(reader.MoveToNextAttribute())
         Format (reader, "Attribute");
       break;
     case XmlNodeType.Text:
       Format (reader, "Text");
       break;
...
static        string lastNodeType = "";

private static void Format(XmlReader reader, string
                                           nodeType)
{
  if (nodeType == "Element")
  {
    if (lastNodeType == "Element")
    {
      Console.WriteLine();
    }
    for (int i=0; i < reader.Depth; i++)
    {
      Console.Write("  ");
    }
    Console.Write(reader.Name);
  }
  else if (nodeType == "Text")
    Console.WriteLine("={0}", reader.Value);
  else
  {
    Console.Write(nodeType + "<" + reader.Name + ">" +
                                        reader.Value);
    Console.WriteLine();
  }

  lastNodeType = nodeType;
}
```

The results resemble the XML that the **DataSet** wrote to a file.

```
AirlineBroker
  Airlines
    Name=America West
```

```
      Abbreviation=AW
      WebSite=www.americawest.com
      ReservationNumber=555-555-1212
  Airlines
      Name=Delta
      Abbreviation=DL
      WebSite=www.delta.com
      ReservationNumber=800-456-7890
  Airlines
      Name=Northwest
      Abbreviation=NW
      WebSite=www.northwest.com
      ReservationNumber=888-111-2222
  Airlines
      Name=Piedmont
      Abbreviation=P
      WebSite=www.piedmont.com
      ReservationNumber=888-222-333
  Airlines
      Name=Southwest
      Abbreviation=S
      WebSite=www.southwest.com
      ReservationNumber=1-800-111-222
  Airlines
      Name=United
      Abbreviation=UAL
      WebSite=www.ual.com
      ReservationNumber=800-123-4568
  Flights
      Airline=DL
      FlightNumber=987
      StartCity=Atlanta
      EndCity=New Orleans
      Departure=2001-10-05T20:15:00.0000000-04:00
      Arrival=2001-10-05T22:30:00.0000000-04:00
      PlaneType=737
      FirstCost=1300
      BusinessCost=0
      EconomyCost=450
  Flights
      Airline=UAL
      FlightNumber=54
      StartCity=Boston
      EndCity=Los Angeles
      Departure=2001-10-01T10:00:00.0000000-04:00
      Arrival=2001-10-01T13:00:00.0000000-04:00
      PlaneType=767
      FirstCost=1500
      BusinessCost=1000
      EconomyCost=300
```

```
PlaneType
  PlaneType=737
  FirstClass=10
  BusinessClass=0
  EconomyClass=200
PlaneType
  PlaneType=767
  FirstClass=10
  BusinessClass=30
  EconomyClass=300
Customers
  LastName=Adams
  FirstName=John
  EmailAddress=adams@presidents.org
  CustomerId=1
```

## Schema with Relationships

If we add relationships to the schema we just created, we can use the schema to create a typed data class to work with our database.

We could do that programmatically by adding constraints and relationships to the dataset, as discussed earlier in the chapter, and then writing out the schema. The **DataSchemaXml** example does just that. You could also create a schema document by hand, or edit the one we generated in the previous example.

The XSD Tool directory has a schema which has been revised to add the relationships between the tables in the AirlineBroker database. The first part of the file, **AirlineBroker.xsd**, looks like the previous version except that the minOccurs=0 attribute has been removed from all the fields because we do not allow nulls in any of them.

```
...
 <xsd:element name="Airlines">
    <xsd:complexType>
    <xsd:sequence>
       <xsd:element name="Name" type="xsd:string" />
        <xsd:element name="Abbreviation"
                         type="xsd:string" />
        <xsd:element name="ReservationNumber"
                         type="xsd:string" />
        <xsd:element name="WebSite" type="xsd:string" />
    </xsd:sequence>
    </xsd:complexType>
 </xsd:element>
...
```

The last section defines the relationships. Here is the definition for the Airlines table primary key. Note the use of attributes in the **msdata** namespace. These attributes are defined by Microsoft using the W3C Schema standard to express additional semantic information about the **DataSet**. These extensions themselves are not a W3C standard. The Schema standard can express constraints with the **unique**, **key**, or **keyref** constructs. Nonetheless, they do not specify which unique key is the primary key.

XPath, which is used to specify relationships to other tables and fields is a W3C standard for locating elements within an XML file. It is used when an XML constraint has to specify to which other element it refers to.

The primary key definition states that the **Airlines_PrimaryKey** is a primary key defined for the **Airlines** element, consisting of the sub element, **Name**. Note how the **msdata:PrimaryKey** attribute is used in conjunction with the standard **unique** construct.

```
    <xsd:unique name="Airlines_PrimaryKey"
                            msdata:PrimaryKey="true">
  <xsd:selector xpath=".//Airlines" />
  <xsd:field xpath="Name" />
</xsd:unique>
```

The next section constrains the Abbreviation column in an Airlines row to be unique.

```
<xsd:unique name="Unique_Airline_Abbreviation">
  <xsd:selector xpath=".//Airlines" />
  <xsd:field xpath="Abbreviation" />
</xsd:unique>
...
```

Reservations_x0020_CustomerId is defined to be a foreign key. The CustomerId field in the Reservations table must be found in the CustomerId field of some row in the Customer table.

```
    <xsd:keyref name="Reservations_x0020_CustomerId"
                    refer="Customers_PrimaryKey"

  <xsd:selector xpath=".//Reservations" />
  <xsd:field xpath="CustomerId" />
</xsd:keyref>
```

The foreign key Flights_x0020_Abbrev has some rules defined for it.

```
<xsd:keyref name="Flights_x0020_Abbrev"
                refer="Unique_Airline_Abbreviation"

                msdata:AcceptRejectRule="Cascade"
                msdata:DeleteRule="SetNull">
  <xsd:selector xpath=".//Flights" />
  <xsd:field xpath="Airline" />
</xsd:keyref>
...
```

## Typed DataSet

An XML schema can be used to generate a dataset that is "typed." Instead of using the index property of a collection to access an element of the dataset, you can use the name of a column. Here is a fragment from the **TypedDataSet** example:

```
AirlineBroker.AirlinesRow UAL = a.FindByName("United");
Console.WriteLine("{0}({1}) ReservationNumber:{2}
    WebSite:{3}", UAL.Name.Trim(), UAL.Abbreviation.Trim(),
    UAL.ReservationNumber.Trim(), UAL.WebSite.Trim());
```

You can assign a meaningful name to rows as well as use strong typing to make sure you are working with the data element you want to. If you try to set the field **UAL.ReservationNumber** to an integer, the compiler will detect the mistake.

A typed **DataSet** inherits from the **DataSet** class, so that everything that is available in a **DataSet** is available in a typed **DataSet**. If the schema of the database changes, however, the typed dataset class must be regenerated.

### Generating Typed DataSets

The XML Schema Definition Tool (Xsd.exe) is used to transform an XML schema (XSD) to a typed data set. The syntax for doing this is:

```
Xsd.exe /d /l:C# filename.xsd
```

The /d switch indicates that a **DataSet** should be generated. The /l switch indicates that a C# class should be generated.

The XSD Tool directory has a batch file that can be used to take the revised AirlineBroker XSD and generate a typed dataset AirlineBroker.cs.

### Fetching Data with a Typed DataSet

The **TypedDataSet** example shows how to use a typed dataset to access the Airline Brokers database. You define your **SqlConnection** as usual and create an **SqlDataAdapter** instance for each table you want to use. You create whatever **SqlCommands** you need to work with the data. A typed **DataSet** is independent of a database, just like the untyped **DataSet**, so it needs **SqlDataAdapter** to handle the database operations.

```
SqlConnection  conn = new SqlConnection(connectString);

SqlDataAdapter  airlinesAdapter = new SqlDataAdapter();
SqlDataAdapter  flightsAdapter = new SqlDataAdapter();
SqlDataAdapter  planetypeAdapter = new SqlDataAdapter();
SqlDataAdapter  customersAdapter = new SqlDataAdapter();
SqlDataAdapter  reservationsAdapter = new SqlDataAdapter();

AirlineBroker airlineBrokerDataset = new AirlineBroker();
```

Next the select commands are defined to fetch the data, just as for use with a regular **DataSet**. For illustrative purposes, constraint checking is enabled even though it is on by default.

```
airlinesAdapter.SelectCommand = new SqlCommand(
                    "select * from Airlines", conn);
airlinesAdapter.InsertCommand = new SqlCommand(
        "insert Airlines(Name, Abbreviation, WebSite,
        ReservationNumber) values(@Name, @Abbrev, @Web,
        @Reserve)", conn);
airlinesAdapter.InsertCommand.CommandType =
        CommandType.Text;

SqlParameter param = new SqlParameter("@Name",
        SqlDbType.NChar, 40);
airlinesAdapter.InsertCommand.Parameters.Add(param);
airlinesAdapter.InsertCommand.Parameters["@Name"].
            SourceColumn = "Name";
...
  airlineBrokerDataset.EnforceConstraints = true;
...
```

Now you can fetch the data. The order is which you do this is important. If Flights data are fetched before PlaneType data, a constraint violation exception will occur, because the PlaneType field in the Flights table does not exist.

```
airlinesAdapter.Fill(airlineBrokerDataset, "Airlines");
planetypeAdapter.Fill(airlineBrokerDataset, "PlaneType");
flightsAdapter.Fill(airlineBrokerDataset, "Flights");
customersAdapter.Fill(airlineBrokerDataset, "Customers");
reservationsAdapter.Fill(airlineBrokerDataset,
                                    "Reservations");
```

## Displaying Data with a Typed Dataset

The strong typing makes it straightforward to display the data:

```
AirlineBroker.AirlinesDataTable a =
                airlineBrokerDataset.Airlines;
```

```
Console.WriteLine(a.TableName);
Console.WriteLine("    {0, -18} {1, -20} {2, -20}
          {3, -15}", "Name", "Abbreviation", "Web Site",
          "Reservation Numbers");
for (int i = 0; i < a.Count; i++)
  Console.WriteLine("    {0, -18} {1, -20} {2, -20}
    {3, -15}", a[i].Name.Trim(), a[i].Abbreviation.Trim(),
    a[i].WebSite.Trim(), a[i].ReservationNumber.Trim());
...
```

It is easy to locate the data:

```
AirlineBroker.AirlinesRow UAL = a.FindByName("United");
Console.WriteLine("{0}({1}) ReservationNumber:{2}
  WebSite:{3}", UAL.Name.Trim(), UAL.Abbreviation.Trim(),
  UAL.ReservationNumber.Trim(), UAL.WebSite.Trim());
...
```

## Modify Data with a Typed Dataset

You modify and update the database with a typed dataset just like a regular dataset. Make sure the correct table is specified in the **Update** method.

```
airlineBrokerDataset.Airlines.AddAirlinesRow("Southwest",
          "S", "1-800-111-222", "www.southwest.com");
NumberRows = airlinesAdapter.Update(airlineBrokerDataset,
          "Airlines");
if (NumberRows == 1)
  Console.WriteLine("Southwest added.");
else
  Console.WriteLine("Southwest not added");
```

## Summary

ADO.NET provides classes that enable you to design and build a distributed data architecture. You can access databases in a connected or disconnected mode depending on your concurrency requirements. The **DataSet** enables you to work with data in a relational manner without being connected to any data source. XML can be used to model relational data inside an XML document that contains nonrelational information. A typed **DataSet** gives you the ability to work in a much easier, type-safe fashion with a **DataSet**, provided you have an XML Schema that defines your data.

# ASP.NET and Web Forms

*A*n important part of .NET is its use in creating Web applications through a technology known as ASP.NET. Far more than an incremental enhancement to Active Server Pages (ASP), the new technology is a unified Web development platform that greatly simplifies the implementation of sophisticated Web applications. In this chapter we introduce the fundamentals of ASP.NET and cover Web Forms, which make it easy to develop interactive Web sites. In Chapter 11 we cover Web Services, which enable the development of collaborative Web applications that span heterogeneous systems.

## What Is ASP.NET?

We begin our exploration of ASP.NET by looking at a very simple Web application. Along the way we will establish a test bed for ASP.NET programming, and we will review some of the fundamentals of Web processing. Our little example will reveal some of the challenges in developing Web applications, and we can then appreciate the features and benefits of ASP.NET, which we will elaborate in the rest of the chapter.

### Web Application Fundamentals

A Web application consists of document and code pages in various formats. The simplest kind of document is a static HTML page, which contains information that will be formatted and displayed by a Web browser. An HTML page may also contain hyperlinks to other HTML pages. A hyperlink (or just "link") contains an address, or a Uniform Resource Locator (URL), specifying where the target document is located. The resulting combination of content and links is sometimes called "hypertext" and provides easy navigation to a vast amount of information on the World Wide Web.

## SETTING UP THE WEB EXAMPLES

As usual, all the example programs for this chapter are in the chapter folder. To run the examples, you will need to have Internet Information Services (IIS) installed on your system. IIS is installed by default with Windows 2000 Server. You will have to explicitly install it with Windows 2000 Workstation. Once installed, you can access the documentation on IIS through Internet Explorer via the URL **http://localhost**, which will redirect you to the starting IIS documentation page, as illustrated in Figure 10–1.

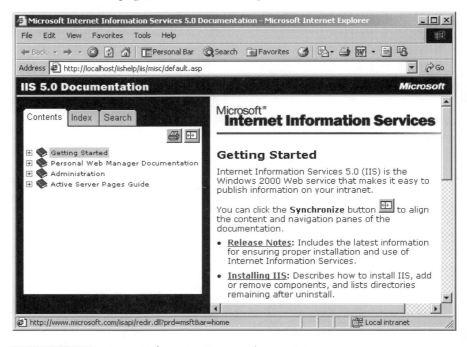

**Figure 10–1**    *Internet Information Services documentation.*

The management tool for IIS is a Microsoft Management Console (MMC) "snap-in," the Internet Services Manager, which you can find under Administrative Tools in the Control Panel. Figure 10–2 shows the main window of the Internet Services Manager. You can Start and Stop the Web server and perform other tasks by right-clicking on Default Web Site. Choosing Properties from the context menu will let you perform a number of configurations on the Web server.

Figure 10–2   *Internet Services Manager.*

The default home directory for publishing Web files is **\Inetpub\
wwwroot** on the drive where Windows is installed. You can change this
home directory using Internet Services Manager. You can access Web pages
stored at any location on your hard drive by creating a "virtual directory."
The easiest way to create one is from Windows Explorer. Right-click over the
desired directory, choose Sharing..., select the Web Sharing tab, click on the
Add button, and enter the desired alias, which will be the name of the virtual
directory. Figure 10–3 illustrates creating an alias **NetCs**, or virtual directory,
for the folder **\OI\NetCs\Chap10**. You should perform this operation now
on your own system in order that you may follow along as the chapter's
examples are discussed.

*Creating a virtual directory.*

Once a virtual directory has been created, you can access files in it by including the virtual directory in the path of the URL. In particular, you can access the file **default.htm** using the URL **http://localhost/NetCs/**. The file **default.htm** contains a home page for all the ASP.NET example programs for this chapter. See Figure 10–4.

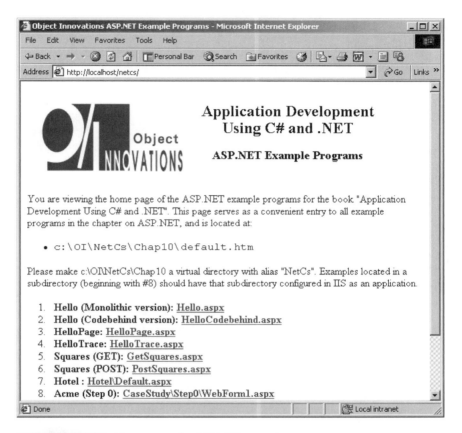

**Figure 10–4**    *Home page for ASP.NET example programs.*

## An Echo Program

The first example program for this chapter is **Hello.aspx**, shown as a link on the home page. The example is complete in one file and contains embedded server code. Here is the source code, which consists of HTML along with some C# script code. There are also some special tags for "server controls," recognized by ASP.NET.

```
<!-- Hello.aspx -->
<%@ Page Language="C#" %>
<HTML>
<HEAD>
    <SCRIPT RUNAT="SERVER">
  protected void cmdEcho_Click(object Source, EventArgs e)
  {
    lblGreeting.Text="Hello, " + txtName.Text;
```

```
    }
    </SCRIPT>
</HEAD>
<BODY>
<FORM RUNAT="SERVER">Your name: 
<asp:textbox id=txtName Runat="server"></asp:textbox>
<p><asp:button id=cmdEcho onclick=cmdEcho_Click Text="Echo"
runat="server" tooltip="Click to echo your name">
</asp:button></p>
<asp:label id=lblGreeting runat="server"></asp:label>
<P></P>
</FORM>
</BODY>
</HTML>
```

You can run the program using the URL **http://localhost/ NetCs/Hello.aspx** or by clicking on the link **Hello.aspx** in the home page of the examples programs. The page shows a text box where you can type in your name, and there is an "Echo" button. Clicking the button will echo your name back, with a "Hello" greeting. The simple form is again displayed, so you could try out other names. If you slide the browser's mouse cursor over the button, you will see the tool tip "Click to echo your name" displayed in a yellow box. Figure 10–5 illustrates a run of this example.

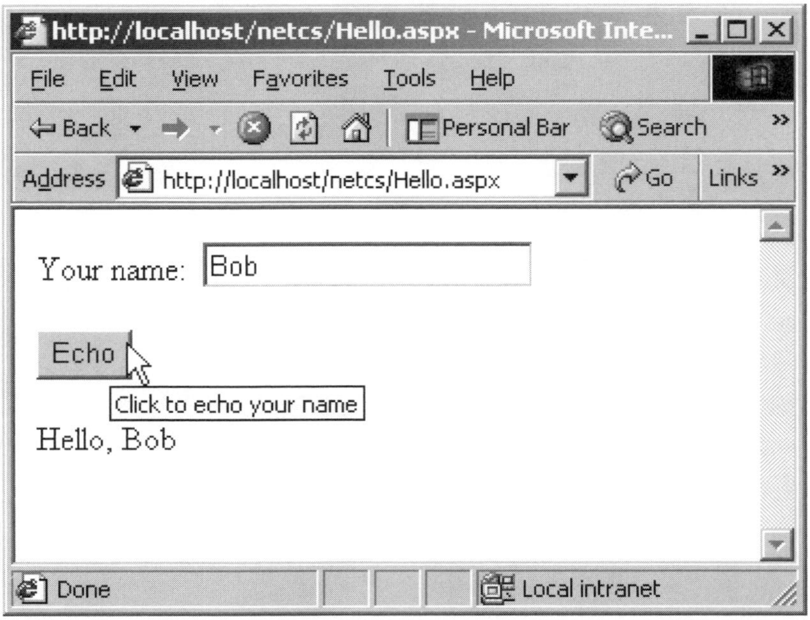

**Figure 10–5**  *Running the Hello.aspx echo program.*

This little program would not be completely trivial to implement with other Web application tools, including ASP. The key user-interface feature of such an application is its thoroughly forms-based nature. The user is presented with a form and interacts with the form. The server does some processing, and the user continues to see the same form. This UI model is second nature in desktop applications but is not so common in Web applications. Typically the Web server will send back a different page.

This kind of application could certainly be implemented using a technology like ASP, but the code would be a little ugly. The server would need to synthesize a new page that looked like the old page, creating the HTML tags for the original page, plus extra information sent back (such as the greeting shown at the bottom in our echo example). A mechanism is needed to remember the current data that is displayed in the controls in the form.

Another feature of this Web application is that it does some client-side processing too—the "tooltip" displayed in the yellow box is performed by the browser. Such rich client-side processing can be performed by some browsers, such as Internet Explorer, but not others.

As can be seen by the example code, with ASP.NET it is very easy to implement this kind of Web application. We will study the code in detail later. For now, just observe how easy it is!

## ASP.NET Features

ASP.NET provides a programming model and infrastructure that facilitates developing new classes of Web applications. Part of this infrastructure is the .NET runtime and framework. Server-side code is written in .NET compiled languages. Two main programming models are supported by ASP.NET.

- Web Forms helps you build form-based Web pages. A WYSIWYG development environment enables you to drag controls onto Web pages. Special "server-side" controls present the programmer with an event model similar to what is provided by controls in ordinary Windows programming. This chapter discusses Web Forms in detail.
- Web Services make it possible for a Web site to expose functionality via an API that can be called remotely by other applications. Data is exchanged using standard Web protocols and formats such as HTTP and XML, which will cross firewalls. We will discuss Web Services in the next chapter.

Both Web Forms and Web Services can take advantage of the facilities provided by .NET, such as the compiled code and .NET runtime. In addition, ASP.NET itself provides a number of infrastructure services, including state management, security, configuration, caching, and tracing.

## COMPILED CODE

Web Forms (and Web Services) can be written in any .NET language that runs on top of the CLR, including C#, VB.NET, and C++ with Managed Extensions. This code is compiled, and thus offers better performance than ASP pages with code written in an interpreted scripting language such as VBScript. All of the benefits, such as a managed execution environment, are available to this code, and of course the entire .NET Framework Class Library is available. Legacy unmanaged code can be called through the .NET interoperability services, which are discussed in Chapter 14.

## SERVER CONTROLS

ASP.NET provides a significant innovation known as "server controls." These controls have special tags such as <asp:textbox>. Server-side code interacts with these controls, and the ASP.NET runtime generates straight HTML that is sent to the Web browser. The result is a programming model that is easy to use and yet produces standard HTML that can run in any browser.

## BROWSER INDEPENDENCE

Although the World Wide Web is built on standards, the unfortunate fact of life is that browsers are not compatible and have special features. A Web page designer then has the unattractive options of either writing to a lowest common denominator of browser, or else writing special code for different browsers. Server controls help remove some of this pain. ASP.NET takes care of browser compatibility issues when it generates code for a server control. If the requesting browser is upscale, the generated HTML can take advantage of these features, otherwise the generated code will be vanilla HTML. ASP.NET takes care of detecting the type of browser.

## SEPARATION OF CODE AND CONTENT

Typical ASP pages have a mixture of scripting code interspersed with HTML elements. In ASP.NET there is a clean separation between code and presentation content. The server code can be isolated within a single <SCRIPT RUNAT="SERVER"> ... /SCRIPT> block or, even better, placed within a "code behind" page. We will discuss "code behind" pages later in this chapter. If you would like to see an example right away, you can examine the second example program **HelloCodebehind.aspx**, with code in the file **HelloCodebehind. aspx.cs**. (These files are in the top-level chapter directory.)

## STATE MANAGEMENT

HTTP is a stateless protocol. Thus, if a user enters information in various controls on a form, and sends this filled-out form to the server, the information will be lost if the form is displayed again, unless the Web application provides special code to preserve this state. ASP.NET makes this kind of state preservation totally transparent. There are also convenient facilities for managing other types of session and application state.

## Web Forms Architecture

A Web Form consists of two parts:

- The visual content or presentation, typically specified by HTML elements
- Code that contains the logic for interacting with the visual elements.

A Web Form is physically expressed by a file with the extension **.aspx**. Any HTML page could be renamed to have this extension and could be accessed using the new extension with identical results to the original. Thus Web Forms are upwardly compatible with HTML pages.

The way code can be separated from the form is what makes a Web Form special. This code can be either in a separate file (having an extension corresponding to a .NET language, such as **.cs** for C#) or in the **.aspx** file, within a <SCRIPT RUNAT="SERVER"> ... /SCRIPT> block. When your page is run in the Web server, the user interface code runs and dynamically generates the output for the page.

We can understand the architecture of a Web Form most clearly by looking at the code-behind version of our "echo" example. The visual content is specified by the **.aspx** file **HelloCodebehind.aspx**.

```
<!-- HelloCodebehind.aspx -->
<%@ Page Language="C#" Src="HelloCodebehind.aspx.cs"
Inherits= MyWebPage %>
<HTML>
   <HEAD>
   </HEAD>
<BODY>
<FORM RUNAT="SERVER">YOUR NAME: 
<asp:textbox id=txtName Runat="server"></asp:textbox>
<p><asp:button id=cmdEcho onclick=cmdEcho_Click Text="Echo"
runat="server" tooltip="Click to echo your name">
</asp:button></p>
   <asp:label id=lblGreeting runat="server"></asp:label>
<P></P>
</FORM>
</BODY>
</HTML>
```

The user interface code is in the file **HelloCodebehind.aspx.cs**,

```
// HelloCodebehind.aspx.cs

using System;
using System.Web;
using System.Web.UI;
using System.Web.UI.WebControls;

public class MyWebPage : System.Web.UI.Page
{
   protected TextBox txtName;
   protected Button cmdEcho;
   protected Label lblGreeting;

   protected void cmdEcho_Click(object Source, EventArgs e)
   {
      lblGreeting.Text="Hello, " + txtName.Text;
   }
}
```

## Page Class

The key namespace for Web Forms and Web Services is **System.Web**. Support for Web Forms is in the namespace **System.Web.UI**. Support for server controls such as text boxes and buttons is in the namespace **System.Web.UI.WebControls**. The class that dynamically generates the output for an **.aspx** page is the **Page** class, in the **System.Web.UI** namespace, and classes derived from **Page**, as illustrated in the code behind page in this last example.

### INHERITING FROM PAGE CLASS

The elements in the **.aspx** file, the code in the code-behind file (or script block), and the base **Page** class work together to generate the page output. This cooperation is achieved by ASP.NET's dynamically creating a class for the **.aspx** file, which is derived from the "code-behind" class, which in turn is derived from **Page**. This relationship is created by the "Inherits" attribute in the .aspx file. Figure 10–6 illustrates the inheritance hierarchy. Here **MyWebPage** is a class we implement, derived from **Page**.

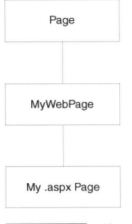

| Page |
|------|

| MyWebPage |
|-----------|

| My .aspx Page |
|---------------|

**Figure 10–6** *Hierarchy of page classes.*

The most derived page class, shown as "My .aspx Page" in Figure 10–6, is dynamically created by the ASP.NET runtime. This class extends the page class, shown as "MyWebPage" in the figure, to incorporate the controls and HTML text on the Web Form. This class is compiled into an executable, which is run when the page is requested from a browser. The executable code creates the HTML that is sent to the browser.

## Web Forms Page Life Cycle

We can get a good high-level understanding of the Web Forms architecture by following the life cycle of our simple Echo application. We will use the code-behind version (the second example), **HelloCodebehind.aspx**.

1. User requests the **HelloCodebehind.aspx** Web page in the browser.
2. Web server compiles the page class from the **.aspx** file and its associated code behind page. The Web server executes the code, creating HTML, which is sent to the browser. (In Internet Explorer you can see the HTML code from the menu View | Source.) Note that the server controls are replaced by straight HTML. The following code is what arrives at the browser, *not the original code on the server.*

```
<!-- HelloCodebehind.aspx -->

<HTML>
  <HEAD>
  </HEAD>
<BODY>
<form name="ctrl0" method="post"
action="HelloCodebehind.aspx" id="ctrl0">
```

```
<input type="hidden" name="__VIEWSTATE"
value="dDwxMzc4MDMwNTk1Ozs+" />
YOUR NAME:  <input name="txtName" type="text"
id="txtName" />
<p><input type="submit" name="cmdEcho" value="Echo"
id="cmdEcho" title="Click to echo your name" /></p>
   <span id="lblGreeting"></span>
<P></P>
</form>
</BODY>
</HTML>
```

3. The browser renders the HTML, displaying the simple form shown in
   Figure 10–7. To distinguish this example from the first one, we show
   "YOUR NAME" in all capitals. Since this is the first time the form is dis-
   played, the text box is empty, and no greeting message is displayed.

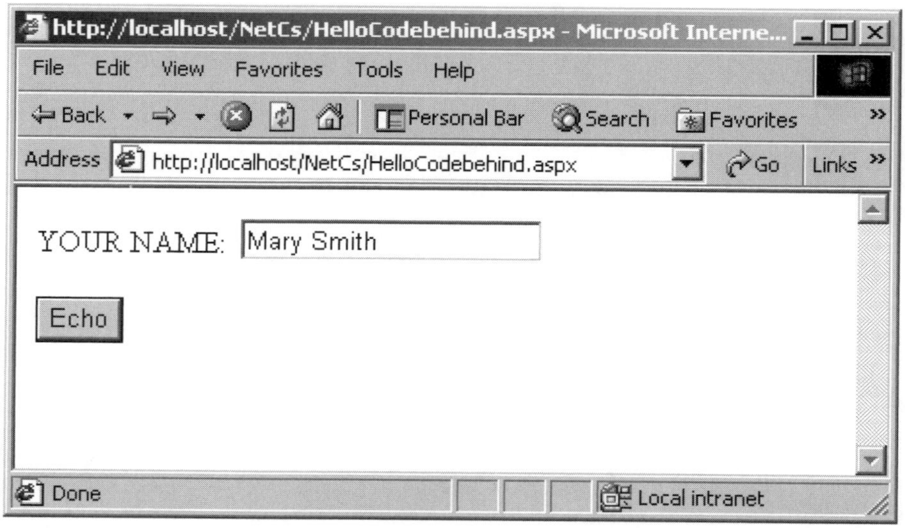

**Figure 10–7**   *The form for the "Echo" application is displayed for the first time.*

4. The user types in a name (e.g., "Mary Smith") and clicks the "Echo"
   button. The browser recognizes that a Submit button has been clicked.
   The method for the form is "post"[1] and the action is
   "HelloCodebehind.aspx." We thus have what is called a "post back" to
   the original **.aspx** file.

---

[1] The HTTP POST method sends form results separately as part of the data body,
rather than by concatenating it onto the URL, as is done in the GET method.

5. The server now performs processing for this page. An event was raised when the user clicked the "Echo" button, and an event handler in the **MyWebPage** class is invoked.

```
protected void cmdEcho_Click(object Source, EventArgs e)
{
    lblGreeting.Text="Hello, " + txtName.Text;
}
```

6. The **Text** property of the **TextBox** server control **txtName** is used to read the name submitted by the user. A greeting string is composed and assigned to the **Label** control **lblGreeting**, again using property notation.

7. The server again generates straight HTML for the server controls and sends the whole response to the browser. Here is the HTML.

```
...
<form name="ctrl0" method="post"
action="HelloCodebehind.aspx" id="ctrl0">
<input type="hidden" name="__VIEWSTATE"
value="dDwxMzc4MDMwNTk1O3Q8O2w8aTwyPjs+O2w8dDw7bDxpPDU+Oz47b
Dx0PHA8cDxsPFR1eHQ7PjtsPEhlbGxvLCBNYXJ5IFNtaXRoOoz4+Oz47Oz47P
j47Pj47Pg==" />
YOUR NAME:  <input name="txtName" type="text"
**value="Mary Smith"** id="txtName" />
<p><input type="submit" name="cmdEcho" value="Echo"
id="cmdEcho" title="Click to echo your name" /></p>
    <span id="lblGreeting">**Hello, Mary Smith**</span>
...
```

8. The browser renders the page, as shown in Figure 10–8. Now a greeting message is displayed.

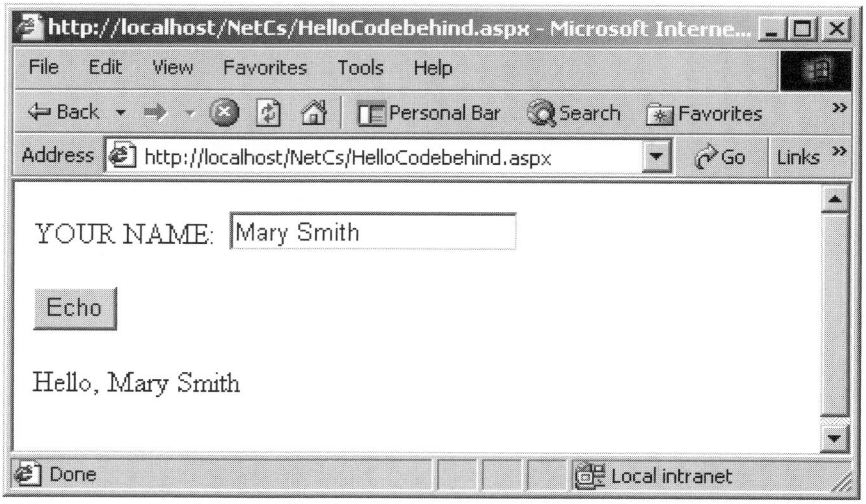

Figure 10–8    *After a round trip a greeting message is displayed.*

## View State

An important characteristic of Web Forms is that all information on forms is "remembered" by the Web server. Since HTTP is a stateless protocol, this preservation of state does not happen automatically but must be programmed. A nice feature of ASP.NET is that this state information, referred to as "view state," is preserved automatically by the Framework, using a "hidden" control.

```
...
<input type="hidden" name="__VIEWSTATE"
value="dDwxMzc4MDMwNTk1O3Q8O2w8aTwyPjs+O2w8dDw7bDxpPDU+Oz47b
Dx0PHA8cDxsPFRleHQ7PjtsPEhlbGxvLCBNYXJ5IFNtaXRoOz4+Oz47Oz47P
j47Pj47Pg==" />
...
```

Later in the chapter we will examine other facilities provided by ASP.NET for managing session state and application state.

## Web Forms Event Model

From the standpoint of the programmer, the event model for Web Forms is very similar to the event model for Windows Forms. Indeed, this similarity is what makes programming with Web Forms so easy. What is actually happening in the case of Web Forms, though, is rather different. The big difference is that events get raised on the client and processed on the server.[2]

---

[2] Some controls, such as the Calendar control, raise some events on the server. Also, the Page itself raises events on the server.

Our simple form with one text box and one button is not rich enough to illustrate event processing very thoroughly. Let's imagine a more elaborate form with several text boxes, list boxes, check boxes, buttons, and the like. Because round trips to the server are expensive, events do not automatically cause a postback to the server. Server controls have what is known as an *intrinsic event set* of events that automatically cause a postback to the server. The most common such intrinsic event is a button click. Other events, such as selecting an item in a list box, do not cause an immediate postback to the server. Instead, these events are cached, until a button click causes a post to the server. Then, on the server the various change events are processed, in no particular order, and the button-click event that caused the post is processed.

## Page Processing

Processing a page is a cooperative endeavor between the Web server, the ASP.NET runtime, and your own code. The **Page** class provides a number of events, which you can handle to hook into page processing. The **Page** class also has properties and methods that you can use. We cover some of the major ones here. For a complete description, consult the .NET Framework documentation. The example programs in this chapter will illustrate features of the **Page** class.

### PAGE EVENTS

A number of events are raised on the server as part of the normal processing of a page. These events are actually defined in the **Control** base class and so are available to server controls also. The most important ones are listed below.

- **Init** is the first step in the page's life cycle and occurs when the page is initialized. There is no view-state information for any of the controls at this point.
- **Load** occurs when the controls are loaded into the page. View-state information for the controls is now available.
- **PreRender** occurs just before the controls are rendered to the output stream. Normally this event is not handled by a page but is important for implementing your own server controls.
- **Unload** occurs when the controls are unloaded from the page. At this point it is too late to write your own data to the output stream.

### PAGE PROPERTIES

The **Page** class has a number of important properties. Some of the most useful are listed below.

- **EnableViewState** indicates whether the page maintains view state for itself and its controls. You can get or set this property. The default is **true**, view state is maintained.

- **ErrorPage** specifies the error page to which the browser should be redirected in case an unhandled exception occurs.

- **IsPostBack** indicates whether the page is being loaded in response to a postback from the client or is being loaded for the first time.

- **IsValid** indicates whether page validation succeeded.[3]

- **Request** gets the HTTP Request object, which allows you to access data from incoming HTTP requests.

- **Response** gets the HTTP Response object, which allows you to send response data to a browser.

- **Session** gets the current Session object, which is provided by ASP.NET for storing session state.

- **Trace** gets a **TraceContext** object for the page, which you can use to write out trace information.

### SAMPLE PROGRAM

We can illustrate some of these features of page processing with a simple extension to our Echo program. The page **HelloPage.aspx** (located in the top-level chapter directory) provides handlers for a number of page events, and we write simple text to the output stream, using the **Response** property. For each event we show the current text in the **txtName** and **lblGreeting** server controls. In the handler for **Load** we also show the current value of **IsPostBack**, which should be **false** the first time the page is accessed, and subsequently **true**.

```
<!-- HelloPage.aspx -->
<%@ Page Language="C#" Debug="true" %>
<HTML>
<HEAD>
 <SCRIPT RUNAT="SERVER">
protected void cmdEcho_Click(object Source, EventArgs e)
{
    lblGreeting.Text="Hello, " + txtName.Text;
}
protected void Page_Init(Object sender, EventArgs E)
{
    Response.Write("Page_Init<br>");
    Response.Write("txtName = " + txtName.Text + "<br>");
    Response.Write("lblGreeting = " + lblGreeting.Text +
                   "<br>");
}
protected void Page_Load(Object sender, EventArgs E)
{
    Response.Write("Page_Load<br>");
    Response.Write("IsPostBack = " + IsPostBack + "<br>");
```

---

[3] We discuss validation later in the chapter, in the section on Server Controls.

```
    Response.Write("txtName = " + txtName.Text + "<br>");
    Response.Write("lblGreeting = " + lblGreeting.Text +
                "<br>");
}
protected void Page_PreRender(Object sender, EventArgs E)
{
    Response.Write("Page_PreRender<br>");
    Response.Write("txtName = " + txtName.Text + "<br>");
    Response.Write("lblGreeting = " + lblGreeting.Text +
                "<br>");
}
protected void Page_Unload(Object sender, EventArgs E)
{
    //Response not available in this context
    //Response.Write("Page_Unload<br>");
}
</SCRIPT>
</HEAD>
<BODY>
<FORM RUNAT="SERVER">Your name: 
<asp:textbox id=txtName Runat="server"></asp:textbox>
<p><asp:button id=cmdEcho onclick=cmdEcho_Click Text="Echo"
runat="server" tooltip="Click to echo your name">
</asp:button></p>
<asp:label id=lblGreeting runat="server"></asp:label>
<P></P>
</FORM>
</BODY>
</HTML>
```

When we display the page the first time the output reflects the fact that both the text box and the label are empty, since we have entered no information. **IsPostBack** is **false**.

Now enter a name and click the "Echo" button. We obtain the following output from our handlers for the page events:

```
Page_Init
txtName =
lblGreeting =
Page_Load
IsPostBack = True
txtName = Robert
lblGreeting =
Page_PreRender
txtName = Robert
lblGreeting = Hello, Robert
```

In **Page_Init** there is no information for either control, since view state is not available at page initialization. In **Page_Load** the text box has data, but the label does not, since the click-event handler has not yet been invoked. **IsPostBack** is now **true**. In **Page_PreRender** both controls now have data.

Click "Echo" a second time. Again, the controls have no data in **Page_Init**. This time, however, in **Page_Load** the view state provides data for both controls. Figure 10–9 shows the browser output after "Echo" has been clicked a second time.

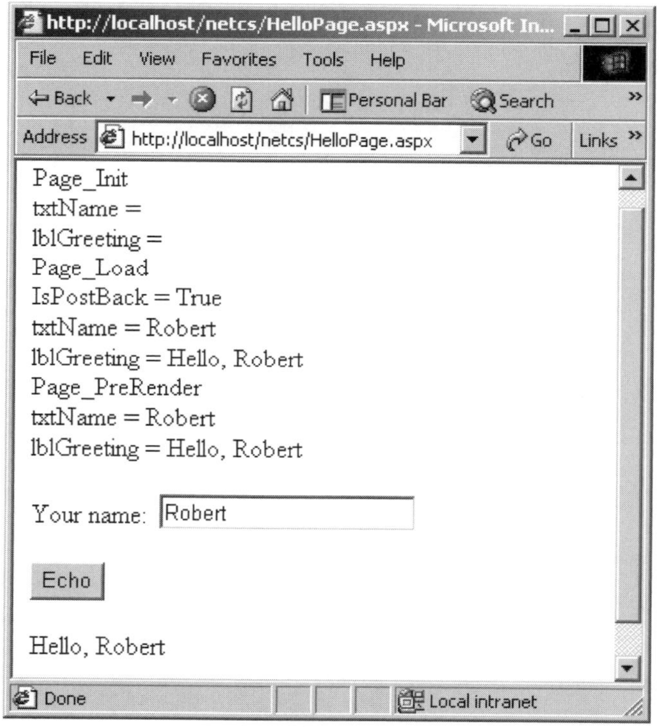

**Figure 10–9**   *Browser output after "Echo" has been clicked a second time.*

## Page Directive

An **.aspx** file may contain a *page directive* defining various attributes that can control how ASP.NET processes the page. A page directive contains one or more attribute/value pairs of the form

```
attribute="value"
```

within the page directive syntax

```
<@ Page ... @>
```

Our example program **HelloCodebehind.aspx** illustrates an **.aspx** page that does not have any code within it. The "code-behind" file **HelloCodebehind.aspx.cs** that has the code is specified using the **Src** attribute.

```
<!-- HelloCodebehind.aspx -->
<%@ Page Language="C#" Src="HelloCodebehind.aspx.cs"
Inherits=MyWebPage %>
. . .
```

### SRC

The **Src** attribute identifies the code-behind file.

### LANGUAGE

The **Language** attribute specifies the language used for the page. The code in this language may be in either a code-behind file or a SCRIPT block within the same file. Values can be any .NET-supported language, including C# and VB.NET.

### INHERITS

The **Inherits** directive specifies the page class from which the **.aspx** page class will inherit.

### DEBUG

The **Debug** attribute indicates whether the page should be compiled with debug information. If **true**, debug information is enabled, and the browser can provide detailed information about compile errors. The default is **false**.

### ERRORPAGE

The **ErrorPage** attribute specifies a target URL to which the browser will be redirected in the event that an unhandled exception occurs on the page.

### TRACE

The **Trace** attribute indicates whether tracing is enabled. A value of **true** turns tracing on. The default is **false**.

## Tracing

ASP.NET provides extensive tracing capabilities. Merely setting the **Trace** attribute for a page to **true** will cause trace output generated by ASP.NET to be sent to the browser. In addition, you can output your own trace information using the **Write** method of the **TraceContext** object, which is obtained from the **Trace** property of the **Page**.

The page **HelloTrace.aspx** illustrates using tracing in place of writing to the **Response** object.

```
<!-- HelloTrace.aspx -->
<%@ Page Language="C#" Debug="true" Trace = "true" %>
<HTML>
<HEAD>
 <SCRIPT RUNAT="SERVER">
protected void cmdEcho_Click(object Source, EventArgs e)
{
    lblGreeting.Text="Hello, " + txtName.Text;
}
protected void Page_Init(Object sender, EventArgs E)
{
    Trace.Write("Page_Init<br>");
    Trace.Write("txtName = " + txtName.Text + "<br>");
    Trace.Write("lblGreeting = " + lblGreeting.Text +
                "<br>");
}
...
```

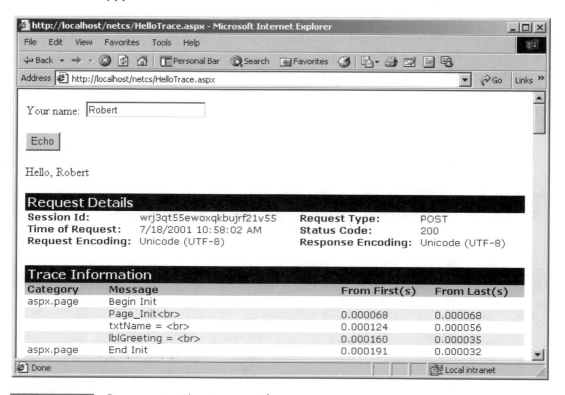

**Figure 10–10**   *Browser output showing trace information.*

Figure 10–10 shows the browser output after the initial request for the page. Notice that the trace output is shown *after* the form, along with trace information that is generated by ASP.NET itself.

# Request/Response Programming

The server control architecture is built on top of a more fundamental processing architecture, which may be called "request/response." Understanding request/response is important to solidify our overall grasp of ASP.NET. Also, in certain programming situations request/response is the natural approach.

## HttpRequest Class

The **System.Web** namespace contains a useful class **HttpRequest** that can be used to read the various HTTP values sent by a client during a Web request. These HTTP values would be used by a classical CGI program in acting upon a Web request, and they are the foundation upon which higher-level processing is built. Table 10–1 shows some of the public instance properties of **HttpRequest**. If you are familiar with HTTP, the meaning of these various properties should be largely self-explanatory. Refer to the .NET Framework documentation of the **HttpRequest** class for full details about these and other properties.

| Table 10–1 | Public Instance Properties of HttpRequest |
| --- | --- |
| **Property** | **Meaning** |
| AcceptTypes | String array of client-supported MIME accept types |
| Browser | Information about client's browser capabilities |
| ContentLength | Length in bytes of content sent by the client |
| Cookies | Collection of cookies sent by the client |
| Form | Collection of form variables |
| Headers | Collection of HTTP headers |
| HttpMethod | HTTP transfer method used by client (e.g., GET or POST) |
| Params | Combined collection of QueryString, Form, ServerVariables, and Cookies items |
| Path | Virtual request of the current path |
| QueryString | Collection of HTTP query string variables |
| ServerVariables | Collection of Web server variables |

The **Request** property of the **Page** class returns a **HttpRequest** object. You may then extract whatever information you need, using the properties of **HttpRequest**. For example, the following code determines the length in bytes of content sent by the client and writes that information to the **Response** object.

```
int length = Request.ContentLength;
Response.Write("ContentLength = " + length + "<br>");
```

## COLLECTIONS

A number of useful collections are exposed as properties of **HttpRequest**. The collections are of type **NamedValueCollection** (in **System. Collections.Specialized** namespace). You can access a value from a string key. For example, the following code extracts values for the QUERY_STRING and HTTP_USER_AGENT server variables using the **ServerVariables** collection.

```
string strQuery =
    Request.ServerVariables["QUERY_STRING"];
string strAgent =
    Request.ServerVariables["HTTP_USER_AGENT"];
```

Server variables such as these are at the heart of classical Common Gateway Interface (CGI) Web server programming. The Web server passes information to a CGI script or program by using environment variables. ASP.NET makes this low-level information available to you, in case you need it.

A common task is to extract information from controls on forms. In HTML, controls are identified by a **name** attribute, which can be used by the server to determine the corresponding value. The way in which form data is passed to the server depends on whether the form uses the HTTP GET method or the POST method.

With GET, the form data is encoded as part of the query string. The **QueryString** collection can then be used to retrieve the values. With POST, the form data is passed as content after the HTTP header. The **Forms** collection can then be used to extract the control values. You could use the value of the REQUEST_METHOD server variable (GET or POST) to determine which collection to use (the **QueryString** collection in the case of GET and the **Forms** collection in case of POST).

With ASP.NET you don't have to worry about which HTTP method was used in the request. ASP.NET provides a **Params** collection, which is a combination (union in the mathematical sense) of the **ServerVariables**, **QueryString**, **Forms**, and **Cookies** collections.

## EXAMPLE PROGRAM

We illustrate all these ideas with a simple page **Squares.aspx** that displays a column of squares. How many squares to display is determined by a number submitted on a form. The page **GetSquares.aspx** submits the request using GET, and **PostSquares.aspx** submits the request using POST. These two pages have the same user interface, illustrated in Figure 10–11.

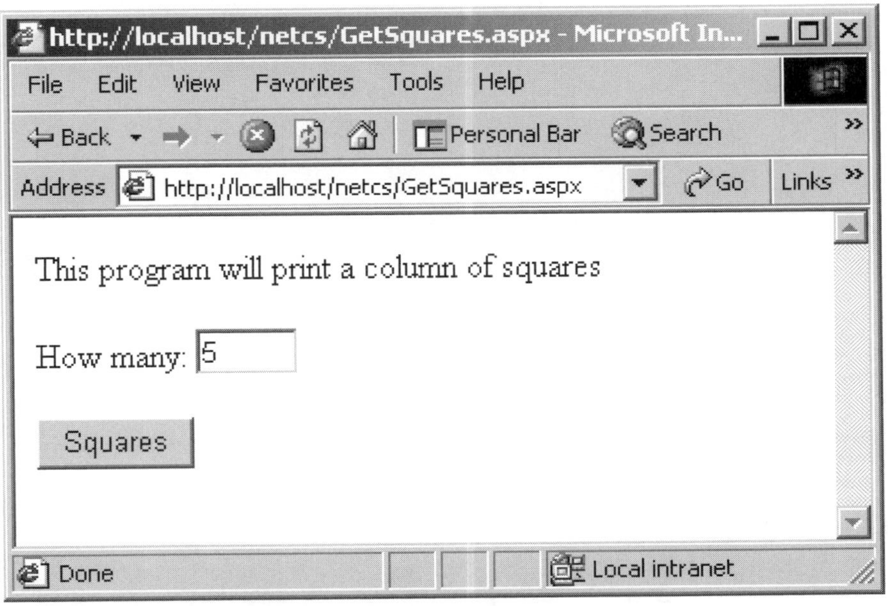

**Figure 10–11**   *Form for requesting a column of squares.*

Here is the HTML for **GetSquares.aspx**. Notice that we are using straight HTML. Except for the Page directive, which turns tracing on, no features of ASP.NET are used.

```
<!-- GetSquares.aspx  -->
<%@ Page Trace = "true" %>
<html>
<head>
</head>
<body>
<P>This program will print a column of squares</P>
<form method="get" action = Squares.aspx>
How many:
<INPUT type=text size=2 value=5 name=txtCount>
<P></P>
```

```
<INPUT type=submit value=Squares name=cmdSquares>
</form>
</body>
</html>
```

The **form** tag has attributes specifying the method (GET or POST) and the action (target page). The controls have a **name** attribute, which will be used by server code to retrieve the value.

Run **GetSquares.aspx** and click "Squares." You will see some HTTP information displayed, followed by the column of squares. Tracing is turned on, so details about the request are displayed by ASP.NET. Figure 10–12 illustrates the output from this GET request.

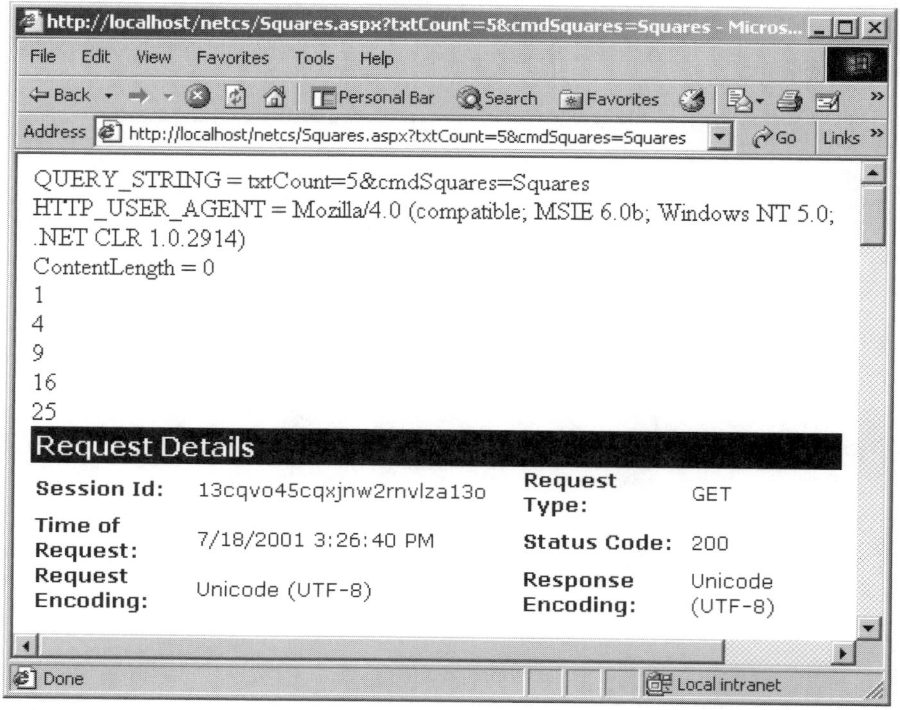

**Figure 10–12**   *Output from a GET request.*

You can see that form data is encoded in the query string, and the content length is 0. If you scroll down on the trace output, you will see much information. For example, the **QueryString** collection is shown.

Now run **PostSquares.aspx** and click "Squares." Again you will then see some HTTP information displayed, followed by the column of squares. Tracing is turned on, so details about the request are displayed by ASP.NET. Figure 10–13 illustrates the output from this POST request.

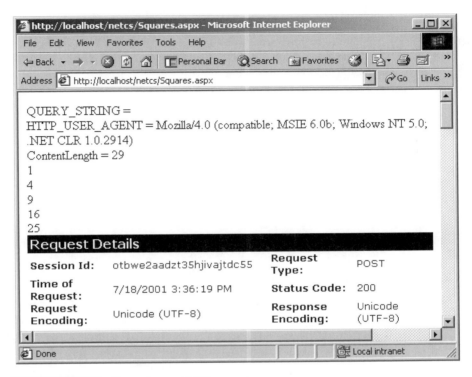

Figure 10–13    *Output from a POST request.*

You can see that now the query string is empty, and the content length is 29. The form data is passed as part of the content, following the HTTP header information. If you scroll down on the trace output, you will see that now there is a **Form** collection, which is used by ASP.NET to provide access to the form data in the case of a POST method.

By comparing the output of these two examples, you can clearly see the difference between GET and POST, and you can also see the data structures used by ASP.NET to make it easy for you to extract data from HTTP requests.

## HttpResponse Class

The **HttpResponse** class encapsulates HTTP response information that is built as part of an ASP.NET operation. The Framework uses this class when it is creating a response that includes writing server controls back to the client. Your own server code may also use the **Write** method of the **Response** object to write data to the output stream that will be sent to the client. We have already seen many illustrations of **Response.Write**.

## REDIRECT

The **HttpResponse** class has a useful method, **Redirect**, that enables server code to redirect an HTTP request to a different URL. A simple redirection without passing any data is trivial—you need only call the **Redirect** method and pass the URL. An example of such usage would be a reorganization of a Web site, where a certain page is no longer valid and the content has been moved to a new location. You can keep the old page live by simply redirecting traffic to the new location.

It should be noted that redirection always involves an HTTP GET request, like following a simple link to a URL. (POST arises as an option when submitting form data, where the action can be specified as GET or POST.)

A more interesting case involves passing data to the new page. One way to pass data is to encode it in the query string. You must preserve standard HTTP conventions for the encoding of the query string. The class **HttpUtility** provides a method **UrlEncode**, which will properly encode an individual item of a query string. You must yourself provide code to separate the URL from the query string with a "?" and to separate items of the query string with "&."

The folder **Hotel** provides an example of a simple Web application that illustrates this method of passing data in redirection. The file **default.aspx** provides a form for collecting information to be used in making a hotel reservation. The reservation itself is made on the page **Reservation1.aspx**. You may access the starting **default.aspx** page through the URL

```
http://localhost/NetCs/Hotel/
```

As usual, we provide a link to this page in our home page of example programs. Figure 10–14 illustrates the starting page of our simple hotel reservation example.

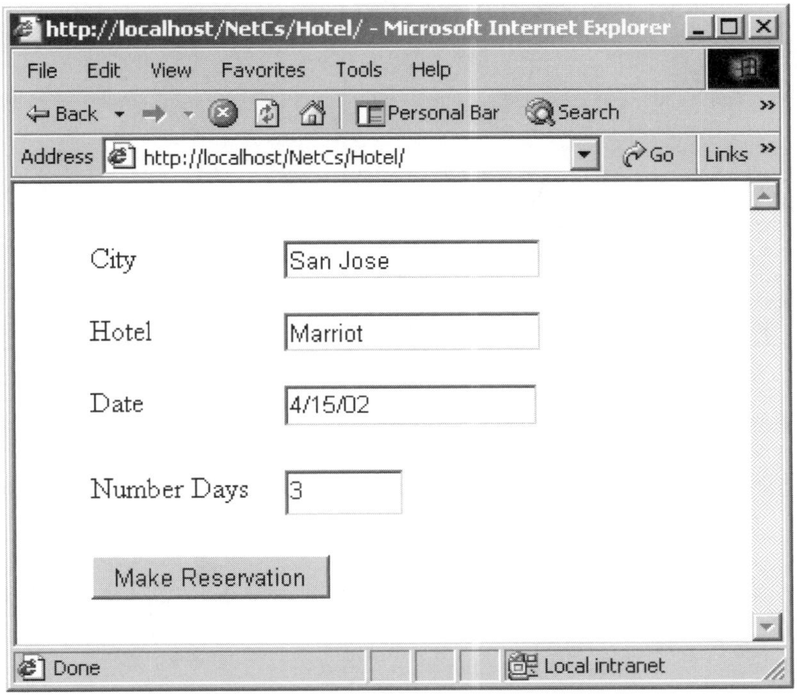

**Figure 10–14**    *Starting page for making a hotel reservation.*

Here is the script code that is executed when the "Make Reservation" button is clicked.

```
private void cmdMakeReservation_Click(
    object sender, System.EventArgs e)
{
    string query = "City=" +
        HttpUtility.UrlEncode(txtCity.Text);
    query += "&Hotel=" +
        HttpUtility.UrlEncode(txtHotel.Text);
    query += "&Date=" +
        HttpUtility.UrlEncode(txtDate.Text);
    query += "&NumberDays=" +
        HttpUtility.UrlEncode(txtNumberDays.Text);
    Response.Redirect("Reservation1.aspx?" + query);
}
```

We build a query string, which gets appended to the **Reservation1.aspx** URL, separated by a "?". Note the ampersand that is used as a separator of items in the query string. We use the **HttpUtility.UrlEncode** method to encode the individual items. Special encoding is required for the slashes in the date and for the space in the name "San Jose." Clicking the button brings up the reservation page. You can see the query string in the address window of the browser. Figure 10–15 illustrates the output shown by the browser. (Our program does not actually make the reservation; it simply prints out the parameters passed to it.)

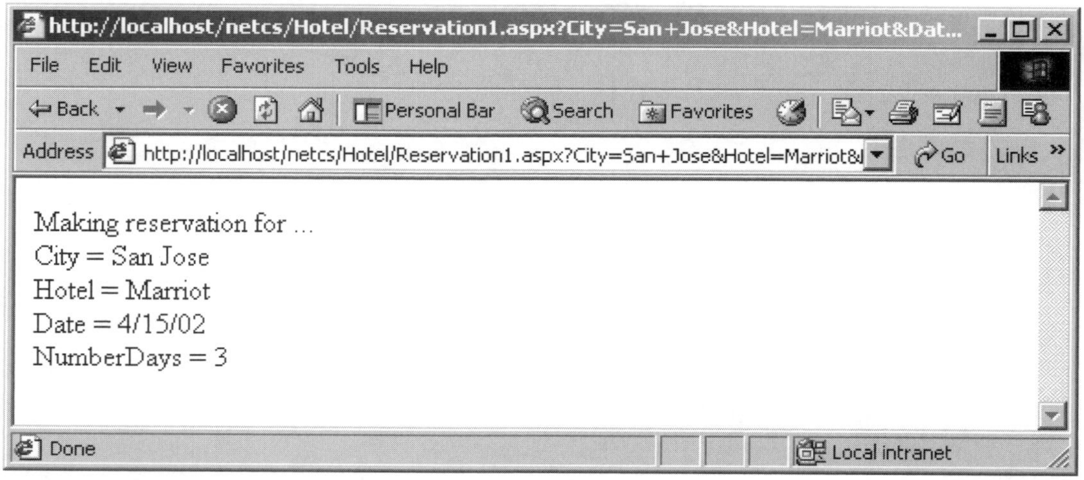

**Figure 10–15**    *Browser output from making a hotel reservation.*

You can turn on tracing, and the trace output should serve to reinforce the ideas we have been discussing about request/response Web programming. In particular, you should examine the **QueryString** collection, as illustrated in Figure 10–16.

| Querystring Collection | |
|---|---|
| **Name** | **Value** |
| City | San Jose |
| Hotel | Marriot |
| Date | 4/15/02 |
| NumberDays | 3 |

**Figure 10–16**    *The query string is used for passing parameters in redirection.*

# Web Applications Using Visual Studio.NET

We have examined the fundamentals of ASP.NET and have created some simple Web pages. To carry the story further it will be very helpful to start using Visual Studio.NET. Everything we do could also be accomplished using only the .NET Framework SDK, but our work will be much easier using the facilities of Visual Studio. A special kind of project, an "ASP.NET Web Application," creates the boilerplate code. The Forms Designer makes it very easy to create Web forms by dragging controls from a palette. We can add event handlers for controls in a manner very similar to the way event handlers are added in Windows Forms. In fact, the whole Web application development process takes on many of the rapid application development (RAD) characteristics typical of Visual Basic.

In this section we will introduce the Web application development features of Visual Studio by creating the first step of our Acme Travel Web site. We will elaborate on specific features of ASP.NET in later sections.

## Form Designers for Windows and Web Applications

The basic look and feel of the Form Designers for Windows and Web applications is the same. You drag controls from a toolbox. You set properties in a Property window. You navigate between a code view and a designer view with toolbar buttons. In the following discussion we assume you have a basic familiarity with this visual paradigm. You may find it helpful to refer back to Chapter 6.

## Hotel Information Web Page (Step 0)

We begin by creating a simple Web page that will display information about hotels. Dropdown listboxes are provided to show cities and hotels. Selecting a city from the first dropdown will cause the hotels in that city to be shown in the second dropdown. We obtain the hotel information from the **Hotel.dll** component, and we use data binding to populate the listboxes. As a source for the **Hotel.dll** and **Customer.dll** components used later, we provide a copy of the GUI application from Chapter 6, **AcmeGui**. The **Hotel.dll** component we need in the following demonstration is in the folder **AcmeGui\Hotel\bin\Debug**.

If you would like to follow along hands-on with Visual Studio, do your work in the **Demos** folder for this chapter. The completed project is in **CaseStudy\Step0**.

## CONFIGURING WEB SERVER CONNECTION

Before getting started you may wish to check, and possibly change, your Visual Studio Web Server Connection setting. The two options are File share and FrontPage. If you are doing all your development on a local computer, you might find File share to be faster and more convenient. To access this setting, select the Visual Studio menu Tools | Options.... Choose Web Settings underneath Projects. You can then set the Preferred Access Method by using a radio button, as illustrated in Figure 10–17.

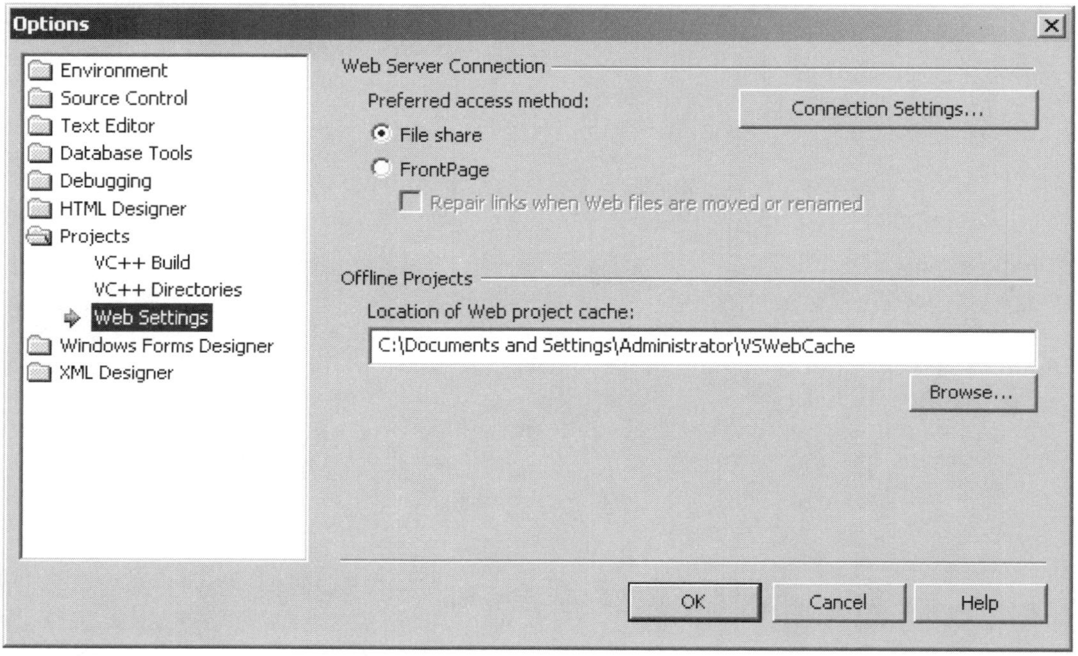

**Figure 10–17**   *Configuring Web server connection preferred access method.*

## CREATING AN ASP.NET WEB APPLICATION

1. In Visual Studio select the menu File | New | Project....
2. In the New Project dialog box choose "Visual C# Projects" as the Project Type and "ASP.NET Web Application" as the Template.
3. Enter "AcmeWeb" as the name of your project. For the location enter an HTTP path to a folder on your server machine. The default will be the IIS home directory **\Inetpub\wwwroot**. If you have made **\OI\NetCs\Chap10** into a virtual directory with alias "NetCs", you

can enter for the path **http://localhost/NetCs/Demos**, as illustrated in Figure 10–18.

*Creating a Visual Studio ASP.NET Web Application project.*

4. Click OK. The project files will then be created in **\OI\NetCs\ Chap10\Demos**. The VS.NET solution **AcmeWeb.sln** will then be created under **MyDocuments\Visual Studio Projects\AcmeWeb**.

## USING THE FORM DESIGNER

1. Bring up the Toolbox from the View menu, if not already showing. Make sure the Web Forms tab is selected.
2. Drag two Label controls and two DropDownList controls onto the form.
3. Change the Text property of the Labels to "City" and "Hotel." Resize the DropDownList controls to look as shown in Figure 10–19.

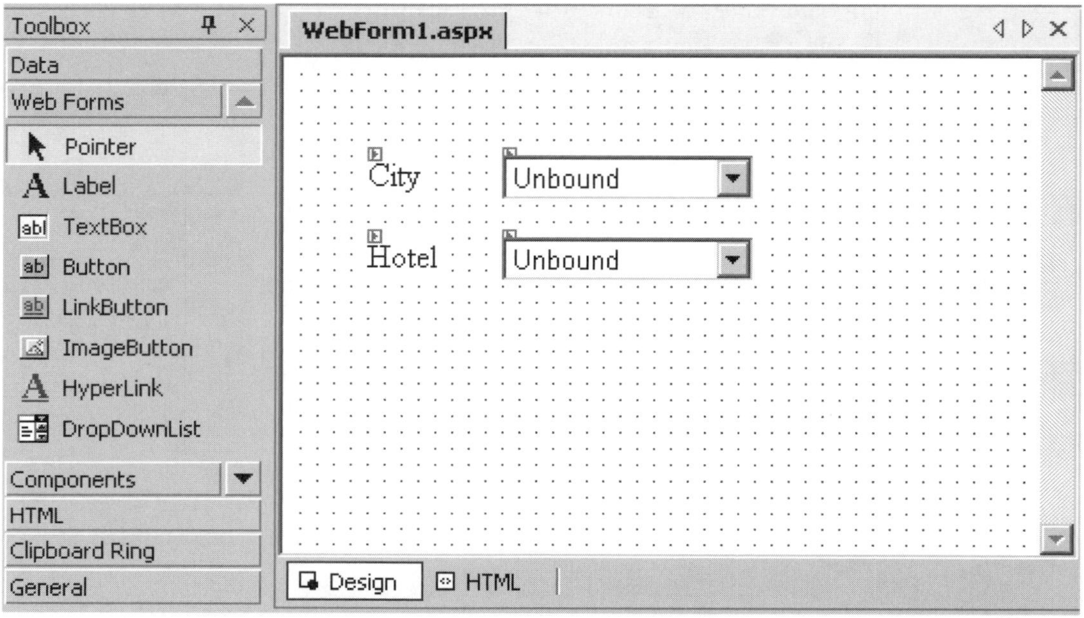

**Figure 10–19**    *Using the Form Designer to add controls to the form.*

4. Change the (ID) of the DropDownList controls to **listCities** and **listHotels.**

### INITIALIZING THE HOTELBROKER

1. Copy **Hotel.dll** from **AcmeGui\Hotel\bin\Debug** to **Demos\ AcmeWeb\bin**.
2. In your **AcmeWeb**, project add a reference to **Hotel.dll**.
3. As shown in the following code fragment, in **Global.asax**, add the following line near the top of the file. (Use the View Code button to show the code.)

```
using OI.NetCs.Acme;
```

4. Add a public static variable **hotelBroker** of type **HotelBroker**.
5. Add code to **Application_Start** to instantiate **HotelBroker**.

```
// Global.asax
using System;
```

```
using System.Collections;
using System.ComponentModel;
using System.Web;
using System.Web.SessionState;
using OI.NetCs.Acme;

namespace AcmeWeb
{
    /// <summary>
    /// Summary description for Global.
    /// </summary>
    public class Global : System.Web.HttpApplication
    {
        public static HotelBroker hotelBroker;
        protected void Application_Start(Object sender,
                                         EventArgs e)
        {
            hotelBroker = new HotelBroker();
        }
        ...
```

6. In **WebForm1.aspx.cs** add a **using OI.NetCs.Acme;** statement, and declare a static variable **hotelBroker** of type **HotelBroker**.

```
...
using OI.NetCs.Acme;

namespace AcmeWeb
{
    /// <summary>
    /// Summary description for WebForm1.
    /// </summary>
    public class WebForm1 : System.Web.UI.Page
    {
        ...
        private static HotelBroker hotelBroker;
        ...
```

## DATA BINDING

Next we will populate the first DropDownList with the city data, which can be obtained by the **GetCities** method of **HotelBroker**. We make use of the *data binding* capability of the DropDownList control. You might think data binding is only used with a database. However, in .NET data binding is much more general, and can be applied to other data sources besides databases. Binding a control to a database is very useful for two-tier, client/server applications. However, we are implementing a three-tier application, in which the presentation logic, whether implemented using Windows Forms or Web Forms, talks to a business logic component and not directly to the database. So we will bind the control to an ArrayList.

The .NET Framework provides a number of data binding options, which can facilitate binding to data obtained through a middle-tier component. A very simple option is binding to an **ArrayList**. This option works perfectly in our example, because we need to populate the DropDownList of cities with strings, and the **GetCities** method returns an array list of strings.

The bottom line is that all we need to do to populate the **listCities** DropDownList is to add the following code to the **Page_Load** method of the **WebForm1** class.

```
private void Page_Load(object sender, System.EventArgs e)
{
    if (!IsPostBack)
    {
        hotelBroker = Global.hotelBroker;
        ArrayList cities = hotelBroker.GetCities();
        listCities.DataSource = cities;
        DataBind();
    }
}
```

The call to **DataBind( )** binds all the server controls on the form to their data source, which results in the controls being populated with data from the data source. The **DataBind** method can also be invoked on the server controls individually. **DataBind** is a method of the **Control** class, and is inherited by the **Page** class and by specific server control classes.

You can now build and run the project. Running a Web application under Visual Studio will bring up Internet Explorer to access the application over HTTP. Figure 10–20 shows the running application. When you drop down the list of cities, you will indeed see the cities returned by the **HotelBroker** component.

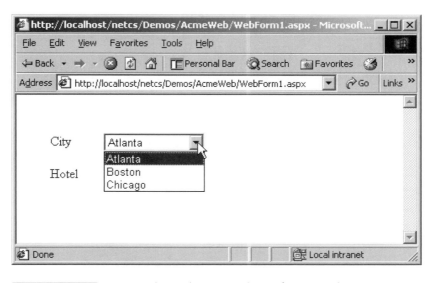

**Figure 10–20**   *Running the Web page to show information about cities.*

### INITIALIZING THE HOTELS

We can populate the second DropDownList with hotel data using a similar procedure. It is a little bit more involved, because **GetHotels** returns an array list of **HotelListItem** structures rather than strings. We want to populate the **listHotels** DropDownList with the names of the hotels. The helper method **BindHotels** loops through the array list of hotels and creates an array list of hotel names, which is bound to **listHotels**. Here is the complete code, which adds the logic for initializing the hotels for the first city (which has index 0).

```
private void Page_Load(object sender, System.EventArgs e)
{
    if (!IsPostBack)
    {
        hotelBroker = Global.hotelBroker;
        ArrayList cities = hotelBroker.GetCities();
        listCities.DataSource = cities;
        ArrayList hotels =
            hotelBroker.GetHotels((string)cities[0]);
        BindHotels(hotels);
        DataBind();
    }
}
private void BindHotels(ArrayList hotels)
{
    ArrayList hotelNames = new ArrayList(hotels.Count);
    foreach(HotelListItem hotel in hotels)
```

```
    {
        hotelNames.Add(hotel.HotelName.Trim());
    }
    listHotels.DataSource = hotelNames;
}
```

## SELECTING A CITY

Finally, we implement the feature that selecting a city causes the hotels for the selected city to be displayed. We can add an event handler for selecting a city by double-clicking on the **listCities** DropDownList control. The is a shortcut for adding a handler for the primary event for the control. In the Properties window you can click on the ⚡ button to see all the events for the control. You can then double-click on the event. The second method allows you to add a handler for any event of the control. Here is the code for the **SelectedIndexChanged** event.

```
private void listCities_SelectedIndexChanged(object sender,
    System.EventArgs e)
{
    string city = listCities.SelectedItem.Text;
    ArrayList hotels = hotelBroker.GetHotels(city);
    BindHotels(hotels);
    DataBind();
}
```

Build and run the project. Unfortunately, the event does not seem to be recognized by the server. What do you suppose the problem is?

## AUTOPOSTBACK

For an event to be recognized by the server, you must have a postback to the server. Such a postback happens automatically for a button click, but not for other events. Once this problem is recognized, the remedy is simple. In the Properties window for the cities DropDownList control, change the **AutoPostBack** property to **true**. (You can get back to a display of properties from a display of events by clicking the ▦ button.) Figure 10–21 illustrates setting the **AutoPostBack** property.

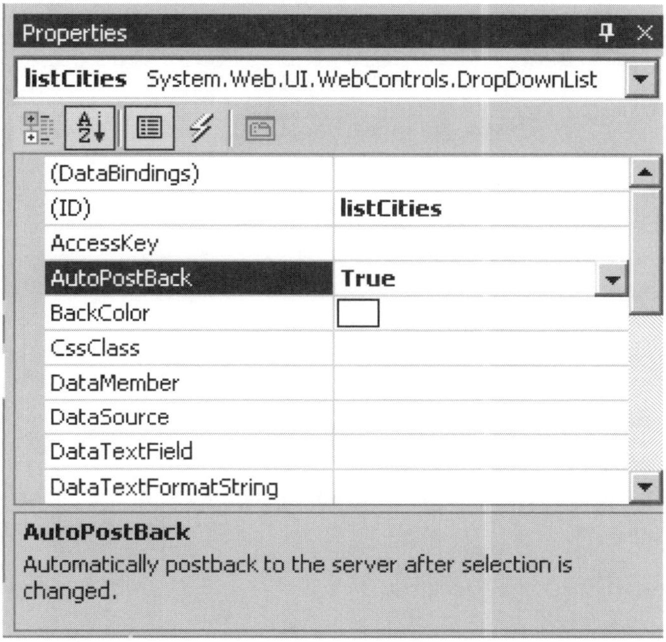

**Figure 10–21**   *Setting the AutoPostBack property of a DropDownList control.*

## DEBUGGING

One advantage of using Visual Studio for developing your ASP.NET applications is the ease of debugging. You can set breakpoints, single-step, examine the values of variables, and so forth, in your code-behind files just as you would with any other Visual Studio program. All you have to do is build your project in Debug mode (the default) and start the program from within Visual Studio using Debug | Start (or F5 at the keyboard or the toolbar button ▶).

As an example, set a breakpoint on the first line of the **SelectedIndexChanged** event handler for **listCities**. Assuming you have set the **AutoPostBack** property to **true**, as we have discussed, you should hit the breakpoint, as illustrated in Figure 10–22.

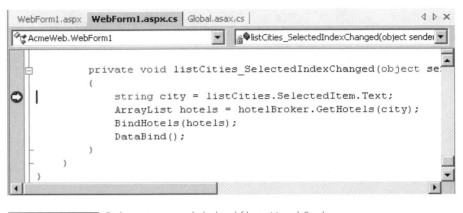

| WebForm1.aspx | **WebForm1.aspx.cs** | Global.asax.cs | ◁ ▷ ✕ |

```
private void listCities_SelectedIndexChanged(object se
{
    string city = listCities.SelectedItem.Text;
    ArrayList hotels = hotelBroker.GetHotels(city);
    BindHotels(hotels);
    DataBind();
}
}
}
```

**Figure 10–22**   *Debugging a code-behind file in Visual Studio.*

## Deploying a Web Application Created Using Visual Studio

Developing a Web application using Visual Studio is quite straightforward. You can do all your work within Visual Studio, including testing your application. When you start a Web application within Visual Studio, Internet Explorer will be brought up automatically. And it is easy to debug, as we have just seen.

Deploying a Web application created using Visual Studio is also easy, but you need to be aware of a few things.[4]

1. The Project | Copy Project... menu can be used to deploy a Web project from Visual Studio.

2. Visual Studio precompiles Web pages, storing the executable in the **bin** folder.

3. The **Src** attribute in the Page directive is not used. Instead, the **Inherits** attribute is used to specify the Page class.

4. The directory containing the Web pages must be marked as a Web application. This marking is performed automatically by Visual Studio when you deploy the application. If you copy the files to another directory, possibly on another system, you must perform the marking as an application yourself, which you can do using Internet Services Manager.

---

[4] This part of the Visual Studio development environment has been the most problematical in working with beta software. A technique we have found useful in the beta is to edit the **.csproj.webinfo** file to provide an HTTP path to a new location where the project has been moved. Then double-clicking on the **.csproj** file will create a new Visual Studio solution, which you can work with. Be sure to consult the **readme.txt** file for this chapter in the code distribution.

### USING PROJECT | COPY PROJECT...

To illustrate using Visual Studio to deploy a Web project, let's deploy the Acme Hotel Information page we have created. We will deploy it to a new directory **AcmeWeb0** in the **Deploy** directory for Chapter 10.

1. Using Windows Explorer, create a new directory **AcmeWeb0** underneath **Deploy**.

2. Bring up the Copy Project dialog from the menu Project | Copy Project....

3. Enter the following information (see Figure 10–23).

   - **http://localhost/NetCs/Deploy/AcmeWeb0** for Destination project folder
   - File share for Web access method
   - **\OI\NetCs\Chap10\Deploy\AcmeWeb0** for Path
   - "Only files needed to run this application" for Copy

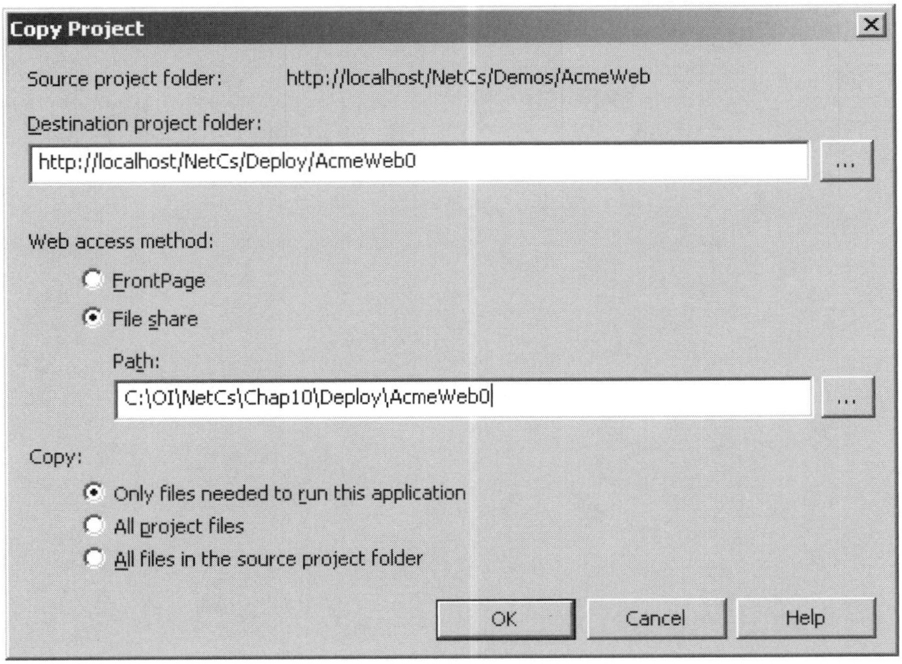

**Figure 10–23**    *Copying Web project files using Visual Studio.*

4. You can test the deployment by using Internet Explorer. Enter the following URL: **http://localhost/netcs/deploy/AcmeWeb0/WebForm1.aspx**. You should then see the hotel information Web page displayed, and

you should be able to select a city from the City dropdown and see the corresponding hotels displayed in the Hotel dropdown.

### PRECOMPILED WEB PAGE

Examining the files in the folder **Deploy\AcmeWeb0**, you will see no code-behind file **WebForm1.aspx.cs**. Instead, in the **bin** folder you will see the DLL **AcmeWeb.dll**.

### INHERITS ATTRIBUTE IN PAGE DIRECTIVE

Examining the file **WebForm1.aspx**, we see there is no **Src** attribute. Instead, the **Inherits** attribute specifies the Page class **WebForm1**, which is implemented in the assembly **AcmeWeb.dll**.

```
<%@ Page language="c#" Codebehind="WebForm1.aspx.cs"
AutoEventWireup="false" Inherits="AcmeWeb.WebForm1" %>
```

### CONFIGURING A VIRTUAL DIRECTORY AS AN APPLICATION

The identical files you copied to **Deploy\AcmeWeb0** are also provided in the directory **AcmeRun\Step0**. Try the URL **http://localhost/netcs/AcmeRun/Step0/WebForm1.aspx** in Internet Explorer. You will obtain a configuration error, as illustrated in Figure 10–24.

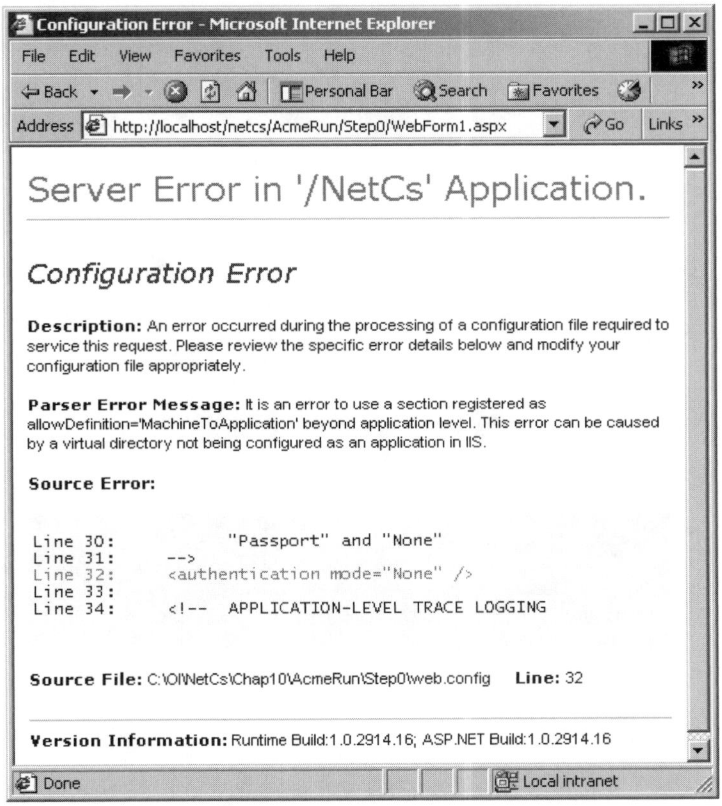

**Figure 10–24**     *Error message when virtual directory is not configured as an application.*

The key sentence in the error message is: "This error can be caused by a virtual directory not being configured as an application in IIS." The remedy is simple. Use Internet Services Manager to perform the following steps.

1. Find the folder **Step0** underneath **AcmeRun** in the virtual directory **NetCs**.

2. Right-click and choose properties. See Figure 10–25. Click "Create."

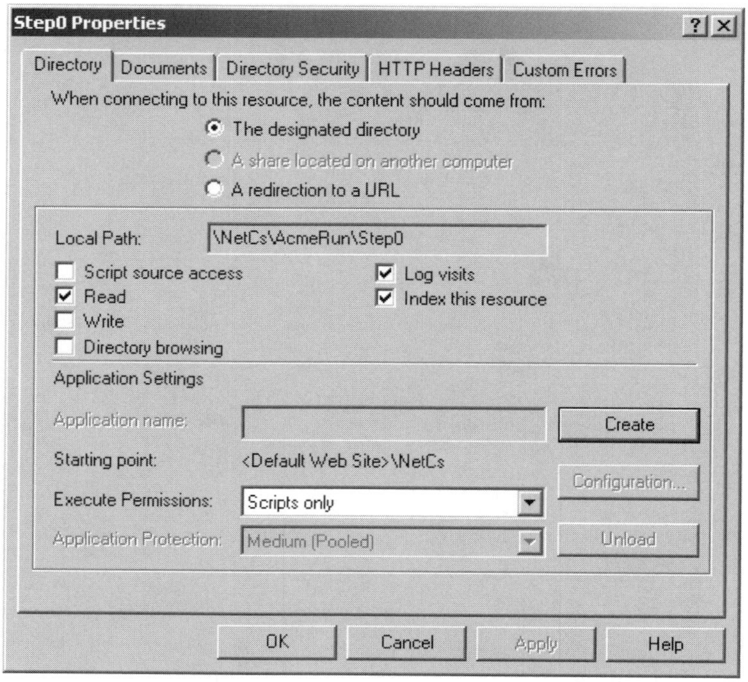

**Figure 10–25**    *Configuring a virtual directory as an application in IIS.*

3. You will then see "Step0" suggested as the application name. Accept all the suggested settings and click OK.

4. Now again try **http://localhost/netcs/AcmeRun/Step0/ WebForm1.aspx** in Internet Explorer. You should be successful in bringing up the application.

### MOVING A VISUAL STUDIO ASP.NET WEB APPLICATION PROJECT

At the time of writing there appeared to be no really clean way to move an entire ASP.NET Web Application project so that you could continue development under Visual Studio. The simplest approach we have found involves copying the source and bin files and editing the **.csproj.webinfo** file. A "brute force" approach is outlined in the **readme.txt** file for this chapter.

    Our illustration will create a copy of the **AcmeWeb** Web application that we have been creating in the **Demos** directory. Our copy will be in a directory called **AcmeWeb0** on the same machine.[5]

---

[5] The detailed steps outlined worked on Beta 2. Please consult the **readme.txt** file for this chapter to check for any changes in behavior in the released product.

1. In Windows Explorer create a new folder **AcmeWeb0** in the **Demos** directory.

2. Close Visual Studio and copy all the source files, except the **.sln** and **.suo** files, from the **AcmeWeb** directory to **AcmeWeb0**. Copy the whole **bin** folder.

3. Edit the file **AcmeWeb.csproj.webinfo** to rename **Web URLPath** to:

```
"http://localhost/NetCs/Demos/AcmeWeb0/AcmeWeb.csproj"
```

4. Double-click on the file **AcmeWeb.csproj**. This should bring up Visual Studio and create a new solution with a project **AcmeWeb**.

5. Remove the (broken) reference to Hotel and add this reference back in, navigating to **bin\Hotel.dll**.

6. Build the solution. When presented with a Save As dialog, save the solution by the suggested name **AcmeWeb.sln**. You should get a clean build.

7. Try to run the project. You will be asked to set a start page. Set the start page as **WebForm1.aspx**.

8. Build and run. If you get a configuration error, use Internet Services Manager to configure the virtual directory as an application in IIS, as previously discussed. You should now be able to run the application at its new location.

You can view what we have done as establishing a snapshot of Step0. You can go back to new development in the main directory **Demo\AcmeWeb**, and if you want to compare with the original version, you have **Demo\AcmeWeb0** available.

## Acme Travel Agency Case Study

Throughout this book we have been using the "Acme Travel Agency" as a case study to illustrate many concepts of .NET. In this section we look at a Web site for the Acme Travel Agency. The code for the Web site is in the **CaseStudy** directory in three progressive steps: Step0, Step1, and Step2. Step0 corresponds to our Visual Studio.NET demonstration from the preceding section. (A final Step3, discussed later in the chapter, is a database version of the case study.)

In this section we will give an overview of the case study, and in the next we will discuss some more details about Web applications, using the case study as an illustration.

## Configuring the Case Study

Links are provided to the three steps of the case study on the ASP.NET exam-ple programs "home page" for this chapter, which you can access through the URL **http://localhost/netcs/**. To be able to run the Web applications, you must use IIS to configure the directories **CaseStudy/Step0**, **CaseStudy/Step1**, and **CaseStudy/Step2** as Web applications. Follow the instructions provided in the previous section. If you want to experiment with any of the steps in Visual Studio, you can double-click on the **.csproj** file to create a Visual Studio solution.

## Acme Web Site Step 1

In Step 1 we provide a simple two-page Web site. In the first page you can make reservations, and in the second you can manage your reservations. We have hard-coded the customer as "Rocket Squirrel," who has a CustomerId of 1.

### HOTELRESERVATIONS.ASPX

The start page for the application is **HotelReservations.aspx**. Figure 10–26 shows this page in Internet Explorer, after a reservation has been booked at the Hotel Dixie in Atlanta.

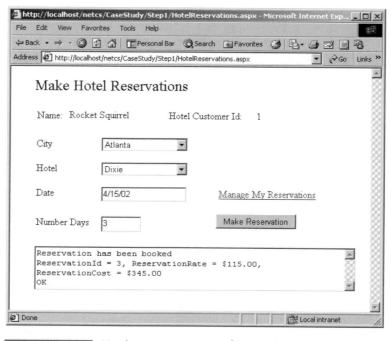

**Figure 10–26**   *Hotel reservations page of Acme Web site.*

The code for initializing the DropDownList controls is the same as for Step 0, as is the code for handling the **SelectedIndexChanged** event for the City dropdown. The key new code is making a reservation. This code should have no surprises for you. It makes use of the **HotelBroker** class, which we already have instantiated for displaying the hotels.

The design of the Web page enables a user to quickly make a number of reservations without leaving the page. We are relying on the postback mechanism of ASP.NET. When done making reservations, the user can follow the link "Manage My Reservations."

### MANAGERESERVATIONS.ASPX

The second page for the application is **ManageReservations.aspx**. Figure 10–27 shows this page in Internet Explorer, after reservations have been booked for Atlanta, Boston, and Chicago.

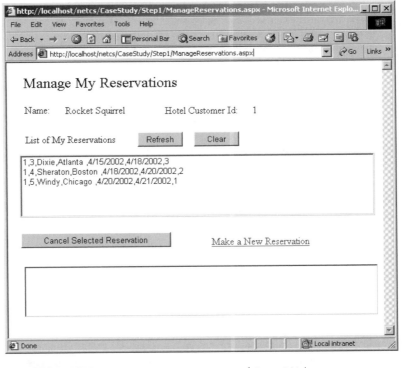

**Figure 10–27**    *Manage reservations page of Acme Web site.*

The user can cancel a reservation by selecting a reservation in the list-box and clicking the "Cancel Selected Reservation" button. A link is provided to the hotel reservations page. The code for this page is quite straightforward, making use of the capability to provide event handlers in a server-side control. Here is the code for a helper method to show the reservations in the listbox. This code is very similar to the Windows Forms code that we looked at in Chapter 6.

```
private void ShowReservations()
{
    int id = Convert.ToInt32(lblHotelCustomerId.Text);
    ArrayList array =
        hotelBroker.FindReservationsForCustomer(id);
    if (array == null)
    {
        return;
    }
    ClearReservations();
    foreach (ReservationListItem item in array)
    {
        string rid = item.ReservationId.ToString();
        string hotel = item.HotelName;
        string city = item.City;
        string arrive = item.ArrivalDate.ToString("d");
        string depart = item.DepartureDate.ToString("d");
        string number = item.NumberDays.ToString();
        string str = id + "," + rid + "," + hotel + "," +
            city + " ," + arrive + "," + depart + "," +
            number;
        listReservations.Items.Add(str);
    }
}
```

## Acme Web Site Step 2

Step 2 is the full-blown implementation of our Web site case study. Acme customers do not interact with the Hotel Broker directly. Instead, they go through Acme's Web site. In order to use the Web site, a customer must register, providing a user ID, name, and email address. Subsequently, the user can log in by just providing the user ID.

### ACMELIB COMPONENT

Internally, Acme maintains a database of user IDs and corresponding Hotel Customer IDs.[6] The interface **IAcmeUser** encapsulates this database maintained by Acme. The class library project **AcmeLib** contains a collection-based implementation of such a database. The file **AcmeTravelDefs.cs** contains the definitions of interfaces and of a structure.

---

[6] The Web site is Acme's, and Acme maintains user IDs for its own customers. Acme connects to various brokers (such as hotel and airline), and each broker will have its own customer ID.

```
// AcmeTravelDefs.cs

using System;
using System.Collections;
using OI.NetCs.Acme;

public interface IAcmeUser
{
    bool Login(string userid);
    bool Register(string userid, string firstName,
        string lastName, string emailAddress);
    bool Unregister(string userid);
    bool ChangeEmailAddress(string userid,
        string emailAddress);
    bool GetUserInfo(string userid, out UserInfo info);
}

public interface IAcmeAdmin
{
    ArrayList GetUsers();
}

public struct UserInfo
{
    public int HotelCustomerId;
    public string FirstName;
    public string LastName;
    public string EmailAddress;
}
```

Login will return **true** if **userid** is found. **Register** will register a new user with the Hotel Broker. Methods are also provided to unregister and change email address. These methods will call the corresponding methods of the **ICustomer** interface. **GetUserInfo** will return a **UserInfo** struct as an **out** parameter. This struct defines an Acme user. The method **GetUsers** of the **IAcmeAdmin** interface returns an array list of **UserInfo** structs.

The class **Acme** wraps access to the **Customers** class, whose methods get invoked indirectly through methods of **IAcmeUser**. The class **Acme** also contains a public member **hotelBroker** of type **HotelBroker**. Thus to gain complete access to the Hotel Broker system, a client program or Web page simply has to instantiate an instance of **Acme**. Here is the start of the definition of **Acme**.

```
public class Acme : IAcmeUser, IAcmeAdmin
{
    public HotelBroker hotelBroker;
    private Customers customers;
    private ArrayList users;
    private UserInfo currentUser;
```

```
public Acme()
{
   users = new ArrayList();
   hotelBroker = new HotelBroker();
   customers = new Customers();
   InitializeUsers();
}
// Initialize users with data from Customers list
private void InitializeUsers()
{
   ArrayList array = customers.GetCustomer(-1);
   foreach (CustomerListItem cust in array)
   {
      string userid = cust.FirstName;
      int custid = cust.CustomerId;
      User user = new User(userid, custid);
      users.Add(user);
   }
}
...
```

The class **Acme** also implements the interface **IAcmeAdmin**.

```
public interface IAcmeAdmin
{
   ArrayList GetUsers();
}
```

The method **GetUsers** returns an array list of **UserInfo**.

## LOGIN.ASPX

To get a good feel for how this Web application works, it would be a good idea for you to register and make a few reservations. You could then try logging in as another user.[7] You can start up the application through the ASP.NET Example programs home page, link to Acme (Step 2), or else direct enter the URL:

`http://localhost/netcs/CaseStudy/Step2/Main.aspx`

The start page for the application is **Main.aspx**. If there is no currently logged-in user, the new user will be redirected to **Login.aspx**. We will examine the logic in **Main.aspx** shortly. For now, let's do the experiment of registering and logging in. Figure 10–28 shows the login page. In our implementation we offer "Rocket" as a possible user ID. Later you can quickly log in as "Rocket Squirrel" by simply clicking "Login." But now click "Register."

---

[7] We are ignoring security considerations in this chapter. Security in ASP.NET will be discussed in Chapter 12.

**Figure 10–28**    *Login page of Acme Web site.*

### REGISTERNEWUSER.ASPX

The "Register New User" page allows the user to pick a User ID and enter some identifying information (first name, last name, and email address). Figure 10–29 shows this page after "John Smith" has entered information for himself. When done entering information, the user should click "Register," which will directly bring up the Acme Travel Agency home page, bypassing a need for a separate login.

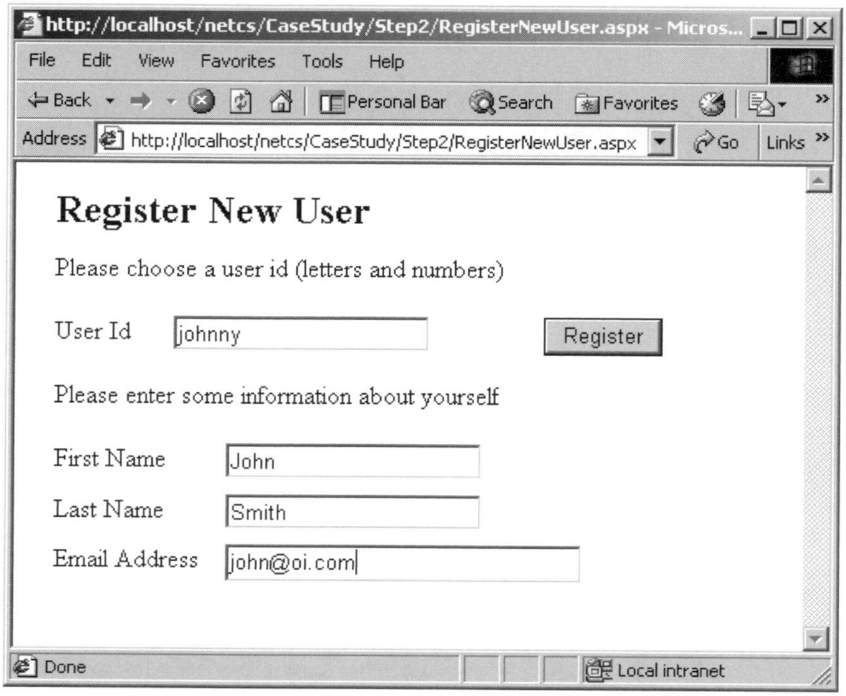

**Figure 10–29** *Register new user page of Acme Web site.*

### MAIN.ASPX

The home page of the Acme Web Site is **Main.aspx**. Figure 10–30 shows this home page for the user "John Smith" who has just registered. A link is provided to "Login" as a different user, if desired. There are links for "Make a Hotel Reservation" and "Manage Your Reservations." These pages are the same as shown previously for Step 1.

**Figure 10–30**   *Home page of the Acme Web site.*

# ASP.NET Applications

An ASP.NET application consists of all the Web pages and code files that can be invoked from a virtual directory and its subdirectories on a Web server. Besides **.aspx** files and code-behind files such as those we have already examined, an application can also have a **global.asax** file and a configuration file **config.web**. In this section we  examine the features of ASP.NET applications. We then investigate the mechanisms for working with application state and session state and for configuring Web applications. Our illustration will be our Acme Case Study (Step 2).

## Sessions

To appreciate the Web application support provided by ASP.NET, we need to understand the concept of a Web *session*. HTTP is a stateless protocol. This means that there is no direct way for a Web browser to know whether a sequence of requests is from the same client or from different clients. A Web server such as IIS can provide a mechanism to classify requests coming from a single client into a logical session. ASP.NET makes it very easy to work with sessions.

## Global.asax

An ASP.NET application can optionally contain a file **Global.asax**, which contains code for responding to application-level events raised by ASP.NET. This file resides in the root directory of the application. Visual Studio will automatically create a **Global.asax** file for you when you create an ASP.NET Web Application project. If you do not have a **Global.asax** file in your application, ASP.NET will assume you have not defined any handlers for application-level events.

    **Global.asax** is compiled into a dynamically generated .NET Framework class derived from **HttpApplication**.

    Here is the **Global.asax** file for our Case Study Step 2.

```
using System;
using System.Collections;
using System.ComponentModel;
using System.Web;
using System.Web.SessionState;
using OI.NetCs.Acme;

namespace AcmeWeb
{
    public class Global : System.Web.HttpApplication
    {
        protected void Application_Start(Object sender,
            EventArgs e)
        {
            HotelState.acme = new Acme();
        }
        protected void Session_Start(Object sender,
            EventArgs e)
        {
            Session["UserId"] = "";
        }
        protected void Application_BeginRequest(
            Object sender, EventArgs e)
        {
        }
        protected void Application_EndRequest(Object sender,
            EventArgs e)
        {
        }
        protected void Session_End(Object sender,
            EventArgs e)
        {
        }
```

```
      protected void Application_End(Object sender,
          EventArgs e)
      {
      }
   }
}
```

The most common application-level events are shown in this code. The typical life cycle of a Web application would consist of these events:

- **Application_Start** is raised only once during an application's lifetime, on the first instance of **HttpApplication**. An application starts the first time it is run by IIS for the first user. In your event handler you can initialize a state that is shared by the entire application.
- **Session_Start** is raised at the start of each session. Here you can initialize session variables.
- **Application_BeginRequest** is raised at the start of an individual request. Normally you can do your request processing in the **Page** class.
- **Application_EndRequest** is raised at the end of a request.
- **Session_End** is raised at the end of each session. Normally you do not need to do cleanup of data initialized in **Session_Start**, because garbage collection will take care of normal cleanup for you. However, if you have opened an expensive resource, such as a database connection, you may wish to call the **Dispose** method here.
- **Application_End** is raised at the very end of an application's lifetime, when the last instance of **HttpApplication** is torn down.

In addition to these events, there are other events concerned with security, such as **AuthenticateRequest** and **AuthorizeRequest**. We will discuss ASP.NET security in Chapter 12.

In the Case Study, we instantiate a single global **Acme** object instance in **Application_OnStart**. This single instance is stored as a static data member of **HotelState**.

```
class HotelState
{
   static public Acme acme;
}
```

In the **Session_Start** event handler we initialize the session variable **UserId** to be a blank string. We discuss session variables later in this section.

# State in ASP.NET Applications

Preserving state across HTTP requests is a major problem in Web programming, and ASP.NET provides several facilities that are convenient to use. There are two main types of state to be preserved.

- **Application state** is global information that is shared across all users of a Web application.

- **Session state** is used to store data for a particular user across multiple requests to a Web application.

## Static Data Members

Static data members of a class are shared across all instances of a class. Hence static data members can be used to hold application state.

In our case study the class **HotelState** has a single static member **acme** of the class **Acme**.

```
class HotelState
{
    static public Acme acme;
}
```

Thus the **hotelBroker** and **customers** objects within **acme** will hold shared data that is the same for all users of the application. Each user will see the same list of hotels.

If you like, you may perform a small experiment at this stage. The directory **HotelAdmin** contains a special version of the Acme Web site that makes available the hotel administration interface **IHotelAdmin** to the special user with user ID of "admin." When this privileged user logins, a special home page will be displayed that provides a link to "Administer Hotels," as illustrated in Figure 10–31.

Browser window titled "Acme Travel System - Microsoft Internet Explorer" showing the page at http://localhost/netcs/HotelAdmin/Main.aspx

> Acme Travel System    Welcome, admin
>
> Lodgings
>    Make a Hotel Reservation
>    Manage Your Hotel Reservations
>
> Flights
>
> Administration
>    Administer Hotels
>
> (If you are not admin, please login)
>
>    Login

**Figure 10–31**   *Home page of the Acme Web site tailored for administrators.*

Run this Web application, either from the "Hotel Admin" link on the example programs home page or else via the URL **http://localhost/netcs/HotelAdmin/Main.aspx**. Log in as "admin" and follow the link to "Administer Hotels." You will be brought to a page showing a list of all the hotels. Select the first hotel (Dixie) on the list and click the "Delete Selected Hotel" button and then the "Refresh" button. You will now see an updated list of hotels, as shown in Figure 10–32.

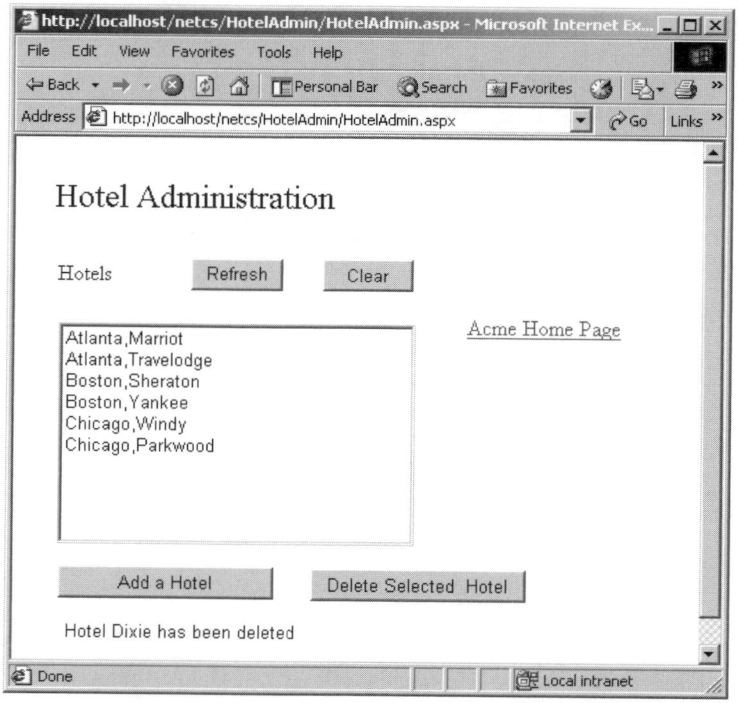

**Figure 10–32**  *Hotel administration page after deleting the Hotel Dixie.*

If your Web server is on a network, you can now try running the same Web application from a different client. Use the URL

```
http://<server-name>/netcs/HotelAdmin/Main.aspx
```

where "<server-name>" is the name of your server machine.[8] Again log in as "admin" and go to the "Hotel Admin" page. You should see the same list of hotels seen by the other client, with Hotel Dixie not on the list.[9]

## Application Object

You can store global application information in the built-in **Application** object, an instance of the class **HttpApplicationState**. You can conveniently access this object through the **Application** property of the **Page** class. The **HttpApplicationState** class provides a key-value dictionary that you can use for storing both objects and scalar values.

---

[8] On a local machine you can use either the machine name or "localhost."

[9] Remember that at this point we are not using a database. Thus our example illustrates application state preserved in memory.

For example, as an alternative to using the class **HotelState** with the static member **acme** that we previously used, we could instead use the **Application** object. We make up a string name for the key—for example, "HotelState." In **Global.asax** we can then instantiate an **Acme** object and store it in the **Application** object using the following code.

```
protected void Application_Start(Object sender,
    EventArgs e)
{
    Application["HotelState"] = new Acme();
}
```

You can then retrieve the **Acme** object associated with "HotelState" by using the index expression on the right-hand side and casting to **Acme**, as illustrated in the code,

```
Acme acme = (Acme) Application["HotelState"];
string name = acme.CurrentUser.FirstName;
```

As a little exercise in employing this technique, you may wish to modify the Step 2 case study to use the **Application** object in place of a static data member. The solution to this exercise can be found in the directory **ApplicationObject**.[10]

## Session Object

You can store session information for individual users in the built-in **Session** object, an instance of the class **HttpSessionState**. You can conveniently access this object through the **Session** property of the **Page** class. The **HttpSessionState** class provides a key-value dictionary that you can use for storing both objects and scalar values, in exactly the same manner employed by **HttpApplicationState**.

Our case study provides an example of the use of a session variable "UserId" for storing a string representing the user ID. The session variable is created and initialized in **Global.asax**.

```
protected void Session_Start(Object sender, EventArgs e)
{
    Session["UserId"] = "";
}
```

We use this session variable in the **Page_Load** event of our home page **Main.aspx** to detect whether we have a returning user or a new user. A new

---

[10] In our current example of a Web application that is precompiled by Visual Studio, it is quite feasible to use a static variable, that can be shared across pages. But if your application is not precompiled, each page will be compiled individually at runtime, and sharing a static variable is no longer feasible. Hence you will have to use the **Application** object to share data.

user is redirected to the login page. (Note that "returning" means coming back to the home page during the same session.)

```
private void Page_Load(object sender, System.EventArgs e)
{
   // Put user code to initialize the page here
   string userid = (string)Session["UserId"];
   if (userid == "")
      Response.Redirect("Login.aspx");
   if (!IsPostBack)
   {
      Acme acme = (Acme) Application["HotelState"];
      string name = acme.CurrentUser.FirstName;
      lblUserName.Text = "Welcome, " + name;
      lblLogin.Text = "(If you are not " + name +
         ", please login)";
   }
}
```

There are some interesting issues in the implementation of session variables.

- Typically cookies are used to identify which requests belong to a particular session. What if the browser does not support cookies, or the user has disabled cookies?

- There is overhead in maintaining session state for many users. Will session state "expire" after a certain time period?

- A common scenario in high-performance Web sites is to use a server farm. How can your application access its data if a second request for a page is serviced on a different machine from that on which the first request was serviced?

### SESSION STATE AND COOKIES

Although by default ASP.NET uses cookies to identify which requests belong to a particular session, it is easy to configure ASP.NET to run cookieless. In this mode the Session ID, normally stored within a cookie, is instead embedded within the URL. We will discuss cookieless configuration in the next section.

### SESSION STATE TIMEOUT

By default session state times out after 20 minutes. This means that if a given user is idle for that period of time, the session is torn down; a request from the client will now be treated as a request from a new user, and a new session will be created. Again, it is easy to configure the timeout period, as we will discuss in the section on Configuration.

### SESSION STATE STORE

ASP.NET cleanly solves the Web farm problem, and many other issues, through a session state model that separates storage from the application's use of the stored information. Thus different storage scenarios can be implemented without affecting application code. The .NET state server does not maintain "live" objects across requests. Instead, at the end of each Web request, all objects in the Session collection are serialized to the session state store. When the same client returns to the page, the session objects are deserialized.

By default, the session state store is an in-memory cache. It can be configured to be memory on a specific machine, or to be stored in an SQL Server database. In these cases the data is not tied to a specific server, and so session data can be safely used with Web farms.

# ASP.NET Configuration

In our discussion of session state we have seen a number of cases where it is desirable to be able to configure ASP.NET. There are two types of configurations:

- **Server configuration** specifies default settings that apply to all ASP.NET applications.
- **Application configuration** specifies settings specific to a particular ASP.NET application.

## Configuration Files

Configuration is specified in files with an XML format, which is easy to read and to modify.

### SERVER CONFIGURATION FILE

The configuration file is **machine.config**. This file is located within a version-specific folder under **\WINNT\Microsoft..NET\Framework**. Because there are separate files for each version of .NET, it is perfectly possible to run different versions of ASP.NET side-by-side. Thus if you have working Web applications running under one version of .NET, you can continue to run them, while you develop new applications using a later version.

## APPLICATION CONFIGURATION FILES

Optionally, you may provide a file **web.config** at the root of the virtual directory for a Web application. If the file is absent, the default configuration settings in **machine.config** will be used. If the file is present, any settings in **web.config** will override the default settings.

## CONFIGURATION FILE FORMAT

Both **machine.config** and **web.config** files have the same XML-based format. There are sections that group related configuration items together, and individual items within the sections. As an easy way to get a feel both for the format of **web.config** and also for some of the important settings you may wish to adjust, just look at the **web.config** file that is created by Visual Studio when you create a new ASP.NET Web Application project.

```
<?xml version="1.0" encoding="utf-8" ?>
<configuration>

  <system.web>

    <!--  DYNAMIC DEBUG COMPILATION
        Set compilation debug="true" to enable ASPX
        debugging.  Otherwise, setting this value to
        false will improve runtime performance of this
        application.
        ...
    -->
    <compilation
        defaultLanguage="c#"
        debug="true"
    />

    <!--  CUSTOM ERROR MESSAGES
        Set mode="on" or "remoteonly" to enable custom
        error messages, "off" to disable. Add
        <error> tags for each of the errors you want to
        handle.
    -->
    <customErrors
    mode="Off"
    />

    <!--  AUTHENTICATION
        This section sets the authentication policies of
        the application. Possible modes are "Windows",
        "Forms", "Passport" and "None"
    -->
```

```
    <authentication mode="None" />

    ...

</system.web>
</configuration>
```

## Application Tracing

Earlier in the chapter we examined page-level tracing, which can be enabled with the **Trace="true"** attribute in the Page directive. Page-level tracing is useful during development but is rather intrusive, because the page trace is sent back to the browser along with the regular response. Application tracing, which is specified in **web.config**, writes the trace information to a log file, which can be viewed via a special URL.

As a demonstration of the use of **web.config**, let's add application tracing to our original **Hello.aspx** application. The folder **HelloConfig** contains **Hello.aspx** and **web.config**. We have added a trace statement in **Hello.aspx**.

```
<!-- Hello.aspx -->
<%@ Page Language="C#" %>
<HTML>
<HEAD>
    <SCRIPT RUNAT="SERVER">
    protected void cmdEcho_Click(object Source, EventArgs e)
    {
        lblGreeting.Text="Hello, " + txtName.Text;
        Trace.Write("cmdEcho_Click called");
    }
    </SCRIPT>
</HEAD>
<BODY>
<FORM RUNAT="SERVER">Your name: 
<asp:textbox id=txtName Runat="server"></asp:textbox>
<p><asp:button id=cmdEcho onclick=cmdEcho_Click
Text="Echo" runat="server" tooltip="Click to echo your
name">
</asp:button></p>
<asp:label id=lblGreeting runat="server"></asp:label>
<P></P>
</FORM>
</BODY>
</HTML>
```

We have provided a trace section in **web.config** to enable tracing.

```
<?xml version="1.0" encoding="utf-8" ?>
<configuration>
```

```
<system.web>
  <trace
      enabled="true"
  />
</system.web>
</configuration>
```

You can run this application from Internet Explorer by simply providing the URL **http://localhost/netcs/helloconfig/hello.aspx**.[11] Enter a name and click the "Echo" button a couple of times. The application should run normally, without any trace information included in the normal page returned to the browser.

Now enter the following URL: **http://localhost/netcs/helloconfig/ trace.axd** (specifying **trace.axd** in place of **hello.aspx**), and you will see top-level trace information, with a line for each trip to the server, as shown in Figure 10–33. If you click on the "View Details" link, you will see a detailed page trace, as we saw earlier in the chapter.

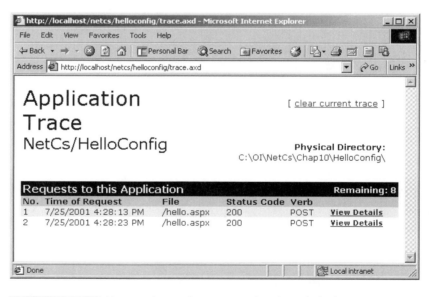

**Figure 10–33**  *Viewing the application trace log through the browser.*

---

[11] If you get a configuration error, try configuring the directory in IIS as an application. See "Configuring a Virtual Directory as an Application" in the section "Deploying a Web Application Created Using Visual Studio."

## Session Configuration

As another example of configuration, modify the **web.config** file for Step 2 of the case study to change the timeout value to be 1 minute.

```
<?xml version="1.0" encoding="utf-8" ?>
<configuration>
  <system.web>
...
    <!--  SESSION STATE SETTINGS
          By default ASP.NET uses cookies to identify which
          requests belong to a particular session. If
          cookies are not available, a session can be
          tracked by adding a session identifier to the
          URL. To disable cookies, set sessionState
          cookieless="true".
    -->
    <sessionState
          mode="InProc"
          stateConnectionString="tcpip=127.0.0.1:42424"
          sqlConnectionString=
             "data source=127.0.0.1;user id=sa;password="
          cookieless="false"
          timeout="1"
    />
...
  </system.web>
</configuration>
```

Now run the application, log in, do some work, and return to the home page. You should be welcomed by your name without having to log in again. Now do some more work, wait more than a minute, and return to the home page. Now the session will have timed out, and you will be redirected to log in again.

# Server Controls

An important innovation in ASP.NET is server controls. They provide an event model that is startlingly similar to Windows GUI programming, and they encapsulate browser dependencies. They integrate seamlessly into the Visual Studio development environment. The end result is an extremely powerful tool for Web development.

We have been using server controls from the very beginning of the chapter, where we presented our "Hello" program. In this section we will look at server controls more systematically, and we will see a number of examples of interesting controls.

## Web Controls

The most important kind of control in ASP.NET is the *Web Forms server control* or just *Web control*. These are new controls provided by the .NET Framework, with special tags such as <asp:textbox>. These controls run at the server, and they generate HTML code that is sent back to the browser. They are easy to work with, because they behave consistently. For example, you can determine the value returned by a control by using simple property notation.

```
string name = txtName.Text;
```

All of our previous examples of server controls in this chapter have been Web controls. In this section, we will look at several additional kinds of Web controls, including validation controls, list controls, and rich controls such as the Calendar control. But first we will look at HTML server controls.

## HTML Server Controls

HTML server controls provide equivalent functionality to standard HTML controls, except that they run on the server, not on the client. In fact, the only way to distinguish an HTML server control from an ordinary HTML control on a Web page is the presence of the **runat="server"** attribute.

Here are two controls. Both are INPUT controls. The first is a server control. The second is of type password and is a regular HTML control.

```
<INPUT id=txtUserId
style="WIDTH: 135px; HEIGHT: 22px" type=text size=17
runat="server"></P>
<INPUT id=""
style="WIDTH: 138px; HEIGHT: 22px" type=password size=17
name=txtPassword>
```

Working with HTML server controls is much like working with the Web Forms server controls we've used already. In server-side code you access the control through a control variable that has the same name as the **id** attribute. However, we are dealing with HTML controls, so there are some differences. You access the string value of the control not through the **Text** property but through the **Value** property. Here is some code that uses the value entered by the user for the **txtUserId** control.

```
lblMessage.Text = "Welcome," + txtUserId.Value;
```

The advantage of HTML server controls for the experienced Web programmer is that they match ordinary HTML controls exactly, so that your knowledge of the details of HTML control properties and behavior carries over to the ASP.NET world. However, this similarity means they carry over all the quirks and inconsistencies of HTML. For example, rather than having two different controls for the somewhat different behaviors of a textbox and a password control, HTML uses in both cases the INPUT control, distinguishing between the two by the **type=password** attribute. Web Forms controls, in contrast, are a fresh design and have an internal consistency. Also, as we shall soon see, there is a much greater variety to Web Forms controls.

### HTML CONTROLS EXAMPLE

Let's look at an example of HTML controls. All of our server control examples in this section can be accessed from the page **ServerControls\WebForms1.aspx**. (As usual, you should use IIS to configure the folder **ServerControls** as an application.) The top-level page gives you a choice of three examples,

- HTML Controls
- Validation
- Calendar

Follow the link to HTML Controls, and you will come to a login page, as illustrated in Figure 10–34.

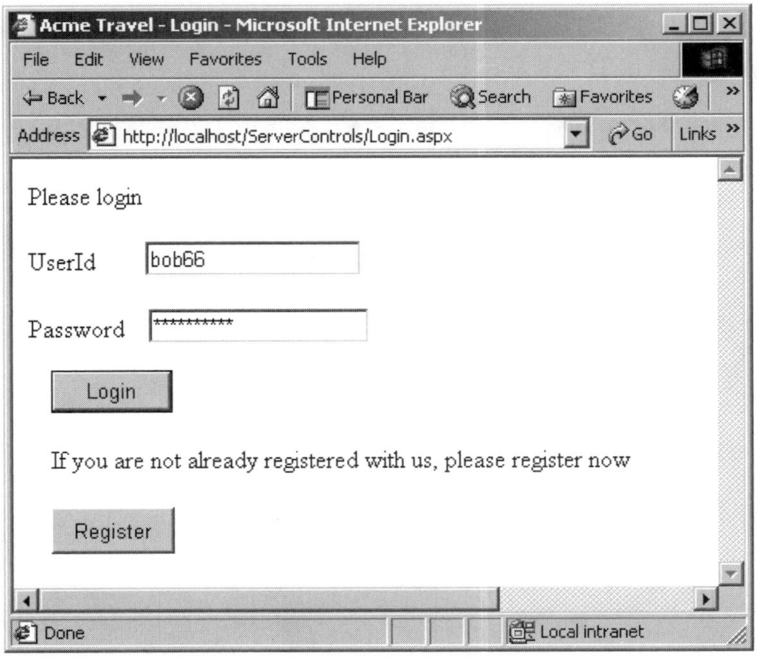

**Figure 10–34** _A login page illustrating HTML server controls._

There is a textbox for entering a user ID and a password control for entering a password. Both of these controls are HTML INPUT controls, as shown previously. The textbox runs at the server, and the password is an ordinary HTML control. Clicking the Login button (implemented as a Windows Forms Button control) results in very simple action. There is one legal password, hardcoded at "77." The button event handler checks for this password. If legal, it displays a welcome message, otherwise an error message.

```
private void Login_Click(object sender, EventArgs e)
{
   if (Request.Params["txtPassword"] == "77")
      lblMessage.Text = "Welcome, " + txtUserId.Value;
   else
      lblMessage.Text = "Illegal password";
}
```

Since the password control is *not* a server control, no server control variable is available for accessing the value. Instead, we must rely on a more fundamental technique, such as using the **Params** collection.[12]

## HTML CONTROLS IN VISUAL STUDIO

It is easy to work with HTML controls in Visual Studio.[13] The Toolbox has a palette of HTML controls, which you can access through the HTML tab. Figure 10–35 shows some of the HTML controls in the Visual Studio Toolbox.

---

[12] We described the various collections earlier in the chapter in the section "Request/Response Programming." The collections are included in Table 10-1.
[13] But it is also confusing, because there is only *one* palette for HTML controls, and you distinguish between classical HTML controls and server HTML controls by **runat="server."** The Forms Designer UI for setting this attribute is described below.

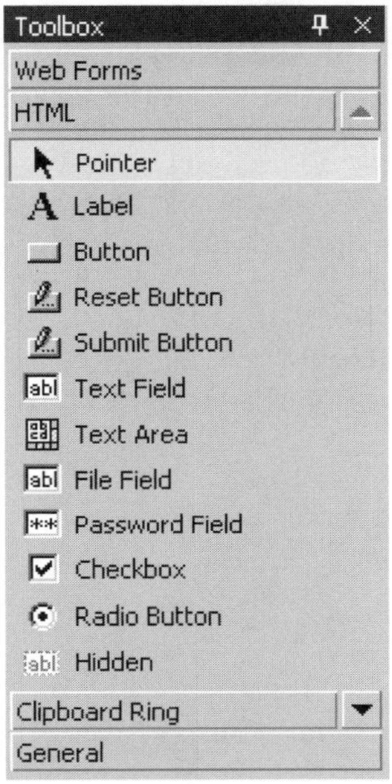

**Figure 10–35**  *HTML controls in the Visual Studio Toolbox.*

You can drag HTML controls onto a form, just as we have done with Web Forms controls. You have the option of using FlowLayout or GridLayout. The default is GridLayout, which enables absolute positioning of controls on a form. FlowLayout is the simplest layout, resulting in elements positioned in a linear fashion. You can set the layout mode through the **pageLayout** property of the form. In our example we used FlowLayout for the two INPUT controls and their associated labels.

The default choice for HTML controls is not to run at the server. To make an HTML control into a server control, right-click on it in the Form Designer. Clicking on "Run As Server Control" toggles back and forth between running on the server and not running on the server. You can inspect the **runat** property in the Properties panel, but you cannot change it there.

## Validation Controls

The rest of our discussion of server controls will focus on Web controls. A very convenient category of control is the group of validation controls. The basic idea of a validation control is very simple. You associate a validation control with a server control whose input you want to validate. Various kinds of validations can be performed by different kinds of validation controls. The validation control can display an error message if the validation is not passed. Alternatively, you can check the **IsValid** property of the validation control. If one of the standard validation controls does not do the job for you, you can implement a custom validation control. The following validation controls are available:

- RequiredFieldValidator
- RangeValidator
- CompareValidator
- RegularExpressionValidator
- CustomValidator

There is also a **ValidationSummaryControl** that can give a summary of all the validation results in one place.

An interesting feature of validation controls is that they can run on either the client or the server, depending on the capabilities of the browser. With an upscale browser such as Internet Explorer, ASP.NET will emit HTML code containing JavaScript to do validation on the client.[14] If the browser does not support client-side validation, the validation will be done only on the server.

### REQUIRED FIELD VALIDATION

A very simple and useful kind of validation is to check that the user has entered information in required fields. Our second server control demonstration page provides an illustration. Back on the top-level **ServerControls\WebForms1.aspx** page, follow the link to "Validation" (or click the Register button from the Login page). You will be brought to the page **RegisterNewUser.aspx**, as illustrated in Figure 10–36. The screenshot shows the result of clicking the Register button after entering a UserId, a Password, and a First Name, but leaving Last Name blank. You will see an error message displayed next to the Last Name textbox, because that is where the validator control is on the form.

---

[14] Validation will also be done on the server, to prevent "spoofing."

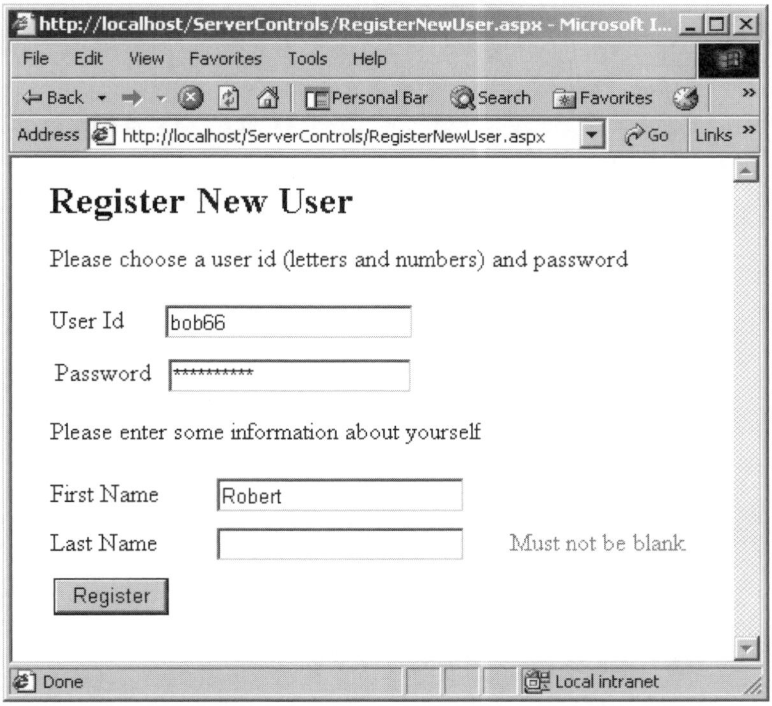

**Figure 10–36**  *Register New User page illustrates ASP.NET validation controls.*

The textboxes for First Name and Last Name both have an associated **RequiredFieldValidator** control. In Visual Studio you can simply drag the control to a position next to the associated control. You have to set two properties of the validator control:

- **ControlToValidate** must be set to the ID of the control that is to be validated.
- **ErrorMessage** must be specified.

Then, when you try to submit the form, the validator control will check whether information has been entered in its associated control. If there is no data in the control, the designated error message will be displayed.

Internet Explorer supports client-side validation using JavaScript. You can verify that ASP.NET generates suitable JavaScript by looking at the generated source code in the browser (View | Source).

This form also requires that the UserId field not be blank. Since the primary validation of this field is done by a regular expression validator, as discussed shortly, we will use another technique for the required field validation. Figure 10–37 shows the location of the various validator controls in the Visual Studio Form Designer.

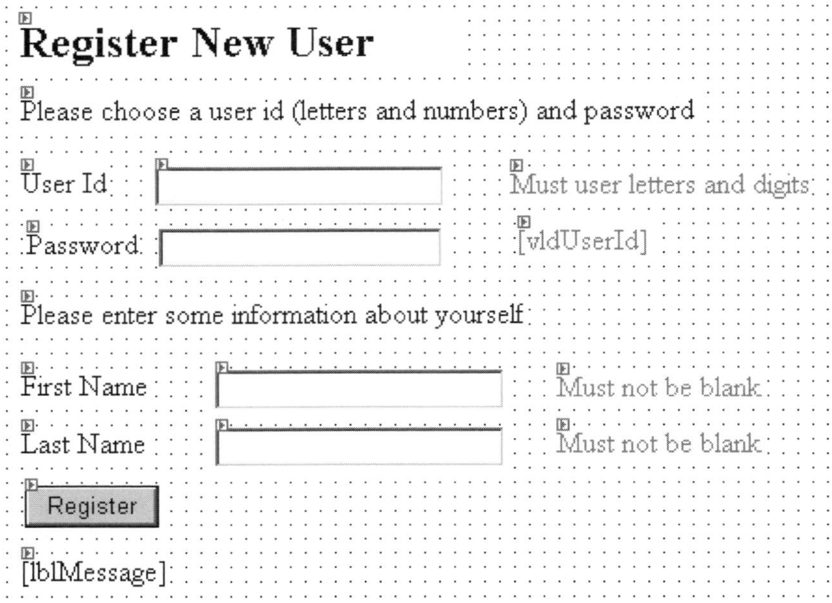

**Figure 10–37** *Layout of validation controls for Register New User page.*

We assign the id **vldUserId** to the required field validator control associated with the UserId control, and we clear the error message. We also set the **EnableClientScript** property to **False**, to force a postback to the server for the validation. The event handler for the Register button then checks the **IsValid** property of **vldUserId**.

```
private void cmdRegister_Click(object sender,
                              System.EventArgs e)
{
   if (vldUserId.IsValid)
      lblMessage.Text = "Welcome, " + txtFirstName.Text;
   else
      lblMessage.Text = "UserId must not be blank";
}
```

If the control is valid, we display the welcome message, otherwise an error message. Note that we won't even reach this handler if other validation is false.

### REGULAR EXPRESSION VALIDATION

The **RegularExpressionValidator** control provides a very flexible mechanism for validating string input. It checks whether the string is a legal match against a designated regular expression. Our example illustrates performing a regular expression validation of UserId. The requirement is that the id consist only of letters and digits, which can be specified by the regular expression

```
[A-Za-z0-9]+
```

The following properties should normally be assigned for a **RegularExpressionValidator** control:

- **ValidationExpression** (the regular expression, not surrounded by quotes)
- **ControlToValidate**
- **ErrorMessage**

You can try this validation out on our Register New User page by entering a string for UserId that contains a nonalphanumeric character.

## Rich Controls

Another category of Web Forms controls consists of "rich controls," which can have quite elaborate functionality. The Calendar control provides an easy-to-use mechanism for entering dates on a Web page. Our third sample server control page provides an illustration, as shown in Figure 10–38.

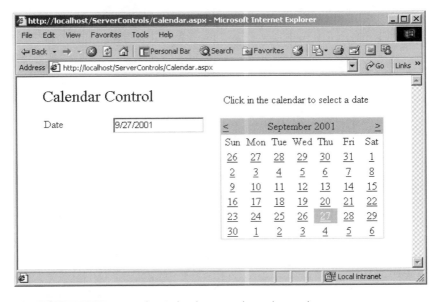

**Figure 10–38**   *Using the Calendar control to select a date.*

The user can select a date on the Calendar control. The **SelectedDate** property then contains the selected date as an instance of the **DateTime** structure. You can work with this date by handling the **SelectionChanged** event. In our example page, the event handler displays the date as a string in a textbox.

```
private void Calendar1_SelectionChanged(object sender,
                                        System.EventArgs e)
{
   txtDate.Text =
      Calendar1.SelectedDate.ToShortDateString();
}
```

# Database Access in ASP.NET

A great deal of practical Web application development involves accessing data in various kinds of databases. A great thing about the .NET Framework is that it is very easy to encapsulate a database, allowing the rest of the program to work with data in a very generic way, without worrying about where it came from. In this section we discuss data binding in Web Forms controls, and we then present a database version of our Acme Travel Agency Web site.

## Data Binding in ASP.NET

ASP.NET makes it easy to display data from various data sources by permitting a Web Forms control to be bound to data source. The data source can be specified in a variety of ways—for example, by directly giving a connection string to a database. This form of data binding is quite convenient in a two-tier type of application, where the presentation layer talks directly to the database. In three-tier applications it is more convenient to bind to some data structure that is returned by a middle-tier component, which does the actual connection to the database. Our Acme case study illustrates this approach. The **Hotel.dll** and **Customer.dll** components encapsulate access to a SQL Server database through the **HotelBroker** and **Customers** classes. Methods such as **GetCities** return an **ArrayList**, and the array list can be bound to a Web Forms control.[15]

We will look at two examples of data binding. The first, mentioned earlier in the chapter, illustrates binding to an **ArrayList**. The second illustrates binding to a **DataTable** through a **DataView**.

---

[15] The component could be hidden behind a Web Service, which will be illustrated in Chapter 11. We can still use data binding in such a scenario, by binding to an array list.

## BINDING TO AN ARRAYLIST

It is extremely simple to bind to an array list. The case study code, beginning with Step 1, provides an illustration. You may wish to bring up Step 1 of the case study and examine the code in **CaseStudy\Step1\MakeReservations.aspx.cs**. When the page is loaded, the **DropDownList** control **listCities** is initialized to display all the cities in the database of the hotel broker. The **GetCities** method returns the cities as strings in an array list. The following code will then cause the cities to be displayed in the dropdown.

```
ArrayList cities = hotelBroker.GetCities();
listCities.DataSource = cities;
DataBind();
```

The **DataBind** method of the **Page** class causes all the Web Forms controls on the page to be bound to their data sources, which will cause the controls to be populated with data from the data sources. You could also call the **DataBind** method of a particular control.

## BINDING TO A DATATABLE

As we saw in Chapter 9, ADO.NET defines a very useful class, the **DataTable**, which can be used to hold data from a variety of data sources. Once created, a data table can be passed around and used in a variety of contexts. One very useful thing you can do with a data table is to bind it to a Web Forms control. Since a data table is self-describing, the control can automatically display additional information, such as the names of the columns. We illustrate with the **DataGrid** control.

To run this example, you need to have SQL Server or MSDE installed on your system, and you should also have set up the Acme database, as described in Chapter 9. The example Web page is **DataGridControl/ShowHotels.aspx**. As usual, you should use IIS to configure the folder **DataGridControl** as an application. This page will display all the hotels in the Acme database in a data grid, with appropriate headings, as illustrated in Figure 10–39. When you work with Web Forms controls you can easily change styles, such as fonts and colors, by setting properties appropriately.

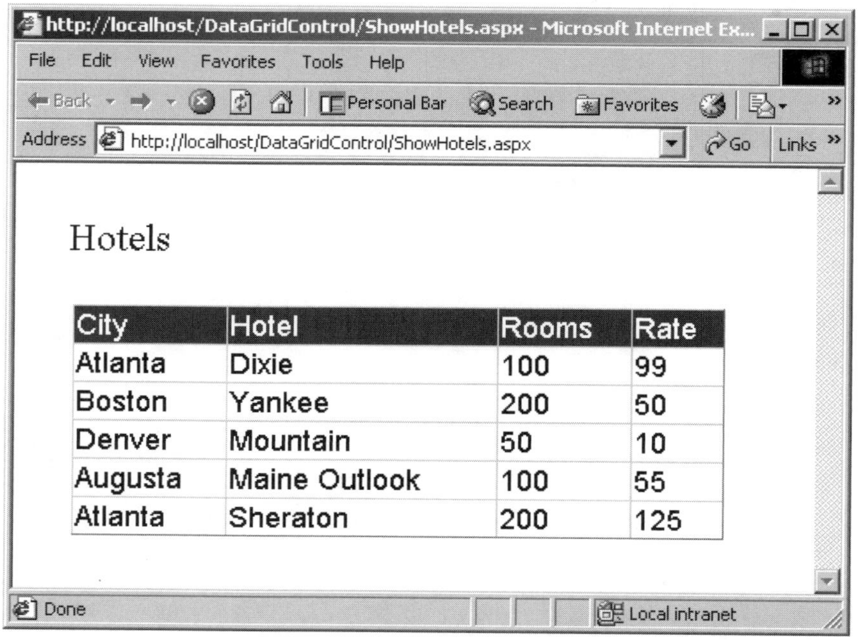

**Figure 10–39**    *Displaying hotels in the Acme database using a DataGrid control.*

The relevant C# code is in the files **Global.asax.cs** and **ShowHotels. aspx.cs**. The first thing we need to do is to create an instance of the **HotelBroker** class. We create a single instance, once, when the application starts up.

```
// Global.asax.cs
using System;
using System.Collections;
using System.ComponentModel;
using System.Web;
using System.Web.SessionState;
using OI.NetCs.Acme;

namespace DataGridControl
{
   public class Global : System.Web.HttpApplication
   {
      public static HotelBroker hotelBroker;
      protected void Application_Start(Object sender,
                                      EventArgs e)
      {
         hotelBroker = new HotelBroker();
      }
      ...
```

In the **Page_Load** method we get the hotels from the Hotel Broker, call a helper method, **CreateDataSource**, to obtain an **ICollection** interface reference (the data binding is very general, and any collection can be used), assign the data source, and bind. We are using the **DataTable** to hold data obtained from the middle-tier component.

```
private void Page_Load(object sender, System.EventArgs e)
{
    if (!IsPostBack)
    {
        // Need to load this data only once.
        ArrayList array = Global.hotelBroker.GetHotels();
        dgHotels.DataSource= CreateDataSource(array);
        dgHotels.DataBind();
    }
}
```

It is in the helper method **CreateDataSource** that the interesting work is done. A data table is created and populated with hotel data obtained from the Hotel Broker.

```
private ICollection CreateDataSource(ArrayList array)
{
    if (array == null)
    {
        return null;
    }
    DataTable dt = new DataTable();
    DataRow dr;
    dt.Columns.Add(new DataColumn("City", typeof(string)));
    dt.Columns.Add(new DataColumn("Hotel", typeof(string)));
    dt.Columns.Add(new DataColumn("Rooms", typeof(int)));
    dt.Columns.Add(new DataColumn("Rate", typeof(decimal)));
    foreach(HotelListItem hotel in array)
    {
        dr = dt.NewRow();

        dr[0] = hotel.City.Trim();
        dr[1] = hotel.HotelName.Trim();
        dr[2] = hotel.NumberRooms;
        dr[3] = hotel.Rate;

        dt.Rows.Add(dr);
    }
```

## Acme Travel Agency Case Study (Database Version)

We have illustrated many concepts of ASP.NET with our Acme Travel Agency case study. For simplicity we used a version of the case study that stored all data as collections in memory. This way you did not have to worry about having a database set up properly on your system, so you could focus on just ASP.NET. Also, the results are always deterministic, since sample data is hardcoded.

Now, however, we would like to look at the "real" case study, based upon our HotelBroker database, and the database version of the **Hotel.dll** and **Customer.dll** components created in Chapter 9.

### ACMECUSTOMERDATABASE

The Acme Travel Agency maintains its own database of customers. Customers register with Acme through the Web site. The following information is stored in Acme's database:

- LoginName
- Password
- HotelBrokerCustomerId
- AirlineBrokerCustomerId

Currently we use LoginName (corresponding to what we called "UserId" earlier in the chapter) and HotelBrokerCustomerId. The AirlineBrokerCustomerId field will facilitate Acme adding an airplane reservation system later. A Password field is also provided for possible future use.

To set up the database, all you need to do is to run the script **acmedb.sql**, which is located in the directory **AcmeScript**. This script assumes you have SQL Server installed on partition **c:**. If your installation is in a different partition, edit the script accordingly.

### ACMELIBDB COMPONENT

The directory **AcmeLibDb** contains a class library project for building an **AcmeLib** component that encapsulates access to the AcmeCustomerDatabase. This component also wraps access to **HotelBroker** and **Customers**, providing the Web pages with a very easy programming model.

### ACME WEB SITE (STEP 3)

The Step 3 version of the Acme Web site is in **CaseStudy\Step3**. As usual, you will need to use IIS to configure this directory as an application. You can start it from the URL

```
http://localhost/netcs/CaseStudy/Step3/Login.aspx
```

You should find the code very easy to understand, because it relies on the same interfaces as the implementation we used earlier based on collections.

## Summary

ASP.NET is a unified Web development platform that greatly simplifies the implementation of sophisticated Web applications. In this chapter we introduced the fundamentals of ASP.NET and Web Forms, which make it easy to develop interactive Web sites. Server controls present the programmer with an event model similar to what is provided by controls in ordinary Windows programming. This high-level programming model rests on a lower-level request/response programming model that is common to earlier approaches to Web programming and is still accessible to the ASP.NET programmer.

The Visual Studio.NET development environment includes a Form Designer, which makes it very easy to visually lay out Web forms, and with a click you can add event handlers. ASP.NET makes it very easy to handle state management. Configuration is based on XML files and is very flexible. There are a great variety of server controls, including wrappers around HTML controls, validation controls, and rich controls such as a Calendar. Data binding makes it easy to display data from a variety of data sources.

In the next chapter we cover Web Services, which enable the development of collaborative Web applications that span heterogeneous systems.

# Web Services

*D*istributing functionality and data beyond the enterprise in which they were developed is the next step in component technology. Developers can integrate into their applications a much more extensive set of services than they could ever hope to develop on their own. Our Acme Reservation System case study is a simple example. The Acme Travel Agency, by using the reservation systems of the airlines and hotels, can provide a wider range of services to their clients.

One vendor will not be able to supply the necessary distributed technology infrastructure. At the very minimum, the worlds of Java, .NET, mobile computers, and legacy systems will continue. Fortunately, TCP/IP and HTTP have established themselves as industry standard networking protocols and can be the basis for any attempt to interconnect heterogeneous systems. HTTP is a text-based protocol, so using the industry standard XML to describe the interactions of these systems makes sense. *Web Services* use XML- and HTTP-based protocols to provide an industry standard to allow diverse systems to interconnect.

Web Services is the second part of the .NET distributed computing story. If all the applications and services that need to interconnect are all based on the Common Language Runtime, .NET remoting can be used. Its advantage is that you can remote any .NET data structure through the remoting serialization. Environments that do not run .NET, however, cannot handle the full range of .NET data types. Hence, Web Services transmit only a much more limited set of data structures that can be expressed in the XML-based protocols that Web Services use today. The versions of the SOAP protocol used by Web Services and by .NET remoting have different programming models. The latter offers full CLR fidelity. The former is constrained by interoperability standards.

Besides the ability of heterogeneous systems to interconnect, Web Services allow business partners to share information or integrate with legacy systems without having to write specialized interconnection applications. Even within a single enterprise you will be able to integrate information from internal and external sources. If Web Services are to be more than just distributed application development, however, the necessary financial, reliability, security, and legal infrastructure have to be developed.

# Protocols

Behind the Web Services technology are several protocols: XML, XML Namespaces, XML Schema, SOAP, and WSDL. Some of these are formal W3C industry standards. Some, like WSDL, are just gaining widespread use without yet being codified in a standard.

## XML

XML is a W3C industry standard[1] that provides a way to structure documents to provide relationships between the basic *elements* of the document. Elements can also have descriptive information called *attributes*. Elements can be composed of other elements, so they can have complex structure. Since such documents can be represented as text,[2] XML can provide a platform-neutral way to represent data that are transmitted over a network. In particular, as text it can go safely through a firewall because HTTP port 80 will invariably be open. Here is an example of an XML document that describes a CustomerList composed of several customers.

```
<CustomerList>
  <Customer>
      <FirstName>John</FirstName>
      <LastName>Smith</LastName>
      <EmailAddress>smith@smith.org</EmailAddress>
```

---

[1] Technically, W3C final documents are called recommendations. However, we will refer to them as standards or specifications. W3C documents that have not reached recommendations status are referred to by their W3C names: proposed recommendations, candidate recommendations, last call working drafts, working drafts, and notes.

[2] But they do not have to be text. You can build programs using the abstractions defined in the W3C proposed recommendation Information Set. Using these abstractions, such as *document, namespace, element, character*, and *attribute*, to represent the hierarchy of an XML document, you are independent of the particular format in which the XML is stored. Mobile solutions will probably use a more efficient binary format for XML encoding rather than text. The XML Schema Recommendation is written based on the Infoset, not the angle-bracket syntax. The Information Set assumes the existence of XML namespaces.

```
  </Customer>
  <Customer>
    <FirstName>Mary</FirstName>
    <LastName>Jones</LastName>
    <EmailAddress>mary@jones.org</EmailAddress>
  </Customer>
</CustomerList>
```

## XML Namespaces

A set of elements and attributes in an XML document can be referred to as a vocabulary. This is particularly useful if this vocabulary can model information that might be reused. For example, we could have vocabularies for financial or chemical information. Namespaces not only allow these vocabularies to be uniquely named in order to prevent conflicts, but allow them to be reused.

The following example XML document uses a namespace attribute to uniquely identify the elements <FirstName>, <LastName>, and <EmailAddress> from any other definitions that might use the same tag names with a different meaning or context. The example also shows that abbreviations can be used with namespaces. This is very convenient if multiple namespaces are used in a document.

```
<Customer xmlns:c=
          "urn:uuid 28833F1C-CBE4-4042-9B35-BF641DFB35DC">
  <c:FirstName>John</c:FirstName>
  <c:LastName>Smith</c:LastName>
  <c:EmailAddress>smith@smith.org</c:EmailAddress>
</Customer>
```

A Uniform Resource Identifier (URI) is used to identify a particular XML namespace. A URI can either be a Uniform Resource Locator (URL) or a Uniform Resource Name (URN). Both represent a unique name. URLs are the familiar Web site addresses, which are unique because they are given out by a central naming authority. A URN is just a unique string. For example, you could use a URN defined by a GUID[3] such as **urn:uuid:28833F1C-CBE4-4042-9B35-BF641DFB35DC**.[4] URIs used for namespaces do not have to resolve to any location on the Web.

---

[3] A GUID, or Globally Unique Identifier, is a 128-bit identifier that is guaranteed to be unique. GUIDs are widely used in COM. You can generate your own GUIDs using the tool **guidgen.exe** (Windows UI) or **uuidgen.exe** (command-line UI). These tools are in the directory …\Microsoft Visual Studio.NET\Common7\Tools.

[4] GUIDs are used in the examples for simplicity and to reinforce the idea that uniqueness, but not existence, is required for a namespace identifier. In real systems URL-based names are used whether or not the URLs actually exist.

## XML Schema

XML with namespaces, however, does not assign any semantics to the data. The XML Schema specification (XSD) defines a basic set of data types and the means to define new data types. In other words, an XML Schema can assign meaning to the structure of a document. The schema itself is written in XML. The CustomerList document described previously could be defined by the following schema:

```
<schema xmlns:xsd="http://www.w3.org/2001/XMLSchema"
        xmlns:c="http://www.acme.com/Customer"
        targetNamespace="http://www.acme.com/CustomerList">
  <xsd:complexType name="Customer">
    <xsd:sequence>
      <xsd:element name="FirstName" type="xsd:string" />
      <xsd:element name="LastName" type="xsd:string" />
      <xsd:element name="EmailAddress" type="xsd:string"/>
    </xsd:sequence>
  </xsd:complexType>
</schema>
```

The targetNamespace element defines the name of the schema being defined. This particular string uses the XSD defined element "string." Using XSD, we can restrict the range of values, specify how often particular instances occur, as well as provide attributes to the elements. The schema itself is written in XML. Both the document and its associated schema can be validated and managed as XML documents. The same document, interpreted by two different schemas, will have two different meanings.

## SOAP

While XML schemas can define the types used by the data, you need a set of conventions to describe how the data and their associated type definitions are transmitted. SOAP, the Simple Object Access Protocol, uses XML as a wire protocol to do just this.

While SOAP can use XML schema types to describe the transmitted types, it was designed before the XML Schema specification was finished, so there are some divergences between the two. The reason is that XML Schema describes a hierarchy or tree structure. SOAP wants to be able to represent objects, and objects can have far more complicated relationships than a hierarchy. Classes, for example, can have multiple parent classes. As we will discuss later, this has some implications for Web Services. The W3C is currently working on reconciling SOAP with XML Schema.

SOAP 1.1 can be used with several transport protocols, not just HTTP.

The use of SOAP for Web Services on Microsoft platforms is not unique to .NET. Microsoft has released the SOAP Toolkit that has allowed

Windows-based platforms to develop Web Services. The support for SOAP, however, is built into .NET. The SOAP Toolkit does contain, however, the SOAP Trace Utility, which is useful for tracking raw and formatted SOAP messages.

## WSDL

Objects contain both state and behavior. Schemas define the data. WSDL, the Web Services Description Language, defines the methods and the data associated with a Web Service. As the simple example we shall describe shortly demonstrates, WSDL is not necessary for writing Web Services. It is important, however, if you want to be able to automatically generate classes that can call Web Services, or do anything that requires automatic machine intervention with Web Services.[5] Otherwise, you would have to craft and send the SOAP messages by hand.

As you will see in the following example, the SOAP that is used to describe the Web Service's transport format is defined in the WSDL. WSDL is a W3C note.

# Web Service Architecture

Besides handling ASP.NET, Microsoft's Internet Information Server (IIS) can handle Web Services, since they come in as HTTP requests. These requests are encoded in the URL or as XML. IIS then creates the required object to fulfill the Web Service request. IIS then calls the object's method that is associated with the request. Any returned values are converted to XML and returned to the client, using the HTTP protocol.

## The Add Web Service Example

To illustrate how this works under Microsoft .NET, we will build a simple Web Service to illustrate this architecture and how the associated protocols are used. Our Web Service will simply add two numbers. To make things clear we will build the Web Service, Add, in the simplest possible way.

By writing code in a file with the suffix **asmx** and placing it in a subdirectory of the IIS root directory we can have a simple Web Service.[6] IIS has the concept of virtual directories, so that the actual directory does not have to physically be under the IIS root directory. The easiest way to do this is to enable WebSharing on the file folder. Select the folder in the NT Explorer,

---

[5] This is similar to VB 6's use of type libraries to make COM programming simpler. Of course, WSDL is a complete description of the Web Service, unlike a type library's incomplete description of a COM object and interfaces.

[6] By default this directory is \inetpub\wwwroot.

right-click on the folder, and select Sharing on the context menu. Use the Web Sharing tab to make the directory a virtual directory for IIS.

The file **add.asmx** first defines the language used to write the Web Service, and the class that has the definitions. That class inherits from the **WebService** class in the namespace **System.Web.Services**. Note the use of the **WebService** attribute to define a namespace for the service. This file is found in the **WebService** subdirectory of the **SimpleWebService** directory for this chapter. You should make **WebService** a virtual directory with alias **SimpleWebService**, as described in the previous paragraph.

A method of that class can be used as a Web Service if the attribute **WebMethod** is applied to it.

```
<%@ WebService language="C#" class="Test" %>

using System;
using System.Web;
using System.Web.Services;

[WebService(Namespace=
        "urn:uuid:10C14FCF-BF4A-477a-BFE7-41B9F2A4514E")]
public class Test: WebService
{
  [WebMethod]
  public long Add(long x, long y)
  {
    return x + y;
  }
}
```

We will put this file in a directory called **SimpleWebService**.[7]

---

[7] You can use a code-behind page here if you wish. WebServices created with VS.NET do reference a code-behind page in the asmx file.

## A Client Program for the Add Web Service

Internet Explorer can be used as a simple client program that uses the HTTP GET protocol's URL encoding of a Web Service request. Using **http:// localhost/SimpleWebService/Add.asmx** as the address, Figure 11–1 shows the result.

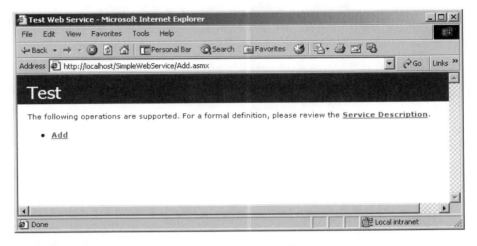

**Figure 11–1**   *Web Service request in Internet Explorer.*

By clicking on the Add link you will get a form enabling you to submit a request to the Add Service. In addition, the form describes the various HTTP protocols that can be used for submitting the request. For our purposes, two protocols are worth mentioning: HTTP GET and SOAP.

The HTTP GET protocol is worth exploring because the form that appears in IE uses it. The protocol has boldfaced placeholders for data that has to be entered:

```
GET /SimpleWebService/add.asmx/Add?x=string&y=string
 HTTP/1.1
...
```

The data entered into the form is added to the URL in the standard way that any HTTP GET request is made. Data are returned as:

```
...
<long xmlns="urn:uuid:10C14FCF-BF4A-477a-BFE7-
                         41B9F2A4514E">long</long>
```

Figure 11–2 shows values entered into the form. By pressing the Invoke button, you can call the Web Service.

*Values entered on the Internet Explorer form.*

An IE window will appear with the part of the HTTP response data generated by the Web Service that contains the actual returned value:

```
...
<long xmlns=
  "urn:uuid:10C14FCF-BF4A-477a-BFE7-41B9F2A4514E">9</long>
```

This is exactly the format that appeared in the description of the protocol with the answer (9) substituted for the placeholder. HTTP GET, however, can handle only simple types.

The more interesting protocol is SOAP. Both the SOAP HTTP POST request and response are described with placeholders for information that has to be provided in the actual call. Those placeholders are in boldface type.

First, let us look at the SOAP HTTP POST request. The first part is a set of HTTP headers. The XML for the SOAP protocol is in the data (entity-body) section of the HTTP request, which is always separated from the headers by a blank line. The content-length header is the length of the data, which is dependent on the size of the parameters in the data section.

The method header identifies the file to which the request is directed. It could also name an object that is to handle the request (endpoint). The

SOAPAction header indicates the name of the method, qualified by a namespace, to be invoked for the Web Service.[8]

SOAP uses XML to specify the parameters of the method.[9] The SOAP body contains the parameters for the method call. In a real method call, the **long** placeholders would be replaced by the actual parameters to be passed to the Web Service method.

```
POST /SimpleWebService/Add.asmx HTTP/1.1
Host: localhost
Content-Type: text/xml; charset=utf-8
Content-Length: length
SOAPAction:
        "urn:uuid:10C14FCF-BF4A-477a-BFE7-41B9F2A4514E/Add"

<?xml version="1.0" encoding="utf-8"?>
<soap:Envelope
   xmlns:xsi="http://www.w3.org/2001/XMLSchema-instance"
   xmlns:xsd="http://www.w3.org/2001/XMLSchema"
   xmlns:soap="http://schemas.xmlsoap.org/soap/envelope/">
  <soap:Body>
    <Add xmlns=
        "urn:uuid:10C14FCF-BF4A-477a-BFE7-41B9F2A4514E">
      <x>long</x>
      <y>long</y>
    </Add>
  </soap:Body>
</soap:Envelope>
```

Next the HTTP response is described. The **long** placeholder will be replaced by the actual value returned.

```
HTTP/1.1 200 OK
Content-Type: text/xml; charset=utf-8
Content-Length: length

<?xml version="1.0" encoding="utf-8"?>
<soap:Envelope xmlns:xsi="http://www.w3.org/2001/XMLSchema-
instance" xmlns:xsd="http://www.w3.org/2001/XMLSchema"
xmlns:soap="http://schemas.xmlsoap.org/soap/envelope/">
  <soap:Body>
    <AddResponse xmlns=
        "urn:uuid:10C14FCF-BF4A-477a-BFE7-41B9F2A4514E">
      <AddResult>long</AddResult>
```

---

[8] For those with a COM background, you can think of the namespace for the method as equivalent to the GUID that identifies and interface (IID).

[9] The parallel to IDL is WSDL, which we will discuss shortly. SOAP is analogous to NDR, the wire format used for DCOM calls. All these parallels to COM appear in Don Box's March 2000 *MSDN* article "A Young Person's Guide to The Simple Object Access Protocol."

```
      </AddResponse>
    </soap:Body>
  </soap:Envelope>
```

## WSDL

SOAP does not describe the Web Service interface. While you could encode the SOAP yourself, it would be nice to be able to generate proxy classes for the client to use. Otherwise you would have to understand all the details of the SOAP specification and how to parse the returned XML.

WSDL provides a description of the Web Service interface. Here is the WSDL description for our **SimpleWebService** which has one method, **Add**. We have omitted the WSDL for invocations of the Web Service that do not use SOAP. The <types> section defines the types:

- **Add** is used in when SOAP invokes the Web Service.
- **AddResponse** is used when the SOAP Web Service invocation returns.

**Add** has two elements, each occurring exactly once. Both are defined with the XSD type long, and they have the names x and y. The return parameter, whose name is **AddResponse**, has one element which occurs once named **AddResult** defined with the XSD type long. Note how these types were used in the SOAP definitions we looked at previously.

```
...
<types>
...
  <s:element name="Add">
    <s:complexType>
      <s:sequence>
        <s:element minOccurs="1" maxOccurs="1" name="x"
                                       type="s:long" />
        <s:element minOccurs="1" maxOccurs="1" name="y"
                                       type="s:long" />
      </s:sequence>
    </s:complexType>
  </s:element>
  <s:element name="AddResponse">
    <s:complexType>
      <s:sequence>
        <s:element minOccurs="1" maxOccurs="1"
                        name="AddResult" type="s:long" />
      </s:sequence>
    </s:complexType>
  </s:element>
  ...
</types>
```

The <message> section relates the types to their use as parameters.

```
<message name="AddSoapIn">
  <part name="parameters" element="s0:Add" />
</message>
<message name="AddSoapOut">
  <part name="parameters" element="s0:AddResponse" />
</message>
...
```

The <portType> section relates the Web Service to the individual Web methods defined by the <operation> elements. If there had been more Web methods in the Web Service, there would have been more operation elements associated with the portType.[10] Each method's input and output operation is associated with the appropriate message defined previously.

```
<portType name="TestSoap">
  <operation name="Add">
    <input message="s0:AddSoapIn" />
    <output message="s0:AddSoapOut" />
  </operation>
</portType>
...
```

The <binding> section defines the encodings and protocols to be used for each operation.

```
<binding name="TestSoap" type="s0:TestSoap">
  <soap:binding
        transport="http://schemas.xmlsoap.org/soap/http"
        style="document" />
  <operation name="Add">
    <soap:operation soapAction=
      "urn:uuid:10C14FCF-BF4A-477a-BFE7-41B9F2A4514E/Add"
        style="document" />
    <input>
      <soap:body use="literal" />
    </input>
    <output>
      <soap:body use="literal" />
    </output>
  </operation>
</binding>
...
```

The <service> section relates the Web Service to its port and how it is invoked.

```
<service name="Test">
  <port name="TestSoap" binding="s0:TestSoap">
    <soap:address location=
            "http://localhost/SimpleWebService/Add.asmx" />
```

---

[10] For those of you keeping score, this is analogous to a COM interface.

```
     </port>
...
</service>
...
```

## Proxy Classes

The **wsdl** tool can be used to read the WSDL description and generate a proxy class that will make the SOAP calls for you. Since C# is the default language, and SOAP the default protocol, the following command will generate a proxy class file with the name **addproxy.cs**:

```
wsdl /out:addproxy.cs
          http://localhost/SimpleWebService/Add.asmx?WSDL
```

The generated proxy defines a constructor and three methods. The constructor sets the URL which this Web Service uses. One of the methods represents a synchronous, blocking call on the Web Service. The other two methods correspond to the asynchronous design pattern discussed in Chapter 8. If you want to call the Web Service asynchronously you can use the BeginXXX and the EndXXX methods associated with the proxy.[11] The proxy class has the same name as the WebService class.

The **Invoke** method of the **SoapHttpClientProtocol** class will make the HTTP request and process the HTTP response associated with the transmitted and received SOAP packets. This example is found in the **SimpleAddClient** subdirectory under the **SimpleWebService** directory.

```
...
public class Test :
    System.Web.Services.Protocols.SoapHttpClientProtocol
{
  ...
  public Test()
  {
    this.Url ="http://localhost/SimpleWebService/Add.asmx";
  }

  ...
  public long Add(long x, long y)
  {
    object[] results = this.Invoke("Add",
                                        new object[] {x, y});
    return ((long)(results[0]));
  }
  ...
  public System.IAsyncResult BeginAdd(long x, long y,
```

---

[11] Of course in this particular case XXX=Add.

```
              System.AsyncCallback callback, object asyncState)
  {
        return this.BeginInvoke("Add",
                new object[] {x, y}, callback, asyncState);
  }

  ...
  public long EndAdd(System.IAsyncResult asyncResult)
  {
        object[] results = this.EndInvoke(asyncResult);
        return ((long)(results[0]));
  }
}
```

You can then write a program to use the proxy classes to issue a Web Service request.

```
public class AddClient
{
  public static void Main(string[] args)
  {
    Test z = new Test();
    long f = z.Add(1, 2);
    Console.WriteLine(f);
    return;
  }
}
```

## Web Service Client with Raw SOAP and HTTP

To show you what the **SoapHttpClientProtocol** class does, the final client program for this example uses sockets to send both the HTTP headers and the SOAP directly and to receive the response from the Web Service. This example is the **RawAddClient** subdirectory of the **SimpleWebService**.

The main routine first reads in a file that has the SOAP headers for the service to be called. It returns the length of the content, which will have to be placed in one of the HTTP POST headers.

```
long contentLength;
StringBuilder contentData = BuildContent("SoapAdd.txt",
                                         out contentLength);
StringBuilder requestHeader = BuildHeader(contentLength);
```

It then connects to the server, sends the data, and receives the response, which it writes out to the console.

```
IPEndPoint endPoint = new
        IPEndPoint(Dns.Resolve(httpServer).AddressList[0],
                                         httpPort);
Socket sock = new Socket(AddressFamily.InterNetwork,
```

```
                        SocketType.Stream, ProtocolType.Tcp);
sock.Connect(endPoint);
...
sock.Send(header, header.Length, 0);
sock.Send(content, content.Length, 0);
...
bytes = sock.Receive(receivedData, receivedData.Length,
                                                   0);
Console.WriteLine(ASCII.GetString(receivedData, 0,
                                                 bytes));
sock.Close();
...
```

The routine **BuildHeader** just builds a standard HTTP POST request with the addition of the SOAPAction header.

```
StringBuilder sb = new StringBuilder(1024);
sb.Append("POST /SimpleWebService/Add.asmx HTTP/1.1\r\n");
sb.Append("Host: localhost\r\n ");
sb.Append("Content-Type: text/xml; charset=utf-8 \r\n");
string line = "Content-Length: " +
                        contentLength.ToString() + "\r\n"
sb.Append(line);
sb.Append("SOAPAction: \"urn:uuid:
        10C14FCF-BF4A-477a-BFE7-41B9F2A4514E/Add\"\r\n ");
sb.Append("\r\n");
...
```

**BuildContent** just reads a file to a buffer and calculates the size of the buffer in bytes.

```
contentLength = 0;

String line;
while ((line = fileStream.ReadLine()) != null)
{
  sb.Append(line);
  sb.Append("\r\n");
  contentLength += line.Length + 2;
}
fileStream.Close();
...
```

Based on our previous discussion, the SOAP file, **SoapAdd.txt**, looks as we would expect it to. The input parameters "9" and "3" appear as the WSDL would dictate.

```
<?xml version="1.0" encoding="utf-8"?>
<soap:Envelope
    xmlns:xsi="http://www.w3.org/2001/XMLSchema-instance"
    xmlns:xsd="http://www.w3.org/2001/XMLSchema"
    xmlns:soap="http://schemas.xmlsoap.org/soap/envelope/">
```

```
<soap:Body>
  <Add xmlns=
       "urn:uuid:10C14FCF-BF4A-477a-BFE7-41B9F2A4514E">
    <x>9</x>
    <y>3</y>
  </Add>
</soap:Body>
</soap:Envelope>
```

The program first writes out the HTTP POST request. First come the standard HTTP headers with a special SOAPAction header, then the SOAP encoding of the request.

```
POST /SimpleWebService/Add.asmx HTTP/1.1
Host: localhost
Content-Type: text/xml; charset=utf-8
Content-Length: 393
SOAPAction:
       "urn:uuid:10C14FCF-BF4A-477a-BFE7-41B9F2A4514E/Add"


<?xml version="1.0" encoding="utf-8"?>
<soap:Envelope
   xmlns:xsi="http://www.w3.org/2001/XMLSchema-instance"
   xmlns:xsd="http://www.w3.org/2001/XMLSchema"
   xmlns:soap="http://schemas.xmlsoap.org/soap/envelope/">
  <soap:Body>
    <Add xmlns=
         "urn:uuid:10C14FCF-BF4A-477a-BFE7-41B9F2A4514E">
      <x>9</x>
      <y>3</y>
    </Add>
  </soap:Body>
</soap:Envelope>
```

The program then writes out the response. Again, the HTTP headers come first, then the SOAP encoding of the result, "12."

```
...
HTTP/1.1 200 OK
Server: Microsoft-IIS/5.0
Date: Mon, 17 Sep 2001 02:11:30 GMT
Cache-Control: private, max-age=0
Content-Type: text/xml; charset=utf-8
Content-Length: 383
<?xml version="1.0" encoding="utf-8"?>
<soap:Envelope
    xmlns:soap="http://schemas.xmlsoap.org/soap/envelope/"
    xmlns:xsi="http://www.w3.org/2001/XMLSchema-instance"
    xmlns:xsd="http://www.w3.org/2001/XMLSchema">
  <soap:Body>
    <AddResponse xmlns=
```

```
            "urn:uuid:10C14FCF-BF4A-477a-BFE7-41B9F2A4514E">
        <AddResult>12</AddResult>
      </AddResponse>
    </soap:Body>
  </soap:Envelope>
```

## SOAP Differences

Before we finish our basic examination of SOAP and WSDL, a more detailed look at the relationship of SOAP, WSDL, and the XML Schema specification is in order. As mentioned earlier, the SOAP encodings used by .NET remoting differ from those used by Web Services and the XML serializer.

To illustrate the differences between the two, we will take the same program and serialize it to disk and use it as a Web Service. The program builds a circular list of two customer items. The two programs are found in the **SOAP Differences** directory.

The first program, **SOAP Formatter**, creates a circular list and then serializes it to disk using the .NET SOAP formatter. Although it is superfluous to do so, we derive the **Test** class from the **WebService** class to demonstrate that what makes the difference is the way SOAP is serialized, not the basic idea of Web Services.

```csharp
using System.Web.Services;
using System;
using System.IO;
using System.Runtime.Serialization.Formatters.Soap;

[Serializable]
public class Customer
{
  public string name;
  public long    id;
  public Customer next;
}

public class Test: WebService
{

static void Main()
{
  Test test = new Test();
  Customer list = test.GetList();
  FileStream s = new FileStream("cust.xml",
                                      FileMode.Create);
  SoapFormatter f = new SoapFormatter();
  f.Serialize(s, list);
```

```
    s.Close();
}

public Customer GetList()
{
  Customer cust1 = new Customer();
  cust1.name = "John Smith";
  cust1.id = 1;

  Customer cust2 = new Customer();
  cust2.name = "Mary Smith";
  cust2.id = 2;
  cust2.next = cust1;

  cust1.next = cust2;
  return cust1;
}
```

This program produces the file **cust.xml** that has the following SOAP encoding. Note the use of the **id** attribute to identify objects and fields, and the **href** attribute that serves as an object reference.

```
...
<SOAP-ENV:Body>
<a1:Customer id="ref-1">
<name id="ref-3">John Smith</name>
<id>1</id>
<next href="#ref-4"/>
</a1:Customer>
<a1:Customer id="ref-4">
<name id="ref-5">Mary Smith</name>
<id>2</id>
<next href="#ref-1"/>
</a1:Customer>
</SOAP-ENV:Body>
...
```

The second version of the program, **WebService**, as its name suggests, is a Web Service:

```
<%@ WebService language="C#" class="Test" %>

using System;
using System.Web;
using System.Web.Services;

public class Customer
{
  public string name;
  public long   id;
  public Customer next;
}
```

```
public class Test: WebService
{
  [WebMethod]
  public Customer GetList()
  {
    Customer cust1 = new Customer();
    cust1.name = "John Smith";
    cust1.id = 1;

    Customer cust2 = new Customer();
    cust2.name = "Mary Smith";
    cust2.id = 2;
    cust2.next = cust1;

    cust1.next = cust2;
  return cust1;
  }
}
```

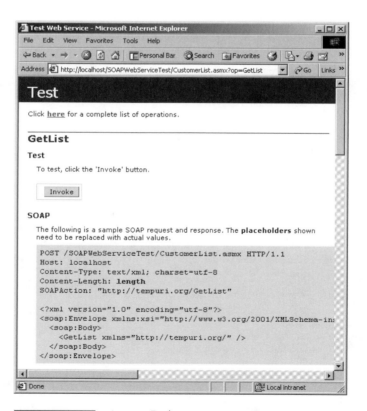

**Figure 11–3**    Internet Explorer recognizes CustomerList.asmx as a Web Service.

If you try to run this Web Service from the Internet Explorer using the URL: **http://localhost/SOAPWebServiceTest/CustomerList.asmx?op=GetList**,[12] Internet Explorer will indeed recognize it as a Web Service. See Figure 11–3.

However, if you go on to Invoke the Web Service, you will get the following error:

```
System.Exception: There was an error generating the XML
    document. --> System.Exception: A circular reference
    was detected while serializing an object of type
    Customer.
 at System.Xml.Serialization.XmlSerializationWriter.
    WriteStartElement(String name, String ns, Object o,
    Boolean writePrefixed)
...
    at System.Xml.Serialization.XmlSerializer.Serialize
    (XmlWriter xmlWriter, Object o,
     XmlSerializerNamespaces namespaces)
...
```

The XML Serializer used to produce the SOAP for Web Services cannot handle the circular reference. If you comment out the line of code: **cust2.next = cust1**, the Web Service will be able to respond with:

```
...
  <name>John Smith</name>
  <id>1</id>
  <next>
    <name>Mary Smith</name>
    <id>2</id>
    <next xsi:nil="true" />
  </next>
...
```

There is no notion, however, of any real relationship between the items, as there was in the remoting case. Why can the SOAP in .NET remoting handle the relationships while the SOAP in Web Services cannot?

SOAP handles the complicated relationships (multiple parents, graphs, etc.) that exist in an object model. XML Schema still reflects the XML heritage of document processing where you can model a document as a tree with a single root, each node having one parent. Since SOAP was being developed before XML Schema was finished, SOAP has some extensions to handle those cases. Since they are in Section 5 of the SOAP specification, they are often referred to as the Section 5 encoding rules.

Those parts of the Section 5 encoding rules that are extensions cannot be incorporated in any XML document that has to be validated against a schema. Hence, the .NET XML serialization classes do not use them. On the other hand, the .NET remoting serializer does not care about schema validation;

---

[12] This URL assumes that you have made the directory **SOAP Difference\WebService** into a virtual directory with alias **SOAPWebServiceTest**.

it cares about the ability to remote full object fidelity and hence uses all the Section 5 rules. In order to maximize interoperability, Web Services implementations tend to use only XML Schema compliant forms that can be validated against a schema.[13] The counterargument can be made that schema validation is not as important when machines are generating the XML, but the industry has not yet taken that approach.[14]

If you want applications and Web Services that reside on different operating system platforms to interoperate, define your Web Services with XML Schema first, then develop the associated WSDL. You can then create an abstract class that can be the basis for an **.asmx** file by using the **/server** option on the **Wsdl** tool.

Starting with an object model and then modeling it with XML Schema might result in incompatible systems. Of course, if only simple types and structures are involved, you are not going to have problems. If you have existing object models, you may need a wrapper layer that translates the Web Services layer and moves it into your existing object model. This is the major technological challenge of Web Services—getting the object models on different platforms to work together.[15]

## Web Service Class

As we have previously demonstrated, a Web Service is nothing but an HTTP request. As such, a Web Service can access the intrinsic objects associated with its HTTP request. These are the same intrinsic objects discussed in the section "State in ASP.NET Applications" in the previous chapter. The **WebService** class has properties that access these intrinsic objects.

You need not derive your Web Service class from the framework **WebService** class. You can derive your Web Service class from a different base class if necessary. In this case you can use the current **HttpContext** to access the intrinsic objects. The **WebService** class inherits from **MarshalByRefObject**, however, so if you want your Web Service class to be remotable, and you do inherit from a different base class, make sure that class also inherits from **MarshalByRefObject**. The **HttpContext** enables you to get information about an HTTP request. By using the static **Current** property, you can get access to the current request.

---

[13] If you have a COM background, think of the work the proxy has to do to handle pointer aliasing if the pointer_default(unique) attribute is not used.

[14] Although we will not discuss them here, there are attributes you can set on your Web Service class and methods to have them use the Section 5 rules.

[15] There is no intent here to slight the security issues associated with Web Services, but if you cannot get the object models to work together in some fashion, security becomes irrelevant because there is nothing to make secure.

We will now build a Web Service inside Visual Studio.NET that will illustrate the use of these intrinsic objects inside a Web Service. As Figure 11–4 demonstrates, choose ASP.NET Web Service from the New Project dialog box in Visual Studio.NET.

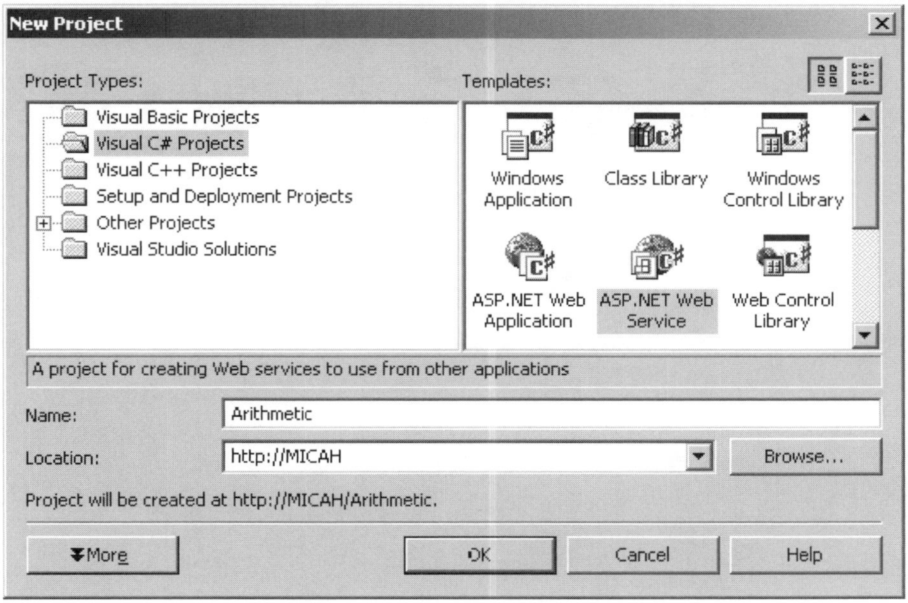

**Figure 11–4**    *Visual Studio.NET New Project dialog with ASP.NET Web Service project selected.*

When you click the OK button, VS.NET will setup a Web Service project for you. By default, the Web Service files are placed in a subdirectory of the IIS directory on your hard drive. By default, projects are placed in a **VSWebCache\MachineName** subdirectory under the **Documents and Settings** directory for the logged in user. Figure 11–5 shows the resulting VS.NET project.

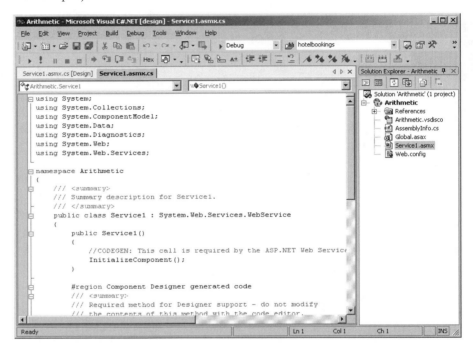

**Figure 11–5**   *Visual Studio.NET Web Services project.*

Our Web Service will have several methods that demonstrate how to use the intrinsic objects. As you will see, this is really no different from their use in ASP.NET. Two of the methods will illustrate the use of application and session state by calculating a cumulative sum of numbers.

In the **global.asax** file we initialize our sum to zero in the appropriate event handlers. **Global.asax** has the same function in Web Services as it does for ASP.NET, as discussed in the previous chapter in the section "ASP.NET Applications." Since the **Global** class inherits from **System.Web.HttpApplication**, it can access the **Application** and **Session** intrinsic objects.

```
public class Global : System.Web.HttpApplication
{
```

```
protected void Application_Start(Object sender,
                                        EventArgs e)
{
  Application["TotalSum"] = 0.0;
}

protected void Session_Start(Object sender, EventArgs e)
{
  Session["SessionSum"] = 0.0;
}
...
```

Renaming the **Service1.asmx** file to **arithmetic.asmx**. we define several Web methods. By setting the **EnableSession** argument to the **WebMethod** constructor to **true**, we turn on session state for the **SessionSum** method. Every time a new session is started, the sum is reset to zero. On the other hand, for the **CumulativeSum** Web method, **EnableSession** is set to its default value or false, so that the sum is reset to zero only when the Web Service application is restarted. The **Application** intrinsic object is used from the **HttpContext** object to show how that class is used.

It should be clear from this code that **HttpApplication**, **WebService**, and **HttpContext** all reference the same intrinsic objects. If you need to save state for the application or session of a Web Service, you can use the collections associated with **HttpApplicationState** and **HttpSessionState** to do so.

```
...
[WebMethod(EnableSession = true)]
public double SessionSum(double x)
{
  Session["SessionSum"] = (double)Session["SessionSum"]+x;
  return (double)Session["SessionSum"];
}

[WebMethod]
public double CumulativeSum(double x)
{
  double sum = (double) Application["TotalSum"];
  sum = sum + x;
  Application["TotalSum"] = sum;
  return (double)HttpContext.Current.Application
                                      ["TotalSum"];
}
...
```

The **GetUserAgent** method show how to use the **Context** object to access information about the request. We return what kind of application is accessing the Web Service. The **GetServerInfo** method accesses the **Server** intrinsic object.

```
[WebMethod]
public string GetUserAgent()
{
  return Context.Request.UserAgent;
}

[WebMethod]
public string GetServerInfo()
{
  string msg = "Timeout for " + Server.MachineName + " = "
             + Server.ScriptTimeout + "; Located at " +
             Server.MapPath("");
  return msg;
}
```

The **ArithmeticClient** console program demonstrates the use of the Web Service. We can create a proxy class from within VisualStudio.NET. On the Project Menu, select Add Web Reference and type in the address of the Web Service in the Address edit box, followed by a carriage return. Information about the Arithmetic Web Service will appear as in Figure 11–6.

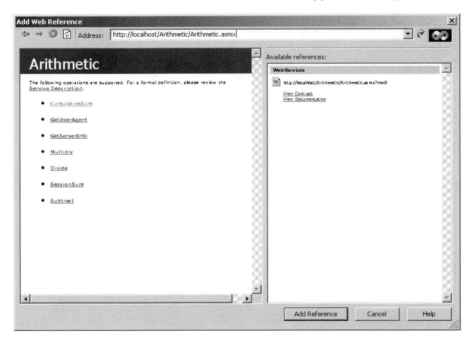

**Figure 11–6**   *Visual Studio.NET display of Arithmetic Web Service information.*

Click on the Add Reference button to add the Web reference. This will add a WebReferences set of subdirectories below the current project that will contain the proxy class and the wsdl file for the Web Service. To the client program we will have to reference the proxy class's namespace:

```
using ArithmeticClient.localhost;
```

We then calculate a sum using the total held by the **Application** intrinsic object. Next we calculate a sum for the total held by the **Session** intrinsic object.

```
Arithmetic a = new Arithmetic();
double sum;
for (int i = 0; i < 5; i++)
{
  sum = a.CumulativeSum(i);
  Console.WriteLine("Adding {0},
                Application sum is now {1}", i, sum);
}

double sessionSum;
for (int i = 0; i < 5; i++)
{
  sessionSum = a.SessionSum(i);
  Console.WriteLine("Adding {0},
                Session sum is now {1}", i, sessionSum);
}
```

This will give us the following output. The exact numbers for the application-based sum will depend on how many times you have run the application.

```
Adding 0, Application sum is now 90
Adding 1, Application sum is now 91
Adding 2, Application sum is now 93
Adding 3, Application sum is now 96
Adding 4, Application sum is now 100
Adding 0, Session sum is now 0
Adding 1, Session sum is now 1
Adding 2, Session sum is now 2
Adding 3, Session sum is now 3
Adding 4, Session sum is now 4
```

We now create another instance of the proxy class and make the same method calls.

```
Arithmetic a2 = new Arithmetic();
for (int i = 0; i < 5; i++)
{
  sum = a2.CumulativeSum(i);
  Console.WriteLine("Adding {0},
                Application sum is now {1}", i, sum);
```

```
}

for (int i = 0; i < 5; i++)
{
  sum = a2.SessionSum(i);
  Console.WriteLine("Adding {0},
                          Session sum is now {1}", i, sum);
}
```

We get the following output. Notice how the application sum continues to increase, while the session bases sum starts again from zero. A new browser session is not the only way to start a new Web Service session.

```
Adding 0, Application sum is now 100
Adding 1, Application sum is now 101
Adding 2, Application sum is now 103
Adding 3, Application sum is now 106
Adding 4, Application sum is now 110
Adding 0, Session sum is now 0
Adding 1, Session sum is now 1
Adding 2, Session sum is now 2
Adding 3, Session sum is now 3
Adding 4, Session sum is now 4
```

Finally we call the **GetUserAgent** and **GetServerInfo** Web methods.

```
Console.WriteLine(a2.GetUserAgent());
Console.WriteLine(a2.GetServerInfo());
```

The output will look something like this:

```
Mozilla/4.0 (compatible; MSIE 6.0; MS Web Services
                        Client Protocol 1.0.2914.16)
Timeout for MICAH = 90; Located at
f:\inetpub\wwwroot\Arithmetic
```

## Hotel Broker Web Service

The next step in the case study is to make the **Customer** and **Hotel** components of the Hotel Broker available as a Web Service. This Web Service is found in the **HotelBrokerWebService** subdirectory of the case study for this chapter. This Web Service will be used both by Acme's customers to make reservations as well as by administrators for maintenance tasks associated with the Hotel Broker.

The proxy classes themselves are built into a **proxies** assembly. Two batch files that can be used to create the proxy classes and build the assembly are located in the **WebServiceProxies** subdirectory of the case study.

In the **HotelBrokerAdministration** subdirectory you will find a version of the admin program that uses the proxies assembly instead of the **Customer** and **Hotel** assemblies. In the **AcmeWeb2** subdirectory for the case study you will find a version of **AcmeLib** that references the **proxies** assembly instead of the **Customer** and **Hotel** assemblies. All references to the **Customer** and **Hotel** components in the Acme reservation Web page and **HotelBrokerAdministration** programs have been removed.

Since at this stage in the book you have a lot of experience with .NET, we do not spell out the details of building the various pieces of the case study. Please consult the file **readme.txt** in the **CaseStudy** directory if you would like some pointers.

## Customer Web Service

To implement the customer Web service we created a file, **CustomerWebService.asmx**, that uses the **Customer** component to implement the details of the Web Service:

```
[WebService(Namespace=
        "urn:uuid:10C14FCF-BF4A-477a-BFE7-41B9F2A4514E")]
class CustomerWebService
{
  private Customers customers;
  public CustomerWebService()
  {
    customers = new Customers("HotelBroker");
  }

  [WebMethod]
  public int RegisterCustomer(string firstName,
                    string lastName, string emailAddress)
  {
    int customerId;
    customerId = customers.RegisterCustomer(firstName,
                              lastName, emailAddress);
    return customerId;
  }

  [WebMethod]
  public void UnregisterCustomer(int customerId)
  {
    customers.UnregisterCustomer(customerId);
  }

  [WebMethod]
  [XmlInclude(typeof(CustomerListItem))]
  public ArrayList GetCustomer(int customerId)
  {
    ArrayList ar;
```

```
    ar = customers.GetCustomer(customerId);
    return ar;
}

[WebMethod]
public void ChangeEmailAddress(int customerId,
                                    string emailAddress)
{
    customers.ChangeEmailAddress(customerId,
                                    emailAddress);
}
}
```

The only new attribute is **XmlInclude**, which allows the XmlSerializer used to create the SOAP protocol to serialize a custom type, in this case **CustomerListItem**. This attribute is found in the **System.Xml.Serialization** namespace. Nonetheless, if you examine the proxy class for this Web Service, which is found in the **WebServiceProxies** directory, you will see that GetCustomer proxy (**customerproxy.cs**) returns only an array of objects.

```
public object[] GetCustomer(int customerId)
```

Although the attribute instructs the serializer to save the custom type, the SOAP protocol understands only how to transmit a generic object type. So the **AcmeLib** code (**Acme.cs**) has to treat the return type as an object and then extract the custom type from it.

```
object[] al = customers.GetCustomer
                            (hotelCustomerId);
foreach(CustomerListItem cust in al)
{
  currentUser.HotelCustomerId = hotelCustomerId;
  currentUser.FirstName = cust.FirstName;
  currentUser.LastName = cust.LastName;
  currentUser.EmailAddress = cust.EmailAddress;
}
```

All the other ArrayLists in the Customer and Hotel Web Services are treated as arrays of objects where the appropriate type has to be extracted. Arrays that use types such as strings and integers, however, need no special treatment by the XmlSerializer.

## Hotel Broker Web Service

For the HotelBroker Web Service, the **Hotel** assembly itself was modified to be a Web Service. The **HotelWebService.asmx file** has to make reference only to the **HotelBroker** class in the **Hotel** assembly, which is located in the **bin** subdirectory of the Web Service.

```
<%@ WebService Language="C#"
            class ="OI.NetCs.Acme.HotelBroker, Hotel" %>
```

The code is the same as the previous version of the component except for addition of the necessary attributes to convert the code to a Web Service. Since Web Service names have to be unique, we had to use the **MessageName** property of the **WebMethod** attribute to give one of the overloaded **GetHotels** methods a unique name.

```
[WebMethod(MessageName="GetAllHotels")]
[XmlInclude(typeof(HotelListItem))]
public ArrayList GetHotels()
```

The code in **Acme.cs** is modified where necessary to handle the generic **object[]** arrays that are returned instead of the CLR specific **ArrayList** type.

## Design Considerations

Network latency is a major performance consideration. Hence, the number of requests made over the network to a Web Service or a database should be minimized. In the HotelBroker Web Service, the reservations for a customer are kept in the dataset as a cache, so that only for database modifications does a database request have to be made. The same is true for tracking the hotels and cities, although there is a trade-off here, since an administrator might add a new hotel. However, that operation is not likely to occur during the relatively short time a customer is making a reservation. Of course, these types of data could be cached inside the Web form itself, so a call to the Web Service would be unnecessary.

HTTP is a stateless protocol and therefore so is SOAP. Minimizing state will help your applications and Web Services to scale better, because objects (such as database connections) can be pooled or reused much more easily, and less memory is required so that more resources are available to handle more requests. This means treating your Web Service objects as endpoints of communication, not as full-fledged objects. Our case study has not really done this, because we wanted to illustrate the use of certain technologies, and the proper way to partition functionality really depends on the details of your actual application and network latencies.

You can also use the **CacheDuration** property on a Web method or the **Cache** property of the **HttpContext** class to cache information to avoid network overhead.

# Summary

Web Services provide a means to extend component functionality across the network between platforms and languages from different vendors. Unlike .NET remoting, however, the types that can be used are much more limited.

Nonetheless, if you start your design from the point of view of the XML Schema specification and then build your WSDL and Web Service classes, you will have a much greater chance of being able to interoperate.

# Security

$W$hile Security considerations are fundamental to application design and should not be left for last, pedagogically it is easier to talk about security once the .NET application model, ASP.NET, and Web Services have already been introduced. This chapter introduces to you the fundamentals of .NET security.[1]

Security prevents a user or code from doing things it should not be allowed to do. Traditionally, security has focused on restricting user actions. .NET allows restrictions to be placed on executing code. For example, you can prevent certain sections of code from accessing certain files. This is particularly useful when you have public Web sites or services where it is impractical to create user accounts, and lock down files or other resources, for an unknown number of users. It is critical when you are executing code that was created by third parties.

It is important to realize that .NET security sits on top of the underlying operating system's security system. For the purposes of this chapter, the underlying operating system is assumed to be Windows 2000. While we will discuss some security issues associated with the underlying infrastructure, including Microsoft's Internet Information Server (IIS), we will go into some detail only with those parts of the security story that are relevant to .NET.[2]

---

[1] Pedagogical reasons also dictate the form of the sample code. It is easier to demonstrate security by starting with an open environment and then showing you how to restrict operations. Real systems should start with the most restrictive security and then open up only as needed.

[2] For more information about secure Web-based applications, read *Designing Secure Web-Based Applications for Microsoft Windows 2000* by Michael Howard.

To give an example of the interaction of .NET security and the operating system, code always runs under some identity, or in other words, as some user id. Irrespective of the file creation .NET security permissions, if the file Access Control List (ACL) denies you the right to create a file, you will be unable to create a file.

*What makes the security story so difficult to tell is that it often seems that you have to understand everything before you can do anything.* For this reason, we will tell the security story several times, each time with a little more detail. At the end you will be able to understand the whole story.

The security story starts with an attempt to answer to two questions. The first is the authentication question: Who are you? The second is the authorization question: Do you have the right to do what you want? Under .NET this story takes two branches, because the "you" can be either a user identity or an identity associated with an assembly.

We start with a brief telling of the security story by showing how both these types of security exist in .NET. Although it is not needed immediately, a brief excursion into Internet security follows, so that we can use that information when we need it. Then we start the detailed narrative with role-based security in .NET.

## User-Based Security

From the perspective of traditional user-based security, the authentication question is: Who is the *identity* attempting to do the action? An identity is typically a user or account name. *Credentials* are what you present to prove who you are; they are evidence presented for verification. A credential might be your password, a smart card, or a biometric device. The user's credentials must be verified with some security authority. An example of this is verifying a user's password against their login name based on a database of user names and encrypted passwords. Systems that allow unverified access are said to allow anonymous access. In security lingo the identity that can be authenticated is referred to as the *principal.*

The authorization question is: Can the identity perform the action they want? The principal is then compared to some list of rights to determine whether access is allowed. For example, when you access a file, your user name is compared with an Access Control List for the action you want to do in order to determine whether you can access the file. Of course, access is not always all or nothing. You might have read, but not modify rights to a file.

In a multitier architecture, the identity under which the server executes is often very powerful, and you want to restrict the ability of the client that makes a request to some subset of privileges the server has. In other cases, such as anonymous access, the server may not know who the client really is.

The server then *impersonates* the client. Code executes under the identity of the client, instead of the server. In the case of anonymous access, the server runs under the identity of some preset user account.

Windows security under .NET, and ASP.NET security, are based on the concepts of user-based security.

# Code Access Security

One of the challenges of the software world of third-party components and downloadable code is that you open your system to damage from executing code from unknown sources. You might want to restrict Word macros from accessing anything other than the document that contains them. You want to stop potentially malicious Web scripts. You even want to shield your system from bugs of software from known vendors. To handle these situations, .NET security includes *Code Access Security* (CAS).

Code Access Security can be applied to verifiable code only. During JIT compilation, the verification process examines the MSIL to verify its type safety. As discussed previously, type-safe code can only access memory locations it is supposed to. Pointer operations are not allowed, so that methods can be entered or left only from well-defined entry points and exit points. You cannot calculate an address and enter code at an arbitrary point. Disallowing pointer operations means that random memory access cannot happen; code can behave only in a restricted manner.[3]

## Security Policy

Code Access Security is based on the idea that you can assign levels of trust to assemblies and restrict the operation of the code within those assemblies to a certain set of operations. Code-based security is also referred to as *evidence-based* security. The name *evidence* stems from the fact that a set of information (or evidence) is used by the CLR to make decisions about what this code is allowed to do. A piece of evidence might be the location from which the code was downloaded, or its digital signature. *Security policy* is the configurable set of rules that the CLR uses to make those decisions. Security policy is set by the machine administrators. Security policy can be set at the enterprise, machine, user, or application domain level.

---

[3] Of course, bugs are still possible, but bugs cannot overwrite the stack, overrun a buffer, or do anything that could be exploited to cause the program to do anything that it does not have the security rights to do. If you give your code unlimited rights, then you do have potential problems. This is especially true of the unmanaged code permission that we will discuss later on.

## Permissions

Security policy is defined in terms of permissions. Permissions are objects that are used to describe the rights and privileges of assemblies to access other objects or undertake certain actions. Assemblies request to be granted certain permissions. Security Policy dictates what permissions will be granted to an assembly.

Examples of the classes that model permissions include:

- **SecurityPermission** that controls access to the security system. This includes the right to call unmanaged code, control threads, control principals, app domain, evidence and the like.
- **FileIOPermission** that controls access to the file system.
- **ReflectionPermission** that controls access to nonpublic metadata and the dynamic generation of modules, types, and members.

All the permission classes inherit from the **CodeAccessPermission** base class, so they all behave in the same way.

Attributes can be applied to the assembly to represent a request for certain permissions. The CLR will use metadata to determine what permissions are being requested. Based on the code's identity and trust level, the CLR will use security policy to determine whether it can *grant* those permissions.

Code can programmatically *demand* (request) that its callers have certain permissions before it will execute certain code paths. If the demand fails, the CLR will throw a **System.Security.SecurityException**. Whenever you demand a permission, you have to be prepared to catch that exception and handle the case where the permission was not granted. Most programmers will not have to demand permissions, because the .NET framework libraries will do that for you on your behalf. You still have to be prepared, though, to handle the exceptions.

Code can also request that permissions it has been granted be restricted or denied. This is important for code that uses third-party components or relies on third-party Web scripts. Since such code may have a lower level of trust than your own code, you might want to restrict the available rights while that code is running. When it is finished running, you can restore the level of permissions back.

Determining the identity of the code is equivalent to the authentication question of traditional security. The authorization question is based on the security permissions that are given or taken away from an assembly.

Many of the classes that support permissions are found in the **System.Security.Permissions** namespace. Some are found in the **System. Net** and **System.Data** namespaces.

# Internet Security

You can use the Internet Protocol Security (IPSec) to restrict access to your computer to certain IP addresses. Of course, you need to know the IP addresses of your clients. The advantage is that you do not have to change your client application, ASP.NET code, or Web Service code to use it. This is impractical for public Web sites or services where you do not know who your clients are.

## Internet Information Server

While the focus of this chapter is .NET security, some knowledge of IIS Security is important. Since both Web Services and ASP.NET use IIS, your IIS settings do affect .NET security.

In the previous chapters on ASP.NET and Web Services, we have used the default settings of Anonymous access. Anonymous access does not require a user name or password to access an account. You run under some default user account. Anonymous access is useful for public Web sites and services that do their own authentication by asking for a user name or password or by some other means. In such a scenario you could use ASP.NET forms-based authentication. You can build forms to get the user name and password and then validate them against a configuration file or database.

Internet Information Services supports the major HTTP authentication schemes. These schemes require you to configure IIS appropriately. These schemes are listed in Table 12–1. In each of these scenarios IIS authenticates the user if the credentials match an existing user account. Secure Sockets Layer (SSL) is used whenever you need to encrypt the HTTP communication channel. SSL can degrade performance. We do not discuss SSL in this chapter.

| Table 12-1 | IIS Authentication Schemes |
| --- | --- |

| Scheme | Type of Authentication |
| --- | --- |
| Basic | User and password information is effectively sent as plain text. This is standard HTTP authentication and is not secure. |
| Basic over SSL | Basic authentication, but the communication channel is encoded, so that the user name and password are protected. |
| Digest | Uses secure hashing to transmit user name and password. This is not a completely secure method because the hash codes stored on the server are reversible.[4] It was introduced in HTTP 1.1 to replace Basic authentication. |
| Windows Integrated Security | Traditional Windows security using NTLM or Kerberos protocols. IIS authenticates if credentials match a user account. Cannot be used across proxies and firewalls. NTLM is the legacy Windows security protocol. |
| Certificates over SSL | Client obtains a certificate that is mapped to a user account. |

You will also have to adjust access to the necessary files (graphics, data store files, etc.) and other resources (i.e., databases) to those user accounts (authorization). For public Web sites and Web services this approach is not useful because users will not have user accounts.

Microsoft has introduced the *Passport* authentication scheme. While ASP.NET does have support for Passport (**System.Web.Security. PassportIdentity** class) on the server side, as of this writing developer tools to handle the client side for Passport authentication do not yet exist. Passport avoids the problem of requiring specific accounts on specific machines. We will not discuss Passport in this chapter.

The security specification for SOAP is being worked on by the W3C. You could create your own custom authentication using SOAP messages. Since XML is transmitted as text, you want to run using Secure Sockets Layer to encrypt the messages (especially if you use tags such as <user> and <password>. In general, secure data has to be encrypted when using SOAP.

---

[4] See the discussion of hash codes in Chapter 7. A message digest is another name for the result of applying a hash code to a message.

# Role-Based Security in .NET[5]

Most people have at least an intuitive understanding of users and passwords. MTS and COM+ have provided an easy-to-understand security system based on *roles*. The best place to start a more detailed look at .NET security is with identities and roles. We will look at this from the point of view first of a Windows application and then of ASP.NET.

## Principals and Identities

Each thread has associated with it a CLR principal. The principal contains an identity representing the user id that is running that thread. The static property **Thread.CurrentPrincipal** will return the current principal associated with the thread.

Principal objects implement the **IPrincipal** interface. **IPrincipal** has one method and one property. The **Identity** property returns the current identity object, and the method **IsInRole** is used to determine whether a given user is in a specific role. The **RoleBasedSecurity** example illustrates the use of principals, identities, and roles.

Currently there are two principal classes in the .NET framework: **WindowsPrincipal** and **GenericPrincipal**. The **GenericPrincipal** class is useful if you need to implement your own custom principal. The **WindowsPrincipal** represents a Windows user and its associated roles.

Since the **RoleBasedSecurity** example is a Windows (console) application, we will have a **WindowsPrincipal** associated with the **CurrentPrincipal** property.

```
. . .6
IPrincipal ip = Thread.CurrentPrincipal;
WindowsPrincipal wp = ip as WindowsPrincipal;
if (wp == null)
  Console.WriteLine("Thread.CurrentPrincipal is NOT a
                                WindowsPrincipal");
```

---

[5] The discussion in this section is relevant for intranets or other scenarios where users will have Windows user accounts on the servers or domains. See the later section "Forms-Based Authentication" for a discussion of security appropriate to the scenario of a public Web site.

[6] The program starts out with a demand for a SecurityPermission and then proceeds to set the AppDomain principal policy. While the reasons for this will be discussed later, the quick answer is to make sure that the example functions properly on your machine. If you get an exception, you will have to set the policy on your local machine to allow you to run the example. On a vanilla system with a standard install, this should not happen. What to do if it does happen is discussed later in the chapter.

```
else
   Console.WriteLine("Thread.CurrentPrincipal is a
                                   WindowsPrincipal");
...
```

An identity object implements the **IIdentity** interface. The **IIdentity** interface has three properties:

- **Name** is the string associated with the identity. This is given to the CLR by either the underlying operating system or the authentication provider. ASP.NET is an example of an authentication provider.

- **IsAuthenticated** is a Boolean value indicating whether the user was authenticated or not.

- **AuthenticationType** is a string that indicates which authentication was used by the underlying operating system or authentication provider. Examples of authentication types are: Basic, NTLM, Kerberos, Forms, or Passport.

### Substitute Name of Your Machine in the Examples

In several of the examples the machine name MICAH is used. You should substitute the appropriate machine or domain name when you run the samples on your computer.

There are several types of identity objects. Since this is a Windows program, we will have a **WindowsIdentity** object associated with the **WindowsPrincipal**. The example next prints out the property information associated with the identity object.

```
IIdentity ii = ip.Identity;
Console.WriteLine("Thread.CurrentPrincipal Name: {0}
           Type: {1} IsAuthenticated: {2}", ii.Name,
               ii.AuthenticationType, ii.IsAuthenticated);
```

On my machine this is printed out:

```
Thread.CurrentPrincipal Name: MICAH\mds Type: NTLM
                                   IsAuthenticated: True
```

The operating system on the machine MICAH using the NTLM protocol has authenticated the user running this program to be "mds." The sample then validates that this is indeed a **WindowsIdentity** object. The **WindowsIdentity** object has additional properties and methods besides those of the **IIdentity** interface. One of them is the Win32 account token id associated with the currently running user.

```
WindowsIdentity wi = wp.Identity as WindowsIdentity;
if (wi != null)
   Console.WriteLine("WindowsPrincipal.Identity Name: {0}
```

```
    Type: {1} Authenticated: {2} Token: {3}", wi.Name,
wi.AuthenticationType, wi.IsAuthenticated, wi.Token);
```

You can use the name of the user to decide (authorize) whether the user has the rights to undertake certain actions by refusing to execute certain code paths.

## .NET Windows Roles

Instead of checking each individual user name, you can assign users to *roles*. You can then check to see if a user belongs to a certain role. The standard administrators group is an example of how a role works. You do not have to individually assign a user identity all the privileges that an administrator has and then check to see if individual users have certain privileges. Instead, you just assign the user to the administrators group. Code then checks to see if a user is in the administrators group before attempting actions such as creating a new user. .NET roles are separate from COM+ roles.

You define roles by defining groups in NT4 or Windows2000. Each group represents one role. Go to the Control Panel and select Administrative Tools. From the Administrative Tools list select Computer Management. In the Computer Management MMC snap-in expand the Local Users and Groups node. As Figure 12–1 shows, if you select Groups you will see all the Groups defined on your machine.

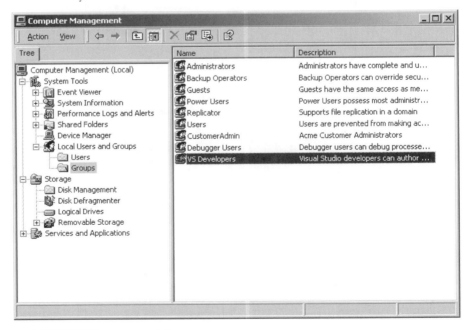

**Figure 12–1**    *Groups defined on a machine.*

Some groups, such as Administrators and Guests, are "built in" because they are predefined for you. CustomerAdmin is a user-defined group that represents administrators who have the right to modify Acme customer information.

To add a new group to the local machine, right-mouse-click on the Groups node and select "New Group." A dialog box you can fill in pops up. Figure 12–2 shows this dialog box filled for a new group entitled "HotelAdmin" which is designed to have all users on the machine who can add or modify information about hotels in the HotelBroker system. Clicking the Create button will add the group to the system. You can use the Add and Remove buttons to add or remove users from the group.

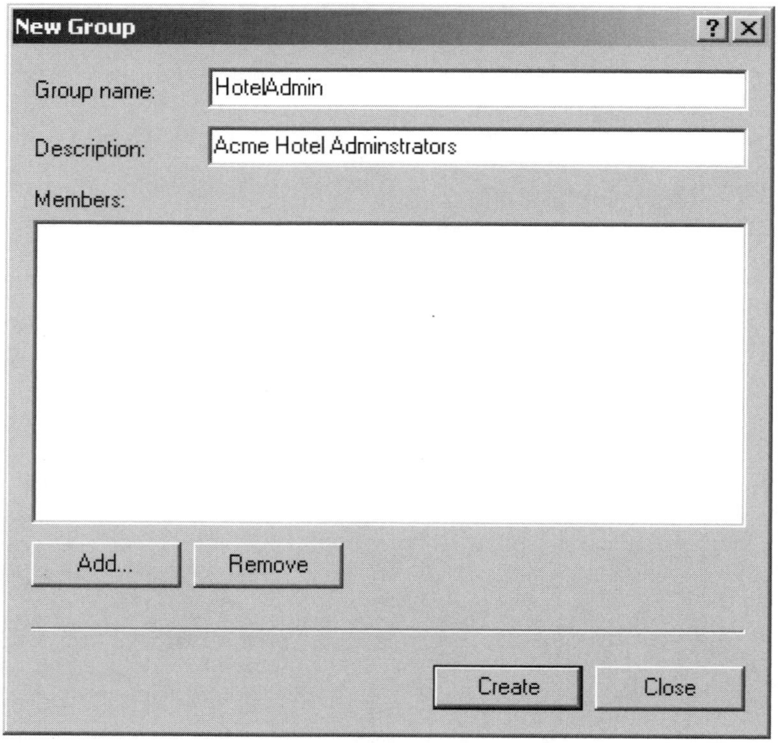

**Figure 12–2** *Dialog to create a HotelAdmin group.*

To modify an existing group, select that group, right-mouse-click, and select Properties. Clicking the Add button will bring up a dialog of all users on the system. You can then select users and add them to the group. Figure 12–3 shows a user about to be added to the HotelAdmin group. The Remove button is used to remove users from the group.

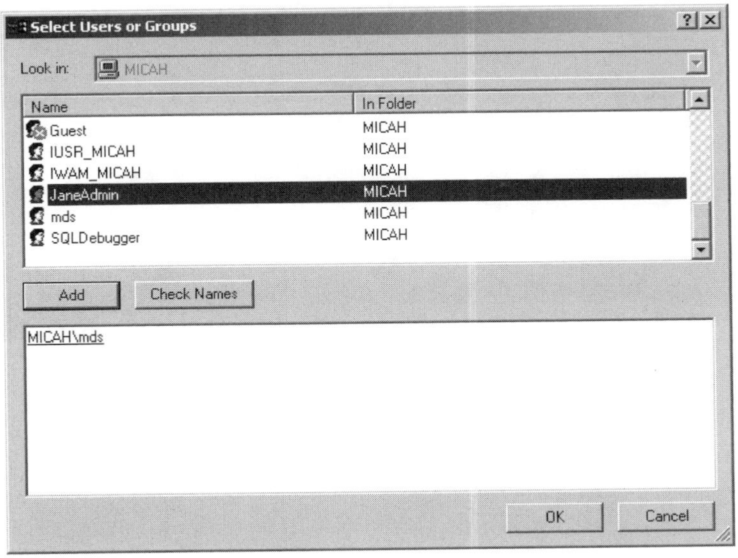

**Figure 12–3**    *User JaneAdmin about to be added to the HotelAdmin group. User mds has already been added.*

In addition to creating a HotelAdmin group, you should also create a CustomerAdmin group with JaneAdmin as a member using the same procedure we just described. Note that the JaneAdmin user need not, and in fact should not, be a member of the Administrators group. Users should run with the minimum privilege required. Within code you qualify the name using the domain or machine name. The CustomerAdmin role is referred to as "MICAH\\CustomerAdmin." For groups that are preinstalled, such as the Administrators group, you use the "BUILTIN" prefix—for example, "BUILTIN\\Administrators." To avoid translation and internationalization problems, the **System.Security.Principal.WindowsBuiltInRole** enumeration can be used to refer to built-in roles. Instead of using the "BUILTIN\\Administrators" string you can refer to the Administrators group as **WindowsBuiltInRole.Administrator**.

The **RoleBasedSecurity** example now checks to see if the current user is in a role. You can either pass the role as a string or use the **WindowsBuiltInRole** enumeration. Remember to modify the programs to use the name of your machine when you run the book samples on your computer.

```
string adminRole = "MICAH\\CustomerAdmin";
bool inRole = wp.IsInRole(adminRole);
Console.WriteLine("In CustomerAdmin role?: {0}", inRole);
inRole = wp.IsInRole(WindowsBuiltInRole.Administrator);
Console.WriteLine("Is in Administrators group: {0}",
  inRole);

inRole = wp.IsInRole(WindowsBuiltInRole.Guest);
Console.WriteLine("Is in Guests group: {0}", inRole);
inRole = wp.IsInRole(WindowsBuiltInRole.User);
Console.WriteLine("Is in Users group: {0}", inRole);
```

## Other Identity Classes

Now let us look in more detail at the other Identity classes. Currently there are four in the .NET Framework:

- **FormsIdentity** is used by the **FormsAuthenticationModule** class. We will discuss this class when we discuss ASP.NET forms authentication.

- **GenericIdentity** can represent any user. This class is used with the **GenericPrincipal** for generic or custom identities and principals.

- **PassportIdentity** is used with Passport authentication. Since we do not discuss Passport, we will not discuss this class.

- **WindowsIdentity** represents a Windows user. A **Windows Principal** instance will have a **WindowsIdentity** instance as its **Identity** property. For authenticated users, the type of authentication used (NTLM, Kerberos, etc.) is available.

Note that the properties of the **IIdentity** interface are read-only and therefore cannot be modified.

Even if your users are unauthenticated, you can get the **WindowsIdentity** for any thread using the static method **WindowsIdentity.GetCurrent** to get the **WindowsIdentity** instance of the current user.[7] You can then use the **WindowsPrincipal** constructor to build a **WindowsPrincipal** instance from this **WindowsIdentity**.

The **HotelBrokerAdminstration** program has been modified so that you cannot run it if you are not in the HotelBrokerAdmin role. See the file **MainAdminForm.cs** in the directory **HotelBrokerAdministration Roles**.

```
static void Main()
{
  ...
  IPrincipal ip;
  ip = Thread.CurrentPrincipal;
```

---

[7] We discuss what this represents in the next section.

```
string hotelAdminRole = "MICAH\\HotelAdmin";
bool inRole = ip.IsInRole(hotelAdminRole);
if (inRole == false)
{
  MessageBox.Show("You cannot run this program since you
                   are not a Hotel Administrator.",
               "Acme Customer Management System",
               MessageBoxButtons.OK,
               MessageBoxIcon.Exclamation);

  return;
}

Application.Run(new MainAdminForm());
}
```

## ASP.NET Roles

Now that we have a fundamental understanding about principals, identities and roles, we can apply it to our AcmeReservationSystem Web site. The Web site has been modified so that you can choose to link to a HotelAdministration page where you can add, modify, or delete the hotels that are part of the HotelBroker system. This example is found in the Step0 subdirectory of the **ASP.NET Roles directory**. To run this example, make sure that the Step0 directory is a virtual directory with the name AcmeWebSecurityStep0. Figures 12–4 and 12–5 show the new Web pages.

Since at this stage in the book you have a lot of experience with .NET, we do not spell out the details of building the various ASP.NET examples. Please consult the file **readme.txt** in the current chapter directory if you would like some pointers.

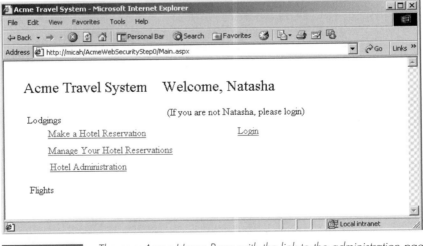

**Figure 12–4**    *The new Acme Home Page with the link to the administration page.*

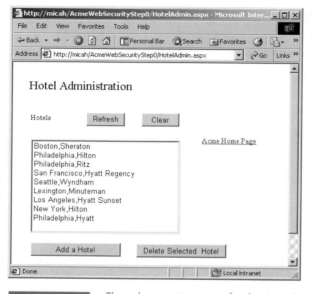

**Figure 12-5** *The administration page for the AcmeReservation system.*

At this point there is no security associated with these pages. Anyone who can log into the Web site can access the administration page and modify the hotel information. We have also modified the login page to print out the current principal and identity information associated with the application as well as the information associated with the current **WindowsIndentity**.

```
string text;

IPrincipal ip;
ip = Thread.CurrentPrincipal;
string principalText = "CurrentPrincipal is of type " +
                                ip.GetType().ToString();

IIdentity ii = ip.Identity;
principalText = principalText + "\n    " +
                        "Is user authenticated?: " +
                        ii.IsAuthenticated.ToString();
text = principalText;

WindowsIdentity wi = WindowsIdentity.GetCurrent();
string identityText = "Current Windows Identity: " + "\n
    " + "Name: " + wi.Name + "\n   IsAuthenticated?:" +
    wi.IsAuthenticated + "\n   AuthenticationType:" +
    wi.AuthenticationType;
text = text + "\n" + identityText;
IdentityInfo.Text = text;
```

As Figure 12–6 illustrates, looking at the information on the login page we find that we have an unauthenticated generic principal for the thread, yet the current **WindowsIdentity** indicates that we are running as the authenticated SYSTEM account. What does this mean? In the previous examples we used the **IsInRole** method associated with the **CurrentPrincipal**. But that user is now not authenticated, so that method will always return false!

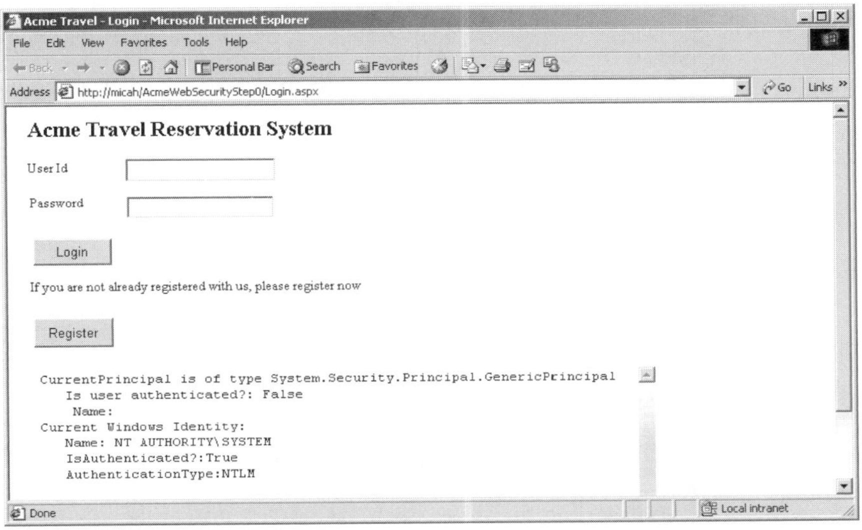

**Figure 12–6**      *Principal and identity information about the Step0 AcmeWebSecurity Web site.*

## Operating System Identity and CLR Identity

As we mentioned at the start of the chapter, .NET security sits on top of the underlying operating-system security. The identity associated with the thread by the CLR and the identity associated with the thread by the underlying operating system are not the same. The identity of the thread from the operating-system perspective is reflected by the setting of the **WindowsIdentity** object returned by the static **Windows.Identity.GetCurrent** method. The CLR identity is reflected by the value of the **Thread.CurrentPrincipal** object.[8] To go back to the example mentioned at the start of the chapter, if

---

[8] The reason why these were identical in the RoleBasedSecurity example is that we set the application domain principal policy in the example to be **PrincipalPolicy.WindowsPrincipal**. With the default ASP.NET settings in the **config.web**, the **PrincipalPolicy.UnauthenticatedPrincipal** policy is used. For that policy, **Thread.CurrentPrincipal** returns an unauthenticated **GenericPrincipal** object. We will discuss principal policy later.

you access a file from within .NET, both the managed and unmanaged identities must have rights to the file within their respective environments.

What values the current **WindowsIdentity** and **Thread.CurrentPrincipal** have are set in two places: IIS Settings and the ASP.NET configuration files.

## UNAUTHENTICATED USERS

Every machine that runs .NET has a **machine.config** file that has the default configuration for the computer. This file is found in the **\WINNT\Microsoft.NET\Framework\v1.0.2914\CONFIG** directory, where **v1.0.2914** would be replaced by the version of Microsoft.NET that is running on your machine. A Web or Web Service application may have a **config.web** file that has the configuration settings for that application. The settings for **config.web** affect all applications in the directory where it lives and all its subdirectories. **Config.web** files in the subdirectories override the settings in the higher-level directories.

If you look in the settings in **config.web** for the Step0 project, you will see the following settings:

```
<identity impersonate="false" />
<authentication mode="None" />
```

The first value sets the unmanaged identity returned by the current **WindowsIdentity**. Since it is set to false, the default operating system identity that ASP.NET runs as will be the SYSTEM account. Since this has broad privileges on the local machine, the Web application can run unimpeded, but this is undesirable from a security perspective, as we will discuss later. The second sets the managed, CLR-based identity returned by **Thread.CurrentPrincipal**. Setting it to "None" means use the default or **GenericPrincipal**. The login page displays the current security configurations, as was shown in Figure 12–6. Here is the relevant output.

```
CurrentPrincipal is of type
System.Security.Principal.GenericPrincipal
   Is user authenticated?: False
   Name:
Current Windows Identity:
   Name: NT AUTHORITY\SYSTEM
   IsAuthenticated?:True
   AuthenticationType:NTLM
```

If you do not have a **config.web** file, the authentication mode set in **machine.config** is "Windows." Now if we set the authentication mode in our local **config.web** to "Windows," we see the following output:

```
CurrentPrincipal is of type
System.Security.Principal.WindowsPrincipal
   Is user authenticated?: False
   Name:
Current Windows Identity:
   Name: NT AUTHORITY\SYSTEM
   IsAuthenticated?:True
   AuthenticationType:NTLM
```

**Thread.CurrentPrincipal** now returns a **WindowsPrincipal**, but it is still unauthenticated and has no name associated with it. Other values for the authentication mode are Forms and Passport.

Let us set the authentication mode back to "None." But now let us set the identity impersonate to "true":

```
<identity impersonate="true" />
<authentication mode="None" />
```

Here are the results:

```
CurrentPrincipal is of type
System.Security.Principal.GenericPrincipal
   Is user authenticated?: False
   Name:
Current Windows Identity:
   Name: MICAH\IUSR_MICAH
   IsAuthenticated?:True
   AuthenticationType:NTLM
```

Where does the identity MICAH\IUSR_MICAH[9] come from? This user is the identity that is set in the properties for this Web application for anonymous access. Select this Web application in the Internet Services Manager, right-mouse-click, and select Properties. Navigate to the Directory Security tab. Click on the Edit button associated with Anonymous access and authentication control. Note that the Anonymous access checkbox is checked. Click the Edit button associated with Account used for anonymous access and you will see this user account listed. Figure 12–7 shows the related dialog boxes. You could change this setting to some other account, but this is the default value set when IIS is installed.

---

[9] As usual, MICAH is the name of my machine. Yours will be different.

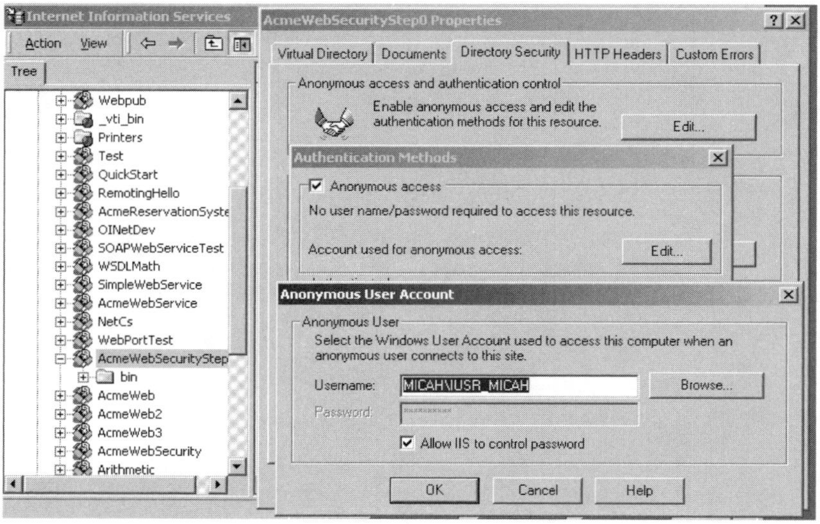

**Figure 12–7** *Internet Services Manager settings for anonymous access.*

Reset the authentication mode back to "Windows" and run again.[10] We still do not see an authenticated principal for the managed **Thread.CurrentPrincipal** identity.

---

[10] To duplicate the results in the next section make sure you reset the authentication mode back to "Windows" now.

## AUTHENTICATED USERS

Now let us use the Internet Services Manager to set our Web application to use Windows Integrated Security instead of anonymous access, as shown in Figure 12–8. Right-click over "AcmeWebSecurityStep0" in the left pane and choose Properties from the context menu. We uncheck the anonymous access box and check the Integrated Windows authentication box.

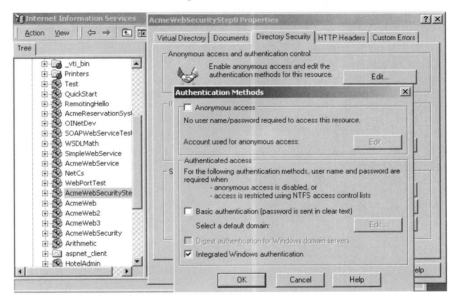

**Figure 12–8**    *Internet Services Manager settings for authenticated access.*

Running our application gets the following results:

```
CurrentPrincipal is of type
System.Security.Principal.WindowsPrincipal
   Is user authenticated?: True
   Name: MICAH\Administrator
Current Windows Identity:
   Name: MICAH\Administrator
   IsAuthenticated?:True
   AuthenticationType:NTLM
```

We now have an authenticated **Thread.CurrentPrincipal** whose identity is the same as the current **WindowsIdentity**. They are associated with whatever user account is currently logged in. Both the managed and unmanaged principals are the same. Now uncheck the Integrated Windows authentication box and check the Basic authentication box in the Internet Services Manager dialog, as shown in Figure 12–9.

*Internet Services Manager settings for Basic authentication.*

If you run the application now, you will have a user and password dialog appear when your run the Web application, as shown in Figure 12–10.

*Dialog for entering a Windows user name and password.*

You now have to enter the user name and password associated with an account on the system. Again, when the login page appears, both the **Thread.CurrentPrincipal** and current **WindowsIdentity** identities are the same, but they are associated with whichever user account you entered into the dialog box, as shown:

```
CurrentPrincipal is of type
System.Security.Principal.WindowsPrincipal
   Is user authenticated?: True
   Name: MICAH\JaneAdmin
Current Windows Identity:
   Name: MICAH\JaneAdmin
   IsAuthenticated?:True
   AuthenticationType:NTLM
```

How did the identity associated with the **CurrentPrincipal** get set to be the same as the **WindowsIdentity**? ASP.NET sets the **CurrentPrincipal** to match the **HttpContext.User** property. In a Windows application you have no choice but to use the **Thread.CurrentPrincipal.** Within ASP.NET it is safer to use the **HttpContext.User** property. Within ASP.NET you can access the **HttpContext.User property** through the **User** object. Step 1 of **ASP.NET Roles** adds the following code to the **Page_Load** method of **main.aspx.cs**:

```
if (User.IsInRole("MICAH\\HotelAdmin"))
  HotelAdminLink.Visible = true;
else
  HotelAdminLink.Visible = false;
```

The Internet Services Manager security should be set to at Windows Integrated security. The following settings are still in **web.config**:

```
<identity impersonate="true" />
<authentication mode="Windows" />.
```

Therefore, any user logged into Windows who is a member of the HotelAdmin group, will see the Administration link, otherwise the link will not appear. Of course, what name you enter into the login page has nothing to do with what you see. It is the identity associated with the thread that matters.

If you want to test your Web application as a different user, you do not have to log out and log in as that user. Navigate to Internet Explorer on the Start Menu, and right-mouse-click while holding down the shift key. You will see a menu item "Run As..." (see Figure 12–11). Select it, and in the dialog box that comes in, log in as the user you want to use. That particular instance of Internet Explorer will be running under that user identity.

| **Figure 12–11** | *RunAs Menu item to run as a different user.* |

### PROBLEMS WITH IMPERSONATION

It would seem that we need only make sure that the user id the thread impersonates is a member of the HotelAdmin group and does not have any more privileges than are needed (i.e., is not System or an administrator, with no ACL rights to any unnecessary files on the server) and then everything will be just fine.

Unfortunately, life is not so simple. Impersonation was designed to be used by a server to alter its rights by running a thread as another user. When the server is done impersonating a user, however, it can revert to its original set of rights by calling the **RevertToSelf** Win32 API. If you call out to a third party or any unmanaged code DLL running in your process, and it made a call to **RevertToSelf**, it would be running as SYSTEM. As SYSTEM this DLL could cause havoc on your system if it were malicious or just buggy.

Step 2 of **ASP.NET Roles** uses the following code to do this:[11]

```
using System.Runtime.InteropServices;
...
[DllImport("Advapi32.dll")]
  public static extern bool RevertToSelf();
...
string text;
```

---

[11] You use the PInvoke interop facility to access the Win32 function. DllImport and PInvoke are discussed in Chapter 14.

```
text = "Windows Identity: " +
                WindowsIdentity.GetCurrent().Name + "\n";
text = text + "CLR Identity: " + User.Identity.Name +
                                                "\n";
text = text + "Calling RevertToSelf()...\n";
bool bRet = RevertToSelf();
text = text + "Windows Identity: " +
                WindowsIdentity.GetCurrent().Name + "\n";
text = text + "CLR Identity: " + User.Identity.Name +
                                                "\n";

txtInfo.Text = text;
```

On the Acme Home Page, calling **RevertToSelf** changes the identity of the thread from the point of view of unmanaged code. The identity from the CLR perspective is unchanged. The HotelAdmin link will be visible or not, depending on the original impersonated identity. Figure 12–12 shows the results.

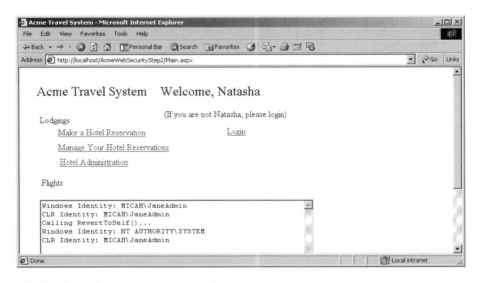

**Figure 12–12**    *Acme Home page showing changes in Thread Identities.*

To avoid running as the SYSTEM account, you can set the identity of the process that your Web application runs under.[12,13] If you look in **machine.config** under the <processModel> tag, you will find the enable, userName, and password attributes.

```
<processModel enable="true"
...
userName="SYSTEM" password="AutoGenerate"
...
/>
```

By default, your application process runs under the SYSTEM account. You can modify this value in the **machine.config** file only. We could change the value to be a specific user name:[14]

```
<processModel enable="true"
...
userName="JaneAdmin" password="xyz"
...
/>
```

---

[12] SYSTEM is the identity of the Process Token for your application. Unless impersonating, all threads in the process would use that token. Calling **RevertToSelf** removes the impersonation from the thread and reverts back to whatever identity the Process Token had.

[13] On IIS 5, the identity is inherited from inetinfo.exe. If you configure inetinfo and iisadmin to run with a different identity, that will be the identity of the aspnet_wp process. On IIS 6 with Windows.NET server, ASP.NET does not run its own process model and inherits identity from the IIS worker process. This worker process is configurable and defaults to Network.Service. This is a much better default then SYSTEM.

[14] You will have to stop and start the WWW service on your machine to make the changes to **machine.config** effective.

Figure 12–13 shows the results.[15] As you can see, the password for this user is written in plain text inside **machine.config**. By default, **machine.config** is readable by everyone, so if you use this approach, rights to that file should be restricted.

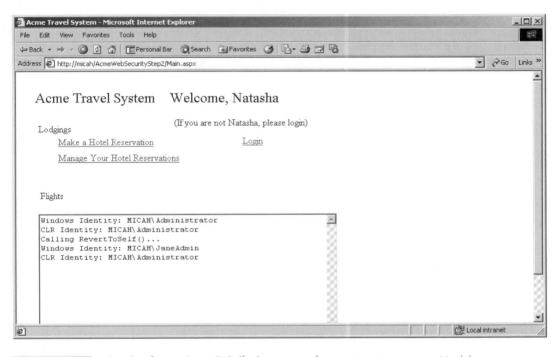

**Figure 12–13**  *Results of using RevertToSelf when a specific user is set in <processModel>.*

---

[15] If you have problems running with a user id you supply here, that id will probably need ACL rights to various system directories on your machine, such as the ASP.NET temporary file directory.

You can also use a setting called MACHINE which uses an account called ASPNET, which is a member of the guest group only and therefore has limited access rights. The ASP.NET setup does add access rights for that user to system directories to enable it to run, such as the **\WINNT\Microsoft.NET\Framework\vx.xxx** directory. Figure 12–14 shows the results of this setting.

```
<processModel enable="true"
...
userName="machine" password="AutoGenerate"
...
/>
```

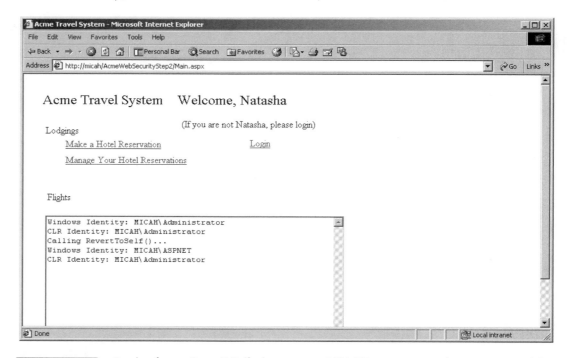

**Figure 12–14**   *Results of using RevertToSelf when generic ASP.NET account is used in <processModel>.*

To summarize, if impersonation is turned off, as Figure 12–15 shows, then you would run as whatever identity is specified in the process model. If you use anonymous access, then Figure 12–16 shows the results you would expect, that the CLR thread identity is unauthenticated.

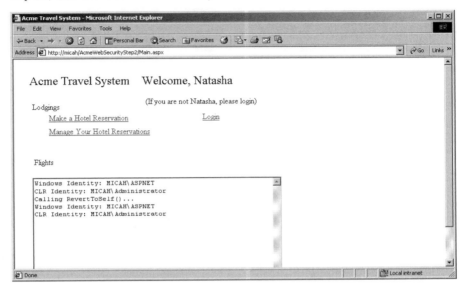

 **Figure 12–15**   *Impersonation turned off, MACHINE specified in <processModel>.*

**Figure 12–16**   *Impersonation turned off, anonymous access, MACHINE specified in <processModel>.*

This discussion also makes clear that the ACLs on **machine.config** and **web.config** should be set so that only administrators can modify the file. Who can read the files should be restricted appropriately. You also have to guard against someone browsing and downloading from those files.

## Specifying Users and Groups for Access in Web.Config

ASP.NET allows you to specify groups and users who are allowed to access the Web site. Inside the <authorization> section of **web.config** you can use the <allow> and <deny> elements with user accounts or groups. To specify groups you use the **roles** attribute; to specify users you use the **users** attribute. The asterisk (*) symbol used with one of those elements means all. A question mark (?) used with a user attribute means "anonymous access."

```
<allow roles="MICAH\HotelAdmin" users="MICAH\Peter">
<deny users="MICAH\John">
```

A reference to a specific user overrides their membership in a group or a wildcard. Deny references take precedence over allow references. These settings do not help you assign users to particular roles or prevent access to different areas of the Web site. Only access to the entire Web site is controlled.

## Forms-Based Authentication

The previous discussion is relevant for intranets or other scenarios where users will have Windows user accounts on the servers or domains. Furthermore, Windows Integrated Security does not work across firewalls or proxies. For public Web sites we need another approach.

The alternative approach is to bring up a login form to authenticate the user. We will look at two of the several approaches to login forms that are possible within .NET. Step 0 of the **FormsBasedAuthentication** example uses the .NET **FormsAuthentication** class and the **config.web** file. Step 1 of the example uses a database login to illustrate using an external database.

### Forms Authentication and Authorization

.NET Forms-based authentication uses **web.config**, login form, and a cookie to authenticate the user.[16] Typically in this scenario you will set up the Web site for anonymous access so that no users will be screened out by IIS. Here is the **web.config** file section for the Step 0 example:

---

[16] You do not have to use a cookie, but it is used for automatic authentication.

```
<authentication mode="Forms">
    <forms name = "HotelBrokerCookie" path="/"
                loginUrl="Login.aspx"
                protection="All" timeout="10">
      <credentials passwordFormat="Clear">
        <user name="Natasha" password="Natasha" />
        <user name="Adams" password="Adams" />
        <user name="peter" password="peter" />
      </credentials>
    </forms>
  </authentication>

  <authorization>
    <allow users="Natasha,peter" />
    <deny users="*" />
  </authorization>
```

The authentication mode is set to Forms. This means that the **User.Identity** object will be a **FormsIdentity** instance if the user is authenticated. The forms element has several attributes that define how the authentication is set up. The name attribute is the name of the cookie. The path attribute indicates where on the site the cookie is valid; "/" indicates the entire site. The loginUrl indicates where the login form resides. The protection attribute indicates how the cookie should be encrypted. "All" indicates that the cookie should be validated and encrypted. Other options are None, Encryption, and Validation. Timeout indicates the number of minutes before the cookie becomes invalid (expires).

The credential elements indicate how the password should be stored in the configuration file. For simplicity we have used clear text. You could also specify SHA1 or MD5 to encrypt the passwords.[17] If passwords are stored in **web.config**, it should be secured against download (which is the default). Passwords for the configuration file can be encrypted with the static **FormsAuthentication** method **HashPasswordForStoringInConfigFile**.[18]

The user elements indicate the user names and passwords. The authorization section, as discussed earlier, determines which authenticated users are authorized to access the Web site.

Since this example uses redirection and cookie validation, a user should attempt to access the main page, **http://localhost/ FormsBasedAuthenticationStep0/default.aspx**, instead of the **login.aspx** file. If a valid cookie does not exist on the system, the user will be sent to the login page. If a valid cookie exists, it will be used to validate the user. If

---

[17] These encryption formats are discussed in Chapter 7.

[18] Storing passwords in a configuration file is convenient for development and testing work. If you do your own validation, as we do with the database example, you do not need to use the **web.config** file.

the user is validated, they will go straight to the **default.aspx** page. If users went straight to the login page, they would have to log in every time, even with a valid cookie.

Here is the code for handling the Login button event:

```
private void Login_Click(object sender, EventArgs e)
{
  if (FormsAuthentication.Authenticate(txtUserId.Text,
    txtPassword.Text))
  {
    FormsAuthentication.RedirectFromLoginPage(
                            txtUserId.Text, true);
  }
  else
  {
    lblErrorMessage.Text = "Could not authenticate user.";
  }
}
```

For simplicity, the Password text box does not hide the password. A password text box that hides the password was discussed in Chapter 10.

The **FormsAuthentication** class's **Authenticate** method validates the user name and password from the **web.config** file. If a valid cookie was on the system, the user is not redirected to the login page. **RedirectFromLoginPage** creates a cookie, and redirects the user to the **default.aspx** page. If the second argument is true, a persistent cookie is placed on the user's system. Persistent cookies are a security risk, because the cookie can be stolen as it is transmitted (hijacked). You should use SSL to protect the cookie. You can remove the session or persistent cookie with the **SignOut** method. The check of the authorization section of **web.config** to see if the user has the rights to access the page is done on each request.

If you run the Step 0 example only Natasha, peter, and Adams will be authenticated. However, only Natasha and Peter will be authorized to use the site. Of course, only Natasha will be found in the database of Acme customers. That test has been moved to default.aspx to distinguish it from the forms authentication done in login.aspx.

**Default.aspx** can refer to the name of the user through the **User** object. The type of identity object is **FormsIdentity**.

```
bool ok = HotelState.acme.Login(User.Identity.Name);
```

If you succeed and log in as Natasha once, subsequent tries will succeed without the login page because we have created a persistent cookie. To avoid persistent cookies, set the second argument to **RedirectFrom LoginPage** to **false**.

The application, however, runs under the identity of the system process or thread, not the identity of the user name that is logged in. Hence, if you want to use role-based security in ASP.NET with Forms authentication, you will have to create your own roles by using a **GenericPrincipal**.

## Database Login Validation

It is fairly straightforward to add password validation against a database as in Step 1 of the **FormsBasedAuthentication** example. When a user is registered, the password is hashed and is stored in the Acme database.[19]

```
string password =
    FormsAuthentication.HashPasswordForStoringInConfigFile
        (txtPassword.Text, "MD5");
bool ok = HotelState.acme.Register(txtUserId.Text,
        password, txtFirstName.Text, txtLastName.Text,
        txtEmailAddress.Text);
```

Before logging in, the password is again hashed and compared with the version stored in the database.

```
string password =
    FormsAuthentication.HashPasswordForStoringInConfigFile
        (txtPassword.Text, "MD5");
bool ok = HotelState.acme.Login(txtUserId.Text, password);
```

With this approach you would have to maintain your own data store to track who is or is not a hotel administrator in order to decide who can see the hotel administration page.

# Code Access Permissions

Code needs permissions in order to access a resource such as a file, or perform some operation. Security Policy (discussed later in the chapter) will give certain permissions to each assembly. Code access permissions can be requested by code. The CLR will decide which permissions to grant based on the security policy for that assembly. We will not discuss how to write a custom permission.

Here are some examples of Code access permissions:

- **DNSPermission** controls access to Domain Name servers on the network.
- **EnvironmentPermission** controls read or write access to environment variables.
- **FileIOPermission** controls access to files and directories.
- **FileDialogPermission** allows files selected in an Open dialog box to be read. This is useful if **FileIOPermission** has not been granted.

---

[19] This assumes that you do not have to mail the password to a user that has forgotten it. Then you have to use two-way encryption.

- **ReflectionPermission** controls the ability to access nonpublic metadata and emit metadata.
- **RegistryPermission** controls the ability to access and modify the registry.
- **SecurityPermission** controls the use of the security subsystem.
- **SocketPermission** controls the ability to make or accept connections on a transport address.
- **UIPermission** controls the user of various user-interface features including the clipboard.
- **WebPermission** controls making or accepting connections on a Web address.

The use of these permissions is referred to as *Code Access Security* because this permission is based not on the identity of the user running the code, but on whether the code itself has the right to take some action.

## Simple Permission Code Request

The **SimplePermissionCodeRequest** example first requests permission to access a file. If the CLR does not grant that request, the CLR will throw a **SecurityException** inside the file constructor. However, this code first tests to see if it has that permission. If it does not, it just returns instead of trying to access the file.[20]

This step is generally superfluous because the CLR will do the demand inside the constructor, but often you want to check permissions before you execute some code to ascertain whether you have the rights you need.

The **FileIOPermission** class models the CLR file permissions. A full path must be supplied to its constructor, and we use the **Path** class we discussed in Chapter 8 to get the full path. We are asking for read, write, and append file access. Other possible access rights are **NoAccess** or **PathDiscovery**. The latter is required to access information about the file path itself. You might want to allow access to the file, but you may want to hide information in the path such as directory structure or user names.

The demand request checks to see if we have the required permission. The **Demand** method checks all the callers on the stack to see if they have this permission. In other words, we want to make sure not only that the assembly this code is running in has this right, but that all the assemblies this code is running on behalf of have this permission. If an exception was generated, we do not have the right we demanded, so we exit the program.

---

[20] We have not yet discussed how you set security policy so you do not yet know how to grant or revoke this permission. By default, however, code running on the same machine that it resides on has this permission. This is another example of how difficult it is to talk about security without knowing the whole picture.

```
string filename = ".\\read.txt";
string fileWithFullPath = Path.GetFullPath(filename);
try
{
  FileIOPermission fileIOPerm = new
        FileIOPermission(FileIOPermissionAccess.AllAccess,
                                    fileWithFullPath);
  fileIOPerm.Demand();
}
catch(Exception e)
{
  Console.WriteLine(e.Message);
  return 1;
}

try
{
  FileInfo file = new FileInfo(filename);
  StreamReader sr = file.OpenText();
  string text;
  text = sr.ReadLine();
  while (text != null)
  {
    Console.WriteLine(text);
    text = sr.ReadLine();
  }
  sr.Close();
}
catch(Exception e)
{
  Console.WriteLine(e.Message);
}
```

Even if the code has the CLR read permission, the user must have read permission from the file system. If the user does not, an **UnauthorizedAccessException** will be thrown when the **OpenText** method is called.

You have to be careful in passing objects that have passed a security check in their constructor to code in other assemblies. Since the check was made in the constructor, no other check is made by the CLR to ascertain access rights. The assembly you pass the object to may not have the same rights as your assembly. If you were to pass this **FileInfo** object to another assembly that did not have the CLR read permission, it would not be prevented from accessing the file by the CLR, because no additional security check would be made. This is a design compromise for performance reasons to avoid making security checks for every operation. This is true for other code access permissions as well.

## How a Permission Request Works

To determine whether code is authorized to access a resource or perform an operation, the CLR checks all the callers on the stack frame, making sure that each assembly that has a method on the stack can be granted the requested permission. If any caller in the stack does not have the permission that was demanded, a **SecurityException** is thrown.

Less trusted code cannot use trusted code to perform an unauthorized action ("luring attack"). The procedures on the stack could come from different assemblies that have different sets of permissions. For example, an assembly that you build might have all rights, but it might be called by a downloaded component that you would want to have restricted rights (so it doesn't open your email address book).

As discussed in the next sections, you can modify the results of the stack walk by using **Deny** or **Assert** methods on the **CodeAccessPermission** base class.

## Strategy for Requesting Permissions

Code should request permissions that it needs before it uses them, so that it is easier to recover if the permission request is denied. For example, if you need to access several key files, it is much easier to check to see if you have the permissions when the code starts up rather than when you are halfway through a delicate operation and then have to recover. Users could be told up front that certain functions will not be available to them. Or, as we will discuss later, you could use assembly permission requests, and then fail to load if the required permissions are not present. The problem is that you may not know what permissions request will succeed because you do not know what assemblies will have callers on the stack when the request is made.

You should not request permissions that you do not need. This will minimize the chances that your code will do damaging things from bugs or malicious third-party code and components. In fact you can restrict the permissions you have to the minimum necessary to prevent such damage. For example, if you do not want a program to read and write the files on your disk, you can deny it the right to do so.

## Denying Permissions

One can apply the **Deny** method to the permission. Even though security policy would permit access to the file, any attempt to access the file will fail. The **SimplePermissionCodeDenial** example demonstrates this. Instead of demanding the permission, we invoke the **Deny** method on the **FileIOPermission** object.

```
...
try
{
  fileIOPerm.Deny();
  Console.WriteLine("File Access Permission Removed");
}
catch(SecurityException se)
{
  Console.WriteLine(se.Message);
}
```

We then try to read the file using the **ReadFile** method. Why we do this inside another method will be explained shortly. Since the permission was denied, the **FileInfo** constructor will throw a **SecurityException**.

```
...
try
{
  FileInfo file = new FileInfo(filename);
  StreamReader sr = file.OpenText();
  string text;
  text = sr.ReadLine();

  while (text != null)
  {
    Console.WriteLine("      " + text);
    text = sr.ReadLine();
  }
  sr.Close();
}
catch(SecurityException se)
{
  Console.WriteLine("Could not read file: " +
se.Message);
}
```

We then call the static **RevertDeny** method on the **FileIOPermission** class to remove the permission denial, and we attempt to read the file again. This time the file can be read. The call to **Deny** is good until the containing code returns to its caller or a subsequent call to **Deny**. **RevertDeny** removes all current **Deny** requests.

```
...
FileIOPermission.RevertDeny();
...
ReadFile();
```

We then invoke the **Deny** method to once again remove the permission.

## Asserting Permissions

The **Assert** method allows you to demand a permission even though you do not have access rights to do so. You might also want to assert a permission because other calls in the call chain do not have the right, even though your assembly does. You can only assert permissions that your assembly has been granted. If this were otherwise, it would be trivial to circumvent CLR security.[21]

The test program code now asserts the **FileIOPermission** and then attempts to read the file.

```
...
...
fileIOPerm.Deny();
...
fileIOPerm.Assert();
...
ReadFile();
ReadFileWithAssert(fileIOPerm);
...
ReadFile();
```

But the file read fails! The assertion is good only within the method that called. The **ReadFileWithAssert** method can read the file because it asserts the permission within the method and then attempts the read. **Assert** stops the permission stack walk from checking permissions higher in the stack frame and allows the action to proceed, but it does not cause a grant of the permission. Therefore, if code further down the stack frame (like **ReadFile**) tries to demand the denied permission (as the **FileInfo** constructor does), a **SecurityException** will be thrown.[22] Similarly, **Deny** prevents callers higher in the stack frame from an action, but not on the current level.

```
 public static void ReadFileWithAssert(FileIOPermission f)
{
  ...
   f.Assert();
   ...
   FileInfo file = new FileInfo(filename);
   StreamReader sr = file.OpenText();
   string text;
   text = sr.ReadLine();

   while (text != null)
   {
     Console.WriteLine("       " + text);
     text = sr.ReadLine();
```

---

[21] You also need the permission to assert.
[22] This is true as well for code above you on the stack frame.

```
    }
    sr.Close();
    ...
}
```

Remember that the assert applies only to IO operations done in this routine for the specific file that was passed the **FileIOPermission** constructor. The call to **Assert** is good until the containing code returns. Hence, **ReadFile** fails again when it is attempted after **ReadFileWithAssert** returns. **RevertAssert** removes all current **Assert** requests.

**Assert** opens up security holes, because some caller in the stack frame might be able to use the routine that calls assert to violate security. Any use of **Assert** should be subject to a security review.

## Other Permission Methods

**PermitOnly** specifies the permissions that should succeed. You specify what resources you want to access. The call to **PermitOnly** is good until the containing code returns, or a subsequent call to **PermitOnly**. **RevertPermitOnly** removes all current **PermitOnly** requests. **RevertAll** removes the effect of **Deny**, **PermitOnly**, and **Assert**.

## SecurityPermission Class

The **SecurityPermission** class controls "metapermissions" that govern the CLR security subsystem. Let us look again at the **RoleBasedSecurity** example from earlier in the chapter. It used the **AppDomain.SetPrincipalPolicy** method to set the application domain's principal policy:

```
AppDomain ap = AppDomain.CurrentDomain;
ap.SetPrincipalPolicy(PrincipalPolicy.WindowsPrincipal);
```

The type of principal returned by **Thread.CurrentPrincipal** will depend on the Application Domain's Principal Policy. An Application Domain can have one of three authentication policies as defined by the **System.Security.PrincipalPolicy** enumeration:

- **WindowsPrincipal** uses the current user associated with the thread. **Thread.CurrentPrincipal** returns a **WindowsPrincipal** object.
- **UnauthenticatedPrincipal** uses an unauthenticated user. **Thread.CurrentPrincipal** returns a **GenericPrincipal** object. This is the default.
- **NoPrincipal** returns null for **Thread.CurrentPrincipal**.

You set the policy with the **SetPrincipalPolicy** method on the **AppDomain** instance for the current application domain. The static method **AppDomain.CurrentDomain** will return the current instance. This method should be called before any call to **Thread.CurrentPrincipal**, because the principal object is not created until the first attempt to access that property.

In order for the **RoleBasedSecurity** example to set the principal policy it needs to have the **ControlPrincipal** right. To ascertain if the executing code has that right, you can demand that **SecurityPermission** before you change the policy. A **SecurityException** will be thrown if you do not have that permission.

```
...
SecurityPermission sp = new SecurityPermision(
            SecurityPermissionFlag.ControlPrincipal);
  try
{
  sp.Demand();
}
catch(SecurityException se)
{
  Console.WriteLine(se.Message);
  return 1;
}
```

We first construct a new **SecurityPermission** instance, passing to the constructor the security permission we want to see whether we have the right to use. **SecurityPermissionFlag** is an enumeration of permissions used by the **SecurityPermission** class. The **ControlPolicy** permission represents the right to change policy. Obviously, this should be granted only to trusted code. We then demand (request) the permission.

As mentioned earlier, you can only assert permissions that your assembly actually has. So rogue components cannot just assert permissions when running within your code. You can either set security policy or use the **SecurityPermission** class to prevent components from calling **Assert**. Construct an instance of the class with the **SecurityPermissionFlag.Assertion** value and then **Deny** the permission. Other actions you can control with the **SecurityPermission** class include the ability to create and manipulate application domains, specify policy, allow or disallow execution, control whether verification is performed, or access unmanaged code.

## Unmanaged Code

Asserts are necessary for controlling access to unmanaged code, since managed code should not call unmanaged code directly.

In order to call unmanaged code you need the unmanaged code permission.[23] Since the CLR performs a stack walk to check whether all the callers have unmanaged code permission, you would have to grant all code the unmanaged code permission. Hence, assemblies other than your own trusted ones could perform operations through the Win32 API calls and subvert the framework's security system.[24]

Better would be to make calls through wrapper classes that are contained in an assembly that has the managed-code right. The code in the wrapper class would first ascertain that the caller has the proper CLR rights by demanding the minimal set of permissions necessary to accomplish the task (such as writing to a file). If the demand succeeds, then the wrapper code can assert the right to managed code.[25] No other assembly in the call chain then needs to have the managed-code right.

For example, if you ask the .NET file classes to delete a file, they first demand the delete permission on the file. If that permission is granted, then the code asserts the managed code permission and calls the Win32 API to perform the delete.

## Attribute-Based Permissions

The **SimplePermissionAttributeRequest** example shows how you can use attributes to make permission requests. This example uses an attribute to put in the metadata for the assembly that you need to have the **ControlPrincipal** permission to run. This enables you to query in advance which components conflict with security policy.

```
[assembly:SecurityPermission(
    SecurityAction.RequestMinimum,ControlPrincipal=true)]
public class pp
{
    public static int Main(string[] args)
...
```

The **SecurityAction** enumeration has several values, some that can be applied to a class or method and some that can be applied to an assembly as in this example. For assemblies these are **RequestMinimum**, **RequestOptional**, and **RequestRefuse**. **RequestMinimum** indicates to the metadata those permissions the assembly requires to run. **RequestOptional** indicates to the metadata permissions that the assembly would like to have,

---

[23] As with all the other "security permissions" this is technically a flag on the **SecurityPermission** class, but the common parlance is to call them permissions.

[24] The underlying operating system identity that is running the program must have the rights to perform the operating system function.

[25] By demanding first, then asserting, you ensure that a luring attack is not in progress.

but can run without. **RequestRefuse** indicates permissions that the assembly would like to be denied.[26]

If you change the attribute in this example to **RequestRefuse** and run it, you will find that the assembly will load, but you will get a **SecurityException** when you attempt to change the policy.

Other values apply to classes and methods. **LinkDemand** is acted upon when a link is made to some type. It requires your immediate caller to have a permission. The other values apply at runtime. **InheritanceDemand** requires a derived class to have a permission. **Assert**, **Deny**, **PermitOnly**, and **Demand** do what you would expect.

Here is an example of a **FileIOPermission** demand being applied to a class through an attribute. **AllAccess** is being demanded of the file. A full file path is required.

```
[FileIOPermission(SecurityAction.Demand,
                        All = "c:\\foo\\read.txt")]
public class Simple
...
```

## Principal Permission

Role-based security is controlled by the **PrincipalPermission** class. The **PrincipalPermission** example uses this class to make sure that the user identity under which the program is being run is an administrator. We do that by passing the identity name and a string representing the role to the constructor. Once again, we use the **Demand** method on the permission to check the validity of our permission request.

```
PrincipalPermission PrincipalPerm = new
                PrincipalPermission(wi.Name, adminRole);
try
{
  PrincipalPerm.Demand();
  Console.WriteLine("Code demand for an administrator
                                    succeeded.");
}
catch(SecurityException)
{
  Console.WriteLine("Demand for Administrator failed.");
}
```

If the running user were an administrator the demand would succeed;

---

[26] An assembly would do this to prevent code from another assembly executing on its behalf from having this permission.

otherwise it would fail with an exception being thrown. The code then checks to see if the user with the name JaneAdmin (not a system administrator, but part of the CustomerAdmin group) and the designated role is running.

```
string customerAdminRole = "MICAH\\CustomerAdmin";
PrincipalPermission pp;
pp = new PrincipalPermission("MICAH\\JaneAdmin",
                                    customerAdminRole);
try
{
  pp.Demand();
  Console.WriteLine("Demand for Customer Administrator
                                    succeeded.");
}
catch(SecurityException)
{
  Console.WriteLine("Demand for Customer Administrator
                                    failed.");
}
```

The **CodeAccessPermission** base class has methods for creating permissions that are the union or the intersection of several permissions. **PrincipalPermission** does not derive from **CodeAccessPermission** because it is based on the identity associated with the code, not on the rights of the code itself. Nonetheless, it shares the same idioms with the **CodeAccessPermission** derived classes.

Next the example code sees if either of these two administrators is the identity of the running code.

```
string id1 = "MICAH\\Administrator";
string id2 = "MICAH\\mds";

PrincipalPermission pp1 = new PrincipalPermission(id1,
                                    adminRole);
PrincipalPermission pp2 = new PrincipalPermission(id2,
                                    adminRole);

IPermission ipermission = pp2.Union(pp1);
try
{
  ipermission.Demand();
  Console.WriteLine("Demand for either administrator
                                    succeeded.");
}
catch(SecurityException)
{
  Console.WriteLine("Demand for either administrator
```

```
                                                     failed.");
  }
```

The code then sees whether any administrator is the identity of the
running code.[27]

```
PrincipalPermission pp3 = new PrincipalPermission(null,
                                                  adminRole);
try
{
  pp3.Demand();
  Console.WriteLine("Demand for any administrator
                                              succeeded.");
}
catch(SecurityException)
{
  Console.WriteLine("Demand for any administrator
                                                 failed.");
}
```

If the users are unauthenticated, even if they do belong to the appropriate roles, the **Demand** will fail.

## PermissionSet

You can deal with a set of permissions through the **PermissionSet** class.
The **AddPermission** and **RemovePermission** methods allow you to add
instances of a **CodeAccessPermission** derived class to the set. You can then
**Deny**, **PermitOnly**, or **Assert** sets of permissions instead of individual ones.
This makes it easier to restrict what third-party components and scripts might
be able to do. The **PermissionSet** example demonstrates how this is done.

We first define an interface **IUserCode** that our "trusted" code will use
to access some "third-party" code. While in reality this third-party code
would be in a separate assembly, to keep the example simple we put everything in the same assembly.

```
public interface IUserCode
{
     int PotentialRogueCode();
}

public class ThirdParty : IUserCode
{
   public int PotentialRogueCode()
   {
      try
```

---

[27] A null user and a role as arguments to mean anyone in that role is not an intuitive
use of null.

```
    {
        string filename = ".\\read.txt";

        FileInfo file = new FileInfo(filename);
        StreamReader sr = file.OpenText();
        string text;
        text = sr.ReadLine();

        while (text != null)
        {
            Console.WriteLine(text);
            text = sr.ReadLine();
        }

        sr.Close();
    }
    catch(Exception e)
    {
        Console.WriteLine(e.Message);
    }

    return 0;
    }
}
```

Our code will create a new instance of the "third party" which would cause the code to be loaded into our assembly. We then invoke the **OurCode** method passing it the "third-party" code.

```
...
public static int Main(string[] args)
{
    ThirdParty thirdParty = new ThirdParty();
    OurClass ourClass = new OurClass();

    ourClass.OurCode(thirdParty);

    return 0;
}
```

Now let us look at the **OurCode** method. It creates a permission set consisting of unrestricted user interface and file access permissions. It then denies the permissions in the permission set.

```
...
public void OurCode(IUserCode code)
{
UIPermission uiPerm = new
            UIPermission(PermissionState.Unrestricted);
FileIOPermission fileIOPerm = new
```

```
                    FileIOPermission(PermissionState.Unrestricted);

PermissionSet ps = new
                        PermissionSet(PermissionState.None);
ps.AddPermission(uiPerm);
ps.AddPermission(fileIOPerm);
ps.Deny();
...
```

The "third-party" code is then called. After it returns, the permission denial is revoked and the "third-party" code is called again.

```
int v = code.PotentialRogueCode();
CodeAccessPermission.RevertDeny();
...
v = code.PotentialRogueCode();
```

The first time, the code execution fails; the second time it succeeds. Each stack frame can only have one permission set for denial of permissions. If you call **Deny** on a permission set, it overrides any other calls to **Deny** on a permission set in that stack frame.

## Code Identity

The characteristics by which a particular assembly can be identified are its identity permissions. An example would be an assembly's strong name or the Web site that generated the code. Based on the evidence provided by the loader or trusted host, identity permissions are granted by the CLR.

### Identity Permission Classes

To identity running code, there are several identity permission classes.

- **PublisherIdentityPermission** models the software publisher's digital signature.
- **SiteIdentityPermission** models the Web site where code originated.
- **StrongNameIdentityPermission** models the strong name of an assembly.
- **ZoneIdentityPermission** models the zone where the code originated.
- **URLIdentityPermission** models the URL and the protocol where the code originated.

These permissions represent evidence that can be used to determine security policy. Identity permissions are not code access permissions.

## Evidence

Security policy is based on a set of rules that administrators can set. The .NET security system can use those rules to enforce the policy. The evidence, represented by the identity permissions, is used to determine which policy to apply.

The **AppDomain** class has a function **ExecuteAssembly** which causes an assembly to run. One argument to the method is an **Evidence** instance argument. This **Evidence** class is a collection of objects that represent the identity of the assembly. This class is a collection of objects that represent evidence.

The **Evidence** example illustrates this. This example gets the collection of evidence associated with a strongly named assembly and prints out the associated values.

```
Evidence ev = AppDomain.CurrentDomain.Evidence;
IEnumerator iEnum = ev.GetEnumerator();
bool bNext;

Console.WriteLine("Evidence Enumerator has {0} members",
                                           ev.Count);
bNext = iEnum.MoveNext();
while (bNext == true)
{
  object x = iEnum.Current;
  Type t = x.GetType();
  Console.WriteLine(t.ToString());
  if (t == typeof(System.Security.Policy.Zone))
  {
    Zone zone = x as Zone;
    Console.WriteLine("    " +
                       zone.SecurityZone.ToString());
  }
  else if (t == typeof(System.Security.Policy.Url))
  {
    Url url = x as Url;
    Console.WriteLine("    " + url.Value.ToString());
  }
  else if (t == typeof(System.Security.Policy.Hash))
  {
    Hash hash = x as Hash;
    byte[] md5Hash = hash.MD5;
    byte[] sha1Hash = hash.SHA1;
    Console.WriteLine("    MD5 Hash of Assembly:");
      Console.Write("        ");
    for(int i = 0; i < md5Hash.Length; i++)
      Console.Write(md5Hash[i]);
```

```
        Console.WriteLine();
        Console.WriteLine("    SHA1 Hash of Assembly:");
        Console.Write("        ");
        for(int i = 0; i < sha1Hash.Length; i++)
         Console.Write(sha1Hash[i]);
        Console.WriteLine();
    }
  else if (t == typeof(System.Security.Policy.StrongName))
  {
        StrongName sn = x as StrongName;
        Console.WriteLine("    StrongName of Assembly is: {0}
                    version: {1}", sn.Name, sn.Version);
        Console.WriteLine("    Assembly public key:");
        Console.Write("        ");
        Console.WriteLine(sn.PublicKey.ToString());
    }
   bNext = iEnum.MoveNext();
}
```

The example's output would look something like this:

```
Evidence Enumerator has 3 members
System.Security.Policy.Zone
   MyComputer
System.Security.Policy.Url
  file:///F:/Book/Chap12/Evidence/bin/Debug/Evidence.exe
System.Security.Policy.StrongName
    StrongName of Assembly is: Evidence version: 1.0.0.0
    Assembly public key:
        0024000004800000940...
        ...D4E1C67A3509E6C9B385EA897BA
System.Security.Policy.Hash
    MD5 Hash of Assembly:
      14332230461041081341241322151846823019516744
    SHA1 Hash of Assembly:
     8213317118447491199915711114314318223823223114 31771
     39171
```

The evidence associated with the **Zone** for this assembly is MyComputer. The **Url** evidence is the location on disk of the assembly. The **Hash** evidence can give us the MD5 and SHA1 hashes of the assembly. The **StrongName** evidence tells us information about the unique assembly name.

Some of this evidence is convertible to the associated identity permissions. For example, the Zone class has a **CreateIdentityPermission** method which returns an **IPermission** interface that represents the **ZoneIdentityPermission** instance associated with this piece of evidence. The **Url** and **StrongName** classes have similar methods.

Another way of looking at the identity permissions is that they answer a series of questions:

- Who published (signed) it?
- What is the name of the assembly?
- What Web site or URL did it come from?
- What zone did the code originate from?

The creator of the application domain (host) can also provide evidence by passing in an **Evidence** collection when the **ExecuteAssembly** method is called. Of course, that code must have the **ControlEvidence** permission. The CLR is also trusted to add evidence, since after all, it enforces the security policy. Evidence is extensible; you can define evidence types and use it in security policy.

# Security Policy

Now that we understand evidence, and how the evidence about an assembly is gathered, we can discuss security policy. Based on the evidence for an assembly, the assembly is assigned to a code group. Associated with each code group is a set of permissions that represent what code associated with that code group can do.

## Security Policy Levels

Security policy is set at several levels. The permissions allowed are defined by the intersection of the policy levels. These levels are enterprise, machine, application domain, and user. If there is a conflict between permissions assigned from a particular level, the more restrictive version overrides. So enterprise policy can override all the machines in the enterprise, and machine policy can override all policies for a application domain or a particular user.

## Code Groups

The enterprise, machine, and user policy levels are a hierarchy of code groups. Associated with each code group is a set of permissions. Code that meets a specified set of conditions belongs to a particular code group.

The root node is referred to as "All_Code." Below this level is a set of child nodes, and each of these children can have children. Each node represents a code group. If code belongs to a code group, it might be a member of one of its children. If it does not belong to a given code group it cannot belong to any of its children.

By evaluating the evidence you assign code a group. By assignment to a group you get an associated set of permissions. This set of conditions corresponds to a named permission set. Since code can belong to more than one group, the set of permissions which can be granted to code is the union of all the permission sets from the all groups it belongs to.

Therefore code policy is determined in two steps. For each level, the permissions for an assembly are determined by the union of all the permission sets to which it belongs. Each level then effectively has one permission set. Then each of these permission sets is intersected so that the most restrictive of each permission setting is the final value. For example, if the machine level gives all access to an assembly, but the user level restricts the file IO permissions to just read, the assembly will have unlimited permissions for everything but file IO, where it will just have the read permission.

Code groups can have two attributes. The **exclusive** attribute dictates that code will never be allowed more permissions than associated with the exclusive group. Obviously, code can belong to only one group marked exclusive. The **level final** attribute indicates that no policy levels below this one are considered when calculating code group membership. The order of levels is enterprise, machine, user, application domain.

## Named Permission Sets

A named permission set consists of one or more code access permissions that have a name. An administrator can associate a code group with this permission set by means of this name. More than one code group can be associated with a named permission set. Administrators can define their own named permission sets, but several are built in:

- **Nothing**: no permissions (cannot run).
- **Execution**: only permission to run, but no permissions that allow use of protected resources.
- **Internet**: the default policy permission set suitable for content from unknown origin.
- **LocalIntranet**: the default policy permission set for within an enterprise.
- **Everything**: all standard (i.e., built-in) permissions except permission to skip verification.
- **FullTrust:** full access to all resources protected by permissions.

Of the built-in named permission sets only the **Everything** set can be modified. You can define custom permission sets.

## Altering Security Policy

Security policy is stored in several XML-based configuration files. Machine security configuration is in the **security.config** file that is stored in the **\WINNT\Microsoft.NET\Framework\vx.x.xxxx\CONFIG** directory. User security configuration is in the **security.config** file that is stored in the **\Documents and Settings\UserName\Application Data\Microsoft\CLR Security Config\vx.x.xxxx** directory.

It is not recommended that you edit these XML files directly. The Code Access Security Policy tool (**caspol.exe**) is a command-line tool that can be used to modify enterprise, machine, and user policy levels.

The .NET Admin Tool introduced in Chapter 7 provides a more friendly interface to changing policy. Figure 12–17 shows the code groups and permission sets defined for the machine and the current user security policy levels as they appear in the left pane in the .NET Admin Tool.

Let us use this tool to examine the current policies in the machine level. First let us look at the named permission sets. As you can see from

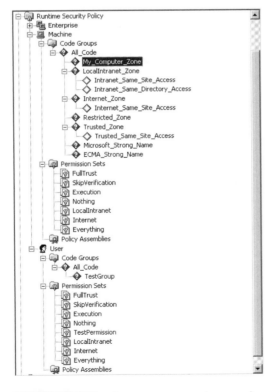

**Figure 12–17**   *Permission sets and groups for machine and user policy.*

Figure 12–18, on the machine level no new named permission sets have been created; only the default ones are present. If you select the Internet permission set and in the right pane select view permissions, you can then select any permission and look at its settings. Figure 12–18 shows the settings for User Interface permission in the Internet named permission set.

Figure 12–19 shows the properties for the Internet Zone code group on the machine policy level. You can see that **Zone** identity permission is cho-

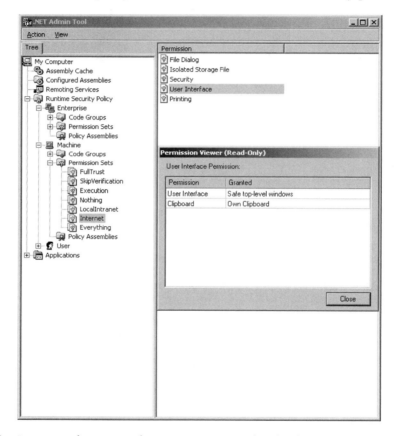

 **Figure 12–18**  *Permissions for User Interface permission in machine-level Internet named permission set.*

sen for this group, and the value associated with it is the **Internet** zone. On the permission set tab, you can view or select the named permission set associated with the **Internet** zone.

To illustrate how security policy affects running code we use a slightly modified version of the **Evidence** example. Besides writing out the associat-

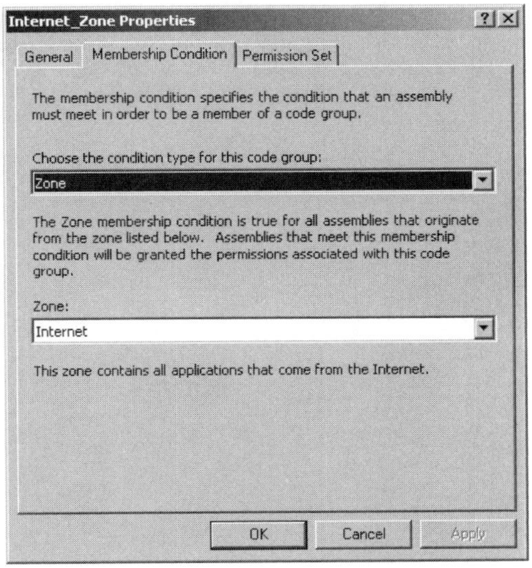

**Figure 12–19**    *Properties dialog for Internet zone, machine policy level.*

ed evidence, the **Policy** example also prints out the contents of a file.

```
string filename = ".\\read.txt";
try
{
  string fileWithFullPath = Path.GetFullPath(filename);
  FileInfo file = new FileInfo(filename);
  StreamReader sr = file.OpenText();
  string text;
  text = sr.ReadLine();

  while (text != null)
  {
    Console.WriteLine(text);
    text = sr.ReadLine();
  }
  sr.Close();
}
catch(Exception e)
{
```

```
    Console.WriteLine(e.Message);
}
```

Figure 12–20 shows the two new code groups and the one permission set we will define at the user policy level to control security policy for this assembly.

We will define a new permission set called **TestStrongName** and two new code groups, TestStrongNameGroup and My_Computer_Zone. The new

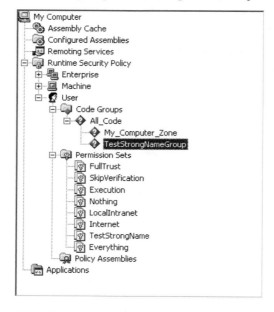

**Figure 12–20**    *Revised user policy level for Policy example.*

permission set definition is in Figure 12–21.

This new permission set is created by selecting the Permission Sets node below the level in which you want to create it (in this case User).

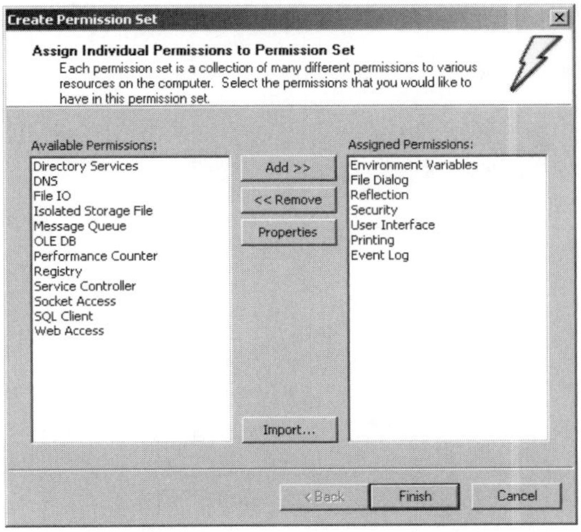

**Figure 12–21**    *TestStrongName permission set definition.*

Right-mouse-click and select New. The initial Create Permission Set dialog comes up and can be filled in as in Figure 12–22.

Clicking the Next button brings up the dialog in Figure 12–23. Use the Add and Remove buttons to define the permissions you want to include in

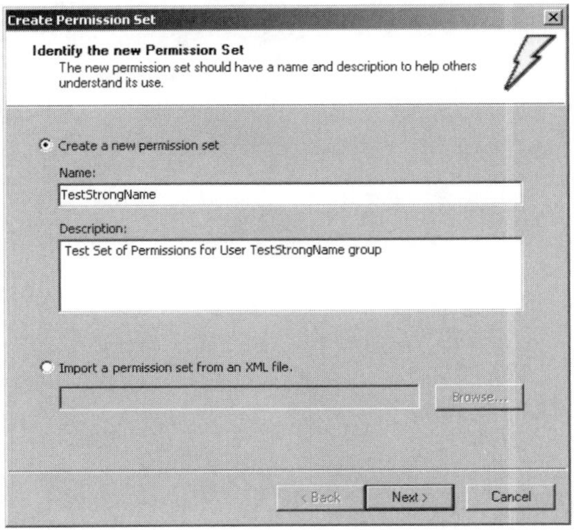

**Figure 12–22**    *Initial Create Permission Set dialog.*

this permission set.

To define the permission itself, select the permission, click the properties dialog, and make the appropriate choices. Figure 12–24 shows the dialog

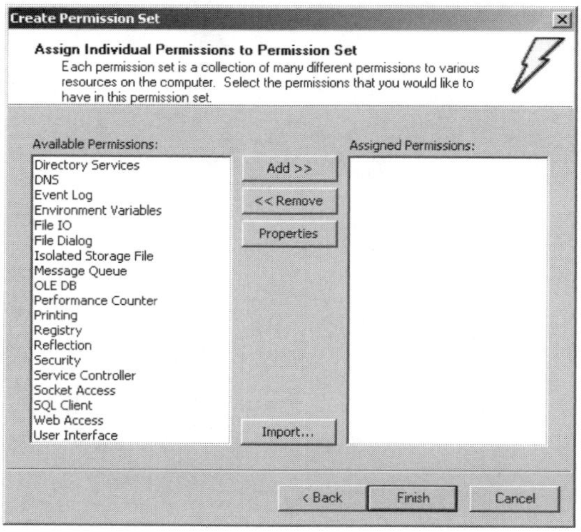

**Figure 12–23**    *PermissionSet definition dialog.*

that appears for the User Interface permission. To modify an existing permission set, select it, right-mouse-click, and select the Change Permissions item. A dialog similar to Figure 12–24 will appear.

Now this permission has to be associated with a code group. How do assemblies get assigned to code groups? We have already explained that each

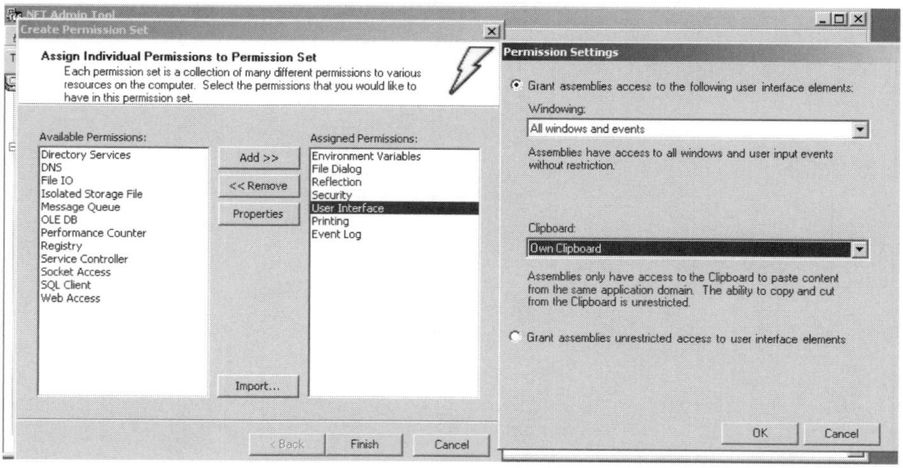

**Figure 12–24**    *Permission modification dialog.*

code group maps to one piece of evidence. Figure 12–25 is a diagram of the User Code Level with its three groups.

Figure 12–26 shows that the TestStrongNameGroup is defined to be the strong name associated with the policy.exe assembly. Figure 12–27

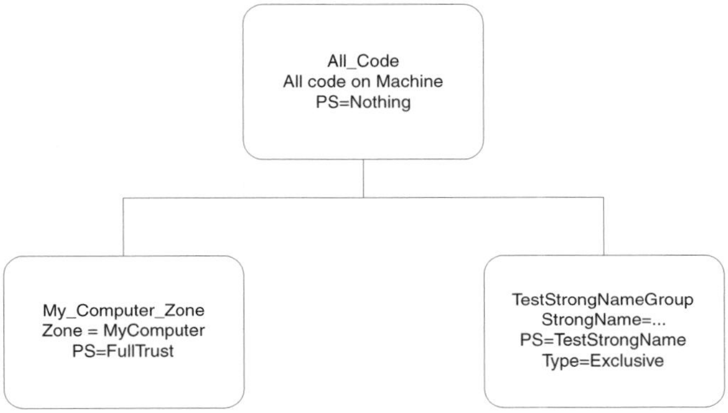

**Figure 12–25**    *Diagram of user-level policy groups.*

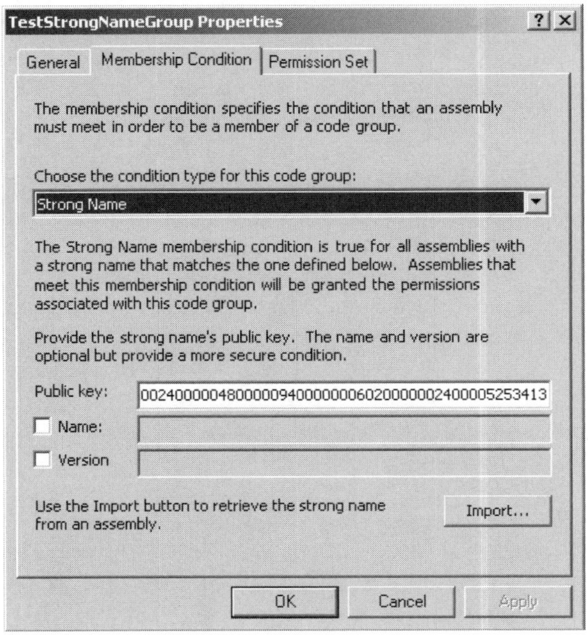

**Figure 12–26**    *Membership condition for TestStrongNameGroup.*

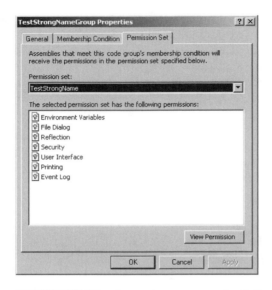

Figure 12–27 *Permissions associated with TestStrongNameGroup from TestStrongName permission set.*

shows the TestStrongName permission set associated with the TestStrongNameGroup. Note that there is no FileIOPermission. This code group was created by selecting the parent group (in this case All_Code) and selecting New from its context menu and filling in the information asked for by the wizard. Dialogs similar to Figures 12–26 and 12–27 will appear.

The My_Computer_Zone group is defined to encompass all code on this computer. It is defined in a similar fashion as the TestStrongNameGroup. The membership condition is Zone, and the MyComputer zone is picked as the associated value. **FullTrust** is selected for its associated permission set. The All_Code group encompasses all code on the machine. It grants no rights to any code. It already existed by default, and we changed its permission set to **Nothing**. It grants no rights.

To find out how an assembly matches the code groups, its evidence its compared with the membership conditions for the group. All code that resides on the current machine (as opposed to another machine on the network or the Internet) matches the All_Code and My_Computer_Zone group. Only policy.exe matches the membership condition for the TestStrongNameGroup. The tree is walked from parent to child node; if a parent node does not match, no further navigation down the tree is done. On a given level the rights assigned to the assembly are the union of all the groups that it matches. In this case, even though **policy.exe** matches a group that does not give it the FileIOPermission, it gets that permission from the My_Computer_Zone group which grants **FullTrust** to code.

A similar analysis of the enterprise and machine levels reveals that they also grant code from this machine FullTrust. So if you run **policy.exe**, it will run.

Now modify the TestStrongNameGroup on its General tab to be exclusive, as indicated in Figure 12–28. This will cause any code that belongs to this group to get its rights from only this group. Since policy is determined by the intersection of all the three levels, **policy.exe** will not have the FileIOPermission. If you try to run it, you will see that it cannot read the file.

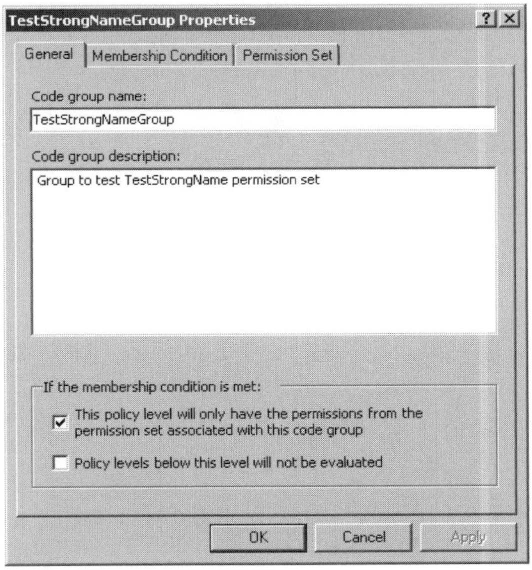

**Figure 12–28**        *Making TestStrongNameGroup.*

## Summary

In this chapter we have attempted to explain the basics of .NET security. .NET security comes in two flavors: user identity security and code access security. The former determines which identity is executing code. The latter determines what rights the executing code has. Between the two you have the basic tools to provide robust applications.

What is missing from .NET security right now is distributed identity and distributed code access security. Remote code cannot use policy information to make decisions, and identity is not automatically transferred through remote calls.

# Tracing and Debugging in .NET

$C$omplicated applications cannot be put under the debugger to find out what went wrong. Duplicating, or even understanding, what conditions are needed to replicate the problem is often difficult. The **System.Diagnostics** namespace has several classes that help you instrument your application.[1]

Instrumenting your application for debugging and tracing will enable you to make your applications more robust. It also illustrates the common pattern of how the framework divides classes into separate tasks (writing the output, controlling the output, and the output destination) so that you can customize parts and still rely on the Framework classes for the rest. The mechanics of instrumenting your application has three aspects.

The **Trace** and **Debug** classes are used to generate the debug or trace output. These classes have identical methods and properties that allow you to write diagnostic output. They do not, however, specify the destination of the output.

The **Listeners** classes are used to direct the output to various destinations, although a default destination does exist.

Finally, there are mechanisms for turning on or off the instrumentation. You can set the DEBUG and TRACE compilation flags to have different tracing for debug or release builds. You can have the output of the **Trace** and **Debug** classes depend on the conditional evaluation of expressions. Or you can control the verbosity of the output, depending on your need for information, using the **BooleanSwitch** and **TraceSwitch** classes.

---

[1] The security of your Web Site or Web Service is enhanced by using tracing and debugging output. You do not want to give out information in an error message that could be used to compromise your system. Capturing that information in a trace or debug log allows the program to generate a generic error message for the user. You could also assign an identifier to the user message that is also recorded with the log message. If necessary that id could be used to help the user diagnose any problems with their system.

## The TraceDemo Example

The **TraceDemo** example illustrates the use of the diagnostic functionality. If you run the example, you will get the following output:

```
Trace Listeners:
        Default

This was compiled with a DEBUG directive!
This was compiled with a TRACE directive!
                Debug Boolean Switch disabled at startup.
                Debug Boolean Switch enabled!
Trace Switch Startup Value = Warning
            TraceError!
            TraceWarning!

Trace Listeners:
        Console.Out Listener
        Output File Listener
```

Refer to this output in the ensuing discussion. You will also find a file called **output.txt** on your computer in the directory where this program ran.

## Enabling Debug and Trace Output

To use the **Debug** class, the DEBUG flag must be defined or else the methods of this class will not be compiled into the executable or library. Similarly, to use the **Trace** class the TRACE flag must be defined. This way you can have different diagnostics for release and debug builds. These constants can be set in the Visual Studio.NET Project | Properties | Configuration Properties | Build Window's conditional compilation constants shown in Figure 13–1.

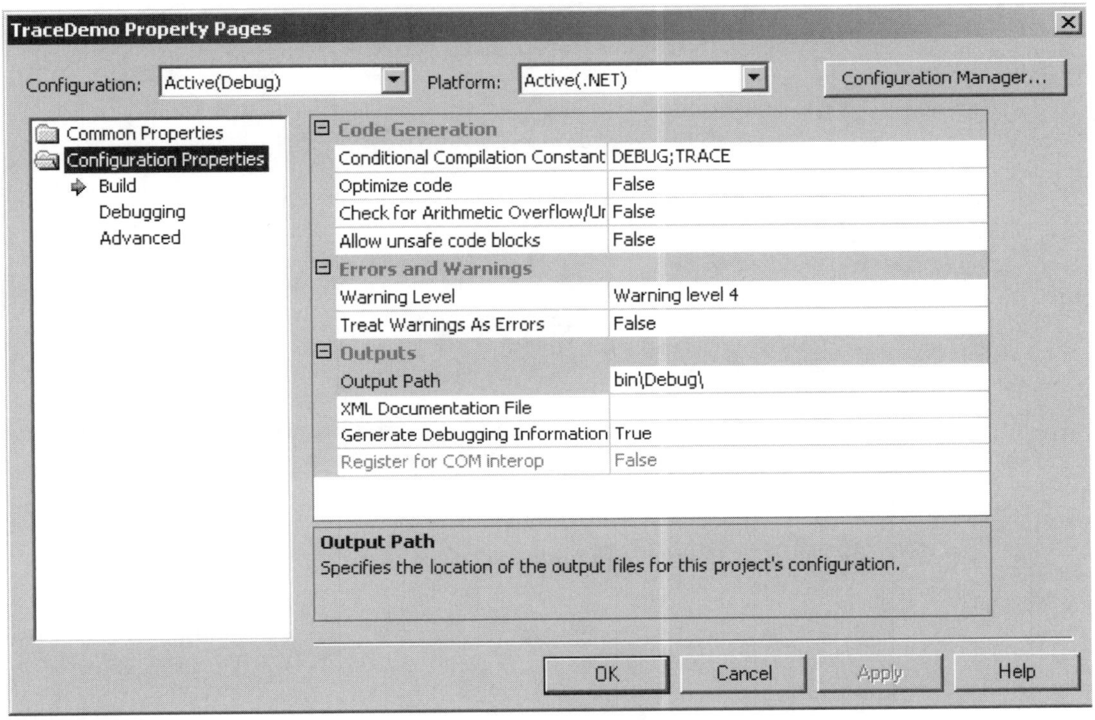

**TraceDemo Property Pages**                                                    ✕

Configuration: [Active(Debug) ▼]   Platform: [Active(.NET) ▼]    [ Configuration Manager... ]

📁 Common Properties        ⊟ **Code Generation**
📁 Configuration Properties    Conditional Compilation Constant │ DEBUG;TRACE
 ➡ Build                       Optimize code                    │ False
   Debugging                   Check for Arithmetic Overflow/U  │ False
   Advanced                    Allow unsafe code blocks         │ False
                            ⊟ **Errors and Warnings**
                               Warning Level                    │ Warning level 4
                               Treat Warnings As Errors         │ False
                            ⊟ **Outputs**
                               Output Path                      │ bin\Debug\
                               XML Documentation File           │
                               Generate Debugging Information    │ True
                               Register for COM interop          │ False

                            **Output Path**
                            Specifies the location of the output files for this project's configuration.

                                        [ OK ]  [ Cancel ]  [ Apply ]  [ Help ]

**Figure 13–1**    *Visual Studio window for setting conditional compilation constants.*

You can also define the constants in your source files or supply the definition to the compiler's command line.

## Using the Debug and Trace Classes

The useful methods and properties are static. The overloaded **WriteLine** and **Write** are used to write debug or trace output. The overloaded **WriteLineIf** and **WriteIf** write output if the condition in their first argument is true.

```
Debug.WriteLine("This was compiled with a DEBUG
                                          directive!");
Trace.WriteLine("This was compiled with a TRACE
                                          directive!");
...
Debug.WriteLineIf(DebugBooleanSwitch.Enabled, "Debug
                 Boolean Switch enabled at startup.");
Debug.WriteLineIf(!DebugBooleanSwitch.Enabled,
             "Debug Boolean Switch disabled at startup.");
```

Output is indented with the **Indent** and **Unindent** methods. The indentation size is controlled with the **IndentSize** property.

```
Trace.Indent();
...
Trace.IndentSize = 10;
```

You can also set the indentation size in the application configuration file.

```
<?xml version="1.0"?>
<configuration>
    <system.diagnostics>
        <trace indentsize="15" />
    </system.diagnostics>
</configuration>
```

The **Assert** method can check an assertion. The **AutoFlush** property and the **Flush** method control the flushing of the output buffer.

## Using Switches to Enable Diagnostics

Switches give you finer grain control over the diagnostic output. You can use the **BooleanSwitch** class to turn output on or off based on the value of its **Enabled** property.

The **TraceSwitch** class gives you five hierarchical levels of control for its **Level** property: **TraceError**, **TraceWarning**, **TraceInfo**, **TraceVerbose**, and **Off**. These values are part of the **TraceLevelEnumeration**. Setting a lower Trace level means that the higher ones are set as well. For example, if the **TraceWarning** level is set, both the **TraceError** and **TraceWarning** levels are enabled.

```
DebugBooleanSwitch.Enabled = true;
Debug.WriteLineIf(DebugBooleanSwitch.Enabled, "Debug
                                Boolean Switch enabled!");
...
Trace.WriteLineIf(TraceLevelSwitch.TraceError,
                                        "TraceError!");
```

The constructors for these switches take two parameters. The first is the name of the switch, the second is a text description of the switch. Both **BooleanSwitch** and **TraceSwitch** classes inherit from the abstract class **Switch**. You can write your own customized switch classes by inheriting from the **Switch** class. Note that the **Enabled** property of the **BooleanSwitch** and the **Level** and named level properties of the **TraceSwitch** are not part of the **Switch** class.

# Enabling or Disabling Switches

You can use settings in your application configuration file to enable or disable a switch at startup. This can also be done programmatically.

## Configuration File Switch Settings

You can set the switch's initial setting in the application's configuration file.

```
<configuration>
  <system.diagnostics>
    <switches>
      <add name="DebugSwitch" value = "0" />
      <add name="TraceSwitch" value = "2" />
    </switches>
  </system.diagnostics>
</ configuation>
```

If no values are found, the initial value of the **Enabled** property of the **BooleanSwitch** with the name **DebugSwitch** is set to false and the **TraceSwitch's Level** property is set to **TraceOff**.

## Programmatic Switch Settings

The **Enabled** property of the **BooleanSwitch** can be set to true or false. The **Level** property of the **TraceSwitch** can be set to one of the options of the **TraceLevel** enumeration: **TraceOff**, **TraceError**, **TraceWarning**, **TraceInfo**, **TraceVerbose**. You can get the level of the **TraceSwitch's** setting by examining the **TraceError**, **TraceWarning**, **TraceInfo**, **TraceVerbose** properties.

## Using Switches to Control Output

You can test the value of the switch before you write, debug, or trace output. You can do this with an if statement, or as an argument to one of the **Trace** or **Debug** classes' methods.

```
Trace.WriteLineIf(TraceLevelSwitch.TraceError,
                                    "TraceError!");
Trace.WriteLineIf(TraceLevelSwitch.TraceWarning,
                                    "TraceWarning!");
Trace.WriteLineIf(TraceLevelSwitch.TraceInfo,
                                    "InfoMessage!");
Trace.WriteLineIf(TraceLevelSwitch.TraceVerbose,
                                    "VerboseMessage!");
```

Since you can set these values outside of your program's code, you can select the circumstances under which you get a particular level of debug or trace output. For example, you can turn on **TraceVerbose** output if you really need a high level of diagnostics, but turn it off after you have found the problem.

## TraceListener

Classes derived from the abstract class **TraceListener** represent destinations for the diagnostic output. The **TextWriterTraceListener** is designed to direct output to a **TextWriter**, **Stream**, or **FileStream**. **Console.Out** is an example of a commonly used output stream. The **EventLogTraceListener** class allows you to send output to an EventLog. You can create your own event logs with the **EventLog**'s static method **CreateEventSource** method. The **DefaultTraceListener** sends output to the debugging output window. Default Debug output can be viewed in Visual Studio.NET's Output window or with utilities (such as DBMon, which is included with this project). You can customize where output appears by implementing your own class derived from **TraceListener**.

## Listeners Collection

Both the **Debug** and **Trace** classes have a static **Listeners** collection. This collection of **TraceListeners** represents a list of **TraceListener** objects that want to receive the output from the **Debug** or **Trace** class. Listeners are added to or removed from the collection just as with any other .NET collection.

```
TextWriterTraceListener ConsoleOutput = new
                    TextWriterTraceListener(Console.Out,
                    "Console.Out Listener");
Trace.Listeners.Add(ConsoleOutput);

Stream OutputFile = File.Create("output.txt");
TextWriterTraceListener OutputFileListener = new
                    TextWriterTraceListener(OutputFile,
                              "Output File Listener");
Trace.Listeners.Add(OutputFileListener);

Trace.Listeners.Remove("Default");
```

In this code extract, the **OutputFileListener** in the example will send the Trace output to a file called **output.txt**. The **DefaultTraceListener** is added automatically to the **Listener** collections. Any of the listeners, including the default listener, can be removed from the collection by invoking the collection's **Remove** method. To list all listeners in the collection:

```
foreach(TraceListener tr in Trace.Listeners)
{
```

```
    Console.WriteLine("\t" + tr.Name);
}
```

## Summary

Instrumenting your application for degrees of debugging and diagnostic output is a common program task. The diagnostic classes exemplify the way .NET provides classes to handle standard programming tasks so you can concentrate on developing the business logic of your programming, not on building infrastructure. On the other hand, they also exemplify how the .NET classes are partitioned so that you can customize the infrastructure using as much or as little of the other classes as you require.

# Interoperability

*M*icrosoft .NET is a powerful platform, and there are many advantages in writing a new application within the .NET Framework. However, a typical application is not a world unto itself, but is built from legacy components as well as new components, and interoperability is very important. We discussed one kind of interoperability in Chapter 11 in connection with Web Services. Using the SOAP protocol it is possible for .NET applications to call Web Services on other platforms, including Unix, mainframes, and mobile devices.

In this chapter we will look at another kind of interoperability, the interfacing of managed and unmanaged code running under Windows. The dominant programming model in modern Windows systems is the Component Object Model, or COM. There exist a great many legacy COM components, and so it is desirable for a .NET program, running as managed code, to be able to call unmanaged COM components. The converse situation, in which a COM client needs to call a .NET server, can also arise.[1] Apart from COM, we may also have need for a .NET program to call any unmanaged code that is exposed as a DLL, including the Win32 API. The .NET Framework supports all these interoperability scenarios through COM Interoperability and the Platform Invocation Services or PInvoke.

In this chapter we assume that you understand the concepts behind the legacy technologies.

---

[1] COM interop is the only mechanism provided for unmanaged code to call managed code.

# Calling COM Components from Managed Code

The first interoperability scenario we will look at is managed code calling COM components. The .NET Framework makes it easy to create a Runtime Callable Wrapper (RCW), which acts as a bridge between managed and unmanaged code. The RCW is illustrated in Figure 14–1.

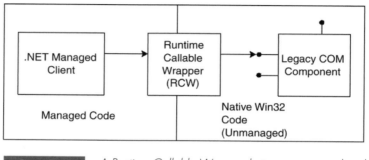

| Figure 14–1 | *A Runtime Callable Wrapper between managed and unmanaged code.* |

You could implement an RCW assembly yourself, using the PInvoke facility (described in a later section) to call into the necessary APIs, such as **CoCreateInstance** and the **IUnknown** methods directly. But that is not necessary, because the **Tlbimp.exe** tool can read type library information, and automatically generate the appropriate RCW for you. Visual Studio.NET makes it even easier when you add a reference to a COM object in Solution Explorer. We will examine both of these facilities, as we look at some examples of COM components and .NET clients.

## The Tlbimp.exe Utility

The **Tlbimp.exe** utility (Type Library to .NET Assembly Converter) program is provided in the **\Program Files\Microsoft.NET\FrameworkSDK\Bin** directory. It is used to generate managed classes that wrap unmanaged COM classes. The resulting RCW is a .NET component (i.e., a managed DLL assembly) that managed client code can use to access the COM interface methods that are implemented in the COM component. The **Tlbimp** tool is a command line program that reads COM type library information, and generates a managed wrapper class along with the associated metadata, and places the result into the RCW assembly. You can view the resulting contents in this assembly using the **Ildasm** tool. The command line syntax for **Tlbimp** is shown below.

```
Tlbimp TypeLibName [options]
Where options may contain the following:
      /out:FileName              Assembly file name
      /namespace:Namespace       Assembly Namespace
      /asmversion:Version        Assembly version number
      /reference:FileName        Reference assembly
      /publickey:FileName        Public key file
      /keyfile:FileName          Key pair file
      /keycontainer:FileName     Key pair key container
      /delaysign                 Delay digital signing
      /unsafe                    Suppress security checks
      /nologo                    Suppress displaying logo
      /silent                    Suppress output except errors
      /verbose                   Display extra information
      /primary                   Make primary interop assembly
      /sysarray                  SAFEARRAY as System.Array
      /strictref                 Only /reference assemblies
      /? or /help                Display help information
```

When the **Tlbimp** tool imports a COM type library, it creates a .NET namespace with the same name as the library defined in the type library (that is the name of the actual library, not the name of the type library file that contains it). **Tlbimp** converts each COM coclass defined in the type library into a managed .NET wrapper class in the resulting .NET assembly that has one constructor with no parameters. Each COM interface defined in the type library is converted into a .NET interface in the resulting .NET assembly.

Consider the typical COM IDL file library statement shown below that would be used to create a type library using **Midl.exe**. The resulting type library (TLB) or DLL file would cause **Tlbimp.exe** to generate an assembly containing metadata, including the namespace **BANKDUALLib**, a managed wrapper class named **Account2**, and a managed interface named **IAccount2**.

```
library BANKDUALLib
{
    importlib("stdole32.tlb");
    importlib("stdole2.tlb");
    [
        uuid(04519632-39C5-4A7E-AA3C-3A7D814AC91C),
        helpstring("Account2 Class")
    ]
    coclass Account2
    {
        [default] interface IAccount2;
    };
};
```

Once you have used **Tlbimp.exe** to generate the wrapper assembly, you can view its contents using the **Ildasm** tool, as shown in Figure 14–2. Note that the namespace shown by **Ildasm.exe** is **BANKDUALLib**, the name of the interface is **IAccount2**, and the wrapper class is named **Account2.**

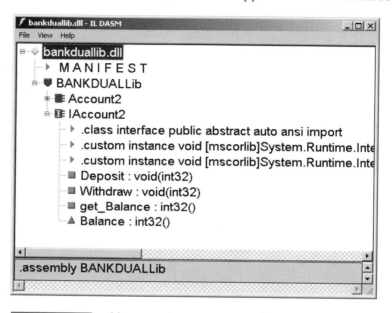

**Figure 14–2**    *Ildasm.exe showing contents of a COM wrapper assembly.*

## Demonstration: Wrapping a Legacy COM Server

The best way to get a feel for how this wrapping process works is to perform the operations yourself. The .NET client program is in the directory **NetClient**. The directory **LegacyComServer** contains the following files:

```
BankDual.dll          COM server DLL
BankDual.tlb          Type library
reg_bankdual.bat      Batch file to register the server
unreg_bankdual.bat    Batch file to unregister the server
BankConsole.exe       Client executable file
```

The source code for the client and server are in the directories **ClientSource** and **ServerSource** respectively. Both programs are written in Visual C++, and project files are provided for Visual C++ 6.0. Unless you have Visual C++ 6.0 installed on your system in addition to Visual Studio.NET, you will not be able to build these projects, but that will not prevent you from running the program and creating an .NET client.

This COM server implements a simple bank account class that has **Deposit** and **Withdraw** methods and a **Balance** property. The simple code[2] is shown in **Account2.cpp** in the **ServerSource** directory.

```
STDMETHODIMP CAccount2::get_Balance(long *pVal)
{
        *pVal = m_nBalance;
        return S_OK;
}
STDMETHODIMP CAccount2::Deposit(long amount)
{
        m_nBalance += amount;
        return S_OK;
}
STDMETHODIMP CAccount2::Withdraw(long amount)
{
        m_nBalance -= amount;
        return S_OK;
}
```

### REGISTER THE COM SERVER

The first step is to register the COM server. You can do that by running the batch file **reg_bankdual.bat**, which executes the command,

```
regsvr32 bankdual.dll
```

You can now see the registration entries using the Registry Editor (**regedit.exe**) or the OLE/COM Object Viewer (**oleview.exe**). The latter program is provided on the Tools menu of Visual Studio.NET. It groups related registry entries together, providing a convenient display. You can also perform other operations, such as instantiating objects. Figure 14–3 shows the entries for the **Account2** class that is implemented by this server. We have clicked the little "+" in the left-hand pane, which instantiates an object and queries for the standard interfaces. You can release the object by right-clicking over the class and choosing Release Instance from the context menu.

---

[2] We will not discuss the somewhat intricate infrastructure code provided by this ATL-based COM server. Such "plumbing" is much easier with .NET. Our focus is on calling COM components, not implementing them.

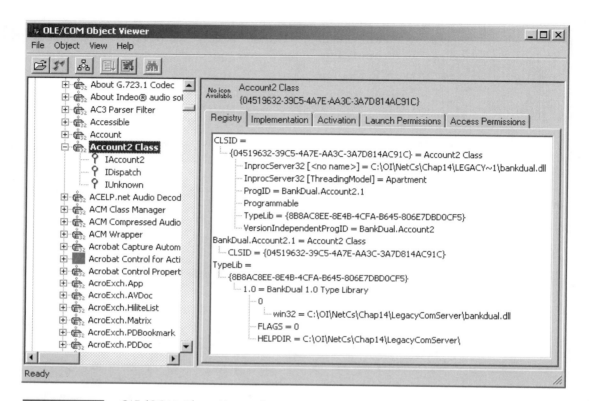

**Figure 14–3**
OLE/COM Object Viewer showing registry entries.

### RUN THE COM CLIENT

You can now run the COM client by double-clicking on **BankConsole.exe** in Windows Explorer. The starting balance is shown, followed by a withdrawal of 25, and the balance is shown again. Here is the source code, in the file **BankConsole.cpp** in **ClientSource**:

```
// BankConsole.cpp

#include <stdio.h>
#include <stdlib.h>
#include <objbase.h>
#include "bankdual.h"
#include "bankdual_i.c"

IAccount2* g_pAccount;

void ShowBalance()
{
```

```
        long balance;
        HRESULT hr = g_pAccount->get_Balance(&balance);
        printf("balance = %d\n", balance);
}

int main(int argc, char* argv[])
{
        // Initialize COM
        HRESULT hr = CoInitializeEx(NULL,
            COINIT_APARTMENTTHREADED);
        // Instantiate Account object, obtaining interface
        // pointer
        hr = CoCreateInstance(CLSID_Account2, NULL,
        CLSCTX_SERVER, IID_IAccount2, (void **) &g_pAccount);
        // First obtain and display initial balance
        ShowBalance();
        // Deposit 25 and show balance
        hr = g_pAccount->Deposit(25);
        ShowBalance();
        // Clean up
        g_pAccount->Release();
        CoUninitialize();
        printf("Press enter to quit: ");
        char buf[10];
        gets(buf);
        return 0;
}
```

For simplicity, no error checking is done. Robust code should check the HRESULT that is returned from each of the COM calls. Here is the output from running the client program:

```
balance = 150
balance = 125
Press Enter to quit:
```

### IMPORT THE TYPE LIBRARY (TLBIMP.EXE)

In order to call the COM component from managed code, we must create an RCW. We can do that by running the **TlbImp.exe** utility that we have discussed. We will run this utility from the command line, in the directory **NetClient**, where we want the RCW assembly to wind up. We provide a relative path to the type library file[3] **BankDual.tlb** in the directory **LegacyComServer**. What we have to type is shown in bold.

---

[3] The file **BankDual.dll** also contains the type library and could have been used in place of **BankDual.tlb**.

```
tlbimp ..\legacycomserver\bankdual.tlb
TlbImp - Type Library to .NET Assembly Converter Version
1.0.2914.16
Copyright (C) Microsoft Corp. 2001.  All rights reserved.

Type library imported to BANKDUALLib.dll
```

The RCW assembly that is created is **BANKDUALLib.dll**, taking its name from the name of the type library, as discussed earlier.

### IMPLEMENT THE .NET CLIENT PROGRAM

It is now easy to implement the .NET client program. The code is in the file **NetClient.cs** in the directory **NetClient**.

```
// NetClient.cs

using System;
using BANKDUALLib;

class NetClient
{
   public static void Main()
   {
      Account2 acc;
      acc = new Account2();
      Console.WriteLine("balance = {0}", acc.Balance);
      acc.Withdraw(25);
      Console.WriteLine("balance = {0}", acc.Balance);
   }
}
```

As with the COM client program, for simplicity we do no error checking. In the .NET version we should use exception handling to check for errors. The RCW uses the namespace **BANKDUALLib**, based on the name of the type library.

You must add a reference to **BANKDUALLib.dll**. In the Visual Studio Solution Explorer you can right-click over References, choose "Add Reference," and use the ordinary .NET tab of the Add Reference dialog.

Build and run the project inside of Visual Studio. You should see the following output:

```
balance = 150
balance = 125
Press any key to continue
```

Once you have added a reference to a RCW, you have all the features of the IDE available for .NET assemblies, including Intellisense and the

Object Browser. You can bring up the Object Browser from View | Other Windows | Object Browser. Figure 14–4 illustrates the information shown.

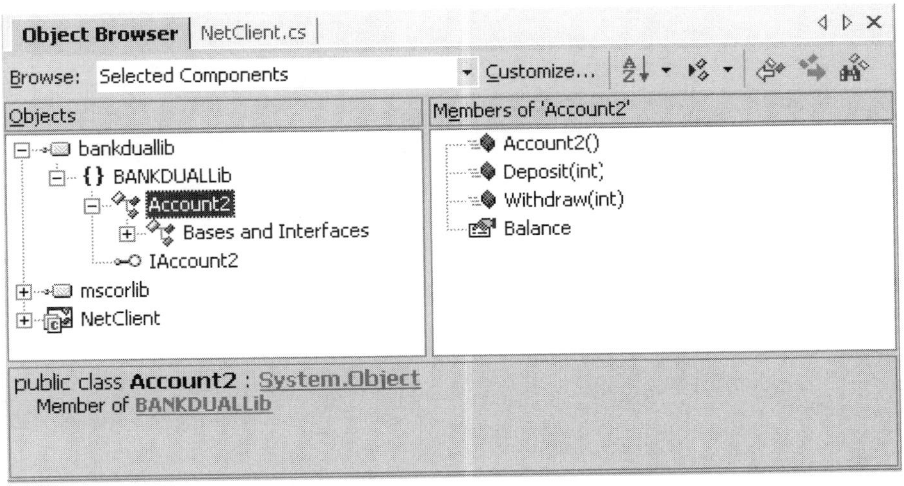

**Figure 14–4**    *Object Browser showing information about the RCW.*

## IMPORT A TYPE LIBRARY USING VISUAL STUDIO

When you are using Visual Studio you can import a COM type library directly, without first running **TlbImp.exe**. To see how to do this, use Solution Explorer to delete the reference to **BANKDUALLib.dll**. In fact, delete the file itself, and delete the **bin** and **obj** directories of **NetClient**. Now right-click over References, choose "Add Reference," and this time select the COM tab from the Add Reference dialog. The listbox will show all the COM components with a registered type library. Select "BankDual 1.0 Type Library," as illustrated in Figure 14–5.

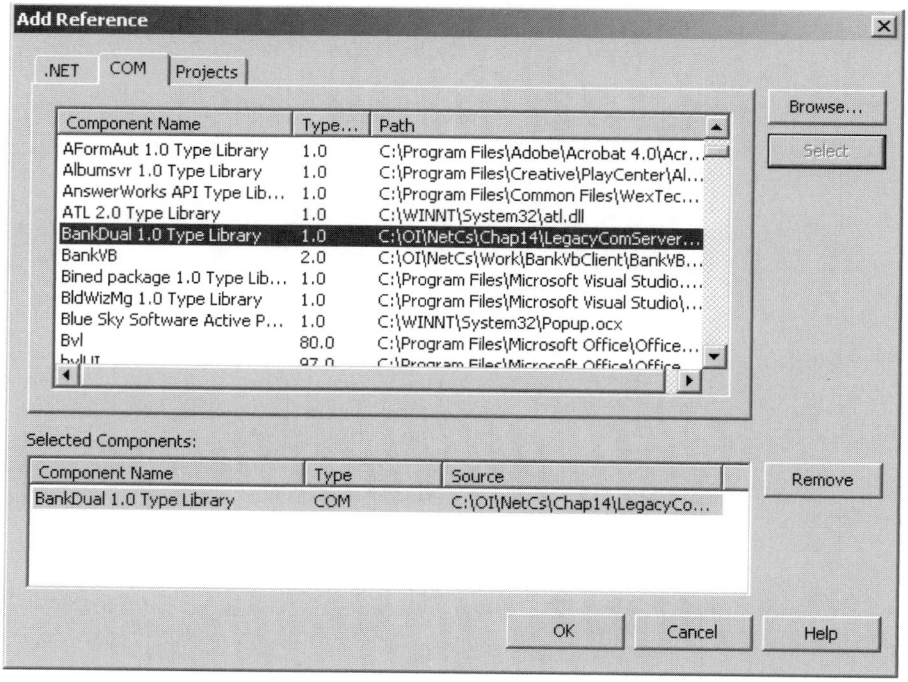

**Figure 14–5**    *Add a reference to a COM component in Visual Studio.*

Now click OK. You will see a message telling you that a "primary interop assembly" is not registered for this type library. You will be invited to have a wrapper generated for you, as illustrated in Figure 14–6. Click "Yes." The generated RCW is the file **Interop.BANKDUALLib_1_0.dll** in the directory **bin\Debug**. You should be able to build and run the .NET client program.

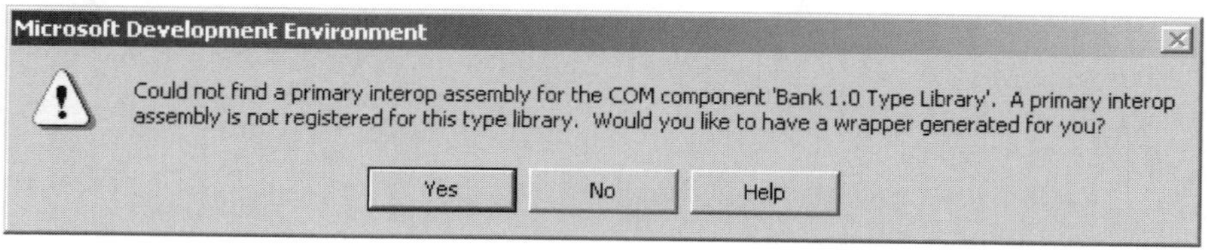

**Figure 14–6**    *Visual Studio will create a primary interop assembly.*

The *primary interop assembly* that was created by Visual Studio is normally created by the publisher of the COM component. This can be done using the **TlbImp.exe** utility with the **/primary** option.

## Wrapping a COM Component with a Pure Vtable Interface

### DUAL INTERFACES

Our example legacy COM component **BankDual.dll** had a *dual* interface **IAccount2**. This means that the interface could be called by both an early-binding COM client using the vtable and also by a late-binding client using **IDispatch**. The IDL file **BankDual.idl** specifies the interface **IAccount2** as dual.

```
[
    object,
    uuid(AAA19CDE-C091-47BF-8C96-C80A00989796),
    dual,
    helpstring("IAccount2 Interface"),
    pointer_default(unique)
]
interface IAccount2 : IDispatch
{
    [propget, id(1), helpstring("property Balance")] HRESULT
Balance([out, retval] long *pVal);
    [id(2), helpstring("method Deposit")] HRESULT
Deposit([in] long amount);
    [id(3), helpstring("method Withdraw")] HRESULT
Withdraw([in] long amount);
};
```

An example of late-binding is VBSCript code for client-side scripting on a Web page. The directory **BankHtml** contains the file **Bank.htm** with an HTML form and VBScript code to exercise our bank account server.

```
<!-- bank.htm -->
<HTML>
<HEAD>
<TITLE>Bank test page for Account object</TITLE>

<SCRIPT LANGUAGE="VBScript">
<!--

dim account

Sub btnCreate_OnClick
        set account = createobject("BankDual.Account2.1")
        Document.Form1.txtAmount.Value = 25
        Document.Form1.txtBalance.Value = account.Balance
End Sub

Sub btnDestroy_OnClick
        set account = Nothing
        Document.Form1.txtAmount.Value = ""
```

```
          Document.Form1.txtBalance.Value = ""
End Sub

Sub btnDeposit_OnClick
      account.Deposit(Document.Form1.txtAmount.Value)
      Document.Form1.txtBalance.Value = account.Balance
End Sub

Sub btnWithdraw_OnClick
      account.Withdraw(Document.Form1.txtAmount.Value)
      Document.Form1.txtBalance.Value = account.Balance
End Sub

-->
</SCRIPT>

<FORM NAME = "Form1" >
Amount <INPUT NAME="txtAmount" VALUE="" SIZE=8>
<P>
Balance <INPUT NAME="txtBalance" VALUE="" SIZE=8>
<P>
<INPUT NAME="btnCreate" TYPE=BUTTON VALUE="Create">
 <INPUT NAME="btnDestroy" TYPE=BUTTON VALUE="Destroy">
 <INPUT NAME="btnDeposit" TYPE=BUTTON VALUE="Deposit">
 <INPUT NAME="btnWithdraw" TYPE=BUTTON VALUE="Withdraw">
</FORM>

</BODY>
</HTML>
```

The **createobject** function instantiates a COM object using late binding, referencing a program ID rather than a CLSID. This is perfectly legitimate, because **BankDual.dll** implements a dual interface on the **Account2** object. Since this is client-side script, we can exercise it locally in Internet Explorer, simply double-clicking on **bank.htm** in Windows Explorer. This will bring up Internet Explorer and show the form. You can click the Create button and instantiate an object,[4] as shown in Figure 14–7. The starting balance of 150 is shown. You can then exercise Deposit and Withdraw, and when you are done, you can click Destroy.

---

[4] Depending on your security settings, you may get a warning message about an ActiveX control on the page. Click Yes to allow the interaction. If you have trouble running the ActiveX control at all, check your security settings in Internet Explorer.

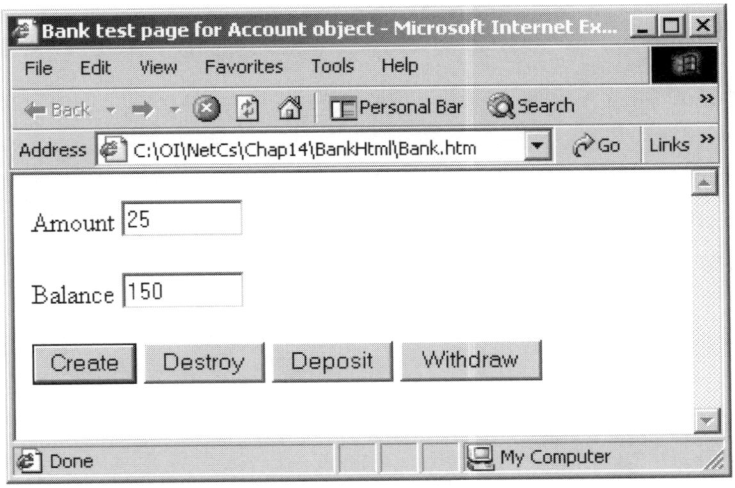

**Figure 14–7**    *Accessing a late-bound COM object in Internet Explorer.*

### PURE VTABLE INTERFACE

Dual interfaces are very common. The default in an ATL wizard generated COM component is dual interface. Visual Basic 6.0 also creates COM components with dual interfaces. However, if there is no occasion for a COM component to be called by a late-binding client, it is more efficient to implement only a pure vtable interface.

There is a slight issue in generating wrappers for COM components with a pure vtable interface. To see the problem, consider the COM component in **VtableComServer**. As with our **LegacyComServer** example, the top-level directory contains the DLL, the type library file, batch files to register and unregister the server, and a client test program. Source code for the COM server and client is provided in **ServerSource** and **ClientSource** respectively. We want to implement a managed client program **VtableNetClient**.

First, verify that the COM client and server work. All you have to do is run the batch file **reg_bank.bat** to register the server, and you can double-click on **BankConsole.exe** in Windows Explorer to run the client.

Next, open up the solution **VtableNetClient.sln** in Visual Studio. Add a reference to the COM type library "Bank 1.0 Type Library." You should get a clean build. But when you run the program, you get an exception:

```
Unhandled Exception: System.InvalidCastException:

QueryInterface for interface BANKLib.IAccount failed.
    at BANKLib.Account.GetBalance(Int32& pBalance)
    at VtableNetClient.ShowBalance() in
```

```
C:\OI\NetCs\Chap14\VtableNetClient\Vtable
NetClient.cs:line 14
   at VtableNetClient.Main() in
C:\OI\NetCs\Chap14\VtableNetClient\
VtableNetClient.cs:line 33
```

The problem is that the .NET client is in a separate apartment, and it needs marshaling. You can use any of the following solutions:

1. Mark the IDL for the interface as *dual*.
2. Mark the IDL for the interface as *oleautomation*, and limit types used to oleautomation friendly types.
3. Build and register the proxy/stub DLL for the interface.
4. Mark the **Main** method in the C# client with the **[STAThread]** or **[MTAThread]** attribute (appropriate to the situation), to place it into the same threading model as the COM server.

Examining the source code for **VtableNetClient.cs**, we see that we commented out the attribute **[STAThread]** in front of **Main**. Uncomment, build, and run again. This time it should work!

As an alternate solution, comment out **[STAThread]** again. Now in the server directory **VtableComServer** run the batch file **reg_bankps.bat** to register the proxy/stub DLL. Build and run the .NET client. Again, it should work!

Notice another feature of this .NET client program. Rather than calling methods on a class object, we go through interface references. We obtain the interface references using the C# **as** operator, as we discussed in Chapter 5. This use of the **as** operator is the analog in .NET of **QueryInterface** in COM.

## Calling Managed Components from COM Client

Obviously, it is much more likely that you will want to write new .NET applications that make use of legacy COM components, however, there may be times when you need to go in the opposite direction. For example, you may have an existing application that makes use of one or more COM components, and you would like to eventually rewrite several of those COM components as .NET components. However, in the mean time, you may want to make use of those new .NET components in your existing COM client applications as well.

COM client programs may use early binding (vtable interface) or late binding (**IDispatch** interface) to access managed .NET components. Early binding requires that type library information is available at compile time. Late binding does not require any type library information at compile time, since binding takes place at runtime via the **IDispatch** interface methods.

However, regardless of whether the client uses early or late binding, a bridge is required between the unmanaged native execution environment of the COM client and the managed execution environment of the .NET component. This bridge is known as the COM Callable Wrapper (CCW), which acts as a proxy for the managed object as shown in Figure 14–8. Only one CCW object is created for any given managed object created for a COM client. The CCW manages object lifetime according to the reference counting rules of **IUnknown**, and it also manages marshaling for the method calls made on the object.

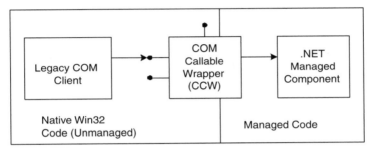

**Figure 14–8**    *A COM callable wrapper between unmanaged and managed code.*

While the RCW assembly is explicitly created as a file, the CCW is created dynamically at runtime by the Common Language Runtime. The CLR creates exactly one CCW for a managed object, regardless of the number of COM clients that request its services, and both COM and .NET clients can make requests on the same .NET object simultaneously.

## A Late Binding COM Client

There are many variations of a COM client calling an .NET component. We will illustrate with just one scenario, a late binding COM client calling a managed component. We will create an .NET component that can be called through VBScript on the **bank.htm** Web page.

Looking at the VBScript code used in **createobject** on **bank.htm**, we see that the ProgId of the COM object is "BankDual.Account2.1." We wish to create an .NET object that can be used in place of this COM object, and that has the same ProgId. To avoid confusion with the COM object, unregister it running the batch file **unreg_bankdual.bat** in the directory **LegacyComServer**. Now if you access **bank.htm** in Internet Explorer and click the "Create" button, you will get an error.

C# code for implementing a compatible bank account object is in the file **Account.cs** in the directory **NetServer**.

```
// Account.cs

using System;
using System.Runtime.InteropServices;

namespace NetServer
{
    [ProgId("BankDual.Account2.1")]
    public class Account
    {
        static private int balance;
        public Account()
        {
            balance = 1000;
        }
        public void Deposit(int amount)
        {
            balance += amount;
        }
        public void Withdraw(int amount)
        {
            balance -= amount;
        }
        public int Balance
        {
            get
            {
                return balance;
            }
        }
    }
}
```

The code shown in bold enables us to assign "BankDual.Account2.1" as the ProgId, making it compatible with the COM object we are replacing. If we left these lines out, we would still be able to call the object through COM. The ProgId would be created from the namespace and the class name, or "NetServer.Account." Other attributes would let us assign various GUIDs, which would be useful in an early binding scenario. Note that to distinguish our .NET component from the COM component it is replacing, we have assigned the starting balance to be 1000.

We are going to deploy our component in the Global Assembly Cache, so we need to create a strong name, as discussed in Chapter 7. We generate a public-private key pair and place them in a file **keypair.snk**, using the command,

```
sn -k keypair.snk
```

In our Visual Studio project we reference this key file in **AssemblyInfo.cs**,

```
[assembly: AssemblyDelaySign(false)]
[assembly: AssemblyKeyFile("keypair.snk")]
[assembly: AssemblyKeyName("")]
```

Our project creates the target assembly **NetServer.dll** in the top-level source directory, where we also have the **keypair.snk** file. We can run all the command-line programs from the directory **c:\OI\NetCs\Chap14\NetServer**. We can then place our assembly in the GAC using the command,

```
gacutil -i netserver.dll
```

You can use the .NET Admin Tool discussed in Chapter 7 to inspect the contents of the GAC, verifying that **NetServer** has indeed been deployed there. See Figure 14–9.

| Figure 14–9 | *Inspecting the GAC using the .NET Admin Tool.* |

In order to make our .NET component available to COM clients, we must provide suitable entries in the Registry. This will enable the COM run-time to locate the appropriate server path and so on. The Assembly Registration Utility, **Regasm.exe**, reads the metadata within an assembly and adds these necessary entries to the Registry, which allows COM clients to use the .NET assembly's components as if they were just old-fashioned registered COM components (via the CCW proxy).

The syntax for using **Regasm.exe** is shown next. This allows COM client programs to create instances of managed classes defined by in the assembly.

```
Regasm AssemblyPath [options]
Where the options may be any of the following.
/unregister          Unregister types
/tlb[:FileName]      Specified typelib
/regfile[:FileName]  Specified output reg file name
/codebase            Sets the code base in the registry
/registered          Only refer to preregistered typelibs
/nologo              Prevents displaying logo
/silent              Prevents displaying of messages
/verbose             Displays extra information
/? or /help          Display usage help message
```

We run this utility on **NetServer** using the command shown in bold,

```
C:\OI\NetCs\Chap14\NetServer>regasm netserver.dll
RegAsm - .NET Assembly Registration Utility Version
1.0.2914.16
Copyright (C) Microsoft Corp. 2001.  All rights reserved.

Types registered successfully
```

We can use the OLE/COM Object Viewer to inspect the entries made in the Registry. Note that there is a special category of COM objects called ".NET Category." Figure 14–10 shows the Registry entries for our "NetServer.Account" object. Note that the ProgId is "BankDual.Account2.1," as specified by the attribute in our C# source code. Note also that the InprocServer32 is **mscoree.dll**, which is the DLL implementing the CLR. As previously mentioned, there is no file created for the CCW. Instead, when the wrapped component is to be instantiated, the CLR creates the CCW on the fly.

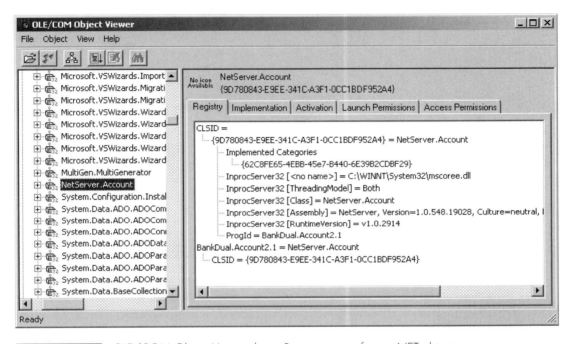

**Figure 14–10**    *OLE/COM Object Viewer shows Registry entries for an .NET object.*

A late-binding COM client can now call our .NET component. That is all there is to it! You can double-click on **bank.htm**, and Internet Explorer will run the VBScript we looked at before. Only this time, the .NET component **NetServer.Account** is invoked, as you can tell by noticing that the starting balance is 1000, as shown in Figure 14–11.

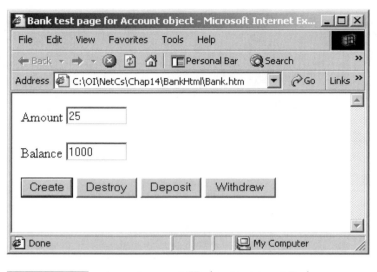

**Figure 14–11**     *Accessing an .NET object in Internet Explorer.*

## Platform Invocation Services (PInvoke)

Platform Invocation Services, also known as "PInvoke," makes unmanaged exported DLL functions available to managed client code. PInvoke allows this to be done from managed code written in any .NET programming language. Notice that PInvoke is not the name of a class, or a method, but is just a nickname for Platform Invocation Services. PInvoke allows marshaling between CLR data types and native data types, and bridges other differences between the managed and unmanaged runtime environments. Although PInvoke is primarily used to access the Win32 APIs, it can be used to call into your own legacy DLLs that you may find are still useful. Unfortunately, PInvoke is in most circumstances a one-way street. You can use it to call from managed code into unmanaged DLL code and of course return back into managed code. PInvoke is used to access global exported DLL functions, so even though it is possible for DLLs to export class methods, they are currently not accessible via PInvoke.

If you are an experienced Windows programmer and have a good knowledge of the Win32 API, you may be tempted, after learning about PInvoke, to call a familiar Win32 API function to perform a task. A secure .NET environment, however, will not give most assemblies permission to call unmanaged code. Usually there will be a native .NET Framework class method that can accomplish your aim, and you should use .NET Framework classes whenever possible. Occasionally it will be necessary to drop down to the underlying platform, and then PInvoke is invaluable.

## A Simple Example

Let's begin with a very simple example of the use of PInvoke, to call the Windows **MessageBox** function. Our sample program is in the directory **SimplePInvoke**.

```
// SimplePInvoke.cs

using System;
using System.Runtime.InteropServices;

class SimplePInvoke
{
    [DllImport("user32.dll", EntryPoint="MessageBoxA")]
    public static extern int ShowMessage(int hWnd,
        string text, string caption, int type);

    public static void Main(string[] args)
    {
        ShowMessage(0, "Hello, World", "From PInvoke", 0);
    }
}
```

The key step is to place a **DllImport** attribute before the prototype of the function we want to call. The function must take ordinary C# data types as parameters, which have natural mappings to the C data types of the native function. The function will be treated as a static method in the class where it is defined. The one required parameter to the **DllImport** attribute is the name of the DLL exporting the function. There are various optional, named parameters, that can be used with **DllImport**. For a complete list, consult the documentation of the **DllImportAttribut** class in the **System.Runtime.InteropServices** namespace. In our example, we use the **EntryPoint** attribute to specify the name by which the function is exported in the DLL. The name of the static method in the class can then be different, and will be the name to be used in the C# code that calls the method. In our example, the Win32 function has the name **MessageBoxA** and our C# code calls the method under the name **ShowMessage**. Figure 14–12 shows the output from this little program.

**Figure 14–12**   *Calling the Win32 MessageBox function through PInvoke.*

## Marshaling *out* Parameters

The previous PInvoke example did not demonstrate how PInvoke automatically marshals **out** parameters for you where there is a clear mapping between Win32 and the CLR types. This is because the **MessageBox** takes only **in** parameters. The next example calls the **GetComputerName** and **GetLastError** APIs via PInvoke. The code for this example is in the directory **PInvoke**.

```
// PInvoke.cs

using System;
using System.Text;
using System.Runtime.InteropServices;

public class Test
{
    [DllImport("kernel32.dll", CharSet=CharSet.Ansi)]
    public static extern bool GetComputerName(
        StringBuilder name, out uint buffer);
    [DllImport("kernel32.dll")]
    public static extern uint GetLastError();

    public static int Main(string[] args)
    {
        bool result = true;
        uint error = 0;
        StringBuilder name = new StringBuilder(128);
        uint length = 128;
        result = GetComputerName(name, out length);

        if (result == true)
            Console.WriteLine(name);
        else
        {
            error = GetLastError();
            Console.WriteLine("Error: {0:x}", error);
        }
```

```
      return 0;
    }
}
```

## TRANSLATING TYPES

Since **GetComputerName** returns a name, **StringBuilder** was used instead of **string**.[5] For input only arguments you can use **string**. An **out** attribute was placed on the length attribute because the second argument to **GetComputerName** is a pointer. Unsigned types were used because DWORD is an unsigned 32 bit quantity. For comparison, here are the proto-types of the corresponding Win32 functions:

```
BOOL GetComputerName(
  LPTSTR lpBuffer,   // computer name
  LPDWORD lpnSize    // size of name buffer
);

DWORD GetLastError(VOID);
```

Some CLR types do not map directly into unmanaged types. You have to tell the Execution Engine (**mscoree.dll**) how to translate to a BSTR. You do that by annotating the declaration with the **MarshalAs** attribute:

```
[MarshalAs(UnmanagedType.BStr)] public string foo
```

The **UnmanagedType** enumeration lists all the translatable types.

# Summary

In this chapter we studied mixing managed and unmanaged code running under Windows. We saw how to call legacy COM components from within the managed .NET environment using a Runtime Callable Wrapper or RCW. We also looked at the use of a COM Callable Wrapper (CCW) to enable a COM client to call a .NET component. Finally, we looked at using Platform Invocation Services (PInvoke), and saw how automatic marshaling is provid-ed for both in and out parameters.

We have come to the end of a long journey, which we hope will be the first of many journeys in the world of .NET. We hope you enjoyed the trip. Good luck on your .NET programming projects!

---

[5] Instances of **string** are immutable, so we use the **StringBuilder** class, which was discussed in Chapter 3.

# Visual Studio.NET

*A*lthough it is possible to program .NET using only the command line compiler, it is much easier and more enjoyable to use Visual Studio.NET. In this chapter we cover the basics of using Visual Studio to edit, compile, run, and debug programs. You will then be equipped to use Visual Studio in the rest of the book. This chapter covers the basics to get you up and running using Visual Studio. We will introduce additional features of Visual Studio later in the book as we encounter a need. This book was developed using beta software, and in the final released product you may encounter some changes to the information presented here. Also, Visual Studio is a very elaborate Windows application that is highly configurable, and you may encounter variations in the exact layout of windows, what is shown by default, and so on. As you work with Visual Studio, a good attitude is to see yourself as an explorer discovering a rich and varied new country.

## Overview of Visual Studio.NET

Open up Microsoft Visual Studio.NET 7.0 and you will see a starting window similar to what is shown in Figure A–1.

**Figure A–1**    *Visual Studio.NET main window.*

What you see on default startup is the main window with an HTML page that can help you navigate among various resources, open or create projects, and change your profile information. (If you close the start page, you can get it back anytime from the menu Help | Show Start Page.) Clicking on **My Profile** will bring up a profile page on which you can change various settings. There is a standard profile for "typical" work in Visual Studio ("Visual Studio Developer" profile), and special ones for various languages. Since Visual Studio.NET is the unification of many development environments, programmers used to one particular previous environment may prefer a particular keyboard scheme, window layout, and so on. For example, if you choose the profile "Visual Basic Developer," you will get the Visual Basic 6 keyboard scheme. In this book we will use all the defaults, so go back to the profile "Visual Studio Developer" if you made any changes. See Figure A–2.

**Figure A–2**     *Visual Studio.NET profile page.*

To gain an appreciation of some of the diverse features in Visual Studio.NET, open up the **Bank** console solution in the **AppA** directory for this Appendix (File | Open Solution..., navigate to the **Bank** directory, and open the file **Bank.sln**). You will see quite an elaborate set of windows. See Figure A–3.

**Figure A–3**    *A console project in Visual Studio.NET.*

Starting from the left are icons for the Server Explorer and the Toolbox, followed by the main window area, which currently is just a gray area. Underneath the main window is the Output Window, which shows the results of builds and so on. Continuing our tour, on the top right is the Solution Explorer, which enables you to conveniently see all the files in a "solution," which may consist of several "projects." On the bottom right is the Properties window, which lets you conveniently edit properties on forms for Windows applications. The Properties window is very similar to the Properties Window in Visual Basic.

From the Solution Explorer you can navigate to files in the projects. In turn, double-click on each of **Account.cs** and **Bank.cs,** the two source files in the **Bank** project. Text editor windows will be brought up in the main window area. Across the top of the main window are horizontal tabs to quickly select any of the open windows. Visual Studio.NET allows you to select the window to show from the Windows menu. Figure A–4 shows the open source files with the horizontal tabs.

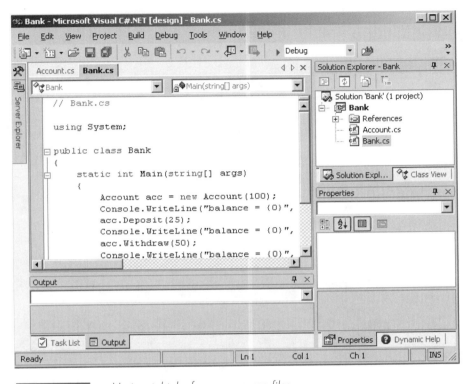

**Figure A–4**    *Horizontal tabs for open source files.*

## Toolbars

Visual Studio comes with many different toolbars. You can configure which toolbars you wish displayed, and you can drag toolbars to position them to where you find them most convenient. You can also customize toolbars by adding or deleting buttons that correspond to different commands.

To specify which toolbars are displayed, bring up the menu View | Toolbars. You can also right-click in any empty area of a toolbar. There will be a check mark next to the toolbars which are currently displayed. By clicking on an item on this menu you can make the corresponding toolbar button appear or disappear. For your work in this book add the toolbars,

- Build
- Debug

## CUSTOMIZING A TOOLBAR

We want to make sure that the "Start Without Debugging" command is available on the Debug toolbar. If it is not already on your Debug toolbar (it is a red exclamation point), you can add it by the following procedure, which can be used to add other commands to toolbars.

1. Select menu Tools | Customize... to bring up the Customize dialog.
2. Select the Commands tab.
3. In Categories, select Debug, and in Commands select Start Without Debugging. See Figure A–5.
4. Drag the selected command onto the Debug toolbar, positioning it where you desire. Place it to the immediate right of the wedge-shaped Start ▶ button.
5. Close the Customize dialog.

**Figure A–5**    *Adding a new command to a toolbar.*

# Creating a Console Application

As our first exercise in using Visual Studio, we will create a simple console application. Our program **Bytes** will attempt to calculate how many bytes there are in a kilobyte, a megabyte, a gigabyte, and a terabyte. If you want to follow along on your PC as you read, you can use the **Demos** directory for this chapter. The first version is in **Bytes\Step1**. A final version can be found in **Bytes\Step3**.

## Creating a C# Project

1. From Visual Studio main menu choose File | New | Project.... This will bring up the New Project dialog.
2. For Project Types choose "Visual C# Projects" and for Templates choose "Empty Project."
3. Click the Browse button, navigate to **Demos,** and click Open.
4. In the Name field, type **Bytes**. See Figure A–6. Click OK.

**Figure A–6**   *Creating an empty C# project.*

## Adding a C# File

At this point you will have an empty C# project. We are now going to add a file **Bytes.cs,** which contains the text of our program.

1. In Solution Explorer right-click over **Bytes** and choose Add | Add New Item.... This will bring up the Add New Item dialog.
2. For Categories choose "Local Project Items" and for Templates choose "Code File."
3. For Name type **Bytes.cs**. See Figure A–7. Click Open.

**Figure A–7**   *Adding an empty C# file to a C# project.*

## Using the Visual Studio Text Editor

In the Solution Explorer double-click on **Bytes.cs**. This will open up the empty file **Bytes.cs** in the Visual Studio text editor. Type in the following program, and notice things like color syntax highlighting to indicate reserved words as you type.

```
// Bytes.cs

using System;
public class Bytes
```

```
{
   public static int Main(string[] args)
   {
      int bytes = 1024;
      Console.WriteLine("kilo = {0}", bytes);
      bytes = bytes * 1024;
      Console.WriteLine("mega = {0}", bytes);
      bytes = bytes * 1024;
      Console.WriteLine("giga = {0}", bytes);
      bytes = bytes * 1024;
      Console.WriteLine("tera = {0}", bytes);
      return 0;
   }
}
```

Besides the color syntax highlighting, other features include automatic indenting. All in all, you should find the Visual Studio editor friendly and easy to use.

## Building the Project

You can build the project by using one of the following:

- Menu Build | Build
- Toolbar
- Keyboard shortcut Ctrl + Shift + B

## Running the Program

You can run the program by using one of the following:

- Menu Debug | Start Without Debugging
- Toolbar
- Keyboard shortcut Ctrl + F5

You will see the following output in a console window that opens up:

```
kilo = 1024
mega = 1048576
giga = 1073741824
tera = 0
Press any key to continue
```

We will investigate the reason for the strange output later. If you press any key, as indicated, the console window will close.

## Running the Program in the Debugger

You can run the program in the debugger by using one of the following:
- Menu Debug | Start
- Toolbar ▶
- Keyboard shortcut F5

A console window will briefly open up and then immediately close. If you want the window to stay open, you must explicitly program for it, for example, by asking for input. You can set a breakpoint to stop execution before the program exits. We will outline features of the debugger later in the chapter.

# Project Configurations

A project *configuration* specifies build settings for a project. You can have several different configurations, and each configuration will be built in its own directory, so you can exercise the different configurations independently. Every project in a Visual Studio solution has two default configurations, **Debug** and **Release**. As the names suggest, the **Debug** configuration will build a debug version of the project, where you can do source level debugging by setting breakpoints, and so on. The **bin\Debug** directory will then contain a *program database* file with a **.pdb** extension that holds debugging and project state information.

You can choose the configuration from the main toolbar ▶ Debug ▼ . You can also choose the configuration using the menu Build | Configuration Manager..., which will bring up the Configuration Manager dialog. From the Active Solution Configuration dropdown, choose Release. See Figure A–8.

Build the project again. Now a second version of the IL language file **Bytes.exe** is created, this time in the **bin\Release** directory. There will be no **.pdb** file in this directory.

## Creating a New Configuration

Sometimes it is useful to create additional configurations, which can save alternate build settings. As an example, let's create a configuration for a "checked" build. If you build with the **/checked** compiler switch, the compiler will generate IL code to check for integer underflow and overflow. In Visual Studio you set compiler options through dialog boxes. The following steps will guide you through creating a new configuration called **CheckedDebug** that will build a checked version of the program.

**Figure A–8**    *Choosing Release in the Configuration Manager.*

1. Bring up the Configuration Manager dialog.

2. From the Active Solution Configuration: dropdown, choose **<New...>**. The New Solution Configuration dialog will come up.

3. Type **CheckedDebug** as the configuration name. Choose Copy Settings from **Debug**. Check "Also create new project configuration(s)." See Figure A–9. Click OK.

**Figure A–9**    *Creating a new configuration.*

**Figure A–10**   *Changing the build settings for a configuration.*

## Setting Build Settings for a Configuration

Next we will set the build settings for the new configuration. (You could also set build settings for one of the standard configurations, if you wanted to make any changes from the defaults provided.) Check the toolbar to verify that the new **CheckedDebug** is the currently active configuration.

1. Right-click over **Bytes** in the Solution Explorer and choose Properties. The "Bytes Property Pages" dialog comes up.
2. In Configuration Properties, select Build. Change the setting for "Check for overflow underflow" to **True** (see Figure A–10). Click OK.

# Debugging

In this section we will discuss some of the debugging facilities in Visual Studio. To be able to benefit from debugging at the source code level, you should have built your executable using a Debug configuration, as discussed previously. There are two ways to enter the debugger:

- Just-in-Time Debugging. You run normally, and if an exception occurs you will be allowed to enter the debugger. The program has crashed, so you will not be able to run further from here to single step, set breakpoints, and so on. But you will be able to see the value of variables, and you will see the point at which the program failed.
- Standard Debugging. You start the program under the debugger. You may set breakpoints, single step, and so on.

## Just-in-Time Debugging

Build and run (without debugging) the **Bytes** program from the previous section, making sure to use the **CheckedDebug** configuration. This time the program will not run through smoothly to completion, but an exception will be thrown. A "Just-In-Time Debugging" dialog will be shown (see Figure A–11). Click Yes to debug.

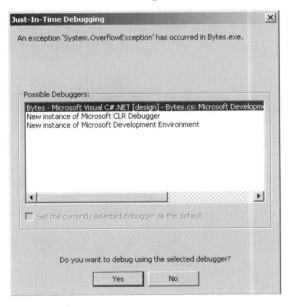

*Just-In-Time Debugging dialog is displayed in response to an exception.*

Click OK in the "Attach to Process" dialog and then click Break in the "Microsoft Development Environment" dialog. You will now be brought into a window showing the source code where the problem arose, with an arrow pinpointing the location.

To stop debugging you can use the ■ toolbar button or the menu Debug | Stop Debugging.

## Standard Debugging

### BREAKPOINTS

The way you typically do standard debugging is to set a breakpoint and then run using the debugger. As an example, set a breakpoint at the first line:

```
bytes = bytes * 1024;
```

The easiest way to set a breakpoint is by clicking in the gray bar to the left of the source code window. You can also set the cursor on the desired line and click the "hand" toolbar button ⊞ to toggle a breakpoint (set if not set, and remove if a breakpoint is set). Now you can run under the debugger, and the breakpoint should be hit. A yellow arrow over the red dot of the breakpoint shows where the breakpoint has been hit. See Figure A–12.

```
// Bytes.cs

using System;

public class Bytes
{
    public static int Main(string[] args)
    {
        int bytes = 1024;
        Console.WriteLine("kilo = {0}", bytes);
        bytes = bytes * 1024;
        Console.WriteLine("mega = {0}", bytes);
        bytes = bytes * 1024;
        Console.WriteLine("giga = {0}", bytes);
        bytes = bytes * 1024;
        Console.WriteLine("tera = {0}", bytes);
        return 0;
    }
}
```

**Figure A–12**    *A breakpoint has been hit.*

When you are done with a breakpoint, you can remove it by clicking again in the gray bar or by toggling with the hand toolbar button. If you want to remove all breakpoints, you can use the menu Debug | Clear All Breakpoints, or you can use the toolbar button ⚒ .

## WATCHING VARIABLES

At this point you can inspect variables. The easiest way is to slide the mouse over the variable you are interested in, and the value will be shown as a yellow tool tip. You can also right-click over a variable and choose Quick Watch (or use the eyeglasses toolbar button 👓). Figure A–13 shows a typical Quick Watch window. You can also change the value of a variable from this window.

When you are stopped in the debugger, you can add a variable to the Watch window by right-clicking over it and choosing Add Watch. The Watch window can show a number of variables, and the Watch window stays open as the program executes. When a variable changes value, the new value is

| Figure A–13 | *Quick Watch window shows variable, and you can change it.* |

shown in red. Figure A–14 shows the Watch window (note that the display has been changed to hex, as described in the next section).

| Watch 1 | | |
|---|---|---|
| Name | Value | Type |
| bytes | 0x40000000 | int |
| | | |

**Figure A–14** *Visual Studio Watch window.*

## DEBUGGER OPTIONS

You can change debugger options from the menu Tools | Options, and select Debugging from the list. Figure A–15 illustrates setting a hexadecimal display. If you then go back to a Watch window, you will see a hex value such as **0x400** displayed.

**Figure A–15** *Setting hexadecimal display in Debugging Options.*

## SINGLE STEPPING

When you are stopped in the debugger, you can *single step*. You can also begin execution by single stepping. There are a number of single step buttons. The most common are (in the order shown on the toolbar):

- Step Into
- Step Over
- Step Out

There is also a Run to Cursor button.

With Step Into you will step into a function, if the cursor is positioned on a call to a function. With Step Over you will step to the next line (or statement or instruction, depending on the selection in the dropdown next to the step buttons `Line ▾` ). To illustrate Step Into, build the **Bytes\Step2** project, where the multiplication by 1,024 has been replaced by a function call to the static method **OneK**. Set a breakpoint at the first function call, and then Step Into. The result is illustrated in Figure A–16. Note the red dot at the breakpoint and the yellow arrow in the function.

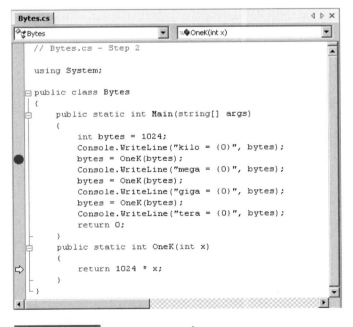

```
// Bytes.cs - Step 2

using System;

public class Bytes
{
    public static int Main(string[] args)
    {
        int bytes = 1024;
        Console.WriteLine("kilo = {0}", bytes);
        bytes = OneK(bytes);
        Console.WriteLine("mega = {0}", bytes);
        bytes = OneK(bytes);
        Console.WriteLine("giga = {0}", bytes);
        bytes = OneK(bytes);
        Console.WriteLine("tera = {0}", bytes);
        return 0;
    }
    public static int OneK(int x)
    {
        return 1024 * x;
    }
}
```

**Figure A–16**     *Stepping into a function.*

When debugging, Visual Studio maintains a Call Stack. In our simple example the Call Stack is just two deep. See Figure A–17.

| Call Stack | | ⯅ ✕ |
| --- | --- | --- |
| Name | | Language |
| ⇨ Bytes.exe!Bytes.OneK(int x = 0x400) Line 21 | | C# |
| Bytes.exe!Bytes.Main(string[] args = {Length=0x0}) Line 11 + 0x8 bytes | | C# |

⊞ Call Stack ｜ 🖑 Breakpoints ｜ ⛶ Command Window ｜ ▤ Output

**Figure A–17**    *The call stack.*

# Summary

Visual Studio.NET is a very rich integrated development environment (IDE), with many features to make programming more enjoyable. In this appendix we covered the basics of using Visual Studio to edit, compile, run, and debug programs, so that you will be equipped to use Visual Studio in the rest of the book. Nonetheless, it is worth spending time to become familiar with many more of the Visual Studio features, because understanding how to use them will make your development work much easier. A project can be built in different configurations, such as Debug and Release. Visual Studio.NET has a vast array of features for building database applications, Web applications, components, and many other kinds of projects. We discuss some of these additional features in the chapters where they are pertinent.

# INDEX

## DEVELOPER TRAINING

OBJECT INNOVATIONS offers training course materials in fundamental software technologies used in developing applications in modern computing environments. We emphasize object-oriented techniques, with a focus on Microsoft® technologies, Java™, and Linux™. Our courses have been used by businesses, training companies, and universities throughout North America. End clients include IBM®, HP®, Dell®, Compaq®, FedEx®, UPS®, AOL®, U.S. Bank®, Mellon Bank®, and NASA. Our courses are frequently updated to reflect feedback from classroom use. We aggressively track new technologies and endeavor to keep our courseware up-to-date.

Founded in 1993, Object Innovations has a long record of firsts in courseware. Our Visual C++ course was released before Microsoft's, we introduced one of the first courses in JavaServer Pages, and our Linux Internals 2.4 kernel course came out several months before Red Hat's course. Now we are leading the development of comprehensive developer training in Microsoft's .NET technology.

## .NET DEVELOPER TRAINING

Object Innovations is writing the premier book series on .NET for Prentice Hall PTR. These authoritative books are the foundation of our curriculum. Each book matches a corresponding course, and the student materials come bundled with the book, so students have comprehensive reference materials after the course. Each core course is five days in length and is very rich in content, containing well over five days worth of material. The courses are modularized, so background information or special topics not needed for a particular class can be cleanly omitted. On the other hand, the courses can be lengthened as required. Thus each course can be easily customized to meet the particular needs and interests of the students. We also have shorter courses.

**The first group consists of shorter, overview courses:**

    401   Introduction to .NET for Developers   (1 day)
    412   Programming C# and .NET   (3 days)
    422   Programming Visual Basic.NET   (3 days)
    452   Introduction to ASP.NET   (3 days)

**The second group constitutes the full-length courses that correspond to the books in the Prentice Hall/Object Innovations book series:**

    410   Introduction to C# Using .NET   (5 days)
    414   Application Development Using C# and .NET   (5 days)
    420   Introduction to Programming Visual Basic Using .NET   (5 days)
    424   Application Development Using Visual Basic.NET   (5 days)
    434   .NET Architecture and Programming Using Visual C++   (5 days)
    440   Programming Perl in the .NET Environment   (5 days)
    454   Fundamentals of Web Applications Using .NET and XML   (5 days)

See our .NET website for complete course listings: www.objectinnovations.com/dotnet.htm

## MICROSOFT DEVELOPER TRAINING

Our Microsoft curriculum is very extensive, with introductory and advanced courses on Visual C++, MFC, COM/DCOM, OLE, COM+, and advanced topics in Visual Basic™. We also provide foundational courses in C++ programming. Selected courses include:

| | | |
|---|---|---|
| 123 | Programming COM and DCOM Using ATL | (5 days) |
| 125 | Programming COM and ActiveX Using ATL | (5 days) |
| 127 | Programming COM and OLE Using MFC | (5 days) |
| 130 | Programming COM and COM+ Using Visual C++ | (5 days) |
| 149 | Distributed COM+ Programming | (5 days) |
| 131 | Programming COM and ActiveX Using Visual Basic | (3 days) |
| 133 | Distributed COM+ Programming Using Visual Basic | (5 days) |
| 142 | Visual C++ Windows Programming for C Programmers | (5 days) |
| 145 | MFC Windows Programming for C++ Programmers | (5 days) |
| 146 | Advanced Windows Programming Using Visual C++ | (5 days) |
| 153 | C++ Programming for Non-C Programmers | (5 days) |
| 156 | C++ Programming for C Programmers | (5 days) |
| 157 | Advanced C++ Programming | (5 days |

## JAVA DEVELOPER TRAINING

Java training courses span the spectrum from beginning to advanced and provide extensive coverage of both client-side and server-side technologies. We emphasize distributed application development using Java. Selected courses include:

| | | |
|---|---|---|
| 102 | Introduction to Java for Non-C Programmers | (4 days) |
| 103 | Java Programming | (5 days) |
| 105 | Using and Developing JavaBeans | (4 days) |
| 106 | Advanced Java Programming | (5 days) |
| 107 | CORBA Architecture and Programming Using Java | (4 days) |
| 109 | Java Server Pages | (2 days) |
| 110 | Java Servlet Programming | (2 days) |
| 111 | Introduction to Java RMI | (1 day) |
| 163 | Enterprise JavaBeans | (5 days) |
| 171 | Developing Web-Based Software Using EJB and JSP | (5 days) |
| 172 | Java Foundation Classes | (5 days) |

## LINUX COURSES

Linux courses range from fundamentals and system administration to advanced courses in internals, device drivers and networking. Selected courses include:

| | | |
|---|---|---|
| 135 | Fundamentals of Linux | (4 days) |
| 136 | Linux System Administration | (4 days) |
| 310 | Linux Internals | (5 days) |
| 314 | Linux Network Drivers Development | (3 days) |
| 320 | Linux Network Administration | (5 days) |

See our .NET website for complete course listings: www.objectinnovations.com/dotnet.htm

# OBJECT INNOVATIONS' .NET TRAINING PARTNERS

*For information about .NET training using OBJECT INNOVATIONS courseware,*
*please check with our .NET Training Partners.*

## ANEW TECHNOLOGY CORPORATION                     www.Anew.net

Specializing in IT consulting, training, mentoring, and development, Anew Technology has been serving many satisfied clients. Our business mission is threefold: to stay at the forefront of IT technologies, to satisfy client needs by applying these technologies, and to provide the best service in our industry. Anew Technology is a business partner with Object Innovations in operations and courseware development.

## COMPUTER HORIZONS                     www.ComputerHorizons.com/Training

For over sixteen years Computer Horizons Education Division (CHED) has been providing on-site, instructor-led IT training and customized workshops for organizations nationwide. We have developed extensive curriculum offerings in Web Technologies, Relational Databases, Reporting Tools, Process Improvement, UNIX™ and LINUX™, Client/Server, Mainframe & Legacy Systems, Windows® 2000, and much more. CHED will design, develop and deliver a training solution tailored to each client's training requirements.

## COMPUWORKS SYSTEMS, INC.                     www.CompuWorks.com

CompuWorks Systems, Inc. is an IT solutions company whose aim is to provide our clients with customized training, support and development services. We are committed to building long term partnerships with our clients in an effort to meet their individual needs. Cutting-edge solutions are our specialty.

## CUSTOM TRAINING INSTITUTE                     www.4CustomTraining.com

Custom Training Institute is a provider of high quality High-End training since 1989. Along with our full line of "off-the-shelf" classes, we excel at providing customized Solutions—from technical needs assessment through course development and delivery. We specialize in: Legacy Skills Transformation, Oracle, UNIX, C++, Java™ and other subjects for computer professionals.

## DB BASICS                     www.DBBasics.com

DBBasics, founded in 1988 as a Microsoft® solution development company, has developed and delivered Microsoft technology training since its inception. DBBasics specializes in delivering database and developer technology training to corporate customers. Our vast development experience, coupled with the requirement for instructors to consistently provide hands-on consulting to our customers, enables DBBasics to provide best of breed instruction in the classroom as well as customized eLearning solutions and database technology consulting.

## DEVCOM                     www.dev-cominc.com

Devcom Corporation offers a full line of courses and seminars for software developers and engineers. Currently Devcom provides technical courses and seminars around the country for Hewlett® Packard, Compaq® Computer, Informix® Software, Silicon Graphics®, Quantum/Maxtor® and Gateway® Inc. Our senior .NET/C# instructor is currently working in conjunction with Microsoft to provide .NET training to their internal technical staff.

## ISRG                     www.isrg.com

The I/S RESOURCE GROUP helps organizations to understand, plan for and implement emerging I/S technologies and methodologies. By combining education, training, briefings, and consulting, we assist our clients to effectively apply I/S technologies to achieve business benefits. Our eBusiness Application Bootcamp' is an integrated set of courses that prepares learners to utilize XML, OOAD, Java™, JSP, EJB, ASP, CORBA and .NET to build eBusiness applications. Our eBusiness Briefings pinpoint emerging technologies and methodologies.

# OBJECT INNOVATIONS' .NET TRAINING PARTNERS

*For information about .NET training using OBJECT INNOVATIONS courseware,*
*please check with our .NET Training Partners.*

## RELIABLE SOFTWARE                                      www.ReliableSoftware.com

Reliable Software, Inc. uses Microsoft technology to quickly develop cost-effective software solutions for the small to mid-size business or business unit. We use state-of-the-art techniques to allow business rules, database models and the user interface to evolve as your business needs evolve. We can provide design and implementation consulting, or training.

## SKILLBRIDGE TRAINING                                   www.SkillBridgeTraining.com

SkillBridge is a leading provider of blended technical training solutions. The company's service offerings are designed to meet a wide variety of client requirements. Offering an integration of instructor-led training, e-learning and mentoring programs, SkillBridge delivers high value solutions in a cost-effective manner. SkillBridge's technology focus includes, among others, programming languages, operating systems, databases, and internet and web technologies."

## /TRAINING/ETC INC.                                     www.trainingetc.com

A training company dedicated to delivering quality technical training, courseware development, and consulting in a variety of subject matter areas, including Programming Languages and Design (including C, C++, OOAD/UML, Perl, and Java), a complete UNIX curriculum (from UNIX Fundamentals to System Administration), the Internet (including HTML/CGI, XML and JavaScript™ Programming) and RDBMS (including Oracle and Sybase).

## WATERMARK LEARNING                                     www.WatermarkLearning.com

Watermark Learning provides a wide range of IT skill development training and mentoring services to a variety of industries, software/ consulting firms and government. We provide flexible options for delivery: onsite, consortium and public classes in three major areas: project management, requirements analysis and software development, including e-Commerce. Our instructors are seasoned, knowledgeable practitioners, who use their industry experience along with our highly-rated courseware to effectively build technical skills relevant to your business need.

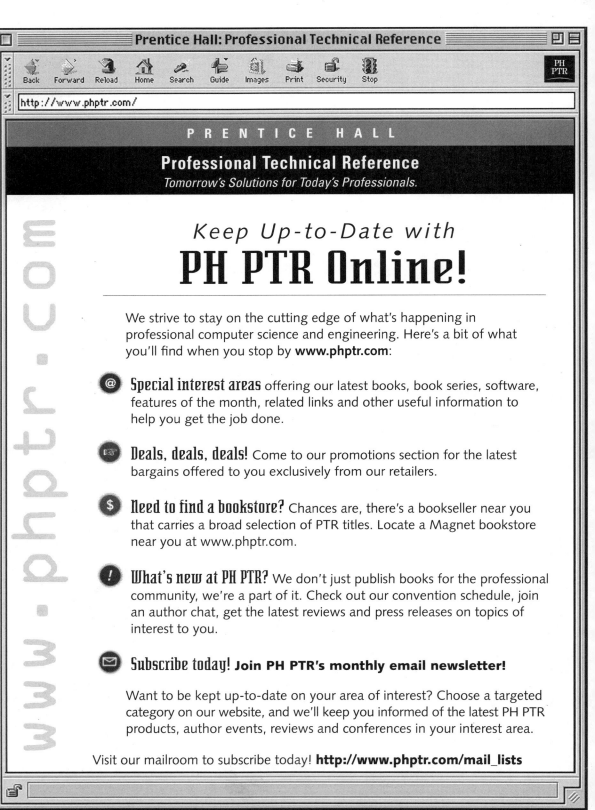